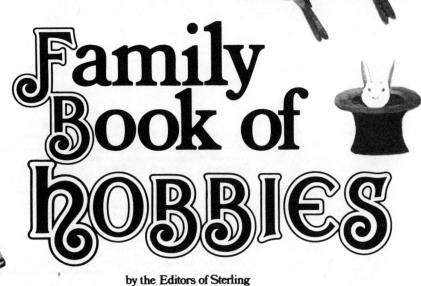

Family Book of HOBBIES

by the Editors of Sterling

STERLING PUBLISHING CO., INC. NEW YORK

Oak Tree Press Co., Ltd. London & Sydney

OTHER BOOKS OF INTEREST

ACKNOWLEDGMENTS

The illustrations in the black-and-white pages of this book are as follows:

"Bird Watching" drawings by Shizu Matsuda and Santa De Haven, photographs from "Bird Life for Young People" and from U.S. Fish and Wildlife Service; Provincial Museum, Victoria, B.C.; Department of Recreation and Conservation, Victoria, B.C.; Michigan Conservation Department; and Australian News and Information Bureau.

"Raising Tropical Fish" photographs from "Tropical Fish in Your Home," Herbert R. Axelrod, Dr. Cliff Emmons, Mervin F. Roberts and G. J. M. Timmerman.

"Indoor Gardening" drawings by Minne.

"Stamp Collecting" photographs from "Getting Started in Stamp Collecting" and from Minkus Publications.

"Coin Collecting" photographs from "Coin Collecting as a Hobby."

"Rock Collecting" photographs from "Treasures of the Earth."

"Shell Collecting" photographs by Gil Murray from "Shell Life and Shell Collecting," drawings by Shizu Matsuda.

"Drawing" illustrations by Chester Jay Alkema and his students; Howard Simon; Gerhard Gollwitzer and his students; Shizu Matsuda, Frank M. Rines, and George B. Bridgman.

"Painting" illustrations by J. Van Ingen, Shizu Matsuda, Frank M. Rines, John F. Carlson and Judith Torche.

"Photography" photographs by Godfrey Frankel from "Short-Cut to Photography," some by courtesy of Eastman Kodak Co. and Standard Oil Co. of N.J.

"Fishing" drawings by Hal Sharp and Dwight Dobbins from "Fishing" by Gil Paust.

"Camping and Backpacking" drawings by Georges Mousson from "101 Camping-Out Ideas and Activities."

"Bike-Riding" illustrations from "BikeWays," some photographs by courtesy of Bicycle Institute of America, Inc., American Youth Hostels, National Park Service, Bike-Toter, Inc., and Potomac Area Council A.Y.H.

"Chess Playing" illustrations from "Chess for Children."

"Handwriting Analysis" illustrations from "The Psychology of Handwriting."

"Fortune Telling with Playing Cards" illustrations from "How to Tell Fortunes with Cards."

"Magic as a Hobby" drawings by Doug Anderson from "101 Best Magic Tricks."

Illustrations on front cover, reading from top and left to right are as follows: Autographs, from "The Psychology of Handwriting," photograph from "Fishing," stamps from "Getting Started in Stamp Collecting," cards from "How to Tell Fortunes with Cards," watercolor from "Aquarelle and Watercolor Complete," chess diagram from "Chess for Children," photograph from "A Bee is Born" by Harald Doering, shell from "Shell Life and Shell Collecting," coins from "Coin Collecting" by Robert V. Masters and Fred Reinfeld, drawing from "Joy of Drawing," tropical fish from "Tropical Fish Identifier." Back cover illustrations: magic from "Magic Tricks" by Guy Frederick, garden drawing from "Herb Magic and Garden Craft," juggling drawing by Shizu Matsuda, bird painting from "Bird Life For Young People."

CONTENTS

BEFORE YOU BEGIN

This book is full of ideas that will enable your family to do things together. All of you need hobbies to give you the feeling of satisfaction that comes with being involved in an activity that supplements the daily routine of home, school or occupation. In an age when our urban-suburban life is becoming more and more stereotyped and sterile, hobbies can provide healthy and enriching diversity, and, as positive activities, can counteract the increasingly passive and sedentary character of modern life.

If your family is like most, all of you spend too much of your time engaged in such inactive pursuits. You sit most of the day on the job or in school, and spend spare moments reading the newspaper, watching television, observing a spectator sport, or going to the theatre. All these are perfectly commendable activities, but they should be balanced by active and creative interests.

Hobbies can provide recreation and exercise, develop your expertise in a special field, give you relief from a dull daily routine, or relaxation from a high pressure routine. If you feel you are under too much pressure or too many other obligations to indulge yourself in such a pastime, you are just the one who would most benefit from having a hobby—or two.

Any hobbies that you choose to take up or encourage in your home will widen your circle of friends, as you will undoubtedly be brought into contact with other like-minded families or individuals with whom you can share these interests.

It is especially important that children develop outside interests at an early age, and not become captives of television. Schools are not always able on their own to reach out to children to develop their individual interests and talents. This is often much better done in the home. What better way for the child to be introduced to the rich and fascinating history of coins, the intriguing world of birds, or the wonders of the woods than through the shared interest of a parent or some other member of the family!

It has been the purpose of the editors to draw together, from many books, information on a score of different hobbies, and to present the information in language that will be easily understood by the whole family. In the few cases where it has been necessary to discuss technical details, it has been done in simple, precise terms, without the use of technical language. The hobbies have been selected to appeal to a wide age group. Naturally, though, some will be more adaptable to the needs of children than others. Wherever possible, suggestions have been given on how to involve children in the activities being discussed.

The hobbies fall into five different categories.

NATURE HOBBIES: These hobbies involve observing and caring for birds, fishes, and plants. The sections on fishes and birds each contain lists describing the different families as well as several pages of color illustrations. You will learn how to develop your garden as a bird sanctuary or how to create and maintain an artistic and healthy environment in a tropical fish aquarium. The indoor gardening section concentrates on the fine points of growing herbs as well as Cacti and other succulent plants in your home.

COLLECTING HOBBIES: These include stamp collecting and coin collecting, both of which foster an interest in history and geography, as well as rock and shell collecting, which increase your knowledge of natural history. With each of these topics, background information is given initially, and then you are told how to begin a collection, what varieties to look for, where and how to find them, how to judge their quality, and how to care for and display them. Wherever appropriate, valuable information is supplied on buying and selling, as well as on trading with other collectors. Excellent examples of each subject have been chosen for illustrations, the stamps, coins, and rocks in black and white, and the shells in color.

CREATIVE HOBBIES: Drawing, painting, and photography are covered here. They each give you the opportunity to express yourself creatively, and to enhance your awareness of your visual surroundings. In compiling the painting and drawing sections the work of a number of famous art teachers has been drawn upon. Their approach is positive and uninhibited, free of exacting rules, and full of ideas for ways in which you can express yourself fully without worrying about whether this is the proper way to go about doing things. The only rule throughout is: if it pleases you, it is right. While you are encouraged to be yourself, you are also given careful guidance, beginning with a comprehensive description of materials you will need (including advice on how to save money) and easily understood explanations of artistic principles. You then progress to suggestions for some simple projects, and eventually, more sophisticated ones. Particularly useful are the illustrations and diagrams which help clarify the text, including two pages of full color, and several charts that should serve as permanent references. The photography section is written by a well-known teacher and photographer who first introduces the beginner to the workings of the camera, and then explains good working techniques, including instructions on setting up and using a dark room.

OUTDOOR HOBBIES: These include fishing, camping, backpacking, and bike riding, all of which provide much needed exercise and a healthy exposure to the out-of-doors, and are increasing in popularity every day. The emphasis in the biking section is on riding as a group activity. Suggestions are given for starting a biking club, taking tours, and camping out. Information about inexpensive hostels is also included. In the fishing section, you will find, among other things, information on casting for trout and bass with artificial and natural bait, as well as tips on how to locate fish. The camping section includes ideas on making your own tepee and wind shelter, as well as helpful advice on how to avoid danger in the wilds. Each of these sections contains information on the special equipment you need or can make at home, and advice on how to keep it in good repair.

PERFORMING HOBBIES: The last part of the book comprises a variety of hobbies which can be thought of as games and done for amusement, or can be taken quite seriously. The first of these is chess, which can be a demanding intellectual exercise if played well, and can be enjoyed at any age. The next two involve the "psychic" endeavors of analyzing handwriting and telling fortunes with playing cards. Both of these sections are written by experts who explain with diagrams and examples, the methods you can use to interpret the character of your friends and acquaintances. The last section is devoted to magic, ventriloquism, and juggling, entertaining hobbies that give children an opportunity to perform for family and friends and develop a certain skill and discipline at the same time.

You probably have already picked up at least one of these hobbies briefly, and then allowed yourself to lose interest, or under the press of other obligations were not able to spend enough time on it. You probably still have your old fishing tackle, a dusty stamp album, or a perfectly good set of oil paints around the house somewhere. This book is just what you need to inspire you to get them out and put them to use again. The authors have such an enthusiastic approach to their respective subjects and the activities they suggest will be so rewarding that this book is certain to help you sustain your interest for a long period of time.

Each section is written with the hope that you will eventually want to pursue this subject in even greater depth, and for this purpose, the authors in many cases have suggested supplementary reading material which is listed in the bibliography in the back of this book.

Nature
Hobbies

BIRD WATCHING

The birds are certainly among the loveliest and most intriguing of the earth's creatures. In addition to providing aesthetic pleasure with their plumage and song, they serve a *vital* role in maintaining the ecological balance of our environment.

Bird watching can be an outdoor pastime pursued in conjunction with camping, backpacking, horseback riding or canoeing, or an indoor-outdoor pastime pursued from your window. It is something you can do individually, or in the company of family and friends.

You are probably already aware of and at least moderately interested in birds—enough so as to recognize some of the species common to your own garden or vicinity. Hopefully, the information you find here will spark that interest. This section will provide you with helpful suggestions on such things as identifying birds, buying equipment, keeping records, photographing, and attracting birds to your garden, by providing proper water, planting, food, and housing for them.

Like any other hobby, bird watching can be pursued on many levels. You may want to go out hiking in swamplands with binoculars and camera in hand, or you may never venture any further than your own garden. This, however, is one of the few hobbies that can provide you with the opportunity to contribute to scientific knowledge. Information is constantly being collected on the habits of birds, particularly their mysterious migrating habits. Almost any information you collect, or records you keep, would be of interest to scientists or ornithologists working in this area.

One of the greatest joys of bird watching is that it can be done with the whole family. There is such pleasure and even excitement in sitting at the breakfast table together and comparing notes and watching for new species. Children, especially, should be encouraged to take up bird watching, as it increases their interest in their natural surroundings and their understanding of our intricately balanced ecology.

FINDING BIRDS

Bird watching should be a year-round activity. It is true that birds are undoubtedly more active in the spring, but each season of the year presents a different panorama of bird life, and the changes can be marked from month to month. Eventually you will be able to categorize the species you observe as year-round resident, summer resident, or spring or fall migrant.

Some people are fortunate enough to be able to go on daily observation walks, but most have to be content with window observation during the week, and reserve observation walks and field trips for weekends and holidays. Most birds are usually active only a few hours a day, in early morning (from sunrise to about 11:00) and late afternoon or evening. Fortunately for those who are confined to window observation on weekdays, these are the very hours which are most likely to be free from school, office, or daily routine.

Particularly during the summer months when food is readily available, there is very little bird activity except during the morning and evening feeding hours; the birds spend the better part of the day quietly perched in shady places. In winter, when food is scarce, they are likely to spend more hours of the day foraging. Certain species, such as ducks and shorebirds, however, can usually be found at any time of the day, whatever the season.

It is difficult to generalize about the best places to observe birds. Bird watchers are of two kinds, those that are interested in seeing and identifying as many different species as possible and those interested in one special aspect of bird watching, such as nesting, migration, or the activity patterns of one particular species. If it is variety which interests you, the best thing to do is seek out observation spots where two distinct kinds of bird habitats meet, such as a woodland bordering on an open field, or wetlands in the vicinity of the shore. The most general advice that could be given would be to learn the preferred

This section prepared especially for this volume by Mary Farrell, and checked for accuracy by Dr. Helmut E. Adler of the American Museum of Natural History.

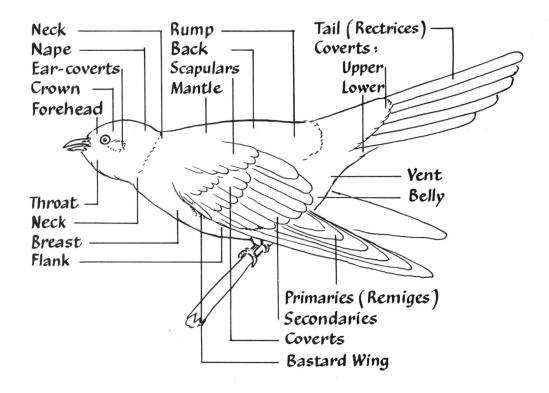

Neck — Nape — Ear-coverts — Crown — Forehead

Rump — Back — Scapulars — Mantle

Tail (Rectrices) — Coverts: Upper — Lower

Vent — Belly

Throat — Neck — Breast — Flank

Primaries (Remiges) — Secondaries — Coverts — Bastard Wing

MAIN PARTS OF A BIRD

habitats of the different species, and you will always have a general idea where to look for those that interest you.

IDENTIFYING BIRDS

A good field guide is an invaluable aid in identifying birds. You may already have one in the house. If not, there are inexpensive, pocket-size ones available in paperback. See the bibliography in the back of this book for a list of recommended bird guides in the United States, England, and Australia.

Many of these guides have color photographs or paintings of birds which provide an excellent means of identification for the bird watcher. Before the advent of color printing, the aspiring bird hobbyist had to learn to identify birds through the study of paintings, colored engravings, stuffed specimens in museums, and species confined in zoos. While all of these sources are still helpful today, the color illustrations in books are certainly more convenient.

In order to identify a bird and its markings and color correctly, you should be certain that the source of light is behind you. If the light is behind the bird, it will, most probably, look completely black. You will find that it is possible to move around until the

light is behind you without frightening the bird if you move slowly and naturally. Many people are under the impression that they must conceal themselves to observe birds successfully, but unless you are watching a nest, this is usually not the case. Birds pay little attention to the motionless bird watcher, and are not ordinarily frightened by slow, natural movements.

If you are observing birds in a group, beware of the over-enthusiastic bird watcher who abruptly points in the direction of a new discovery. Nothing will frighten birds faster than a fast jerky motion. However, they will not react unfavorably to the sound of low conversation. If you want to point something out to a companion, you needn't be afraid to speak in a moderate tone of voice.

BIRD CHARACTERISTICS

These are the characteristics that you should watch for when trying to identify birds.

COLOR: Coloring is not always the best key to identification. Even in the best light, colors can be deceiving. Learn to distinguish carefully between the greys, browns, and olives of the more subtly-shaded species. Note the color of the legs, eyes and bill which will often provide the key to distinguishing one species from another.

MARKINGS: Watch for distinguishing markings such as wing bars, lines on the head, rings around the the eyes, stripes, spots, mottlings.

SIZE: At times you will be able to differentiate between similar species only by noting their comparative sizes. It is difficult to judge the size of a bird unless it is still, and can be measured against an object of known size. The evident size of a bird in flight is often misleading, particularly if it is a small bird with a wide wing spread. For the most part, you needn't worry about mistaking a young bird for one of a smaller species. Birds grow very quickly and most song birds in particular are practically full grown by the time they leave the nest.

SHAPE: After you have observed birds closely for a time, you will begin to notice that species you had always thought quite similar vary greatly in details of shape, in the size and shape of the bill, neck, wings, tail, legs, and feet. It is useful to know that the shape of the bird's body changes with the weather, because the feathers are fluffed out in cold weather to provide warmth, and allowed to lie flat in warm weather. The same bird is often not recognizable in shape from season to season. Some field guides contain very helpful silhouetted drawings of the shapes of different species, when perching and in flight.

HABIT OF MOVEMENT: This is another aspect which you will begin to notice with practice, and which will be a great help to you in differentiating between species. You will note, for example, that birds assume different postures when perching: One will remain completely motionless, another will twitch its tail; one will hop on two feet, while another will walk with one foot after the other. Flying habits of birds differ greatly too. Once you begin to recognize this you will be able to identify a species by watching a flock in flight.

HABITAT: By learning the preferred habitats of the various species, you can, by the process of elimination, narrow down the number of possible species in a given area.

SONGS AND CALLS: You needn't see the bird at all in order to identify it from its distinctive songs and calls. In some cases these will provide a more decisive clue to the bird's identity than the plumage. There are now phonograph records of bird calls available to those who would be interested in using them as study aids. If you own a tape recorder, you may be interested in recording songs and calls yourself. Birds will often answer tape recordings of their own calls.

Dotterel

Lark Sparrow

Rock Sparrow

LINES ON THE HEAD

Solitary Vireo

Kirtland's Warbler

American Robin

RINGS AROUND THE EYES

Golden Crowned Kinglet

Ruby Crowned Kinglet

Acorn Woodpecker

HEAD PATCHES

Bird Characteristics ■ **13**

MARKINGS

Wood Thrush

Rock Thrush

SPOTS

MOTTLINGS

Brown Thrasher

STRIPES

Bearded Tit

WING BARS

Yellow-Throated Vireo

Chaffinch

Rufous Warbler

TAIL PATTERNS

Isabelline Wheatear

Eastern Kingbird

Snow Finch

SHAPE

Wood Ibis

Common Egret

SIZE

Black Vulture

Red-Tailed Hawk

IN FLIGHT

Woodpecker

Tawny Pipit

Sedge Warbler

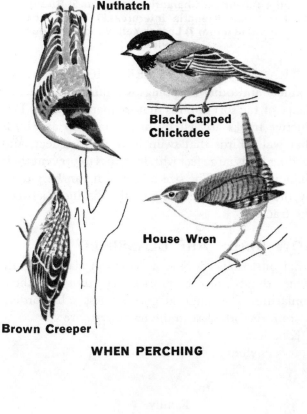

HABIT OF MOVEMENT

White-Breasted Nuthatch

Black-Capped Chickadee

Brown Creeper

House Wren

WHEN PERCHING

ON THE GROUND

Sparrow

Crested Lark

Bird Characteristics ■ 15

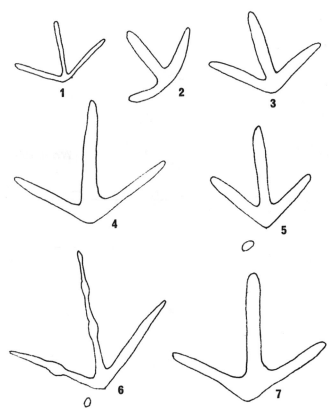

A small selection of shorebird tracks from the extensive records compiled by Charles Anderson Urner of Elizabeth, New Jersey. 1) Least sandpiper *Erolia* *minutilla* 2) Piping Plover *Charadrius* *melodus* 3) Sanderling *Crocethia* *alba* 4) Killdeer *Charadrius* *vociferus* 5) Ruddy Turnstone *Arenaria* *interpres* 6) Woodcock *Philohela* *minor* 7) Lesser Yellowlegs *Totanus* *flavipes*.

TRACKS AND OTHER SIGNS: Tracks, feathers and other droppings will often provide evidence of the sort of birds that frequent an area. Distinctive tracks are left by birds that hop and birds that walk. Birds that swim have webbed feet, and wading birds large feet with long toes to prevent their sinking in mud. The size of the bird can be judged by the length of the feet and the distance between the tracks.

HOW BIRDS ARE CLASSIFIED

Scientists have devised a system of classifying all living things into categories according to their similarities. The major categories in descending order, or from the broadest to the narrowest, are:

Kingdom
   Phylum
      Class
         Order
            Family
               Genus
                  Species

This system of classification serves to clarify the relationship of one species to the other and to place each on the evolutionary tree. It also provides a suitable Latin name by which each species can be identified. In addition to its Latin name, each bird has a popular or common name, but these frequently vary with locality. For this reason, the national ornithological societies generally decide on one name which is to be used in all publications referring to that species.

Birds are classified as follows:

Kingdom—Animalia (as distinguished from plants and one-celled organisms)

Phylum—Chordata (meaning animals with a backbone)

Class—Aves (meaning birds, as distinguished from fish, amphibia, reptiles, and mammals)

The following is a list of *most* of the orders of birds found in the United States, Great Britain, and Australia, and a breakdown of *some* of the bird families within those orders. The purpose of this list is to give you an idea of the geographic distribution of the different bird families and demonstrate how certain birds have developed and retained the same characteristics as they evolved over the centuries. In ornithology, as in other fields of natural science, there are few areas of complete agreement, so this list may not be entirely consistent with other lists.

LOONS (order *Gaviiformes*): This order is limited to one family. Loons are diving birds with large webbed feet, which feed on fish, crustaceans, and some water plants. They are usually seen on or over water, as they only come ashore to breed and nest. The flight of the loon is characterized by rapid wing beats with the head held lower than the body, rather than gliding. Found throughout the world, they are called "divers" in some regions.

GREBES (order *Podicipediformes*): Also limited to one family, grebes comprise another order of diving birds, but are smaller than loons with short legs, tails, and wings, and lobed toes. They feed on small water animals, and are almost always seen on or over water as they nest on floating vegetation. They are found throughout the world.

TUBE-NOSES (order *Procellariiformes*): These birds are so called because they have external tubular nostrils. They are seabirds that come ashore on remote islands and shores only to breed. All have hooked beaks, and feed on marine life. This order includes the shearwater-fulmar family, and the stormy petrel family, both of which are found throughout the world, the diving petrel family found only in the southern hemisphere, and the albatross family found only in the southern hemisphere and north Pacific.

PELICANS AND THEIR ALLIES (order *Pelecaniformes*): These are large aquatic, fish-eating birds with four webbed toes. The order includes the pelican family, found only in tropical and temperate regions, and the cormorant family and the booby-gannet family, both of which are found throughout the world.

HERONS AND THEIR ALLIES (order *Ciconiiformes*): These are wading birds with long necks, legs, and bills. Most feed on aquatic animal life in shallow water, and some have long plumes in breeding season. The order includes the heron-bittern family, the stork-jabirus family, and the ibis-spoonbill family, all three of which are found throughout the world, as well as the flamingo family found only in temperate and tropical regions.

WATERFOWL (order *Anseriformes*): These are aquatic birds with webs between the three front toes. They have long necks and narrow, pointed wings, and most have short legs. They differ from loons and grebes in having flattened bills with tooth-like edges that serve as strainers. This order includes the duck-swan-goose family found throughout the world.

BIRDS OF PREY (order *Falconiformes*): These are flesh-eating birds with heavy, sharp, hooked bills, and toes with strong curved talons used to seize and hold their prey. Scientists characterize them as *diurnal* or daytime birds to distinguish them from the nocturnal birds of prey, such as the owl. The order includes the hawk-Old World vulture-harrier family, the osprey family, and the falcon-caracara family, all three of which are found throughout the world, as well as the New World vulture family found only in the Americas.

GALLINACEOUS BIRDS (order *Galliformes*): These are heavy-bodied, chicken-like land birds, with short, heavy bills and rather long legs. They forage on the ground for seeds and insects, and are more likely to be seen walking or running than flying. They fly with rapid wing-beats and seldom more than a few hundred yards at a time. This order includes the grouse or partridge family and the quail-pheasant-peacock family, both of which are found throughout the world, the megapode family found only in the Australian region and the East Indies, and the turkey family, native to the western hemisphere but introduced into other parts of the world.

CRANES AND THEIR ALLIES (order *Gruiformes*): These are wading birds, with long legs, which vary greatly in size. The order includes the rail-coot-gallinule family which is found throughout the world, the crane family, which is found everywhere but South America, the bustard family and the bustard-quail family found only in the eastern hemisphere, and the collared hemapode family found only in Australia.

SHOREBIRDS, GULLS, AND AUKS (order *Charadriiformes*): This order is comprised of a large and diverse group of birds all of which either swim or wade in water. It includes the oystercatcher family, the snipe-woodcock-sandpiper family, the avocet-stilt family, the skua-jaeger family, and the gull-tern family, all of which are found throughout the world, as well as the skimmer family found in the Americas, southern Asia and Africa, the thick-knee family found everywhere but North America, the phalarope family found everywhere but Australia, and the pratincole-courser family found only in the eastern hemisphere, the painted snipe family found everywhere but North America and Europe, the sheath bill family found only in the southern hemisphere, and the auk-auklet-murre family found only in the northern hemisphere.

SAND GROUSE, PIGEONS AND DOVES (order *Columbiformes*): These are medium-sized, rather heavy birds, which frequently have long tails. The order includes the sand grouse family, which prefers, as its name implies, dry, flat, sandy habitats, and is found only in the eastern hemisphere, and the pigeon-dove family which is found throughout the world.

PARROTS AND THEIR ALLIES (order *Psittaciformes*): These birds are distinguished by a stout, curved, hooked bill, and zygodactyl feet (having toes in pairs, two in front and two behind), and a short square tail. The order includes the lory-parrot-macaw family, which is found only in the tropical and warmer temperate zones of the world.

CUCKOOS AND THEIR ALLIES (order *Cuculiformes*): These are medium-sized, long-tailed birds with pointed wings, some of which leave their eggs to be incubated in the nests of other birds. The order includes the cuckoo-roadrunner-anis family which is found throughout the world.

OWLS (order *Strigiformes*): These are large-headed, short-necked birds of prey, most of which are nocturnal. They have flat, round or heart-shaped faces concealing large external ear flaps. Their large eyes are fixed in their sockets, requiring the bird to move his whole head when looking from side to side. The order includes two families, the first consisting of the barn owl only, and the second made up of all other owls. Both families are found throughout the world.

GOATSUCKERS (order *Caprimulgiformes*): These are nocturnal insect-eaters with large flat heads and small bills. The order includes the owlet-frogmouth family found only in the Australian region, the frogmouth family which ranges from India to Australia, and the goatsucker family, also called the nightjar and nighthawk, found everywhere but the eastern Pacific. (The American whip-poor-will species is included in this family.)

SWIFTS AND HUMMINGBIRDS (order *Apodiformes*): These are birds with short legs, small feet, narrow wings, and long primaries. The order includes the swift family, which is found throughout the world, the crested swift family found from India to New Guinea, and the hummingbird family found only in the Americas.

KINGFISHERS AND THEIR ALLIES (order *Coraciiformes*): This order is comprised of a highly diversified group of very picturesque birds, including the kingfisher family, which is found throughout the world, and the bee eater family, the roller family, and the hoopoe family, all three of which are found only in the eastern hemisphere.

WOODPECKERS, JACAMARS, BARBETS, AND TOUCANS (order *Piciformes*): This is another brightly-colored, diversified group of birds comprising several tropical bird families and the woodpecker–piculet family found everywhere but Madagascar and Australia.

PERCHING BIRDS (order *Passeriformes*): This is the largest order of birds, including more than half the birds in the world. Chiefly songbirds of perching habits, they range in size from the smallest titmouse to the largest raven. Because the birds of this order are so numerous, you will often hear scientists and ornithologists categorize species according to whether or not they belong to this order by referring to them as passerine or non-passerine.

A partial list of the songbird families and the geographic areas in which they are found, follows:

lark family—throughout the world
swallow family—throughout the world
cuckoo shrike family—in the eastern hemisphere only
Old World oriole family—in the eastern hemisphere only
crow-magpie-jay family—throughout the world
bird of paradise–bower bird family—in the Australian region
titmouse family—in Europe, Asia, Africa and North America
nuthatch family—in the northern hemisphere and the Australian region
creeper family—in Europe, Asia, North America and Australia
wren tit family—in the western United States only
babbling thrush family—in the eastern hemisphere only
bulbul family—in the eastern hemisphere only
dipper family—in the northern hemisphere
wren family—throughout the world except Africa and Australia
thrasher–mockingbird family—in the western hemisphere only
thrush family—throughout the world
Old World warbler family—everywhere but the Americas
Old World flycatcher family—in the eastern hemisphere only
accentor–hedge sparrow family—in Europe and northern Asia
wagtail–pipit family—throughout the world
waxwing family—in the northern hemisphere only
wood swallow family—in Africa, India, and the Australian region
shrike family—everywhere except South America
starling–glossy starling family—native to the eastern hemisphere but introduced into North America
honey eater family—in the Australian region
sunbird family—in Africa, Asia, and the Australian region
flowerpecker family—in Africa, Indo-Malaya, and the Australian region
white-eye family—in Africa, southern Asia and the Australian region
vireo family—in the western hemisphere only
wood warbler family—in the western hemisphere only
weaver finch family—in Africa, Europe, Asia, and Australia (one form, the English sparrow introduced into America)
blackbird–troupial family—in the western hemisphere only
tanager family—in the western hemisphere only
grosbeak–finch–bunting family—everywhere but Australia

The families mentioned here are then further divided into genus, species, and even subspecies. For the most part you will not want to concern yourself with anything but the identification of the species by their common name as they appear in the field guides of your county. Other categories are important only to the ornithologist. The details that distinguish subspecies, for example, are so minor that most bird watchers ignore them.

An Eared Grebe _Podiceps nigricollas_ (right) nesting in the Lower Souris National Wildlife Refuge in North Dakota; a Red-footed Booby _Sula sula_ (above) photographed on Nidoa in the Hawaiian Islands, and Double-crested Cormorants _Phalacrocorax auritus_ (below) on Gallingal Island, British Columbia. Grebes, diving birds with partially-webbed feet and lobed toes, make up the order _Podicipediformes_. The booby and the cormorant are both _Pelecaniformes_, an order of fish-eating, rather large birds, possessing webbed feet with four toes, the most familiar of which is the pelican.

Black-necked Storks <u>Xenorhynchus</u> <u>asiaticus</u> (upper left) and Royal or Black-billed Spoonbills <u>Platalea</u> <u>regia</u> (bottom right), all photographed in Australia; a Great Blue Heron <u>Ardea</u> <u>herodias</u> (lower left) at the Great Bear National Wildlife Refuge, Utah; and a brood of young herons (upper right). All these birds are <u>Ciconiiformes</u>, an order comprised of rather large birds which have long legs and bills, and feed on fish and/or other animal prey.

Canada Geese <u>Branta</u> <u>canadensis</u> (above) photographed in Michigan; a Mallard <u>Anas</u> <u>platyrhynchos</u> (right) and young nesting in a tree at Little Scioto River, Ohio; and Snow Geese <u>Anser</u> <u>coerulescens</u> (below) at the Sacramento National Wildlife Refuge, California. These three species all belong to the order <u>Anseriformes</u>, the members of which all lay unspotted eggs, have young covered with a thick down, and have three webbed front toes and a fourth small hind toe.

Immature Goshawks <u>Accipiter</u> <u>gentilis</u> in Michigan. Like most of the other birds that belong to the order <u>Falconiformes</u>, Goshawks are hunters of live prey, and have the curved, pointed bills and strong, gripping feet clawed with talons that are characteristic of the order. These birds are grey with white markings and piercing yellow eyes. They grow to a length of 19 to 23 inches, and are capable of killing another bird as large as a pheasant. Because they are such stealthy and ferocious hunters, particularly well-suited to shrub and woodland areas, they have traditionally been used in the sport of "hawking" or falconry.

A Sharp-tailed Grouse <u>Pedioecetes phasianellus</u> (left) photographed at Two Ocean Lake, Wyoming; and a White-tailed Ptarmigan <u>Lagopus leucurus</u> (right) in Colorado. Both birds belong to the family <u>Tetraonidae</u> in the order <u>Galliformes</u>, made up of chicken-like birds, generally of medium size, sometimes referred to as game birds. They are, for the most part, ground-feeding birds, but some are partly arboreal or of tree-dwelling habits. The White-tailed Ptarmigan is found on the mountain tundras of Western North America. Like other birds of this family, they acquire the protective coloration of their surroundings. During the winter they turn snow white, and develop "snow shoes," a thick mat of feathers on the toes.

Whooping Cranes <u>Grus</u> <u>americana</u> at the Aransas National Wildlife Refuge, Texas. The crane belongs to the order <u>Gruiformes</u> made up of essentially ground-living birds. Most of the families in this order live in marshes and grasslands or other areas near water. As these wetland habitats disappear, so do the creatures that inhabit them. The Whooping Crane is presently considered an endangered species.

Kittiwakes <u>Larus</u> ("<u>Rissa</u>") <u>tridactylus</u> (left) nesting at the Ardiguen Rookery in Alaska; a California Gull <u>Larus</u> <u>californicus</u> with young on a nesting island in Tule Lake National Wildlife Refuge, California; Horned Puffins <u>Fratercula</u> <u>arctica</u> (above) on St. Paul Island, Alaska. All these birds, as well as those illustrated on the next three pages, are <u>Charadriiformes</u>, a large and diverse order, the members of which are often referred to as "shorebirds" or "waders." They are ground-living birds, most of which are found in the vicinity of water.

Common Murres <u>Uria</u> <u>aalge</u> on the cliffs of Bogoslof Island, Alaska. Hovering above are gulls waiting to prey on eggs and baby birds. Murres, like the puffins pictured on the opposite page, belong to the <u>Alcidae</u> or Auk family in the order <u>Charadriiformes</u>. Auks are stocky, short-legged, wing-propelled, diving birds with three webbed toes, a vestigial first toe, and bills that vary greatly in form. Generally found in the colder parts of northern oceans, these birds feed on fish and crustaceans which they pursue while entirely submerged, using their wings to propel them and their feet to steer.

A black tern Sterna ("Chlidonias") nigra (left) nesting with young and an American Woodcock Philohela minor (above), both photographed in the state of Michigan; a Long-tailed Jaeger Stercorarius longicaudus (below) at Hooper Bay, Alaska. Each represents a different family of the Charadriiformes, the Laridae, the Scolopacidae, and Stercorariidae families respectively.

Purple Sandpipers <u>Calidris</u> <u>maritima</u> along the shore at False Pass, Alaska; a Killdeer <u>Charadrius</u> <u>vociferus</u> (below) and a Black-necked Stilt <u>Himantopus</u> <u>mexi-canus</u> (below) both photographed at the Bear River National Wildlife Refuge in Utah. All three species are <u>Charadriiformes</u>, the sandpiper belonging, like the woodcock pictured on the opposite page, to the <u>Scolopacidae</u> family, and the killdeer and the stilt belonging to the <u>Charadriidae</u> and the <u>Recurviro-stridae</u> families respectively.

A Black Swift **Cypseloides niger** (left) of the order **Apodiformes** photographed in Victoria, Canada; and Kookaburras (also called Laughing Jackasses) **Dacelo novaequineae** ("**gigas**") (above) of the order **Caraciiformes**—photographed in Australia.

Spotted Owl **Strix occidentalis** watching its nest, photographed in the vicinity of San Mateo, California. Owls belong to the order **Strigiformes**, nocturnal birds of prey, easily recognized by their disc-like face, large eyes, and hooked bill. Owls seldom, if ever, build their own nests, but move into holes in trees or rocks, or nests deserted by other birds. The Spotted Owl is distinguished from others by the horizontal bars on its underparts.

Swainson's Warblers Limnothlypis swainsonii (above) photographed in Duval County, Florida; White-necked Raven Corvus cryptoleucus (below) perched on a fence post in Spur, Texas; a Tree Swallow Iridoprocne bicolor at the Lower Souris Wildlife Refuge in North Dakota. These three species, as well as all those illustrated on the next three pages, belong to the order Passeriformes, perching and singing birds with feet having four toes well-adapted to gripping. This order includes more than half the birds in the world. The warbler shown here is of the family Parulidae, the New World warbler family having nine primaries, which is to be distinguished from the Old World warbler family, Muscicapidae, having ten primaries.

A female Rufus-sided Towhee **Pipilo erythrophthalmus** (top left) incubating her eggs—photographed in the vicinity of Buffalo, New York; Song Sparrow **Melospiza melodia** (bottom left) nesting in debris on the shore of Lobstick Island, Alberta, Canada; and a House Wren **Troglodytes aedon** (below) entering its nest with food—photographed in Marshalltown, Iowa. All the species illustrated here are **Passeriformes**. The towhee and the sparrow belong to the family **Emberizidae** which includes the buntings of the Old World. The wren belongs to **Troglodytidae** family which comprises about sixty different species.

A Cedar Waxwing <u>Bombycilla</u> <u>cedrorum</u> (right) with young at Douglas Lake, Michigan (note the banded leg of the adult); and a Loggerhead Shrike <u>Lanius</u> <u>ludovicianus</u> (below) photographed in Iowa watching over its nest. Both species are <u>Passeriformes</u>. Waxwings are handsome crested birds belonging to the family <u>Bombycillidae</u>. They are considered to be quite tame and even a little peaceful, as they will defend no territory other than their own nest. Fruits, berries, and, occasionally, insects make up their diet. Shrikes, on the other hand, are highly aggressive, essentially carnivorous birds belonging to the family <u>Laniidae</u>. Some eat only insects, others prey on small birds, mammals, and reptiles. Because of their habit of impaling their victims on thorn trees or barbed wire before eating them, they are called "Butcher Birds" in England.

An abstract pattern created by great numbers of Starlings _Sturnus_ _vulgaris_ roosting in trees in Washington D.C. _Passeriformes_ of the family _Sturnidae_, these birds are native to the Old World but have been unwisely introduced into other parts of the world where they have often become agricultural pests and have driven off other more desirable native birds. Starlings tend to gather and move in great masses, covering the surrounding trees or roosting in every available nook on the facades of city buildings.

BUYING BINOCULARS

Bird watching requires very little in the way of equipment, as compared with many other hobbies. The most worthwhile investment the prospective bird watcher could make would be a good pair of binoculars. The sizes recommended as most practical for observing birds are the 6x30 and the 7x35 binoculars. The first figure indicates the magnifying power of the glasses, the second figure indicates the size of the objective or front lens. For example, a six power (6x) glass is one that magnifies an object six times, or brings it six times closer. In other words, if a bird were 600 feet away, it would seem to be only 100 feet away when viewed through the glasses.

The figure 30 gives, in millimeters, the diameter of the objective lens. This measurement is important because it determines the amount of light the glass is able to collect. For birdwatching purposes, the diameter of the objective lens should be five times the magnifying power of the glass, hence, 6x30 and 7x35.

Don't jump to the conclusion, as some beginners do, that the magnifying power of the glass is most important, and as a result invest in 10- or 12-power glasses. The greater the magnifying power of the glasses, the more difficult it is to hold them steady, and the more bulky and cumbersome they are to handle. The light-gathering capacity of the glasses is particularly important to the bird watcher, as the best time to observe birds is early morning or late evening when the light is apt to be poor.

"Field" and *"central focussing"* are two other important factors to take into consideration when buying binoculars. If the manufacturer gives the *field of view* as 150 yards at 1,000 yards, this means that when viewing an object at a distance of 1,000 yards,

you will have a field of view 150 yards wide. For purposes of bird study you are interested in obtaining glasses with the widest possible field of view, in order to enable you to do such things as pick up a flock of birds in flight and follow it. This would be difficult to do with glasses having a narrow field of view or individual focussing.

With individual focussing, each lens has to be focussed separately. Binoculars of this type are frequently less expensive, but are at the same time a little impractical for the bird watcher who must be able to focus quickly, frequently on a moving object.

One last word of advice. You may see advertisements for surprisingly inexpensive "field glasses." These are, for the most part, of very little value. Their magnifying power is seldom more than 4x, and their light-gathering power is very poor. When you look into them you will see two images side by side rather than the single image you would see with binoculars.

RECORD KEEPING

Keeping records of your observations can be the most rewarding aspect of bird watching. You can begin by keeping a notebook handy in which you can jot down notes and sketches that will aid you in remembering identifying characteristics such as the coloring, markings, and habits of the birds you observe. You can also use this notebook to record your phonetic impressions of bird calls, such as "hoo hoo" for the horned owl's call or "see tow hee" for the towhee's call.

When you have enough confidence in your ability to identify species correctly, you can start keeping observation records of the number and kinds of species observed and their location and behavior. As these records accumulate over a period of years and patterns develop, they become increasingly interesting and useful.

There are several ways to set up and maintain these records. Some birdwatching societies provide pre-printed check lists of birds in a given area as well as more elaborate record-keeping systems of pre-printed filing cards.

If you prefer to devise your own method of record keeping, you might try a variation on the following. List all the species common to your area in the left-hand margin of a notebook and then rule off the rest of the page with vertical lines one half inch or so apart. Across the top line you can enter the dates you made your observations and then check off or indicate the quantity of each species you observed that day, or enter a code for the activities observed,

such as "nb" for nest building, "s" for singing, or "n4e" to mean nest with four eggs.

If you are interested in accumulating data in specialized areas, you may want to conduct migration studies, nesting studies and surveys, or a life-history study of a particular species, or you may want to get involved in a bird banding project. All these activities will require specialized forms of record keeping. The important thing to keep in mind when devising a system is that it should be consistent and easily interpreted.

If you are consistent and conscientious in collecting data, you will get a great deal of satisfaction out of analyzing the results and sharing the information with fellow bird-watching enthusiasts, ornithological publications, and the scientific world. Because of the important rôle that birds play in maintaining a balanced environment, such information is invaluable to scientists working in the field of ecology.

BIRD PHOTOGRAPHY

You can also create a visual record of your bird experiences with a camera. Bird photography requires a certain amount of skill and patience as well as some special equipment, but it can be an excellent means of improving your expertise in two fields at the same time.

If you would like to explore this possibility, but have little or no knowledge of photography, read over the section on photography as a hobby in this book for a start. Since bird photography is such a growing field of interest you will find books as well as numerous articles advising you on appropriate camera equipment, black-and-white and color films, and the best camera settings (aperture opening and shutter speed) for this type of photography.

Whatever your make of camera or your choice of film, you *will* need a tripod and a telephoto lens.

PHOTOGRAPHING NESTS: Birds are particularly protective when nesting. It was necessary to use a blind to photograph this Australian caterpillar-eater (Edoliosoma tenuirostre) feeding its young.

A flash attachment is also helpful because so much bird photography is done in subdued light.

Your object when taking most bird pictures will be to get as close as possible to the bird without disturbing it. To do so you will either have to set up your camera within close range of the subject and trigger the shutter by remote control from a concealed place, or set up a bird blind or observation hide-out near the subject in which you can conceal both yourself and the camera. Most bird photographers prefer the latter method as it allows them to control the focus and composition of the photograph, which they would not be able to do if they were shooting by remote control.

Portable and easily assembled bird blinds can be purchased, but such an investment is not recommended for the beginner as perfectly serviceable blinds can be made at home. You can carefully construct one by covering a frame made of aluminum poles or wood with a fabric such as canvas or muslin, or you can quickly improvise one by throwing some burlap or other material over a beach or lawn umbrella which has been driven into the ground. However the blind is constructed, if the fabric is not secured tightly and is allowed to flap in the breeze, its movement will frighten the birds away.

CREATING A BIRD SANCTUARY

As each year passes, more wetlands, woodlands and wilderness areas are claimed by man—built upon or destroyed by industry—and the natural resources upon which birds depend diminish. If you, personally, work toward creating a place of sanctuary for birds in your own back yard or garden or somewhere in your community, you will be helping to counteract this destructive trend.

The ideal sort of bird sanctuary would be one that provided sufficient food, water and shelter by natural means. Birds will eat food provided in trays and live in man-made shelters, but as wild creatures, they would naturally prefer to feed on wild fruits, seeds, and insects, and nest in trees, shrubs, or open fields. If you are interested in developing your own garden as a wildlife sanctuary, you should set out plantings with this in mind. A few trees and shrubs that provide natural food for birds are dogwood, elderberry, wild rose, blueberry, blackberry, raspberry, and holly. Those that provide excellent cover include evergreens, such as hemlock, cedar, spruce, and yew, as well as rambling roses. These are only a few suggestions which may or may not not be appropriate to the area in which you live. Your local or national bird-watching association would be happy to provide you with a similar list of trees and shrubs adaptable to the climate of your area.

NATURAL FOOD AND SHELTER: A Pied Woodpecker (Dendrocopos macei) feeding on a nut which it has wedged into the crevice of a tree.

A good bird sanctuary should have a source of water. If there is no natural source, such as a brook or a pond, in your garden, you can contrive any number of different kinds of bird baths. It needn't be any more complicated than the top of a trash can placed on a post to catch the rain. But if you are feeling industrious and creative, you may want to design a more elaborate bird bath, possibly even one with running water or a fountain. You can, in any case, always find the conventional pedestal bird bath at a garden shop. When installing a bird bath, it is a good idea to place a large stone or some other device in the water to enable the birds to perch on something while they drink or bathe. The bath should be situated near trees or shrubs to which the birds can resort quickly if threatened by danger, as it is difficult for them to fly too fast or too far when they are wet.

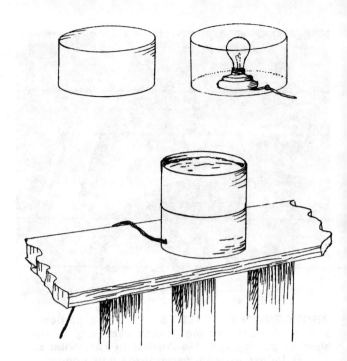

ANTI-FREEZE BIRD BATH: This simple warmer, made with two coffee tins, is one way to provide water for the birds that visit your garden during the freezing winter months.

BIRD BATHS

If you live in an area with freezing winter temperatures, you should remember to provide water for the birds during the cold months. One way of doing this would be to create an anti-freeze bird bath. You can make one quite easily with an electrical socket on a cord, a 40-watt bulb, and two shallow 1-pound coffee cans. Punch a hole in the side of one of the cans, put a bulb in the socket, and place it in the can with the cord extending out the hole in the side. Fill the other coffee can with water and tape it to the top of the first one, as illustrated. The finished bird bath will then have to be placed in a spot within reach of an electrical outlet, such as a window or a porch.

During the late autumn and winter, when many of the natural sources of food are scarce, you can attract great numbers of birds to your garden by maintaining well stocked bird feeders. However, once you start winter feeding, and the birds learn to rely on you, be consistent and don't neglect them.

Birds that visit your garden during winter months generally fall into two categories, seed-eaters and insect-eaters. You can provide mixed seed, such as hemp, millet, kaffir corn, cracked corn, and sunflower seed for the seed-eaters, and suet for the insect-eaters. In addition, there will be some birds that will appreciate fruits such as raisins, currants, bayberries, and small pieces of apple and banana, as well as bread crumbs, doughnuts, and cold cereal. Like the bird bath, the feeder should also be placed near protective cover, as some birds won't venture into an open area to feed.

A great many kinds of bird feeders are available for purchase, but if you like doing things with your hands, you may prefer to make your own. Some very simple varieties are illustrated here, but if you feel inclined to make something more elaborate, several books and brochures are available through bird associations and libraries which will provide you with ideas and instructions for bird feeders and for bird houses as well.

If not enough natural nesting places exist in your garden, you may want to provide bird houses. It will

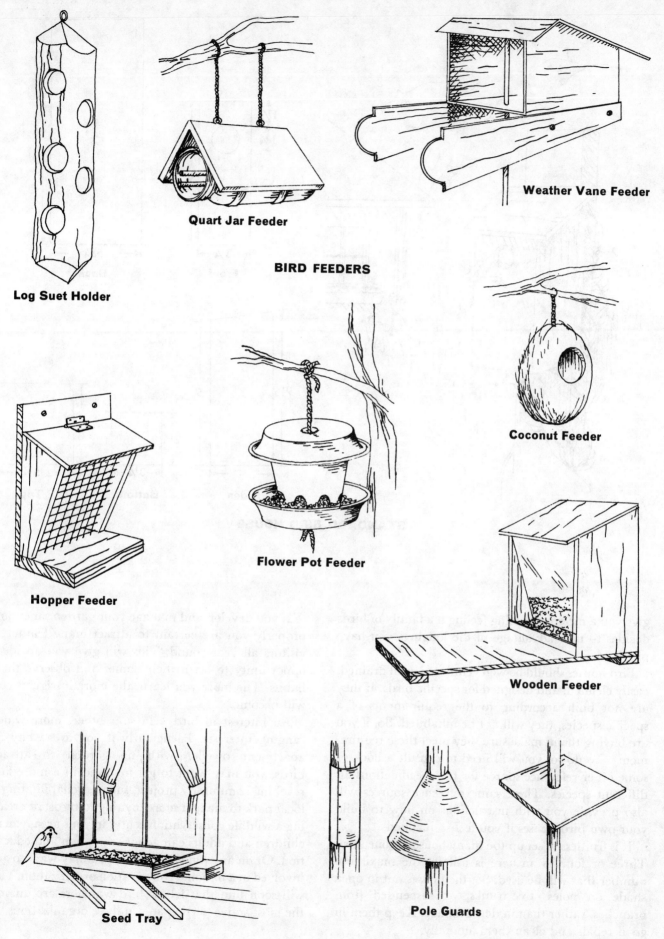

Log Suet Holder

Quart Jar Feeder

Weather Vane Feeder

BIRD FEEDERS

Coconut Feeder

Hopper Feeder

Flower Pot Feeder

Wooden Feeder

Seed Tray

Pole Guards

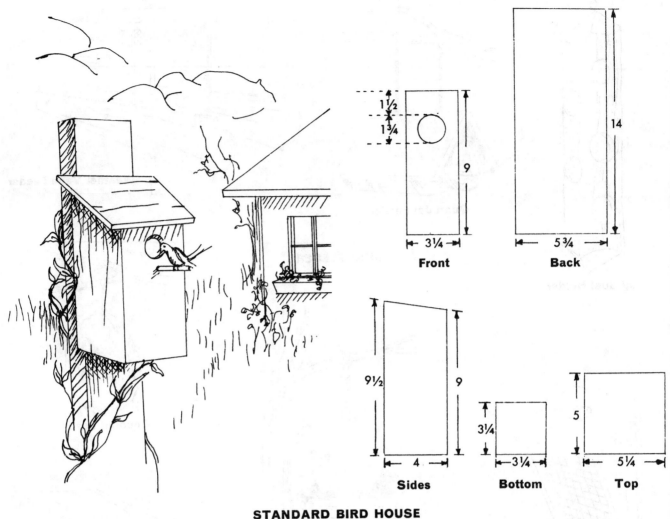

STANDARD BIRD HOUSE

give you a nice patronizing feeling if a family of birds decides to take advantage of the lodgings you have provided.

Bird houses should be well ventilated, well drained, easily cleaned, and designed for specific birds. If they are not built according to the requirements of a specific species, they will not be inhabited. So, if you are buying them, make sure they meet these requirements. To do so, you will need to consult a book or some other reference source for the specifications for different species. These same reference sources will also provide you with instructions on how to build your own bird houses if you feel so inclined.

It is fruitless to set up too many houses in one area. Three or four to an acre is usually the maximum number that will be used. Set the houses out in open shade on poles, tree trunks, or suspended from branches, rather than in dense foliage. Keep them in good repair and clean them annually.

If you develop and manage your garden sanctuary properly you are certain to attract many feathered visitors all year round. This will give you an ideal opportunity to learn their names and observe their habits. The more you learn, the more intrigued you will become.

An interest in birds can spur other, more wide-ranging interests. Particularly if you are a city or apartment dweller with no garden to attract birds, you may want to get involved in a more far-reaching community project, such as rehabilitating a local park to make it more inviting to birds, or creating a wildlife conservation center in your area, where children and adults can go for recreation and education. Or on an even wider scale, you may want to get involved in a national conservation organization. You will soon find that fellow bird watchers are among the most active participants in these organizations.

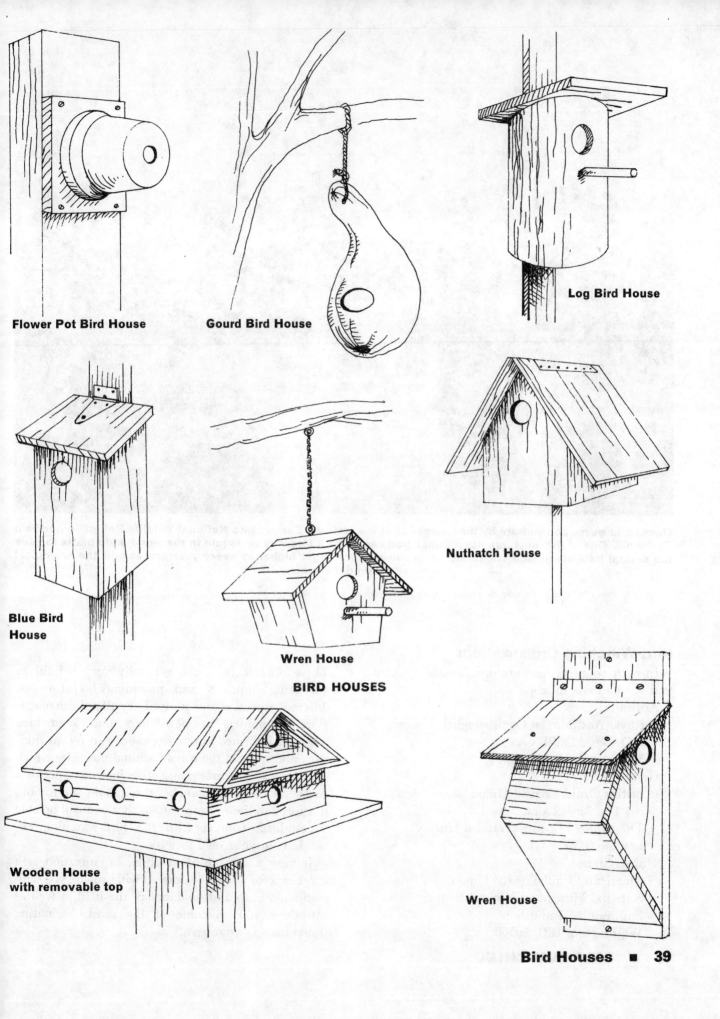

Flower Pot Bird House

Gourd Bird House

Log Bird House

Blue Bird House

Wren House

Nuthatch House

BIRD HOUSES

Wooden House with removable top

Wren House

Ducks and geese concentrate by the thousands at the restored Sacramento National Wildlife Refuge in northern California. One of the most important things you can do as a birdwatcher is join in the world-wide battle to save the natural habitats of wild creatures. Stakes in this battle get higher as every year passes and the ecological situation deteriorates.

Bird-Watching Organizations

In each country there are ornithological societies that are national in scope.

Australia:
   Royal Australasian Ornithologists' Union
   P.O. Box 5236BB
   Melbourne, Victoria 3001
Great Britain:
   British Ornithologists' Union
   c/o The Bird Room
   The British Museum (Natural History)
   London SW7
United States:
   American Ornithologists' Union
   National Museum of Natural History
   Smithsonian Institution
   Washington, D.C. 20560

These organizations are generally very helpful in answering inquiries and providing literature on different aspects of bird study. They all publish magazines, pamphlets or newsletters that keep bird watchers informed of current issues and recent findings, and most of them hold annual meetings which are open to all members and other interested persons. As they have local branches throughout the nation, it is through these organizations that you will be able to establish contact with the bird-watching enthusiasts in your own locality.

Joining a local bird-watching organization is a good idea for several reasons. It will provide you with companionship and guidance in the field as well as introduce you to some of the most fascinating individuals in your area.

RAISING TROPICAL FISH

A LIVING PICTURE

Beautiful jewels of color and motion, graceful courtship amidst rich green plants, fascinating habits and exotic personalities—all in a single aquarium. That is reason enough for some 20 million people in America to maintain tropical fishes in their homes, but there are other reasons, too.

Doctors and dentists have long known the value of having an aquarium in their waiting rooms. It helps relax their patients and soothes their nerves. Some psychologists even prescribe the hobby for nervous people, or for those whose ailments require them to take long rests. Patients with eye trouble who must exercise their eye muscles have often been given an aquarium with some very active fishes, such as the Danio species, to watch. This has been found much less tedious and boring than long series of eye exercises, and has in most cases given better results.

The aquarium hobby is also a fascinating and simple approach to teaching natural history to children. Parents, instead of using the "birds and bees" lecture, which they often do not tell easily, can present the so-called "facts of life" in a natural and even fascinating manner by letting the children have an aquarium and a few pairs of inexpensive and colorful live-bearer fishes. More often than not, the parents too are ensnared by the charm of the fishes.

It is the purpose of this section to introduce you to the tropical fish aquarium, its inhabitants, its plants, and to the easy way in which it can be maintained.

SOME FALLACIES

There are many mistaken notions about aquarium keeping. Let us take up the prevalent ones, and see if there is any truth to them.

Fallacy Number One:

First of all, there is the fellow who looks at a large aquarium and says:

"What a lot of mess and bother it must be to change all that water!"

Well, if you had to, it would be. However, a properly kept aquarium need *never* be changed. True, there is a certain amount of evaporation which has to be compensated for now and then by adding fresh water. Naturally, if you wish to move the aquarium from one place to another, you must remove most of the water. If this is done, it is best to save the water that was taken out and put it back after moving. Changing water is done only in extreme cases: if the water has become fouled or is laden with disease bacteria, but generally not otherwise.

Fallacy Number Two:

"I wouldn't want one of those smelly tanks in my house!"

If they were smelly, no one would want them. An aquarium which gives off an unpleasant odor has something very much wrong with it—the result is that the water becomes foul. This may be due to a number of things, but about 90 percent of the time the fault lies with the misplaced generosity of the Lady (or Lord) Bountiful who dispenses the good things to eat. A fish can go a long time without being fed. Overfeeding to the extent that there is uneaten food left is a practice which is sure to bring on disaster, and quickly, too.

Fallacy Number Three:

"Aren't they beautiful! I'll bet they're awfully expensive!"

Wrong again! If they were expensive, would so many people be able to afford them? Almost any

Condensed from the book "Tropical Fish in Your Home" by Herbert R. Axelrod and William Vorderwinkler © 1956 by Sterling Publishing Co., Inc., New York

popular aquarium fishes can be bought for less than the cost of a lamb chop. Some cost considerably less. True, there are a few rare species which represent a much bigger outlay, but these are the less attractive fishes. Here's how it works: a beautiful species of fish which is easy to breed is bound to be kept and bred by a great many people; the brisk demand for this beautiful fish is also the green light for the hatcheries to produce the species in large quantities. Suddenly this fish, beautiful as it is, becomes so commonplace that it is no longer a novelty, the demand lessens rapidly, and the price becomes ridiculously low.

The Neon Tetra, before people found out how to breed it, was a very expensive item imported from far up the Amazon. This little beauty, easily the most brightly colored of all aquarium fishes, is now bred extensively and the price is as low as for almost any species. Like all collectors' items, aquarium fishes are more apt to be priced according to their rarity rather than their beauty.

Fallacy Number Four:

"You can't keep those things! I had a friend who had a lot of fish and they died one after the other!"

This man's friend probably didn't believe in taking advice, either from a book or from someone who could tell him what he was doing wrong. You don't have to be a trained biologist, ichthyologist or any other sort of "-ologist" to maintain an aquarium successfully, and even be able to breed and raise most of the fishes available today. All you need is to

follow a few common-sense rules, and your chances of success are almost certain. The thrill of seeing your fishes propagate under conditions which you provided is a never-ending source of satisfaction, one which never palls.

There are other fallacies which you may hear about aquarium keeping. Some of these might be hangovers from the days when the aquarist had much less equipment to work with, and when the equipment he had was much less dependable and more expensive. The fact still remains that the fish hobbyist has much more fun per dollar than any other hobbyist you could name. Many aquarists make enough profit on the surplus stock of fishes they raise to offset all expenses. How many people have a hobby which pays for itself?

SETTING UP THE AQUARIUM

The kind of aquarium you should be concerned with is the show tank. This is an aquarium in which effort is made to create a beautiful background for beautiful fishes. The fishes are selected for their colors or other interesting characteristics, and the aquarium is to show them off to the utmost.

If several species of fishes (used plural, "fishes" refers to two or more varieties; if many of one variety, the word is "fish," plural) are grouped, this becomes what is known as a "community aquarium." There are some fussy people who insist that, in order to conform with a true natural setting, you should confine your tank to fishes which are native to the same area. This gives you a rather narrow scope, however, and you can generally put together fishes from all corners of the globe, as long as they get along with each other.

There are some fishes whose beauty or interesting characteristics make them desirable in spite of their somewhat disagreeable habits when placed with strangers. These should be kept in separate tanks, if your interest in them is great enough to warrant keeping them at all.

UTILITY AQUARIA

There are special tanks also which are set up with a utilitarian purpose in mind. For instance, if you want to be sure you are not contaminating your aquarium with disease when new fishes are purchased, set up a "quarantine tank." Here keep new purchases for a week or so. If the fishes remain healthy, then consider them safe to join the others.

Then there is the so-called "hospital tank" where fishes which contract disease are put in an effort to cure them.

Another type of aquarium is the "breeding tank." Here you set up conditions which will permit your fishes either to give birth to their young or to lay their eggs in the manner to which they are accustomed. Sometimes this breeding tank is not large enough to accommodate the youngsters when they begin to grow; they are then placed in a "raising tank."

The proper way to set up these utility aquaria varies, and will be taken up later.

PLACING AND LIGHTING THE SHOW TANK

In the first place, you must consider location. The ideal way to see a fish in all its colors is to have the sunlight shining on the tank from behind the observer. If it is at all possible to place your aquarium in such a location, and if the light is not too strong, you have perfection. Some of the color which you see when you look at a fish is refracted or bounced back; if the light is in a position where it will not bounce back, these delicate shades are lost. Remember, a diamond looks like a piece of glass unless it is held so that you can see its refracted colors.

Lighting the aquarium at night presents less of a problem. There are reflectors made to fit across the front of the aquarium, which come equipped with either incandescent or fluorescent lights. The incandescent lights are very satisfactory. Avoid getting the so-called "daylight" blue-tinted tubes if you purchase a fluorescent fixture, as this gives a cold light which washes out many of the attractive blues and yellows in the fishes. There is a fluorescent tube

known as "warm white" which will give a much better result.

Another thing you must check before filling the aquarium is whether or not it is standing level. The pressure is unevenly divided in a tilted aquarium, and leaks can be the result.

If you have a good, solid table for your aquarium, fine and dandy; if you decide to get yourself an aquarium of large capacity, say 15 or 20 gallons (10 gallons is the usual beginner's size), you will probably want to get a matching stand, which fits the bottom of the aquarium perfectly, and provides a good, solid foundation. A stand usually has the added feature of having a shelf underneath, where another aquarium may be added, if desired.

SHAPE OF THE TANK

There are torture chambers which come under the heading of "fish-bowls." Many thousands of these are still in use, many of them with goldfish in them, gasping at the surface for air. A bowl which bulges at the sides gives a smaller surface at the top than at the widest point, and is a trap for carbon dioxide gas. A fish breathes oxygen and gives off carbon dioxide, just as humans do, and when there is an oversupply of carbon dioxide, the fish is in trouble. Oxygen is absorbed by the water at the surface, but when the surface is small, the oxygen content of the water is greatly reduced.

The most sensible aquarium is a rectangular, metal-framed receptacle. This provides a water surface which is exactly even from top to bottom, and there are no curved glass surfaces to distort the shape of the fishes. You may be tempted to purchase an aquarium at a "bargain" price. This will get you an aquarium with a frame of thin, galvanized iron which has been painted; it may also have a weak, possibly flawed slate bottom. A tank like this may give satisfactory service for years, but sooner or later the paint will scratch off and give way to ugly rusty spots. A slightly higher outlay will give you a tank which has a stainless steel frame, a heavier slate bottom and better glass. Don't forget, you are buying something which will give you pleasure for many years.

GRAVEL FOR THE TANK

Now your aquarium is ready to be filled. Your first concern is to provide gravel as an anchor for the plants which you intend to use. A happy medium is called for here. If you use gravel which is too fine, the plant roots will have trouble pushing their way through it. On the other hand, if you use coarse

GRAVEL: When setting up your aquarium, choose a medium-sized gravel (above). If the grain is too fine, the plants will not root properly; if too coarse, uneaten food particles will not decay. After the gravel has been washed in a clean pail, pour it into an unfilled aquarium (right) so you can mold it without stirring up the debris in the water.

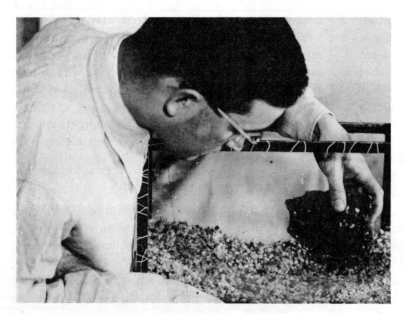

SETTING IN THE ROCKS: Do not use rocks of a limestone nature in the aquarium. Rocks of a basaltic nature, or non-metallic rocks such as sandstone or granite, may be used safely. They should be set in after the gravel has been molded.

gravel, fish detritus and uneaten food will settle down through it resulting in foulness. A medium gravel, with grains about the size of the small "o" in this print, is about right.

Take enough of this gravel to cover an even inch of bottom, and pour it into a dishpan or a bucket. Set it where the receptacle can overflow and turn on your hose or faucet just enough so that you can push the nozzle or stream of water around in the gravel and loosen the dust-fine particles enough to overflow with the water. When the water comes clean, your washing chore is done. Pour the wet gravel into the aquarium, pushing it back from the front center so that it is deeper at the sides and back. There is a double reason for this: it will allow deeper rooting for the plants which you will put in later, and secondly, all the trash will gather at the front, where it can be seen easily and removed by siphoning. When pouring water in, place a sheet of white paper over the gravel and pour the water gently into a cup on the bottom, letting it overflow onto the paper, so as not to disturb the gravel. Then remove the paper.

DECORATING THE TANK

Decorating is a matter of taste. In the old days, it was fashionable to put a lot of marbles, small castles, porcelain mermaids, and the like, into an aquarium. We still see many with decorations—divers, sunken ships, treasure chests—on the bottom. However, most aquarists prefer to landscape or "aquascape" their tanks by creating a natural setting with rocks and plants.

You have a large selection of plants from all parts of the world to work with. A living picture can be created which equals any underwater scene in beauty. Of course, here again the purists might disapprove if the plants in one aquarium come from widely varied places. You can still create a lovely picture and limit your plants to those from certain areas, as well as fishes from the same areas.

Where rocks are concerned, there are a few words of warning which must be heeded. A rock should not add anything to the water. Therefore those which contain minerals or those which are of a limestone nature will make the water very alkaline and are definitely "out." Rocks of a basaltic nature, or non-metallic rocks such as sandstone or granite, may be used safely. Here is a chance to give scope to your artistic ability by creating a background, using the rocks to set off the plants.

PLANTS AND "AGED" WATER

Your aim in setting up your aquarium is to try to imitate the natural surroundings of the fish you are keeping for pets.

In general, use the taller plants in back, and the shorter ones in the foreground, leaving an open space where the fish can show themselves.

Plant your aquarium when it is about one-quarter full of water. (If you already have your tank set up, remove some of the water and keep it in a container to add back later.) Push your rooted plants down so that the roots are well spread in the gravel and all buried. The unrooted plants should have the cut ends buried about one half inch in the gravel, where they will soon anchor themselves. Once the planting is done, add back the "aged" water by pouring it gently into an old saucer or cup standing in the open part of the aquarium. This will deflect the wash of

A NATURAL SETTING: It was at one time the fashion to decorate aquariums with marble castles, mermaids, and such things, but the natural setting seems to be preferred by most today. Depending upon how much of a purist you are, you can create an underwater environment similar to the native surrounding of a particular group of fish, or you can mix together species of plants and fishes from all over the world.

the water upward instead of washing out the roots you have just buried and spoiling all your work.

Don't ever shock your tropical plants by using cold water! Temper it to about room temperature before pouring it in. Never add fresh water! It must always be "aged." Water is too fresh if used out of the tap and will give you trouble, especially if it is chlorinated for drinking. Chlorine will kill fish and plants alike. Water, unless from a clean pond, must be allowed to set at least three days in some other container before it is used in the tank. This aging process may be speeded up with the help of tablets which de-chlorinate the water, available from most dealers.

SELECTING YOUR PLANTS

Different plants grow well in different types of aquarium settings. The depth to which they are planted, as well as the light they are to receive, is very important to consider before they are purchased. Take a look at the various plants which are available for the home aquarium:

Cabomba caroliniana, commonly called simply "Cabomba," is native to the southern part of the United States. It is usually available at low prices from most dealers. Cabomba is a lovely plant that can be bunched with 5 or 6 strands. The fan-shaped appearance of the leaves may have suggested its popular name, "Fanwort." This plant needs plenty of light and gets stringy when light is not available. If a tank is placed near a window where north light is always available during the daylight hours the plant will do very well.

When planting, snip off the bottom inch or so of the plants and place them about an inch into the sand so they may take root and not float up.

Elodea, or more scientifically, *Anacharis canadensis,* is another popular plant in home aquaria. This is one of the most common North American aquatic plants, and has been introduced in European waters. Cultivated plants are priced reasonably, are usually available, and will be found to be more attractive and grow better than wild plants.

Since *Elodea* and *Cabomba* grow to very long lengths under the proper conditions, it is wise to plant them to the rear of the aquarium so they will not grow in front of the smaller plants.

Milfoil, or *Myriophyllum spicatum,* is a plant closely resembling Fanwort, but is much more delicate in its lacy leaves. It, like all plants, will grow toward the light, so it is best to plant it in the back or on the sides of the aquarium where the most light is allowed to enter. It is fast-growing and is widely used to help egg-laying fishes to spawn. This plant has a wide distribution throughout the warmer portions of North and South America. Usually available at low prices.

Vallisneria spiralis is the most popular species of aquatic tape grass. It is native to the southern United States and is also found in southern Europe. It grows very well in a moderate light, and when conditions are to its liking will propagate freely by sending out runners from the base. These runners take root at intervals and result in a whole series of new plants. Usually sold by the dozen at a moderate price.

Sagittaria natans resembles *Vallisneria,* but has wider, sturdier leaves. It is a little more difficult to grow and propagates in the same manner as *Vallisneria,* but not as rapidly or as readily. Native to the southern United States, it is usually available at moderate prices.

The *Cryptocorynes* comprise a family which includes about 40 species of plants, some narrow-leaved, and some wide-leaved. They are native to the Malay Archipelago, and usually sell at a fairly stiff price. The reason is that these plants grow and propagate very slowly. This fact is offset by the beauty of these plants. They grow best in about one-half the light required by other aquatic plants. When well established in conditions to their liking, these plants will live for years and propagate regularly by sending up shoots from their root-stock.

Echinodorus intermedius, or more commonly the Amazon Sword Plant, is an ideal centerpiece for a tank deep enough to maintain it. It is senseless to place an Amazon Sword Plant in a tank less than 12 inches deep. The plant will grow to 2 or 3 feet tall, depending on the depth of the water. It should be planted with the crown above the sand line and it sometimes needs to be weighted with a piece of lead until it roots.

It is truly the prince of aquarium plants and a good reproducer. The Amazon Sword Plant will make an attractive setting as it grows daughter plants all around it. When a runner starts going out, it is wise to weight the runner into the sand with a small rock or a piece of lead. The daughter plants may be severed from the parent plant as soon as they root.

Some floating plants like *Lemna minor* and *Spirodela polyrhiza,* the familiar Duckweed, are usually only a nuisance and should be avoided. Sometimes they, as well as *Riccia, Salvinia, Utricula minor* and *Eichhornia crassipes,* the Water Hyacinth, are used when one is trying to encourage the fishes to spawn.

1. *Myriophyllum* (Milfoil); 2. *Echinodorus intermedius* (Amazon Sword Plant); 3. *Salvinia*; 4. *Cabomba caroliniana* (Cabomba or Fanwort); 5. *Sagittaria natans*; 6. *Vallisneria spiralis.*

ROOTING PLANTS: Be certain that the water level is low so that it will not overflow when you are working in the tank. When setting the plants in, consider the source of light in order to anticipate the direction in which they will grow.

CARE OF PLANTS

Never use humus or soil of any kind to "fertilize" your plantings. The fish will take care of that job. If the plants begin to lose their green and get stringy this simply means that they are not getting enough light and more light should be offered them.

ACIDITY AND HARDNESS TESTS

As we all know, water is composed of two parts of hydrogen, and one part of oxygen. This is water in its pure state, distilled water. In its natural state, there are many impurities mixed in, just as in the air we breathe. For fishes, you must keep the impurities under control.

There are two conditions to watch for: one is whether the water is acid, neutral or alkaline; the other is whether the water is hard or soft.

In order to determine acidity or alkalinity, there are several types of kits on the market known as pH kits. The usual kit consists of a small vial into which a sample of aquarium water is poured, and then dyed with a special preparation. The water is then compared with a color chart which goes from blue through green to yellow. Blue water shows alkaline, green neutral, and yellow acid. Fishes need neutral or slightly acid conditions.

Whether water is soft or hard can be determined roughly without the aid of a kit. If the water from the tap does not lather readily, or leaves a ring in the bathtub which is difficult to remove, you have hard water. Most fishes require soft water, so if your water is hard you must do something about it. But first you must know more exactly how hard the water is.

There are two types of test kits which determine the amount of hardness in water. The simpler of the two consists of a graduated beaker and a bottle of liquid soap. A measured amount of aquarium water and a specified number of drops of the soap are placed in the beaker and the mixture is shaken up vigorously. The height to which the suds rise in the beaker is an accurate indication of the degree of hardness which the water has.

Another kit consists of three solutions and a small vial. The water to be tested is poured into the vial, and a specified number of drops of the first two solutions are added. This results in a deep purple solution. Then the third solution is added drop by drop. The water which was purple will suddenly turn blue, and the number of drops which it took to do the trick gives you the number of degrees of hardness of the water. The ideal aquarium water for all-around use should show no more than 10 degrees of hardness.

CONTROLLING WATER CONDITIONS

Suppose your water is hard and alkaline, as many tap waters are. You have one of two courses to choose: you can look for a natural source of soft water, such as an uncontaminated pond or brook, or you can correct your water artificially. If you seek a natural source, take your kit along, and make a test on the spot. A body of fresh water which has a fish population can be assumed to be fairly free of contamination.

There is another source of good aquarium water, and that is Jupiter Pluvius. Rain water is usually quite acid, and very soft. If you gather rain water, wait for a heavy fall, and do not catch it until it has rained for a while. The dust on a roof and in the air can be a real source of contamination, and should be allowed to wash away first. The rain water you finally collect should then be allowed to stand in a non-metallic container until clear. Then it can be separated from any settlings by pouring it off or siphoning it out. If a test shows that the resulting water is highly acid still, add alkaline tap water until the mixture is only slightly acid.

For most fishes, between 5 and 10 degrees of hardness is proper. A few species require less or more for breeding. (These will be pointed out later.) You will probably find that as your water gets softer, it turns more acid. If it does not, it may be necessary to add a little acid solution. The least harmful, it has been found, is a brew made by boiling a handful of peat moss in about a quart of rain water and then allowing the result to settle. The boiling should be done in either an enameled or Pyrex container. The clear, dark-brown fluid can be bottled and kept indefinitely, and should be added to the tank water a little at a time until the proper acidity is attained. It may stain the water a light amber color, which is not unpleasant once you have become accustomed to it.

Adding tap water generally will turn your water to the alkaline side. You are aiming to get neutral or slightly acid tank water.

CHLORINE AND OTHER PROBLEMS

Tap water usually contains some chlorine, which could do harm to your fish if they are added to tap water too soon. But chlorine soon leaves the water as it is allowed to stand, especially if the water is agitated by means of aeration or a filter. This is the big reason why water should be "aged" before putting fish into it.

In some districts, sodium fluoride is now being added to water as a means of preventing tooth decay. Fluoride does not leave the water as a gas as chlorine does.

There are several chlorine and fluoride neutralizers on the market which do a good job chemically. These should be used where there is fluoridation, and may be used to speed up the de-chlorination process where there is only chlorine in the water.

When letting the water stand, be sure to use a wide-mouthed container. If a large bottle of the carboy type is used, fill it only to the point where it begins to narrow toward the neck.

Sometimes it happens that water will turn cloudy. A microscopic inspection will show that it contains immense quantities of protozoan life. This sometimes happens in a newly set-up tank; however, it will clear up in a day or two. Protozoan life requires

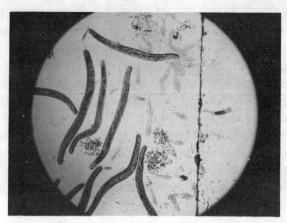

INFUSORIA: Here is a microscopic view of one of the protozoan life forms that can multiply in your aquarium and cause the water to become cloudy.

food, and in an empty tank this is rapidly exhausted and starvation clears them out.

Cloudy water in an established tank is a different matter. Here there must be a cause. The most common one is over-feeding; the uneaten food decays and provides sustenance for the swarms of protozoan life which cloud the water. A neglected tank with too much debris on the bottom is also very likely to develop this condition. A dead fish lodged somewhere out of sight can also be the culprit. In any case, the cure is the same: remove the cause. Siphon the decayed matter off the bottom and replace the water which was removed in the process with clean water. Dead fish, snails or plant leaves should, of course, be removed.

AQUARIUM ACCESSORIES

Now that you have the aquarium set up and ready for its finny occupants, you have to take stock of your other necessary equipment. In the first place, you will need a net. Don't get a very small one. One which is large enough to make fish-catching easy will save much wear and tear on the fishes, and on your own nerves.

An enameled pail is often very handy, as is a 6-foot length of rubber or plastic hose. The pail is for transporting water, and the hose for siphoning water when you give your tank the occasional cleaning or change of water which it requires. If your aquarium is a small one, all you need for a satisfactory cleaning job is a dip-tube—a tube with a chamber on one end. You push down the chamber end to the bottom with your finger closing the upper end. Lifting your finger causes the water to rush into the chamber, carrying with it the dirt you want to pick up. Then you lift up the chamber and dump the dirty water into the waiting pail.

Certain fishes are adept at jumping out of the water. In order to curb this exuberance, you will find it necessary to cover the exposed top part of your aquarium with a piece of glass. If you are using a reflector with incandescent lamps for lighting, do not use a cover glass which extends all the way over the top. If the reflector is placed on top of the glass, a great deal of heat will be generated and the glass will crack. So, bring your glass up to the edge of the reflector. If you use a fluorescent light reflector, much less heat will be generated, and you can put the reflector on top of the glass.

HEATERS

The next problem is how to heat your aquarium comfortably for your fishes. This is usually no problem in the summer months, when there is heat aplenty. In the winter, however, you must provide your aquarium with an artificial source of heat. Before the days of electricity, tanks were heated by little lamps or gas flames under the base, and woe betide the aquarist who forgot to fill the lamp on a chilly night! Available now are dependable electric heaters with thermostatic controls which can be set so the water is heated to exactly the right temperature.

Heaters come in various wattages, for different sizes of aquaria. To figure the wattage required, multiply the gallon capacity of your aquarium by 5 watts; for example, a 10-gallon aquarium requires a 50-watt heater.

The over-all temperature range at which practically all tropical aquarium fishes are comfortable is 76° to 78°F (24° to 25°C). This brings us to another piece of necessary equipment: an aquarium thermometer. This either floats in the water or is set on the bottom. (Do not expect an accurate reading from a floating thermometer which is near a light bulb.)

AIR PUMPS

Now we come to the question of whether or not to have aeration in the tanks. Consider the difference it makes, and then decide whether you want an air pump. Without aeration, a limited number of fish can be accommodated in your aquarium, averaging 2 inches of fish for each gallon of water. Now, what happens when you move this water by pumping a gentle air stream into it? The moving water immediately doubles its capacity to contain fish, because of the fact that a great deal more oxygen is now absorbed by the moving surface. Another thing also happens: the heat generated by the heater is distributed evenly throughout. Cool

THE FILTER: In order to work efficiently, a filter must be cleaned regularly. The one pictured here is easily cleaned by replacing the fiberglass when it becomes discolored.

water has a tendency to be heavier, and without circulation in your tank, it might be several degrees cooler on the bottom than at the surface.

An air pump used to be a high-priced luxury. This is no longer the case; for a small amount, you can get a model which works from a vibrator, and gives years of satisfactory service.

FILTERING

An air line lets you do one more thing: filter the water, and remove the unsightly suspended matter which sometimes prevents your water from being crystal-clear. There are many different types of filters, but they have only one job: to remove dirt. You do not need a large filter for a small aquarium, and a small one is not adequate for a large aquarium.

In order to work efficiently, a filter must be prevented from becoming clogged. Clean it regularly. Glass wool may be removed and rinsed in running water until clean, and if the filter uses charcoal or gravel, a brisk rinsing under the tap will do the trick.

FOODS

Now that your aquarium is set up with its equipment, you can begin to turn your thoughts to what to feed your fishes.

Feeding is not a simple matter of shaking out a few grains from a box every day, as the fishes thrive and grow and grow. While fishes are far from being finicky where food is concerned, you just can't keep on feeding them the same things day after day, year in and year out. In the first place, no matter what the claims are on the box, no food is *that* perfect. In the second place, no matter how you like steak, you wouldn't want it exclusively every day in the week, would you?

There are many prepared dry foods on the market;

practically all are very good, but none are perfect. They don't cost much. Buy three or four varieties, and then try varying these from day to day. If some are rejected, or consumed with reluctance, go easy on them, or throw them away. You will soon see what your fishes' preferences are, but don't narrow down to one food.

OVERFEEDING

The next paragraph should be in capital letters, because it is by far the most important piece of advice in this whole section:

Your fishes have a limited capacity for food, even though they are gluttons. When they have reached this capacity, they stop eating. Whatever food is left over spoils quickly, contaminating the water and providing sustenance for billions of harmful bacteria. If there is any food left on the surface or on the bottom 10 minutes after your fishes are fed, you are overfeeding. Avoid this and you will scarcely ever have any trouble with sick fish.

LIVE FOODS

Prepared fish foods are never a substitute for living foods; they are merely a supplement. True, some fishes can be kept in good health for a long time on an exclusive diet of dried foods. However, if you want to keep your fishes in really top-notch condition, you must give them an occasional meal of living food. Some of these foods are not difficult to come by:

DAPHNIA: Although these look like insects, these little creatures are actually crustaceans, and lead a completely aquatic existence. They are red, and about the size of a pin-head. Swimming is performed in hops, and for this reason and their flea-like shape, they are often called "water-fleas." They occur in huge swarms in some bodies of fresh water which are rich in decaying vegetable matter, and have little or no fish population. If you are fortunate enough to be within travelling distance of one of these ponds, you have a valuable source of what is one of the best possible foods you can provide.

BOSMINAE: Some ponds will be found to contain an organism which is very similar to daphnia, but much smaller and black in color. These are bosminae, and are often found along pond edges. The swarms give the water the appearance of having black pepper suspended in it. This tiny food is just the ticket for baby fishes. They gorge themselves with it until they seem ready to burst.

MOSQUITO LARVAE: A walk through swampy terrain will sometimes disclose pools which are swarming with mosquito larvae; these swim with a wriggling motion, and spend a good deal of time on the surface, where they must come for air. A meal of these is just about the greatest treat you can give to your fishes, but too much generosity on your part with these will backfire: the warm water will speed up the larval growth, and every uneaten larva will result in a mosquito in your house.

ENCHYTRAE (WHITE WORMS): Here is a food which is excellent for your fishes, and can be raised with very little trouble. For this you require a wooden box about 2 feet square, with humus in it about 4 inches deep. Humus can be purchased at a garden supply store or nursery. In this box, place a culture of white worms, such as can be obtained from your dealer, if you do not have a friend with a box of worms going.

Moisten the soil slightly. This does not mean to make mud; just moisten the soil as you would for plants. A sheet of glass on top of the box will keep the soil from drying out, and will also permit you to see how things are going. To feed your worms, place a slice of wet white bread on top of the soil. This will disappear in a surprisingly short time, and turning over the soil will disclose the fact that the worms have multiplied. An old fork is a handy tool for this job, as it can also be used for removing the worms, which form balls.

For feeding worms to the fishes, a worm feeder is a handy piece of equipment. This consists of a cup of glass or plastic which is perforated in the lower area, and arranged to float on the surface. The worms wriggle through the perforations, to be gobbled up by the hungry fishes.

TUBIFEX WORMS: Many ponds which daphnia inhabit are also home for aquatic worms known as tubifex worms. These worms gather in clusters along the pond edges, where there is soft mud and a certain amount of decay. The clusters may be recognized by their bright red color. Gathering often proves to be quite a messy job, but if the worms are thick, the clusters may be felt as lumps in the mud and pick up almost intact. However, it is sometimes necessary to gather a whole bucketful of oozy, smelly mud in order to extract from it a handful of tubifex worms.

For those who do not care to go to all this trouble, there are professional worm men who ship to most dealers, and a cluster can be bought at a pet shop at very little expense. The tubifex worms can be fed with a worm feeder in a similar manner to white worms.

BRINE SHRIMP: Fishes should be fed live food as often as possible, as they cannot survive indefinitely on packaged dry food. The Brine Shrimp shown here, magnified many times, is one of the most convenient live foods.

BRINE SHRIMP (*Artemia salina*): Here is what is doubtless the most convenient live food of all. Brine shrimp come in egg form, and are collected in two places, San Francisco and Ogden, Utah. They are equally fine foods, the only difference between them being that the Utah eggs are a bit larger. The embryos remain dried up inside the eggs for an indefinite period of time, ready to hatch when placed in salt water. All you need do when you want a supply of living food is to follow the easy directions which come with the eggs. (These directions vary for the two types.) The newly hatched nauplii, which resemble very small daphnia, should be removed from the salt water in which they hatch by using a fine-meshed net. They will live for a short time in the fresh water of the aquarium. For obvious reasons, avoid pouring salt water into the fresh water when transferring the eggs.

There are also some substitutes for living foods which you should know about. When you come home from a successful fishing trip, give your pets a bit of fish roe or chopped-up fish liver which they will accept with enthusiasm. A piece of fish may also be frozen in the refrigerator, and an occasional meal provided by shaving off a slice with a razor blade and chopping it up into bite-size pieces for your fish. Shrimp, clams, oysters and other shellfish may also be used in this fashion.

SPAWNING FISHES

"I don't know why it is, but Joe Smith seems to be able to spawn any fish he wants to!"

You will often hear this statement made by a fellow aquarist.

In the first place, an aquarist who says *he* "spawned" a certain species is guilty of misstatement. What he should say is that a certain species of fish spawned *for him*. He may have helped by creating conditions which were to the fish's liking, but the credit for spawning still belongs to the fish.

The first thing is to find out whether you have a pair or not. This may sound silly, but a busy store clerk anxious to make a sale could easily be tempted to catch two immature fish and assure you that you are getting a pair, meaning a male and a female. Also, some fishes are difficult to "sex" (determine sex of) when fully-grown, and impossible to sex when half-grown.

Another important thing is the *age* of the fish. Select a young, healthy couple in the prime of life. Even a mature pair, new to your tank, may have trouble adapting themselves to the new environment, so avoid purchasing mature fish for breeding purposes.

Rather than choosing a large pair, try to get a half-dozen youngsters which are only half to three-quarters grown. You will then be in a position to observe them and become acquainted with their habits and food preferences. When they are ready for spawning, you may select the best specimens. In the case of Cichlids, you need not even select, as there is a tendency for males to pick females of their preference and "pair off." Your fish are almost certain to spawn in these cases.

THE "EASIEST" EGGLAYERS

Many aquarists who would like to try their hand at breeding egglaying fishes want to know which ones are easiest to breed. Try a few pairs of White Cloud Mountain Fish, *Tanichthys albonubes*. Beyond feeding them, give them no other attention, and in two weeks you may have several hundred fish of all sizes swimming about in little schools.

For something almost as easy to breed, try a pair of small Danios. The fry (young) are very hardy, and easy to raise on prepared as well as live foods.

Most of the Barb family are easily spawned as well. If a well-conditioned pair are put together, things are almost bound to happen.

THE BREEDING TANK

Any small, well-planted aquarium will serve as a "maternity ward" for live-bearing fishes. The female is put there when her bulging sides warn that her time is near. When her babies have all arrived, return her to the original tank, and let the youngsters get a start in the place where they were born. Larger quarters are then in order, where they will have plenty of room for growing. Of course, match the temperatures of the two tanks before transferring.

A breeding tank for egglaying fishes is a slightly more complicated thing. Here you must take the fish's breeding habits into consideration and plant or furnish the tank accordingly.

For fishes which spawn in bushy plants, such as most Barbs or Tetras, a tank of no less than 10 gallons for the smaller species, and 15 to 20 gallons for the larger ones, is recommended. Plant one side generously with *Myriophyllum* or *Nitella*, or if you prefer, a bundle of Spanish moss.

Cichlids usually require some rocks or similar retreats. Flower pots are often used, and are excellent. Dwarf Cichlids can be spawned easily in a 5-gallon tank, but the larger Cichlid varieties will require 15 to 20 gallons. Some of the really large ones like *Astronotus ocellatus* would require larger accommodations yet.

It is always advisable to let the youngsters get a start in the same tank where they hatch. Newly-hatched fry cannot stand any amount of moving; make sure the breeding tank is large enough so that they will not be crowded for the first few months, and leave them there. After this time they will be in much better shape for moving to other aquaria.

FISH PREFERENCES

Now comes the point when you must observe and study your fish a little. Do your fish prefer to swim in the open, or are they always hiding? Do you find them in sunny spots, or do you have to look for them in dark corners? What is the nature of the terrain from which they come? Are they native to clear, running streams or sluggish, muddy-bottomed ponds? Do they come from far inland or from coastal waters?

How can you as an aquarist duplicate the conditions in which the fish feel at home? You cannot duplicate, but the conditions can be approximated.

First of all, keep in mind that a pond or stream does not resemble an aquarium. The glass sides let in a great deal of light where Mother Nature does not. Some fishes love sunlight, while others instinctively avoid it. Simple observation on this point will tell you whether it is better to select a bright or shady location for your spawning fish.

If you force a timid fish to show himself by taking away some of his hiding places, this increases his timidity and keeps him in a constant state of terror. How can a fish spawn under these conditions? It is better to provide such a fish with *more* plant thickets into which he can dodge. You may be surprised to see that he puts in an appearance more often when he knows that there are places where he *can* hide if something frightens him.

Fishes which are native to running streams, such as Danios or White Clouds, will not tolerate dirty water or very high temperatures. On the other hand, pond or lake dwellers, such as Cichlids, might pick a spot in shallow water near the shore for spawning, as Sunfishes do. Here the sun is bright and the water warm. In the case of other Cichlids, the presence of enemies forces them to hide in pockets along the shore, or in reed growths, or in rock piles. If you approximate these conditions, and make your fish feel at home, your battle for breeding is usually won.

As for the water itself, it will be found that a species of fish which comes from brackish, coastal water will require the addition of a little salt for its well-being. Rain-fed inland streams have an almost neutral, very soft water, while fishes from swampy regions require water of definitely acid character. They will survive without perfect water conditions, but they probably will not breed.

Don't be misled by the apparently careless procedure of the successful breeder who declares he has no trouble; just uses tap-water. There are all kinds of tap-water, and his kind may be just right for the fish he is breeding. He also is well aware of the other requirements of his fish, and supplies them too. Remember that the successful breeder will tell you of his successes; you don't often hear of his failures. Don't let failure discourage you; the "experts" have them too!

But don't try breeding salt-water fishes, and don't start with a salt-water aquarium until you think of yourself as an expert.

DISEASES OF FISHES

Here are the major causes of trouble, but you are not likely to encounter more than one or two:

ANCHOR WORM (*Lernaecera* species)

Symptoms: Heavy whitish spots of curled-up, imbedded worms (actually this is not a worm but a crustacean).

Treatment: Remove with a sharp, fine needle. Paint spot with mercurochrome.

BLACK SPOT DISEASE (*Diplostomiasis*)

Symptoms: Spots are usually black, though in light-colored fishes the spots take on a brownish cast, and contain a slowly moving worm rolled up inside the cyst. The cyst is surrounded by heavily pigmented cells; thus the color symptom. In time the fish will be nearly covered with these parasites.

Treatment: Life cycle of this parasite is dependent upon a snail, though new fishes may carry it into an otherwise clean tank. Treat infected fish by adding 20 ml. of a 1:100 solution of picric acid and water

FUNGUS INFECTION: The large cotton-like growths on each of these fish are symptoms of fungus infection. The infected areas should be painted with iodine or mercurochrome. In addition, the water in the tank may be treated.

to a gallon of water and bathing fish for an hour. You may remove the fish sooner due to distress.

CONSTIPATION

Symptoms: Loss of appetite, slight abdominal swelling, few, heavy feces.

Treatment: Soak dried food in medicinal paraffin oil, glycerin or castor oil. If fish refuses this food it must be taken off dried food diet and fed Daphnia, mosquito larvae or Cyclops. *Do not use white worms* as they are a chief cause of constipation.

DROPSY (Caused by the basterium *Pseudomonas punctata*)

Symptoms: Bloating of the belly as though the fish were egg-bound.

Treatment: There is no known cure for dropsy. The antibiotics are of no value. Some suggest tapping the liquid from the body of the infected fish, but this is of little value.

EYE FUNGUS

Symptoms: This is a true fungus infection which might easily be fatal. The eye appears to be covered with a whitish scum; cottony appearance in later stage.

Treatment: Paint infected eye with 1 per cent silver nitrate solution obtained from drugstore. (Tap water should not be used in mixing solution.) Then bathe fish's eye in a 1 per cent potassium dichromate solution. The red precipitate which forms on the eye is harmless to the fish. The infected fish should be isolated in an aquarium containing 2 grains of potassium dichromate per gallon of water, until the eye heals, though the disease is not infectious.

FISH LOUSE (*Argulus foliaceus*)

Symptoms: An external visible parasite about as large as a Daphnia, it attaches itself to the skin of the host by two suckers and lives off the blood sucked from the host.

Treatment: Parasite may be removed with a pair of forceps or tweezers and the spot painted with mercurochrome or peroxide of hydrogen. If parasites are difficult to remove, touch them with a piece of salt.

FLUKE (*Gyrodactylus and Dactylogyrus*)

Symptoms: Fish loses color and grows pale, fins close, skin becomes slimy and small blood-spots appear on the body and base of fins. Breathing is more rapid.

Treatment: Treat fish with 5 drops of 5 per cent methylene blue per gallon of water or a 1:100 formalin-water solution. Use aeration when treating with formalin.

FUNGUS INFECTION (*Saprolegnia*)

Symptoms: A cottony growth about a single or multiple site. Area usually will first show signs of being bruised or torn, as fungus cannot attack a healthy fish.

Treatment: Paint infected areas with a diluted (1:10 solution of commercial strength) preparation of either iodine or mercurochrome. Entire aquarium may be treated with a 1 per cent potassium dichromate solution, or 1 gram of crystalline potassium dichromate to $7\frac{1}{2}$ gallons of water. After fish is cured water should be changed. Treatment should last about a week.

ICH: A close-up of a fish infected with ich, a parasite that takes the form of small white spots. Ich cannot be treated while still on the fish, but the spots will fall off if the water temperature is raised. Once the fish is clean of spots, it should be put in treated water for at least three hours.

ICH (*Ichthyophthirius multifiliis*)

Symptoms: White spots of pinhead size pepper the body and fins of the fish. Fish gets sluggish, closes fins, and gradually dies.

Treatment: Ich is a parasite which cannot be treated while still in the skin of the fish. Raising the water temperature will hasten the departure of the Ich from the host for reproductive purposes. Then you can easily get rid of it. Use 50 mg. of quinine hydrochloride per gallon or bathe infected fish in a brine bath, 4 tablespoons of salt per gallon of water. Leave fish in either bath for at least 3 hours *after* each fish is clean of white spots.

KNOT or PIMPLE DISEASE (*Morbus nodulosus*)

Symptoms: Not really a specific infection but rather a series of parasitic sporozoa. Looks like Ich but is really little knots, or pimples. "Stubborn Ich" might well be name of this disease.

Treatment: No known cure. Remove infected fish immediately and treat for Ich. If this treatment fails, infected fish should be destroyed.

LEECH

Symptoms: External parasite visible as it is attached to the host, sucking its blood.

Treatment: Place the infected fish in a 2½ per cent salt solution for ½ hour. Remove remaining parasites with forceps and paint area with mercurochrome.

LOSS OF COLOR

Symptoms: Fish becomes pale and its colors are not sharp. Normally active live-bearers lose sexual interest.

Treatment: This is strictly a food problem. The diet deficiency is due to a monotonous, unbalanced diet. Feeding of tubifex, daphnia and other live foods usually remedies the situation within 24 hours.

NEON TETRA DISEASE (*Plistophora hyphessobryconis*)

Symptoms: Blemish or spot forms along the "neon" blue-green line on Neon Tetras and related species. As disease progresses the area becomes extended.

Treatment: No known cure, though treatment with 500 mg. *each* of terramycin and aureomycin per 15-gallon aquarium helps considerably.

POP-EYE; EXOPHTHALMIA

Symptoms: The eye starts to bulge as though it were being forced out by an accumulation of fluid behind it.

Treatment: Antibiotics are of no value. No known cure. May be caused by *Pseudomonas punctata* (dropsy).

SCALE PROTRUSION (Either *Mibrio piscium* or *Bacterium lepidorthosae*)

Symptoms: Scales of fish start to protrude all over the body. Fish moves slower, frequency of breathing increases, tail becomes paralyzed and fish stays near top of water.

Treatment: As soon as scales begin to protrude, treatment should begin. Aureomycin, 250 mg. per gallon of water helps at times, but isn't a "sure cure." There is no known absolute remedy. Once this infection has been observed all members of the infected tank should be sterilized by adding 2½ grains of potassium dichromate and two teaspoonsful of salt to each gallon of water. Change water completely after two weeks.

SLIMY SKIN DISEASE (*Cyclochaete domerguei*) (*Chilodon cyprini*) (*Costia necatrix*)

Symptoms: There is a slimy secretion seen on the fish's skin. The fish loses its color, grows paler as the slime covers the entire outside of the fish.

Treatment: 30 minute bath in a $2\frac{1}{2}$ per cent salt solution; repeat in 48 hours, and every two days after that until all symptoms are gone. At least three known organisms are responsible for the symptomatic slimy skin disease. If the salt treatment fails, 2 grains of quinine hydrochloride should be added to a gallon of water and the infected fish should be maintained in this treated water until it is cured. A bath in 2 ml. of formalin per gallon of water, for 15 minutes is a last-resort treatment.

SPOTTINESS OF THE SKIN IN LABYRINTH FISHES (*Pseudomonas fluorescens*)

Symptoms: Whitish or bloody patches appear on the skin and fins of the infected fish.

Treatment: There seems to be no known cure for this disease. *Pseudomonas* seems to thrive in an antibiotic environment. Since labyrinth fishes are usually involved, a high temperature plus a heavy salt bath might work, though it has shown positive results in only a few cases out of many. Try 90° F (32° C) for 2 hours in a 5 per cent salt solution.

SWIM BLADDER DISEASE

Symptoms: Fish has difficulty swimming. It falls head-over-tail or cannot maintain itself on an even level in the water. May rest on the bottom.

Treatment: Not a fatal disease, but crippling. Fish seldom recovers. It is caused by physical factors such as poor diet, chilling, sudden changes of temperature or pressure.

TAIL-ROT AND FIN-ROT, often called TAIL-FUNGUS, MOUTH FUNGUS

Symptoms: None of these are true fungus infections. They are caused by slime bacteria and are easily seen by the whitish appearance of the infected area. The sooner the disease is observed the easier it is to cure. Water changes are often responsible for weakening the fish's resistance to bacterial infections of this sort.

Treatment: Aureomycin is ideal for treatment. Single fish may be treated with a 10 mg. tablet of aureomycin in a quart of water. Entire aquarium may be treated with a dose of 250 to 500 mg. of aureomycin per gallon. Sometimes cures are effected with a 500 mg. dosage per 15 gallons of water, but this only removes the symptoms while the cure is in doubt. Bathe the fish in a strong salt solution after the aureomycin treatment. Use 4 tablespoonsful of salt per gallon.

TUBERCULOSIS

Symptoms: Loss of appetite, sluggishness, progressive thinness and gradual wasting away. Yellow spots at the base of the caudal peduncle in Tetras are also a sign.

Treatment: Treatment with streptomycin and PAS (para-amino-salicylic acid) are possible cures in the early stages. 10 grains per gallon of water is the recommended dosage. Prolonged overcrowding might be the cause of this disease. No "sure cure" known.

VELVET DISEASE (*Oodinium limneticum*)

Symptoms: May resemble Ich, but a closer look will show smaller spots, which, when viewed from reflected light, have a velvet-like appearance on the fish's skin. Often the skin looks as though it were peppered with fine powder. White Clouds seem especially susceptible to this disease.

Treatment: Add 2 drops of 5 per cent methylene blue solution per each gallon of aquarium water. Acriflavine, same strength, may be substituted for methylene blue. Keep tank in complete darkness. Remove and sterilize, or throw out, plants. Treatment lasts for 5 days; then a 3-day rest and complete water change, then another treatment.

FISHES FOR THE AQUARIUM

Many species owe their continued existence to the efforts of hobbyists who after an intensive study of the habits of certain fishes, were able to solve the riddle of how they bred in the wild and made greater numbers of these fishes available. In spite of these, there are still some fishes which have rarely or never bred yet while in captivity. One of the most fascinating facets of this hobby is to get to work on these "difficult" fishes and get results. However, for the aquarist who is content to take the easier ones and get the satisfaction of seeing young fishes in his aquaria which he raised, there are many species which are not very finicky in their requirements and will spawn readily if given half an opportunity. It would take a heavier volume than this to present to you all the fishes which it is possible to keep and breed in aquaria.

The newcomer generally gets his biggest surprise when he finds out how inexpensive most fishes are.

The greatest paradox in aquarium fish prices is the best-known fish of all: the Guppy. A common Guppy can be bought for a few cents, while a pair of fancy, line-bred show Guppies may bring astronomical prices, if they can be bought at all.

Other live-bearing fishes are comparatively inexpensive. Prices vary with the size and quality of the stock, but you generally buy a pair of live-bearers, with the possible exception of large Black Mollies, for very little.

With the egglaying fishes, prices vary considerably, but practically all of the easily bred species can be purchased inexpensively. This group would include the Danios, Barbs, many of the Tetras, the young of most Cichlids, many of the Catfishes, and others.

Some fishes are not so easy to breed, grow slowly, or require other special attention. Avoid these at the start. The Siamese Fighting Fish, for instance, presents a problem for breeders. In order to keep the beautiful, flowing fins of the males intact, it is necessary to raise each fish individually in its own glass jar.

Other fishes, such as the Cyprinodonts, also present problems. The eggs take about two weeks to hatch, and each female will lay only a few eggs per day. The result is that you get a group of young which varies greatly in size and must be sorted frequently to prevent the big ones from eating the little ones.

Don't concern yourself at the beginning with where the fish came from, or their exact Latin names. Just be sure the fishes you put together will get along in a community tank—don't put long-tailed fishes who are slow-moving with speedy nipping species. And remember their popular names.

LIVE-BEARERS

Best to start with is the family of live-bearing Tooth-Carps which includes the well-known Guppy, Platy and Swordtail. Keeping and breeding them is usually a simple matter of putting a healthy male and female together and waiting for Nature to take its course. The bulging abdomen of the female is the signal for her to be moved to a maternity tank, which should be heavily planted to give the newly-born young plenty of places to hide from their mother, who might easily mistake them for edible tidbits.

By means of selective breeding, it has been possible to produce many beautiful strains.

As soon as they begin to show signs of becoming males, the youngsters should be separated, until

GUPPY: Selective breeding of this popular and hardy species has led to the development of many beautiful strains of various shapes and colors.

nothing but females are left in the breeding tank. The males have long tails and are brightly colored. The females drab. The best of the second generation females are then mated back to their father, and then there is a fairly well-established strain.

The important thing is to use only the *healthiest* specimens from each generation.

The Guppy is one of the hardiest of fishes; it demands nothing more than fairly clean water, and a temperature of 76° F (24° C). It thrives in the smallest aquarium, and a healthy female thinks nothing of giving birth to as many as 60 or 70 offspring. Feeding is no problem; it is fond of living foods, but is also satisfied with the prepared ones.

Another of the popular live-bearing species is the Swordtail. The male is distinguished by an unusual

SWORDTAIL: In this example, the "sword" tail is not particularly exaggerated in length, but it is sometimes as long as the body. (See color section.)

PLATY: Many color varieties of this fish have been produced through selective breeding. The grown female Platy is 3 inches long; the male is considerably smaller and has more intense coloration. This is an excellent, peaceful, community fish.

tail formation, the lower caudal rays being greatly elongated into a sword-like point. The female has almost as much color, but no sword. Top size for tank-raised females is about 4½ inches, with the males about an inch shorter.

A peaceful fish, it is a favorite for the community aquarium. It is a jumper, and the tank should be kept covered.

The Platy is another of the very popular family. A large female measures 3 inches, and the male is considerably smaller. By selective breeding, many color varieties have been produced, such as the Red, Black, Blue, Tuxedo, Gold Wagtail, Red Wagtail, Gold, Berlin, Salt-and-Pepper, Bleeding Heart, and others.

The Platy is very peaceful and desirable in the community aquarium. If you wish to use Platies for selective breeding, remember that they will interbreed if put together, and one fertilization will produce anywhere from 4 to 7 batches of offspring.

CARP-LIKE FISHES

The Cyprinidae (egglayers) are the carp-like fishes of the world, of which many of the smaller members make excellent aquarium inhabitants.

Pearl Danios are among the most active of aquarium fishes. They are always scurrying about busily, in search of food or each other, and will add a great deal of life to any community aquarium. A small, slender fish, the Pearl Danio never exceeds 2½ inches in length. Its sides are of a mother-of-pearl iridescence.

Here is a good fish for anyone who wants to try his hand at breeding egglayers for the first time. An all-glass aquarium of one to two gallons capacity is covered with pebbles or glass marbles on the bottom, and then fresh tap water is added to the depth of about 3 inches. This is allowed to stand for a day, and then a heavy female and two healthy males are added. Almost at once a wild chase begins, and eggs are scattered all over. Eggs are non-adhesive, and drop down between the pebbles. When the female is depleted, the parents are removed. The eggs may be seen by placing a light above the pebbles and looking up through the glass bottom. Hatching takes place in 48 hours, and the young become free-swimming in another 48 hours, when they may be fed with fine foods. Temperature, 76° to 78° F (24° to 25° C).

The most popular of the group, the Zebra Danio, like the Pearl Danio, is 2 inches in length, and just as active. The body is silvery, with wide blue horizontal stripes running from the gill-plate all through the sides, the tail, and even the anal fin. Fullness of body is not an infallible guide to sex; a depleted female can look just like a male. However, the background on the anal fin of the female is silver, and on the male, gold.

Breeding procedure is exactly similar to that for the Pearl Danio.

The Spotted Danio, smallest member of the family, 1½ inches in length, comes from Burma. The sides are adorned with several greenish blue stripes across the upper half of the body, and rows of spots

SPOTTED DANIO: At 1½ inches, this is the smallest member of the cyprinid family. It can be identified by greenish blue stripes and rows of dots across its body.

on the lower half. It is as active as the others, and may be spawned as easily in the same manner.

For all its size, the Giant Danio will not molest any fish it cannot swallow. The size is a respectable one for an aquarium fish: 6 inches.

The body is blue, with a few short vertical bars just behind the gill-plate. From here back to the tail, there are two yellow horizontal stripes. The fins are orange in the female, and almost red in the male.

The genus Puntius includes a great number of fishes. For a long time, the generic name was known as *Barbus* and this name, although incorrect, will probably stick for a long time. Most of the Barbs are peaceful; they are valuable aquarium fishes because in addition to their beauty, they have excellent appetites and prefer to feed on the bottom and clean up a lot of food which would otherwise spoil.

All conform to the same breeding pattern. They require a large aquarium, but the smaller species will spawn in a smaller space.

The Rosy Barb is one of the medium-sized Barbs, which is fully grown at 4 inches. Its disposition is peaceful. Normally, it is a silvery, large-scaled fish with a black spot. The males are a bit slimmer, and the fins just a shade darker than those of the females, whose fins are plain. At breeding time, however, a great change takes place: the male's entire body becomes suffused with a deep rose-pink color, and the fins become black. Young, immature specimens never show these colors, and when a male gets them it is a good indication that he is ready for spawning. Put him with a female whose sides are well rounded and you can be fairly sure of success.

A tank of about 15 gallons is right, and a temperature of 80° F (27° C). The tank should be well planted on one side with thickets of bushy plants. When conditions are right, driving begins shortly, the male trying busily to coax and cajole the female into the plants. Her coyness soon disappears and they swim into the thickets together, occasionally stopping side by side and quivering as about 4 to 6 eggs are dropped to be fertilized at once by the waiting male. This Barb is prolific, and 300 to 400 fry from one spawning is not at all unusual. Hatching time is a little under 2 days, and the fry absorb their yolk-sacs in another 2 days. At this time they must be fed. Be guided by the amount of fry as to the amount of food given.

Many people who buy the Clown Barb when still young, at a size of 1½ inches or so, are astonished when they see how big it gets. Five inches is not an unusual length. The fish is gaily colored, the sides being rosy pink and the fins red. There is a saddle on the shoulder, and another halfway between the dorsal fin and the tail.

To breed this large member of the family you need an aquarium of at least 20 gallons.

Carp-like Fishes ■ 59

BLACK SPOT BARB is most attractive when only half grown because its gold, red, and black coloration fades somewhat as it grows to its full size of 7 inches.

Like the Clown Barb, the Black-Spot Barb is one of the big ones; 7 inches is usually the full size. Half-grown specimens are particularly attractive. The sides are golden, with an indistinct band vertically just in front of the dorsal fin, and a large black spot halfway between the dorsal fin and the tail. The dorsal fin is red, as well as the outside rays of the tail, which are tipped with black. As the fish becomes older, the colors fade somewhat.

When the male is ready for spawning, his face becomes covered with sexual tubercles, which resemble pimples. The female makes apparent her readiness for spawning by bulging with eggs. Spawning is similar to the Clown Barb, and results are sometimes astronomical. When broods are large, they should be spread out to extra tanks as they grow, to prevent excessive crowding.

In its spawning colors, the Black Ruby Barb is second to none in the Barb family. As with the others, the male has the lion's share of the bright hues. This is one of the medium-sized Barbs, which does not exceed 2½ inches in length. The male's body is suffused with a deep, cherry red at spawning time, and there are 3 broad black bars on the sides, which extend into the dorsal and anal fins. The scales each carry a golden dot, and the head is purple in color. The female has the bars, but the deep red of the male is only palely reflected here.

Breeding is the same as for the Rosy Barb, but the pair should be well conditioned and in the best of health.

The large, shining scales and attractive colors of the perky little Checkered Barb make it an attractive addition to any collection. It barely reaches a length of 2 inches. The back is olive green; there are two horizontal rows of alternating black and light scales. Each light scale is topped by a dark scale, giving a checkerboard pattern. The male's fins are a brownish red, edged with black; the female has light brown fins and less body color.

BLACK RUBY BARB: This medium-sized barb grows to a length of 2½ inches. Its head is purple, and its body red with three broad black bars. The male's coloration is much deeper than the female's.

SUMATRAN OR TIGER BARB grows to a length of 2 inches. Its short stocky body is silver with a light rosy tinge and three thick black vertical bars across it. The female's coloration is only slightly less intense than the male's, but she is easily identified by her greater girth.

This peaceful little fish has the added attraction of being very easily bred. Standard procedure as for the other small Barbs is followed.

The Cherry Barb is another of the popular small Barbs. In size it barely attains 2 inches, and in disposition it is peaceful. A broad black horizontal line characterizes both sexes, and another golden line borders it on top. The male has a brown back, and below the black line has a reddish ventral region, which becomes brilliant cherry red at spawning time. Fins and tail are also red. The female is chocolate brown on the sides, with a silvery belly and little or no color in the fins.

The species is prolific and easy to spawn in the regular manner for small Barbs.

The Sumatran or Tiger Barb is by far the most showy member of the family, which accounts for its widespread acclaim. Body length is usually under 2 inches. This fish is sometimes guilty of nipping an occasional fin, and it would be unwise to keep it in

the company of such long-finned species as the Angelfish or any of the Gourami family.

Although there are many species of *Rasbora*, the Harlequin Fish is so much better known than others that it is usually called simply "Rasbora." In an aquarium, they leave nothing to be desired: they are peaceful and colorful. They have an unusual velvety black triangle against a red background on the posterior half of the body. The anterior half has a violet iridescence. With red dorsal and tail fins, the *R. heteromorpha* is one of the most handsome of the smaller aquarium fishes.

Spawning this little beauty is not the easiest of tasks.

The White Cloud Mountain Fish from China, since its introduction in 1932, has been popular with fanciers the world over. A small fish, its maximum size is 1½ inches, and it has a slender body, deep blue on the back, with a golden stripe on the side, followed by a blue one below and a silvery belly.

HARLEQUIN FISH OR RASBORA: Because of its unusual appearance and peaceful nature, this is the most popular of the Rasbora species. Note the distinctive black triangle which marks the posterior half of its 2-inch red and violet body.

MARBLED HATCHET FISH: This deep-keeled beauty has mottled mother-of-pearl coloration and attains a length of 2 inches. Like other hatchet fish, it has proven difficult to breed, and thus far no one has been able to do so successfully.

The tail has a red area in the middle, and the dorsal fin is red with a blue edge.

This is probably the easiest of all egg-laying fishes to breed; a well-fed pair in a well-planted aquarium will produce great numbers of offspring, and seldom eat them unless pressed by hunger. The horizontal blue stripe in the youngsters is very bright. This species comes from slightly cooler waters than most of our tropicals, and a temperature of 70° F (21° C) is ample for them.

CHARACINS

The Characins are egg-layers and their breeding habits are diversified. In most cases eggs are deposited haphazardly among plant thickets, where the parents will eat most of them if not removed after spawning is completed. However, this is generalizing; individual spawning habits are discussed when the fish is described. Some habits are unique.

The Hatchet Fishes are among the more oddly-shaped fishes in this group; they have a keeled belly and huge pectoral fins. The Black-Winged Hatchet Fish is the smallest member of the family, and probably the easiest to keep. As these fish are top-feeders, probably jumping out of the water for insects in their natural habitat, this diet is not an easy one to duplicate. They are fond of swatted flies. You can train them to take floating dried foods, however. Breeding them is still an accomplishment which has not been realized. Keep the tank covered, or you are likely to find them in another tank or on the floor.

The Marbled Hatchet Fish is a bit larger than its preceding cousin, attaining 2 inches. The mottled pattern of wavy lines on a mother-of-pearl body distinguishes it from all the other Hatchet Fishes. Habits are similar, and this beauty has never been spawned either.

Like the other Hatchet Fishes, the Silver is attractive and oddly shaped. The body has the same deep keel, and the entire fish is silvery, with the exception of a black horizontal line. It attains a size of 2½ inches, and has never been bred in captivity. It is not one of the hardiest fishes to keep.

The Black Tetra is one of the larger Tetras, attaining a length of 3 inches. When large, they may cause some trouble if kept in a community aquarium with smaller fishes. Young specimens are especially attractive, with the posterior half of the body a deep black. This gradually fades to a grey as the fish gets older. The males are slimmer and smaller than the heavier-bodied females.

Breeding is easily accomplished if the sexes have been separated and well conditioned. The breeding aquarium should be at least 10 gallons in capacity; 15 or even 20 gallons is even better, because spawnings are large. Water should be partly fresh and nearly neutral, and there should be plenty of bushy plants. At about 78° F (25° C) driving will begin, the female often taking the initiative. Eggs are scattered all over the plants, and the parents should be removed immediately after spawning is completed. Fry should be given adequate feedings as soon as they become free-swimming.

Probably no other aquarium fish has caused the excitement that the Neon Tetra did when it was first introduced in the 1930's. They are aptly named for their bright flashy red stripe.

Body size of this slender fish is 11 inches. The upper half of the body, from the eye almost to the tail, is brilliant greenish blue. The belly is white, and the lower posterior half of the body is bright red. Females have a slightly deeper body.

The Neon Tetra is not an easy fish to breed; it is still one of the so-called "problem fishes," but it can be done.

The Glow-Light, a peaceful Tetra, made its appearance in the United States about the same time as the famous Neon Tetra, and has shared its popularity. It attains a length of 1¾ inches, and is

SILVER HATCHET FISH: As its name implies, this fish is silvery with one black stripe. It grows to a length of 2½ inches.

BLACK TETRA: At a length of 3 inches, this is one of the larger Tetras, and it can sometimes be a troublemaker if kept in a community aquarium. As is often the case, this species fades as it ages and the handsome dark black coloration of its posterior half turns to grey. The female's larger size helps to distinguish between the sexes.

NEON TETRA: Discovered in the 1930's in the Peruvian headwaters of the Amazon, this very popular, small, slender fish is a bright, greenish blue with white and red or black markings.

GLOW-LIGHT TETRA: Another small Tetra which grows to only 1¾ inches; its outstanding characteristic is the glowing red stripe along the side of its body.

characterized by a glowing red line through the center of the body which resembles nothing so much as a lighted neon tube. The male is considerably more slender than the female.

Water for spawning this fish should be slightly acid and quite soft. At a temperature of 78° to 80° F (26° to 27° C), the pair will soon be observed swimming closely together into the plants, which should not be too closely bunched. Here they lock fins and do a sort of "barrel roll," at the same time expelling a few eggs, some of which fall to the bottom. After the spawning is completed, the aquarium should be

GOLDEN TETRA: A shy and peaceful species, this bright golden tetra grows to a length of 1½ inches.

covered to shade it until the fry hatch; this takes place in about 48 hours. Parents should of course be removed when their work of spawning is done.

The Golden Tetra is an attractive little fish that looks as if it had been dipped in gold. It is only 1½ inches in length. Sexes cannot be distinguished by color, but the females have the deeper, heavier body. They have a peaceful, rather shy disposition.

Breeding is similar to the Black Tetra, but a smaller tank may be used.

The Head-and-Tail-Light is one of the old perennials among tropical aquariums. It is a sturdy, good-looking Tetra which is easily kept and bred. There is a bright red spot at the top of the tail base, which is matched by the upper half of the eye. When lighted from above, it looks as if it had lights glowing fore and aft. Males can be distinguished by a white spot in the anal fin.

Spawning is done in a manner similar to the Black Tetra but a smaller tank may be used, about 3 to 5 gallons in capacity.

The Feather Fin resembles the Head-and-Tail-Light a great deal in body form. The difference is that the bright spots are lacking, but the dorsal fin is adorned with a black spot, and the anal fin is edged with black. The female of this species is considerably heavier than the male, and sexes are easy to distinguish in mature pairs.

The same method given for spawning the Head-and-Tail-Light may also be used for this fish.

The Flame Tetra or Tetra from Rio has everything to recommend it: color, peaceful disposition, hardiness, and ease of breeding. It rarely attains a length of 2 inches; most adult specimens are nearer 1½ inches. The posterior half of the body is a bright red, as are the dorsal, tail, anal and ventral fins. Two short black bars adorn the sides in the front half of the body. The male is easily distinguished by the fact that his anal fin and the front half of the dorsal are edged with black.

Breeding is the same as for the Black Tetra, but smaller aquaria may be used.

The Lemon Tetra in the bare tanks of a dealer seems almost colorless, but this is not the case when it is transferred to a planted aquarium, where it becomes a thing of beauty. The body length is 1¾ inches when fully grown. There is a streak of lemon yellow in the upper half of the dorsal fin, as well as the front edge of the anal fin, which is further adorned with a black streak behind it, and a black edge. The eye is a brilliant red. Females have a deeper body and slightly less color.

Spawning is similar to that of the Black Tetra.

HEAD-AND-TAIL-LIGHT TETRA: Named for the bright red spot at the base of its tail and the red upper-half of its eye, this Tetra is easily kept and bred.

FEATHER FIN TETRA is similar to the Head-and-Tail-Light in size and shape, but its markings are black rather than red.

FLAME TETRA is so called because of its bright red coloration. Other distinguishing markings are the two black bars on the front half of its body. This fish rarely grows any longer than 1½ inches.

BLACK-LINED TETRA: A large silver tetra that attains 3 inches in length, this fish is distinguished by the dramatic black stripe that runs along its side and ends in a diamond at the tail.

The Black-Lined Tetra is one of the larger Tetras, which grows to about 3 inches in length. It is a silvery fish, with a prominent black horizontal line crossing the body from the gill-plate to the tail, where it ends in a triangular spot. The female is considerably deeper-bodied than the male.

These fish are easily propagated in the same manner as the Black Tetra. They are so hardy that it is possible for the breeders in Florida to raise them in huge quantities the year round in pools.

The first thing you notice about the Rosy Tetra is the large, showy dorsal fin of the male. It reaches a size of 1¾ inches. The body is a bit deeper than most members of this family, and healthy specimens have a rosy tint. The ventral and anal fins, as well as the outer edges of the tail are bright red, and the dorsal fin carries a large black area with white margins. The male's dorsal fin is about twice as long as that of his mate, making it an easy task to distinguish him.

It is easily bred in the same manner as the Black Tetra.

CICHLIDS

The Cichlids are another very large family which includes many aquarium fishes. Some have the drawback of being rather vicious, but all are interesting in their breeding habits; they are usually devoted parents, lavishing extreme affection on their young, but at times, for no apparent reason, they make a meal of them.

To breed the average Cichlid a tank of at least 20 gallons is required, with gravel and a few rocks in it. Separate the breeders for a time, until the female is heavy with roe, then place the pair in the tank. When they have become accustomed to their surroundings, the male begins to clean off one of the rocks. When this job is done to their mutual satisfaction, the female begins to glide over the rock. As her vent touches it, she releases a row of eggs which adhere there. The male follows just behind and fer-

tilizes the eggs. Row after row of eggs are laid and fertilized. The male usually takes charge of guarding them, although the female sometimes guards them too. When the eggs hatch, the parents dig holes in the gravel and move the young about. When the fry become free-swimming, they are constantly herded until such time as they revolt against this parental supervision. By this time the parents are often ready to spawn again. Brine shrimp or sifted daphnia should be provided when the fry begin to swim; the best food for the parents is cut-up garden worms or some other form of worm food.

There is something about the way an Angelfish moves that appeals to all who watch this most dignified of aquarium fish. It attains a size of 5 inches, has 4 vertical bands on a silvery body, and the dorsal is as high as the diameter of the body. The anal fin is the same length, with a long ray which extends back much further. The ventral fins consist only of a few rays, one of which is also very much elongated. The first and last rays of the tail fin are extended as well. The eye is red.

Eggs are laid Cichlid fashion, usually on the leaf of a large plant. Parental care is divided, and a well-mated pair will seldom eat their young, from which they should be removed as soon as they begin to swim.

An all-black variety has been developed which is one of the most popular aquarium fishes. Don't keep Barbs in the tank with Angelfishes.

The Discus is a beauty but hard to feed, hard to keep and almost impossible to breed. The body is shaped like a pancake stood on end, and attains a diameter of 9 inches. The main color is brown, and there are 9 vertical bars. The fins are blue, mottled with bright red. The male has some of these blue and red markings in the back and belly regions as well. The ventral fins are edged with bright red.

They spawn in a very similar manner to the Angelfish, whose habitat they share.

The Flag Cichlid is one of the really peaceful Cichlids, although it is a large one which sometimes

FLAG CICHLID is recognized by the black area that runs on a diagonal along the top of its body, as well as by the indistinct black bars that mark its side, and the black spot surrounded by a golden halo at the base of its tail. This species is quite large (6 inches) but of a peaceful disposition. (See also color section.)

grows to 6 inches. Its mark of distinction is an oblique line which begins at the mouth, travels upward through the eye, and ends at the tip of the dorsal fin. There are indistinct vertical bars, and a black spot at the tail base which is ringed with yellow.

There is no mistaking the large Fire-Mouth Cichlid: a fiery red area extends from the chin through the entire belly. The body is dark brown, with indistinct vertical bars and a horizontal line which ends in a large black spot in the middle of the body. There is another black spot in the red area at the bottom of the gill-plate. The male has the more pointed dorsal fin. A word of warning: this fish should not be kept in a community aquarium with smaller fishes. It is safe only in the company of big fellows like itself.

It breeds in Cichlid fashion.

The Agassiz Dwarf Cichlid is referred to as a "dwarf," being 3 inches in length at most. The shape of the tail is an easy means of identification: it comes to a single point. Body color is a yellowish brown. There is a black horizontal line from the mouth to the tip of the tail, and the fins are blue, edged with red. The female has plain round fins, and is a bit more yellow in body color.

Breeding is Cichlid style, but a much smaller aquarium may be used; 5 gallons is sufficient. There is one important difference, however: after spawn-ing, the little female begins to attack her much bigger mate, and may injure or even kill him if he is left with her. He should be removed, and the female will take over all parental duties herself.

Ramirez's Dwarf Cichlid, or Butterfly Cichlid, is blue, with a number of brown vertical bars, especially noticeable in the female. The body is sprinkled with gleaming light-blue spots. The high, saddle-shaped dorsal fin is blue, edged with orange, and the first rays are black. These first rays are elongated in the male. Large specimens sometimes attain 3 inches, but most are a bit smaller.

A temperature of 80° F (27° C) is recommended for their breeding, and they follow the procedure of the preceding species. They are a bit timid, however, and are apt to eat their eggs. Dense planting may help somewhat.

ANABANTIDS

Some very interesting and colorful fishes are included among the Anabantids, which are unusual in that they must occasionally come up for a gulp of air, and have a special breathing mechanism known as a "labyrinth" which handles this air. These fishes include the Betta, the Gouramis, and others. Most of them make nests at the surface by blowing bubbles; the eggs are placed into these and guarded.

The Siamese Fighting Fish are used in a gambling game in their own country. The males, while not

AGASSIZ DWARF CICHLID: The heart shape of the tail, the long ventral fins, and the dark stripe running along its side from the eye to the base of the tail are the distinguishing characteristics of this fish. Its body coloration ranges from brownish yellow to greenish blue and its size is 3 inches.

THREE-SPOT OR BLUE GOURAMI: In spite of its name, this fish has only two spots, one on its center and one at the base of its tail. Its body coloration is pale blue and its fins and tail transparent with white dots. Though a fish of generally peaceful habits, the Blue Gourami should not be put in a breeding tank because it will kill and eat the fry.

particularly vicious when alone, become hellions when another male is placed in close quarters with them. A good fighter fish, like a fighting-cock in Mexico, can be a valuable asset to its owner.

There is very little resemblance between the short-finned, not particularly colorful fish which the Siamese use and the long-finned, brightly-colored beauties which have been developed from them. The body is slender and 2½ inches long, with long, flowing tail and anal fins, and a high dorsal. Color varieties are numerous, with many combinations of blue, green, red, and a white-bodied fish with red or blue fins. There is even an albino with a white body and fins, and pink eyes. The females have shorter fins and heavier abdomens. They thrive on living foods, but can be carried over for quite a time on prepared foods also.

The breeding behavior of this fish, as well as the other members of the family, is an interesting procedure. Fill a 10-gallon aquarium to a depth of about 5 inches with water which has been aged a few days, and is about neutral. No gravel is required on the bottom, and there is no need for plants. First place the male in the tank. When he signifies his willingness to spawn by blowing a mass of bubbles, introduce a female whose abdomen is bulging. After many tries, the male will lure her under the bubbles, where he wraps his body around hers and squeezes a few eggs out of her, which he fertilizes at the same time. This act is repeated over and over, until the female is depleted, at which time she is driven away. The male then takes full charge of the bubble-nest, and the female should be taken out. In about 30 to 40 hours the eggs hatch, and the male keeps busy retrieving fry which fall out of the nest to the bottom. When the fry become free-swimming, they leave the nest and begin to search for food, at which time the male's work is done, and he should be removed. Dust-fine foods may be fed at this time, to be followed by freshly hatched brine shrimp, which the youngsters soon learn to tear to pieces with their sharp teeth.

Probably the best-known of the Gouramis is the Dwarf Gourami. It is a small fish, the male about 2 inches in length, and the females slightly smaller. They are a peaceful species. As is usual with fishes, the male comes in for the lion's share of the colors. There are alternating slanting vertical bars of bright blue and red which pass through the entire length of the body, and the fins are orange, sprinkled with red. At spawning time, the region from the chin to the belly is suffused with bright deep blue. The female has pale bars and plain fins. The ventral fins are unique: they consist of one long ray, which is very flexible. These fins are used as "feelers" and the fish touches everything within range with them.

Breeding is the same as for the Siamese, except that these fish like to weave some plant leaves into their nest so a few floating plants are welcome.

The Three-Spot or Blue Gourami has only two spots on each side of the body. It grows as large as 5 inches, at which size it should be kept with large fishes only. The entire body of the male is suffused with blue, and there are many irregular wobbly vertical dark bars. The fins are a lighter blue, and covered with large white dots.

They breed like Siamese, and are easily raised.

Many people consider the peaceful Pearl or Mosaic Gourami the most beautiful of all the Gouramis. It grows to 5 inches. The body is covered with a fine, reticulated pattern, and the ground color is silvery with a mother-of-pearl sheen, which often shows as a pale violet. At spawning time, the male develops an orange-red area from the chin all through the belly area. Another way to distinguish him is by the deeper anal and higher dorsal fins. Both sexes show a heavy black line which begins at the mouth and fades out about three-quarters of the way down the body.

This fish breeds like the Siamese.

MYERS' CORYDORAS is distinguished by the heavy black stripe that runs along its back much like that of the Arched Corydoras, except that the stripe starts at the back of the head rather than at the mouth. Its coloration is pinkish brown.

CATFISHES

The Armored Catfishes are identified by a series of bony plates on the sides in lieu of scales. They spend their time on the bottom grubbing around for some bit of food the others missed, a habit which makes them extremely valuable to the aquarist. Not only do they clean up otherwise uneaten food, but they also keep the gravel loose around the plant roots, thereby cultivating them. Seldom is their digging vigorous enough to dislodge rooted plants.

These bony fishes require calcium, so give them slightly alkaline water in the breeding tank. Not much planting is required; most of the eggs are deposited on the glass sides. A 10-gallon aquarium is ample for all *Corydoras* species. The breeding act is interesting. The pair become unusually active, and chase about a great deal. Finally the male stops, and rolls over on his side. The female attaches herself to him by sucking her mouth to his belly; at the same time 4 or 5 eggs are expelled into a pocket which the female makes by pushing together her ventral fins. She then lets go and swims to a previously selected site, usually a spot on the glass sides, and first rubs the spot with her mouth, and then pushes the sticky eggs there. This process is repeated frequently. At 80° F (27° C), which is the proper spawning temperature, the eggs hatch in 72 hours. The parents seldom bother their young, but there is no point in tempting them, so they should be removed. Dust-fine food should be stirred into a small jar full of water, to allow it to soak and sink to the bottom; live foods may follow when the youngsters grow.

The Arched Corydoras is easily distinguished from the rest of the family by a wide black stripe which runs from the mouth up through the eye and along the back all the way to the bottom of the tail base. Its size is 2½ inches. It hasn't been spawned.

The Bronze Catfish is the most popular member of the family. The sides have a slight greenish bronze tinge, and the maximum size attained is 3 inches. Sex can be easily distinguished by looking down from above: the males are smaller, and the females are wider. Spawning occurs as described for the genus.

Myers' Corydoras is very similar to *C. arcuatus*. It has a darker, pinkish-brown body, and the wide black line, instead of curving from the mouth through the eye, starts just behind the head.

This fish breeds as described for the genus, but there is a peculiarity in the offspring: the front half of the body is red, the back half bright green and the fins are pink. As the fish grows up, the green area gradually becomes the black line, and the pink area spreads out over the lower half of the body.

The Dwarf Catfish, the smallest member of the family, at maturity is 1½ inches and it is easily recognized. The body color is brown, with a horizontal stripe of black which ends in a triangular spot at the caudal base. Spawnings are numerous but small in number, and the young are not eaten if the parents are well fed. Fry are large, and well able to fend for themselves.

DWARF CATFISH: This species has brown coloration with a black stripe and black tail markings. As its name would suggest, it is the smallest member of the catfish family.

BLACK-SPOTTED CATFISH: This species has flesh-pink body coloration, a black "mask" over its eyes, and a black patch spreading out from the base of the dorsal fin. It grows to a length of 2½ inches.

The Black-Spotted Catfish has a pinkish body peppered with small black spots, as is the tail. The face is black, and there is a black area in the dorsal fin which extends down a little way into the body. For spawning, they require a well-planted aquarium in a spot which is partly shaded; otherwise they are inclined to be very nervous and shy.

This introduction to tropical fish has, up to this point, purposely avoided the use of Latin names. But since these names are an invaluable aid in making exact identifications, and since you will certainly encounter them in other literature on the subject, the following reference list has been included, giving the Latin name of each species mentioned in this section or appearing in the color pages of this book. It is not to be mistaken for a complete list of all tropical fish, as there are many other species in addition to those discussed here. Also, keep in mind when using the list, that scientists are not in complete agreement on all these names, because taxonomy—the science of naming and classifying living things—is constantly changing as new species are discovered or known ones are reclassified.

In principle, the names of fishes, as well as the names of all plants and animals, are made up in much the same way as those of people. The only difference is that the more important name (which relates to the surname) takes the first position. It is as if Harry Jones, for instance, were to be called Jones Harry, which is, to be sure, the way he is listed in the telephone directory. Now take, for example, the Latin name of the Pearl Danio. The more important name, called the "generic" name— that is, the name of the genus—always begins with a capital letter, thus: *Brachydanio*. The "specific" name—that is, the name of the species to which the fish belongs—follows, as *albolineatus*. The specific name begins with a lower-case letter.

The *full*, scientific name of a fish consists of four parts: the name of the genus, the name of the species, the name of the "author," and the year. The year (which does not appear in this list) marks the time of the *first* scientific description of the fish. The author is the scientist (often the discoverer) who wrote up and published the first description. The specific name is given by the author in accordance with factors characterizing and distinguishing this particular specimen from other species of the same genus which have already been described and published.

Agassiz Dwarf Cichlid, *Apistogramma agassizi* Steindachner
Angelfish, *Pterophyllum eimekei* Ahl
Arched Corydoras, *Corydoras arcuatus* Elwin
Black Ruby Barb, *Puntius nigrofasciatus* Günther
Black Clown Upside-Down Catfish, *Synodontis angelicus* Schilthuis
Black-Finned Pacu, *Colossoma nigrippine* Cope
Black-Lined Tetra, *Hyphessobrycon scholzei* Ahl
Black-Spot Barb, *Puntius filamentosus* Cuvier and Valenciennes
Black-Spotted Catfish, *Corydoras melanistius* Regan
Black Tetra, *Gymnocorymbus ternetzi* Boulenger
Black-Winged Hatchet Fish, *Carnegiella marthae* Myers
Bronze Catfish, *Corydoras aeneus* Gill
Checkered Barb, *Puntius oligolepis* Bleeker
Cherry Barb, *Puntius titteya* Deraniyagala
Clown Barb, *Puntius everetti* Boulenger
Clown Loach, *Botia macracantha* Bleeker
Jack Dempsey Cichlid, *Cichlasoma octofasciatum* Regan
Discus, *Symphysodon discus* Heckel
Dwarf Catfish, *Corydoras hastatus* Eigenmann
Dwarf Gourami, *Colisa lalia* Hamilton-Buchanan
Feather Fin, *Hemigrammus unilineatus* Gill
Flag Cichlid, *Cichlasoma festivum* Heckel
Fire-Mouth Cichlid, *Cichlasoma meeki* Brind
Flame Tetra or Tetra from Rio, *Hyphessobrycon flammeus* Myers
Giant Danio, *Danio malabaricus* Jerdon
Glass Catfish, *Kryptopterus bicirrhis* Cuvier and Valenciennes
Golden Tetra, *Hemigrammus armstrongi* Schultz and Axelrod
Glow Light Tetra, *Hemigrammus gracilis* Reinhardt
Guppy, *Poecilia reticulata* Peters
Half-Lined Leporinus, *Leporinus nigrotaeniatus* Schomburgk
Harlequin Fish or Rasbora, *Rasbora heteromorpha* Duncker
Head-and-Tail-Light Tetra, *Hemigrammus ocellifer* Steindachner
Leaf Fish, *Monocirrhus polyacanthus* Heckel
Lemon Tetra, *Hyphessobrycon pulchripinnis* Ahl
Marbled Hatchet Fish, *Carnegiella vesca*
Myers' Corydoras, *Corydoras myersi* M. Ribeiro
Mystus Catfish, *Schilbe mystus* Linnaeus
Neon Tetra, *Hyphessobrycon innesi* Myers
Ornate Catfish, *Chrysichthys ornatus* Boulenger
Pearl Danio, *Brachydanio albolineatus* Blyth
Pearl or Mosaic Gourami, *Trichogaster leeri* Bleeker
"Pimelodella angelicus," *Pimelodus pictus* Steindachner
Platy, *Xiphophorus maculatus* Günther
Red Hook, *Myloplus rubripinnis* Müller and Troschel
Rosy Barb, *Puntius conchonius* Hamilton-Buchanan
Rosy Tetra, *Hyphessobrycon rosaceus* Durbin
Siamese Fighting Fish, *Betta splendens* Regan
Siamese Tiger Fish, *Datnioides microlepis* Bleeker
Ramirez's Dwarf Cichlid *Apistogramma ramirezi* Myers and Harry
Silver Hatchet Fish, *Gasteropelecus levis* Eigenmann
Spotted Danio, *Brachydanio nigrofasciatus* Day
Sumatran or Tiger Barb, *Puntius tetrazona* Bleeker
Swordtail Helleri, *Xiphophorus helleri* Heckel
Three-Spot or Blue Gourami, *Trichogaster trichopterus* Palas
White Cloud Mountain Fish, *Tanichthys albonubes* Lin
Zebra Danio, *Brachydanio rerio* Hamilton-Buchanan

INDOOR GARDENING

There are few things so gratifying as planting something and watching it grow.

You may have discovered this and may be a great gardening enthusiast already. If so, you probably have a few house plants such as geraniums, bulbs, African violets, or philodendrons in your home. But you may not have considered growing herbs or Cacti, both of which are practical, attractive, and easy to care for.

This section will introduce you to the different kinds of fragrant herbs and Cacti and other succulent plants that you can grow indoors, and will tell you how to care for them. If you have never tried any indoor gardening, this may be the time to start, particularly if you are a high-rise dweller or someone who has little or no land on which you can garden. Gardening indoors in pots and window boxes is also the answer for those people living in areas which have overly long winters.

YOUR INDOOR HERB GARDEN

No longer think of herbs only as bits of dry seasoning, bottled and hidden on the kitchen shelves. There isn't a room in any house or apartment that won't be more attractive with fragrant herbs growing there.

If you are an apartment dweller, surrounded by concrete out-of-doors, you can have an indoor herb garden. In fact, you can grow almost as many varieties of herbs indoors as you could in an average-sized outdoor garden. On the other hand, if you have a herb garden outdoors, you will enjoy being surrounded by herbs inside too. For example, why not have a sweet scented geranium in your living room? These lovely plants were often found in Victorian parlors. Dittany of Crete (*Origanum dictamus*), immortalized by Virgil, was also popular. Both will fit into your home.

There are several ways to begin your indoor herb garden. You may bring plants in from your outdoor garden, if you have one; start plants from seeds, from cuttings or you may acquire the plants themselves from a friend, a florist or nursery, and then pot them as described later in this section.

Starting on page 74, there is a list of herbs that will grow well indoors, with descriptions and instructions for starting them. But here, to give you an idea of the wide choice you have, is a quick rundown.

HERBS TO GROW INDOORS

Perennials	Annuals	Perennial Shrubs
Burnet	Anise	Dittany
Chives	Basil	Geranium,
Germander	Borage	scented
Lemon balm	Chervil	Lemon verbena
Marjoram,	Dill	Rosemary
sweet	Lavender	
Mint (pepper-	Parsley	
mint and	Savory, summer	
spearmint)		
Sage		
Tarragon		
Thyme		

The following perennials should be bought as plants, or the plants raised in the garden and brought into the house when they are well established:

Chives	Lemon balm	Lemon verbena	Mint
Rosemary	Sage	Tarragon	Thyme

If you are starting new annuals to bring indoors, plant them late in the season outdoors and transplant before the first frost.

You may plant seeds of sweet marjoram, parsley, basil, dill, anise and coriander directly in your indoor containers. However, there is never any trouble bringing plants of parsley and basil in from the

Condensed from "Herb Magic and Garden Craft" by Louise Evans Doole © 1972 by Sterling Publishing Co., Inc., New York

garden. Choose small plants of basil, since they are apt to grow quite tall, and small parsley plants, since otherwise the taproot would be too deep to transplant.

If you want to grow chives and do not wish to divide your outdoor clump, buy another clump and set it in a bulb pan or low pot filled with light, sweet soil. Cut back the foliage and let new growth start. There is no need to waste the trimmings; chop and freeze them. Put the chives in a sunny window where they will not get too warm—55° to 60° F (13° to 16° C) is best—and keep them on the dry side. One reason that so many people have trouble keeping chives growing through the winter is the heat of the kitchen.

In your outdoor garden you may have had some perennials such as rose geranium, rosemary and lavender which need the protection of the house during the winter. These plants are not easy to start from seed, nor are the plants themselves readily available. So, once started, you will not want to take the chance of letting them winter-kill. Bring them inside.

If your house space is limited, try this idea. Keep one rose geranium indoors and let it grow as large as it wishes, so that you can cut slips from it. Let the geranium be the focal point of the planter instead of the more usual cut-leaf philodendron, which almost every house plant owner has climbing up a center pole of spagnum moss. Why not be different? Fasten the leggy branches of your rose geranium to the pole, and put your smaller herbs around it. Give the planter a place on the floor or on a low table by a sunny window.

CONTAINERS

In general, pots are more successful than boxes for herb growing. Glazed pottery makes good containers since the roots do not dry out as quickly as they will in clay pots. Plastic is satisfactory for the same reason. However, there is one danger with non-porous containers. The plants, if overwatered, may become waterlogged and rot. So if you prefer, you

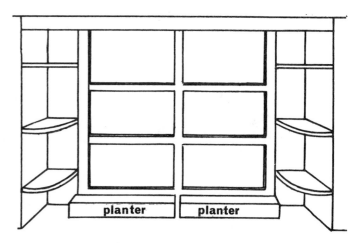

You can use this arrangement for a dining room or breakfast room window. If you are building a new house or remodelling your kitchen, consider this built-in herb garden. A planter at the sink will hold half a dozen herbs, which will thrive happily in sun and moisture. And how convenient for you when you need a bit of seasoning or a sprig for garnishing!

may set unglazed pots in the more decorative containers of glazed pottery or metal.

The trouble with miniature pots is that they will not keep herbs alive for more than a couple of weeks. With 5-inch pots, you can use your herbs all winter, and set them out again in the spring if you also have an outdoor garden. So, if you use this idea, choose a larger container or fill it with fewer individual pots.

If you do not have enough pots for all your herbs, paint tin cans in bright shades, and letter the names of the herbs in gold or some other paint that contrasts. You may punch a few holes in the sides near the bottom for drainage. Instead of painting, you might prefer to cover the cans with the attractive paper which sticks to any surface and can be kept clean by wiping with a damp cloth.

When you start looking for pots or containers in which to plant your herbs, you will find interesting ideas all round you. Poke into storage shelves, the attic and basement, the kitchen cupboards. A big iron skillet will make an attractive planter when filled with small pots of herbs. First, line it with heavy aluminum foil so that it will not rust, and fill the spaces between the pots with damp peat moss or vermiculite. This suggestion is just to get you started. You will enjoy creating planters or containers out of whatever is handy.

If you planted a terra cotta jar or strawberry jar for your terrace, it can come indoors for the winter. Some of the plants should be cut back to ensure vigorous growth before frost, while other plants may need to be replaced. Your family room or basement

When you are in a remodelling mood, consider a window set at an angle to catch the sun and double the sill planting space.

recreation room would be a pleasant place to put the jar. If sun is lacking, consider fluorescent lighting.

Rose geraniums and lemon balm make interesting bathroom decorations. Keep them trim by pinching off fragrant leaves for your bath water.

A small pot of herbs, or a group of several arranged on the dining table, will make a charming scented decoration—and you will enjoy clipping a few leaves to add to salads or drinks.

POTTING

Most herbs do best in an alkaline soil. Here is a potting mixture for those which are to be kept indoors:

2 parts good garden loam
1 part leaf mold or peat moss
1 part sharp sand (not the smooth, fine variety).

To each half-bushel of this mixture add:
1 pint raw crushed limestone or finely crushed plaster
½ pint bone meal
1 quart well rotted or commercial manure.

Make up the mixture at least two weeks ahead of time so that the soil will have time to become alkalized before you pot the plants.

You may have another potting soil that you prefer, but whatever you use, remember to mix in some limestone. As to the quantity of manure, it is difficult to be exact. Use your judgment, and keep notes for another season. Keep in mind that if you wish to have lush greenery, you should use a rich soil. But for richness and fragrance, use a fairly poor potting soil.

Drainage is extremely important. If you decide to use nonporous containers, start with a few bits of broken clay pot or bits of brick, then add a layer of coarse gravel.

Partially fill the container with potting soil. Set the plant in gently, making a hole in which to lower the root if necessary. Then gently pack more soil about the roots, making sure not to cramp them or to cover the crown, the junction of stem and root. The soil should come to within about one-half inch of the top of the pot. Sprinkle well with water and keep in the shade until the plant sends up leaves.

If you set the pots in saucers, elevate them a bit so that the water can drain out easily.

ARTIFICIAL LIGHT

If your house or apartment lacks sunlight, consider fluorescent lighting. Artificial light for growing plants is becoming more widely used all the time.

You can set up a miniature garden in any corner of your house with the use of fluorescent lighting. A strawberry jar, a china cabinet, a bookcase, a table top or set of special shelves can be made into an indoor garden merely by mounting two 40-watt fluorescent tubes in a fixture over the area. This will be sufficient for a growing area of about 3 x 4 feet, and the tubes should come within a foot of the plants. Keep the lights on for approximately 14 hours a day; the cost will be very little.

If you prefer to use incandescent light bulbs, use 60- or 75-watt bulbs and keep the plants about 2 feet away. This is important since the bulbs give off heat. You will not want to wilt your tender herbs.

WATERING

All of your herbs like moisture in the air but not too much in the pots. A weekly watering plus an occasional misting with a fine spray will keep them in good condition.

Water only when the top soil feels dry. Then do not merely sprinkle the top, but wet down thoroughly until you can see water seeping out of the hole in the bottom of the pot. Do not water again until the soil seems dry. Plants may be as easily ruined by too much water as by too little. Keep them damp but not wet.

One of the worst conditions with which house plants must contend is the excessive dryness of the air. A good way to provide the extra moisture they need is to set the pots in shallow trays filled with pebbles. You can use a baking pan or a plastic tray. The heavy aluminum foil pans in which some baked goods or frozen foods are packed are excellent for this purpose, and you can find almost any size and shape you need.

If your plants are to be set in the same windows each year, it may pay you to have special trays made to fit the sills. They should be the length and width of the sill and about 2 inches high. If your window sills are narrow, you can buy or make extensions which can be attached and removed easily.

After these trays or pans are filled with pebbles, add water until it just shows and keep it at that level. Good news: the moisture provided for the plants will be good for your family, too.

HEALTH HINTS

Indoor gardening is a healthful hobby. Not only will the herbs stimulate your appetite, but their habits will also help you keep a check on your own. They are fresh-air enthusiasts, and once a day, unless the temperature is far below freezing, open the window and let them breathe. You can breathe right along with them unless you are a softie.

Keep your herbs in a south or southeast window if possible. They are sun worshippers, and the more sun they get, the more they will show their appreciation by vigorous growth. If you don't expect them to do as well indoors as out, you won't be disappointed. Apartments are often kept much too warm for healthy plants, and unless you have a seldom-used room or a sun porch, you may have to choose between an overheated room and healthy herbs.

The temperature which all but the most tender perennials like best is between 50° and 55° F (10° and 13° C), although some take to warmer rooms. Do not be afraid to try any herb you choose, however. If you turn the heat down at night and keep the plants near a window during the day, they are very likely to survive.

Herbs do not need much fertilizer, but after six weeks you may give them a little balanced plant food once a month if they seem to need it.

Plant lice are not too great a problem with herbs. But if you are moving outdoor plants inside for the winter, it's a good idea to spray them with a soapy solution containing some nicotine insecticide before bringing them into the house. Repeat this at intervals of two or three weeks if you think it necessary.

The automatic pruning as you cut leaves for cookery will keep new foliage coming on, and will encourage a thick and bushy growth. With herbs, you see, you may have your plants and eat them, too!

HOUSE-HAPPY HERBS

Here are some of the herbs which will grow well indoors. Choose as many of these as you can find room for. They will bring fragrance to your home, exciting taste to your foods, and a little fillip to your imagination.

 ANISE

Hung over your bed, anise may not make you as fair and youthful as our ancestors believed, but surely the new interest which it brings to foods will keep your appetite young. Although anise is generally grown for its sweet seed, the fresh leaves are appetizing in fruit salads, soups, stews and herb teas.

Start anise from seed or bring in a young plant from the garden and let it have plenty of sunlight.

 BASIL

This herb grows particularly well in the kitchen, for it doesn't mind the heat. Keep the plants trim by using the leaves generously in salads, stews, ground meats, poultry stuffings and fruit cups. It is a necessity in any dish containing tomato, or with fresh tomatoes. If you have enough basil, sprays are beautiful in bouquets.

Start basil from seeds or bring in healthy small plants from the garden. You can put three or four light green, smooth-leaved basil plants in the same container. In the spring, set the basil plants back in the garden. These plants can be counted on to produce seed. This is not always true of those raised the first year from seed, especially if your growing season is too short for seeds to ripen thoroughly.

 BORAGE

Although borage is more attractive in the garden than in the house, a pot containing three or four plants will furnish young cucumber-flavored leaves for salads and cool drinks. If it blooms, the blue flowers are worth the space given this somewhat coarse, hairy-leafed plant. Borage loses its flavor when dried, so use its young, tender leaves.

Start the borage from seed or bring in young plants from the garden.

 BURNET

Burnet trails its feathery leaves when grown indoors. It is one of the prettiest plants, and the dainty, cucumber-flavored leaves are delicious in salads. A sprig is attractive in cool drinks.

Because of their trailing stems, burnet, santolina (French lavender), and sweet marjoram are good choices for hanging pots or those placed on shelves at cupboard ends or alongside windows.

Bring burnet in from the garden or buy a plant.

CHERVIL

LAVENDER

This fine-leaved herb resembles parsley in looks but not in taste. It is too lovely to look at and too good to eat to be left out of the kitchen herb garden. Bring in a plant and use the fresh anise-flavored leaves for garnishing and to season sauces, soups and salads. The white blossoms are small and fragile. It will germinate rapidly and may be grown from seed.

CHIVES

If you have both an outdoor and indoor garden, divide a large purchased clump and bring part of it to the kitchen window. The spiky leaves are excellent wherever a delicate onion taste is desired.

DILL

The Orientals used dill in brewing up charms. We "charm" our guests by using its seeds in pickles, fish sauces and salads, and use the leaves, too, in cooking. Why not try them?

Sow dill seed in a large pot and do not thin it out. It makes a pretty feathery plant. Dill grows rapidly, even indoors, so it may produce its yellow flowers in fairly large umbrels.

GERMANDER

Germander makes a handsome house plant. Its low branching growth is luxuriant with dark green, glossy leaves and small purplish-rose blooms. However, it is not likely to bloom indoors since it needs a great deal of sun if it is to produce flowers. Start germander from seed, cuttings or root division.

The fragrant lavender makes an especially pleasant house plant. You will have to buy plants to start with. Give them a dry and sunny home. If you have managed to establish lavender in the outdoor garden, it is best to bring the plants indoors for the winter unless you live in a very mild climate.

LEMON BALM

One of the most fragrant of all herbs, lemon balm is worthy of a place in practically any room in the house. Planted outdoors, it grows erect, but when you bring it indoors, the stems tend to trail over the sides of the pot in a lovely effect. Use lemon balm in potpourris, sachets, in the bath water, in floral bouquets, teas, fruit salads and drinks.

If you have lemon balm in the garden, dig up a generous number of plants for the house. Otherwise, get seeds or roots from a nursery.

MARJORAM

Sweet marjoram is one of those herbs which *must* be included in the kitchen window garden. Either dig up a plant, or start a fresh one from seed. Better yet, try both methods. You'll find marjoram well worth the trouble.

MINT

Most popular among the 40 varieties are spearmint and peppermint. Mint will thrive indoors if kept in a temperature of not more than 65° F (18° C) and out of the hot sun. It likes filtered sunlight for part of the day. What a joy to drop a few fresh leaves of mint into a cup of hot tea when you are tired or out of sorts. In winter, minced fresh mint in carrots or peas may help you forget that garden-fresh vegetables are still months away.

In the autumn, pot a clump in heavy soil. Keep it well soaked and let it remain outdoors (on your window sill if necessary) until after the first heavy frost. You can then cut back the tops and bring it inside. Beg a root or cutting from a friend, or buy one at a nursery. The cuttings root rapidly in a glass of water.

PARSLEY

This herb, one of the oldest known to man, is as popular today as always. When grown in a sunny window in a glazed or metal pot so that the roots will not dry out, it will thrive for a long time. Use rather small plants, for the taproots of mature plants are long. Parsley does better in a cool temperature. Do not use fertilizer. Although parsley will do well inside, it will not be as strong and full as when it grows outdoors. The curly-leafed variety is the prettiest, the flat-leafed type the tastiest.

If you do not have a plant to bring in from the garden, it should be easy to get one from a nursery.

ROSE GERANIUM

Best-known and easiest to find of the fragrant-leaved geraniums is the rose geranium. The leaves are useful in potpourris, sachets and in bouquets, and they are soothing in the tub. A bit of leaf in a cup of tea gives an indescribable fragrance. Use it in apple jelly and cakes.

Start new plants with cuttings from an established plant. Since they are sensitive to cold, you must bring rose geraniums indoors in the winter.

ROSEMARY

Rosemary, the herb of poetry and legend, is not easy to grow, but it is worth the trouble. Grown in a pot as a house plant, it may be less than a foot tall and its lower branches will fall gracefully over the sides of the pot. The leaves resemble long, oval pine needles, particularly when dried. The leaves of rosemary are more fragrant than the flowers, and when gently crushed, they will give off the warm aroma of pine.

Rosemary is a tropical plant, and it must be cut back, potted and brought indoors before frost. Your first plant should be purchased from a nursery as it is hard to start rosemary from seed.

SAGE

If you can find a small sage bush, it may be brought indoors. Its furry grey-green leaves are attractive and its fragrance pleasant. Although you will probably use sage which you dried during the summer, a growing plant gives a nice variation in hue to your indoor garden.

TARRAGON

Tarragon must be brought in for the winter in most climates, and may be set back in the garden in the spring. Early in the summer, start new plants from cuttings, for tarragon does not set seed which will germinate. Plunge the new plants in the earth, pots and all, and let them grow during the summer. When the first heavy frost causes the leaves to fall, you can trim back the stems and transfer the plants to larger pots for wintering indoors. Its young leaves are delicious in eggs, fish, meat and poultry dishes and salads.

Plants must be purchased at a nursery.

THYME

Thyme will thrive in your window. Use it sparingly, in poultry stuffings, stuffed peppers, onions, zucchini squash, in meat and fish dishes.

Start thyme from seed, and make sure that it has a sunny spot in which to grow.

FLOWERING CACTI AND OTHER SUCCULENT PLANTS

The two words "succulent plant" are probably well known to you, and in any event are very simple to define. They indicate plants which, from an anatomical and structural point of view, have undergone modifications in order to accumulate reserve substances, and thus present a fleshy appearance. Such modifications are not always carried out in the same part of the plant. Sometimes it is the leaves which become thick; in other plants the stems swell and take on a peculiar appearance, reaching enormous dimensions in diameter, and bearing no resemblance to other kinds of plants. In other cases, the base of the stem forms a sort of protuberance from which normal stems and leaves develop every year. Or the stem may thicken and carry thinly spreading branches.

Why has nature produced plants with such strange shapes? The reason lies in the kind of existence such plants lead in nature. Living in very unusual regions they have developed an organism which permits them to withstand the hazards of the climate. In fact, as these regions are usually situated in tropical and sub-tropical zones, and have very limited rainfall, it is necessary for the plants to store reserves of water during the wet season, so that they may survive during the long dry season. It is because of this acclimatization that succulents can be grown indoors in dry, overheated apartments.

CACTUS FAMILY CARE

Cacti are among the best-liked house plants because they are basically undemanding and they delight the eye with their bizarre shapes as well as with their lovely blossoms. Their care is much simpler than that of orchids, for instance. Two main misconceptions, however, lead to many a failure in the care of Cacti. During their period of growth, their need for water is easily under-estimated; and during their winter resting period, they are often kept too warm. Nearly all Cacti love the open sun in summer. Leaf Cacti such as the Christmas Cactus and Phyllocactus (*Epiphyllum*), quite to the contrary, are damaged by it. They go through a less pronounced resting period than the Cacti from arid regions and have greater need for water. It is important to water Cacti with soft water and to use a fertilizer that is low in nitrogen. It goes without saying that they are hardly watered at all during their resting period.

Without going into the details of systematic botany, succulent plants are represented by more than 400 species belonging to some 20 families. Let us look at the most typical, and those most frequently encountered. The Cactaceae family, whose individual representatives everyone knows under the name of Cactus, consists essentially of succulent plants. Without going into great detail concerning every family, it is certainly worth while noting a few striking examples. There is, for instance, the Ampelidaceae family—and who does not know it, having eaten its delicious fruit and sipped its rare vintages? This is simply the Vine family. Another kind appears within the range of succulent plants, the Cissus, in the Cucurbitaceae family. It is the Melon, of which three or four kinds make this family eligible for classification as a succulent.

There are two other families whose plants are well known. The Aloe, which is quite frequently confused with the Agave by many people, belongs to the Liliaceae family, like the Leek. The Agave, a more widespread species, belongs to the Amaryllidaceae family. The Geranium (more properly known as Pelargonium) has, besides those varieties which decorate our gardens and balconies, several examples of quite different form, which are also classed as succulents.

It can be appreciated that the adaptation of plants to life in arid conditions is because they have one purpose—to live and to endure. Planting them in your home will give you great pleasure, especially when they flower.

Some Cacti are only of decorative interest, but there are others which are, surprisingly, a prime necessity. These plants live in arid regions, in a dry and pebbly soil devoid of other vegetation. By their presence, such Cacti manage to change the appearance of these regions. By casting shade on the ground they prevent too much desiccation, and promote condensation of dew during the night. The plants themselves even eject a little water from their reserve—

a form of sweating. All this contributes in lightly tempering the climate of these regions. The roots, many of which are found near to the surface of the earth, conserve what soil there is. If they were not there, the soil would be swept away by the wind, or by the rain during the rainy season. Even dead plants are of some importance, for valuable humus is formed by the decomposition of Cactus fruits, broken branches and dead plants. Plants with decaying leaves more rapidly modify those regions where they install themselves. Other less specialized plants develop, and these regions begin to take on an almost normal aspect. Thus one can say that Cacti maintain animal and plant life in regions where nothing, at first, seemed able to exist. It is important to know this when you cultivate Cacti at home.

Succulent plants do not involve great expense. Their shapes harmonize well with contemporary décor in the home, and, not least, they are hardy plants. They can be left out of doors during the entire summer, they survive drought (especially Cacti), and so one does not have to worry about watering them when away from home; and even when not away, how many people forget to water their plants, and are quite surprised to see them wither! At least with succulent plants these inconveniences are greatly diminished.

HOW TO GROW SUCCULENTS

Several courses of action are possible in order to obtain plants for making a collection.

The easiest is to buy plants at a responsible florist's. Among these some may be the flowering type, and others purely decorative by reason of their silky hairs or the coloration of their spines. A second method consists in taking cuttings from the plants of a friend.

The last method is to buy seed. To grow from seed, however, is a long process, and sometimes disappointing; yet there is much satisfaction when such plants flower for the first time. It is a fitting reward for patience, and let us admit, one is always happy to have been successful in one's own cultivation.

Sowing is a procedure, widely used by growers of Cacti, which can be employed by the amateur. A flower pot and a sheet of glass are sufficient. The pot must be drained and filled with a light sandy soil, peat moss for example, or a mixture composed of half river-sand and half leaf mold, the whole being finely sieved. The seeds sown on the soil should be lightly packed down. The smallest should not be covered, while the largest need to be covered with a layer of soil, equal to their size. The pot should be

lightly watered, care being taken not to disarrange the seeds. Then place a plate of glass on top of it.

If the sowing is done near the end of spring, the pot can be placed on a window sill, where the warmth of the sun will be sufficient at this time of year to ensure germination. The main things are to keep the soil slightly damp, and watch the sun, which is sometimes too strong at this season, and may therefore burn the young plants through the glass. To shade the pot place a sheet of paper on the glass during the hottest part of the day. As the tiny plants develop they should gradually be given air by raising the glass a little, and finally removing it completely. Planting in a window box (or outside) takes place after a lapse of time, and according to the species, varying from two to three months from the date of sowing.

Growing succulents from cuttings is a very widespread method, and nearly always proves satisfactory for the amateur. For cuttings of Cacti, the wound resulting from a cut must be allowed to dry for several days. Cuttings of other succulent plants can be planted out as soon as the cuttings are made. The soil for cuttings must be light and sandy. Moderate watering at the beginning must become more frequent after rooting. The best time is the period stretching from the end of spring to early autumn.

Grafting is a process specially employed for Cacti, either for the multiplication of the cristate forms, or to obtain more rapid growth in certain species with slow vegetation, when cultivated from their own roots.

To cultivate and care for succulent plants is a complex problem, because the wide variety of plants forming this group require different care; we shall restrict ourselves merely to a few words of advice. But if your passion for cultivation becomes increasingly strong, consult specialized works on the subject. Which plants are used most often for interior decoration? Generally Cacti, and some of the other

succulent plants, such as the Aloe and Agave. The too delicate plants naturally rule themselves out.

There is a rule common to all these plants: they like the sun! During winter months, the period when plants have to be brought indoors, the best possible place for them will be near a window, and in a place where the temperature fluctuates around 10 to 12 degrees. During the autumn period, watering should be very moderate, rarely, if ever, in the winter, and only lightly again in the spring. About the middle of spring, the plant can be placed on a window ledge in full daylight. For people with a garden, the pots should be put in a well-cleared spot, and buried up to the middle, which prevents the soil drying up too rapidly during very hot weather. Those placed on a window sill should stand in a box containing sand. As the summer months draw near, water must be distributed more frequently so as to keep the soil more moist. A Cactus should only be watered when the soil in the pot has dried out.

The repotting of plants is as important an operation as that of watering. The soil should be composed of a mixture, in equal parts, of leaf mold, compost, garden soil, and river-sand. The pots must be well drained, as drainage facilitates the seepage of water after watering. The best time for repotting is at the moment of departure of the vegetation, generally during the spring. The dimension of pots is also of importance. Many people imagine that the bigger the pot, the more chance the plant will have for nourishment, and the quicker it will grow. In reality almost the opposite happens.

These hints are valid for Cacti Euphorbias, and some of the better well-known succulents. The Epiphyllum and the Phyllocactus, frequently seen indoors, are also Cacti, but for these two genera the treatment is different. They are plants used to semi-shade, and require much more watering, especially in winter and spring, when they flower. Soil for repotting them should consist of a mixture of peat moss and leaf mold.

(See color section for illustrations in full color)

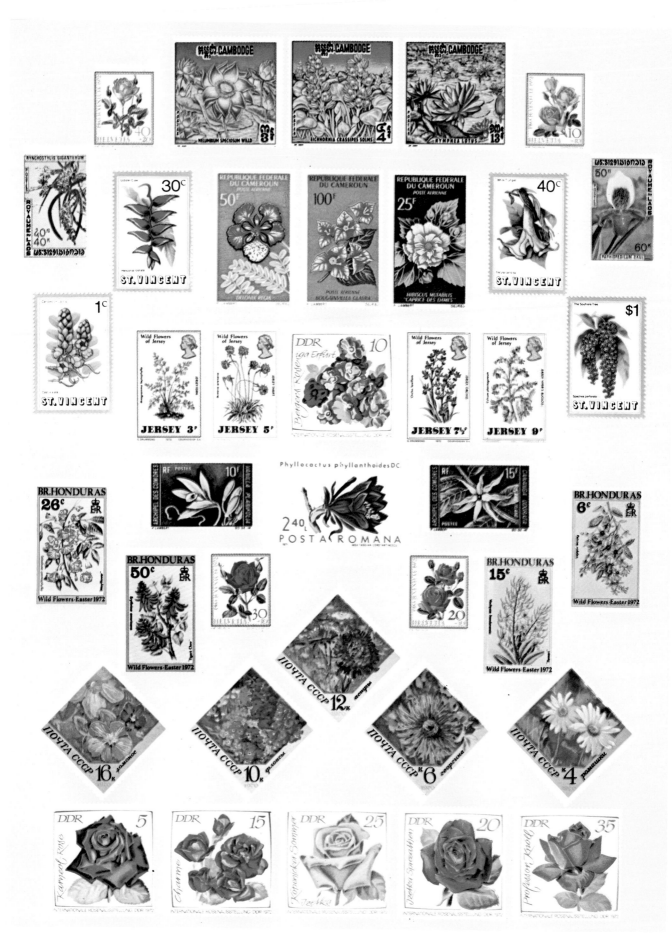

TOPICAL COLLECTING: If you are interested in collecting stamps on a particular subject or theme, you might have a page in your album that looks something like this.

This page from Minkus Stamp Journal and used by permission.

A

SPANISH COLONIAL GOLD: This gold 4 escudos from the Mexico City mint is typical of the coins that were shipped back to Spain from the New World each year in the great treasure fleets. The mintages were so huge that many coins of the Spanish colonial era are still available today.

RELIEF AND INCUSE: One of the most widely circulated gold coins of all time is the British Sovereign or pound. The obverse carries the portrait of the reigning monarch, the reverse shows St. George slaying the dragon. The U.S. 2½ and 5 dollar gold pieces struck between 1908 and 1929 are unusual in that the design is incuse or cut down into the planchet instead of standing up in relief as on most other coins. The idea was that the coins would wear better in circulation.

MODERN ISRAEL: This Israeli commemorative 20 pound piece was struck in 1960 to mark the anniversary of Dr. Theodor Herzl's death.

BLACK CLOWN UPSIDE-DOWN CATFISH (<u>Synodontis</u> <u>angelicus</u> **Schilthuis): Usually less than 6 inches long; generally peaceful, but occasionally fights with other fish of the same genus.**

SIAMESE TIGER FISH (<u>Datnioides</u> <u>microlepis</u> **Bleeker): 6 t 8 inches long; aggressive, best kept alone or with othe fishes able to take care of themselves.**

BLACK-FINNED PACU (<u>Colossoma</u> <u>nigripinne</u> **Cope): Usually less than 2 feet long when aquarium bred; keep with other large fishes of gentle disposition.**

ORNATE CATFISH (<u>Chrysichthys</u> <u>ornatus</u> **Boulenger) 6 inches long when aquarium bred; competitive but otherwis peaceful with most fishes too large to be swallowed.**

JACK DEMPSEY CICHLID (<u>Cichlasoma</u> <u>octofasciatum</u> **Regan): Attains length of 6 to 8 inches if kept in large aquarium; rather pugnacious disposition.**

MYSTUS CATFISH (<u>Schilbe</u> <u>mystus</u> **Linnaeus): 5 to 6 inches long when aquarium bred; preferably kept in groups of several; a free swimmer, preferring a sparsely planted aquarium.**

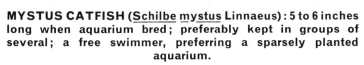

These pages of tropical fish photographs from "Tropical Fish Identifier" by Braz Walker.

C

BRONZE CORYDORAS (Corydoras aeneus Gill): 3 inches long; efficient scavengers in a community aquarium—search out uneaten scraps of food unnoticed by other fishes.

LEMON TETRA (Hyphessobrycon pulchripinnis Ahl): 1¾ to 2 inches long, should be kept in schools in a well planted, moderately to brightly lit aquarium.

CLOWN LOACH (Botia macracantha Bleeker): 5 inches long when aquarium bred; keep in well-planted, large community aquarium provided with caves, roots or rocks for seclusion.

ZEBRA DANIO (Brachydanio rerio Hamilton-Buchanan): 2 inches long; an excellent, hardy, and lively community fish.

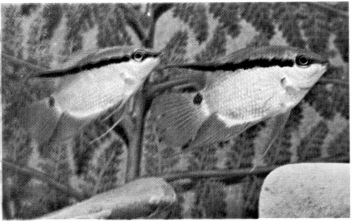

FLAG ACARA (Cichlasoma festivum Heckel): 5 inches long; a shy cichlid requiring good cover; eats soft-leaved plants, such as Sagittaria and Amazon sword plants.

GREEN SWORDTAIL (Xiphophorus helleri Heckel): Less than 5 inches when aquarium bred; excellent community fish in well planted aquarium with other similar-sized fishes.

D

GLASS CATFISH (<u>Kryptopterus bicirrhis</u> Cuvier and Valenciennes): 4 inches long; should be kept in schools in community or other sizeable well planted aquarium.

WHITE CLOUD MOUNTAIN FISH (<u>Tanichthys albonubes</u> Lin): 1½ inches long; excellent community aquarium fish; best kept in schools in the presence of other small, active, and harmless fishes.

"PIMELODELLA ANGELICUS" (<u>Pimelodus pictus</u> Steindachner): 3 to 4 inches long; an undemanding and lively addition to well planted community aquarium containing medium sized to medium large fishes.

LEAF FISH (<u>Monocirrhus polyacanthus</u> Heckel): 2½-3 inches long; best kept with own species in well planted aquarium provided with cave-like hiding places.

HALF-LINED LEPORINUS (<u>Leporinus nigrotaeniatus</u> Schomburgk): 6 inches long when aquarium bred; sneakily aggressive and an excellent jumper; keep covered in large aquarium with other sturdy fishes such as cichlids.

RED HOOK (<u>Myloplus rubripinnis</u> Müller and Troschel): 4 to 6 inches long (or less); omnivorous; will eat any plants in aquarium; should be kept in groups if possible.

E

SEA JEWELS : (1) Glorious Scallop (<u>Pecten</u> <u>gloriosus</u>): 3 inches. (2) Purple Sea Snails (<u>Janthina janthina</u>): 1½ inches. (3) Hump Back Cowrie (<u>Cypraea mauritiana</u>): 3 inches. (4) Orange Spider Conch (<u>Lambis crocata</u>): 4 inches. (5) Calico or Checkerboard Clam (<u>Macrocallista maculata</u>): 2½ inches. (6) Tapestry Turban (<u>Turbo pentolatus</u>): 3 inches. (7) Striped False Limpet (<u>Siphonaria pectinata</u>): 1 inch. (8) Bleeding Tooth Nerite (<u>Nerita peloronta</u>): 1½ inches. (9) Florida Fighting Conch (<u>Strombus alatus</u>): 3 to 4 inches. (10) Haitian Tree Snail (<u>Liquus fasciatus</u>): 2 inches. (11) Pink-

This page from "Shell Life and Shell Collecting" by Sonia Bennett Murray.

mouthed Murex (<u>Murex erythrostomus</u>): 6 inches. (12) Triton's Trumpet (<u>Charonia variegata</u>): 12 to 18 inches. (13) Marlinspike (<u>Terebra maculata</u>): 10 inches. (14) Turret Shell (<u>Turritella terebra</u>): 4 or 5 inches. (15) Harp Shell (<u>Harpa conoidalis</u>): 4 inches. (16) Nutmeg (<u>Cancellaria reticulata</u>): 1 to 1¾ inches. (17) Atlantic Winged Oyster (Pteria colymbus): 3 inches. (18) Common Fig Shell (<u>Ficus communis</u>): 3 to 4 inches. (19) Limpet, interior view (<u>Patella</u>) (<u>Celana</u>): ¾ inch. (20) Striped Bonnet (<u>Phalium strigatum</u>): 3 inches.

This page from "Shell Life and Shell Collecting" by Sonia Bennett Murray.

G

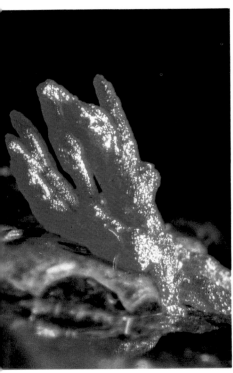

Cinnabar (10×)

Chabazite (3×)

Axinite (3×)

THE COLOR AND STRUCTURE OF MINERALS: You don't have to be a trained mineralogist to enjoy rock collecting any more than you have to be an ornithologist to enjoy bird watching. There are about 2,000 known minerals, but only about 120 of those are considered common, and many of them can be identified by their color. Sometimes, however, color can be deceiving, because a very small amount of impurity can strongly alter the color (but not the other properties) of minerals. The crystal structure of minerals is the best key to their identity. This is often impossible to determine without sophisticated laboratory equipment, but many minerals have forms that do exhibit such characteristic crystals that identification can be made on sight. These photographs have been magnified as shown in order to bring out the full color inherent in the mineral as well as to reveal characteristic shapes and forms.

Mimetite (5×)

Atacamite (10×)

Lazulite (5×)

H

This page from "Colorful Mineral Identifier" by Anthony C. Tennissen—photographs by Werner Lieber.

Tom Thumb Cactus   **Bird's Nest Cactus**   **Spiny Mammillaria**

FLOWERING CACTI: Why has nature produced plants in such strange shapes? The reason lies in the kind of existence they must lead. Living in regions of very limited rainfall, they have developed an ability to store reserves of water during the wet season, so that they may survive during the long dry season. In addition, many species are covered with numerous prickles or tiny scales which serve to protect them from direct exposure to the sun. Other species possess a root that will contract under conditions of extreme drought and pull them down into the ground, until they are almost completely buried. So in addition to their intriguing shapes, Cacti are very hardy and require little care as house plants. Which is not to say they can be ignored completely. They do, for example, need to be watered during periods of growth, and certain species, such as the Christmas or Crab Cactus (<u>Lygocactus</u> <u>truncatus</u>) and the Epiphyllum (<u>Epiphyllum</u> <u>hybridus</u>) pictured below, are basically forest plants and require a limited amount of shade.

Epiphyllum   **Prickly Pear**   **Crab Cactus**

This page from "House Plant Identifier" by Helmut Bechtel.

1

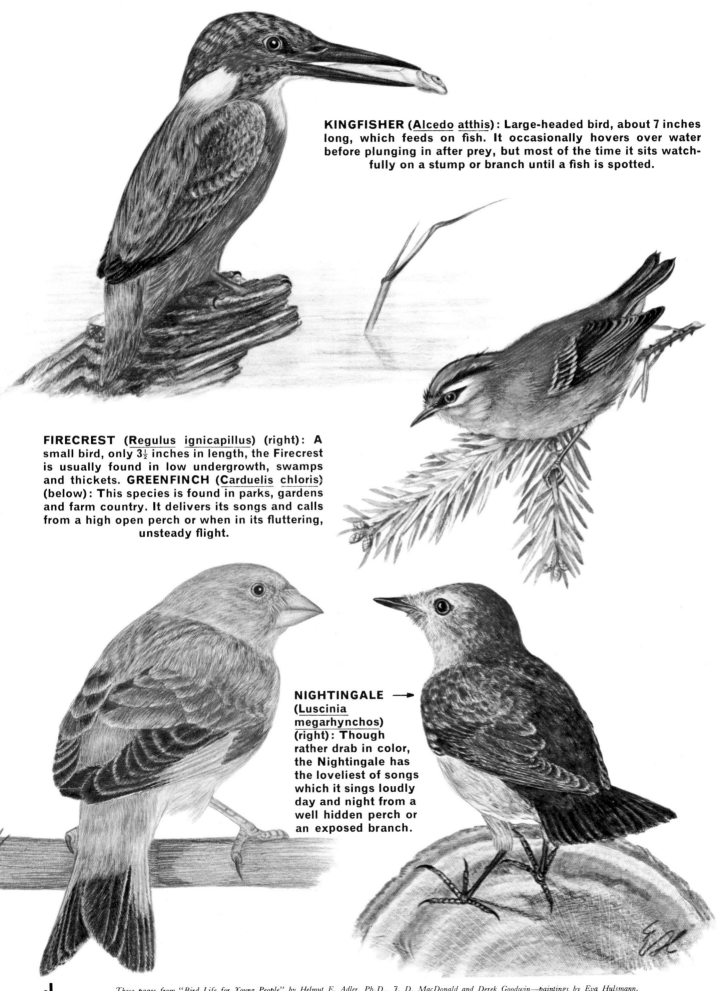

KINGFISHER (Alcedo atthis): Large-headed bird, about 7 inches long, which feeds on fish. It occasionally hovers over water before plunging in after prey, but most of the time it sits watchfully on a stump or branch until a fish is spotted.

FIRECREST (Regulus ignicapillus) (right): A small bird, only 3½ inches in length, the Firecrest is usually found in low undergrowth, swamps and thickets. **GREENFINCH (Carduelis chloris) (below):** This species is found in parks, gardens and farm country. It delivers its songs and calls from a high open perch or when in its fluttering, unsteady flight.

NIGHTINGALE → **(Luscinia megarhynchos) (right):** Though rather drab in color, the Nightingale has the loveliest of songs which it sings loudly day and night from a well hidden perch or an exposed branch.

J   *These pages from "Bird Life for Young People" by Helmut E. Adler, Ph.D., J. D. MacDonald and Derek Goodwin—paintings by Eva Hulsmann.*

MALLARDS (Anas platyrhyn-chos) (right): Common dabbling ducks, mallards are found on almost any body of water, even in city parks. The male (right) and the female (left) differ in breeding plumage but both can be easily identified by the blue speculum or patch of color on the wings. The Mallard is the ancestor of the domesticated duck.

SANDWICH TERN (Thalasseus sandvicencis) (left): A rather large tern (15 inches long), with a yellow-tipped black bill and a black crown during the winter, this species is a powerful flier, and is able to catch its fish far off shore. It nests in dense colonies in sand dunes with other terns.

BARN OWL (Tyto alba) (right): A large earless owl quickly distinguished from other owls by its heart-shaped face and light-colored breast. It is strictly nocturnal and nests in barns, ruins, belfries, cavities in trees, and burrows and tunnels.

K

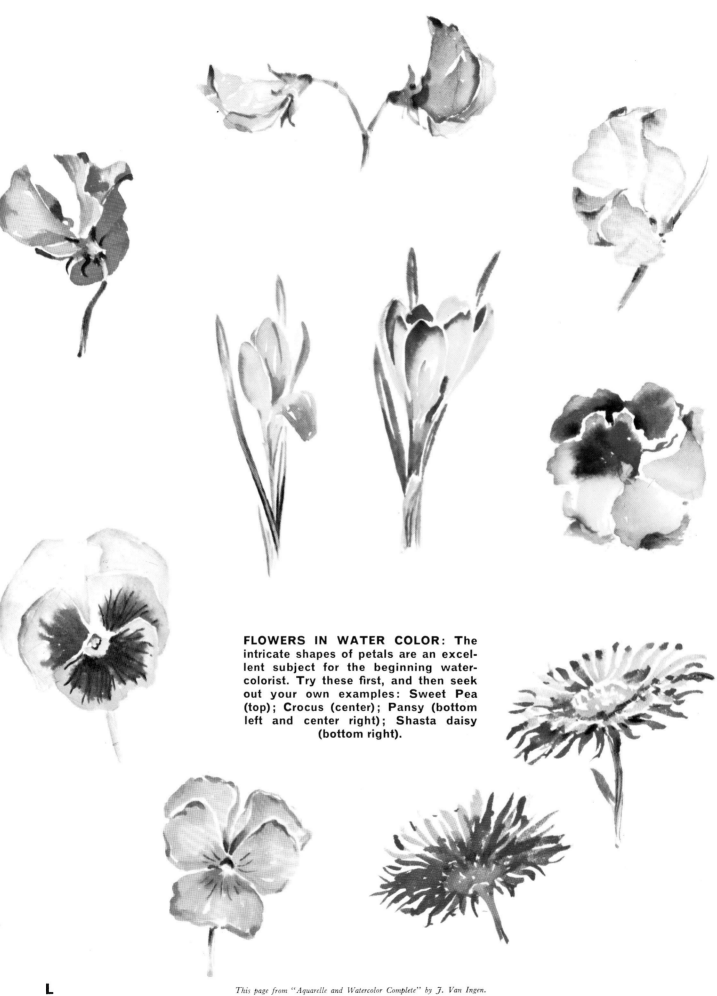

FLOWERS IN WATER COLOR: The intricate shapes of petals are an excellent subject for the beginning watercolorist. Try these first, and then seek out your own examples: Sweet Pea (top); Crocus (center); Pansy (bottom left and center right); Shasta daisy (bottom right).

This page from "Aquarelle and Watercolor Complete" by J. Van Ingen.

Collecting hobbies

STAMP COLLECTING

The urge to collect things is an instinctive part of human nature. Collecting—and there is no limit to the kinds of things one can collect—is rewarding on many levels. All the different aspects of building up a stamp collection—searching for stamps; sorting and identifying new acquisitions; arranging and mounting them in your album; studying reference books and catalogues to learn about each one—provide for a varied and gratifying pastime.

Prior to the invention of the postage stamp, the sender of a letter did not pay postage; the recipient had to pay cash-on-delivery for the service before he knew what the letter contained. This was an unsatisfactory procedure, but it endured until the middle of the nineteenth century. The first postage stamp, called the "Penny Black," was used in 1840, when Rowland Hill of Great Britain (later awarded a knighthood for his achievement) succeeded in establishing a uniform penny rate for letters sent anywhere within the United Kingdom. The penny postage scheme applied only to letters that were paid for in advance and the adhesive postage stamp was introduced as a sort of receipt to show clerks and carriers that the postal fee had been collected. The idea was so successful that the United States adopted it in 1847, and by 1860 the use of adhesive postage stamps had spread to most of the civilized nations of the world.

With the help of stamps you can wander through lands, time and history. The important events of the past, including the history of our own countries, are recalled by special commemorative issues. A stamp collection presents a picture gallery of great people of all times—rulers, statesmen, warriors, explorers, artists and scientists—as well as their achievements and adventures. Stamps invite further study—you will want to know about the people,

(Left) The Penny Black, the world's first adhesive postage stamp, on its 100th anniversary was reproduced on a stamp of Mexico.
(Right, above) Another early stamp, the "Post Office" Mauritius issue, also shown on its centennial. Originals of the 1847 issue are worth about $50,000!

where on the globe the countries are, why the pictures on the stamps were selected, and what their significance is.

Stamp design has become a highly developed art form. The first stamps were very plain. They showed the portrait of a sovereign or president, the coat of arms of a nation, while some had merely a mark of value. Most modern issues, however, are beautiful, multi-colored pictorials. Because great care and expense goes into their design and production, they are often miniature works of art.

The formal term for stamp collecting is philately, and those who collect stamps are known as philatelists. Joining a stamp club is one way to ensure a lively, continuing interest in your collection.

Exhibits and displays are an important feature of club meetings; as a fellow hobbyist, you can appreciate the effort others put into their collections and you will discover the pleasure of displaying and telling about your own possessions. Besides the educational merit of belonging to a club, there is the valuable opportunity of trading duplicates—getting rid of excess stamps in exchange for stamps you want.

Condensed from "Getting Started in Stamp Collecting" by Burton Hobson, © 1970, 1965, 1963 by Sterling Publishing Co., Inc., New York

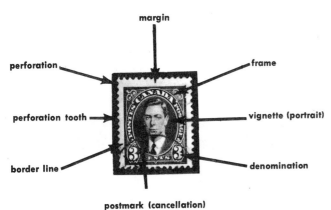

margin

perforation

frame

perforation tooth

vignette (portrait)

border line

denomination

postmark (cancellation)

The arrows show the principal features of a typical stamp.

TERMINOLOGY

The diagram above will help to acquaint you with some of the things that the stamp collector looks for.

DENOMINATION: The first function of a stamp is to indicate the prepayment of a fee to the postal clerks so, of course, there must be an indication of its value.

MARGIN: The "margin" is the unprinted area outside the border of the design. As you will learn, collectors value accurately centered stamps with equal margins.

PERFORATIONS: Most stamps have a series of "teeth" or "holes" along the edge. These "perforations" allow the stamps to be separated easily. Some countries use a series of slits between stamps rather than punched holes, and such stamps are referred to as "roulette." No means of separation was provided for the earliest stamps and they had to be cut from the sheet with scissors. There are still occasional issues of "imperforate" stamps, without roulettes or perforations between them.

POSTMARK: As mail passes through the post office, stamps are "cancelled," that is, invalidated to prevent their reuse. These cancellations are usually in the form of wavy ink lines or postmarks showing the name of the city where the cancellation was applied. Beginners generally get used stamps for their collection; cancelled stamps no longer have face value and cost less than "mint" or unused stamps. In many ways, used stamps are more interesting; you can be sure they have fulfilled their purpose of carrying mail and the cancellation usually shows when and where they were posted. On the other hand, a heavy cancellation interferes with the full appreciation of a stamp as a work of art.

VIGNETTE: The picture portion of a stamp is called the "vignette." On most issues, the vignette

is enclosed within a frame. On many modern issues, the picture covers the whole stamp. Stamps are often used on international mail, so the name or some device indicating the country of origin appears, except on the stamps of Great Britain. The national name has never appeared on English stamps, presumably because Britain was the first nation to use stamps (beginning in 1840) and there was no need to differentiate them from stamps of other countries.

WATERMARKS: When you become an experienced collector you will often refer to the back side of a stamp for information. Two stamps are not necessarily identical just because they look alike on the surface. The back side of a stamp will tell you about the kind of paper it is printed on, whether the paper was watermarked and, if it is an unused stamp, you can see the gum. In judging the condition of a stamp you will soon find it very important to check the back side for thin spots and old hinges.

The beginner is usually not concerned with these minor variations. Many collectors never do bother with anything more than "face-different" stamps. There are some technical things beyond the scope of this book and of most collectors. As you go on to advanced collecting you will learn how to recognize and identify watermark varieties. When you first take up the hobby, however, it is enough to know that if you have the time and inclination to study and examine your stamps there can be more to collecting than getting one of each kind and putting it in an album.

A postage stamp represents the promise of a government to perform a certain postal service, but the modern postal system provides a variety of services and sometimes different stamps are used for each one. Many stamp catalogues and albums have separate listings for each group of stamps so you will have to learn to recognize the various classifications.

GENERAL ISSUES: General issues are stamps that can be used for regular mail or any other service. In the United States, for example, general issues may be used for regular mail or a service, such as special delivery, even though there are distinctive special delivery stamps. (Special delivery stamps, however, cannot be used for regular service.)

AIRMAIL: The design of airmail stamps usually has wings or an airplane or some other symbol of flying. Special stamps that are readily identified for airport service speed the dispatching of mail to the airport.

Early stamps (above) were usually very plain. Recent issues (below) are usually colorful pictorials; some are "modern design" compositions.

These stamps from Greece, Italy, Nyassa (now part of Mozambique) and Egypt show the Colossus of Rhodes, the Parthenon, Caesar Augustus, Vasco da Gama's ship "San Gabriel," the pyramids, and the Battle of Salamis—all recalling bits of history.

One of the most famous stamp collectors was Franklin Delano Roosevelt, shown here at his hobby.

Famous people from all walks of life appear on stamps. (Left) Actress Grace Kelly and Prince Rainier. (Center) Author Robert Louis Stevenson. (Right) Inventor Thomas A. Edison.

Stamps come in all shapes.

Stamps come in many sizes. (Right) Reproduction of a Japanese print by Sharaku. (Below) Reduced size South African wartime issue.

These Formosa butterflies are shown in full color on the actual stamps. Multicolor pictorials add to the appeal of collecting and the appearance of your album pages.

All of the above stamps were taken from incoming mail. You can see how easy it is to gather an attractive stamp display without spending a cent.

The amount to be collected is the prominent feature of most postage due stamps.

This is called a general issue.

(Left) An early biplane shown on a 1919 German airmail stamp. (Right) This recent stamp from Israel shows a modern jet transport.

SPECIAL DELIVERY: These stamps show payment of the fee for the special service of having a letter taken from the receiving post office straight to its destination by a postal messenger ahead of the regular delivering postman.

POSTAGE DUE: Stamps in this class are used on letters or parcels which were mailed without sufficient postage, or are being returned to the sender because of a faulty address, refusal to accept, or some similar reason. They show the postman how much he must collect before handing over the item.

In addition, you will occasionally come across stamps for other special services such as parcel post, registered or certified mail, special handling for parcel post, newspaper stamps, and pneumatic post stamps from Italy for letters sent through underground tubes.

The stamp collector should also be acquainted with the following varieties of stamps and the purposes for which they are issued.

DEFINITIVE ISSUES: The basic stamp issue of a country is called the "definitive issue." The defini-

Special delivery stamps frequently use the motorcycle as a symbol.

(Left) Two-centavo stamp of the 1928 Guatemala definitive issue. (Center) UN CENTAVO surcharge reducing the value of the stamp to fill a need for the lower denomination. (Right) A bisected half of the two-centavo value used provisionally as a one-centavo stamp.

tives include a wide enough range of denomination to prepay the lowest unit rate or the highest. The stamps are usually of convenient size and are intended for use over an unspecified period of time. They are available concurrently with special commemorative or semi-postal issues.

PROVISIONAL STAMPS: Temporary issues of stamps placed in use pending completion of a regular issue are called "provisionals."

COMMEMORATIVE STAMPS: Commemorative stamps are issued in limited numbers and, when sold out, are seldom reprinted. They have pictures and inscriptions calling attention to the person or event being commemorated and are usually larger than normal stamps to allow more area for the design. The beauty and historic significance of commemoratives often create an interest among people who are otherwise indifferent to stamps.

SEMI-POSTAL STAMPS: Semi-postal stamps provide a government-supported means of raising money for worthy projects. Semi-postals are sold to the public through post offices for more than their postal value; the difference is turned over to the selected cause. Semi-postal stamps are imprinted with both values—the amount for valid prepayment of postage and the surtax the purchaser pays. After a specified time these stamps are declared obsolete for postal use. The public can still buy regular stamps for their mail at no premium, but semi-postal designs are particularly handsome to encourage their use. Funds raised are usually for child-welfare, the Red Cross or other organizations of undoubted merit. Issues like the French stamps for unemployed intellectuals may be open to question. The United States and Great Britain are two countries that have never used semi-postals.

OVERPRINTED STAMPS: In every assortment of stamps you will find some that have an "overprint," not a cancellation but a mark, inscription or design on the face that was not part of the original design. These overprints are especially interesting because they alter the value, use or locality of the stamp to fill a temporary need. Others may show a lost war or a change in government. A few overprints commemorate an occasion or a person and were probably made because there was not time to design and print a regular commemorative stamp. Most overprints are to change the value of a stamp; this kind of special overprint is called a "surcharge." Collectors, of course, consider an overprinted stamp completely different from the original stamp without the overprint.

The U.S. Dag Hammarskjold memorial stamp received world-wide publicity because of an unusual color error. (Left) Yellow color plate inverted—note color in left and right margins, white area around building. (Right) Normal stamp.

Semi-postal stamps are often issued as surtaxes for tuberculosis fund, Red Cross and child health. The black borders show mourning for Queen Astrid, killed in a car accident.

(Left) Commemorative overprint produced on short notice. (Right) Surcharge changing the postal value.

Stamps overprinted to limit their use to official mail. The stamp at the right was further restricted to official army business.

OFFICIAL OR DEPARTMENTAL STAMPS: In many countries, "official" stamps used on government business are overprinted with that word to prevent unauthorized use. They are usually for general use of all branches of government but sometimes "departmental" stamps are overprinted with the name of a department for the exclusive use of that particular department.

OCCUPATION STAMPS: When a foreign army moves into captured territory, "occupation stamps" may be issued for use in the conquered territory. Some nations produce whole new issues for occupational use, but more often stamps of the victorious nation are overprinted for use in the conquered area. Collectors can follow the fortunes of war by studying their stamps.

PRECANCELLED STAMPS: City names overprinted on the face of U.S. stamps do not alter the use of the stamps. These are "precancelled" stamps which have been invalidated before being applied to mail. They are used only under permit by large firms to save a step in processing their mail. Canada, France and Belgium are other countries using precancelled stamps.

Air raid propaganda overprint on Chinese airmail stamp issued during the final days of Japanese occupation.

The following are specialty items that add impressive touches to a display of stamps.

STAMPS ON COVER: A whole envelope, a cover, shows more of the postal markings than can appear on single stamps. The postmark shows the city and date where and when the cover was mailed. Many countries use special commemorative slogans. If you are specializing in the stamps of one area, you will certainly want to keep up with current events as reflected on their mail.

FIRST-DAY COVERS: These are covers carrying a new stamp cancelled on its first day of use with an appropriate inscription. This is a different way of adding the new issues of your chosen country to your collection. Many first-day covers have attrac-

tive printed cachets (legends) pertaining to the purpose of the issue.

MAXIMUM CARDS: Collectors use stamps on the picture side of postcards with designs similar or related to the design of the stamp as an outstanding way to complement and call attention to the beautiful designs of the stamps.

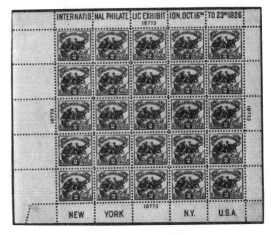

SOUVENIR SHEETS: With stamp collectors in mind, many postal departments, including the U.S., issue small sheets. The margins of most of these sheets contain printed legends relating to the event or purpose for which the sheet was issued.

BLOCKS OF STAMPS: If one stamp looks good, wouldn't four stamps be four times as attractive? Some collectors mount unsevered blocks, usually four stamps, in their album. This is common practice among those who buy for investment. Investors buy every new issue in blocks of four in the hope that they can some day sell three of the stamps for the price they paid for the block of four. In the meantime, a block of stamps makes quite a showing in their album.

First Day Cover of the 4¢ Project Mercury commemorative. This is the only U.S. commemorative issued without advance notice. The stamps were prepared in secrecy and released in honor of the successful completion of the first American orbital flight.

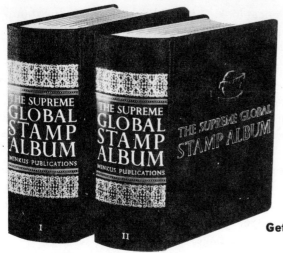

Get an album that is printed and bound in loose-leaf form.

PLATE-NUMBER BLOCKS: This term especially applies to U.S. and Canadian stamps. It refers to a block that has the part of the margin that shows the number of the printing plate from which the stamps were printed. Plate-number blocks are scarcer than regular blocks or single stamps since the number appears only once on each pane (usually 50, 70, or 100 stamps).

The number is that of the plate from which the stamps were printed. It appears on each pane of 50, 70 or 100 stamps and four panes with the same number are printed from each plate. The number can appear in four different positions, lower right (shown), lower left, upper left and upper right. A plate block of the same number from each of the four positions is a "matched set."

EQUIPMENT

The tools of the stamp collector are relatively few and comparatively inexpensive. The first and most important of these is an album.

ALBUM: There are two "musts" in choosing your album—get one that is printed, and be sure it is loose-leaf. Printed albums are arranged by country and many of the spaces have illustrations that are useful for identifying stamps and serve as guides for mounting them on the pages. With a loose-leaf album you can always add pages to take care of new issues or other stamps for which no space is provided. Some manufacturers publish periodic supplements that can be inserted in their albums to provide spaces for recently issued stamps.

Transferring a collection of even a few thousand stamps from one album to another is a big job, so buy one right away that is large enough to ensure your not outgrowing it too soon. Adding extra pages to a loose-leaf album will take care of some overflow, but you won't like having more stamps on blank pages than in the printed spaces. Albums are made to accommodate anywhere from about 3,000 to nearly 100,000 stamps. To determine what size is best for you, estimate how many stamps you think you will get in the next 3 or 4 years. No album will provide spaces for just exactly the stamps you will get, so make some allowance for that. A rule of thumb is to buy an album that has spaces for about twice the number of stamps you expect to have.

Albums with fewer than 6,000 spaces are only for the youngest collectors, probably someone who is "helping dad" with his collection. Fewer than 5% of the stamps issued can be accommodated in an album this small, so no matter how modestly you collect, you will get too many stamps for which there are no spaces.

Boys and girls who are serious about collecting will find an album with 10,000 to 20,000 spaces just about right. This size should provide enough spaces to hold all of the stamps you are likely to accumulate for quite a while although, if you spend 50¢ a week on stamps, you will need a bigger album in 3 or 4 years. Enough stamps are illustrated for you to identify what you have and to guide you in making orderly arrangements on the pages. Remember that only stamps issued before the album was printed are illustrated, so get one that has been revised within the past year or two and be sure to buy the loose-leaf edition so you can add blank pages for new stamps.

Adult collectors generally start with a bigger album. The next group has about 25,000 to 40,000 spaces. This sounds like a lot of stamps when you are just starting out, but if you spend $2–3 a week on stamps for the next 3 years you can build a collection of 20,000 different. A great proportion of the stamps you will get will be illustrated in larger albums, and there are likely to be spaces for all but the rare early issues, high values and minor varieties. Even though you later limit your collection to some special field, you will probably maintain an interest in your general collection.

Still larger albums are available—the very biggest having spaces for nearly every stamp issued. Besides face-different stamps, they accommodate perforation, watermark, paper and minor design varieties. Just as you must be sure to get an album large enough for your needs, you should also beware of buying one that is too big for a beginner. Even 5,000 or 10,000 stamps get lost in a set of albums with 100,000 spaces. The biggest albums should be a second purchase made only after you have been collecting for a while and gone as far as you can with a smaller album. An experienced collector who is seriously maintaining a world-wide, general collection must have a large, comprehensive album.

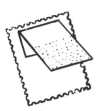

This shows how a hinge is properly attached to the back of a stamp. Be especially careful not to moisten the gum on the back of unused stamps or you will find them sticking to your album page when you want to remove them.

STAMP HINGES: The only sensible way for a beginner to mount stamps is with stamp hinges. Hinges are small pieces of semi-transparent paper coated with special peelable gum. You can peel them off the back of your stamps without damaging the paper.

You can buy hinges prefolded (which save time) or flat in packages of 1,000. If you buy them flat, fold the hinge a third of the way down with the gummed side out. Moisten the short side with the tip of your tongue and attach it to the back of the stamp. The fold goes toward the top of the stamp just below the row of perforations. Next, moisten the bottom half of the long side of the hinge and place the stamp in the proper space in your album.

For a neat looking job, take care to place the stamp squarely in its space. If you are working with unused stamps be careful not to moisten the stamp's gum before or when you put it in the album or you may find it will stick to the page when you try to take it out again. A special warning—never try to remove a hinge from the back of a stamp while it is still damp. Hinges aren't "peelable" until the gum is completely dry.

If you find pieces of old hinges on the back of a stamp, be sure to remove them before you attach the new one. Too many layers of hinges make a stamp bulge when it lies in an album under the weight of other pages.

This Czechoslovakian stamp illustrates the proper use of stamp tongs.

STAMP TONGS: Picking a stamp up with your fingers is often awkward. You can handle stamps easily and safely, though, with a pair of tongs, which are like household tweezers except they have flat blades at the end; these let you get a firm grip on a stamp without tearing it. With your tongs you can hold the stamp straight as you place it on the page. Also, you are less likely to soil or crease it.

INTERLEAVING: To pack in as many stamps as possible, an album must be designed with spaces for mounting stamps on both sides of each page. As the album fills up, stamps mounted on facing pages sometimes catch and pull out as the pages are turned. Putting glassine or acetate interleaving between the pages will prevent this. Glassine interleaves cost only about half as much as acetate. Albums bulge a bit as your collection grows, but extra binders are usually available. If your album becomes too full, you can get an extra binder and divide the pages.

CATALOGUES: World-wide catalogues give listings and illustrations, by country, of every recognized variety of stamp. With a catalogue you can verify the identification of a stamp, determine its date of issue and find the value of used and unused copies. The prices listed in catalogues are intended merely as guides. The market value of a stamp is often less than its catalogue value, often in the vicinity of 60–75% of the figure shown. Contrary to suggestions often given, it is not essential for a beginner to have a catalogue. While it is a most useful tool, it is a substantial investment that you can defer for a while, since you can make do by using your album pages for information and using free dealers' price lists for values.

WORKING METHODS

SOAKING: Stamps still on paper from mixtures or on envelopes that come in the mail must be soaked off before you can do anything further with them. Don't make the mistake of pulling them off because you will surely tear them or create a thin spot in the paper. Soaking the pieces in cool water for about 15 minutes will loosen the gum enough for you to slide the stamps right off the scraps of paper. Dry the stamps by putting them face down on a clean blotter or other absorbent paper. If they curl up as they dry, press them in a heavy book overnight to flatten them out again. Be careful to hold the stamps flat as you close the book on them. If a corner of a stamp gets turned under, it will be permanently creased. Stamps stuck to pieces of colored paper should be soaked apart from the others, because the color can run and stain the other stamps. You may want to save the full postmarks sometimes though, as they often tell when and where the stamp was used.

Stamps are usually soaked off paper before they go into an album. You may want to save the full postmarks sometimes though, as they often tell when and where the stamp was used.

SORTING: When all of your stamps are "off paper" you are ready to start sorting them out. This is your first chance to look at them individually, to see what you have, and begin arranging them for mounting in your album. A large table is a good place to work; you need plenty of room to spread your stamps out and the family can gather around and enjoy the fun too. Separating them by country is the first and most difficult step toward turning an accumulation of stamps into an orderly collection.

You will have to separate them in stages if you have any quantity at all to sort, since an assortment of 2,000 stamps can easily represent 150 or more different stamp-issuing nations and colonies. It's impossible to make individual piles for each country the first time through. Make your first division according to the alphabet, A B C, etc. Of course you

These stamps show the names of the issuing countries in English even though English is not their native language.

will have to make an extra pile at one side for the stamps whose country of origin you don't know. The first few times you sort stamps, this will probably become the biggest pile of all.

Once the assortment is broken down into smaller groups, take them one at a time and separate the stamps by country. Have a supply of plain envelopes on hand and label one for each country. You can use the same envelopes later for storing duplicates. One sitting is seldom enough to finish a sorting job, but with envelopes handy it is easy to pick up your work and keep it in order until next time.

IDENTIFYING: After all the stamps you can recognize are sorted into envelopes by country you can turn your attention to that pile of stamps you haven't identified. Most stamps are easy to attribute; the only problem is knowing what to look for. Because there are a great many British colonial issues, a sizable proportion of the world's stamps show the name of the issuing country in English.

Then, too, many countries are known in English by the same name as their native languages. In most of the nations of Central and South America, Spanish is the official language but you will recognize the stamps of Argentina, Bolivia, Chile,

The names of several countries are exactly the same in English as in their native language which makes identification easy.

Colombia, Cuba, Ecuador, Guatemala, Honduras, Mexico, Nicaragua, Panama, Paraguay, Peru, El Salvador, Uruguay, Venezuela and others right away because we use their Spanish names when we speak and write English. The same is true too of some other countries that use languages besides Spanish.

Another large group of countries issue stamps on which the name of the country in the native language is similar enough to what we call them in English for you to guess where they are from. Here are some foreign names that you will recognize: Belgique (Belgium), Brasil (Brazil), Ceskoslovensko (Czechoslovakia), Eire (Ireland), Republique Francaise (France), Norge (Norway), Polska (Poland), Espana (Spain), Sverige (Sweden).

Other countries issue stamps that are not so easily identified. You may need help to know that "Deutsches Reich" is Germany and that "Helvetia" is Switzerland and it's almost certain that you won't recognize "ΠOYTA" on Russian stamps or "CPbNJA" as Serbia. A few stamps like these do not have lettering or identifying elements that can even be expressed in English characters. Before you can put these stamps in your album you will have to do a little detective work to find out what country they are from. First, read through the table of contents or index of your album to acquaint yourself at least slightly with the names of the past and present stamp-issuing countries of the world.

Then, study the design and wording of your unknown stamps for clues to their identity. When you have more experience with stamps, you will recognize most of them on sight from key words or familiar characteristics of the design. Check first of all to see whether the name of the country appears anywhere in English. For example, a stamp with the inscription AFRIQUE OCCIDENTAL GABON is from the former French West African country, Gabon. You may not have known before that Gabon was a stamp-issuing territory, but seeing the name on the stamp in a position following the other words (which appear on many stamps) can be the clue you need.

Be careful not to pass over the name of some small country printed plainly on the face of a stamp without realizing it is the very thing you are trying to uncover. Most people have never heard of Fiume, for example, yet it had its own postage stamps for a few years and there are spaces for them in your album. FIUME appears clearly on its stamps.

A stamp identifier or a chart of key words such as the one in "Getting Started in Stamp Collecting" by Burton Hobson (Sterling, 1970) will help you identify stamps without recognizable words. If you are still not able to identify some, put them aside and watch for illustrations of them in your album as you work.

Whenever you tentatively identify a stamp and want to verify your hunch, turn to the pages in your album or catalogue for the country in question and compare the stamp with those illustrated. Look at all of the stamps from the country; there may be separate sections for Post Offices Abroad, Occupation Stamps, etc. If you are right, you should find either an exact picture or one similar enough to convince you that your attribution is correct. Don't mount the stamp in your album just yet though. Even if you find a picture of the exact stamp it is best to wait until you have all of your stamps sorted. You may find that you have more than one copy of the same stamp, in which case you should select the one in best condition for your album.

BEGINNING AND BUILDING A GENERAL COLLECTION

Nearly everyone starts with a general collection—stamps of all kinds from all countries. This is the best way, as beginners should get acquainted with all

These stamps show different designs; yet, they are obviously part of the same "set" and should go together in your album.

kinds of stamps, not just a particular kind. Besides, it is the least expensive way to begin—you get the most stamps for the least money. Later on you may want to limit your collecting, but don't be in a hurry to specialize. Take enough time to find out what stamps really interest you. Plunging right in on a specialized collection without some general experience may result in an unfortunate choice, and you will spend time and money on a project only to find that you really have no interest in finishing it. A general collection lets you preview the possibilities for specialization and provides the basic stamp knowledge a collector needs to build a worthwhile advanced collection.

Mixtures and packets are for sale in all kinds of places; department and variety shops, hobby shops, card shops and, of course, there are stamp dealers all over the world. Stamp dealers are collectors at heart and have put in lots of time studying stamps. They can be very helpful to you in getting started. At the stamp shop you will find stamps for sale in mixtures and packets, used and unused sets, even individual stamps of every description. A few sets and a handful of single stamps are not much of a start; you will be more interested in buying a world-wide assortment. Handling costs are much lower on assortments than on single stamps so you will get many more stamps for your money.

There are two kinds of world-wide assortments, "mixtures" and "all-different packets." Mixtures are just that, a supposedly unpicked and unsorted combination of stamps from a variety of sources. They contain many duplicates. You will be fortunate to get 200 different stamps from a mixture of 500, but the packet is very inexpensive, nevertheless. Most of the stamps in a mixture are "on paper," still stuck to a corner of the original envelope.

The best investment for a new collector is an all-different packet. You will only mount one copy of a stamp in an album and you can use every stamp in an all-different packet. Duplicates do have value as trading material, but it is best to avoid the unnecessary accumulation of duplicates this early in collecting. There will be enough time later when they can't be avoided. All-different packets are not expensive either. Packet prices vary somewhat depending upon how many countries are represented in the assortment, how many pictorials, high values and "mint" (unused) stamps they contain. Nearly all of the stamps in packets are "off paper."

Packets come in sizes ranging from 100 to 50,000 different. The price per stamp goes up in proportion

International stamp mixtures give you the greatest number of stamps for the least cost. Buying packets of all different stamps from individual countries is the least expensive way of filling out your world-wide collection.

to the size of the packet. A packet of 10,000 different costs four times as much as two packets of 5,000 different. A packet of 5,000 contains the commonest stamps of a wide range of countries. Scarcer stamps of the same countries have to be added to the original 5,000 to make the bigger packet. The second 5,000 cost about three times as much as the first 5,000.

Don't be too ambitious at first. You want enough stamps to have an interesting variety, but not more than you can handle or absorb. Boys and girls should start with a packet of 2,000 or 3,000 different. Adults will probably want 3,000 to 5,000 different. If you get more than that, the stamps will be difficult to identify and sort (unless you buy them already sorted and mounted in booklets, but that takes away the fun of working with them yourself).

If you decide to start with 2,000 different, buy that size right away. It won't work to buy a packet of 1,000 now and 1,000 later, because they will contain just about the same assortment. Starting with a packet that is too large on the other hand, will result in many duplicates later when you begin building up your collection with packets from individual countries.

After identifying and mounting a few thousand different stamps, you will get a good idea of what kinds of issues each country has. Most of the pages in your album will contain at least a few stamps, and the majority of stamp-issuing countries will be represented. But what about the remaining spaces? Packets are still the least expensive way to build up a general world-wide collection.

There is no point, however, in buying another world-wide packet if you bought one to start with. Another packet of the same size will contain just

Try to avoid torn and creased stamps, "perfins" (stamps with perforated initials), straight edge, badly off-center and heavily cancelled stamps.

about the same stamps you already have; a bigger packet will have some new stamps, but only the number by which the second packet exceeds the first. You will have to buy packets now of individual countries or groups of countries. When you buy a packet of just one country you must at the start buy the biggest packet you ever plan to get, because the bigger packets always duplicate the contents of the smaller ones.

Most dealers have packets of British, French and Portuguese colonial stamps. Sometimes you can get packets by areas, such as Asia or Latin America. These packets combine many inexpensive stamps so the unit cost per stamp is low. Don't buy one of these area packets if they include countries from which you might want to buy individual packets later.

Going through your album from A to Z with packets is possible if you would enjoy doing it that way. You may have found some countries more interesting than others as you worked your way through the first world-wide packet and you may prefer to build up your collection of those countries first. If this is so, you will probably want to get the bigger, more expensive packets of just these countries rather than smaller packets of many countries.

On the other hand, you may be anxious to increase the number of stamps in your album. The unit cost per stamp is much less for countries that have issued lots of stamps than for countries that have not used so many. Even though Great Britain was the first nation to use postage stamps, its issues have been conservative and a packet of 200 different costs

Look at your stamps carefully as you sort them out! These three German stamps look very much alike at first glance. Can you spot the differences in the inscription and the background behind the figure?

considerably more than a similar packet from Hungary which has issued a great many stamps. You can buy as many as 1,000 different Hungarian stamps in a packet for less than the unit cost of English stamps. Looking at it another way, for the cost of adding 200 English stamps to your collection, you can add 800 Hungarian stamps. If you are more interested in stamps of Great Britain than in the Hungarian issues you should buy the English stamps: they cost more and are worth more. However, if your goal is primarily to build up the number of stamps in your collection, the unit cost per stamp is an aspect that you should consider. Other countries whose stamps are available in large packets at small unit cost are Austria, Belgium, Czechoslovakia, France, Germany, Italy, Netherlands, Poland, Rumania, Russia, Spain and Turkey.

The country packets will have some duplicates of the stamps of each country you got in your worldwide packet. Save the duplicates as trading stock; be sure to compare the condition of the newly acquired stamp with the one already in your album. If the old one is not as good, replace it. Try to "upgrade" the condition of your stamps this way every chance you get.

After you have added the contents of an individual nation's packet to your album, you should have a good showing on that country's pages. If you want to fill the remaining spaces, you will have to purchase specific sets or singles from dealers' catalogues or stock books, or look through approval selections for the stamps you need, or trade duplicates with your stamp pals.

Older, scarcer stamps are sold as singles from dealer's stock books.

By the time you exhaust the possibilities for packet material, though, you will probably decide to confine your activities to building up some special country or group of countries or to a topic that appeals to you. After you have gone through the initial stage of general collecting and handled the stamps of many countries, you will probably want to concentrate on a project that holds promise of being completed within a reasonable length of time.

Most collectors sooner or later do decide to limit

their serious collecting, although most of them maintain their world-wide collection to some extent.

MOUNTING

When all of your stamps are sorted out by country, the next step is to get them into your album. You can start with any country you like, although it is a good idea to begin with those from which you don't have so many stamps and work up to those where you have a great many. Open your album to the pages for the country you are going to mount and look through the pictures. This will give you an idea of the kinds of stamps the country has and the order in which they are to be arranged on the pages. Now, spread out the stamps you have from that country and note which ones obviously "go together." They may be exactly the same designs but with different values, or they may show pictures of the same person, or be distinctive because of unusual size or shape.

Get any duplicate stamps together at this point. When you find duplicates, be sure to put the stamp in finest condition in your album. It's best not to mount any stamps until you have checked for duplicates; otherwise, as soon as you have a stamp hinged in place a better copy may turn up. Tears, heavy cancellations, creases and folds, faded colors, missing perforation teeth, poor centering, all detract from the attractiveness of a stamp. Few of your stamps will be perfect in every respect, but when you have more than one to choose from, be sure to mount the best you have.

Use your tongs to pick up a stamp and move it along the rows of illustrations in your album until you find the picture that is exactly the same or close enough so that you know it is part of the same set. The lower value stamps are usually the ones illustrated, so when you pick up a stamp to mount, start with the lowest value if it is one of a series. When you locate the right space for the stamp, attach a hinge and put it down squarely in its space. Put the stamp right on top of the illustration, if identical. If it is a different value of the same set, mount it in one of the spaces to the right of the illustration. The spaces to the right may have printed descriptions of the value or color of the stamp that can go there. If not, make your own arrangement in the extra spaces with the lowest value to the left, the highest value to the right.

After a little trial and error, you should find spaces for all the stamps from your first country. If you do have a few stamps left over, check the unfilled spaces again to make sure you haven't overlooked the right

Unused blocks of stamps make an attractive showing on an album page. It is also a way to hold extra stamps as an investment.

space. Then look at the stamps you have mounted to be sure the loose stamps don't duplicate any stamps already in place. If you still don't find a place, check your stamp again to be positive you have it with the proper country. If it is the right country, and there is really no space for it, then it is either a scarce issue or a high value that the editors of the album left out, or a new issue released after the pages of your album were designed and printed. Add a page if you have a loose-leaf album, or mount the extra stamps in the margins near the other stamps of the country. You run into this problem most frequently with small albums since the editors can only provide spaces for a small percentage of the world's stamps and must leave out many stamps that even beginning collectors easily acquire. With small albums you will often find that spaces have been provided for only the lower values of a set. If you find yourself with too many extra stamps for which there are no spaces you can be pretty certain the album you have is not adequate for your collection.

BUILDING A SPECIALIZED COLLECTION

Nearly everyone looks forward to completing a project. The need to specialize if you want to complete anything becomes apparent as you advance through the introductory phase of general collecting. You can set a reachable goal for yourself by concentrating on stamps of one country or a group of countries, or in one kind of stamp, such as airpost issues or topical stamps that are related to one another by pictorial design, such as animals on stamps.

U.S. issues make a fine specialized collection; they cover almost the whole period of time that adhesive postage stamps have been in use. There are rarities, but every issue has some common stamps and can at least be represented at modest cost; the commemora-

One of the advantages of limiting your collection is that you have time to learn the story behind each of your stamps. These two Danish stamps refer to the Hans Christian Andersen fairy tales, "The Ugly Duckling" and "The Little Mermaid."

tives cover a wide range of important subjects; and there are many new issues every year to sustain your interest. The stamps of Canada and Mexico and the other American republics are also popular countries for specialization. European stamps arouse the interest of many collectors because of our common heritage. On the other hand, your taste may run toward the lesser known countries of Asia or Africa. Newly independent nations have a special appeal—you can easily begin with their first stamps and maintain a complete collection.

These maps show the extent of the British and French colonial empires.

By specializing in colonial issues, you can have a world-wide but still limited collection. British and French colonial issues especially are extensive, but there are also stamps of Portuguese, German and Belgian colonies and others. The "Benelux" countries, Belgium, Netherlands and Luxembourg, are often grouped together as a specialized collection. Other popular groups are British North America, the West Indies, Scandinavia, Oceania and Central Europe.

You will be glad to find that special albums are available for individual countries and for some groupings. The specialized albums have a space for every stamp issued by the country. Rarities, varieties and high values are not left out as they are in world-wide albums. Every space has an illustration or a description of the stamp intended for it. The pages present a perfect guide for you to follow in developing your collection.

Begin your specialized collection by transferring the stamps for the chosen country from your world-

wide general album to your new specialty album. With a general collection, you concentrate on the stamps you have; with a specialized collection, you will be more and more aware of empty spaces, the missing stamps.

Another form of specialized collecting is that of topical collecting, which often appeals to those who might not otherwise be interested in stamp collecting. Here is a kind of collecting without any "do's and don'ts." You choose a subject that appeals to your own interest, gather stamps from the nations of the world whose designs are related to your topic, and display them in whatever manner is most pleasing to you. In a topical collection, stamps are associated according to the subjects illustrated; the people, places or things pictured are somehow related to the subject you are collecting. Nearly every popular subject has been featured on stamps of many countries so your collection will have world-wide representation, yet be held within workable limits.

Choosing a subject to be developed is the first step. One may suggest itself from your work or some other personal interest—for example, athletes often select stamps with sports designs, doctors collect stamps on medicine, teachers and students can assemble stamps related to education. Every important human industry or resource is represented on postal issues.

Topical collecting in its simplest form is based entirely on the objects pictured on stamps. A design featuring an elephant or beaver or dog obviously belongs in an animals-on-stamps collection. Sometimes, though, your subject appears as just a small part of the over-all design.

More elaborate topical collections are based on the themes expressed by stamps. Religion on stamps is a popular theme, and such a subject can be developed to include many kinds of stamps. Surely, stamps picturing churches and holy places belong in a religion-on-stamps collection, but you can add to these the hundreds of stamps picturing saints, religious leaders, composers of sacred music, reproductions of paintings of religious scenes and stamps such as the U.S. Christmas issue—in other words, any stamps which refer to events of religious significance.

Topical collections are displayed on blank album pages. Part of the fun of topical collecting is making pleasing arrangements of stamps on the pages. Most topics can be divided into groups and sections and the stamps of each group mounted together. If you collect animals, you might have one group for domestic animals, another for wild animals. Within

Birds on stamps

**TOPICAL
COLLECTING**
(See color section for
additional illustrations
in full color)

**Religion
on stamps**

Sports on stamps

This stamp fits into a collection of animals on
stamps but it could also go into a collection of
agriculture, plants or landscapes on stamps.

Flowers on stamps

Building a Specialized Collection ■ 97

each group, you might have a separate page for each animal. A collector of trains on stamps would divide his collection into groups for steam engines, electric trains and diesel locomotives. Similar divisions suggest themselves for other topics.

Learn as much as you can about your topic and write a little caption below each stamp in your album. Your write-up should tell briefly the story behind the stamp as related to your particular topic. A world-wide stamp catalogue will give you information about the designs. To learn the historical background of your field, you will have to consult an encyclopedia and other such reference books.

Finding what stamps have been issued, getting the stamps you want, learning about them and mounting them in an album requires a great deal of time and study. Topical collecting can easily be your only collecting interest. On the other hand, it can provide an entertaining sideline to another specialty. You can keep busy with an elaborate topical collection or be equally pleased by the fun, attractiveness and interest of even a single simple topical project.

JUDGING A STAMP'S CONDITION

Your first concern as a specialist collector will be filling in the empty spaces. Improving the appearance of your collection by upgrading the condition of your stamps will be the second. If the issues of the country you have chosen are at all extensive, you will find you have blank spaces not only for "face different" stamps but for "varieties" as well. Perforation and watermark varieties occur in the issues of many countries. Nearly all stamps have perforations and a good many are printed on watermarked paper. These two factors become important when you have to differentiate between otherwise identical stamps. Two stamps can be exactly alike except for a difference in their perforation measurement or the watermark in the paper on which they are printed.

PERFORATIONS: The number of holes within a space of 20 millimeters (this is about $\frac{3}{4}$ of an inch) along the side of a stamp is the "gauge" of the per-

These three stamps show the same design but are differently perforated: (1) compound perforation, perf 11 x 10, (2) coil stamp, horizontal perf 8½, (3) coil stamp, vertical perf 10.

forations. Determining the gauge is easy: just run the edge of a stamp along the face of a metal gauge finder (called a perforation gauge) until the perforations match one of the rows of dots. Stamps are described as "perf 10, perf 10½, etc." The horizontal (top and bottom) gauge is customarily given first if it is different from the gauge of the vertical edges (sides), for example, "perf 11 × 10½." Much experimenting with perforation was done in earlier years and you are more likely to find perforation varieties on older stamps. Most countries now have a standard perforation which they use on all issues. "Coil stamps" are a special type produced in roll form for stamp-vending machines. They are perforated on two edges only, either the two horizontal or the two vertical edges.

With a watermark tray and fluid you can detect the watermarks in the paper on which stamps are printed. When a stamp is put in the tray and covered with fluid its watermark might show up like the drawing at the right.

WATERMARKS: Watermarks, too, create varieties. Stamps that are identical in design may have been printed on sheets of paper with different watermarks or sometimes on watermarked and un-

Perforation gauge

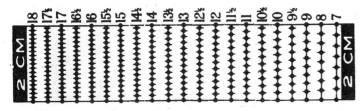

watermarked paper. Designs or lettering are impressed in the paper during its manufacture. The paper is thinner where the design has been impressed and it shows up when the paper is held in front of a light. The outline that you see is called a watermark. Once the paper has been printed on, it is not so easy to see the watermark clearly. You can use a watermark tray, a shallow black dish, to bring it out again. Dealers sell the trays for very little. Place your stamp face down in the tray and pour in a little benzine or one of the trade name detector fluids. Carbon tetrachloride will work as a detector fluid, but using it can be dangerous since its fumes are harmful when inhaled. As the paper absorbs the fluid, the thin part (the watermark) appears dark in contrast to the rest of the paper. Waving the stamp in the air with your tongs will dry it in just a few seconds.

Popular watermarks are small devices, such as crowns, crosses, flowers and monograms, and at least one complete design shows up on each stamp. A few stamps are printed on sheets of paper with an overall watermark—wavy lines or lozenges which are still clear enough on individual stamps. Other watermarks, such as coats of arms or a series of letters, spread over a whole sheet, but only a small portion shows on any one stamp. Your album or catalogue will tell you what to look for.

Collectors use the following terms to describe the condition or state of preservation of stamps. By studying these terms you will know what to expect when you buy stamps; by applying your own stamps to these standards you can judge the condition of your own collection.

SUPERB: A stamp described as superb must be perfect in every respect. The color must be bright, clean and unsoiled. The centering must be perfect, with even margins all around. No perforation teeth may be missing. Imperforate stamps must have ample margins on all sides. The slightest thin spot, a crease or a tear would disqualify a stamp. Mint stamps must have their full original gum (o.g.). Used stamps must be clearly, lightly and neatly cancelled. Many issues, particularly older stamps, are virtually unobtainable in superb condition.

VERY FINE: Very fine stamps are well above average and highly desirable. The color must not be faded and such a stamp must be unsoiled. It will be well centered, with ample margins all around, although not necessarily perfectly even. The perforations must be intact and the stamp free of any defects in the paper. Mint stamps have full original gum; used stamps have reasonably light cancellations.

FINE: The term, fine, describes an attractive stamp that is not quite as bright or as well centered as a Very Fine copy. The margins are usually uneven, but the perforations should not cut into the frame line of the printed design at any point. It may have a few short perforations, but none should be missing completely. The paper should be free of defects. A mint stamp must have gum, but it may show some heavy hinge marks. Used stamps may be heavily cancelled, but not so heavily that important parts of the design are obliterated.

GOOD: The average stamp found in packets, mixtures and approval books falls into this category. Good stamps are often far off center, heavily cancelled but not obliterated, even lightly creased. They must not, however, have tears or bad thin spots.

POOR: Not much is expected of stamps in this

category. Poor stamps may be heavily cancelled and perforations may cut far into the design. Some perforations may be missing; the stamp may be slightly torn or heavily creased.

BAD and DAMAGED describe stamps that are highly undesirable. They usually have tears or other extreme faults and are best left out of your album.

BUYING STAMPS

Dealers of all sorts are spread across the country and around the world. Larger cities all have stamp shops and literally thousands of mail-order dealers solicit business. Some carry a general line, others specialize, many ask for want lists, most will send approval assortments, and a few sell only at auction.

Check your classified telephone directory under "Postage Stamp Dealers" for the addresses of local shops. At stamp shops you can buy stamps in mixtures, packets and sets, as well as single stamps. You will also see many specialty items such as covers, maximum cards and souvenir sheets. No doubt you are already well acquainted with packets and will be more interested in the stock books. This is the place to look once you have assembled the bulk of your collection and are trying to fill in spaces. Stock books are usually arranged by country and the dealer puts in all of the miscellaneous stamps he gets from the collections he buys and breaks up. You will find both mint and used stamps in these books and frequently more than one copy of the same stamp. If the dealer lets you pick the one you want, remember what you have learned about condition and look for the best one. Don't be too long in looking them over, though, or the dealer will feel he's wasting time waiting for you to choose and will just hand you one stamp. If the dealer is doing the selecting, don't hesitate to ask if he has another copy, if you don't like the first stamp he offers.

Collectors who specialize may not be able to get all the stamps they want from general dealers. No one dealer can possibly have every variety of every stamp of every country. Topical collectors especially run into trouble since many of the stamps showing the subjects they're interested in are in the middle of sets and regular dealers are reluctant to break them. Dealers specializing in topicals stock individual stamps.

If you collect stamps from just one country and want varieties or older issues, you may have to get them from a specialist. Other specialist dealers feature covers, precancels, plate blocks; whatever your collecting interest, there is a dealer to serve you.

Mail-order dealers advertise in newspapers,

This jumbo-sized 10¢ airmail stamp picturing an astronaut stepping onto the surface of the moon marks the lunar landing on July 20, 1969.

national magazines, even on match-book covers. Stamp ads often offer premiums or loss-leaders to attract new customers. Ads offering attractive assortments for just a few cents generally specify "with approvals" or "approvals accompany" which means that in addition to the item you order the dealer is going to send you a selection of other stamps at regular prices that he hopes you will buy.

Looking through approval selections is a good way to fill in empty spaces, once you have assembled the bulk of your collection from packets. There is no difficulty in finding dealers who will send you stamps "on approval." Don't request them from too many companies at the same time, though; you get much better service and assortments when you are known as a regular customer. If you are more interested in stamps of certain countries or if you want only new or used stamps (used are generally less expensive), be sure to tell the approval dealer—he will prepare his selections to suit your wants. The big advantage of approval buying is that you have the privilege of examining many stamps before you pay for any. The disadvantage is that it is costly for dealers to prepare and process approvals, and this is reflected in the prices you have to pay.

Approval stamps are usually mounted on sheets with the catalogue number and price of each stamp clearly marked. Sometimes the prices are for sets of stamps which are not to be broken. Remove the stamps you want to buy and return the rest along with payment for the ones you keep. Beginners' lots usually contain stamps priced from 2¢ to 10¢ each. You are expected to make your return and remittance within 10 days. You must pay for any stamps that are lost or damaged while in your possession, and it goes without saying that you are not to trade or substitute stamps.

Some dealers offer "penny approvals." Stamps at this price are haphazardly mounted on sheets or loose in envelopes. They are not identified by catalogue number and there are none of the data you sometimes get with more expensive approvals.

Doing some of the dealer's work yourself, however, brings the price down low. Stamps in these selections are usually not in as good condition as regular approvals and many dealers are now charging 2¢ for their "penny approvals"—still inexpensive enough.

As a result of answering ads or sending for a price list, your name may get on a mailing list and you will receive approval selections without having ordered them from companies you've never heard of. Sending "unsolicited approvals" is a practice many collectors condemn, but you may be interested in the stamps and appreciate the service. Keep in mind that you are not under obligation to buy from an approval selection if you don't want to, especially if you haven't asked for it. If the dealer who sends you unsolicited approvals doesn't include return postage, you legally don't have to return them. However if you receive approvals that you don't request and aren't interested in buying, the best idea is to return them, whether postage is provided or not, with a note telling the dealer you are returning the stamps this time, but not to send any more. If more are sent after this, just put the lot aside and ignore it until the dealer sends you postage for its return. If you don't buy, you will soon enough be off the prospect list. As you might imagine, dealers in this business have a high rate of loss and must charge sufficiently high prices for the stamps they do sell to make up for the ones that are never paid for.

Ordering specific stamps from ads or printed price lists is about the best way to fill spaces at low cost. Paid-in-advance orders for special stamps can be handled at much lower cost than approvals and the saving is passed on to the customer. The dealer has invested money in his ad or price list and will make his prices low enough to ensure getting enough business as a result. Not only that but prices listed in print are easily compared with what other dealers charge for the same stamps, so the dealer will be sure the prices he quotes are as low as anyone's. To order from ads, you must subscribe or have access to stamp papers or magazines, and you need a catalogue to know what is being offered. Lengthy descriptions are costly so the dealer usually gives just the catalogue number, the condition and the price asked. Unless they specify otherwise, the numbers used in American ads are taken from the Scott Standard Postage Stamp Catalogue and in English ads from Gibbons. You are expected to send payment with your order and to keep the stamps unless they are not as advertised. Any unsatisfactory stamps should be returned without delay.

Many collectors find it convenient to place standing orders for all new issues from "their" countries and their dealer sends stamps automatically as he gets them in stock. Dealers' first stock of new issues frequently sell out; by placing a standing order, you are assured of getting every issue you want at the lowest first price.

Mint sets of related stamps issued at the same time are sold as a complete unit with every value from the highest to the lowest. If the set contains expensive high values, dealers usually offer a modestly priced alternative, a "short set" complete except for the top values. Before you buy a complete set, check to see whether your album has spaces for all values or just the short set. Complete sets of mint stamps, especially commemoratives, have the best investment potential.

If the stamps you want don't turn up in approval selections and you cannot find them in dealers' ads and price lists or their stock books, you can try leaving your dealer a want list. Give him a list of stamps that you're looking for—catalogue number and condition wanted, whether new or used, premium copy or average stamp—and he will try to get them for you from other dealers, and will also watch for them among the stamps passing through his hands. As they are available, he will submit stamps against your list. You can return any that do not suit you because of condition or other factors, but you are under a little more obligation to buy when you ask for specific items as opposed to general approvals. The dealer has devoted more time to finding your particular stamps and you should repay him with a purchase whenever possible. Topical collectors often must use want lists to get the stamps they want.

Some clubs assist the collector in buying and selling. Members mount duplicates in books provided by the club, a price is put on each stamp by its owner and the books circulate among the other club members who remove any stamps they wish to buy. The book plus remittance is then returned to the club member in charge of books. A small percentage goes to the club to defray the expense of handling. This works well for the seller because he gets money for his duplicates but is even better for the buyer since the prices are well below what he would pay at retail.

Stamp auctions are conducted frequently but feature only medium- or high-priced stamps. If there are common stamps included, they are lumped together in lots. Sales are well advertised in advance and you can write for a catalogue if you are interested.

Stamps in the Fine Arts series are reproduced in color: (left) "The Smoke Signal" by Frederic Remington and (right) "Breezing Up" by Winslow Homer.

At public auctions you can enter bids from the floor. Mail bidders fill out a bid sheet showing their maximum offer per lot. To bid intelligently you must be familiar with stamps and their values and be able to estimate how lots will sell. All sales are final, unless you can show a lot was improperly catalogued (which seldom happens), so auctions are a little risky for beginners.

How do you know whether a dealer's prices are fair?

Catalogues provide a par value for each stamp. The market price may be over or under the catalogue value, according to its current popularity. A great many stamps can be purchased below catalogue. If they're far below, it's because there is little demand for them and they are likely to stay about the same price over the years—which means they are poor investments if you want to make a profit. It also means that you can take your time about buying such stamps if you want them for your collection.

Prices of some stamps seem to advance out of all proportion to their catalogue values. The only explanation for this is that they are in vogue at the moment. The majority of stamps, however, advance normally in keeping with the increasing number of collectors.

Here are some worthwhile thoughts to keep in mind when buying stamps.

Stamp values are determined by supply and demand. If a new issue is in short supply and demand for the stamps is strong, its price invariably goes up. On the contrary, if too many of a stamp are printed or if too many people buy up the same issue, the likelihood of making a profit within a reasonable time is poor.

Don't be carried away by a wave of popularity for certain issues. Some recent issues hit a peak price while they were in the spotlight and interest was heavy. As collectors moved on to the next new issue, interest lagged and prices dropped. Too often, highly promoted issues are popular today, forgotten tomorrow. Be cautious, especially about issues with paid publicity behind them. The smart buyer bides his time, passing the highly touted issues in preference to bargains that are being overlooked in the excitement of getting on the bandwagon.

Sets of mint stamps have the best investment potential. Commemoratives or other limited issues are better than regular issues which may be produced for years. Commemoratives are generally released just once in predetermined limited quantity, the plates then destroyed, and no more is ever printed. The original printing minus the number used for postage is the total number of stamps available to satisfy the demands of collectors forever. Each day new collectors take up the hobby, and this creates a growing demand for a steadily diminishing supply of stamps, a sure omen of price increases ahead.

Stamps from popular countries are likely to remain in demand over the years. It's not wise to invest unless there is a steady demand for a country's issues because there won't be anyone to buy them when you are ready to sell. If the designs show animals, flowers, sports or other popular subjects, you will have a two-fold demand for them—from collectors of that country's issues, as well as from topical specialists. Color and design have nothing to do with a stamp's historical significance, but it is a fact that bright, attractive stamps are in greater demand than plain ones. If you are buying for investment, the event a stamp commemorates becomes secondary to its attractiveness, the number issued and the demand for it.

These jumbo stamps of 1969 honor the late President Dwight Eisenhower and American artist William M. Harnett.

SELLING STAMPS

Offering stamps for sale is often a disillusioning experience for collectors. It shouldn't be, if you remember certain facts. Every time you buy a stamp the price you pay includes a mark-up for the dealer to provide him with a reasonable profit on the transaction after covering the cost of his services, and his overhead in maintaining a business. Unless the value of your stamps has gone up, you can't resell them for the price you paid. A dealer buying from you must allow for the same expenses of overhead, and of carrying the purchased stamps in stock until a buyer is found. Also, he has the cost of advertising, plus the need for a profit for the time he will spend incorporating your collections into his stock.

Selling a collection outright to a dealer is the fastest way to get your money. Be sure your stamps look their best before you offer them. Pull out any torn, mutilated, heavily cancelled or otherwise undesirable stamps. You won't get a cent for them and they will make your good stamps look worse. Give the impression of being a collector who bought only good stamps and the dealer will have more respect for you and your collection. Be sure every stamp is in its proper place as the buyer will be much more interested if he notes that he can put your material right into stock without further checking.

In an outright cash sale to a dealer, you should not expect more than about 50% of the selling price of complete mint sets and as little as 20%–25% of your cost if you have a general collection made up of packet material. Much of what you paid for packets went towards the cost of making them up.

It is foolish to sell for a small fraction of your cost, especially if your only reason for selling is that your interest in collecting has lagged—in a few years you may wish you had your stamps back.

Stamps sold on consignments are catalogued and priced by their owner and turned over to a dealer who in turn offers them to his regular customers. At the end of a specified period, the dealer returns any remaining stamps and pays for the ones sold. He deducts his commission at a rate which has been agreed upon in advance. Dealers ask a commission ranging from 10% to 25% of the selling price depending upon how valuable and readily saleable your stamps are.

The advantage of consignment selling is that you can get the price you want for your stamps if they are sold at all. The disadvantage is that you have to wait for the final settlement to get your money. For another thing, you may find only your best stamps were sold and what is left over isn't worth anything without the better items to attract some interest.

The auction is the most important means for disposing of valuable stamps. The competition among bidders sets the price, so that only those stamps in considerable demand sell well at auction. Common stamps that are normally offered by any dealer sell at very low prices when put up at auction since nothing about them excites the bidders' enthusiasm.

For selling valuable stamps, auction is best since the catalogue circulates to a wider audience than one dealer can possibly reach. The owner gets more in the long run since the commission for cataloguing and selling is only 20% and good stamps sell at the highest possible price. However, there may be a delay of as much as six months from the time the material is submitted, until the auction is held and payment received from buyers. You also must agree to sell to the highest bidder and you must accept the risk of a disappointing sale price.

Recent issues are available from dealers in unused sets.

TRADING

Stamps are generally traded on the basis of catalogue value rather than one for one. Joining a stamp club is one of many ways to contact people who will trade duplicates with you. It's also possible to correspond with collectors here and in foreign countries who will trade stamps. Stamp papers have subscribers all over the world and inserting a small classified ad will surely get some response—or you can watch for ads that other collectors run. You can also write to the U.S. government's People-to-People Letter Exchange Program, Box 1201, Kansas City, Missouri 64141, or the People-to-People Hobbies Committee, 153 Waverly Place, New York, N.Y. 10014, for the names of people in other countries who want to exchange stamps.

Foreign embassies here or our embassies abroad may give you the names of people in other countries who will trade stamps—or at least they may reward your inquiry by using foreign stamps on their reply envelope.

Ships on stamps

COIN COLLECTING

Collecting rare coins as a hobby has been a popular pastime of men of means since the days of the Greeks and Romans. This interest, in modern times, has spread to all segments of the population. Tens of thousands of housewives, schoolchildren, grandparents, working men and professional people are actively building coin collections, starting by selecting from their daily change. New collectors are joining their ranks every day. There are many reasons to account for the popularity of the hobby and the enthusiasm of its adherents.

WHY COLLECT COINS?

The collecting urge seems instinctive in human nature and it is not surprising that coins should be the object of so much attention. Many coins are associated with interesting events or people. The coins that pass through our hands daily, seldom getting little more than a glance, have portraits of six of the best known men of American history—Franklin, Washington, Jefferson, Lincoln, Roosevelt and Eisenhower. The dates on coins recall significant years in our history: 1812, 1849, 1861, 1898, 1918, 1929 and 1941. A whole series of special commemorative coins was designed and struck for the purpose of recording important events, anniversaries, and so forth. Foreign and ancient coins can take us much farther back in time. In our hands we can hold coins from the time of the early Greeks, the Roman legions, bygone Byzantium, the Crusades, the Holy Roman Empire, Imperial Russia, or just about any time and place we choose.

Coins are miniature works of art. Gifted artists have been responsible for their designs, and the preparation of the dies and the striking of the coins have been the work of skilled craftsmen. On coins we find the likenesses of many famous people, some from centuries ago. The collector of foreign coins soon encounters some of the intricacy and beauty of heraldry. American coins, particularly issues such as the walking Liberty halves, Standing Liberty quarters and Mercury dimes introduced in 1916, carry attractive designs. The collector trains his eye to observe acutely and in doing this he uncovers many interesting facts about his coins.

Coins invite study in related fields. Historians and archeologists often use coins to illustrate points of history. The coin collector tries to discover as much as he can about his coins and uses history to add background interest to his collection. It is a pleasure to hold an old coin in your hand, but often what is seen in the mind's eye is more interesting than the coin itself.

Collecting can fill odd moments or occupy long hours, depending upon the time you can devote to your hobby. There is considerable activity involved in building up a collection—arranging and classifying the coins; searching for additional coins; studying reference books, price lists and catalogs. You can take pride in displaying your work. There is a keen sense of pleasure in owning a well organized collection of fine coins. There are many museums and other places where great collections can be seen, but it is really more satisfying to look through even the simplest collection if it belongs to you. You will derive more pleasure from handling one coin of your own than a whole collection of someone else's.

MOST POPULAR SERIES for beginners is often either Lincoln Head cents or Jefferson nickels or both, coins which can be taken from circulation. The pre-1964 silver dimes, quarters and halves, however, have just about disappeared from circulation.

(See color section for additional illustrations in full color)

Condensed from "Coin Collecting as a Hobby" by Burton Hobson © 1972, 1969, 1967 by President Coin Corp., Port Washington, N.Y.

NEW SERIES: Britain, Australia and New Zealand have all recently adopted decimal coinage. In Britain, the old 1 shilling piece (left) is equivalent to 5 new pence (right). In Australia and New Zealand, the shilling became 10 cents.

Coin collecting appeals to our gambling instinct as well. There is always the chance of a good bargain, the unrecognized rarity or a great find. Valuable coins do turn up unexpectedly. The story is told that the only known specimen of the 1870-S three-dollar gold piece was worn on a watch fob for years before it was discovered. Everyone feels that someday luck will come his way and there is no more likely opportunity than that provided by coin collecting.

Coins and the necessary supplies can be easily purchased. Nearly every city has at least one professional coin dealer and leading department stores all over the world have sections devoted exclusively to the needs of the coin collector. An extensive mail order business is conducted in the coin field so even those living in remote areas can be served.

Coin collecting is a convenient hobby. With the albums available, even large collections can be stored in small spaces. Coins have a lasting interest, they are fun to search for and arrange, and they become more precious to their owner as he becomes familiar with each one and learns more about them. Coins are durable and with the simplest precautions can be preserved practically forever.

Too often, people who have been exposed to coin collecting and like what they have seen have been heard to say that they would like to collect if only they knew more about it. No special talent is needed other than the capability of enjoying your hobby and the best advice for the would-be collector is to start right in and collect something. There is no "only way" to collect coins and you can let your interest lead you where it will. This section will give you useful information on arranging, classifying, displaying and acquiring coins. It will tell you about some of the methods other collectors have used and the kinds of collections they have built up. You can test your own interest and plan a goal for yourself. Remember, though, that there is a difference between a *collector* and an *accumulator*. You will want to plan and build your collection in an orderly, intelligent manner. You will enjoy collecting from the moment you put aside the first coin, but your pleasure will grow along with knowledge and experience of your own.

SERIES COLLECTING

Series collecting, the practice of acquiring a complete date and mint mark set of a given series of coins such as U.S. Lincoln Head cents or British farthings, has long been the traditional way to begin. The collector could start with current or recently issued, lower denomination coins and build a collection with coins right out of his own pocket. This has become more difficult, however, in recent years, since the circulating money in most countries has completely changed. In many countries the intrinsic metal value of the coins began to exceed the face value, and the earlier issues all disappeared from circulation to be replaced by base metal issues. In the British Commonwealth nations, the old shillings and pence have given way to new decimal coins. While the older coins are readily enough available, many at just a small premium over face value, many collectors have decided that if they must purchase coins, they should get older or more interesting coins for their money.

If you do want to collect the available series from circulation, there are two things that you must try to do. The first is to find one coin of each different date, from each different mint. Your second goal must be to find the coins in the best possible condition. Superior-condition coins are certainly more pleasing to own and display. The finer they are, the more desirable, and hence more likely to become valuable in the future.

The secret of finding coins with scarce dates in circulation is to be consistent. If you are watching your coins, watch all of them. If you only look at the date when you "think it might be a good one," you are bound to let most of the scarcer ones slip right by.

When you are ready to check coins against your collection, sit down near a strong light. Pick up one of the coins to be checked and read the date and mint mark. Turn to your check list or the space provided in your album for that particular coin. If the space is empty, you have made a "find" and you place the coin in it. If the space is filled, compare the condition of the new coin with the one already there and retain the better of the two pieces.

You may wish to search through more coins than come your way in daily change. It is possible to purchase rolls of coins from banks and you may also

MODERN HISTORICAL COINS (left to right) Elizabeth II on the obverse of the 1965 British Crown memorializing Winston Churchill; President Dwight D. Eisenhower memorial dollar of 1971, with the Apollo 11 moon-landing team insignia on the reverse.

RARITY: When collectors of U.S. coins think about rare items, the first piece to come to mind is this 1804 silver dollar. It has sold for as much as $77,500 in 1970.

RAPID RISING VALUE: This 1959 Bermuda crown was originally available for 70¢ in Bermuda, but recently specimens have sold for as much as $15 (£6). Issued to commemorate the 350th anniversary of the islands as a colony, it has proved popular beyond expectation.

INTERESTING DESIGN: Canada's 1958 dollar with its totem pole reverse was widely available for a small premium during its year of issue.

CELLINI is believed to have engraved the dies from which this portrait coin, a silver testone of Florence, was struck in the 1530's.

TRAVEL DREAMS are evoked when a collector looks at a coin such as this 50 franc piece from French Polynesia (Tahiti) with the scene of palm trees, beach, native hut and outrigger canoe.

A COMBINATION of the allure of faraway places and a familiar figure in literature occurs on this coin from Western Samoa where Robert Louis Stevenson spent his last four years.

SPORTS ON COINS are not unusual. This Austrian 50 schillings of 1964 takes you ski jumping. Collecting coins by topics is becoming increasingly popular.

Series Collecting ■ **107**

be able to arrange to go through coins taken in at local stores, from parking meters, vending machines, collection plates, etc.

If you save duplicates, remember always to save the ones in best condition. Some collectors like to work on a "second set" of each series which they keep exclusively for "trade bait." If you are fortunate enough to find extras of any of the really scarce dates, you can easily sell them to a coin dealer at a good price.

JUDGING A COIN'S CONDITION

Condition—how well a coin is preserved or how badly it is worn—has a great deal to do with its value. Collectors set great store by condition and like to get coins in the best possible condition. When you are buying coins, you will find that the asking price for a superior condition specimen can run ten or more times as much as for exactly the same coin in poor condition.

On each difficult coin design there are certain key points to inspect in order to assign a condition grade to any given specimen. The most important parts of a coin design, so far as the process of grading is concerned, are the points of highest wear. Every coin has certain features of the design that stand out from the remainder of the coin and these are the first areas to bump or rub against other coins or objects. The absence or presence of wear on these high points determine whether a coin is uncirculated or used. The relative amount of wear on a used coin determines its exact grade as shown on the opposite page in the enlarged photographs of Lincoln cents over a range of conditions.

By accepting specimens in less than perfect condition, a collector can get many more coins for the same amount of money. Of course, a somewhat worn coin has actually been in use, and there is always the intriguing possibility that it may have been in famous hands or a witness to important scenes. It is for this reason that many collectors find it a rewarding and pleasant experience to own an ancient in any condition.

In the case of ancient Greek coins, for example, a coin in superb condition may easily cost ten times as much as the same item in lesser but still presentable condition, but the chances of significant historical participation are greater for worn coins than for those in better condition.

Most Roman coins circulated extensively during their period of use in ancient times. Consequently, many of them that have come down to us are not in as fine a state of preservation as the numismatist might desire. On the other hand, part of the charm of having an ancient coin is the consideration of where and by whom it may have been used in its earlier days.

Some of the bronze coins, over the years, have taken on a lustrous, smooth, green coating called "patina." Collectors of this series usually consider "patinated" pieces especially desirable. The new collector may or may not care for patinated pieces but is cautioned not to refer to the condition as a blemish in the presence of experienced collectors.

In buying coins, especially by mail, you must understand the terms dealers and collectors use to describe the condition of coins. With this information, you will know what to expect (and what not to expect) if you buy a coin described as "fine." Since the price varies with the condition, you want to be sure to get as good a coin as you have paid for. On the other hand, you must not expect to get an "uncirculated" coin for the "very fine" price. Not surprisingly, in buying, selling, or trading coins there is often more dispute over the grading than the price. Grading is the process of assigning the proper label to a given coin. Here in generalized terms are the accepted standards for each condition.

UNCIRCULATED (Unc.): In perfect, new condition. All lettering, the date, and details of the design must be extremely clear. An uncirculated coin must show no sign of wear or serious damage at any point. New coins, unfortunately, are often packed and shipped loose in bags, so even an uncirculated coin may show a few light scratches, abrasions, or scuffs, called "bag marks," from this rough handling.

An absolutely perfect coin is often described as Gem Uncirculated or FDC (Fleur de Coin). Uncirculated coins are often brilliant but not necessarily so.

EXTREMELY FINE (EF or XF): Nearly as well preserved as uncirculated except that the very highest points of the design will show just the slightest signs of wear or rubbing. All fine detail is still clear and coins in this condition may even still show a little mint sheen.

VERY FINE (VF): Design still quite clear although the coin will show definite signs of wear. The lettering may be worn, but the complete outline of every letter must still be clear. The highest points of the design will show smooth spots of wear.

FINE (F): A considerably worn but still desirable coin. The basic outline must still be clear, but much of the fine detail is lost. Portions of some of the lettering may be worn away.

COIN CONDITIONS

UNC

EF

VF

F

Very good

ROOSEVELT DIMES begin to show wear first at the hair just above the ear.

Uncirculated

Extremely fine

Very fine

Fine

Judging a Coin's Condition ■ 109

VERY GOOD (VG): A much worn but not altogether unattractive coin. Coins in this condition should be free of serious gouges or other mutilations, but they may be somewhat scratched from use.

GOOD (G): A really minimum-condition coin. The date and mint mark must be legible and major portions of the design distinguishable.

FAIR: Coins this badly worn are usually not acceptable to collectors. They may have only partial dates and be dark in color, and parts of the design may be completely worn away. Fair coins are generally used as "space fillers" in a collection, only until such time as a better coin can be obtained.

POOR: Coins in poor condition are usually highly undesirable. They may be bent, corroded, and completely worn down.

Searching for better specimens, that is, upgrading the coins already in your collection, will give you just that much more opportunity to work with your coins. The challenge is greater and so is the feeling of accomplishment when the series finally measures up to a high standard.

If you are buying coins, you will want to get only coins in satisfactory condition right away. It usually works out best to buy the first time a coin that you will be happy with later.

TYPE COLLECTING

The plan of a type collection is to let one coin represent many others, since it is difficult today to collect coins from circulation. Usually this means that one of the commonest and thus least expensive dates or varieties is used to represent all the other coins, including expensive rarities that are of the same design style or "type." Nearly every collector of older coins soon abandons series collecting—having a specimen of every date and variety—and instead collects a single coin of each type.

Collectors are seldom in agreement as to just how much or how little alteration of the design creates a different type. If your interests are wide, if you collect coins of all the world or a fair portion of it, you will probably be concerned only with major, obviously different types. On the other hand, if you limit your activity to the coins of just one country, you will surely want some of the minor types and varieties to fill out your collection.

Specially designed albums are available for the type coin collections of several different countries. Non-collectors particularly enjoy looking at type collections because every coin is different and has a separate story to go with it. By collecting types

JEFFERSON NICKELS begin to show wear first on his eyebrow, cheekbone, and lower part of the back of his hair. On the reverse, wear shows first on the steps and on the outline of the lintel above the doorway of Monticello.

you can own and learn about many older, historically interesting coins, yet keep the cost at a level that is not prohibitive.

A similar plan can be used to collect the coins of any nation by type. The independent coinages of many countries are fairly recent, but others date back for centuries. The cost or scarcity of the early coins may force you to choose an arbitrary starting point for your collection. Usually you can find a logical starting point in a nation's coinage history. For the European nations, the Napoleonic period draws a line between what might be called "old" and "modern" coins.

The type-collection approach can be applied to rulers as well as design types. You can use one coin to represent all the coins issued by the same ruler. This sort of collection is especially pleasing to those who are interested in the political history of a country. Early English coins are frequently collected this way. A set of English shillings is shown of one of each of the British monarchs back to Henry VIII, who first regularly issued the denomination. Coins of diverse denominations could just as well have been used to add variety, but some collectors prefer to show coins more nearly uniform in size, which demonstrates again how well coin collecting can suit the individual.

Draped Bust of Liberty—a. 1795-98 standing eagle reverse; b. 1798-1804, heraldic eagle reverse.

1794-95 Liberty Head with Flowing Hair.

1840-73 Seated Figure of Liberty.

1878-1921 Liberty Head with Cap and Wreath.

1921-35 Radiant Head of Liberty. The collection would be rounded out with the Eisenhower head of 1971, shown on page 107.

OBSOLETE COINAGES: Including issues of former nations will greatly increase the number of countries in your collection. Serbia (above) and Naples and Sicily (below) are two nations no longer in existence.

GENERAL GEOGRAPHIC COLLECTING

Collecting coins from as many different coin-issuing states as possible is extremely interesting and will teach you a great deal about geography. You will come to know the identifying features of each nation's coinage, develop a familiarity with words in various languages, and pick up quite a bit of history. About one hundred and fifty nations and colonies issue coins at the present time, but hundreds of other cities, principalities, duchies, former kingdoms, and former colonies have had their own coinage in times gone by.

Latvia, Lithuania, and Estonia disappeared as coin-issuing nations at the start of World War II. Serbia and Montenegro disappeared in World War I. The Kingdom of the Two Sicilies ceased issuing coins upon the unification of Italy in 1861. There are hundreds of similar examples back over the centuries; yet coins of these places still exist, many in sufficient quantity to turn up frequently in collections and dealers' stocks.

BUILDING A SPECIALIZED COIN COLLECTION

Eventually, almost every collector finds that one phase of collecting has a particular appeal so he decides to concentrate his attention on that area. He may, of course, pursue a specialty in conjunction with the more usual date and mint mark collections. Through years of interest in numismatics, it is not unusual for a collector to concentrate at different times on various phases of the hobby.

ANCIENT COIN COLLECTING

The remarkable age of the Greek and Roman coins in itself makes these pieces appealing to experienced collectors and beginners alike. The beauty of workmanship and the artistry of style is readily apparent. The ancient coins are essential to any comprehensive numismatic study as all subsequent coinages are to some extent based on the ancient series.

BEAUTIFUL COIN: One of the most sought-after of all ancient coins is this silver dekadrachm of the Greek city-state of Syracuse (*c.* 400 B.C.). The head is of Persephone, and the charioteer on the reverse is driving a <u>quadriga</u> (of four horses) with a winged figure of Victory flying above.

The people of the ancient world were great hoarders. There were no banks as we know them today, so coins were often buried in the ground or sealed up in walls. Deposits of ancient coins are still being dug up today and there are many hoards still to be found. Because of these finds, many coins of the Greeks and Romans are not nearly as scarce or expensive as might be expected in relation to their antiquity.

The Greek people were the first to utilize coins in the form we think of—portable objects, reasonably round and flat, of standard weight and fineness, having an intrinsic value of precious metal.

The very earliest coins were made about 700 B.C. by the kingdom of Lydia (in what is Turkey on our

THE TURTLE COINS of Aegina, dating back to 650 B.C., are among the first known coinages.

maps today) followed soon after by the turtle coins of Aegina (a Greek island). The Persians had a large coinage by the 6th century B.C. and their silver siglos were the first coins to be widely circulated. These first coins had designs on one side only, the reverse having only "incuse squares" from the anvil. The later coins have designs on both sides, often in beautiful high relief.

ROMAN REPUBLIC COIN: Head of the goddess Roma, and Castor and Pollux, the heavenly twins.

By about 300 B.C., Rome was supreme in Italy and the first series of true Roman coins made their appearance. In some respects, the reverses of the Roman coins are more interesting, varied and significant historically than the obverses which nearly always show a bust of the ruler or member of his family. These coins circulated throughout the empire which was made up of many diverse groups of people and thus had great propaganda value. The coinage proclaimed the universality of Roman law and rule and was designed to inspire loyalty to the empire. The reverse designs fall into three main groups: gods and goddesses; allegorical personifications; designs relating to the emperor or to events in the empire.

THE COLOSSEUM is on the reverse of this sestertius of the emperor Titus (79-81 A.D.). Historians have learned about Roman buildings by studying coins.

A great variety of types refer to deeds of the emperor. His entries into cities, journeys through the provinces, victories and triumphs, presents to the people and army and happy events in the Imperial family are all recorded. Coins were issued showing buildings such as the Circus Maximus, the Colosseum, temples, bridges, aqueducts, etc.

STANDARD COIN OF THE EMPIRE was this denarius of Caesar Augustus, the first Roman emperor.

No two ancient coins are ever precisely alike. The coins were created one at a time by workmen using only an anvil, punch and mallet. Size and shape vary greatly because the lump of metal would spread out differently each time. Many ancient coins are weakly struck or off mark. Sometimes more than one blow from the mallet was required to attain the desired relief and detail. If the punch slipped a little between blows, "double struck" coins occurred. This lack of uniformity is one of the charms of the ancient coinages.

TOPICAL OR THEMATIC COLLECTING

Coin collectors can borrow a technique that is very popular among stamp collectors—"topical" or thematic collecting. In a topical collection, the coins are related to one another on the basis of their design and the people or objects shown. Coins do not present quite the diversity of design found on stamps, but several subjects, such as animals and birds, are especially well represented. The range of the animal kingdom, from elephants to bees, can be found on coins. The new African nation of Mali gave us the first hippopotamus on a coin in 1961.

Looking through a coin catalogue will suggest various subjects for a topical collection. By combing the listings and illustrations in a world-wide catalogue, and by watching the new issues of the world for appropriate designs, you will add to your collection and keep your enthusiasm high.

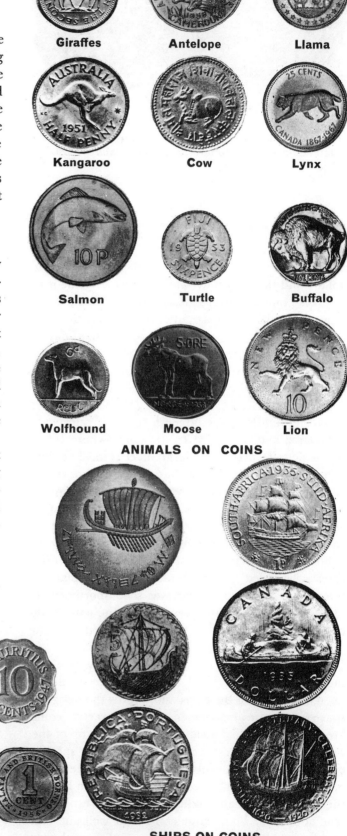

Giraffes Antelope Llama

Kangaroo Cow Lynx

Salmon Turtle Buffalo

Wolfhound Moose Lion

ANIMALS ON COINS

UNUSUAL SHAPE COINS

SHIPS ON COINS

CROWN AND JOACHIMSTHALER: Edward VI (left) in mail on horseback adorns the 1551 British crown piece, while St. Joachim (father of the Virgin Mary) is shown on the Bohemian thaler of about 1520.

CROWN OR TALER COLLECTING

Collectors use the word "crown" to describe coins approximating the size of the U.S. and Canadian dollars and the British five-shilling piece. While it is true that many crowned heads are shown on these large coins, the name actually derives from the fact that the first English silver coins of this size, dated 1551, were struck from fine silver (90% or more of the precious metal) called "crown" silver. The coin itself was equal in value to five shillings and was called a crown.

By the middle of the fifteenth century, European commerce had expanded to the point where there was a definite need for a large silver coin. The first dated issues of these new, large-size crowns were struck in 1486 by Archduke Sigismund at a mint in the Tyrol. Dollar-size coins were struck in quantity after the discovery in 1516 of a rich silver vein at Joachimsthal (Joachim's Valley) in the county of Schlick of the Kingdom of Bohemia. These large coins were called Joachimsthalers after their place of origin, but the coin's name was soon shortened to "thaler," then as coins spread across the continent, changed to "taler" to "daalder" to "daler" to "dollar."

Crown collecting has become a very popular numismatic branch. The large size of crowns allows for more detail on the coins and affords the designer space for artistic arrangement. These attractive coins are often rich in historical significance. Many of the recently issued pieces commemorate some specific event. Besides their beauty and historical connections, one of the attractions of coins is that you can handle them and enjoy their solid feel, and this is especially true of crowns. These large coins wear well and can usually be obtained in the better conditions. Large

quantities of many issues were struck and these can be purchased at moderate prices.

Special albums are on the market to accommodate this kind of collection. If you collect in this manner, you may want to stretch your budget as far as possible and select the least expensive issue of a country as an automatic choice without considering the others. You should, however, at least find out about all the available issues because you will sometimes find that a considerably more interesting or significant coin can be obtained for just a little extra expense.

You can also specialize in the crowns of one country or area. There have been more crowns from Germany than from any other nation. Many of the quite early coins can still be purchased for less than the cost of some of the modern coins issued within the past ten years.

DOUBLE COMMEMORATIVE: Both Denmark and Greece issued wedding commemoratives when Princess Anne-Marie married the then King Constantine of Greece.

COMMEMORATIVE COIN AND MEDAL COLLECTING

Many commemoratives have been issued as crown-size coins, but other sizes have been used just as frequently. Commemoratives have designs and legends that mark important occasions, recall historic events, or glorify famous men. A few examples of modern coins issued to record events at the time they happened are those struck for the reopening of the Vienna Opera House in 1955, the World Fairs— in Belgium in 1958 and Japan in 1970—and the Olympic Games—in Finland in 1952, Japan in 1964, Mexico in 1968 and Germany in 1972. Sometimes more than one country will commemorate the same event.

Most modern commemoratives recall events of

CENTENNIAL COINS, celebrating the 100th anniversary of the founding of a nation, are the most often issued commemoratives. This 1961 coin memorialized the unification of the Italian states in 1861.

times past; they are frequently issued to celebrate the anniversary of some military or political achievement. The centennial (one-hundredth anniversary) of an event is perhaps most often celebrated with a coin as, for example, the 1961 Italian 500-lire piece struck to commemorate the 1861 unification of the individual Italian states into the nation of Italy as we know it today. Events commemorated on recent coins are as far distant in time as 544 B.C., recalled on the 1957 coins of Ceylon struck on the 2500th anniversary of Buddha's attainment of Nirvana.

Finally, commemoratives pay respect to famous men and mark events in the lives of people as well as of nations. Birth years, death years, weddings, wedding anniversaries, anniversaries of the reign—all have been celebrated with coins. Great Britain issued a special crown in 1953 for the coronation of Queen Elizabeth II and another in 1965 in memorializing Winston Churchill. A Danish 5-kroner piece piece of 1960 commemorates the silver wedding anniversary of King Frederick and Queen Ingrid. Besides statesmen and rulers, coins have recognized

discoverers and explorers, builders, physicans and scientists, writers and musicians, religious leaders and saints.

Medal collecting has become a field of widespread interest within the past few years. Especially in America, where no commemorative coins have been issued since 1954, many collectors have turned to various officially authorized medals to take their place.

MEDAL: The official Pony Express centennial medal issued in 1960 shows the founders of the service on the obverse and a rider on the reverse. The medals were struck in both bronze and silver, with silver limited to 5,000 pieces.

Many of the new medal issues have been available in both bronze and silver. A few have been struck in platinum and gold. Current regulations prohibit gold medals from entering the United States. The quantities of each medal issued in the precious metals has been limited to a handful in platinum, a few hundred or less in gold and a few thousand pieces in silver. The limited quantities have made these issues especially sought after.

NON-CIRCULATING LEGAL TENDER

Coins struck especially for collectors are not new on the numismatic scene—nearly all official government proof coins, for example, are in this category. In England, minting special varieties of tradesmen's tokens for collectors was a common practice nearly two centuries ago. The last decade, however, has brought a tremendous growth in this kind of activity. Several private organizations, often in conjunction with recognized governments, are producing issues that are declared to be legal tender coins even though they are not intended for circulation and usually do not correspond to the denominations in actual use. These pieces are nearly all beautifully struck, their designs are attractive and they deal with popular subjects. Nevertheless, there is a great deal of controversy as to whether these constitute bona fide numismatic issues. They are, however, widely advertised and many collectors are buying them.

LIMITED ISSUES: This Panama-Pacific $50 gold piece of 1915 with head of Minerva and owl on reverse came in two varieties—645 pieces of the octagonal shape, and 483 pieces round.

Building a Specialized Collection ■ 115

FAO COIN: Uganda was one of the first nations to issue a coin to publicize the U.N.'s Food and Agriculture Organziation's drive to grow more food. This 5-shilling piece of 1968 features livestock and was issued in a quantity of 100,000 for general use and an additional 5,000 in proof.

FAO COINS

A brand new possibility for collecting opened up in 1968 with the start of the first international coin issue. Launched under the auspices of the Food and Agriculture Organization of the United Nations, the FAO coin plan is intended to draw attention to one of the great problems of our times—that of providing food for the expanding world population. Where they are used in circulation, these special coins serve as daily reminders of the problem. Their purchase by collectors provides funds for agricultural development. The "profit" on the coins comes from the difference between the intrinsic metal value and their higher face value (called seignorage). The coins themselves carry messages such as "Grow More Food."

More than 40 nations have authorized coins under the FAO coin plan and more than 250 million pieces have already been released. All of the coins are legal tender in the country of issue and many are low denomination coins released into normal circulation. A few issues, however, were produced in small numbers primarily for collectors. Individual FAO coins are available from dealers and various agencies. The FAO organization has also assembled special albums which are sold by the page as the coins are released.

PROOF COIN SETS

These are special products of a mint made for coin collectors or for official presentations. They are generally available as full sets often attractively boxed or packaged. Proof coins might be described more meaningfully as "specimen" or "display" sets. The metal blanks for proof coins are carefully selected and cleaned. They are struck from dies which are kept clean and polished. The result is a coin with a brilliant mirror-like surface, sharp edges and perfect detail. At all stages, the coins are carefully handled, never allowed to come into contact with one another.

IDENTIFYING COINS

The first step toward identifying a coin is to determine its country of origin. During the past hundred years alone, more than three hundred different nations, states, colonies, and cities have issued distinctive coins. And the farther back we go, the more diverse the coin issues become. Literally hundreds of areas and cities that are now absorbed into modern nations were once independent or under different authority and, as such, issued coins under their own names. Although the authority that produced the coin may no longer exist, many coins have survived even from centuries ago and the collector's aim is to attribute them as nearly as possible to the locality that produced them. In most cases, the inscriptions on the coins themselves are the means of accurate identification.

Most modern world coins are easy to attribute. A sizable proportion of them, including those from most of the British colonies and Commonwealth nations (but *not* Britain itself) show the name of the issuing country in English. Then, too, many countries are known in English by the same name as in their native languages.

Other countries issue coins that are not so easily identified until you know certain key words. It is almost certain you will not recognize "Euzkadi" as the Viscayan Republic, "Suomi" as Finland, or "Shqipni" as Albania. Some of these key words are written on coins with the Greek or Cyrillic alphabets and can only be approximated using English characters. You may also encounter coins from Moslem and oriental countries which do not have any recognizable words.

A large proportion of the coins issued in the past hundred and fifty years are from British, French, and Portuguese colonies. Be sure to read the complete inscription on coins that seem to be from Britain, France, or Portugal to determine whether they are from the country itself or one of the colonies.

As mentioned earlier, coins of Great Britain do not show the name of the country in English. Except for the denomination, British coin inscriptions are in Latin. The key word in identifying them is BRITANNIARUM (of Britain), although on most recent issues, it is abbreviated to BRITT. or even BR.

When you have an unknown foreign coin, study its design and inscriptions for clues to its identity.

Afghanistan (mosque) · Burma (lion) · Ceylon (lion) · China (dragon) · Egypt (fez) · Ethiopia (lion)

India (Asoka pillar) · Iran (lion) · Iraq (grain) · Israel (Hebrew inscription) · Japan (chrysanthemum) · Korea (flower)

Mongolia (emblem) · Morocco (star) · Muscat (crossed daggers) · Nepal (trident) · Pakistan (crescent) · Saudi Arabia (palm)

Thailand (coat of arms) · Tibet (design) · Sudan (camel) · Syria (eagle) · Thailand (elephant) · Turkey (toughra)

Check first of all to see whether the name appears anywhere in English or is close enough to English to be recognizable. Be sure not to pass over the name of some small colony or new nation without realizing it is the very name you are seeking. If reading the inscription on a coin doesn't tell you what country it is from, pick the word that looks most promising and look it up.

There is an excellent identification chart in the book *Coin Collecting as a Hobby* by Burton Hobson, which will provide you with the heading under which you are likely to find the coin described in standard coin catalogues, as for example, Braunschweig—Brunswick (Germany).

From the standpoint of coin identification, there are three factors to bear in mind in regard to coins issued before 1800: First, nearly all legends on pre-1800 coins were in Latin and many of the words were engraved in abbreviated form. On small-size coins of rulers with long titles, the legends are sometimes abbreviated to the point of being little more than a string of initials. Second, the republics we know today had not come into existence by 1800 and nearly every coin was issued in the name of an emperor, king, duke, or other noble. The sovereign's name, especially if the piece is dated, can be very useful in identifying a coin. By referring to a biographical dictionary or dated lists of rulers, you can often verify or add to your supposition about a coin.

Finally, a great many states, provinces, etc., that

were later consolidated, were still issuing independent coinages, as for example, the provinces of The Netherlands—Gelderland, Holland, Overijssel, Utrecht, West Frisia, and Zeeland.

Coins of the Middle Ages are more difficult to identify than those struck after 1500, mainly because the legends are so often blurry or even partially illegible. The greatest problem for beginners is the recognition of letters in their medieval forms. The important points to remember are that the letter U is invariably shown as a V, that J is shown as I, that letters are sometimes reversed (especially N's and C's), and that two letters are sometimes joined into one (ligated) such as AE. Be careful not to confuse B's and E's, H's and N's, and K's and R's, G's and 6's, which look very much alike if not sharply engraved.

MEDIEVAL COIN: This gros tournois of Cologne has the inscription **WALRAM ARCHIEPCS COLONIE** (Walram Archbishop of Cologne) on the obverse. The reverse inscription, **MONETA TVVCIEN XPC VICIT**, etc. is explained in the text.

During the Middle Ages all coins were inscribed with the Latin names of the towns and cities issuing them. To further complicate identification, these names were usually in abbreviated form. The earlier issues show only words, monograms, and crude designs. By the thirteenth century, however, as larger-size coins came into use, representations of saints, rulers, and coats of arms began to appear. The key to attribution, however, is still the legend. Occasionally letters are repeated in words, such as TVVCIVM instead of just TVCIVM, the Latin word for Deutz, one of the mint cities of Cologne in Germany.

The starting point of the legend is often marked with a small cross. The ruler's name nearly always comes first in its Latin form, abbreviated more often than not. The name is usually followed by DG (Dei Gratia—by the Grace of God) and the ruler's title (REX, DVX, COMES, EPIS—King, Duke, Count, Bishop). The ruler's title is followed by the names of his domains, also in abbreviated Latin. The territories are usually listed in order of importance.

In attributing coins struck by foreign rulers for territories over which they had jurisdiction, allot them to the area in which the coins were intended to circulate. On their coins, many monarchs claimed sovereignty to territory long after the fact. Lengthy legends sometimes start on the obverse and continue on to the reverse of a coin. The reverse also often carries the name of the specific mint city (MONETA NOVA CIVIT IMPER TREMONIENSIS—New Money of the Imperial City of Tremonia—Dortmund, Germany). On larger coins, we often find religious mottoes as part of the reverse inscription (XPS REGNAT XPS IMPERAT XPS VINCIT—Christ reigns, Christ commands, Christ conquers).

Dated coins are much easier to locate in catalogs and the dates are often helpful in verifying a coin's attribution. Dates on coins came into general use about 1500, although many coins struck later are not dated. A few coins dated according to the Christian era are known from the late fourteenth century. The earliest dates are shown in Roman numerals. Arabic numeral dates did not appear until a century later, toward the end of the fifteenth century, the earliest known being 1484.

Ancient coins often cannot be dated as precisely as more modern issues. Most Greek coins, however, can be assigned reasonably accurate dates of issue that scholars have arrived at by studying the style, symbols and workmanship of the coins.

MOSLEM COIN: The date 1321 does not make this a medieval issue for it signifies A.H. (after Hegira) and not A.D. (Anno Domini). It is actually the 1903 Moroccan 5 mazunas piece.

Some very modern-looking coins carry dates in the 1300's, but these are from Moslem countries dated according to the Mohammedan calendar, which begins with their year 1, equivalent to our year 622 A.D. The year 622 is the date of Mohammed's flight or "Hegira" from Mecca; the Moslems number their years from this point. Moslem dates are given as A.H., meaning "After Hegira." To convert Moslem dates into Christian-era dates, a small computation is necessary because the Mohammedan calendar is based on a lunar year of 354 days rather than our solar year of 365 days. To convert

Mohammedan (A.H.) into Christian (A.D.) dates, it is necessary to deduct 3 per cent from the A.H. date (compensation for the difference in length of years) and add 622 to arrive at the A.D. equivalent. Thus, a coin of Morocco dated 1321 was actually struck in 1903 according to our method of reckoning (1321 minus 3 per cent, or roughly 40, plus 622 equals 1903). These A.H. date coins turn up fairly regularly, and to avoid being fooled into thinking you have a coin that is very much older than is actually the case, bear in mind that the earliest Arabic-numeral full-dated coin of the Christian era is from 1484.

BUYING AND SELLING COINS

While certain rare coins are in great demand and do bring high prices, the vast majority of coins sell for much less. A leading coin retailer in the United States recently computed that his average transaction was about $3.75 and recalled individual sales over the preceding year ranging from 10¢ to $6,000. More than half of the coins he sold were priced at a dollar or less. Literally thousands of different coins can each be purchased for less than the price of a cinema ticket and the entertainment factor is infinitely more lasting!

Since coins, except for the relatively few that can be found in circulation, do cost something, one of the first things a potential collector wants to know is whether coins are wise purchases and what profit or loss he can expect on his investment. In one sense, and assuming that we are talking about moderately priced coins, most collectors feel that just the pleasure alone of owning an unusual coin repays its cost.

Every coin has a market value, the price that dealers are currently charging for it. This price is determined by supply and demand—the available quantity of a coin and the number of collectors and degree of interest they have in owning it. If there are enough coins to go around, the price will be moderate, because coin dealers compete sharply for collectors' business. On the other hand, if a few coins have to be divided among many collectors, rivalry bids the price up quickly.

If you ask a non-collector his opinion of what makes a coin valuable, he will answer unhesitatingly, "Rarity!" It is true that rarity is a large part of the answer, but it is not the whole answer.

Again in the eyes of a non-collector, the age of a coin is also a prime factor in determining value. This is true to some extent but again it is not the whole story. The coin trade has other standards besides age and rarity in assessing coin values.

The value of a given coin is a complex thing. The

ODDITY: This "cracked skull" Lincoln cent is caused by a break in the die used in minting.

number of pieces struck during the year of issue naturally has much to do with it. As you would expect, an 1877 Indian Head cent with a mintage of fewer than one million pieces is worth about ten times as much as the older 1867 of which nearly ten million were made, and approximately 100 times as much as the 1887 with a coinage of 45 million pieces.

Low mintage alone, however, is not enough to make a coin valuable. A coin may be scarce, but if there is little or no demand for it, then it will not be valuable. Lack of demand leaves prices on a fairly even keel. Many of the world's coins and certainly most of the ancient coins are rare and the supply is limited, to be sure. But the demand for them is nothing like the demand for certain coins of the U.S., Britain and other popularly collected countries, which is why these coins sell for several times the price of actually scarcer and older coins.

As we have seen, another key element is the physical state of a coin—its condition. A coin in brilliant, uncirculated condition can easily be worth ten times as much as the identical coin in used condition. On the other hand, mutilation or damage to a coin detracts from its value. Unless it is a rare date, a coin in poor condition is worth little or nothing to a collector.

Collectors have the "law" of supply and demand working for them. The supply of most coins is constantly decreasing as more and more coins go into collections, and demand is building as more and more people take up the hobby. Population growth and increasing leisure time alone should assure ever more collectors. Thus a collector may very likely find that after he has held on to a coin for a few years, its price will have gone up to the point where fifty per cent of the market value is more than his original purchase price. Coin collecting is one of the few hobbies one can enjoy over the years and still stand to make a profit. Profits are especially likely if a collector concentrates on coins that are readily available now, but are likely to gain more and more popularity with the passage of time.

PRACTICES OF THE COIN TRADE

As used here and as generally understood among coin collectors and dealers, "value" means the price you are likely to have to pay for a given coin when you buy it from a dealer. *It does not mean the amount you can expect to realize if you want to sell the coin to a dealer.*

The dealer's *buying* price averages around half of his *selling* price. This is understandable, since his selling price has to include his cost of doing business plus a reasonable profit.

A small firm cannot afford to keep a great deal of money tied up in its stock of coins. Consequently its purchases from an individual have to be resold to a larger dealer and the cost of handling must necessarily be allowed for in setting the purchase price. A large firm, on the other hand, keeps an extensive inventory —a costly burden which can tie up considerable sums of money. This, too, places a limitation on the amount the larger dealer feels justified in paying for the coins he buys.

Still another motive influences the dealer. When presented with the opportunity to buy a small or miscellaneous collection, his general experience is that it contains a few highly desirable coins that he can resell very quickly. However, the bulk of the collection will be items that will probably move slowly. And so what the dealer really does is pay for the coins he can dispose of readily; the rest of the collection must come as part of the "package."

Selling at auction is recommended by some authorities. This type of sale is suitable, however, only for the disposal of collections which are quite large and contain a great many highly desirable items.

TRADING WITH OTHER COLLECTORS

One of the best ways to dispose of duplicate coins is doubtless through trading with other collectors. You naturally want to keep the coins which are in better condition and dispose of those in inferior condition. If you are on friendly terms with other collectors, the chances are you can arrange swaps that will please both parties.

While it may be possible to do a certain amount of business with other collectors, don't minimize the dealer's role! The bulk of a collector's transactions will always be with dealers, who render a service that cannot possibly be matched by collectors.

HOW COINS ARE MADE

Knowing a little about how coins are made—in earlier times as well as now—helps a collector to understand about such things as die varieties and flaws and especially about errors and mis-struck pieces.

Sometimes, due to such minute variations, flaws, cracks, errors, recutting, etc., it is possible to identify and distinguish between coins struck from different sets of dies even though the coins bear the same date and design. This is particularly true of the older coins made in the handcraft days before the mints were highly mechanized. Variations of this sort, known as die varieties, are the concern of collectors specializing in a given series.

To strike a coin, a pair of dies, obverse ("head") and reverse ("tail"), are required. For the design to stand up in relief on the finished coin, it must be cut (incused) into the die. Occasionally, a die will crack or chip while still in use. When this happens the crack impresses itself on to the coins as a line, an unintentional addition to the design.

A chip in the die appears as a dot on the coin. Working the other way, waste material can clog up part of a die. When part of the die if filled in, that portion of the design (usually a letter or numeral) is not impressed on the coin.

Even in the most modern mints, coins are made today in much the same way they have been produced since steam power was first applied to minting nearly two centuries ago. The basic idea, that of impressing blank pieces of metal between two dies, dates back to the time of the ancient Greeks. Many of the world's mints have guided tours or observation windows for visitors. Seeing a mint in operation is a great treat for anyone interested in coins.

Errors can occur at several steps in the coining process and varieties can be created in preparing the dies. Interest in varieties causes collectors to study their coins, to inquire about how they are made and how varieties and errors come about. You are sure to hear more soon about varieties, as they are added to catalogue listings and given spaces in albums. They are worth knowing about, since a growing demand for this kind of material will definitely result in significant price increases.

ROCK COLLECTING

Collecting rocks and minerals (rocks are aggregates of minerals) may give you an absorbing, lifelong interest and will certainly bring you into healthful surroundings out in the open. The lure of new discoveries always provides an attractive goal. If you collect as most people do, in a group or with a person of similar interests, it will foster good companionship and perhaps lasting friendship.

Pictures of rocks and minerals are interesting, but they cannot begin to approach the attractiveness of "the real thing" itself, in its natural surroundings. A visit to the museum is enjoyable, but again it lacks the pleasures of a field trip. And then there is joy and pride of personal ownership in treasured objects that may have cost you a good deal of toil and trouble.

How do people start collecting rocks and minerals? Often such a collection starts with attractive pebbles that happen to catch the eye. This might occur on a hike, on a beach, or on a summer holiday trip—anywhere, in fact, out in the open. Charles Darwin's scientific career started with his interest in the pebbles on his father's doorstep. Eventually that interest took shape in a memorable voyage of scientific discovery around the world.

Sometimes people become interested in collecting in the course of school or college field trips in the country, or through seeing a sample collection at a summer camp. (Collecting is a popular activity for winning the Boy Scout merit badge.)

Those who are lucky enough to have a friend or relative or teacher with this hobby may easily become fascinated by the pleasures of collecting. A visit to a museum may inspire a lifelong interest in minerals.

WHERE TO COLLECT

To the beginner the problem of finding specimens may seem to be very difficult, but actually there are many possible sources. Cliffs, ravines, abandoned ore piles or old mining towns, ancient glacier beds, and river banks are ideal for finding minerals.

So are places where roads and railway tracks have been cut through. The vicinity of mines and quarries is also rich in material for you. Fields often contain boulders and smaller stones that will swell your collection. The seashore, too, is a good place to find attractive specimens.

But even if you don't live near any such areas, your case is far from hopeless! You may visit one of these places or pass them during a vacation trip or excursion, and thus get a chance to do some rewarding collecting.

You can always pick up interesting minerals around excavations, where old houses are being torn down, or where new ones are being built. (That adds a new interest to being a "sidewalk superintendent.")

Even when all these suggestions cannot help you, there are still other sources. You can buy specimens,

SPLITTING A ROCK: This often provides useful information about a specimen.

Condensed from "Treasures of the Earth" by Fred Reinfeld © 1954 by Sterling Publishing Co., Inc., New York

INSPECTING CRYSTALS: This is a task for father and son together.

many of them very reasonably priced, from the dealers who advertise in magazines devoted to natural history hobbies.

Very often collecting takes a specialized turn. You may collect (or buy) rocks containing fossils—a good way to make even more vivid the fascinating story of creatures that lived on this earth millions of years ago. Minerals with beautiful crystals make an absorbing hobby, too.

Some collectors specialize in flint arrowheads, catlinite pipes, obsidian knives, soapstone dishes, and other things made by primitive peoples. Collecting minerals for samples of various kinds of cleavage, or lustre, is still another fascinating hobby. The more advanced collector may specialize in a classified collection of igneous, sedimentary, and metamorphic rocks.

OUT HUNTING FOR SPECIMENS: This is basic to rock collecting.

EQUIPMENT FOR COLLECTING

To begin with, you need tools for breaking off bits of rock, or for prying them loose. You can get these from a hardware store or from scientific-supply houses which advertise in the hobby magazines.

Most important is a geologist's or prospector's hammer or pick. This type of tool has a broad head for hammering and breaking open rocks, and also a pick with a narrow point for prying out specimens. By using such a tool and a chisel you may often make attractive finds that were not visible on the surface.

Hammers   **Pick**

A chisel, about one inch wide—or a little less—will help you pick out smaller crystals and fragments.

A pocket knife is easy to carry and is helpful in checking "hardness" (page 124) of specimens.

A pocket magnifying glass is also needed; some magnifiers provide four grades of magnification, the maximum being 20 times, although 8 to 10 is all that will usually be needed.

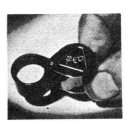 

Magnifying Glass   **Storage Cabinet**

To carry your specimens you might do best to obtain a canvas or plastic knapsack or backpack. You can carry your equipment and stones in this bag.

You will find out by experience that it is advisable to number the items you collect. Adhesive tape is very useful for this purpose. Take a strip of adhesive tape before leaving on your trip and cut it up into 20 small pieces. Stick them onto some wax paper (to keep them moist) and number them with black India ink from 1 to 20. On your trip you can then stick a numbered piece of adhesive tape on each specimen.

You will also need a loose-leaf notebook and a

pencil. When you find your first specimen, you number it and record the number in the notebook, giving the date, the locality, and a careful description of the stone—including its name and type. Make the entry at the time of discovering the stone. Don't rely on your memory.

Such descriptions may sometimes be the key to finding something of real value, or to indicating accurately where certain kinds of deposits may be found. You may want to return to search the area, and this information will be valuable to you and to your fellow collectors.

A diameter of about 2 inches is roughly right for each specimen. If larger, the items will be too heavy and bulky; if smaller, some interesting detail might be lost. There may be special reasons for wanting a stone of a different size. Soft specimens can be cut with a knife; hard ones can be handled with a chisel.

It is a good idea to take along some old newspaper or wrapping paper to wrap each item separately. In this way you will avoid losing the smaller items, and you will protect the softer ones from getting scratched by the harder rocks and minerals.

Some collectors like to pick up two pieces of each stone. They use the duplicate for swapping or testing. (In that case, they take along a duplicate set of numbers.) However, this has the drawback of limiting the variety of specimens that you can bring home.

HOW TO STORE YOUR COLLECTION

Once you have your stones, follow through on the idea of keeping them properly numbered and identified.

Offhand the problem of maintaining a collection of stones seems to involve some difficulty and awkwardness. Actually, there are many ways to store a collection—in old cigar boxes, shirt boxes, old dresser drawers, or even trays, shelves, and cabinets. (Egg cartons are fine for smaller items. Cuff-link boxes and similar containers of jewelry are likewise suitable.) The space you have can be divided by wooden or cardboard partitions. You can also buy trays from the minerals supply houses.

Where available, an old bookcase or a cabinet with interchangeable drawers is probably the best to use. A good material for the shelves is plywood, which can be bought very reasonably from any retail lumber yard. A 2-foot length for the shelves is advisable.

As a matter of fact, you don't need a bookcase in order to use shelves. You can build a very serviceable "bookcase" or cabinet with crates obtained from a supermarket. Allow plenty of height between shelves so that you can pile one box or tray on another if necessary. Once you paint or varnish the finished job, you will be proud of its appearance.

(It's a good idea to check in advance on the probable size of your trays or other containers, and work out the size of your shelves accordingly.)

The labelling and cataloguing of your stones will add greatly to the pleasure and knowledge you derive from your collection. Instead of the adhesive tape technique mentioned before, you can put the information on paper and attach it to the stone with household cement. Still another way is to clean a small part of the stone and paint some white enamel

CATALOGUING AND LABELLING: If you don't keep proper records of your collection, you will lose half the enjoyment of the hobby, and will never be able to display your rocks with accurate descriptions.

TESTING for hardness (left) and for streak (right) are the standard methods of identification.

over that section. Then, with a fine camel's hair brush and black enamel or black India ink, you can supply the number and name of the stone.

Near the tray you can pin or paste up a sheet of paper (or an index card) repeating the information in written or typed form. On all such records, you keep using the original number assigned to the stone. If any record is lost, you can check the information in your notebook.

This notebook should be in loose-leaf form because if you find a better specimen of a certain type of rock or mineral, you will want to insert a page for a new description. (You may want to replace the older specimen and set it aside for trading purposes.) Also, a loose-leaf record always allows room for unforeseen expansion—for photographs, for example, of striking formations of column lava, and the like.

IDENTIFYING MINERALS

One of the most useful aids to identifying minerals is the standard hardness scale, called the Mohs' scale, which has ten grades of hardness.

A stone of Grade 10 (the hardest) can scratch all the lower grades without their scratching it. A stone of Grade 1 will be scratched by all stones of Grade 2 to 10, without scratching any of them.

Each stone scratches stones belonging to lower grades of hardness, but does not scratch minerals belonging to higher grades of hardness. In the case of two stones belonging to the same grade of hardness, they will scratch each other.

The standard hardness scale uses ten representative minerals, beginning with the softest and ending with the hardest:

1	talc	6	feldspar
2	gypsum	7	quartz
3	calcite	8	topaz
4	fluorite	9	corundum
5	apatite	10	diamond

Here are some examples of how the scale is used,

with explanations of the first seven degrees of hardness:

Hardness 1: stones so soft they can be scratched with a fingernail.

Hardness 2: these stones do not feel soft but they can still be scratched with a fingernail.

Hardness 3: these stones cannot be scratched by a fingernail, but they are scratched by a penny.

Hardness 4: these stones resist the penny, but a knife will scratch them with no trouble.

Hardness 5: these stones can just barely be scratched by a knife.

Hardness 6: these stones will scratch the blade of the knife and will just barely scratch glass.

Hardness 7: these stones scratch glass easily and will scratch the vast majority of common minerals.

Hardnesses 8, 9, and 10 are not very common.

Some degrees of hardness may be in between; more than 6, say, and less than 7.

Another help in identifying a mineral is finding out the color of its "streak." The surface color of a mineral specimen is often different from the color you find if you scratch the mineral with a piece of bathroom tile. (This is the kind of tile used on bathroom floors. It is also used under hot plates to keep them from damaging a table top.) The color brought out by the tile is the mineral's streak. The table on page 125 shows the hardness and streak of common minerals.

This table also gives the lustre of common minerals. Lustre is the quality of reflecting light. In the case of metals and ores, this lustre is metallic as a rule. In the non-metals, the most common lustre is glassy.

Another help in identifying minerals is to test their cleavage—the way they split. Feldspar, for example, splits cleanly in three directions. If you have a mineral that barely scratches glass (Hardness 6), splits in the manner just described, and has a glassy to dull lustre, the mineral you are testing is

HARDNESS POINTS (left) and STREAK PLATES (right) are valuable aids in identifying minerals.

Mineral	Hardness	Streak	Lustre	Remarks
AMPHIBOLE	5.5	white to pale green or pale brown	satiny or glassy	group of minerals ranging from white to green, brown, or black, with six-sided long slender crystals; common in metamorphic rocks
APATITE	5	white	glassy	white, green, or brown; found in many igneous or metamorphic rocks
AZURITE	4	light blue	glassy	azure blue; copper ore; bubbles in acid
BERYL	7.5	white	glassy	commonly found in pegmatite; generally green or bluish green
CALCITE	3	colorless	glassy to dull	colorless and transparent in pure state; yellow, brown, green, red or blue from impurities; uniform cleavage in 3 directions; bubbles in hydrochloric acid; clear calcite provides a double image; also known as "Iceland spar"
DOLOMITE	3.5	white	glassy	white, pink, or grey; contains magnesium; resembles calcite, but bubbles only in warm hydrochloric acid
EPIDOTE	6.5–7	white	glassy	pistachio to very dark yellow-green; found in igneous and metamorphic rock
FELDSPAR	6	white	glassy to dull	feldspar group makes up 60 per cent of the earth's crust; all form crystals with 2 good cleavage planes and 1 imperfect one; mostly white, yellow, pink, but also green, brown, grey
FLUORITE	4	white	glassy	colorless or violet, green, yellow, or rose; cubic system crystals; 4 perfect cleavage directions
GALENA	2.5	lead-grey	metallic	lead-grey color; opaque; brittle; lead ore; perfect cubic cleavage
HALITE	2.5	white	glassy	common salt; colorless to white; test by taste; cubic cleavage
HEMATITE	6	red to dark red	metallic, glassy, or dull	ocher red to black; iron ore; streak test is the definite one
LIMONITE	5.5	yellow-brown	metallic to dull	yellow-brown to black; iron ore; looks like rust; streak test important
MAGNETITE	6	black	metallic	steel-grey to black; magnetic iron ore; found in igneous or metamorphic rocks
MALACHITE	3.5	light green	silky or dull	vivid green; copper ore; bubbles in acid
MICA	2–3	white	glassy to pearly	group of minerals; white (muscovite), black (biotite), also grey, pink, yellow, green, brown; always crystalline, with some crystals 3 feet in diameter; splits in sheets sometimes less than 1/1000th of an inch thick; these sheets are flexible, elastic, transparent, shiny
PYRITE	6	greenish-black	metallic	brassy yellow, called "fool's gold"; sulphur and iron compound; found in igneous and metamorphic rocks; the hardest metallic mineral
PYROXENE	5.5	white to greyish-green	glassy	group of minerals; common with feldspars in granite, gneiss, and lava

(continued on next page)

Mineral	Hardness	Streak	Lustre	Remarks
QUARTZ	7	white	glassy	group of most common individual minerals, forming 12 per cent of the earth's crust; crystals usually 6-sided with six-sided pyramid at one or both ends; many varieties are semi-precious; quartz is common in sedimentary, igneous, and metamorphic rocks
SALT				see HALITE
SERPENTINE	2.5-3	white	greasy or waxy	yellowish or green; never occurs in crystals; generally found in metamorphic rocks

feldspar. Mica, with a hardness of between 2 and 3, splits into very thin, flat, flexible and elastic layers.

Another common mineral, calcite, may be identified in a number of ways. It bubbles when hydrochloric acid is spilled on it. It scratches a penny and is also scratched by it. This places it in the Hardness 3 group. And finally, calcite breaks cleanly in three ways.

Dealers in mineral supplies sell sets for measuring hardness, which provide all the materials you need for this purpose.

MINERAL CLASSIFICATION

Approximately 2,000 minerals are known; about 120 are considered common, and the remaining 1,880 are considered rare or very rare! The more common ones make up the bulk of the rocks and occur in large quantities. Many are found only as deposits in small concentrated aggregates, and are therefore valuable. Some are found in small quantities in unusual or selected types of deposits, and are relatively rare.

Generally, minerals are classified according to the chief *ion* (or ion group) which serves as a mineral's fundamental unit. The minerals are generally grouped in the order of these classes. This list follows that order:

1. NATIVE ELEMENTS: Only one element required to make a mineral.

2. SULFIDES AND SULFOSALTS: Sulfur ion (S) is fundamental ion.

3. HALIDES: Fluorine (F) or chlorine ion (Cl) is fundamental unit.

4. OXIDES AND HYDROXIDES: Oxygen (O) and hydroxyl ion (OH) is fundamental unit.

5. CARBONATES: Carbonate ion (CO_3) is fundamental unit.

6. BORATES: Borate ion (BO_4) is fundamental unit.

7. SULFATES: Sulfate ion (SO_4) is fundamental unit.

8. CHROMATES, TUNGSTATES, MOLYBDATES: Chromate (CrO_4), Tungstate (WO_4), Molybdate (MoO_4) ions are fundamental units.

TYPES OF CLEAVAGE: Mica (top left) splits into very thin layers; halite (top right) is an example of cubic cleavage; fluorite (bottom left) goes in four perfect cleavage directions; sphalerite (bottom right) has a highly perfect cleavage of 12 plane faces.

FELDSPAR (left) is one of the commonest minerals. An ACID TEST (right) is used by geologists to test drilling samples for limestone. Hydrochloric acid will bubble if limestone is present.

9. PHOSPHATES, ARSENATES, VANADATES: Phosphate (PO_4), Arsenate (AsO_4), Vanadate (VO_4) ions are fundamental units.

10. SILICATES: Silicate ion (SiO_4) is fundamental unit.

The most abundant minerals making up *igneous* rocks are the silicates: quartz, feldspars, micas, augite, hornblende, and olivine. In *sedimentary* rocks, clay minerals, quartz, feldspars, calcite, and micas are abundant. However, many other minerals occurring in minor quantities in small deposits often are more interesting, more colorful, and more sought after by collectors.

SEDIMENTARY ROCKS

LIMESTONE is made up mostly or entirely of calcite (calcium carbonate). It may contain a little sand or clay as well. In the pure state it shades from white to light grey. When impurities are present, it ranges from near-black through grey to reddish-brown to buff.

The standard test for limestone is to spill some drops of hydrochloric acid on it, which will make it bubble. Varieties of limestone include:

Chalk—a soft and porous variety formed from tiny sea animals.

Shell limestone—formed from broken shells.

Coquina—formed from small marine shells. It is crumbly and porous.

Encrinal limestone—formed from the shells of creatures which are relatives of the starfish.

Coral limestone—formed from corals.

Tufa—found chiefly in hot springs.

Travertine—found chiefly around the hot springs. It is a banded form of tufa ranging from white to red.

SANDSTONE is composed of grains of sand which were formed by erosion of rocks. Some sandstone contains only quartz, but it may also have feldspar, magnetite, garnet or other minerals. Sometimes sandstone is soft and crumbly, so that surface particles break off to the touch. Other times the stone is solid enough to make fine building material.

In the pure state sandstone is creamy white. Impurities color it yellow, pink, or red.

SHALE, which was originally formed from mud, is a clayey rock that is usually grey, although green, buff, and red are also seen. It is usually soft and crumbly.

CATLINITE is a clay that is soft when it comes out of the ground and turns hard later on. It varies from grey to red. The Plains Indians used it to make their smoking pipes, and for this reason it is also known as "pipestone."

TRACHYTE PORPHYRY: This igneous rock is mostly feldspar mixed with other minerals.

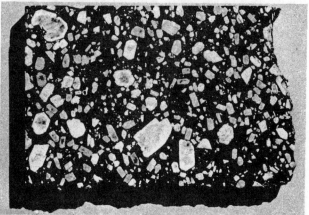

Granite

Obsidian

Basalt

CONGLOMERATE ("pudding stone") is a mixture of pebbles and sand held together by clay, silica, or some other material.

IGNEOUS GRANITIC ROCKS

GRANITE is the commonest of all the igneous rocks and the one with the coarsest grains. It was formed from magma (the molten material in the centre of the earth) that cooled very slowly, and is often exposed to view by erosion of upper layers of rock. Granite always contains quartz and feldspar; it may also contain mica or amphibole. It is a light-colored rock, running to grey, pink, buff, and green.

Pegmatite, or "giant granite," often contains fluorite, mica, topaz, or beryl in addition to quartz and feldspar.

Diorite, which contains little or no quartz, is a grey or grey-green rock. It has a good deal of feldspar, with other minerals—generally amphibole and mica.

Syenite has a great deal of feldspar, but differs from granite in the complete absence of quartz.

Diabase is a dark, hard rock containing feldspar, magnetite, and pyroxene. It is grey, green, or black.

Gabbro is also dark. It contains mostly feldspar, with some pyroxene that gives it a dark color—grey, black, or green. Some gabbro contains copper or nickel ores.

Anorthosite is mostly grey feldspar with some magnetite and pyroxene. The chief colors are white, grey, yellow, brown.

Porphyry refers to texture rather than the name of any specific mineral. It is an igneous rock containing two generations of the same mineral, with the minerals of one generation usually distinctly larger than those of the other.

IGNEOUS VOLCANIC ROCKS

ANDESITE is the characteristic rock of lava in the Andes Mountains of South America; hence its name. It is a common rock, generally grey or pink, sometimes red, brown, or purplish.

BASALT is one of the commonest igneous rocks. It is lava that cooled in flows to form lava columns or "ropy" lava. It usually contains lime and magnetite, and its color ranges from dark grey to black. When it is weathered, its color is apt to be brown.

OBSIDIAN is a volcanic rock that cooled too rapidly to leave any time for the formation of crystals or coarse grains. Obsidian therefore is smooth and glassy—and breaks sharply, like glass. The Aztecs and other Indians used it for arrowheads and knives. Chemically it is two-thirds feldspar and one-third quartz. Black is the usual color, though it may also be grey, red, or brown.

RHYOLITE is pink, red, or brown. It may have quartz or feldspar crystals, and it is often found with bands of various colors.

PUMICE is obsidian that contained a lot of gas bubbles when it was hot. The bubbles formed holes that made this mineral very light. The light weight of pumice makes it float quite a distance from the

Pumice

Tuff

Slate

scene of an ocean eruption. In color, pumice ranges from white and grey to red.

TUFF is made up of volcanic ash or cinders that have formed into a fairly soft stone that usually has holes in it. White, grey, or brown are the most usual colors.

AGGLOMERATE, as the name indicates, is a mixture of volcanic matter. It is coarse-grained and its color is determined by the main mineral it contains.

METAMORPHIC ROCKS

Heat and steam plus pressure of magma produce changes in rocks. These rocks become even harder and their originally coarse grains take on a smooth, sometimes glassy, appearance.

GNEISS ("nice") is coarse-grained made-over granite, shale, or sandstone. Whatever its origin, it is harder than the original. Gneiss comes in many different colors, depending on the color of the original rock. The new colors may be white, grey, or black; pink, red, or green; and there are other possibilities.

Gneiss

The heat and pressure exerted on gneiss force the light and dark parts to separate from each other. Gneiss has wavy bands of light and dark colors running through it. Some rocks have undergone so much change that it is impossible to tell what they were originally.

SCHIST ("shist") has more mica or dark minerals than gneiss. It is made up of thin, flaky or scaly crystallized layers that split easily. Schist is a made-over rock, chiefly shale and sandstone.

Colors of schist are determined by the rocks it is formed from. For example, mica schist, a fairly common variety, is mostly mica and quartz and is generally dark grey to brown. Sometimes it is lighter grey, sometimes it is dark enough to be black.

MARBLE is made-over limestone or dolomite. Its calcite bubbles when hydrochloric acid is spilled

PECTOLITE: This silicate mineral, which is either whitish or greyish, has a fanlike structure.

on it. Pressures on the rock may create cloudy, wavy lines in it. Pure marble is white, but various impurities will affect the color. Thus, graphite can make some parts black; iron results in red or pink. Mica, amphibole, or pyroxene are other minerals that are likely to be present.

QUARTZITE is made-over sand or sandstone. You can no longer feel the grains of sand because they are so compactly pressed together. Quartzite is hard enough to be used as paving material.

When quartzite is made up of pure (or nearly pure) quartz, it is white. When impurities are

MARCASITE: This mineral, which contains iron, was used in earlier times to strike a light.

Metamorphic Rocks ■ 129

present, they impart red, yellow, green or other colors. When the proportion of quartz in sandstone is relatively low, it will metamorphose into schist rather than quartzite.

SLATE is made-over shale. The original shale was grey, but organic carbon usually turns the slate dark; hematite may make it red or green. Brown and purple are also seen sometimes.

SERPENTINE is made-over basalt or dolomite. When it contains little iron, it is white. But some shade of green is more usual.

ICELAND SPAR: This is a name often used for clear calcite, because one of its early discoveries was in Iceland.

MUSEUM STUDY

Your own field work will take first place in your new hobby, and museum study comes next. In museums you can see rocks that have already been classified and are properly displayed in their showcases. In this way you can learn to recognize the rocks and minerals you are especially interested in finding.

Maybe you don't live in a big city, but your town museum probably has a geological section. These may be of even more interest to you, as you can use them to become an expert on the rocks and minerals of your own district. Moreover, the museum

exhibits will help you to learn how to classify and label the rocks in your own collection. Try to get to every important museum exhibition and to learn when the displays are being changed. Your town museum will probably also have a collection of geological maps and handbooks that you should consult before every field trip into an area you have not covered before.

YOUR ROCK CLUB

Many rock collectors—young and old alike—find it helpful to belong to clubs that plan and organize nearby or distant outings. In this way, everyone has a chance to learn quickly, and by actual *doing*, how to find and identify rocks. Often these clubs will provide you with the guidance of an adult who knows rocks well. Or maybe you and some interested friends can form your own club. If so, here are some rules you should follow:

1. Plan your work beforehand and obtain as much information as possible about the area you will be searching.

2. Wear clothes that are suitable for the climate and ruggedness of the area and carry food along with you in the knapsack that holds your rock-taking equipment.

3. If you are going into remote country, leave information of your route with someone at home or at headquarters of your club.

4. Do not expose yourself or others to danger—at the sea coast watch the tides and beware of dangerous cliffs; when you are searching near rivers and lakes, acquaint yourself with their currents; do not go into caves alone and if your site is a railway cut, be on the watch for unexpected or off-schedule trains.

5. Protect all wildlife in the area.

6. Observe the same personal code of conduct you would follow in your own home or neighborhood. That is,

(a) don't be a litterbug;

(b) ask permission before you go onto private property.

Finally, report all important finds to your local museum.

(See color section for additional illustrations in full color)

SHELL COLLECTING

Ages ago a primitive human being first foraged a beach and satisfied his hunger with raw shellfish. Since that day people have used shells, originally for food, and later for commercial and aesthetic purposes. The story of man and mollusk is absorbing, though its earliest chapters are irretrievably lost. In those days, lore and legend were passed down from generation to generation by word of mouth, becoming blurred and forgotten with time. Shells, however, are concrete things not easily destroyed; they afford clear evidence of prehistoric events to those who can read the tale they have to tell. Much of the story has been uncovered by archeologists, and every few years they make a discovery that helps to fill in its gaps.

They have found, for instance, seashell necklaces in France, far inland, at the grave sites of Cro-Magnon, a race that lived some 30,000 years ago. It is reasonable to think that the necklaces were made by people who lived near the sea, and then traded to other tribes; they may have changed hands repeatedly on their journey inland before being bartered to Cro-Magnon people.

Far later in prehistory, about 5,000 years before the birth of Christ, shellfish became a staple food in Europe when a group of nomadic hunters realized that the Oyster beds on the coastlines of northern Europe could support a more settled form of existence. They are called the "Kitchen-Midden People" because the sites of their villages are marked by enormous middens (refuse heaps) of empty shells and bones. As the centuries passed they became expert fishermen and skilled flint-workers. Later on, in the Stone Age, colonists began to migrate from the east, bringing with them a knowledge of agriculture; their skills, combined with those of the fisherfolk, brought an improvement in the standard of living. These people also used shells for ornamental purposes, and some of the shells came from far away. Shells from the Red Sea and Indian Ocean have been found with their bodies, entombed in the cold earth of northern Europe.

The next advance in man's use of mollusks came a thousand years later. Shells were highly valued for their beauty during this period. When the royal tombs were discovered at Ur, an ancient Sumerian city in the Euphrates Valley, the remains of Sumerian queens were found, decked in headdresses of gold inlaid with shells and lapis lazuli. Sumerian lapidaries were famous for their inlay work; the tombs yielded a rich treasure of golden jewels, sculptures, ladies' dressing boxes and gentlemen's gaming boards, all inlaid with mother-of-pearl shell and lapis lazuli. Even today, nearly 5,000 years after they were made, the colors are still fresh and bright.

The mollusk had other uses in addition to providing food, decoration, and a means of exchange. A certain species of mollusk, called Murex, was found to squirt ink to form a protective screen when alarmed. The ancients soon discovered that this ink could be used to color fabric a rich purple. Tradition says the first dye was made from Murex ink at the famous Phoenician seaport of Tyre; in any event, an industry sprang up there that was to make "Tyrian purple" a household word around the Mediterranean. The word "purple" comes from *purpura*, one of three species of Murex that the Tyrians processed into dye.

During the Middle Ages a shell came to be the symbol of pilgrimage. About A.D. 1000, European pilgrims frequently banded together to visit the Holy Land, which was under Mohammedan rule. Later, after the crusades to win back the Holy Land for Christianity began, the Scallop shell became a symbol of service in the Holy Wars, and as such, it was incorporated into the coat of arms of many families. This is why, today, many of England's leading families bear on their crest the outline of a common seashell.

Archeologists have also found much evidence that

(See color section for additional illustrations in full color)

Condensed from "Shell Life and Shell Collecting" by Sonia Bennett Murray, © 1969 by Sterling Publishing Co., Inc., New York

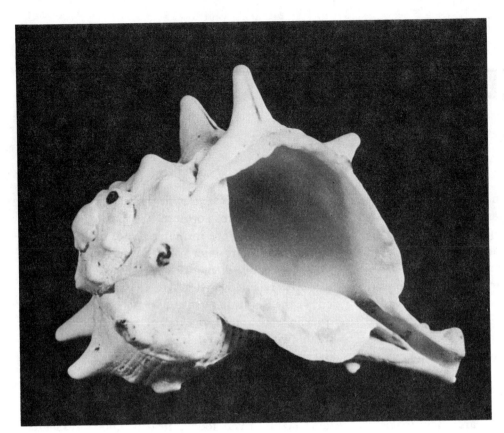

DYE MUREX: A purple ink is released into the water as a smoke screen by this shellfish in escaping from its enemies. In ancient times this Murex was treasured by kings and queens because it was from its ink that "royal purple" dye for cloth was made. The Phoenician city of Tyre on the eastern Mediterranean shore became the hub of an industry devoted to making the popular dye.

the early peoples of the Americas used and valued shells. For example, the fossilized remains of a young girl who lived during the Ice Age were discovered in the area that is now the state of Minnesota. Around her neck the girl had hung a Conch shell from waters far to the south—evidence that "interstate commerce" had already begun!

Many tribes used shells to decorate their pottery or to inlay the surfaces of wooden dishes. Other tribes used the famous shell coinage, wampum. Wampum was made of tubular beads ground out of the shell of a Common Clam which we call by its Indian name, Quahog. The valves are mostly white, but there is a purple splotch on the inside, near the rim. Only a few purple beads could be obtained from each shell, so purple wampum was valued more highly than white. The Indians also used to keep records of important events by weaving meaningful patterns into the belts of wampum beads. In general, white designs indicated peaceful events, with purple denoting death or war. Each collection of belt records had a keeper, an Indian historian who was versed in the sign language used and could interpret the events recorded on old belts long after those who made them had died and been forgotten.

Further south in the Americas, two great civiliza-

tions were flowering—the Aztec in Mexico and the Inca in Peru. Although both of these peoples were rich in precious metals and semi-precious stones, they still valued seashells for their beauty, and frequently used them in creating mosaic ornaments. There is, for example, among the outstanding collection of Aztec art in the British Museum in London, a ceremonial mask made of cedarwood inlaid with turquoise, the eyes and teeth of which are made of white shell.

We live today in an age of plastic beads and paper money; yet mollusks retain their usefulness to man. Each year in the Mississippi Valley, 7,000,000,000 fresh-water Mussels are put through machines which turn them into mother-of-pearl buttons. In Florida, houses are built of coquina, a building material composed of Coquina shells and Coral bound with cement. And along the Gulf Coast, roads are built on Oyster-shell foundations. Many species are valued for their meat.

The sea-food industry is big business, and is likely to get bigger, for the world's population is expected to triple by the end of the century and it is already pushing at the limits of its food supply. While most arable land is already being used, only a tiny fraction of the protein-rich food which the seas have to offer us is currently harvested.

Then too there are few people who can resist the appeal of a fine pearl necklace or fail to admire a cameo ring, both of which are produced from mollusks, the pearl produced primarily by Oysters and cameo carved from Conch shells. As there are few people of any age who can see a collection of exquisite shells without a feeling of wonder and awe, shell collecting has a definite appeal. Delicate colors and fanciful shapes combine in infinite variety to captivate the beholder. Fashions in jewelry come and go, but so long as people respond to beauty, seashells will be collected and cherished; for now, as in the past and future, the shells on our beaches are truly jewels of the sea displayed free for the taking. Happy shelling!

THE EVOLUTION OF MOLLUSKS

The study of shells that lived millions of years ago helps geologists to determine the age of rocks, and paleontologists to learn how living things evolved.

There are very few places on earth where mollusks do not dwell: both arctic and tropic zones, both mountains and deserts, both rocky shores and sandy bays have a population of highly specialized shell dwellers that cannot survive in any other environment. Yet these creatures, so diverse in appearance and habitat that few people realize they are kin, have all evolved from jelly-like blobs that somehow acquired the ability to take the mineral content of their food and convert it into a hard outer covering.

When these first shells were made, perhaps

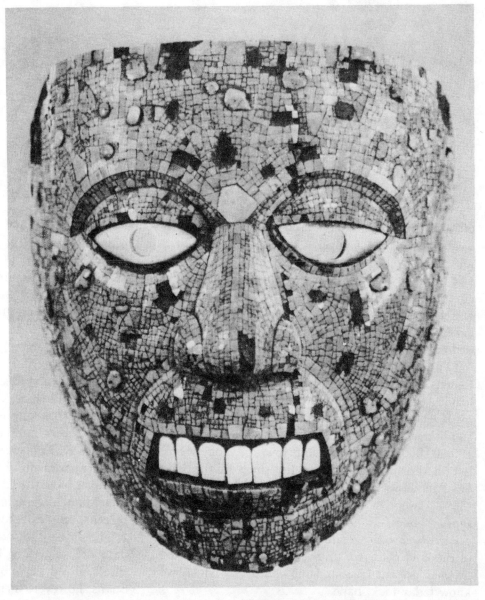

CEREMONIAL MASK:
Once used by the Aztecs of Mexico to represent the god Quetzalcoatl, the mask has eyes and teeth of white shell. The mosaic is made of shell and turquoise.

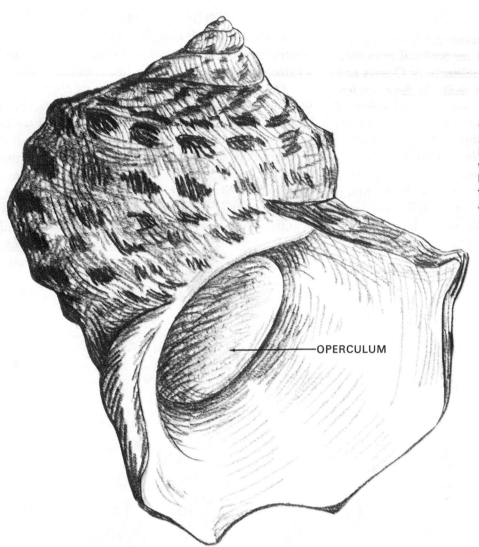

GREEN TURBAN SNAIL: About 8 inches high, this Snail has a trapdoor (or operculum) when alive. The operculum is a limey plate at the base of its foot. In this picture, it is shown as it was replaced in the shell after the death of the Snail.

OPERCULUM

600,000,000 years ago, the land masses of the world today were partially covered by shallow seas. Then, and for 2,000,000 years to come, much of the world was largely under water. Mollusks found ideal conditions in the vast expanses of shallow water, and flourished and multiplied. As generation after generation lived and died, their empty shells drifted down to the sea bed.

Centuries passed away and the land, still unstable, folded and buckled and rose; the waters receded, leaving their ooze high and dry to be slowly covered by layers of dust. Reptiles were suited to the new conditions, and flourished in their turn; for 100,000,000 years their footprints and bones were left in the mud and above the shells of the long dead mollusks. At last the land settled once more, the sea swept in, and marine debris entombed the reptile bones. In some places land and sea succeeded each other again and again as the contours of the land changed, until at last the seas retreated to their present level and the continents which we know today took shape.

The dust and debris of a day weighs little, but over the centuries tons were deposited. Beneath this weight the lower layers were compressed, hardening at last into solid rock. Minerals carried by seeping water replaced the shells and bones, gradually turning them to stone. Hardened mud preserved an indelible record of footprints and leaves.

All these petrified and preserved traces of bygone life are known as fossils. Like many of our words, the term "fossil" comes from Latin; originally it meant "that which is dug up." Fossils are of interest here because great numbers of seashells were preserved in this way. From studies of these ancient shells, and from experiments with living animals and plants, scientists have traced the evolution of mollusks from their simple beginnings in the primeval seas to their present complexity and diversity of form.

The oldest fossil mollusks that have been found to date look something like our modern Snails. Among the fossilized shells of the descendants of these first Snails, however, there are slightly different species.

These new varieties resulted from a genetic change, or mutation, which occurred in their parents.

Mutation and natural selection of the mutants best adapted to survive have done much more than produce different species: these processes have enabled mollusks to climb out of the sea and conquer a whole new world, the world of the land. Early mollusks were sea creatures, taking their oxygen from the water through primitive gills in order to breathe. Then a few Gastropods (next column) adapted to life at the margins of the sea, the rocks and shallow bays.

The rocks of the seashore proved to be a bridge to the land. Snails living there had to find a way of breathing during periods of exposure. One can only wonder how many Snails lived there briefly, only to die during far-ebbing tides, for how many thousands of years, or hundreds of thousands of years, before one mutant Snail that could take oxygen from the air through slightly modified gills came along. That it happened we know. Many adapted in another way, learning to creep into tidepools or survive buried under wet seaweed; today these species still exist, having found a satisfactory mode of existence without completing the transition from gills to lungs which their kin accomplished so long ago. The descendants of that first mutant air-breather went on to the land; after countless generations they lost the ability to breathe by extracting oxygen from water, and became true Land Snails. Place a Garden Snail in water and it drowns.

Every part of the body has been modified to allow mollusks to colonize different habitats. Even within family groups, shells are of slightly different construction and composition, giving the most suitable combination of strength and weight and shape for the way of life of each species.

THE FIVE CLASSES OF MOLLUSKS

The animal kingdom, the one that concerns us here, was found to contain creatures with backbones and creatures without backbones—vertebrates and invertebrates. Then these subdivisions were broken down into races (phyla) of similar animals. One such race of invertebrates, the phylum Mollusca, contains the animals which make shells. *Mollusk* merely means soft-bodied. Like many other words you will meet in shell study, it is derived from Latin.

All mollusks possess an organ called the FOOT, which has evolved into five radically different forms. All the species which have the same kind of foot are grouped together into a class. The foot is only

one of several anatomical differences which set the members of the five classes apart from each other. Their external appearance is distinctive, too.

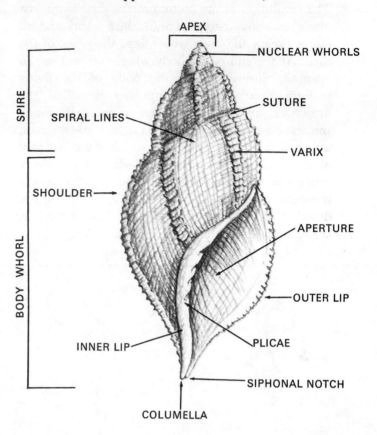

I. GASTROPODA

The largest and most important of the five classes contains the Snails, Slugs, and Conchs (pronounced "conks"). These mollusks, and all the others in this class, each possess a large foot, located directly below the head, on which they crawl or glide. This unusual form of transportation gives the class its name, GASTROPODA, meaning "belly-footed." A Gastropod moves along in a series of ripples; it extends the tip of its foot, presses it down against the ground for an anchor, and contracts it to pull the rest of its body forward. It has eyes mounted on two fleshy stalks, which children call horns, at the tip of its foot, where its head is located. Most Gastropods make shells that circle around an AXIS or COLUMELLA, spiralling to the right. These right-handed species are called DEXTRAL. Occasionally species which make dextral shells form a shell which spirals to the left instead; some Gastropods always make left-spiralling or SINISTRAL shells. All Gastropods make their shells in one piece, and for this reason they are often called UNIVALVES, meaning they have one valve only.

Take a look at a Conch shell. The first complete

revolution, at the apex or tip, is called the NUCLEAR WHORL; it was the original shell of the baby mollusk, later added to and extended to fit its growing owner. The revolution at the bottom of the shell is the last made, or BODY WHORL. The nuclear whorl and all others except the body whorl form the SPIRE of the shell. At the end of the body whorl you will see an opening, through which the body of the living mollusk protruded. This opening is called the APERTURE, and its edge the LIP of the shell. Some species have a horny trapdoor, the OPERCULUM, attached to the tip of the foot, which is the last part of the body to be withdrawn when the mollusk retreats into its shell. When the foot is pulled in, the trapdoor closes the aperture tightly, as raising the drawbridge seals a castle doorway. The operculum is also used as a claw to pull its owner along.

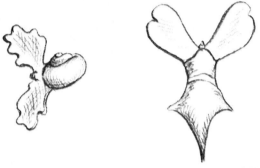

SEA BUTTERFLY: This mollusk has a coiled Snail-type shell which it loses soon after it hatches. It is replaced by wing-like fins.

Gastropods vary greatly in size, from tiny species too small to be seen with the naked eye to Giant Conchs 2 feet or more in length. The heavy shells of these larger species afford excellent protection, but like any other form of armor plate they are heavy and awkward to carry around. Some Univalves, such as Slugs, have lost their castles and learned to rely on darkness to hide them from their enemies, staying under leaves or stones in daylight and coming out to feed at night; others, for example Sea Slugs and Sea Hares, depend on speed and smoke screens rather than fortresses to keep them alive.

Sea Slugs or Nudibranchs (the name means "naked or exposed gills") are often very beautiful, having gaily colored mantles which undulate as they move through the water. The MANTLE is a vivid, delicate envelope of flesh enclosing a mollusk's soft inner parts, comparable to our skin. In many species the GILLS, which are equivalent to the lungs of higher animals, have disappeared, being replaced with capillary veins close to the surface of their bodies which extract oxygen from the water. Other species have gills, carrying them in feathery rosettes on their backs; these exposed gills give the group its name.

II. PELECYPODA

Now let us take a look at the second great class of mollusks. This class, PELECYPODA, contains such common species as Clams and Oysters, which make two-piece or BIVALVE shells. The word Pelecypod means "hatchet-foot," and as one might expect, many Pelecypods do have a hatchet-shaped foot. In this class the foot is used to burrow and dig in mud and sand, rather than for crawling. Pick up an empty Clam shell and look at it. You will see that the VALVES were held together in three ways: by interlocking ridges or TEETH around the margins, by similar teeth at the apex (between the two prominent humps, or UMBONES), and by the powerful pull of the Clam's ADDUCTOR muscle or muscles which have left a scar where they were attached to the inside of the valves. An elastic cartilage called the HINGE joins the valves together between the umbones, but this cartilage tends to pull the valves apart. When the Clam wants to open its valves it does so by relaxing its muscles and letting the powerful spring of the hinge pull its shell open.

The Clam's valves are known as right and left; it is fairly easy to tell which is which, since the umbones usually point to the front and the twin breathing tubes, called SIPHONS, toward the rear of the shell. Look at the inside of a valve: scars marring its smooth finish tell a great deal about the anatomy of the animal that lived there, and are often described in handbooks as a means of distinguishing between similar species. There are large scars where the adductor muscles were attached to the shell; the MANTLE or PALLIAL LINE connecting these scars shows where the tissue of the mantle rested. The PALLIAL SINUS, a v-shaped dent in this line dipping toward the margin of the shell, marks the place where the bulky siphons protruded between the folds of the mantle. Collectors call a bivalve shell with its valves still joining at the hinge a PAIR.

Bivalves are lower down on the scale of life than Univalves; they have little or no head, and usually lack eyes. With the exception of a few free-swimming species, they are sedentary (stationary), finding a permanent homesite early in life and settling down to a peaceful existence. Their sedentary way of life

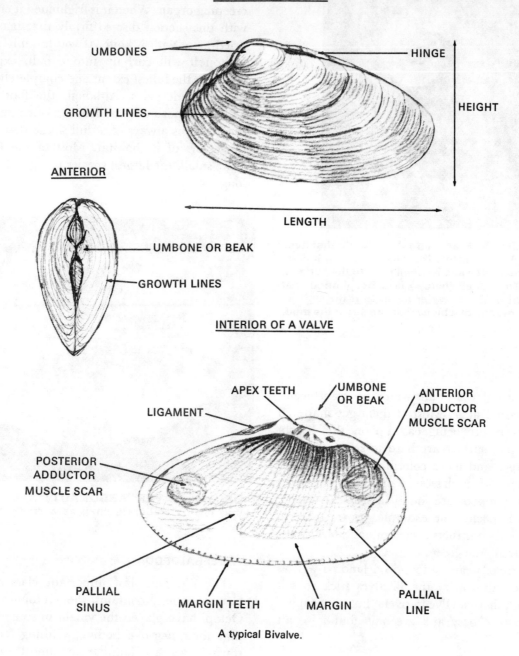

EXTERIOR OF VALVES

UMBONES

HINGE

GROWTH LINES

HEIGHT

ANTERIOR

LENGTH

UMBONE OR BEAK

GROWTH LINES

INTERIOR OF A VALVE

APEX TEETH

UMBONE OR BEAK

LIGAMENT

ANTERIOR ADDUCTOR MUSCLE SCAR

POSTERIOR ADDUCTOR MUSCLE SCAR

PALLIAL SINUS

MARGIN TEETH

MARGIN

PALLIAL LINE

A typical Bivalve.

probably accounts for the fact that Pelecypods grow larger than Gastropods; a shell that is thick and heavy is good protection for a mollusk that spends its life in one place, but it would be a fatal handicap to an animal that had to move about quickly in search of food. There are a few microscopic species, but most of the Bivalves reach a fair size and some of them are massive, the largest species being a 5-foot Giant Clam found in the South Seas. The valves of this monster often weigh 400 or 500 pounds, and are often used to form ornamental basins for outdoor fountains or lights.

III. SCAPHOPODA

The small class SCAPHOPODA make strange little shells that look like the tusks of carved ivory elephants. Because of this similarity the Scaphopods are often called Tusk shells, or Elephant Tooth shells. They are more closely related to the Univalves and Bivalves than to the other mollusks, for they have the one-piece shell structure of the former and the bilaterally symmetric body of the latter. Tusk shells are not often found; some collectors think them rare. Actually they are present around American coastlines in considerable numbers, but the North

TINY SHELLS: The Spinula (top) is a Squid that lives from 600 to 3,000 feet below the surface. When it dies, its body disintegrates and its shell rises to the surface. The Texas Tusk shell (below) is a Scaphopod that dwells in mud. It draws water down to it through its shell, the narrow end of which sticks up out of the mud.

another way: it serves as a suction disc as well as a creeping organ. When it is frightened it clamps down with this suction disc so firmly that it can only be pried loose with a knife. If you forcibly remove the Chiton it will curl up into a ball, expanding its armor to the fullest extent and completely protecting its soft underparts. Although the foot and body, which are normally hidden, are often gaily colored, the armor is always of a dull shade that blends into the colors of its habitat. Most of the Chitons are quite small, the largest species being about 10 inches long.

BROWN PAPER ARGONAUT: This Cephalopod makes this elaborate shell as a cradle for its eggs.

American varieties are all white or translucent, small, and very fragile. Most of them get shattered to fragments before being cast up on the beach, while those that survive are hard to see among the heaps of larger and more colorful specimens. As is true with the other classes of mollusks, the most beautiful Scaphopods are found in tropical waters. One tropical species, for example, grows to be 6 inches long and constructs a shell of delicate, beautifully sculptured jade green.

The Gastropods can be found on land as well as in fresh and salt water; the Bivalves stick to salt water, though they can live in rivers; but the Scaphopods are more choosy and are only found in salt water.

IV. AMPHINEURA

The Chitons, which make up the class AMPHINEURA, have shells formed by eight overlapping plates joined together by a muscular girdle. This plate-and-girdle armor, which gives the Chitons their popular name of Coat-of-Mail shells, is ideally suited to their way of life because it allows them to expand and contract their protective coating along with their bodies to fit snugly against the irregular surfaces of the rocks on which they live. If you have visited a rocky shore you have probably noticed these little animals or found detached segments of their shells washed up on the beach.

The foot of the Chiton has been modified in still

V. CEPHALOPODA

The fifth and last important class of mollusks, CEPHALOPODA, contains the Octopus and Squid. Octopi have played the villain in so many tall tales that their bag-like bodies, writhing tentacles, and staring eyes are familiar to almost everyone. Although these animals have no external shell and are very different in appearance from their relatives the Snails and Clams, they are true mollusks: at some time in the remote past their ancestors made coiled or conical shells as much as 15 feet long, and even now some species carry a vestigial remnant of shell within their bodies. The tough skin of the Cephalopod—the name means "head-footed"—is equivalent to the delicate mantle tissue of other mollusks. The head and foot are close together in Cephalopods, and the edge of the foot has evolved into a number of sucker-covered tentacles, which now ring the animal's mouth. As the name Octopus suggests, this creature has eight tentacles; Squids are decapods, having the eight tentacles plus two more extremely long, flexible arms. Squid and Octopi have similar saclike bodies, but the Squid is longer and more cylindrical in shape than his cousin.

There are three other Cephalopods which are of interest to shell collectors: the Paper Argonaut, the Nautilus, and the Spirula. The first of these, the Paper Argonaut, makes a fragile, finely sculptured white shell as a cradle for its eggs, discarding the shell after the eggs hatch out. The collector who finds this shell on a beach has a treasure indeed. The Nautilus carries its tentacles sheathed within an oddly developed foot and shelters its body in the end of a flat coil of pearly material. As it grows too big for its old home it seals off the vacated space with a thin partition called a SEPTUM, and builds larger

walls for itself. The Spirula makes a similar home, but its shell is small, white, and partially hidden within its body. The Cuttlefish is a Cephalopod, but it is of commercial interest only: it makes a flat, internal, limey plate which is hung in bird cages to provide the birds with lime. Its ink is sepia, the pigment used by artists.

As you can see, the basis for grouping these animals together is their body plan rather than their appearance. Various organs have been developed or lost in the members of the five classes we have discussed, making them very different in appearance from each other, but they all have basic similarities such as the foot and shell which distinguish them from members of any other class, and even greater differences which set them apart from members of other phyla.

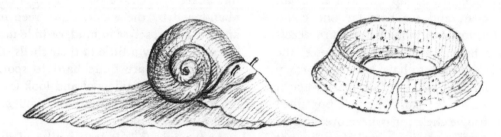

ATLANTIC MOON SNAIL: This mollusk extrudes its eggs embedded in a gelatinous ribbon which hardens when it meets the water. The egg mass is shaped by the foot and base of the shell. The flared base of the "collar" (right) lodges firmly in the sand, anchoring it. As it hardens, sand sticks to it and acts as a camouflage.

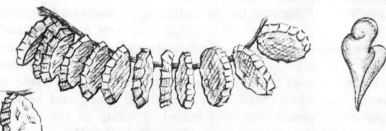

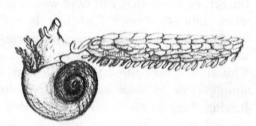

½"—1"

LIGHTNING WHELK: Egg "ropes," yard-long egg cases such as these are common on European and American shores.

JANTHINA and its egg float.

PURPLE WINKLE: Shaped like tiny bottles, the egg cases of the Purple or Dog Winkle are found in rock crevices. Each little capsule holds from 20 to 40 baby Purples.

BUCCINUM WHELK: These egg cases served as sailors' "scrub balls" in olden times.

EQUIPMENT

Now that you have learned something about shell dwellers you will find a greater interest in the shells you already have or will collect. Shell hunting is fun: every stretch of beach teems with hidden life; every weed-covered rock may hide a beautiful or rare species you have never seen before. But a good collection is not easy—it results from many hours of happy hunting, and a little planning. To pick up beachworn shells is easy, but after a time you will find yourself looking at them critically, and wanting better specimens. The most perfect shells are found on living mollusks, and the search for them has all the fascination and thrill of a treasure hunt.

Most advice to shell collectors starts with a list of things to take along on shelling expeditions. It would be interesting to add up the weights of all these pieces of gear, and see how far one could stagger under the load! Although there are accessories which are helpful for certain purposes, the only thing you really have to have is a bag to carry your shells in—one that will not fall apart when it gets wet. It helps, too, to carry a small box filled with cotton, for fragile shells; it is heartbreaking to find a delicate, perfect specimen and then have it crushed to fragments on the way home.

In rocky areas a pointed bar (pinch bar), for turning over stones, and a pocket knife for prying mollusks off rocks will be useful. A shovel and a bucket, or a can that will hold water, are necessary when hunting Clams that live buried in mud. Tongue depressors or similar flat strips of wood, together with lengths of soft string, are needed for Chiton hunting. Most shell collectors keep these simple tools in their cars, to have them handy, leaving them in the trunk until needed. Whatever the old manuals may say, you don't have to drag along a pickaxe every time you walk down a beach!

There is one other accessory which will be a great help to you: a glass-bottomed box or bucket with the inside painted black. The surface of the sea is rarely smooth, for even the smallest breeze causes ripples, making a bewildering dance of light and shade. Trying to see the bottom through this is like trying to see through a frosted glass window. A glass-bottomed box, floated on the water, gives a porthole view of the sea bed. You can make the box yourself, or buy it fairly cheaply from a marine supply company. A skin-divers' face mask for surface use is a fair substitute, but the rippling water around it causes glare and distraction and it has a very limited viewing area.

Dredging for shells is a pleasant way to spend an afternoon. Your dredge may be an expensive professional job installed aboard a yacht. But it can also be a home-made bag of chicken wire, supported and held open at the neck by coat hangers bent into a rectangle, and towed behind a rowboat with a length of clothesline! In shelling, simple tools get excellent results.

COLLECTING SHELLS

Experienced collectors plan their shelling trips to coincide with the lowest of low tides. Tables listing the times of high and low tide are published in the newspapers of coastal towns. At low tide, Bivalves are left stranded on the beach by the retreating water, to be had for the taking by birds and collectors alike. The Univalves are always harder to find; abandoned by the water, they creep into tidepools and bury themselves in mud, or hide under seaweed. They leave only a little of their shells sticking out of the mud, and are quite hard to spot. Float your viewing box in a tidepool and look for little bumps on its bottom; then prod, and you may come up with a buried Snail!

As the tide falls it leaves piles of driftwood and rubbish behind. Lift the pieces up and look them over. Crumbling wood may contain Teredos. Wharf pilings and stone piers are exposed at low tide; they provide homes for many kinds of shell dwellers. Float your box in shallow water and look for tracks in the sand. Short, wide tracks are made by Sand Dollars and long, wandering ones by horseshoe crabs; but if you find a trail that is fairly short and ends in a little hummock you may have found a Moon Snail. Poke the mound gently and he will move away, still buried. A bump on the bottom that moves along slowly indicates a Conch on the prowl.

Shells you want to keep should go into your bag at once. If you pile them on the beach while you look for more you may find your choicest specimens have walked away! This is because empty mollusk shells do not always remain empty: the Hermit Crab, a lazy little animal that will not bother to build a home of his own, often moves in.

Mollusks usually move fairly slowly on land, or are too timid to come out of their shells at all when taken from the water; even so, it is best to put them in the bag promptly, for the one you most want to keep is sure to be the one that disappears!

The mud flats and sand bars exposed at low tide are pitted with holes leading to buried clams, crabs,

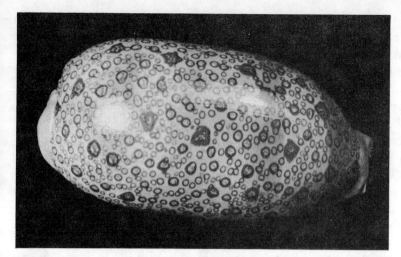

EYED COWRIE: An excellent example of shell camouflage. Pigments absorbed from the Cowrie's food are used by the mantle to make circles and blobs of color, which extend through the thickness of the shell.

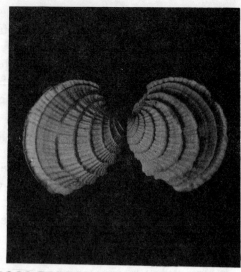

CROSS-BARRED VENUS: This perfectly sculptured shell shows the Venus' radial ribs, prominent concentric ridges, and an interior of rich purple.

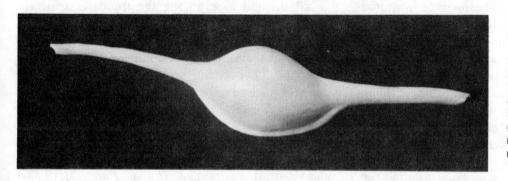

SHUTTLE SHELL: The most perfect shell specimens are found on live mollusks. This shell is unmarred and glossy. Rolling in breakers, beating against rocky shores, and bleaching in the sun—all combine to wear and chip the ridges and striations, resulting in a "dead" shell.

FURBELOW CLAM: You are not likely to discover as beautiful a frilled shell as this unless you go to the South Pacific. Found on coral reefs, all Giant Clams have this general structure. This specimen came from the Sulu Archipelago of the Philippines.

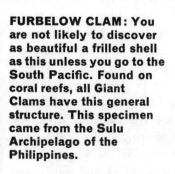

and worms. Deciding which hole leads to which animal is quite a problem. Worms often leave casts of mud at their doors, or build tubes covered with bits of broken shell and tiny stones that stick up an inch or so above the sand. Other holes may not display these nameplates, but digging will turn up only a large, vividly colored sea worm, or a crab. The only way to be sure a Clam made a particular hole is to see its siphons. It is easy to see siphons when there is water over them, but as the tide falls the necks are retracted underground. If you try to dig up a Clam when there is water above it you will stir up huge clouds of mud and the hole will fill in as you dig it; the only thing to do is to try to remember where you saw the necks and dig later, when the sand is high and dry.

If you are lucky and persevering enough to get one of the fragile Angel Wings, or any other delicate-valved Clam, it must go into a bucket of sea water at once, or it will contract violently and shatter its shell to pieces.

If you find sun-bleached Olive Shells or Coquinas in the debris on the beach you will know there are colonies living nearby. These mollusks are very common on sandy beaches around southern U.S. coastlines, living buried just beneath the surface. A little shallow digging may turn up hundreds of them. Try taking along a kitchen colander one day, shoveling mud into it, and then swirling it in the sea to wash away the mud; you may be surprised at what you have sieved out!

Sea grasses on mud flats shelter large numbers of shell dwellers, just as seaweed and kelp do in rocky areas. Wade or row out and look among the roots as well as on the stems. Pull up a frond or two; some species like to cling around the holdfasts. Thousands of little green Nerites can sometimes be found just below the water line on reeds. Along the southern U.S. Atlantic coastline (and other places) the beautiful Star Shells can be found, clinging to blades of kelp. Mangrove roots submerged at high tide shelter Coon Oysters, and the Conchs which feed on them; high in the mangrove branches are Snails making the transition from sea to land. If you have a boat, try drifting in the shallow water above mud flats and fishing around with a long-handled rake. Hard-shell Clams are sometimes collected in this way.

Every rocky coast hides an abundance of life. High on the shore are species that breathe air and drown if they are immersed in water for very long. These creatures stand dry air and lack of moisture well, drying out and becoming comatose if necessary until wet weather or high tides revive them. (There are many stories of Periwinkles accidentally left uncleaned coming to life after years in display cabinets; one was found crawling around a tool shed three months after it was collected and stored as an empty shell.)

Living farther down on the rocks are mollusks which require a daily bath if they are to survive. Even closer to the low-tide marks, species dry out and die in a few hours of strong sunlight; species living below the low-water mark cannot stand the sun at all, and die in an hour or two if they are not submerged. The underside of stones in these areas has a rich coating of weeds and algae that makes a pleasant habitat for shell dwellers. When stones are overturned and not replaced, the sunlight destroys this growth, and mollusks cannot shelter there for months, until it grows again. So when you move rocks, replace them as they were. Next year you may want to collect in that area again!

Lift up and look among the fronds of seaweed. Some Snails are so perfectly camouflaged that you may have trouble seeing them when you are looking directly at them. All the Amphineura (Chitons) live on rocks. They attach themselves very firmly, and you will have to use a knife to remove them. As you slide one from the rock, slip a wet tongue-depressor under it and tie it to the wood with string. This is important because otherwise the Chiton will roll up into a ball, and a rolled-up Chiton does not make a good collection specimen. If it does manage to curl up, drop it into the bucket of salt water and try again after it relaxes and straightens out. A Chiton in a bucket is wary, however, and curls at the first disturbance; it is far easier to tie it flat to begin with.

A word of warning here about collecting in areas where steep cliffs fall to the sea. In such areas there may be no beach uncovered at high tide, and the water may rise to considerable depth at the base of the cliffs. Every year visitors forget the CAUTION signs usually posted by the steps giving access to the beach. They wander too far to get back before the rising tide cuts them off, and spend hours on narrow strips of sand or sit cramped on rock ledges waiting for the tide to recede. In places where the cliff rises sheer and is swept by breakers at high tide they may drown. It is easy to lose track of time when you are far out on the rocks hunting shells and having fun, so check the tide-tables in the paper before starting, to be sure the tide is falling, not rising, and allow yourself plenty of time to get back.

CHANNELLED DUCK CLAM: This Clam's bleached white shell is thin and fragile compared to other Clams. Note the drill hole, evidence that this specimen fell prey to a Snail.

ROYAL COMB VENUS: The most beautiful of the American Venus Clams, this species is found from Texas to the West Indies. An uncommon specimen is this ivory-white Venus with spines marked with violet and purple.

LONG-SPINED STAR SHELL: This specimen has shorter than average spines. Found in shallow, grassy bays and on eelgrass in the Florida Keys, this mollusk is either brownish yellow or greenish on the outside, and pearl colored inside.

ANGEL WING (left) and **FALSE ANGEL WING** (right): From deep mud flats come the True Angel Wings (up to 5 inches long) among the most beautifully sculptured shells known. Most specimens are pure white. The False Angel Wings bear a strong resemblance, but are much smaller—only 2 inches long.

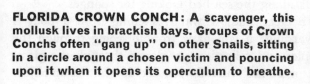

FLORIDA CROWN CONCH: A scavenger, this mollusk lives in brackish bays. Groups of Crown Conchs often "gang up" on other Snails, sitting in a circle around a chosen victim and pouncing upon it when it opens its operculum to breathe.

Rocks on California coastlines may harbor Abalones. These creatures, like Limpets, have a suction-disc foot to secure them to the rock and must be pried loose with your knife blade. Abalones have a wide range; in Australia they are known as Mutton Fish, and in England the local species are called Ormers, or Ear Shells. The European species have the same shape and pearly lining as American, but they are much smaller. Abalones are protected by California law against overcollection; size and weight limits vary for different species, so check the current regulations in the area in which you plan to hunt them.

In some areas the shells you take, like the rocks they are found on, are covered with small, white, shell-like cones. These are barnacles; in spite of the shell-like covering they are not mollusks. For centuries educated people thought the long stemmed or "goose" barnacles were the eggs of migratory birds!

Harbors have large populations of wood- and rock-boring mollusks, but they are poor hunting places because their waters are full of decaying refuse, and are highly acid; the acid pits and dulls the shells exposed to it, making good specimens hard to find. Harbor bottoms have large scavenger populations which live on the refuse.

Florida fishermen sometimes catch Scallops by accident. If a line happens to fall between the open valves of a Scallop, the valves snap closed, and the Scallop can be drawn from the water attached to the line. It is doubtful that a collector would have such luck; dragging a home-made dredge behind a boat in shallow water would almost certainly get better results than dangling a line on the off-chance of it touching a Scallop.

Coral reefs are home to a wide variety of shell dwellers. The water around them is very clear, and if you look in the crevices and pools with a glass-bottomed box you may get some fascinating glimpses of underwater life.

When you are exploring a coral reef, be careful. Potholes and tidepools are hard to tell apart in the clear water; you may start to wade across what you think is a shallow pool and find yourself out of your depth without warning. The coral is razor sharp, so it is wise to wear thick-soled shoes and handle it carefully. Some of the creatures living on reefs have poisonous spines hard enough to pierce a thin-soled sandal. The light which bounces off white coral and sparkling water can cause a bad sunburn, even on a less than perfect summer day, so it is best to wear clothes that afford some protection. Shorts and sleeveless tops are ideal for shell hunting in most areas, but not for coral.

Skin-diving is a wonderful way to collect fine specimens, if you are a good swimmer. Sponge-divers in many places, especially Greece and Florida, pick up rare and lovely deep water mollusks as they walk along the sea bed looking for sponges.

In clear shallow water, shelling from a boat is rewarding; if you have trouble seeing through the ripples and reflections, a glance through the glass-bottomed box will help you decide whether an object on the bottom is worth diving for. A face mask helps once you are under water.

Storms are the ill winds that blow shell collectors

good. After a hurricane the beaches are littered with choice shells, some of them rare species from deep water, that have been blown ashore. As a general rule, the worse the weather the better the shelling!

FLORIDA HORN SHELL: A useful scavenger that lives in shallow water, this little mollusk is a valuable food source for waterfowl and fish. Also called a Florida Cerith.

Some coastlines are incredibly rich in shells. Sanibel Island, on the west coast of Florida near Fort Myers, has been famous among conchologists for years. It is hard to see the sand for the shells, here; there are drifts of shells 3 feet deep, extending the length of the Gulf side of the island. At Clearwater, Florida, the shells do not cover the beach in drifts and heaps and piles as they do at Sanibel: instead they are deposited individually on the sand as if laid out in a jeweler's window for one to pick and choose. You can find the delicate Tusk Shells there, the Winged Oysters (*Pteria*) with linings of lavender and pink and silver, and pairs of Yellow and Rose Teilins. Sanibel has varieties not found at Clearwater, and vice versa. St. Petersburg and the Ten Thousand Islands are recommended by many collectors. In Europe, the Algarve coast of Portugal and the Costa del Sol of Spain are worth a visit. Their climate compares with Florida's. In the Pacific, the Philippine Islands are a shell collector's heaven. Beautiful specimens can be found in Australian waters. Many fine deep-water shells are taken off the coasts of Japan.

The Florida Keys are rich in shells, though not Key West, which has been so built upon that there are few public beaches left. The Middle Keys, however, are worth a trip.

On all the beaches you will notice that most of the shells are heavy white Bivalves with horny outer coverings, members of the Ark family. There are more Ark shells on American beaches than shells of all other species put together! There are tremendous numbers of miniature shells, too, but collectors rarely notice these because they are so small. Go through a drift of shells and small debris one day with a magnifying glass, and you may add some unusual little specimens to your collection.

You will probably also add a few fossilized shells to your display as the years go by. Fossils can be found in the most unlikely places; a 400,000,000-year-old Brachiopod was found in the gravel in front of a drive-in restaurant in Kentucky, and a fossil Clam was collected from the road bed at Naples, Florida. Brachiopods look like modern seashells, and there are in fact some species of Brachiopods to be found in the ocean today, though they are rare; but they do not belong to the phylum Mollusca. The ancient Brachiopods lived side by side with the ancestors of modern mollusks, but they did not spring from the same stock (so far as can be determined now). Their body plans are dissimilar from those of mollusks.

FOSSIL CLAM found in a road bed in Golden Gates, Florida. Fossil shells, which may be many thousands of years old, are fun to collect and to compare with modern shells.

Many of the Snails that live on land are quite beautiful; the delicate rose-pink *Euglandina Rosea Bullata Gould* (so little known that it has no popular name, though it is very common) can be found in many parts of the southern United States, while the Garden Snails, like the yellow and brown Banded Snails of Europe, deserve a place in any collection. Look in your own back yard at night with a flashlight, for many species are nocturnal, and you may be surprised at what you find! Snails live everywhere; in woods on the slopes of Alpine mountains, and in cracks in the old stone walls of Agamemnon's city, Mycenae.

The finest shells are usually found on living mollusks; and though very few species have any legal protection against shell hunters, the vast majority of collectors see no reason to kill unnecessarily and take only those they really want.

It is a good idea to sit down at the end of each shelling trip and sort out your shells. You will almost certainly find you have duplicates in your bags, and specimens that are not worth the trouble of carrying home and cleaning. Now is the time to put back those you do not intend to keep for your collection or for trading with other collectors. One or two specimens of each species are all you will need in your own collection, unless of course there are great varieties of form or coloring within a species which you would like to display. There is little point in collecting a lot of shells you have no use for, to take up storage room!

CLEANING SHELLS

Often the specimens you bring home will be muddy, or have their beauty hidden under a coat of green algae. Those taken alive must be cleaned at once, for shellfish decay rapidly. Don't postpone this chore or your catch will probably end up in the garbage, for the stench of rotten shellfish at close quarters is unendurable.

The best place to clean shells is the kitchen sink, as running water is a necessity. You will need an old toothbrush, a saucepan, a can of scouring powder, and a little detergent. A pair of tweezers and a crochet hook will also be useful, though toothpicks can substitute for these.

Shells that have been washed by the surf and dried in the sun until there are no traces of their builders left inside need little cleaning. Soap and water or a little scouring powder will take off any mud or algae the waves have left. Sometimes these "dead" shells are encrusted with barnacles, which can be removed by soaking the shells in water for a few hours and then tapping the barnacles sideways, quite gently, with a knife handle. If one is stubborn, place the blunt edge of the knife blade across its top and press down lightly; it will split and come away in pieces. The whitish rings left at the site of the colony can be removed by scratching them away gently with the point of your crochet hook. This treatment would break a fragile shell, but for some reason barnacles prefer to build on strong, chunky foundations.

Shells taken alive are more of a problem. Bivalves will open up if you drop them into water which has been boiled and allowed to cool. Boiling removes the oxygen from the water so that mollusks suffocate when placed in it. After a few minutes their adductor muscles will relax, allowing their valves to spring apart. Scoop them out, scrape the meat out with tweezers, and wash the shells in soapy water. Shells containing hermit crabs get the same treatment; once the crab relaxes its grip on the shell it can be eased out with tweezers. Be gentle or the end of the tail will break off and remain hooked to the core of the shell, out of reach.

There are several methods of cleaning Univalves taken alive. The procedure least likely to damage their shells is very simple: leave them to soak in water, out of doors, until they rot and come out in bits. The water must be changed daily, or the acids from the rotting meat will accumulate and pit the shells. After the soft parts have disintegrated, a thorough rinsing is needed to make the shells sweet-smelling and fit to come indoors. To avoid getting operculums mixed up, put similar-sized shells in separate containers. Be sure your specimens are out of reach of dogs, cats, and children while they are soaking! This method of cleaning is called "spoiling out"; but it is rather smelly and unpleasant.

Some collectors clean large shells by putting them in ant heaps and letting the ants do the work! If you try this, remove the operculum first, and number it and the shell with ink, so you can unite them again. Ants do a thorough cleaning job, but they pull small shells down into their nests and separate them from their trapdoors. Once small specimens are buried it is hard to find them again, so this lazy way of cleaning them is rather risky.

Perhaps the best way is to put your shells in a pan of warm water and bring it to a boil. Remember, though, that sudden changes in temperature will crack and spoil the surface of glossy shells like Olives and Cowries; when cleaning this type of shell the water must be heated very slowly and allowed to cool gradually. The length of time the shells must be boiled depends on their size. Err on the side of too much boiling rather than too little; large specimens may take half an hour.

When they have cooled to the touch take them from the water one at a time and ease the meat out with a crochet hook. Insert the hook at the siphonal canal and work it well up into the flesh before you start to pull it out, turning the shell as you pull, to gently "unscrew" the dead mollusk. As the flesh cools it shrinks, pulling away from the walls of its home, so it is easy to pull out; but as it shrinks it also retracts from the aperture, making it harder to reach

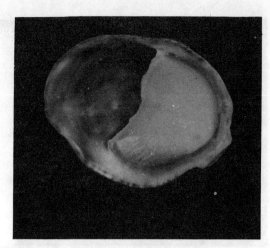

COMMON ATLANTIC SLIPPER SHELL: This mollusk changes its sex sometimes. It lives in colonies in shallow water, often attached to its mates in piles. As the young males mature, they release a hormone into the water which causes the males underneath them to undergo a sex change and become females.

with the hook. If you wait until it is quite cold you may not be able to see the flesh through the aperture at all. Sometimes, however careful you are, the meat will break off deep within the shell and it will be necessary to spoil out the piece left behind.

Snails with only a few whorls will come out easily if you freeze them and then let them thaw slowly. The meat shrinks away from the shell under this treatment. Many spiraled shells, though, cannot be cleaned in this way, as the meat shrinks back out of reach into the upper spirals.

If a delicate specimen needs algae and dirt removed, it is wise to clean it before removing meat, as the animal's solid flesh supports the shell and makes it less likely to break. When handling frail shells be careful to avoid pressure on the lip, which has little structural support and will crumble almost at a touch. It is safest to spoil out these shells. Tiny specimens can simply be left exposed to the air in a covered pan, far away from the house and out of reach of animals, until all objectionable odors are gone; then a few hours soaking in a pan of alcohol will make them fit for display.

Alcohol dries out the shell as well as the flesh within, so rinse your shells thoroughly to remove it or it may dull their finish. A 70 per cent alcohol solution will preserve a mollusk's soft body if you wish to keep it for study; needless to say, the flesh will spoil unless it is kept in its alcohol bath.

If you ever forget to clean a shell for several days after collecting it, don't attempt the task. Let it sit well away from the house for a couple of months, until Nature has taken care of the matter. Cleaning live shells sometimes poses a problem; if you are staying in a motel without kitchenette while on vacation, for example, you cannot boil water, and the live shells you find will not wait to be cleaned until you get home! It is a good idea to plan for vacation shelling by keeping a small, inexpensive camp stove in the trunk of your car, and taking an old saucepan and your crochet hook along.

Chitons will curl up if they are unbound before cleaning, and their empty shells tend to curl as they dry, so it is best to keep them bound flat as much as possible. Drop them, with the strips of wood they are on, in the boiled water you used for Bivalves and shells containing hermit crabs. Leave them for an hour, unbind them, and scrape out their flesh carefully to avoid damaging the girdle that holds their plates of shell together. Re-tie them to the wood and let them dry thoroughly in this position before adding them to the collection.

Thick deposits of lime or coral on a shell will come off in a 20 per cent or stronger solution of laundry bleach. This solution will fade the colors if shells are left to soak for very long, however. After bleaching, they will need an extra thorough rinsing. Some handbooks suggest using caustic soda or muriatic acid to remove lime deposits. This will certainly brighten the colors of some species, but acid treatment gives a shell an unnatural appearance and ruins it as a specimen.

If you want to experiment, remember that acid burns clothing and fingers as well as shell. Use a weak solution to start with, and work on poor or worthless specimens for practice. Apply the solution to a small area at a time with a paintbrush and rinse immediately. Wear rubber gloves and old clothes, hold the shell with tweezers if it is not too large, and stay near the faucet. If you do splash the acid on you, rinse it off as quickly as you can and keep the water running over the skin for several minutes to make sure every molecule is flushed away.

Most collectors leave the epidermis on their shells, feeling that it is a natural part of the mollusk and it would be a mutilation to remove it. Some like to clean it off so they can see more of the sculpture and colors of the shell. Often the epidermis, or periostracum, is quite attractive; the pitchy black "whiskers" of some of the Ark shells are prettier than the plain white shell beneath. In some families, such as Cones, the epidermis is drab and hides the beauty of the glossy patterned shells it covers. We usually leave the periostracum on if it is pretty or unusual, or if there is no reason to remove it. If you plan to keep more than one specimen of each species you might leave one its epidermis, and clean the other specimen off.

Now that your shells are clean, you may notice that some of them are not so pretty as they were when you found them on the beach. Boiling, scrubbing, and soaking in alcohol all tend to make shells look parched and dried out. A thin coat of mineral oil, wiped on gently with a soft rag, will restore their original good looks and also keep the hinges of Bivalves and periostracums of all species from growing brittle over the years.

IDENTIFYING SHELLS

Every collector wants to know the names of his shells. The color section of this book shows pictures of various shells to get you familiar with their types and colors. As you progress, you will need a really comprehensive identification guide, containing photos of as many different species as possible, to avoid the frustration of trying to match your shell to a poor picture, or worse, the misery of trying to identify a species not pictured at all. As you get experience, too, you will want to call your shells by their Latin names, which are more specific than their popular names.

To identify a shell, look through your large identification guide until you find a picture of one similar to yours, and then look up the description of that species in the text. Species within families are listed together, so if you have not found the exact description of your shell look up descriptions of close kin of the shell that most nearly resemble yours; you will probably find your specimen listed there. Remember that specimens vary in size and coloring; the shell photographed may not be an exact match to the one you have. Shells found on the beach are not always seashells, for storms wash mollusks from the swamps and low ground out to sea and cast them up on the shore; so if you find a Univalve which cannot be identified it is worth trying a guide to Land Snails of the area.

From time to time every collector finds a shell he simply cannot identify. Museum shell collections are a help here; every shell in such a collection is labelled and it is usually fairly simple to find the name of your problem shell. If it is not on display, the museum workers may be able to help you to identify it. As a last resort, and only after you have exerted every possible effort to identify the specimen yourself, the

WEST INDIAN WORM SHELL: While most of these mollusks live a solitary life, some varieties attach themselves to rocks or twine inextricably together to form colonies.

staff of the Smithsonian Institution in Washington, D.C. will help you if you send them the shell, with a letter stating when and where it was found. It is a courtesy to send one or two duplicate specimens which they may keep for the Smithsonian's collection in the event that the problem shell turns out to be a new species, or of interest to science in some other way; your note should say whether or not you want the duplicates returned. Busy, world-renowned scientists are frequently courteous and helpful; but their kindness must not be abused.

Once you have identified your shells, which should be done as soon as they are cleaned, get a notebook or make an index card file and write down where and when they were found. Scientists and collectors alike feel that shells without this information are of little interest, and if you wish to exchange shells with other collectors later on you will find that you cannot remember where they were found; so write it down!

The number is assigned to each shell as it is found to avoid mixing up specimens. The first shell entered will be #1, and so on. Put the number on the shell itself, with a fine nibbed pen and India ink, in an inconspicuous place. Make your location entry as accurate and exact as possible. The Latin name is useful when exchanging specimens; it will save you from sending Butterflies and receiving the same shells called Pompanos or Coquinas in exchange (all of them local names for the same shell, *Donax variabilis*). Under remarks, note who collected the specimens if you did not, and anything unusual or interesting about the find.

A shell catalogue may look like this:

Number	Date	Place found	Name	Remarks
405	1 May 1973	Bay side Sanibel Isl. ½ mile from west end	Common Slipper Shell (*Crepidula fornicata*)	Live, on live oyster

STORING AND DISPLAYING SHELLS

Your shells are now ready to be displayed. Too often, people do this haphazardly. Don't start out this way. Those who don't arrange their shells usually stop collecting after a while, saying "What's the use use of getting any more? I can only show off so many shells, you know." This is quite true if the shells in your display are duplicates. As a general rule you should only display one or two specimens of each species. There are many reasons for breaking this rule, though: you might wish to display 20 pairs of the gaily marked Coquinas to show the range of

colors and variety of markings that can be found. Always display only your best specimens, and try to keep the families together. Then, when you show the collection to friends, you can point out the differences between Arks from New England and Florida, and between shells from America and another country halfway round the world. You may wish to specialize in shells of one particular family, Cowries or Tellins, for example. If you wish, you can trade specimens with other collectors, extending the range of your collection. The duplicate shells which are your storage headache will be the pride and joy of a

(1) A Hawk-Wing Conch and (2) back view of the same shell. (3) A Laciniated Conch with a thickened flare. The mature animal continues to lay down conchiolin at the edge of its mantle even after its body has stopped growing. In this way, the lip grows larger and larger. (4) An Arthritic Spider Conch: here the conchiolin grows into spikes.

HEART COCKLE: Cockles live in mud, like clams. This one comes from the Indo-Pacific region.

an hour's work to find a particular shell you want in the jumble. Cigar boxes make good storage units for all but the large species; they should be labelled with their contents ("Cones," "Murex," "Janthinas" etc.), to simplify locating what is needed.

LACE MUREX: Common in Florida, this delicate Murex is a carnivore. Using its powerful suction foot as a lever, it pries with its spiky outer lip, and can force open the skull of an Oyster or Clam.

conchologist in Japan or Australia, while his spares will enrich your display.

Some collectors feel that buying shells is unsportsmanlike; this, of course, is a matter of opinion, but it does seem that there is more fun in building up a fine collection by your own efforts than in paying for professional help. Your collection can be anything you care to make it. There are some people who would not pick up the rarest Cone in the world if it were washed up at their feet because they are only interested in fossilized Snails that lived a million years ago. Others want only the prettiest shells, or the oddest shells. Whatever you choose to collect, you should build the collection on orderly lines, grouping your specimens according to species and family, and country of origin.

Duplicate specimens intended for exchange or gift should be stored in orderly fashion, or it will take you

Some collectors display their shells in cotton-lined drawers, while others prefer shelves or boxes containing several trays resting on one another. Any sturdy container, a cigar box, shoe box, or an old fishing tackle box, for example, can be used to begin with. Stacks of empty matchboxes, glued together and lined with cotton, provide storage for miniature shells. A coating of adhesive-backed plastic makes such a "chest" more presentable. A metal cabinet with plastic drawers, designed to hold small items, and with a label-holding slot on the front of each drawer is ideal for smaller species. Bivalves can be shown off in flat, velvet-lined butterfly boxes obtainable from museum shops. These boxes, or ordinary flat cardboard boxes with clear acetate tops, are handy for exhibiting shells as they keep dust and curious fingers out.

A few of your choicest specimens can grace the shelves of a room divider in your living room, or be displayed in a recess under a glass-topped coffee table. Artificial light will not damage shells, but strong sunlight will fade them in time, so don't put them on a window sill unless they are easily replaceable. Don't be so afraid of harm coming to them, though, that you keep them forever hidden in cotton-packed boxes. Like all lovely things, they deserve to be seen and admired.

SPINY COCKLE: Some Bivalves, like this one, secure their castles against the hungry outside world with interlocking teeth.

SNIPE'S BILL MUREX: The spikes, ridges and siphonal canal of the Murex provide stability in rough seas by acting as anchors into muddy bottoms. This prevents the mollusk's being swept out to sea, away from its food supply.

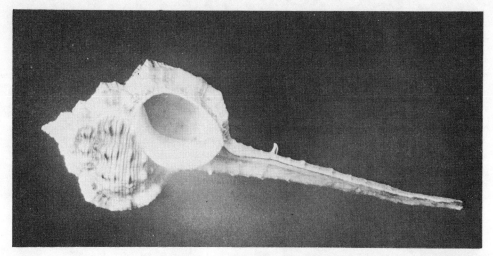

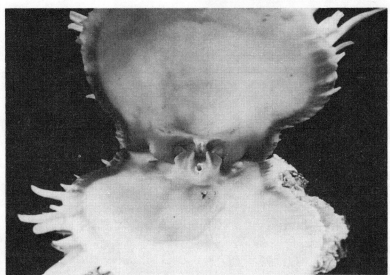

PENNSYLVANIA LUCINE: Dwelling in sand 3 feet below the surface, the Lucines construct a mucous-lined sand tube which serves in place of an incurrent siphon. This Lucine is found from North Carolina south to the Caribbean, while others are found in the Pacific.

THORNY OYSTER: Its intricate hinge, which operates like a ball and socket joint, together with its powerful adductor muscle, protects this Oyster from any attempt to wrench its valves apart.

FLORIDA SPINY JEWEL BOX: After spending all its life attached to a small bit of shell or rock, this mollusk will have its attachment broken and get washed up on the beach. You will find a scarred spot close to the beak of the right valve.

GEOGRAPHY CONE: This pretty South Pacific Cone has a deadly sting with which it kills its prey. It apparently has a built-in immunity to its own venom as it eats the meal it has poisoned.

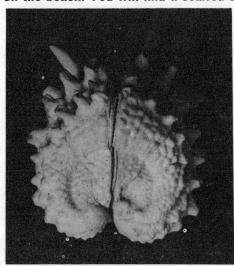

Creative hobbies

DRAWING

Almost everyone wants to draw. The fact is anyone can. Drawing can be simply an occasional exercise in self-expression or an all-consuming career. For those who draw as a hobby, it is usually something in between the two.

Drawing is a hobby that can easily be enjoyed by the whole family. The purpose of this section is simply to introduce you to the basic concepts, the materials, and the various approaches recommended to beginners by several different art teachers. Therefore, while you can find here a fairly comprehensive survey of the things a beginner needs to know, you won't find an outline for the perfect approach to drawing, simply because there is no perfect approach. It will be up to you to choose the approach that best suits you. Even if you are not a beginner you are certain to find some helpful suggestions here.

Drawing is a very personal creative expression, much like handwriting. If the results of your efforts please you, then you have done a "good" drawing.

So let's begin—you and the whole family. You may discover a great artist in your midst. But even if you don't, you're certain to enjoy yourselves. Just keep in mind that the only rules are those of observation, relaxation, and self-expression.

INTRODUCING CHILDREN TO ART

Professor Chester Jay Alkema, a teacher of art teachers and students, feels that it is particularly important to keep these thoughts in mind when introducing children to drawing.

To start with, you might ask three children to draw a cat. Do not say any more. Each child will draw upon his own experience in the creation of his cat. One might create a small, pencil-drawn, stick kitten; another, a great colorful jungle beast. The third might paint his own family cat. No one will draw an adult's conception of a simple cat shape. Supposing you had instructed these youngsters by drawing a big ball with another, smaller ball on top of it, two ears, a long tail, and told them to copy it. You would have had three rather poor imitations of *your* idea.

Children's standards are not the same as adults'. They *do* see and feel things differently. In these three examples, the children were drawing upon experience; they were motivated by their experience to express themselves. Exaggerations of form, emphasized proportions, skylines, baselines—all represent truthful statements based on the children's own personal lives. The perceptions of children are just as valid as the perceptions of adults.

It is very important that a toddler is not inhibited from making random strokes and scribbles. Very often parents or other adults grab the pencil from a 2- or 3-year-old and say, "That's not how you make a person, Johnny. Here, let me show you." Anyone who has observed this situation knows that Johnny watches momentarily and wanders away. Johnny knows perfectly well that he is not capable of rendering such perfect circles and lines. He is more than likely hurt and confused that his efforts were "wrong."

Encourage a child to be individual and original in expressing ideas. This causes the child to make discoveries, to experiment, to make "mistakes." The child comes to believe that it is his ideas that are wanted above all else. He is drawing upon his own world, limited as it might be in adult eyes. Instead of being told, "Do this, do that,"—like the game, "Simon Says"—he is free to do what *he* wants and is capable of doing.

Condensed from the following books: "Alkema's Complete Guide to Creative Art for Young People" by Chester Jay Alkema, published by Sterling Publishing Co., Inc., New York/"Joy of Drawing" by Gerhard Gollwitzer © 1961 by Sterling Publishing Co., Inc., New York/"Drawing from Nature" by Gerhard Gollwitzer © 1970 by Sterling Publishing Co., Inc./ "Techniques of Drawing" by Howard Simon © 1963 by Howard Simon/"Bridgman's Complete Guide to Drawing from Life" by George B. Bridgman © 1952 by Sterling Publishing Co., Inc., New York.

FIVE-YEAR-OLD'S CONCEPTION OF MOTHER rendered in the geometric fashion typical of this age group. The figure is lacking arms and legs, but it expresses the essence of a happy person better than many drawings of a more finished nature would be able to do.

There are many ways of selecting stimulating topics to inspire young people to express themselves. The important thing to bear in mind is that probably not more than one in thirty children will assume the rôle of an adult, practicing artist. You should not attempt to train children to become skilled artists in the fullest sense of the word. Rather, allow each child to respond to his environment and to draw upon his experiences in his own childlike way. The expression of an idea is far more important to a child's development than the acquisition of specific art skills.

The creative art experience does not happen in a vacuum. You "set the stage" and a child will take it from there.

Watch children in the playground, back yard or playroom and take note of the various activities and interests they are pursuing. Observe how these activities change from season to season, from sunny day to cloudy day. Discuss these activities with a child and you will inspire him to recapture the magic moments of his daily life.

One of the best ways to provide meaningful experiences for a child would be to take him or a group on an excursion.

An excursion can be as simple as going into the garage, into a flower garden or visiting a bakery. The world is so full of details that we often see things without *really* seeing them. We have impressions of our daily environment, but if called upon to describe in detail a certain tree in the back yard, the result would be sketchy.

A group of young fourth-graders were told by their teacher simply to draw a picture of a house and to color all areas of their papers. This was the only instruction given.

A week thereafter the same children were taken on a "looking walk" down a familiar block in the town, during which details of houses such as shapes and types of windows, doors, porches, chimneys, garages, and roofs, as well as surrounding shrubs, street signs, and so forth, were pointed out to them. When they returned to school and again drew their conceptions of a house, the results were much richer in detail.

It is not difficult to find opportunities to increase children's awareness of their surroundings or to help them visualize and represent their experiences. Try, for example, pointing out the details of objects in nature, such as trees and flowers, or encouraging them to capture on paper the feelings that a poem, fairy tale, or a piece of music elicit. In doing these things, you will, of course, stimulate your own creative awareness and cultivate your own powers of observation.

TEACHING YOURSELF

Professor Alkema's theories about the importance of self-expression and observation in drawing hold true for people of any age. These same basic principles are expounded by other art teachers as well, such as Howard Simon, George Bridgman, and the German professor, Gerhard Gollwitzer.

You can learn drawing in many ways and for many purposes. The method suggested next leads you from the elements of creative drawing to nature studies, to stimulating and enriching your imagination. These exercises have been developed from experience, and to encourage the beginner, the illustrations are largely student work. To be sure, they are frequently imperfect, but they are examples, suggestions pointing out the way.

From experience, we know that people, especially when they draw from nature, usually tend to become too picayune. Also, they are usually cramped when drawing. In addition, they take for granted those things which one first has to master: the drawing surface and drawing materials. They frequently only copy; that is, they reproduce only the *exterior* image and not the *essence* of objects.

These first doodling exercises serve to make you bold, to loosen you up, and to let you master the drawing surface, the formats, the media, and the language of forms. Then later everything will go much easier and better.

DOODLING WITH A PURPOSE

Use cheap paper at the beginning—newsprint, inexpensive writing paper, or thin drawing paper. Get yourself a pad or substantial supply of large sheets about 12 inches x 16 inches, so that your work can proceed without interruption. For the time being, use soft pencils, charcoal pencils or sticks, ball-point pens, or brushes for your drawing. Put a sheet (with a pad underneath for protection) on a table and *stand* in front of it: then you will work with more freedom than if you sat down.

Now, hovering over the paper like a bird of prey, draw a few squares with rounded corners in the air until you land with your pencil (or brush) on the paper. Don't lift the pencil from the paper, but let it continue long enough to get a real feeling of the square drawing surface. Then move towards the inside of the square with horizontal and vertical lines. Repeat these with broader and narrower spaces or with more verticals or more horizontals.

Starting the same way, draw a circle and then spiral inwards to the middle. On the next sheet, start in the middle and draw the spiral outwards, emphasizing the final circle by redrawing it several times. Let your pencil run along the inside edge of the circle in either large or small spirals. Always draw everything without lifting your pencil, and draw it boldly.

Always hold your pencil or brush loosely in your hand. Hold it with the ends of your fingers and with your thumb—that is, don't hold it as if you were writing. Always draw from the center of your body, from where guidance can be given, rather than from the wrist. The power should run from the center of your body through your shoulder and arm to the point of the pencil.

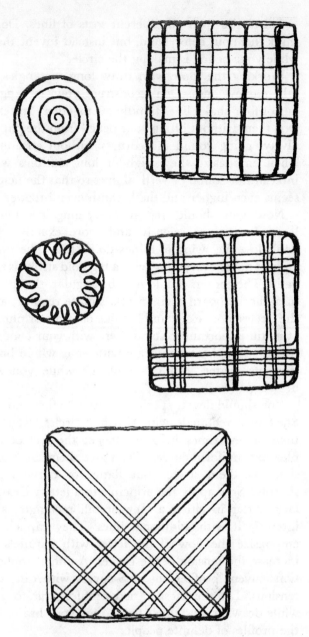

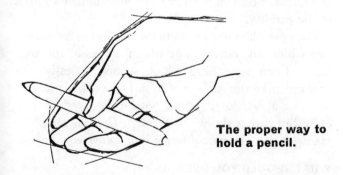

The proper way to hold a pencil.

Start as you did before and fill a square with diagonals and their parallels.

From circles you can progress to the figure 8, drawing both horizontal and vertical 8s. Develop figures out of them.

DON'T LIFT THE PENCIL from the drawing surface. Draw from the center of your body rather than from the wrist.

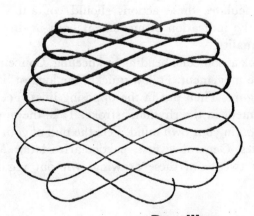

Fill circles with all different sorts of lines. Don't think them out beforehand, but instead invent them while your pencil is making the circle.

Working the same way, draw long rectangles or tall, narrow ones. Don't construct your rectangles out of four shaky lines timidly set together. Instead, *form* them without lifting your pencil from the paper, always going round the corners without straining. Then emphasize these high or long outlines with interior horizontal or vertical lines so that the height seems even higher and the breadth even broader.

Now you should repeat everything previously learned more consciously and more exactly. But don't lose the swing of things doing this. The principle of doing everything with a big bold stroke is still valid. The corners should now be angular, the spaces in a checkerboard division of a square regular, and the circles more exact and less like potatoes or plums. It is still important to stand there with your concentrated strength and to draw with your whole body from its center. Don't "stammer" while you are drawing.

You should devote special attention to the S-curve. Start in a rectangle with two half-circles. Redraw them a few times in order to get the feel of the pleasant, uniform curves. Then give them some tension: let them stretch out flatter or curve more sharply. Now apply the principle to a letter. Draw a large letter in either a long or tall rectangle, and intensify it with additional lines. They can either emphasize the flow of the letter with parallels or increase the tension of the curves. Another application: invent profiles out of S-curves with different tensions. Let the most varied profiles *occur* to you while drawing, and don't try to rack your brains for the profiles of definite people.

Now, without losing that same feeling of freedom, attempt to articulate movement, such as a person bending to pick up an object, a tree bent by the wind, or clouds driven across the sky. Even a road "winds" or "moves" across a picture. The line that describes or articulates these actions should contain within itself the indication of movement both in direction and quality.

Look at someone bending or kneeling. Concentrate on the movement. Follow quickly the longest line in the figure. Then put in the opposing lines. Feel the movement in the rhythmic stroke. Take the model's position in your own mind. Feel the pull of your own muscles. Generalize first, particularize later. Make about twenty of these drawings without regard to detail.

An oval for the head and broad-stroke indications of movement alone will suffice. Soon the line itself will take on a rhythm of movement. Scarcely take your pencil off the paper during this exercise. Let the line weave back and forth, following the movement. Concentrate on the weight by neglecting the details.

RULES OF THUMB

The following suggestions may be helpful when you decide to proceed to drawing from nature.

Never lose an overall view of the whole sheet. Look at the sheet from as vertical a position as possible. Either lean the drawing surface against the edge of a table and hold it on your knees, or lay it on a table with a rising slant, or work at an easel. *Always leave your body free to move and keep your distance from the sheet.*

Do not work *too small*; it is better to draw small things enlarged. And, at first, always leave yourself a margin about two or three fingers wide. You will find a need for it often enough.

Start with light, boldly sketched strokes and hold your pencil in the way described previously. In general, draw loosely; don't "dig in."

At the *beginning*, always have the *end* in sight; with the detail in mind, think of the whole. When you are drawing the head of a figure, look at the feet, and when you are drawing the feet, look at the head.

Never lose yourself in the details and never start with them. Therefore, stand off and look at your drawing from a distance again and again while you are working, or else look at it in a mirror or by turning the drawing upside down.

At the outset, always draw in all those non-existent lines which contribute to the clarification of the forms. You continually have to visualize an idea of the totality.

Every stroke must *say* something. Do not mistake a line which suggests, for one which is merely approximate. Even something which seems restlessly disordered (like the surface of a ball of wool, a maze of wire, or a meadow) should not be rendered chaotically but rather should be formed. *Drawing something entangled does not mean drawing it in a disorderly fashion.*

WHAT SHOULD YOU USE?

The medium has an active effect on the final results. Drawing does not start with the first stroke on the paper, but rather with the choice of materials. Each paper has a definite surface and a certain shade of white tending either towards grey or yellow. Like-

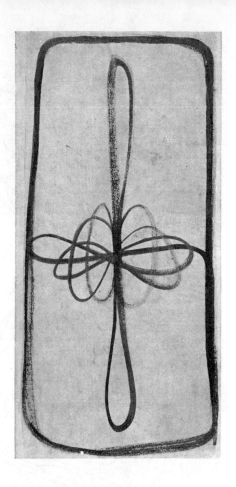

DON'T THINK OUT THE DRAWINGS beforehand, but invent them while your pencil is moving.

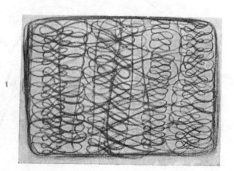

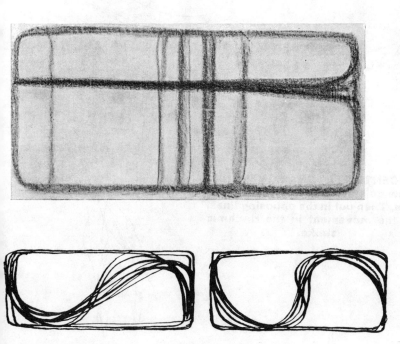

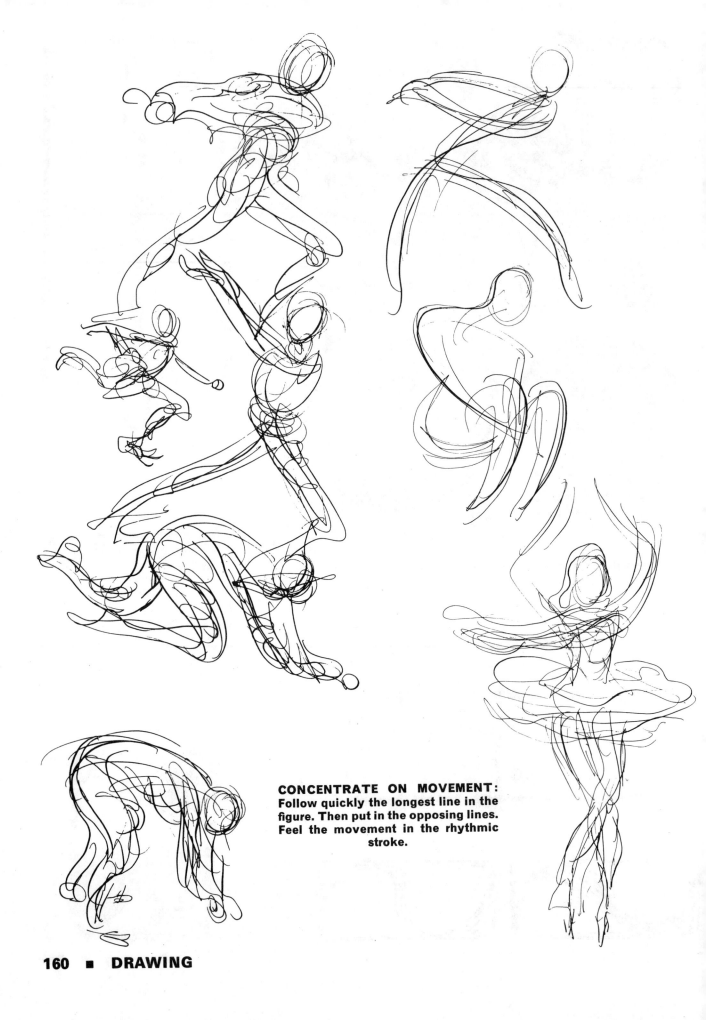

CONCENTRATE ON MOVEMENT:
Follow quickly the longest line in the figure. Then put in the opposing lines. Feel the movement in the rhythmic stroke.

wise, there is no single drawing stroke, but rather lines made with a pointed stiff pen or lines drawn with a soft brush. Here is a survey of the most important materials.

PAPER: We distinguish between smooth and rough paper, between "sized" and absorbent, grained and stippled, heavy and thin. Collect and try out different papers, everything from paper napkins to the precious hand-made Japanese papers. Everyone quickly finds the ones he especially likes. Primarily, you need three types of drawing paper. First of all, you need a lot of inexpensive "scrap paper" for exercises and sketches, something like newsprint. Secondly, you need either single sheets or pads of good drawing paper (with a plate finish for pen). A pretty, somewhat rough paper for use with charcoal, reed pen, or brush is "Ingres paper," which can be purchased in all shades. Third, you need a pocket-sized sketchbook—this you can easily get or make for yourself.

PENCILS: There are many degrees of hardness, which are indicated by a standard code. H, 2H, 3H, and so on indicate increasing degrees of hardness; B, 2B, 3B, etc. show increasing softness; and HB is medium hard. For the first exercises, a soft drawing pencil between 2B and 4B is best. Later you can use HB. There are also "drawing leads," that is, leads which fit into special adjustable lead holders and are always ready to use. For fine work, however, the traditional wooden pencil is preferable. The paper has to have "tooth" enough (a sufficiently rough surface) so that the pencil will leave a mark, and the surface must be hard enough so that the pencil does not dig into it. The blackness and density of a stroke depend on the paper. The same pencil will write dark on grainy paper and grey on smooth paper. But don't try to achieve too much depth by gouging into the paper. For bold drawing, a large-lead carbon or charcoal pencil is recommended—it can be used either pointed or on the broad side.

CHARCOAL: This is a soft material appropriate for shaded drawings. A charcoal line is deep, velvety black, and dull even in the deepest layers. Such a line is much coarser than that of a pencil, but it has a greater range from black to light grey. However, charcoal all too easily leads one astray into pretentiousness and smearing. Charcoal can be bought in wooden holders or as long square sticks. It is better to use the sticks; you can break them into pieces a half-inch to an inch long and use the corners for line work, the sides for large areas. Sanguine (a red crayon) and sepia (brown) are similar to charcoal.

CONTÉ CRAYON: You draw with the square-shaped Conté stick by using a corner for line work or using a whole side for broader strokes. Besides velvety black Conté sticks, you can obtain red or brown ones. The softness and shape of the material allows more freedom of movement than pencil or pen and ink, and you should use larger sheets of paper.

DRAWING TOOLS: Try them all, learn the advantage of each.

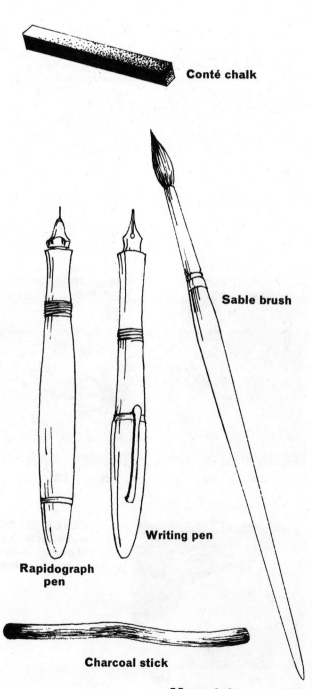

Conté chalk

Sable brush

Rapidograph pen

Writing pen

Charcoal stick

B

2B

3B

4B

F

HB

H

2H

3B 4B

B 4B H

HB 2B

2B 2H

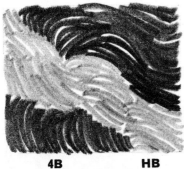

4B   HB

PENCIL STROKES: A few examples of the infinite number of textures and effects that can be achieved using varying strokes and different grades of pencil, B—soft (top), HB and F—medium (center left), and H—hard (center right), or combinations of several (bottom two rows).

162 ■ DRAWING

FIXATIVE: Since soft pencil and charcoal are easily smeared, they have to be "fixed." A good fixative is a 5 per cent solution of white, bleached shellac in alcohol. You can buy it ready to use, either in bottles or spray cans. There are two types of fixatives available. Workable fixative allows you to add to your drawing after spraying, whereas non-workable creates a surface that you cannot draw over. Apply it carefully at a distance of about 12 to 18 inches from the drawing. It is better to spray several thin coats of fixative rather than one heavy coat, since drops or little puddles leave ugly spots. First try a few test sprays into the air. If you are using a bottle with a mouth-type atomizer, the less fixative in the bottle the harder it will be to apply, because the liquid has to be drawn up by the flow of air.

PENS: Pens are also good drawing tools. You can use the holder-type writing pen, and the smaller and finer drawing pen, or the specially designed rapidograph. The advantage of the rapidograph is that you can move it forwards and backwards, enabling you to draw in all directions. Its disadvantage is that the stroke always has the same thickness and cannot be made to swell or shrink. Exchangeable points of different widths are available, but can be expensive. The rapidograph is recommended for your first exercises and for sketches in the open air.

For all pens, you can choose inks which range from heavy, waterproof kinds, including India ink, to thinner, fountain-pen types. The rapidograph is good for outdoor work because it has an ink reservoir and does not have to be dipped continually.

With a brush and diluted ink, you can "wash" a drawing, that is, give it various shades of grey by applying the ink-and-water mixture in different strengths. Try the wash technique with two types of brushes; with a round, hair brush of $\frac{3}{8}$ inch (9 mm.) diameter and with a flat, hair brush of $\frac{1}{2}$ inch (12 mm.) width. You can use washes to touch up a pen or a chalk drawing or give it accents. But you may also start courageously with wash and subsequently touch up and add to your composition of lights and darks with strokes of the pen.

ADDING TEXTURE

Continue your exercises in the language of drawing by trying to bring out through the drawing media the essential substance of various objects.

Start by inventing different modes of expression with a pen by filling up two-inch squares with dots, checks, curlicues, wavy lines, circles, and latticed or pulsing lines. Put all sorts of really dissimilar things together—a piece of wire screen, a feather, a piece

PEN AND INK: Examples of the various surface textures you can achieve with this medium.

of bark, a polished knife—and study the charm of the surface of each one.

Draw a number of uniform objects, that is, objects which are scarcely different in contour but which are decidedly different in surface texture; for example, an apple, a lemon or an orange, an egg, a rubber ball, a marble, and an onion.

Then, after the pen, try out the same exercises with other media—pencil, charcoal, brush. You will discover that there is an especially suitable medium for each type of surface.

A FEELING FOR PROPORTION

Getting a feeling for proportion, for the relation of the parts to the whole and of the parts to each other, must become part of your flesh and blood. Study proportions wherever you go. In the façade of a

PLEASING PROPORTIONS: Whether drawing a tulip or a wine glass try to get a feeling for the relationship of the parts to the whole.

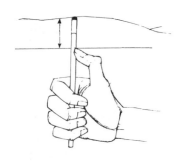

SIGHTING with a pencil to determine the proportionate height of the hill in the distance.

ADDING SHADES AND TONES

Up to now you have been working primarily with lines. Now you should become acquainted with the tonal media and the language of toned areas on the drawing surface. For this purpose use charcoal without a holder or a large brush with some water color or with ink and water. You can use non-absorbent drawing paper as well as absorbent paper for a drawing surface or even newsprint or strong paper napkins. Begin with the outline of a square or a

CREATING SHADES AND TONES with charcoal on tinted paper (center) and ink washes (top and bottom).

house, for example, note the relation of the width to the height, of the height of the windows to the height of the building, of the foundation-work height to the height of the house. Compare different façades. Compare the height of a tree to that of its crown.

Or compare the three parts of a face: the forehead, the nose, and the mouth-chin part. Compare a slender boy to a fat man with short legs, a slim girl to a plump matron. Compare the relationship of head to body with a one-year-old child, a six-year-old, and a man. How many times does the head go into the length of the body? Let the expressive language of proportions everywhere have its effect on you.

"Sighting" will sharpen your eye for proportions, for conscious understanding and comprehension of relationships. For this, hold a long pencil or a stick or rod like an umbrella in your hand; stretch your arm out horizontally with the stick held vertically; now line up the end of the rod with the highest point of the object to be measured—that is, get your eye, the end of the stick, and the upper limit of the object in a straight line. Then run your thumbnail so far down the rod that your eye, your thumbnail, and the lowest point of the object are also lined up.

By the "sighting" method of measurement you can take the dimensions of the whole thing. For example, with the measure of the foundation-work you can determine the height of the whole building. How many times does the part go into the whole? What is the proportion of the parts to each other?

With horizontal measurements, repeat the same process but from left to right. What is the relation of the width to the height? To be sure, when you are "sighting," you always have to stand on the same spot and keep your arm stretched out. The slightest change causes large errors.

Only use "sighting" of the comparative dimensions as a help—as a self-check and as encouragement in order to perceive the greater, more definite tension in nature—then do it only *after* you have sketched the whole thing.

164 ■ DRAWING

rectangle and make the surface vibrate with light and dark tones.

Try going from the outside to the inside, getting lighter until you have an untouched spot of the original paper in the middle. Or start at the top with dark, horizontal stripes and let them get lighter until you have a white stripe in the middle; then let them get dark again towards the bottom edge.

You will soon notice that the danger is in making *everything* too light or *everything* too dark. Then there is no true modulation and the tones swim into each other. Therefore, you have to divide the shading clearly into three or four steps. Distinguish between black, dark grey, medium grey, light grey, and white. Each tone should touch the next one *without* a black dividing line and *without* even a tiny white stripe between them.

During these exercises, pay attention to light and shade everywhere in nature. Notice the graceful, weightless, silvery nuances of a foggy morning, the strong contrasts at high noon, or the tension at night between the brightness of a house door, the semi-darkness of the wall, and the blackness of the sky.

WHAT IS LINEAR EDGE?

There is no flatness in nature. Everything has a third dimension. The linear edge must express this dimension. The line you draw to express dimension in space must travel around the form. This means the line in your drawing travels not in one direction alone. The line of your drawing must travel down and around, in and out of the figure.

Set up a still life with variety of size and shape. For example, use a vase, a lemon and a grapefruit; or a sugar bowl, an apple and a banana; or three other diverse forms. Set the objects against a simple white background and arrange them so that the forms overlap each other. Look directly at the objects and study them carefully. Do not look at the paper.

Using a pencil, begin to draw the linear edge slowly. Following the longest line you see, go around the outer edge. As soon as you reach a place on the drawing at which the line changes direction, look at your paper. Then continue in the new direction. Be sure the drawing is directly in front of you. The proportion will doubtlessly be wrong at first try. Do not be discouraged. Try again. Repeat this exercise until skill in rendering the linear edge is evident to you.

Try to remember the shape of the objects you have just drawn without looking at them. Drawing from

OUTLINE DRAWING: You can express a third dimension in a simple line. Remember to look directly at the objects you are drawing rather than at the paper.

memory helps you draw imaginatively and releases you from complete dependence on the model as a source of subject matter.

RECOGNIZABLE SHAPES

You have already been introduced to the concept of value. The terms, dark, half-tone, light and highlight are all descriptive of value. Three or four distinctive values placed properly on the drawing of a cylinder will communicate the sense of its form. The sense of form is the recognizable shape of a thing, a person, a rock, a tree. It is its weight added to its height and width and depth. It is also what is revealed to the observer when light strikes that object in a particular way.

THREE-DIMENSIONAL FORMS take shape through distinctive shading.

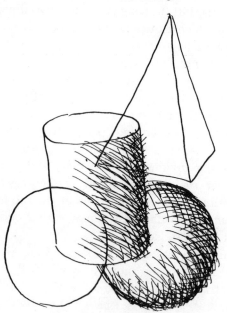

Recognizable Shapes ■ 165

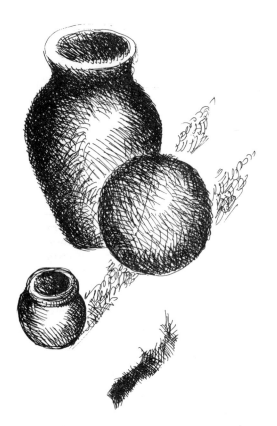

MODELLING: Darken towards the outside edge those forms which are round as well as any flat or receding planes.

It is almost impossible to discuss form without recourse to the terms of sculpture. One refers to weight, modelling, pressing back forms, and other terms which have to do with the appearance of actual solid forms, but drawing remains a two-dimensional art form which can convey a third dimension to the observer through the use of proper shading and highlighting of the forms.

Once again create a still life composition by placing three diverse forms on a table. Then if you possibly can, relax the tension that results from the search for accuracy in finding perspective and correct outline. Concentrate on achieving a sense of form by building up the different light and dark tonal values, or *modelling* the form. Darken towards the outside linear edge those forms in the model which are round. Also darken the planes that recede and are flat in the model.

Set up at least four such compositions, with three objects in each, or more as your skill increases. Concentrate on giving the forms reality, substance, weight.

ORGANIZING THE MOTIF

There are rules for composition but they are mechanical and at best are only measurements. It is sometimes better to discard them entirely. Later, they can serve for critical analysis of your picture, but before all else, your natural instinct to design must be given a chance to assert itself. You cannot create a picture with warmth and interest entirely by rule.

If you base your composition or arrangement on something experienced or observed, it will be simpler than something of an imaginative character.

Leave out all unnecessary detail. Keep rearranging until the major subject is dominant. Don't let the eye move out of the picture—it must travel within the space of the drawing.

Often the word organization is used to supersede the older term composition. To organize is really the work of the artist. The elements may be found in objects or in human beings or even in ideas. But the way lines and forms are distributed on the paper and where and what to put in or leave out— this is *organizing the motif*.

In organizing the drawings there are a few points to guide you, in order to organize more skilfully:

EYE PATH: The lines in a drawing ought to direct the observer from subject to idea and from pattern to plan without allowing his eye to stray from the area of the picture.

BALANCE OF SHAPES: For purposes of interest, shapes should vary in size and kind. Variety is a necessary ingredient of organization.

RHYTHM: This is obtained by repetition of similar shapes or lines.

DOMINANCE: This refers to a shape to which the other elements of design are related but subordinated.

USE OF THE ENTIRE SPACE: It is as important to conceive the composition in terms of the entire picture area.

CONTRAST: The pattern of lights and darks should be considered.

If you are careful to compose your picture, organization soon becomes instinctive and second nature. Selectivity and arrangement are not so conscious as you may think at first.

ABSTRACTING

These guide lines can be used in creating abstract compositions as well. Begin by freely moving your pencil within a given space on the paper. Develop the movement into a suggestion, then carry on by adding, more consciously, stroke upon stroke until

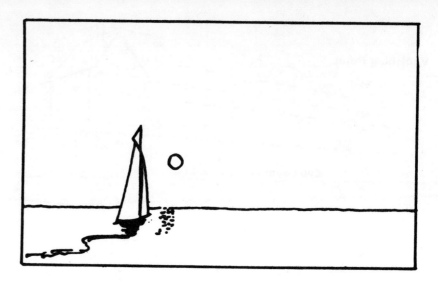

COMPOSITION: Notice how the shifted position of the boat redirects the eye towards the center of interest.

the composition takes on a purposeful form. This is a very interesting exercise and one that is practiced consciously or otherwise by most artists when searching for a pictorial idea.

QUESTIONING THE COMPOSITION

Study the composition of paintings. Ask yourself questions when standing in front of a well-composed picture. What format is used? What is the proportion of height to width? What path does the eye follow? What is the central object? Where is it situated? How is it related to the format? What are the main directional forces? the minor ones? How are the shades of light and dark distributed? Where are the dark spots concentrated? the light spots? How are the edges of the picture drawn into the picture itself?

Answer these questions for yourself while looking at a fairly uncomplicated picture. Check your understanding of a composition by recomposing its basic features from imagination. Then repeat this process of re-creation in front of the picture itself.

Do you sense how all the parts of a good picture are involved with each other, not just placed side by side? Do you feel the organized unity with its inner tension? Do you understand how the empty space "carries" the meaning and why it does not "float?" Do you sense the difference between a slice of nature and a picture?

Try to learn from this how to place even a simple drawing on the surface correctly. If your first attempts do not succeed right away, or if after a time, you have not thought it out well, there is still a chance to make up for the mistake by cutting down the sheet.

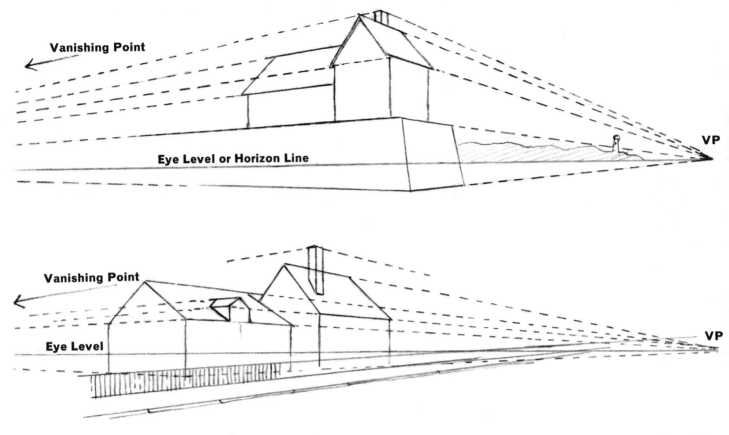

Vanishing Point

Eye Level or Horizon Line

VP

Vanishing Point

Eye Level

VP

PERSPECTIVE: Keep in mind that (1) the important line is the horizon line; (2) objects become smaller as they recede into the distance; (3) horizontals do not run parallel but always toward their respective "vanishing point"; (4) vertical lines remain vertical; (5) objects lose detail as they recede into the background. This last is called "aerial perspective."

WHERE IS THE VANISHING POINT?

In most Western art since the 16th century, perspective is used in a more or less scientific manner. There are mathematical formulae to tell you with exactness how much a form diminishes in size as it retreats into the picture plane, and there *are* instances in which such information is of great importance.

But for purposes of beginning drawing, a few simple guide lines can be used. For instance, the horizon line is imaginary but few representational pictures can do without it. The shape of an object will vary as one sees it either above or below the horizon or at eye level.

Vertical lines remain vertical.

Horizontals do not run parallel, but always towards their respective "vanishing points." That is, horizontal lines above the horizon descend towards it and those below the horizon rise. Lines converge as they recede from the eye. Therefore, width, heights and distances between objects are "foreshortened."

Remember that, theoretically, perspective drawings can be made from one viewpoint only, but that drawing in a creative sense often makes use of more than one viewpoint, and that sometimes it is necessary to distort both perspective and proportion in order to produce expressive effects.

Try simple examples of perspective: a street lined with buildings, a building of uncomplicated form from different angles, a drawing of figures in the street. Relate the figures to the buildings. If your figures are in the foreground you will have a perfect example of how forms diminish in size as they retreat from the eye. If your eye is close to the figure, a doorway 20 feet away from that figure seems far too small to admit it.

LIFE DRAWING, BRIDGMAN STYLE

Before you make a line you must have a clear conception of what the figure to be drawn is doing. Study the figure from different angles. Sense the nature and condition of the action, or inaction. This conception is the real beginning of your drawing.

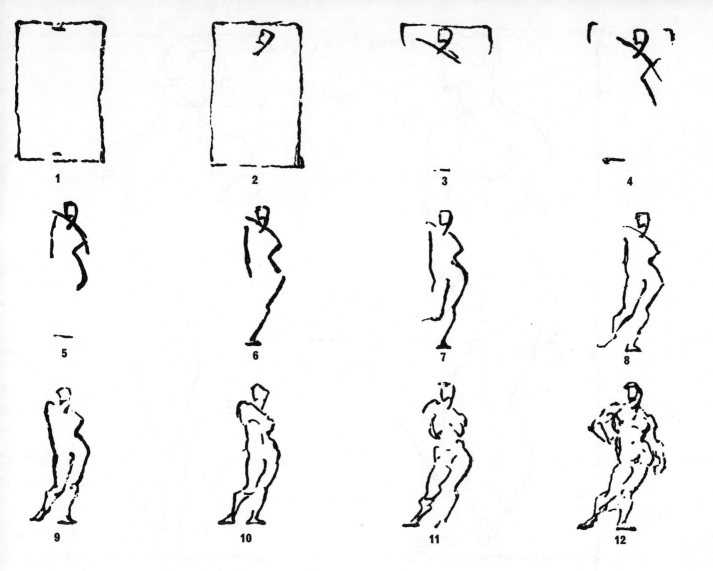

1.   Consider the placement of your drawing on the paper, for balance and arrangement. Make two marks to indicate the length of the drawing.

2.   Block in with straight lines the outline of the head. Turn it carefully on the neck, marking its center by drawing a line from the Adam's apple to the pit between the collar bones.

3.   From the pit of the neck make one line giving the direction of the shoulders, keeping in mind the marking of its center, which should be the pit between the collar bones.

4.   Indicate the general direction of the body by outlining to the hip and thigh, at its outermost point, the side that carries the weight.

5.   Follow this by outlining the opposite inactive side of the body, comparing the width with the head.

6.   Then, crossing again to the action side of the figure, drop a line to the foot. You now have determined the balance, or equilibrium of the figure.

7.   Carry the line of the inert side to the knee, over and upwards to the middle of the figure.

8.   On the outer side, drop a line to the other foot.

9.   Starting again with the head, and thinking of it as a cube with front, sides, top, back and base, draw it on a level with the eye, foreshortened or in perspective.

10.   Outline the neck and from the pit of the neck draw a line down the center of the chest.

11.   At a right angle to this line, where stomach and chest join, draw another line and then draw lines to indicate the rib cage as a block, twisted, tilted or straight, according to its position.

12.   Now draw the thigh and the leg which support the greatest part of the weight of the body, making the thigh round, the knee square, the calf of the leg triangular and the ankle square. Then draw the arms.

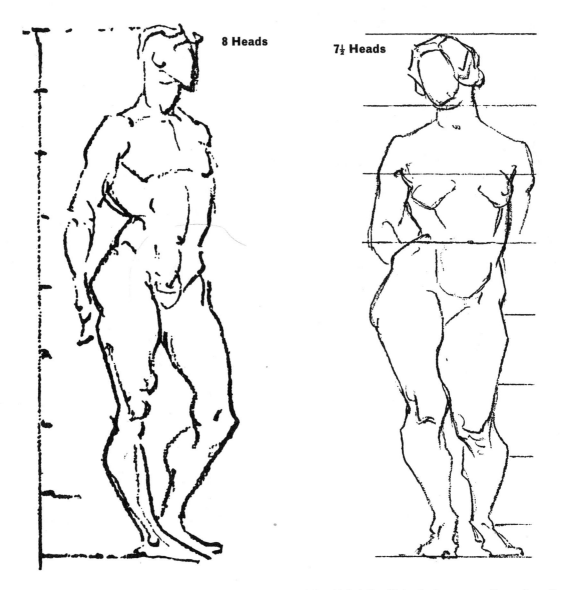

8 Heads

7½ Heads

PROPORTIONS OF THE HUMAN FIGURE: You can use the "sighting" technique mentioned earlier to judge the proportions of a human figure. Measure the size of the head, and mark off that length 7½ or 8 times. It would be best, however, to develop a feel for the proper relationships, and not to rely on mechanical means.

These few simple lines place the figure. They give its general proportions, indicating its active and inactive sides, its balance, unity and rhythm.

Bear in mind that the head, chest and pelvis are the three large masses of the body. They are in themselves immovable. Think of them as blocks having four sides, and as such they may be symmetrically placed and balanced, one directly above the other. In this case, the figure would have no movement. But when these masses bend backwards, forwards, turn or twist, the shifting of them gives action to the figure.

Whatever positions these three masses may assume, no matter how violently they may be drawn together on one side, there is a corresponding gentle-ness of line on the opposing, inert side and a subtle, illusive, living harmony flowing through the whole, which is the rhythm of the figure.

One method of arriving mechanically at the proportions of the human figure is the measurement by which the head is used as a determining factor in proportion. The usual formula is seven and one-half heads to the length of the figure, with eight heads a bit closer to the modern ideal.

This and other mechanical methods have the serious fault of making the student depend upon them to the detriment of his power of observation. Besides which they halt the search for rhythmic movement.

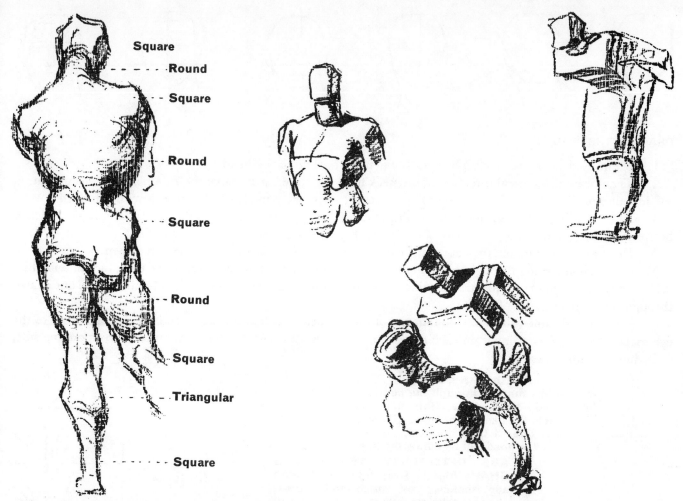

Square
Round
Square

Round

Square

Round

Square

Triangular

Square

BALANCE AND SHADING: If you visualize the human body as a series of geometric forms, it will help you judge where the light and shade should fall. Note the sense of balance achieved in the standing figure on the left. The center of gravity passes from the head down through the supporting leg creating a sense of balance even though the figure stands with all the weight shifted to one side.

BALANCE

In a drawing there must be a sense of security, of balance between the opposite or counteracting forces, regardless of where the center line may fall. This is true no matter what the posture may be. A standing figure whether thrown backwards or forwards, or to one side or the other, is stationary or static. The center of gravity, from the pit of the neck, passes through the supporting foot or feet, or between the feet when they are supporting the weight equally.

LIGHT AND SHADE

Shade with the idea that light and shade are to aid the outline you have drawn in giving the impression of solidity, breadth and depth. Keep before you the conception of a solid body of four sides composed of a few great masses, and avoid all elaborate and unnecessary tones which take away from the thought that the masses or planes on the sides must appear to

be on the sides, while those on the front must appear to be on the front of the body. No two tones of equal size or intensity should appear directly above one another or side by side; their arrangement should be shifting and alternate.

There should be a decided difference between the tones. The number of tones should be as few as possible. Avoid all elaborate or unnecessary tones and do not make four tones or values where only three are needed. It is important to keep in mind the big, simple masses and to keep your shading simple, for shading does not make a drawing.

DISTRIBUTION OF THE MASSES

It is not granted many of us to remember complex forms. So in considering the human figure it is better, at first, to think only of those major forms of which it is composed, and these may be thought of and more easily remembered by a simple formula such as the one illustrated here.

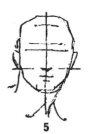

1   2   3   4   5   6

DRAWING THE HEAD

1.   Begin by drawing with straight lines the general outline of the head.

2.   Then draw the general direction of the neck from its center, just above the Adam's apple, to the pit, at the junction of the collar bones. Now outline the neck, comparing its width and length with the head.

3.   Draw a straight line through the length of the face, passing it through the root of the nose, which is between the eyes, and through the base of the nose where the nose centers in the upper lip.

4.   Draw another line from the base of the ear at a right angle to the one you have just drawn.

5.   On the line passing through the center of the face, measure off the position of the eyes, mouth and chin. A line drawn through these will parallel a line drawn from ear to ear, intersecting, at right angles, the line drawn through the vertical center of the face.

6.   With straight lines, draw the boundaries of the forehead, its top and sides, and the upper border of the eye sockets. Then draw a line from each cheek bone at its widest part, to the chin, on the corresponding side, at its highest and widest part.

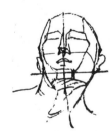

THE HEAD AS A CUBE (left): Think of a line running through the center of the head from ear to ear. If the head is tilted back, the base of the nose will be above that line; if tilted forward, the base of the nose will be below the line.

AGE DETERMINES THE HEAD'S SHAPE (right): From infancy, through adolescence, to adulthood, great changes take place in the upper, as well as the lower, portion of the face. The face lengthens, the nose and cheekbones become more prominent, and the teeth add width and depth to the lower part of the face. The forehead recedes, the jaw bones become more angular and pointed, the masseter or chewing muscles more evident, and the chin more square.

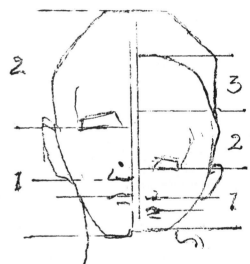

If the head you are drawing is on a level with your eyes, the lines you have just drawn will intersect at right angles at the base of the nose and if both ears are visible and the line from the ear extended across the head, it will touch the base of both ears.

Consider the head as a cube, the ears opposite each other on its sides or cheeks and the line from ear to ear as a spit or skewer running through rather than around the head.

If the head is above the eye level, or tilted backwards, the base of the nose will be above this line from ear to ear. Or should the head be below the eye level or tilted forward, the base of the nose will be below the line from ear to ear. In either case, the head will be foreshortened upwards or downwards as the case may be and the greater the distance the head is above or below the eye level the greater the

distance between the line from ear to ear and the base of the nose.

You now have the boundaries of the face and the front plane of the cube. The features may now be drawn in.

In an adult, from the extreme top to the bottom, the eyes, roughly speaking, are in the middle. The head and face of an infant may be divided in three parts, the eyes placed on the line marking the upper third, from the chin up. In all heads the base of the nose is placed halfway between the eyes and chin; the mouth two-thirds the distance from chin to nose. Ages between these two necessarily range somewhere between.

There is also a marked difference in the formation of the head with varying ages. The forehead of an adult recedes, the cheek bones become more prominent, the jaw bone more angular, the whole head in fact more square. In infancy the head is more elongated and somewhat oval in form. The forehead is full, it recedes down and back towards the brows; the jaw bone and other bones of the face are diminutive; the neck is small compared to the head.

In youth the face is lengthened and is less round than in the infant. The head above the brows however, is not enlarged in proportion to the increase of the lower part of the face.

AN OUTDOOR EXCURSION

When you proceed to landscape drawing, you will have the opportunity to co-ordinate and utilize all the various elements of drawing discussed so far.

There is no need to go out on a landscape drawing excursion encumbered with a great many materials. Take along only some charcoal, pen and ink, or a set of drawing pencils, as well as a sketchbook or some loose sheets of paper and a drawing board. Just be certain the texture of the paper is appropriate for the medium you have chosen. You might also need a kneaded eraser.

Now let us concentrate on one of the essential elements of landscape drawing, the tree. For anyone who is going to draw or paint out-of-doors, a thorough acquaintance with the anatomy of trees is just as important as the knowledge of human anatomy when working from the figure. Each species of tree has certain distinctive characteristics, and so does each individual tree within the species, just as each individual of the human race does.

Sit before a tree, at a great enough distance so that it can be seen as a whole. With a pen, search out the linear edge of the forms of trunk and branches, starting at the roots, following the forms slowly, watching where the direction of the branches changes, how some come towards you in space while others retreat. Remember one rule of thumb: "At the beginning, always have the end in sight; with the detail in mind, think of the whole." Feel the power of the structure as you draw. Search for the character in the movement of the great branches. Notice the movement upwards or downwards. It is this insistence on feeling the form which will give character and individuality to your drawing. Try to draw many trees and allow yourself to enter the mood of each one. Some trees have a quality of lithe movement in their branches, others are stiff and uncompromising and thin-branched. All are studies in rhythm and expressive line.

In summer when the leaves cover much of the

DRAWING A TREE: When drawing trees in summer, do the foliage first, then draw in the branches.

structure, trees present another form problem. Now your attention will turn to the difference between the *silhouettes* of trees, the growth of different kinds of foliage. You will soon notice that the silhouette is usually related to the leaf form.

Draw the foliage in great masses; do not try to detail each leaf. While concentrating on the silhouette, also see the form or structure on which it rests. You will find the same quality of depth in the leafed tree that was present in the visible branches; so keep the edges of the masses of foliage soft and lacy in order to maintain the impression of separate leaves through which the wind can blow and sun can shine.

As you work, remember to relate background material to the tree. Find the lines behind and in front that suggest the forms of hill and grass. A

Outdoor Excursion ■ **173**

LANDSCAPE IN PENCIL: Notice how strong compositional elements in this drawing are created. Also observe how objects lose detail as they recede into the background.

tree grows within an environment. It does not stand alone.

After you have had some practice with individual trees or groups of trees, try doing some quick landscape sketches, keeping in mind the composition guide lines discussed earlier. Choose subjects that are simple, but in some way unique or inspiring to you. Try to determine what it is that you find striking or interesting about each. Formulate an idea or feeling about the subject, and then plan your composition in such a way as to express this idea.

Your immediate problems here are those of choosing a focus of interest, placing the horizon line and the other elements of the picture in such a way that they emphasize this focal point, and eliminating extraneous detail.

Another very important element to take into consideration when composing a landscape drawing

is that of lighting. The prevailing light will determine the areas of light and dark, as well as the length, intensity and direction of shadows, and all these masses and tones can be used to heighten and strengthen the composition. You will probably find that you have to experiment with several different compositions until you find the one that is strongest and best embodies the idea you are trying to express.

After you have done some quick sketches and developed an awareness of the problems of landscape composition, you may be interested in trying some more finished drawings, such as those illustrated here. When you have found a pleasing subject and arrived at a composition that satisfies you, draw in very carefully the main lines of each object as well as the shadow shapes and masses, so that when the rendering is started, you can concentrate wholly on the values and technique, and not have to be concerned with drawing. The more preliminary drawing that is done, the better the final results are bound to be. Here you should recall another rule of thumb: "A drawing should be finished in every stage of completion." Never lose yourself in details and never start with them.

In doing the outline drawing, the sighting technique discussed earlier will help you judge proportions and distances. Remember, though, the slightest movement in the sighting arm can cause distortion. This is also true of your position. Having once begun a drawing, if you alter your position only slightly, you will find you are looking at things from a completely different viewpoint. You won't, for example, be able to start a drawing in a standing position and sit down halfway through it. Just that minor change in your position would alter your view of the subject considerably.

When you have finished outlining the main masses and details, you are ready to begin adding tones and modelling or rendering the forms. The way in which you go about this will be determined very much by the medium you have chosen. Pencil strokes, for example, should never be rubbed or "stumped" as charcoal is, as this always destroys the fresh appearance, and creates a greasy-looking tone.

While rendering the landscape, keep in mind that contrast is essential to an interesting drawing. One way to provide contrast is to avoid monotonous strokes. The character of the stroke may largely be determined by the nature of the medium and the object being represented. When working with a pencil, a short or choppy stroke is not, as a rule, desirable; yet at times, if used with proper discretion,

it may serve as a relief from too many sweeping lines. Refer back to page 162 for a helpful chart demonstrating some of the pencil strokes that can be used to suggest different textures. With pen and ink, you need only change the pressure of your stroke or switch to a broader or narrower pen point to achieve a variety of strokes. You also have the advantage of being able to use washes to obtain different tones when working in this medium.

Using dark masses against light, and light against dark, at the focus of interest, also affords an excellent means of contrast. Remember that the parts of a drawing that are left white, in other words, not rendered, are just as necessary as the parts that are given tone. Only by leaving certain areas white can sunlight or sparkle be added to the scene. It is always easier to go back and tone a space which seems too light, than it is to lighten up an area that is too dark; therefore, leave plenty of white paper until the final touches are being applied. If you are working in pencil, charcoal, or Conté crayon, a kneaded eraser can be used for purposes of highlighting dark areas.

Here are a few last suggestions: When rendering water, take great care that the strokes are either absolutely horizontal or absolutely vertical; otherwise the water will give the appearance of travelling uphill. Often the importance, as well as the proportion of a comparatively insignificant growth or object in the foreground has to be exaggerated in order to give a feeling of distance to the scene. It is usually the clearly delineated detail in the foreground and the lack of much detail in the background that gives aerial perspective to a drawing. Be sure the foreground, as the name implies, comes forward.

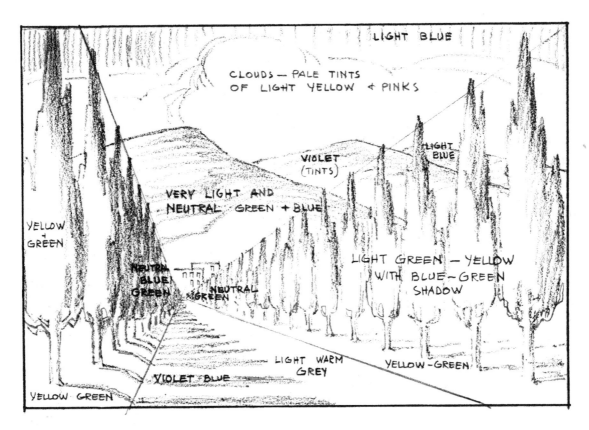

Labels within the image:
LIGHT BLUE

CLOUDS — PALE TINTS OF LIGHT YELLOW & PINKS

VIOLET (TINTS)

LIGHT BLUE

VERY LIGHT AND NEUTRAL GREEN + BLUE

YELLOW + GREEN

LIGHT GREEN — YELLOW WITH BLUE-GREEN SHADOW

NEUTRAL BLUE GREEN

NEUTRAL GREEN

LIGHT WARM GREY

YELLOW-GREEN

VIOLET BLUE

YELLOW GREEN

RENDERING: First outline the main masses and details, and then begin rendering or modelling the forms. The technique you use will depend upon the medium you have chosen.

When you feel that you have attained a measure of proficiency in drawing, it may be time to go on to painting.

PAINTING

The first and best advice that could be given someone considering painting as a hobby would be to acquire first the basic drawing skills. But, if you are anxious to get right into painting, it might be a good idea at least to read over the previous section, particularly the parts on composition and landscape drawing.

An understanding of the principles of composition, as well as those of line and form, tone and value are essential to the beginning painter. Since they have been discussed rather fully in the previous section, they will be touched upon only lightly here. This section will concentrate on introducing you to some very basic color theory and to the tools and techniques of the different painting media. The media discussed here are water color, oil, acrylics, and gouache. They all vary in the way they handle, in the skill required to use them successfully, and in the initial outlay required for appropriate materials. Read the entire section through before deciding which media to experiment with first. If you experience difficulty with one, don't be discouraged, just go on to the next. Many teachers would warn you away from beginning with water color, as it is generally thought that it requires a fairly accomplished painter to use it successfully. But this needn't necessarily be the case.

Before you begin to paint, get yourself a good sketchbook. This is one of the painter's most essential tools. Buy the best you can afford. They are graded from 9H, the hardest, down to 7B, which is extremely soft. To start with you might buy a 2B and a 4B or 5B.

COLOR THEORY

Over the centuries many artists have concerned themselves in practice and in theory with the use of color in painting. In the past fifteen years alone, an entire school of painting has grown up around the study of color. These "color painters" devote themselves exclusively to experimenting with the way in which colors affect one another and the way the human eye reacts to these effects. Their paintings are simply color studies, usually consisting only of stripes or squares of different colors.

Obviously, it is a fascinating area that can be explored in great depth, but for the purposes of getting started, it will be sufficient to be exposed to a few basic principles. It is not necessary to absorb them all now. As you begin mixing and using colors, you will begin to discover things on your own, and at that time you may want to refer back to these charts and guide lines for assistance.

PRIMARY AND SECONDARY COLORS

The term, primary, is used to denote any color that cannot be broken down, one that is not made up of a combination of other colors. The three primary paint pigments are red, yellow and blue. By combining the two paint primaries, red and yellow, you get orange. Adding equal amounts of two primary colors results in a secondary color, in this case, orange. By combining yellow and blue paint primaries, you obtain green. By combining red and blue paint primaries equally, the result is a violet. When the three primaries are combined the result is black. This is said to be a subtractive process; when one color is added to another color, part or all of the light it reflects is subtracted.

Color Primaries	Color Secondaries
Red + yellow =	orange
Yellow + blue =	green
Blue + red =	violet

From the primary and secondary colors—and in fact from all colors—you can make innumerable *tints* by adding different quantities of white. You can make innumerable *tones* by adding varied quantities of black-and-white (grey) and you can make innumerable *shades* of colors by adding varied quantities of black. The important point to remember is not so much the terms—tint, tone and shade—

Condensed from the books, "Carlson's Guide to Landscape Painting," by John F. Carlson © 1958, 1953 by Sterling Publishing Co., Inc./"Color in Oil Painting" by Maria and Louis Di Valentin © 1966 by Sterling Publishing Co., Inc./"Acrylic and Other Water-Base Paints for the Artist" by Dr. Judith Torche, © 1969, 1967 by J. H. Torche, Ed. D./"Aquarelle and Watercolor Complete" by J. Van Ingen © 1972 by Sterling Publishing Co., Inc., New York. Taken in part from "Instructions for Young Artists" © 1968, 1960 by John Mills

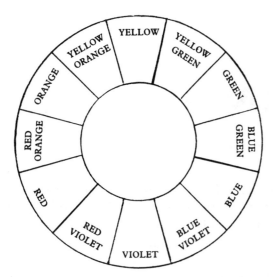

THE COLOR WHEEL: "Cool" colors are on the right, "warm" colors on the left; complementary colors are opposite one another, and analogous colors are any three next to each other on the wheel.

but the fact that proportions of mixtures and/or addition of pigments will give you an unlimited number of tints, tones and shades.

COMPLEMENTARY AND ANALOGOUS COLORS

The color wheel illustrated here includes the primary and secondary tints as well as the intermediaries. It is very useful and will provide a ready guide when "cool" and "warm" colors are mentioned: those on the blue side of the circle are said to be cool while those on the red side are warm. Colors which are opposite each other in the color wheel are called *complementary* colors. Many painters have worked with these complementaries, notably the French Impressionists and the later Post-Impressionists. An artist employing this method places two complementary colors together to produce the maximum effect from both. For instance, yellow and purple or red and green will produce the strongest effect when used in combination. This is called *complementary harmony*.

The color wheel can also be used to produce a second form of color harmony called *analogous*. This means that when three colors next to each other on the wheel are placed together in a picture, they will produce an effect of concord rather than discord. Blue, green-blue, and green are a good example of *analogous harmony*.

You can also paint in monochrome. This simply means using different tones of one color. Dark brown, for example, when intermixed with varying degrees of white, will produce a vast range of tints.

BASIC PIGMENTS

Before too long you will realize that you must learn something about the chemistry of colors. You must know what the colors are made from, which have a chemical affinity for each other, and which should not and must not be mixed together.

The most essential colors are listed in the chart on the next page. Your choice of colors will depend upon the medium in which you choose to work, and separate lists of suggested pigments to use with each medium will appear later on.

The basic pigments are generally the same in the various media. Cadmium yellow pigment, for example, is identical in water color with the pigment used in a cadmium yellow oil, pastel or gouache.

Water color contains the basic pigments ground in water. It is then mixed with various gums and other substances to provide a different consistency for each of the three forms available, cake, stick or tube. Oil colors are ground straight into oil. Gouaches, or poster colors, are ground into gum. In acrylics, however, you will not be able to find some of the basic colors. The term "acrylic" is usually used to describe the "plastic" paint made with acrylic and vinyl resins, with which certain traditional pigments will not mix successfully.

The substance into which the pigments are ground to create the painting media is called a vehicle.

PAINTING IN WATER COLOR

Water color is often said to be the most difficult medium, yet this is not completely true. Even when used by a beginner its wonderful spontaneity and brightness of effect can express what the new artist is seeking.

MATERIALS

When you buy your set of colors, you will have to choose between tins containing tablets and tubes. Stick colors are also available, but they are intended primarily for use by draftsmen and architects. Whether you decide on pan color in a paintbox, or a collection of tubes is a personal matter, and one on which it is hard to advise. In some ways the tubes do have an advantage over the paintbox type, for you can squeeze an appreciable amount of color onto your palette. Thus, when painting out of doors speedy mixing is possible. It takes a little longer when

MIXTURE CHART

Color	Derived from	Permanency	Mixability
Alizarin Crimson	coal tar	not permanent	do not mix with lead, copper or earth colors
Rose Madder	the madder root	not permanent	can be mixed with all other colors
Vermilion	mercury and sulphur	not permanent	do not mix with copper blues or copper greens, lead or earth colors
Cadmium Red	cadmium sulphide and cadmium selenide	permanent	do not mix with copper greens or blues
Sienna	earth	permanent	can be used burnt and raw in all mixtures
Venetian Red	earth	permanent	can be mixed with all other colors
Umber	earth (manganese oxide and iron hydroxide)	permanent	can be mixed burnt and raw; its manganese content makes it an excellent dryer
Cadmium Yellow	cadmium sulphide	permanent	do not use with copper colors; because it is a sulphide, in mixtures with copper it turns black
Chrome Yellow	lead (chromate)	not absolutely permanent	do not mix with copper or sulphur colors
Yellow Ochre	earth	permanent	when free from impurities can be used in all mixtures
Cobalt Blue	cobalt and aluminium oxides	permanent	useful in all mixtures; lightproof; dries fast; must be used over dry surface, otherwise will cause cracks
Ultramarine (natural)	lapis lazuli	permanent	rarely used today, very expensive
Ultramarine (artificial)	sulphur, soda, carbon	not permanent	do not use with copper colors like emerald green (reddish blue)
Cerulean	(related to) cobalt	permanent	useful in all mixtures, durable (blue)
Viridian	(based on) chromium oxide	permanent	renders all copper greens unnecessary; useful in all mixtures, mixes with cadmium and madder
Emeraude	same as viridian	permanent	same as viridian
Terra Verte	contains silicic acid and ferrous hydroxide	permanent	useful in all mixtures
Ivory Black	carbon	permanent	useful in all mixtures
Lamp Black	carbon	permanent	used generally for drawing purposes
Titanium White	titanium dioxide	permanent	opaque, can be cut with zinc white
Zinc White	oxide of zinc	permanent	transparent, useful in all mixtures
White Lead or Flake White	carbonate of lead	not permanent	compatible with all colors except alizarin and ultramarine

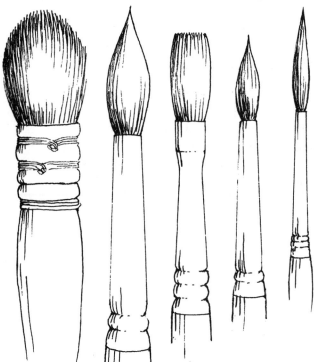

WATER-COLOR BRUSHES: This selection of brushes (shown in actual size) should be adequate to begin with. Sable brushes are a good investment—they will last indefinitely if well cared for.

you have to stroke your tablet of color with a brush again and again to obtain the strength you wish.

The next question is the selection of colors. Usually paintboxes are ready-filled with a choice based on the advice of professional artists, and generally these boxes are entirely reliable. If you prefer, you can ask for a selection of your own choosing. This is a simple matter, especially if you are buying tubes.

The best thing to do, of course, would be to limit yourself at first to the basic primaries. This is the best way to gain an understanding of the art of mixing colors. Try working with just these three for a start:

Rose Madder Deep
Yellow Ochre, light
Cerulean

After buying colors you will have to select some brushes. The water-colorist ordinarily uses a soft hair brush. The best of these are made from sable and, in the very finest grades, can be extremely expensive. However, a good sable brush is a wonderful tool which will last a lifetime. Cheaper grades of sable are available, as are coarser hairs. The brush shapes available include the round, which is self-descriptive; the flat, which may be up to an inch

wide, with hairs about three-quarters to one inch long; the sword, which is shaped so as to provide a head that will draw a long, crisp line with considerable control; and lastly, a mop. This is a rather large-headed brush meant solely for applying areas of wash. If you wish, you may buy brushes already packaged in sets.

To start with, four or five brushes will be enough: a large mop for the wash, a No. 12, a No. 8, a half-inch flat and perhaps a sword will give you all the effects you require when beginning.

The material you paint on is called a ground. Water colors are usually painted on paper, and you will find a variety of papers to choose from at your dealer's. The humblest of all is a rough paper which is produced from wood pulp and comes in many different thicknesses or weights. Paper is sold in definite sizes, the most popular of which measures about 30 by 22 inches. Generally you will have to buy a whole sheet, but sometimes a good-natured dealer will cut one of these in half for you.

After the rough inexpensive papers come the handmade varieties, which undoubtedly are the best for water-color painting, as they are extremely strong, and offer a considerable choice of rough, smooth or shiny textures on which to work. These papers are all watermarked. The way to find the right side on which to work is to hold them up to the light and read the maker's name and the date of production; you should paint on the side on which the wording reads from left to right.

Other papers for the water-colorist include a pleasant buff-toned, speckly, rough-textured paper. There is also a range of tinted papers (sometimes called Ingres) that can be used not only for water color but also for gouache. Besides these, you will come across many other less known but perfectly reliable kinds of paper. Water-color papers as a whole are completely suitable for any form of painting other than oils. Although some artists have successfully used oils on this form of ground, it is not really an advisable practice.

As to a palette, you can of course use the lid of your specially designed paintbox or a form of white tile with low divisions for the various colors. Another type is the white plastic with six or more wells. Saucers, plates, enamelled screw caps from jars—anything of this nature will serve quite adequately.

Blotting paper is extremely useful for mopping up excess color, taking out a highlight or stopping one color from running into another if it gets out of control. Other useful accessories are a piece of clean white cotton or linen rag; a small sponge to assist in blending colors and mopping out areas; a gum eraser, a razor blade and a piece of sandpaper.

HOW TO GET STARTED

Although many different positions are used when holding the brush for various purposes, there are two basic positions: For precise work and firm control of little lines and spots of color, hold the brush fairly close to the ferrule and use your little finger as a support, as shown. This will prevent your hand from moving too quickly and spoiling the effect you are trying to achieve. For looser, more fluid, or impressionistic effects, hold the brush farther up the handle. How far up depends upon the degree of freedom of movement you desire. Practice this in as many positions as possible so you will become familiar with each position and its results. Here, your hand or wrist must never touch the paper or you will immediately constrict your brush movement and spoil the work.

Before starting to paint, get to know your colors. Try out different mixtures on some odd scraps of paper. From the recommended three you will be able to produce many different colors. Try out various brush strokes too. See what you can produce with your brushes fully loaded, moist and almost dry.

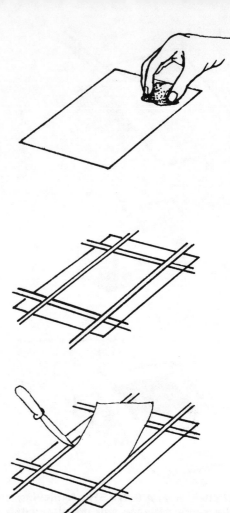

STRETCHING THE PAPER: In order to prevent your water color from buckling after it has dried, the paper should be stretched, taped, and dried before you begin, preferably a day in advance, since it takes about 6 hours to dry. The finished, dry painting can then be cut free with a knife.

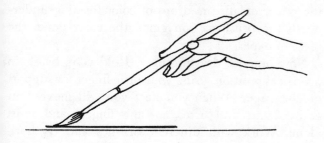

HOLDING THE BRUSH: Use the first position (upper) when you need firm control, as when doing line or detail work; use the second position (lower) for freer work such as applying a wash.

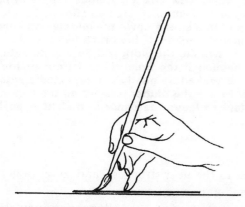

Unless you are using a very thick, heavy paper or a strong cardboard, it is an excellent plan to stretch the paper ahead of time. Lay it face downward on your drawing board or piece of hardboard on which you are going to work, and thoroughly moisten the back by means of a sponge or piece of absorbent cotton. Next, turn the paper over and repeat the process on the reverse side. As the paper expands and buckles, you have to remove the bubbles and ridges that form. Lift one end and then smooth it down again with the sponge until you have it absolutely flat. After you have gotten rid of all the irregularities, fasten the paper to a drawing board with masking tape. You will probably have to prepare your paper the day before you intend to start work; it takes about 6 hours to dry.

Water color ∎ 181

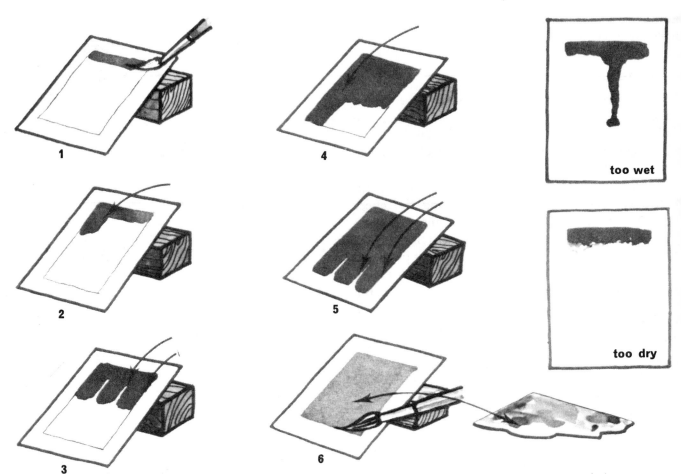

PAINTING A FLAT WASH: Achieving an even-toned flat wash is not as simple as it would seem, and will require some patience and practice. First, tack or tape your paper to a drawing board or something that will serve as a substitute. Pencil off the area you intend to use, and then rest the board on a slant against something in order to allow the paint to flow naturally down the paper as you work. Now mix a generous supply of paint, and using a mop, run a ridge of color across the top of the paper, and down each side as shown. Before the paint has had time to begin drying, add more color to your brush and run a stroke down the middle and connect the four masses; then continue down the page with smooth, downward strokes. If the brush has just the right amount of color, and there is enough moisture in the first horizontal swatch, the work will flow quite naturally down the paper. The examples on the far right show what will happen if the brush is wet (top) or too dry (bottom). A puddle of color will form at the bottom, which should be soaked up gently and repeatedly with the brush that has been cleaned and dried on a blotter. Do not attempt to use the blotter directly on the paper, but use it instead to absorb the moisture from the brush. It is important to leave the paper in a slanted position until the wash is dry.

APPLYING THE COLOR

It is best to apply water color as lightly and directly as possible. The accompanying illustrations show the method for applying a flat wash such as you might need for a distant sky or a large expanse of sea. Mix your color beforehand on a palette or in a series of old saucers. Always mix more than you will need. If you have to stop to remix in the middle of a wash, it will be impossible to achieve a smooth satisfying effect. Ugly ridges will undoubtedly form. If you want a graded effect, mix two or three different strength solutions and work so that as you go down the piece of paper you can work from the

strongest to the next strongest, and so on to achieve the lessening in your tone.

As you can see from the illustration, you should apply plenty of color. Keep a ridge of liquid moving down the paper as you work. Apply your brush with the lightest possible touch. It should hardly touch the paper at all, the drops of color forming underneath the brush as you guide the color down the piece of paper.

Now practice drawing lines. Hold your brush in a vertical position, using your little finger for support on the paper. When you start you will move your entire hand and arm, not the fingers and wrist alone. Work with different brushes and try horizontal and vertical lines; thick ones and thin ones. To gain control, keep the lines evenly spaced.

Also try lines that are not completely straight, that is, ones that jut off at angles and cross each other as shown here.

Experiment with control of lines by means of varying pressures on the brush. By using light pressure you will produce thin lines; using heavier pressure will produce thick lines. Make a series of lines showing as many gradations of thickness as you can achieve with one brush.

Paint a line pattern of varying thickness, color tones, and spacing. Then, as a test of your control and proper handling of the brush, try experimenting with spirals and curves.

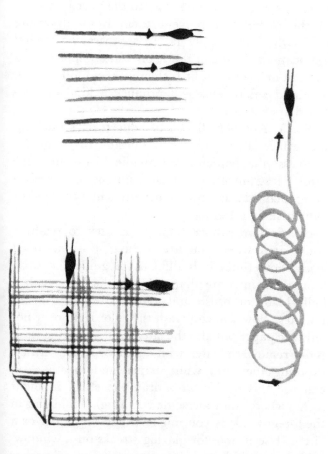

THICK AND THIN LINES like these can be achieved by holding the brush in the upright position illustrated on page 181 and using the little finger as a support. Practice and you will get brush control.

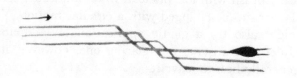

SMALL AREAS OF COLOR: First try making patches of every color on the color wheel. When doing these, hold the brush toward the end, changing the angle at times to create different effects. When you begin to develop some control, try painting individual flower petals, and then whole flowers.

Handling small areas of color requires a different position when holding the brush. Firmly grip the end of the handle, and lightly and surely make a number of color spots on your paper.

By lowering the angle of the brush, you can make use of the side of it when doing small-area painting. Try arranging your spots of color so that they give an impression of a flower.

Find a picture of a flower similar to the Clematis shown here. Work out the color range and practice diffusing the colors. Use light transparent tints to capture the delicacy of the petals and contrast them with dark "eyes" and stems. See color page L of this book for more examples of flowers painted in water color.

BEGIN WITH A LANDSCAPE

You are now ready to begin, and as water color is essentially a medium which is spontaneous—one that calls for quickness in application—a suitable subject can be a landscape.

LANDSCAPE: From flat washes of color to painting a landscape is just a short step. You will find, however, that if you attempt only simple compositions at first, such as the one illustrated here, you will have more success than if you undertake a more elaborate project.

You will probably want to indicate the drawing lightly in pencil, or, for a more free and enjoyable approach, paint it in. Mix a very thin neutral grey and draw with this. Concentrate on getting your basic lines.

In the second stage, don't attempt any fine detail. Keep your feeling broad; obtain the masses first, and strive to achieve the right tone values. Tone values or depths of color (regardless of hue) are the most important elements of any picture. You can also begin the sky. Vaguely suggest it and bring along the blue areas and the patchy clouds.

In pure water color you should not use white or thick opaque colors. The whole picture should be in transparent colors and you should *work from light to dark,* the opposite of oils, where you tend to work from dark to light.

Having brought your picture to the second stage, proceed to the final touches, but resist the temptation to take the water color too far. It is easy to go on fiddling with a small brush, picking up tiny details here, accentuating this or that. In a very short time you can spoil the freshness of your picture. It is much better to leave a water color (for that matter, an oil, or any form of picture) slightly unfinished. If you work at it too long, you may become tired unconsciously and will lose a sense of what you are doing. Try to train yourself to stop painting at just the right moment.

CREATING SPECIAL EFFECTS

There are a number of simple tricks which you can use successfully with water color.

No. 1: You can use a rubber or gum eraser on the paper to remove any amount of paint, to weaken a certain area, or, most effectively, to indicate rays of light from a lamp or sunbeams coming through a window into a dark room.

No. 2: You can use a razor to create highlights, but you must be a bit careful with this method if the paper is thin. If you are using a thick paper, you will be surprised how strong an accent you can achieve.

No. 3: You can scrape sandpaper across the surface of the color to simulate such effects as rays of light, texture on a field, or rough stone. Of course, different grades of sandpaper will produce different effects.

No. 4: You can produce a speckled appearance by means of a wax resist. Rub a piece of ordinary paraffin or a wax candle lightly over the surface of rough paper. It will stick only to the raised portions of the paper and prevent them from absorbing color when you apply it. This process has many applications. You can use it on white paper or you can put one color on first, then wax and follow with a second color. This will produce a kind of two-toned appearance.

No. 5: Another effect is produced by scratching the surface of the paper with a needle, the point of a compass, the point of a penknife blade, or some similar instrument. Use this technique for accentuating such things as rough, dry grass in a hayfield or light striking a railing.

No. 6: Use rubber cement or latex to retain a white area when you are making a strong-toned wash. Sometimes it is difficult to guide the wash around an intricate shape. Apply the latex with a knife blade or brush and allow to set for 5 or 10 minutes. Now you can wash the color right over not only the paper but also the latex itself. After the wash is dry remove the latex with a gum or rubber eraser, exposing the pure white paper underneath. You can use this device with dramatic effect in night scenes where you want some very bright highlights in the foreground, as you might in painting a fair or a circus. Use it, too, for glazing streaks on a window, or for an immediate contrast of dark and light tones which would be difficult to obtain by normal methods.

Water color is essentially a strong, bright method of painting which succeeds best if it is done directly and kept broad in treatment. Correction is nearly impossible to achieve, but if you want to attempt it, use a brush with lots of clean water and softly scrub the area to be changed with a circular motion. You might also try a gentle application of sandpaper. Unless the mistake is a glaring one, however, it is generally best to leave it.

Always remember that to achieve the sparkle and purity which make watercolors so delightful it is essential to keep your brush as clean as possible all the time. Always have a large quantity of clean water on hand. If you go out-of-doors to paint from nature be sure to take plenty of water with you.

PAINTING IN OIL

After you have explored some of the possibilities of water color, you will undoubtedly wish to try oils. No other way of painting can give quite the richness and the range in color, tone and effect that oils produce. Perhaps that is why the majority of great pictures of past and present have been painted in this medium. You may even wish to start with oil painting before trying other methods.

Oil paint lends itself to a great variety of uses. For example, you can paint it on thinly, almost like water color, diluting the pigments with turpentine. You can paint in the standard method, using bristle brushes to spread fairly thick layers of paint, or using both hair and bristle brushes for a combination of effects. You can create pictures using only little trowel-like palette knives. Like many contemporary artists, you can use thick ridges of paint, called impasto, to achieve various textures. With oil paint you can use almost any type of brushwork you wish.

BUYING COLORS

When you purchase your oil paints, you can either buy a ready-filled box or choose your own colors. As with other methods of painting, it is the best policy to start with as few colors as possible. Many of the finest artists of the past worked with a very limited palette. If you buy two or three dozen different colors, the chances are that you will buy some which will not work satisfactorily together or, even worse, may be harmful to each other, causing darkening, cracking or some other form of discoloration. Second, you will have far more colors than you can quickly master.

The following pigments will serve you well for a long time and are quite capable of producing all the different effects which you may desire: cadmium yellow, yellow ochre, cadmium red, sienna, alizarin crimson, ultramarine, viridian and raw umber. Besides these you will need a large tube of white, preferably titanium. This is a satisfactory, powerful clean white which is non-poisonous, covers well and is a good mixer.

If you are buying loose tubes, it is economical to buy them as large as possible, because they are cheaper that way. Also, it will tend to encourage you to paint thickly and get the most from this exciting medium.

Tube colors, while convenient, can of course still be wasteful if left on the palette because they lose their adhesive power. Remember that painting media are best when simple and that the more substances introduced into the paint, the more the danger of unsatisfactory reaction. The same media should be used throughout a painting, in all of its paint layers. By mixing your own oil colors you have the assurance that no stabilizers, thickeners or adulterants have been added.

MIXING YOUR OWN COLORS

Artists' oil colors are a mixture of dry colored powder (pigment) and linseed oil. You have to use the proper amount of linseed oil in order to give the colors the best workable consistency, and the appearance you want. (The linseed oil also contributes to the adhesion between the paint layers.) A painter can mix his own colors, not only for the sake of economy, but to acquire experience and to become aware of materials. In addition, creating your own color mixtures will give your work a charm that is often lacking when you use manufactured, already-mixed tube colors.

With experience you will come to realize that each color mixed with linseed oil requires a different percentage of oil. Dense colors, such as white, require the least amounts of oil, while colors like raw sienna and ivory black require much more.

Oil has to be added to the powdered pigment very gradually. Do not *pour* oil on the color. Use a low, glass custard cup, and stir the mixture thoroughly with a spatula or palette knife. If the color is too thin, add more dry pigment. The mixture should not be either watery or too thick, but must allow free brush strokes to be handled easily. The final consistency should be that of paste or whipped cream. Linseed oil color dries the hardest and most thoroughly and is the least susceptible to cracking. Maximum pigment should be combined with minimum linseed oil.

The pigment of course is of paramount importance and must be of the best quality. The linseed oil should be the stand oil or boiled linseed oil available in art supply shops, rather than the raw variety.

Be sure you store your jars of powder in a dry place. The colors you mix can be protected from the effects of the atmosphere by making lids of aluminum foil for the cups. If you have mixed more pigment than is required for the session, you can store the cups, tightly covered.

The disadvantages of factory-mixed tube colors are that (1) some are too finely ground, (2) they often contain slow-drying oils to keep them in saleable condition, or (3) they contain other substances (fillers or adulterants) which are detrimental to the eventual preservation of the artist's work, and (4) they contain an overabundance of binding media.

PALETTES, BRUSHES, AND GROUNDS

There are different kinds of palettes: wood, paper, glass. They come in brown, silver-grey, white, transparent. The brown is the least desirable since one is forced to translate color values from a brown palette to a white or grey canvas ground. A practical inexpensive palette is the pad palette, made of white non-porous paper which is disposable.

The glass palette is best if you have a definite and permanent place to work, such as your own studio, but is not for outdoor work. When the colors are placed on this glass (ideally against a neutral background) there is no interference at all. Another advantage of the glass palette over the wooden or paper one is that the old dried painting mixtures can eventually be neatly taken off with a scraper, leaving a perfectly clean glass with which to begin a new painting session. Also because it has a permanent resting place, it leaves the left hand unencumbered for wiping off brushes.

The oil painter's brushes should be made of a fine white bristle; as his color is ordinarily stiff, the softer brushes used in water coloring are unsuitable for controlling the paint. The brushes are round, flat and filbert, the latter being a cross between a flat and a round, a carefully shaped brush, which can give great delicacy of stroke. One other type can be included for oil painting where fine detail is required; that is a sable rigger.

After you have finished painting, rinse your brushes thoroughly two or three times in turpentine and then in lukewarm water. Soak them well and scrub them around on the palm of your hand until all traces of pigment are removed. If oil paint hardens at the base of the bristles where they enter the metal ferrule, the brushes will lose their elasticity and their color-carrying capacity, and will very soon be quite useless for painting.

When you visit your art dealer's you may see some small trowel-like knives. These are painting knives. After you have begun to master the manipulation of paint with a brush, buy one or two of these

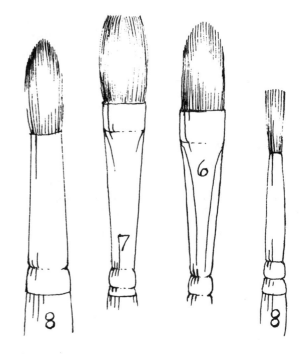

BRUSHES: The four basic types used for oil painting. Clean them thoroughly after each painting session or they will soon deteriorate to the point where they are useless.

knives and attempt painting with them. It can be quite a useful exercise in directness.

The cheapest ground is an oil-painting paper with a canvas-like texture which has been sized to reduce the degree of absorption and primed with some form of white undercoat. This is perfectly suitable for the beginner and you can obtain most of the effects of real canvas. The sheets come in pads. Before you paint, stretch them, stick them down with masking tape on a piece of cardboard, or at least pin them to a drawing board.

Somewhat more expensive are canvas boards. These are thick sheets of cardboard on which thin canvases have been glued. In many ways they resemble the final stretched canvas which most painters use. They have the same tooth and grip as a real canvas, and make excellent painting grounds.

The professional painter generally uses a real canvas tightened across a frame which is called a stretcher. The corners of the stretcher have little wedges to keep the canvas taut. You can either buy stretched canvases ready-made or make your own. This is undoubtedly the most pleasant material on which to paint, but you may find it too expensive.

Besides the grounds that you can buy, there are several that you can prepare for yourself. The simplest of these is a piece of thick cardboard covered with several coats of acrylic gesso (see page 194). You can apply the same treatment to a piece of three-ply wood or to hardboard. Which side you use, the rough or the smooth, is a personal choice, but it is advisable to start on the smooth side. The mechanical reverse patterning on the rough side tends to absorb a great deal of color, making the application of the paint difficult.

For your first work, oil-painting papers will be quite satisfactory. They will enable you to get most of the effects which are possible on a canvas board or stretched canvas. Since pads of these papers are inexpensive, you can use them freely. Later, you will graduate to canvas on board and eventually to stretched canvas on a wooden frame.

Besides colors, brushes, palette and ground, you will need a small bottle of either linseed oil or copal oil medium for diluting colors; a bottle of turpentine for washing the brushes and palette at the end of the day; a bundle of rags and, lastly, an easel. True, you can arrange a makeshift easel indoors by putting a box on the table, against which to lean your canvas board, or out-of-doors, by propping your board against the trunk of a fallen tree, a branch, a wall or a gate. But as soon as you can, get some form of easel for yourself. For then you can go to work wherever you want. An easel can be adjusted and will hold your canvas steady.

BEGIN WITH A STILL LIFE

For oil painting, it is wisest to start with an indoor subject. As we have seen, landscape painting poses the problem of changing light and its effect on color. Since oils are not particularly fluid, managing them will take a great deal of concentration. For a while you will have to give more effort to manipulating the paint than to capturing your subject dramatically.

Before you start any serious painting, spend some time experimenting with your various brushes and also with all your different colors. Try out different mixes to see what they will produce, so that, when you begin to paint, you will quickly be able to get the particular tones and tints you are seeking.

As an elementary exercise which will give you practice in composition, in mixing colors, in using color to create a sense of volume, and in manipulating the paint, try painting a simple still life made up of household objects with basic geometric shapes, such as an apple, a banana, and a blue vase of a triangular shape, using only the three primary colors.

Using cadmium red, cadmium yellow, and ultramarine blue, place the colors on the palette in this order: red, yellow, blue. Keep each color mound perfectly pure and clear. Keep some rags or a roll of paper towels nearby for wiping brushes clean of color and oil. This is an important convenience, and helps to avoid muddying up the colors.

Besides the three primary colors, you will need to add another container with thoroughly mixed white. Use three medium-size flat brushes, one for each color.

When you have set up your group, you are ready to begin painting. Your paper, prepared board, or canvas board is in place on the easel, or leaning against a box on the table.

Take your palette in your hand, or stand close to your sheet of glass on the table. In your left hand hold your spare brushes and your rag. Stand back from your model; look at it carefully and for quite a long time until you feel the basic shapes of the composition which you have arranged imprinted on your mind. With your brush well moistened with turpentine, mix up a thin, diluted neutral grey, almost of watercolor consistency. Go right ahead and draw the principal shapes in boldly.

At this stage any attempt to capture minute details would only worry you and might cause the picture to lose balance.

Many artists and teachers advocate the preparation of a very careful pencil or charcoal underdrawing, correct in every detail, before applying any oil. This may have advantages, but it also has disadvantages. For instance, if you draw with charcoal, you will have to "fix" it before you paint; otherwise, it will mix with the colors. Second, careful drawing does tend to constrict the painting that will follow. To be successful, oil painting must be direct.

After you have sketched in the brush drawing, swiftly brush in the principal areas with color slightly diluted with turpentine. Painting with color that is diluted in this way rather than with a heavy oil, such as linseed, copal or poppy, is said to be "lean," and the rule is to paint "fat over lean." The reason is that if you put two layers of thick oil color one upon the other, they are likely to dry at different speeds, thus causing eventual severe cracking. So dilute your underpainting with turpentine and brush it in quickly. It will dry in a short period of time, and you can begin overpainting.

Underpainting in this manner serves, too, to

point up any error of judgment in the placement of shapes and objects at the drawing stage. Often when the picture is partially colored, such errors will stand out. If a correction is needed now—or at the earlier drawing stage—it is very simple to moisten a corner of your rag with turpentine and to rub out the undesired parts.

First work at your background. Whatever the method of painting you are using, it is always the wisest course to paint the distances first, gradually working forward. Use white mixed separately on your palette with the three primaries. This will result in a neutral grey which will set off the colors of the still life.

Since you have grouped the three objects in such a way that they form a pleasing composition, the objects are not isolated and therefore touch each other or overlap. In filling in the shapes, where the yellow overlaps the red circle, remember that the two colors will become orange; and where the red circle touches the blue triangle the mixture will become purplish. (To some extent you will want to maintain and use this effect since colors do cast reflections on one another.) Since you are painting one color on top of another while still wet, wipe off your brushes carefully each time before you pick up new paint.

In order to give roundness to the apple, the curves which go to the back must be darkened. So, in shaping the apple you darken the receding sides. You must do this at the edges of the object, to create the impression that the object has another side behind. Use a little yellow and blue, which will darken the dominant red. Pick up a bit of each color with the tip of the brush for that color, apply the paint, then wipe the brush off, as you cannot help picking up some of the wet paint beneath in overpainting.

Next, in order to show that the banana has a cylindrical dimension, you shape it by adding a bit of red and blue to the dominant yellow. Shape the vase by adding a bit of yellow and red to the dominant blue as the vase recedes and curves around to the back.

This neutralizing of the dominant color by adding a bit of the other two primaries (complementaries when mixed) is a simple way of giving the object the illusion of roundness, of receding to the back, of being further away in the visual sense. It creates an illusion of form, by calling attention to distance or space occupied by form.

Paint the foreground glowing white. Add to the brush, after you pick up the white pigment, just the smallest amount of yellow by touching it to the yellow mound. This will spark the white and bring it forward. To that part of the table which is behind the object, add a small amount of blue.

While applying the true colors, watch for tone. As pointed out on page 165, tone is in many ways more important than color. To get the relationships correct, look at your painting with half-closed eyes.

Finally, at this stage, when your tones and colors presumably are correct, you can concentrate on trying to achieve the different textures of the various objects you are painting.

You should be able to complete a still life in a couple of sittings. On the first day, try to finish the underpainting and the rough drawing. Then on the second day your picture will be dry, and you can apply your thick paint. Work at getting your tone values correct and put in the texture, highlights and the final little flicks of color which will bring a picture to life.

PROCEED TO LANDSCAPE

After you have painted two or three still lifes or flower pieces indoors, you can proceed with landscape. Use the technical hints you have learned for brushwork and mixing colors.

Because of the ever-changing light, there is no stable form in landscape painting. There can only be a temporary effect. It is therefore best to come out-of-doors and paint at the same time each day or else paint out-of-doors on rather grey days.

Before you start to paint, however, concentrate on the scene until you can see it with your eyes closed. Study the trees, their line, their color, their texture, their structure. Study the patterns in the trees and rocks and buildings, the areas of light and dark, the composition, the relationship of one to another.

After close observation and concentrated attention to light and dark masses, you decide on the color, line and form, the structural and compositional elements with which you will organize your painting. Make several preliminary sketches, experimenting with different compositions. You can begin by planning your composition so that both forms and colors work together to unify. You select and arrange, you simplify and give your impression or interpretation. Remember that you should not try to imitate, but to present essentials.

It is also a good idea to take written notes or mark up your sketch, putting in semi-permanent form your observations of colors and masses and darks and lights. Begin systematically with the dark

COMPOSING THE LANDSCAPE: When making the preliminary sketches for your painting, make an effort to select and rearrange elements of the landscape in such a way that they form a pleasing composition and convey your feelings about the scene before you as well. Your purpose is not to imitate, but to create from nature.

and light masses, then the colors, the gradations, etc. Writing down serves another purpose—it forces your attention and concentration on the points that change as the sun moves. It also enables you to carry on your work indoors after the light has failed or changed to the extent that you cannot continue to work from nature.

You are already acquainted with the two kinds of harmonies—analogous and complementary. These are the keys which you will use to determine your color scheme. Your aim is to choose and proportion your colors so that they can be distributed pleasingly, with one color combination or group of colors dominating.

Line as such, of course, is subordinate to mass, to the light and dark of color. In a landscape, the masses are the trees, the clouds, the distant hills. There will be large masses and small masses, light and dark masses, all relative in color value. Both line and mass can serve a painter well—one may be used to dominate the other, but one need not exclude the other.

In a landscape in which you want to convey a feeling of rest and calm, use horizontal lines rather than diagonals or broken lines. However, if you are depicting a stormy scene, use scattered, whirling waving lines to express tree movement caused by wind, etc.

Lines, like color, can through their character express feeling. They can, like color, also represent objects. Lines and color are suggestive, they create impressions: continuity, flow, direction, movement, dignity, strength, as well as shape, form and structure.

When you have arrived at a satisfactory composition and taken sufficient notes, you may begin to set up your palette. Arrange the colors in an orderly sequence from warm to cold and from light to dark, with your white placed in the most convenient place since it is used most often. The following limited, but perfectly adequate selection of colors is suggested: white, raw umber, cadmium red, cadmium yellow, ultramarine, viridian.

Before you begin to paint, mix *generous* quantities of color in approximately correct tones. Then, using a medium-sized bristle brush or some charcoal, proceed to draw in roughly the main masses of the composition. This accomplished, take a larger brush, and using colors of a fairly thin consistency, fill in the main masses. Don't worry about achieving exact hues or nuances, but about obtaining the proper relative values between the masses. The accompanying diagrams illustrate what these values might be on a typical sunny day.

You may notice at this point that a composition which worked well as an outline needs to be re-adjusted now that the masses have been colored in. Redistribution of these masses should be an easy matter at this stage.

You should now have a poster-like, colored design made up of four or five flat tones of unequal weight and value—for example, the blue of the sky, the darker violet or blue green of the mountains, the still darker green of the trees, and the semi-light, yellower greens of the ground. You should strive to maintain this simplicity while you are adding the local color, the gradations of form, and the final details. Remember throughout to keep your brushes and colors clean.

You can create the roundness or third dimension of various objects by broad use of complementary colors, also by the direction of your brush strokes, as you did in the still life.

The following will help you to understand how to add local color, highlight and shadow to your painting.

THE REFLECTION OF COLORS

Daylight is merely diffused sunlight. The sky is blue because fine particles of dust and smoke in the atmosphere decompose the sunlight and scatter its violet, blue and green rays. The clouds are white because they are composed of moisture-laden particles which reflect sunlight as white light. The air is densest closest to the earth, and the bluest part of the sky will be directly overhead (unless the sun is burning through it).

A landscape is always tinged with the colors of the sky, sun and clouds. Just as the trees, foliage, and rocks will take on yellowness, so will they take on blueness as the amount and direction of sunlight changes.

THE PALETTE

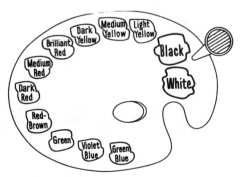

Sky

Mountains

Trees

Ground

LIGHT AND DARK VALUES: Before you concern yourself with achieving exact nuances of local color, be certain you have established the proper relative values between the elements in the landscape. The chart at the top illustrates the range of values which might prevail on a typical sunny day; the middle diagram shows how this chart can be applied to an actual landscape; the bottom diagram demonstrates that it is possible to maintain these relative values when you begin adding modelling to your painting.

Blueness is especially apparent on a white surface. A shadow on a white surface has a blue character; on a red surface a shadow takes on a purplish character. The color of shadows depends upon the color of the sky, and the position of the sun. The winter sky reflecting on snow will make shadows look violet blue because the sky is blue. The snow may reflect colors from the sky, the clouds and the sun— all three—varying from pale blue to violet to purple.

Most water has its own color—brown, aquamarine, blue, blackish, gold yellow, orange—depending not only upon its mineral and vegetable content, but its shallowness or depth. Reflections on sand will be governed not only by the quality of the sun, the clouds and the sky, but also by the water near it. There is a constant interplay of colors near the sea, a splashing of one color on to another.

"A landscape is always dominated by the sky," any landscape artist will tell you. Everything under it shows its influence. In painting your landscapes become familiar with the relationships of colors, the way they mingle, the way one color reflects upon the others, the special kind of light above, next to, and around an object which will influence and affect its own color. And, of course, note how each color contributes some of itself to the color alongside.

THE EFFECT OF DISTANCE ON COLOR

Even though you may already understand linear and aerial perspective, you will now have to take into consideration the effect that distance has on color value.

You know, of course, that as distance increases, size decreases. But colors and their values are also modified by perspective. The decrease in size of objects as they recede into the distance also makes their color less vivid. Objects have practically no color at a distant vanishing point. Make sure that your first sketches follow the principles of linear perspective as to parallel lines reaching a vanishing point.

How does aerial perspective, the result of the atmosphere, affect color? It causes objects to change gradually as they recede, to take on a haziness, a single tone, a greyness or blueness. Where particles of dust and water are suspended in air, it breaks up the violet and blue light waves and makes distant mountains appear blue, for example. The use of cooler colors, together with a decrease in size, will create an illusion of depth and distance.

A final word of advice: You should strive, above all, to achieve a "landscape sense," the ability to

LANDSCAPE IN ART: Examine this painting, keeping in mind the things you have learned about composition, aerial perspective, and the effect of light on relative color values.

capture the "*float* of a cloud," the *weight* and *solid* massive form of the ground, the growth and reach of the trees, each a graceful personal thing. *This* is what will bring your painting to life. A sense of color, line, and form is not enough.

VARNISHING AN OIL PAINTING

Leave your completed picture to dry leaning against a wall face inward so that dust won't fall on the sticky paint. When it is "skin-dry," the surface of the paint dry to the touch, it is safe to frame it and hang it. At this stage don't attempt to varnish the surface even though it appears dry to the touch, for the oil in the thickest areas will not have hardened completely. An oil painting should not be varnished for at least nine months; it is better to leave it for a whole year. At that time, dust it and wipe it with a swab of absorbent cotton dipped in turpentine. Varnish it on a warm, dry day either with a mastic, damar, or better still one of the new clear synthetic varnishes.

If for some reason such as an exhibition or some other special event, you wish to brighten up your picture before it has been varnished, you can lightly brush it with "retouching varnish." This is a weak solution of resin which will brighten up the colors, but will not put an impervious seal over them which would prevent the oils from drying out properly. Retouching varnish or medium is also useful if you begin a picture and have to leave it for a few days; when you come back to the painting, brush this varnish over the areas which have dried out in an unpleasantly flat manner.

PAINTING IN ACRYLICS

The creative possibilities of this medium defy the imagination. Acrylic, more properly referred to as acrylic polymer emulsion, is a relatively new, water-soluble plastic medium. Created and perfected sometime after World War II, it has become increasingly popular since the early 1960's, when contemporary artists and students began to discover its unique and highly flexible qualities.

The brilliance of acrylic color is much greater than that of oil, and it can dry in as little as twenty minutes, making it possible to overpaint almost immediately, instead of having to wait for hours or even weeks. This medium may be thinned with water, but becomes resistant to water when dry. In addition, it is adaptable to any painting technique imaginable. All these qualities make acrylics the ideal medium for the beginning or weekend painter. If you begin by working with it, you may never feel the desire to work with anything else.

A great deal of confusion exists, even among professional artists, as to what constitutes an acrylic medium. Put simply, the answer is, any of the plastic, water-based paints using acrylic as a binder to hold the pigments together.

ACRYLIC MEDIA

There are several different acrylic substances available which can be mixed with pigments or combined in innumerable ways with one another to enable you to work in a wide range of techniques, from the traditional techniques of water-color and oil painting to the more contemporary techniques of staining canvas with transparent colors and of building collages. The following is a brief description of the characteristics of some of these different media and some of the ways in which they are used.

BASE MEDIUM: This is a milky white liquid which can be used by itself or used as a vehicle in which to grind pigments. It can also be used as a thinner for the ready-mixed acrylic colors which are available in jars or tubes, or it can be mixed with acrylic colors to make transparent glazes. It can be combined with other acrylic media to produce many varied textures, and can serve as an adhesive for collage materials as well. The most remarkable thing about the base medium is its quick-drying quality. (Depending upon the consistency of the paint, it can take anywhere from twenty minutes to several hours to dry.) Finally, when applied to a finished painting, the base medium can serve as a varnish and protective coating. It is obtainable in a gloss or matt finish. In addition to all these versatile characteristics, the base medium is non-flammable and will not irritate the skin. For this reason, acrylic is an ideal medium for use by children as well as adults.

GEL MEDIUM: This is a transparent acrylic medium, with a viscous or sticky, paste-like consistency. It is used most frequently as an additive to thicken acrylic paint and slow down its drying process, in order to allow the artist to work longer and at a more leisurely pace. It is also used under, in, and over, other acrylic substances to create three-dimensional or transparent, stained-glass effects. Like the base medium, it can also be used as an adhesive in doing collage.

MODELLING PASTE: Acrylic modelling paste is pigmented with finely ground marble dust. It dries and hardens rapidly, becoming resilient and durable. It can be shaped, modelled, and textured while still wet, and then carved, cut, and sanded when dry. It can also be used to build three-dimensional forms and to produce heavy impastos.

GESSO: Gesso (pronounced jesso) is a sizing and priming agent applied to the painting surface in order to provide a smooth, level, white ground. Traditionally gesso has been composed of plaster of Paris and glue, but since it is a time-consuming chore to mix this sort of gesso and then wait several days for it to dry, most artists now prefer to use acrylic gesso which will dry in less than an hour. It has an intense whiteness that will not discolor with time, but if you prefer a slightly toned ground, it can be tinted with acrylic color before being applied. Acrylic gesso can be applied to virtually any surface, including old used canvases or other painted surfaces, after they have been sanded to remove the gloss of the existing paint. Used in this way, gesso can provide considerable savings for the weekend painter or student.

Each acrylic manufacturer uses the same binder in all its products from gesso to varnishes. Therefore, any combination of acrylic materials of a specific brand name can be made without weakening the structure of the paint film.

ACRYLIC COLORS

As has already been mentioned, the acrylic base medium will not mix successfully with certain traditional pigments. There are, however, other pigments that can be used as substitutes, which are quite permanent and reliable. They can be purchased in powder form and mixed with the acrylic base medium or they are also available in the ready-to-use jars or tubes. The following is a partial list of acrylic colors that are made by one manufacturer. The same colors can be made transparent or opaque depending upon which acrylic substances you mix with them.

YELLOW	Yellow light, Hansa
	Yellow medium, azo
	Yellow orange, azo
	Cadmium yellow light
	Cadmium yellow medium
	Yellow oxide
ORANGE	Cadmium orange
RED	Indo orange red
	Napthol ITR red light
	Napthol ITR crimson
	Quinacridone red
	Cadmium red light
	Cadmium red medium
	Red oxide
BLUE	Cerulean blue
	Phthalocyanine blue
	Ultramarine blue
	Cobalt blue
GREEN	Hooker's green
	Light green oxide
	Chromium oxide green
	Phthalocyanine green
PURPLE	Quinacridone violet
	Dioxazine purple
BROWN	Burnt umber
	Burnt sienna
	Raw sienna
	Raw umber
BLACK	Mars black

The tube color has a paste-like consistency as well as handling qualities similar to those of oil color. When it dries, it looks much as it did when first applied; it has an even, low sheen that adds to the brilliance of the color. It also remains wet much longer than the jar color and is easier to handle on the palette.

The jar color has a liquid consistency that facilitates rapid handling. This type of color is particularly well adapted to detail line work and covering large areas with smooth color. It also dries more quickly than the tube color.

PALETTES, BRUSHES AND GROUNDS

Depending upon the consistency of the paint you choose to mix, you may use brushes of any variety with acrylics: standard bristle, sabeline, high-grade ox hair, red sable, nylon, or large house-paint brushes. You may also want to use a palette knife and other similar tools when applying heavy impastos.

It is a good idea to wet your brush in water before dipping it into the acrylic medium and to keep the brush wet while working. Be careful not to allow the medium to dry on the brush. It is preferable to use more than one brush, and to keep both constantly wet. If the medium dries on the brush, a remover should be used to clean it. Wet brushes can be cleaned with soap and water.

Any smooth, non-absorbent surface could provide an acrylic palette. A sheet of glass or plexiglass would be excellent. In view of the rapid-drying, waterproof, and highly-adhesive properties of acrylics, the conventional method of laying out colors on a palette may not be the best alternative. An arrangement of cups, ice-cube trays, jars, or tin-foil muffin cups might be more useful. The use of small, disposable, and easily-cleaned containers saves waste and facilitates storage of the paint. Individual containers can be covered to prevent the color from drying out, and stored away between painting sessions. A thin skin may form on the top of the colors, but the paint underneath will remain fresh and usable for some time.

If you prefer to set up your palette in the more conventional way on a flat surface, set out only as much paint as you anticipate using. Remember that once it has dried out completely it is worthless. Colors that have thickened but are not dry can be made workable by adding water or the base medium. But colors that have become thoroughly dry cannot be reworked or made fluid again.

A palette that has not completely dried can be cleaned with soap and water. It is sometimes helpful first to soak it in water for about an hour, or to leave a soaking-wet newspaper on it overnight.

Acrylic materials adhere to almost any ground or surface, including: canvas, linen or cotton; rag linen paper and cardboard; gesso panels; plaster; cement; *untempered* Masonite wall board; textiles, preferably linen; acetate; tile; wood; illustration board; masonry; textiles; mortar; or any non-oily or non-greasy surface.

Acrylic media are water-thinned and water-compatible, but when using water to thin acrylics, do so with moderation. Overly-thinned paint will lose body to the point where a coherent film cannot be produced.

VARNISHING AN ACRYLIC PAINTING

An acrylic painting can be washed with water and does not have to have a final varnish. However, to provide a protective surface which will absorb physical wear and protect thin glazes, or to adjust the degree of surface gloss, the base medium can be used in the gloss or matt variety as a final varnish.

This may be done as soon as the painting is completely dry. First thin the varnish with a *small* amount of water. Then, with a soft hair brush, apply the varnish in a continuous film from one side of the painting to the other. A partially dried varnish should not be retouched. If it is necessary to go over the painting, wait until it is completely dried. The wet varnish gives a cloudy appearance which will disappear when it dries. The varnished surface, like the painting itself, can be cleaned with soap and water.

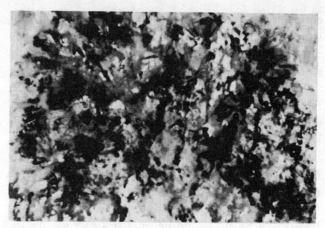

ACRYLIC PAINTING, with wax resist, bleach and dye.

PAINTING IN GOUACHE

The handling qualities of gouache make it one of the easiest media in which to work. It has been found to be particularly adaptable to the purposes of commercial art and for this reason it is sometimes referred to as "poster color." It is also occasionally called "show card color" and "opaque water color." However, it is a good medium for weekend painters to experiment with.

It is a water-based medium, the components of which are nearly identical to those of water color, with the exception of some additional ingredients to give it an opaque quality rather than the transparent quality of water color. As a result, in working with gouache, the texture you achieve will depend on the consistency of the paint you mix rather than, as in water color, on the quality of the paper. Depending upon the amount of water and the quality of white gouache used, the effects of this medium can range from those of a translucent water color to an oil painting done in heavy impasto.

MATERIALS

The materials you need will not necessarily run into great additional expense. To start with, you can use ordinary water colors with one of the thick opaque whites which are available. If you want to supplement these colors, you can buy gouache colors in cakes, tubes or jars. If you decide to buy the latter, remember to avoid sticking the brush in the jar, as this can alter the color or dilute the thickness of the paint. Instead transfer the color from the jar to the mixing palette with a tool such as a palette knife. If the paint hardens in the jar, it can be softened by adding a small amount of *boiled, not boiling* water. The color in tubes tends to stay moist longer, but once it does dry out there is no remedy for it.

Unless you are working with gouache in a heavy

consistency, the best brushes to use are sable, or watercolor brushes. There are also times when you may want to paint with a palette knife or a spatula to achieve certain effects.

You can use the same papers used for watercolor, from inexpensive coarse ones to art cover papers, which come in bright colors, often an effective background for this medium. Generally though, when using gouache, the paper should be fairly heavy, matt finish, sufficiently absorbent, and of medium grain. A very smooth grain, such as Bristol board, will not do, since it repels water. But poster board, kid finish, would be fine. In other words, the thicker the paper, the better.

As a palette you may use a muffin tin, a piece of glass, palette cups of metal or porcelain, saucers, or anything which will hold a large amount of color. The essence of this type of painting is the use of plenty of paint. Mix large quantitites, because if you run out of a color you will never be able to match it again.

WORKING IN GOUACHE

You can control vividness of color over a great range by regulating the amount of opaque white you mix with a pure color. To lighten a color, add white, *never water*. In mixing colors, such as red and yellow to make orange, always mix them on the palette, never directly on the paper as you could do with oil paints or water colors. Add small amounts of each color to your palette, testing until the desired shade is obtained. Add water only to thin the paint, never to lighten the color. Avoid combining too many colors at one time, or the effect will be muddy. If the colors "over-puddle" they will lose their bright, vigorous tints and become drab.

Then, when you have a sufficient quantity of the desired color, the desired consistency, try it out with the brush on a piece of paper. Only then begin to paint with it. Although this medium can be used in many different consistencies, the one recommended for the use of weekend artists is relatively thick, rather like that of heavy cream.

Gouache shares with the other water-base paints the quick drying characteristics which help them to attain freshness and spontaneity. The opaqueness of the pigment also permits you to work over previous layers of paint when dry, adding and changing details easily. For this reason many people find it easier to work with than water colors.

These fast-drying characteristics, while they are very helpful in some respects, are a drawback in others. For example, you can never "patch" a tone, since it will unavoidably remain a patch. You must instead wait for the entire area to dry and then repaint it. At the same time if you need to cover a large area in one tone, as for a background, you must work quickly, because if one part of the area dries before you are finished covering it, you will not be able to go back and finish or retouch it without creating a patched effect. Be sure to prepare a sufficient quantity of color and always *work wet* to achieve an evenness of tone.

Almost any gouache color, however light and clear it may be, can completely block out a darker color underneath. Because of this quality it is generally recommended that you work from *light to dark*, rather than from dark to light as you did with water colors.

This same quality also permits freedom of execution and modifications during and after execution.

There are innumerable ways in which gouache can be used, by itself, and in combination with other media. You might try, for example, slightly strengthening a normal water color by mixing opaque white with other colors to achieve darker and richer tones. At first you can attempt slight accents of strength here and there. Later you can use these intense colors on buildings, or trees. You will be surprised at how vividly they stand out against the more limpid tones of the water color.

VARNISHING A GOUACHE PAINTING

Finally, a word about varnishes and fixatives: These are not always useful with gouache. In fact at times they are dangerous: they tend to "show up" the mistakes made during execution which would have disappeared if the painting had been allowed to dry by itself. It is especially wise to avoid them rigorously if you have used burnt sienna, a color that "bleeds" or runs when varnish is applied on top of it.

If you apply varnish, do so with a broad, flat brush, uniformly, rapidly and softly. You can also varnish with wax: simply rub a piece of candlewax lightly over the surface.

The best way to apply fixative is with an atomizer or spray can. This a fairly expensive technique, but you have only to push a button and the fixative comes out in vaporized form. Avoid allowing an excessive quantity to fall on the painting: it could cause circular stains. The best plan is to tilt the painting vertically and spray it from a distance in a consistency resembling light rain.

PHOTOGRAPHY

Taking pictures is fun—that is why photography has become one of the most popular hobbies in the world today.

It's quite likely you already know how to take photographs, but the purpose of this section is to teach you more about what makes a good photograph, and thereby increase your enjoyment and appreciation of photography as an art.

Here you will learn all the fundamental photography techniques, how to recognize good picture material, how to compose it in your viewfinder, how to photograph it under less than ideal conditions, and finally, how to make your own prints. Most important, you will learn how to make a statement or convey an emotion through your photographs. There is enough technical information here to get you started and this should inspire you to go on to advanced amateur photography or even make a career of this hobby.

LET THERE BE LIGHT!

Photography begins with a source of *light* (either natural or artificial) which illuminates a *subject*. The subject, in turn, reflects some of the light. How much it reflects depends upon:

1. The strength of the light source and the angle at which its rays fall upon the subject.

2. The size, color, and shape of the subject itself.

A white fence, for example, reflects *direct* sunlight more strongly than it reflects either slanting sunlight, or the weak light of a cloudy day. Moreover, since the fence is large, white, and presents a flat reflecting surface, it naturally reflects more light than would a small green shrub. Water, snow, sand, or pavement likewise reflects more light than dark buildings, lawns, or heavy forests.

If light can be described as being the first key to photography, the second key is a camera, a device to allow just the right amount of reflected light to register on a piece of material capable of producing an image.

HOW A CAMERA WORKS

Essentially, a camera is a dark box having a hole in one end covered by a glass *lens*. Either inside the lens, or in back of it is a shielding device called a *shutter*. At the back of the box is a piece of light-sensitive material (film) on which images can be recorded.

The purpose of the shutter is, first of all, to keep the inside of the box in pitch darkness so that the film will not be *fogged* (spoiled) by too much light. The only time the shutter is open is when an *exposure* is being made.

This is what happens when the lever on the outside of the camera is released for making an instantaneous exposure:

1. The *shutter* opens to permit light to enter the camera.

2. Rays of light reflected by the subject pass through the *lens* and through a circular opening called a *diaphragm* on their way to the film.

3. The shutter closes automatically.

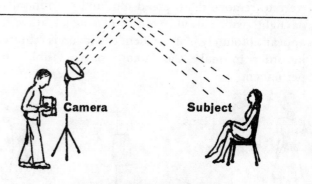

How bounce light works

Condensed from "Short Cut to Photography" by Godfrey Frankel, © 1961, 1954 by Sterling Publishing Co., Inc., New York, and revised especially for this volume by the author.

POISED JUST RIGHT: The photographer had interesting subject matter to start with in this picture that won the grand prize in the National High School Photographic Contest for Jane Lankford of Oakland, California.

In the fraction of a second that elapses between the opening and closing of the shutter, the "working heart" of the camera does its job. The shutter controls "how long" the light will be permitted to enter the camera. The diaphragm opening controls "how much" light will be allowed to enter during the given interval of time. The lens bends the rays of light so that they converge to produce images on the light-sensitive emulsion of the film. If you were to remove the exposed film and examine it in daylight (which would ruin it, of course), it would appear absolutely blank. Chemical action is required in order to make the latent images visible and permanent.

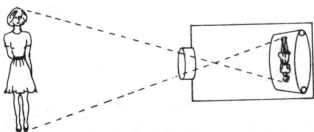

THE THREE MAGIC BATHS

Three very simple baths or solutions, all done in the dark, are required to convert a roll of exposed film into a negative from which black-and-white photographs can be printed.

The first solution is the developer. When a ray of light strikes the film in the camera, it releases an atom of silver from the silver bromide crystals in the film emulsion. When the film is submerged in the developer bath, the silver turns to a black substance, metallic silver, rendering the images on the film visible.

After the developer has acted upon the emulsion for a given length of time at a certain temperature, the film is transferred to a "short-stop" bath containing a weak solution of acetic acid. The purpose of this bath, as its name implies, is to "stop" further development immediately by neutralizing the developer.

After a moment or so in the stop bath, the film goes into a "fixing" bath which dissolves any unaltered silver particles that remain after development. At the same time, the fixing bath (usually a solution called "hypo") removes other chemicals and renders the images permanent. All that remains is to wash the film thoroughly, and dry it.

When you hold a negative to the light, you see images in reverse shades of black, grey, and light or clear areas. In other words, everything that was white in the original subject is dark grey or black in the negative; everything that was jet black in the original subject will appear as either a clear area or a very light tone of grey in the negative. A negative is the reverse of the original scene; therefore to reproduce the original scene as a photograph, you have to reverse the negative. This brings us to the subject of printing.

"Contact prints," the exact size of the negatives, are usually made to help determine what prints you may want to enlarge. This process helps save time when the negatives come out poorly.

HOW CONTACT PRINTS ARE MADE

Photographic printing paper, like film, is sensitive to white light; therefore prints are always made in a darkened room in which the only illumination for most of the printing process comes from an orange-yellow "safelight." Light of this color has no effect upon the paper—that is, it does not "fog" the paper or cause it to turn black in the developing solution as would ordinary white light or daylight.

To make what is known as a "contact print," a negative is simply placed over a sheet of paper which has been coated with a light-sensitive emulsion. The paper, with the negative on top, is generally placed beneath a piece of glass in a frame which holds them both in perfect "contact."

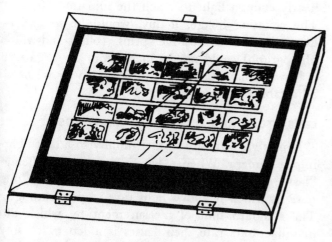

Contact frame

Then a certain amount of white light is allowed to pass through the negative for a calculated length of time. Although the paper still appears blank at this point, the action of the light passing through the negative has, nevertheless, produced a *positive* latent image. In other words, the latent image has again been reversed from that appearing on the negative, and the original subject matter will now appear in shades of black, white, and grey, much as it looked at the time the shutter was snapped.

Contact prints must be developed in this order. First place in short-stop. Second, fix in hypo and then wash. The solutions are identical to those used in developing the original film into negatives.

ENLARGING AND CROPPING

To make a "blow-up" or enlargment of a negative, the negative is placed in a device (enlarger) which projects it through a lens onto a sheet of sensitized paper.

If desirable, the whole negative can be enlarged, but generally only the most interesting portion of the negative is used to fill the sheet of sensitized paper. Sometimes the negative itself is partially "masked" with tape so that only a portion of it can be projected; in other cases, the entire negative is projected, but the sides of the easel holding the enlarging paper flat are adjusted so that the light from only a certain portion of the negative can actually reach the paper.

When only a part of the original negative is printed (or when a portion of the picture has been trimmed off the print), the picture is said to have been "cropped." Cropping can be judged at first in the camera viewfinder, and performed later during enlargement, or after the picture has been developed, washed and dried. It is a very important part of producing a pleasant result.

THE CAMERA AS A TOOL

Remember this always: YOU create the picture; a camera simply records it. In order to use any tool skilfully, however, you must know when and how to make use of the various controls at your command. Thus far we have briefly discussed the way in which various mechanisms (the shutter, diaphragm, lens, etc.) control the amount of light permitted to reach the film. In order to understand the functions of these mechanisms still better, let's compare them with the human eye.

EYE	CAMERA	
Pupil	Lens	Opening through which light rays enter
Iris	Diaphragm	Opening which controls "how much" light can enter during a given interval of time
Eyelid	Shutter	Keeps interior dark when closed; also controls "how long" light can enter during an exposure
Retina	Film	Where light rays record their impressions

THE THREE VARIABLES

In making *any* picture, you must be acquainted with "the three variables" and reckon with them. The variables are:

1. The proper shutter speed to be used.

2. The proper aperture, or diaphragm opening, to be used.

3. The distance between the camera and the subject.

A very simple camera of the "box camera" type restricts these variables automatically. It has what is called a "fixed" shutter speed, a "fixed" diaphragm opening, and a "fixed" focus. In other words, the shutter was pre-set at the factory to operate *only* at a speed of about 1/25th of a second. Similarly, the circular opening in the diaphragm is of a certain size (usually between f/11 and f/16) and nothing can be done to increase or decrease the size of this opening. The focus has also been set at the factory so that all objects 8 feet or more in front of the camera will be recorded with reasonable sharpness on the film.

Better cameras have controls which make it possible to adjust the shutter speed, diaphragm opening, and focus. The better the camera, as a rule, the more mechanical "know how" it takes to operate the controls.

SHUTTER SPEEDS

For making snapshots under satisfactory light conditions, a shutter speed of 1/25th second is fine. That is why simple cameras operate automatically at this speed. If a longer exposure is needed because of very poor light, a box camera must be placed on a tripod or some other firm support so that the shutter can be operated on "T" (Time) or "B" (Bulb). For a Time exposure, the marker on the side of the camera must be placed at "T." When the shutter-release lever is pressed down, the shutter

remains open until the lever is pressed a second time. For a Bulb exposure, the marker is placed at "B." When the shutter-release lever is pressed down, the shutter remains open only so long as the lever is held down. If the lever is released, the shutter closes automatically.

In addition to a "T" and/or "B" arrangement, the shutters on more expensive cameras provide a number of other speeds at which the shutter can be operated. A typical shutter with an adjustable "speed-control," for example, may provide speeds of 1 second, 1/2 sec., 1/5 sec., 1/10 sec., 1/25 sec., 1/50 sec., 1/100 sec., 1/250 sec., and 1/500 sec. Some cameras even have speeds ranging up to 1/1000 sec. or faster.

Naturally there are valid reasons why so many different speeds have been built into the better shutters. A speed of 1/25 second is the slowest that can be used when a camera is being hand-held, and even then the resulting picture is likely to have images which appear slightly blurred from camera-movement. At a speed of 1/50 sec. to 1/100 sec., the danger of camera-movement blurring the images is considerably less, but if the *subject* is moving, the image may still appear blurred. A shutter speed of 1/100 second, for example, definitely wouldn't stop or "freeze" an athlete sprinting across the camera's field of view. To obtain a sharp image of the runner, a shutter speed of up to 1/500 second might be required—the exact speed depending somewhat upon the camera-to-subject distance involved.

Suppose, however, you had a shutter that could be adjusted to operate at a speed of 1/500 second, but the size of the diaphragm opening in the camera was "fixed" at f/12 (the size of opening generally built into a box camera designed to operate at 1/25 sec.). Obviously a diaphragm opening of this size would not, under normal circumstances, allow nearly enough light to reach the film in 1/500 sec. The resulting image, if any, would be so under-exposed that a positive print (black-and-white photograph) could not be made from the negative.

Now we have uncovered the reason why we need adjustable diaphragms!

LENS STOPS AND DIAPHRAGM MARKINGS

Lenses vary greatly in their ability to admit light into a camera. When a lens is described as being "fast" or "slow," reference is being made to the *speed* at which it allows light rays to pass through. The standard unit of measurement by which all manufacturers rate their lenses is a letter "f" followed by a number. The next time you look at a camera (other than a box camera), note the "f" number marked on the lens.

The *lower* the f number, the *faster* the lens is; the *higher* the f number, the *slower* it is.

This f number on the lens represents the fastest speed at which it can be used. But while you can't increase its speed, you can slow it down. This is done by means of the adjustable diaphragm.

The diaphragm markings on a camera always begin with the fastest f number the lens has. This may be f/2.5, f/3.5, or even f/8. Each succeeding marking on the diaphragm control ring is a different "lens stop." Each succeeding lens stop allows only *half* as much light to pass through it as the stop before.

Suppose you have a camera with diaphragm markings (lens stops) which run like this: f/3.5, f/5.6, f/8, f/11, f/16, f/22. If you want to shoot a picture with the lens "wide open" to admit just as much light as possible, you use the lens stop of f/3.5. If you want to cut in half the amount of light coming through, you "stop down" the lens by moving the diaphragm control so that the marker points to the next stop, f/5.6. If you move the marker one more stop, to f/8, the circular opening in the diaphragm will close ("stop down") until only half as much light can pass as the opening of f/5.6 will admit.

LENS OPENINGS

Opening Largest (most light)	⬤	◦	Opening Smallest (least light)

| | f/4 1/500 | f/16 1/25 | |

These lens openings each allow the same amount of light to enter the camera, because with the wider opening at f/4 a speed of 1/500th of a second is used, while at f/16 a speed of 1/25th of a second is used.

THE SHUTTER AND DIAPHRAGM TEAM

We have already discovered that one of the main functions of a shutter is to control "how long" light will be allowed to reach the film. We have also determined that a diaphragm opening has the say-so about "how much" light can enter while the shutter is open. Since both the shutter speed and the lens or f stops (diaphragm openings) are adjustable on a good camera, they can be worked beautifully as a team when a picture-problem is at hand.

You can give the same exposure to a negative by using any of a number of different shutter-speed and f-stop combinations.

Suppose, for example, you knew the proper exposure for a picture to be 1/50 second at f/11. If you had reason to fear that slight movement on the part of the subject might impair the sharpness of the resulting image, you could set your shutter speed at 1/100 sec. (or twice as fast), and the diaphragm opening at f/8 (twice as wide). Thus, while cutting in half the length of *time* that light could enter the camera, you would be doubling the *amount* of light that could pass through the diaphragm opening during that interval. If you chose, you could slow the shutter down to 1/25 second (half as fast as 1/50 sec.) and use a diaphragm opening of f/16 (half as wide as f/11)—with exactly the same results as far as the exposure of the negative is concerned.

sec.	f-stop
1/25	f/16
1/50	f/11
1/100	f/8
1/250	f/5.6
1/500	f/4

HOW TO DETERMINE A BASIC EXPOSURE

Again, we have *three* major things to consider in determining the right lens stop and shutter speed for a picture. These are:

1. The kind of film in your camera (for example, tri-x, fast; plus-x, slower).
2. The amount of light being reflected by your subject.
3. Whether the subject is stationary or in motion.

Some films are coated with emulsion that reacts to light much faster than other emulsions. "Fast" films require shorter exposures than "slow" films.

There are a number of devices for "measuring" the amount of light being reflected by a subject. If you have access to a photo-electric exposure meter, by all means give it a try, for it is the most accurate measuring device of all. Some cameras have built-in exposure meters. Many photographers, however, get along very nicely with cheaper devices—or even by simply following the directions which come with each roll of film.

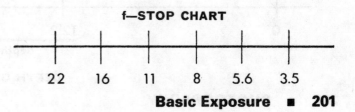

f—STOP CHART

| 22 | 16 | 11 | 8 | 5.6 | 3.5 |

A stationary subject is no problem at all because you can, if necessary, photograph it with a "Time" exposure if the light is too poor for using regular shutter speeds. A moving subject normally means that your first problem is to choose a shutter speed fast enought to "stop" the action. With a shutter speed decided upon, you next select a diaphragm opening or lens stop which will provide adequate exposure for your negative, and *at the same time* give you as much *depth of field* as you need in order to obtain sharp images. Let's explain this.

DEPTH OF FIELD

Depth of field is the range of distance over which near and far subjects in a picture will appear *in sharp focus*.

Every camera lens is of a definite *focal length*. Don't worry about what focal length *is* at this point; you have bushels of pictures to make before you will be interested in any lens other than the one that happens to be on the camera you use. What you should do is to obtain a *depth of field* chart for the lens on your camera.

Let's imagine that you are using a camera having a lens of 80 mm. focal length. You wish to photograph a friend standing 15 feet away at a shutter speed of 1/100 second at a lens aperture of f/4.

A glance at your depth of field chart will show that at an aperture of f/4, your 80 mm. lens can be focussed for 15 feet and will produce a *sharp image* of all objects from 12'2" in front of the camera to 19'5". Therefore, if you focus at 15 feet, you have nothing

to worry about; the image of your friend is bound to be in focus—and so will all objects several feet in front of and in back of him.

Now let's complicate the problem a little. You want to include *two* friends in the same picture, one standing 15 feet away, the other standing 5 feet behind him, or a full 20 feet from the camera. The chart has told you that 19'5" is the maximum distance at f/4, and the lens simply won't produce a sharp image of the person standing 20 feet (or ½ foot farther) away. So back you go to the depth of field chart which tells you that if you "stop down" the lens to f/5.6, all objects from 11'4" to 22' in front of the camera will be in sharp focus. Here's your answer so far as finding the right aperture is concerned.

But in closing the lens diaphragm one full stop (from f/4 to f/5.6), you have cut in half the amount of light that will be permitted to enter the camera. Remember? If you decrease the lens aperture, you must either compensate for it in some other way, or risk "underexposing" the negative. How do you compensate? By cutting the shutter speed in half. Instead of shooting at 1/100 second, you must shoot at 1/50 second, thus allowing light to enter the camera *twice* as long. In other words, a negative exposed at f/5.6 for 1/50 second will receive exactly the same amount of light as a negative exposed at f/4 for 1/100 second.

As a general rule, the more you "stop down" (decrease the size of) a lens aperture, the greater the depth of field or overall sharpness you can obtain.

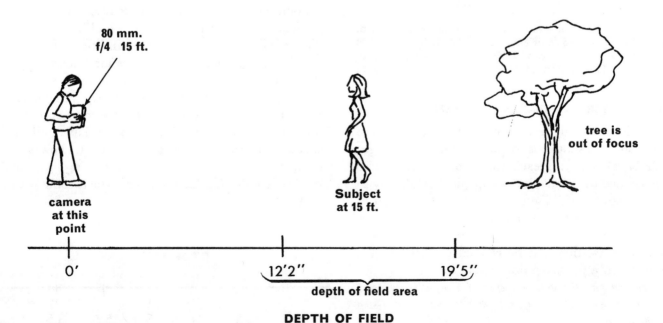

80 mm.
f/4   15 ft.

camera
at this
point

Subject
at 15 ft.

tree is
out of focus

0'   12'2"   19'5"

depth of field area

DEPTH OF FIELD

Conversely, the larger the diaphragm opening you use because of poor light conditions (or for special optical effects), the less depth of field or overall sharpness you will obtain.

If this sounds pretty complex, after you've shot a few rolls of film, you'll begin to forget there are such things as depth of field charts. You'll be setting your lens aperture to the right opening for various shots as naturally as you reach for the right fork when your salad is served! Now let's get started:

1. Study your three camera controls: diaphragm, shutter speeds, and distance.

2. Know and practice (without film) how to use these three controls together.

3. Start shooting with film, making pencil notes of the three camera controls used for each picture taken, such as (picture 1, 1/50th, f/8, 15 feet).

4. Study picture results with notes and try to discover what you did wrong and right in each case.

Only with practice can you learn new techniques.

WHAT CAMERA TO BUY

A camera is like a suit of clothes or a new dress—it has to fit your individual needs and tastes. Take your time about making a choice. Look over the cameras your friends are using and ask them what they like or dislike about their cameras. Talk to the salesmen in photo shops, to camera club members, or to anyone who is capable of advising you. But try to reach *your own* decision based upon the kind of pictures *you* want to make.

Whatever you do, start simply. It doesn't pay to buy an expensive camera right away, and it doesn't pay to buy lots of gadgets. Just remember that a box camera in the hands of an experienced photographer will produce better pictures than the most expensive equipment in the hands of a novice.

Once you have pretty well decided which *type* of camera is best suited to your needs, the next thing to consider is how to get the most for your money. If you can afford a brand new camera, fine. If not, there are thousands of good used cameras on the market. But don't trust your own judgment alone in picking out a second-hand camera. Take someone along who knows inside out the type of camera you are looking for. Do your shopping *only* in established camera shops which have a reputation for honest dealings to maintain. If possible, arrange to have the camera tested by an expert before you buy; if this isn't possible, pay for the camera with a provision that after a reasonable test period you can turn it in (undamaged, of course) for full allowance on some other camera. Reputable dealers will co-operate with you all the way.

The following survey lists some of the advantages and disadvantages of the better type cameras. You will want to consult it when you are ready to buy one of the more advanced cameras.

MINIATURE CAMERA
(35 mm. negative)

Advantages: Easily portable. Easy to handle for fast action. Uses roll film. Light in weight. Pictures have wide depth of field. Film inexpensive per exposure, therefore allows freer experimentation. Camera is inconspicuous. Interchangeable lenses make it possible to take wide angle, telescopic and other shots.

Uses: For travel, hobby, candid and color.

Disadvantages: Negatives are so small that everything must be enlarged. Enlargements are magnified so much that some lose sharpness and definition.

REFLEX CAMERA
(120 size; $2\frac{1}{4} \times 2\frac{1}{4}$ negative)

Advantages: Most are light enough to be carried for some distance. Permits exact picture size viewing and aids composition. Uses roll film. Pictures have wide depth of field, but not as wide as miniature cameras. Negatives are large enough so that contact prints can be seen easily and used.

Uses: For travel, hobby, candid, color, and some commercial work.

Disadvantages: Lens not interchangeable, limiting camera's use. Sometimes enlargements suffer in quality from magnification, but not as much as with miniature cameras.

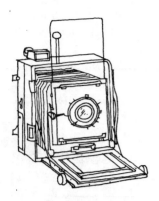

PRESS CAMERA
(4 × 5 negative)

Advantages: Flexible viewing at eye level or through ground glass. Large negative assures sharp print. Can develop one film sheet as soon as it is exposed instead of waiting for an entire roll to be exposed. Interchangeable lenses for wide angle and other use. Swing adjustments eliminate vertical and horizontal distortions.

Uses: For newspaper, magazine, commercial work, and hobby.

Disadvantages: Too heavy to be carried far by hand. Often need tripod for pictures without flash. Larger film more expensive; can't experiment as freely. Must use film pack or cut film, which means more handling. Less depth of field than smaller cameras.

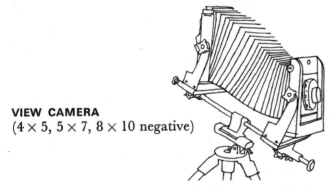

VIEW CAMERA
(4 × 5, 5 × 7, 8 × 10 negative)

Advantages: Large negative assures ultimate in sharpness and definition if used as contact print. Interchangeable lenses for wide angle and other uses. Easier to compose pictures through ground glass of same size as print. Swing adjustments eliminate vertical and horizontal distortion.

Uses: For commercial copy and studio work; not used much by hobbyists.

Disadvantages: Too heavy to carry far. Must always use tripod. Not suitable for pictures that call for rapid action. Takes more time to assemble and operate. Little depth of field unless "stopped down." Film is expensive.

FILTERS

You don't have to have a filter to take a good picture; hundreds of thousands of fine photographs were made before anyone ever heard of a filter.

A filter can, however, help record a scene a little more the way you have seen it. As you probably know, all colors in black-and-white photography are recorded in the various shades of grey, somewhere between snow white and jet black. The red colors tend to photograph darker than they really are, and the blues tend to come out lighter. This is because the emulsion on film does not always distinguish between one color and another.

A blue sky, for example, often registers as white on film. If a medium or dark yellow filter is placed over the lens, however, the effect is to "correct" the blue sky. In other words, the film then registers the blue sky as a dark shade of grey against which fluffy white clouds stand out by contrast. Without the filter, the white clouds would be invisible in the final picture, because the sky itself is white.

A medium yellow filter is the only one you will need for quite some time. It is well to know, however, that there are other special purpose filters to acquire as you grow more experienced, *if* your need for them arises. A dramatic, moonlight effect, for instance, can be obtained by using a red filter over the lens when your camera is loaded with panchromatic film.

A simple rule to follow in using a filter of any color is this: To render a colored object in a scene *light* in tone on the final print, use a filter the same color as the object itself; for example, use a green filter to cause green vegetation to appear *lighter* in the final photograph than it would appear without a filter. Look at your scene of colored objects through a filter. If one color looks darker than the adjacent colors, it will also record that way if you put that filter in front of your lens.

Panchromatic film should be used with a red filter. That is because *panchromatic* film is more or less sensitive to all colors. *Orthochromatic* film, on the other hand, *is not* sensitive to red. This means that anything red in a picture—red dress, for example—will register as black on orthochromatic film. There are two general kinds of film to choose from: "pan" film which records all colors in tones of grey; "ortho" film which records *most* colors in shades of grey, but "sees" red as black.

A filter absorbs part of the light that passes through it, and by absorbing part of the light, it permits less light to reach the film. To avoid under-

HOW FILTERS AFFECT A PICTURE: These two photographs were taken a few moments apart. The top one was shot with a red filter, the bottom without a filter. Note particularly the differences in the cloud formations.

exposing the negative when you use a filter, you have to compensate in some way for the amount of light the filter will absorb.

FILTER FACTORS

Filter manufacturers know how much light each filter produced by them will absorb. Thus, when you buy a filter, you will receive a slip of paper saying that the "factor" for that filter is "2", "3", or any numeral up to "6" or more. This means that because of the filter, you must increase the exposure "X" number of times (according to the number or factor involved). If, for example, your yellow filter has a factor of "2", you must allow *twice* as much exposure for the picture as you would if no filter were being used. Thus, if a normal exposure without a filter called for a lens opening of f/16, a filter with a factor of "2" would require the lens opening to be increased one full stop to f/11. Each stop larger

lens opening, you will recall, admits twice as much light as the opening which precedes it.

Suppose that for some technical reason you don't want to increase the size of your lens opening from f/16 to f/11, but you *do* want to use a filter having a factor of "2". Are you stymied? Certainly not! Instead of opening the lens diaphragm one full stop, you can use the next *slower* shutter speed on your camera. If, in other words, the exposure for a scene *without* a filter is 1/50 second at f/16, you can add a filter having a factor of "2" and compensate by using a shutter speed of 1/25 second. The slower shutter speed will then pass twice as much light as before, but the filter will absorb half of it. The result will be exactly the same as though you opened the lens diaphragm twice as wide.

Don't forget that the lens stops and shutter speeds work together as a team. They provide the "give and take" you need in order to produce a properly exposed negative.

HOW TO MAKE FLASH PICTURES

The nice thing about flash pictures is that you can carry your light source with you. No matter how dark your surroundings may be, you can flood nearby objects with light long enough to record an image on film.

Flash can be used with any camera—even a simple camera that has no provision for flash. To produce a flash picture with a non-flash kind of a camera, you simply buy an inexpensive gun designed for "open flash" operation. Your photo dealer will be able to supply you with the right kind of flashgun and a supply of bulbs. The procedure in making an "open flash" picture is this:

1. Place the camera on a steady support, such as a tripod or a table.

2. Choose a subject that will remain still. When you are ready to make the picture, either dim the room lights or turn them off entirely.

3. Open the camera shutter on either Time or Bulb.

4. Fire the flashbulb.

5. Close the shutter.

That, essentially, is all there is to open flash.

Many cameras nowadays have what is called "built-in synchronization." This means that the flashbulb is automatically fired in the interval that the shutter is open to admit light. Synchronized flash is much more desirable, of course, than using open flash. If you have "sync" flash, you can shoot any time and any place insofar as existing light and

FLASH captured the action and grace of this struggle for the ball with great clarity. Taken by Robert Tomsil, 17, of Cleveland Heights, Ohio, it won an award in a Scholastic-Ansco Contest.

moving subjects are concerned. Moreover, you can hand-hold the camera instead of using a tripod.

The best way to learn how to use flash illumination well is to practice with a floodlight or electric bulb on an extension cord. Hold the single bulb in front of your subject and move it from side to side, watching the effect of the light and shadows on your subject's face. Notice that a single light produces rather harsh illumination with large white areas and pitch black shadows. Because of this harshness and "flatness" (or lack of the illusion of roundness called *modelling*), a single flash directed straight towards a subject is seldom used except by necessity.

BOUNCE LIGHT AND FILL-IN LIGHT

In order to get better gradations of tone and/or modelling, many photographers illuminate their subject with "bounce" light. Instead of aiming the flashbulb (or photoflood bulb, as the case may be) directly towards the subject, the light is turned towards a white ceiling or a light-colored piece of cardboard or wall. The light which illuminates the subject is then reflected light, or *bounce light*. The

effect is much more uniform illumination with no extreme contrasts between black and white. Having more grey tones than harsh, direct light, bounce light provides better modelling.

Some photographers also use a second flashbulb (or even a whole string of extra flashbulbs) to illuminate a subject. The extra lights, called *extension flash* are usually used farther away from the subject than the main or "key" light which supplies most of the actual subject illumination. A single extension light is generally used to "fill in" (illuminate) the areas of the subject which would otherwise be thrown into inky shadows by the action of the key light. Multiple extension lights are used to illuminate other areas within the scene for specific purposes. One light, for example, might be used to illuminate only the subject's hair, another to illuminate only the background, and so on. Naturally extension lights are fired at the same time (and by the same triggering device) as the key light.

In using *any* type of artificial illumination, exposure is based upon the distance between the *key light and the subject*. The distance between the camera and subject can be disregarded.

1. Practice with a short extension cord and electric light bulb until you can judge how flash will illuminate a subject.

2. If possible, use "bounce" flash to obtain a more even distribution of light, hence better modelling.

3. Follow the instructions which come with each carton of flashbulbs *carefully* in order to obtain the proper lens stop and shutter speeds at any *light-to-subject* distance.

4. Use a sunshade over your lens to eliminate the danger of flare (unwanted light) reaching the lens and spoiling your negative.

COMPOSITION OR "ARRANGEMENT"

Good composition in a picture is nothing more than a pleasing arrangement of subject matter. There are many ways to control the position of a subject on film. If you are working with small objects, you can often move them physically into a more attractive arrangement. If you are photographing people, you can sometimes direct their positions and poses. If you are photographing a building or landscape, you can move the camera until a pleasing composition appears in your viewfinder.

A well-composed picture invariably "hangs together." In other words, all the objects in the picture appear in their proper balance and relationship. All

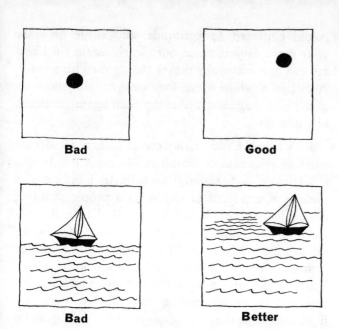

Bad   Good

Bad   Better

the minor objects, moreover, help point up or emphasize the object the photographer has selected as his *center of interest.*

BEGIN WITH A CENTER OF INTEREST

There can be *only one* center of interest in a good picture. This can be a single object, or many objects presented as a single subject—but if there is more than one main subject in a picture, the picture falls apart.

Suppose you have a small table, the top of which represents your picture area. The edges of the table represent the margins of your picture. Suppose, also, you have four white buttons which represent any kind of subject matter you choose—people, jet planes, buildings—or just buttons!

If you place one button anywhere on the table, your eye will be drawn to it and it will unquestionably become the "center of interest." There simply isn't anything else in the picture area to look at.

But what happens if you place one button in each corner of the picture area? Your eye can't decide which button to look at; therefore your picture falls apart!

To arrange the four buttons so they once again become a single center of interest (as a unit, this time), you have only to group them together so they touch, or form a design small enough so that the eye automatically "bridges" the gap between them. In this case, you have physically shifted your subject matter about in order to create a center of interest.

Suppose the buttons represent four trees growing close together, and you want the viewer to see something about just *one* tree that interests you. How do you make one tree—or even a part of one tree—

become the undisputed center of interest in your picture?

1. LIGHT. The human eye, like a moth, is attracted to light. In a picture, the eye notices light-colored objects first, shadowy and dark objects last. If the tree you want to emphasize stands in a shaft of sunlight which does not reach the other trees, it will dominate the picture. The same thing will happen if you spotlight one person in a crowd. Or suppose you are making a portrait of a subject whose outstanding feature is a pair of beautiful eyes. If you illuminate the eyes in some way, and leave the rest of the face in shadows, the eyes will become the center of interest.

2. POINT OF VIEW. The camera can only record the image of whatever happens to be reflecting light in front of it when the shutter is snapped. Unlike your eye, it does not see selectively—and it does not attach meaning to what it sees.

Let's say that in studying the four trees, you notice that one tree has a lightning-blasted limb. The stump of the limb reminds you of a twisted gargoyle—and that is what you want a viewer to see in your picture.

If you shoot from a distance, no one will notice what you intended to be the center of interest. So you move in closer, studying the gargoyle from every angle. Finally you discover that you can see it quite clearly in your viewfinder—but that one of the remaining trees creates a splotchy background. You experiment some more and find that by pointing the camera upward from a crouching position, your gargoyle is clearly outlined against a plain blue sky. This is your picture! You have created it by finding a camera angle or a point of view that does everything possible to emphasize and interpret your center of interest.

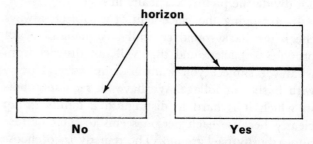

horizon

No   Yes

3. PLACEMENT OF THE SUBJECT. Whether you are making a head portrait or photographing a landscape, your center of interest should occupy a spot where it appears pleasing to the eye. Usually this is *not* the dead center of the picture area. A subject located in the center of a picture appears static, hence dull and uninteresting. It is almost always

Composition or "Arrangement" ■ **207**

Courtesy of Standard Oil Co. (N.J.)

PERSPECTIVE: The line of trees carries the eye deep in the photo to the vanishing point. Take a sheet of paper, cover the tops of the trees, and notice how the picture flattens out. It needs to be a vertical.

best to locate your main subject a little to one side of the vertical center of a picture, and a little above or below an imaginary line which bisects the picture area horizontally. A horizon line crossing a picture should, for example, be located above or below the center of the picture area; a telephone pole should not divide the picture vertically in half.

In arranging the placement of a subject, always check the background carefully. A plain blue sky provides a background that will not distract from whatever subject you want to emphasize. Not so with bushes or foliage. We have all seen snapshots in which it is hard to distinguish a family group clearly because each person seems to melt or fuse into a bushy background. The remedy is to choose either a plain background, or to pose the family group so far in front of the bushes that the foliage appears completely out of focus and blurred in the background.

Another error in arranging the placement of subject matter is to have a telephone pole or tree appear to be growing out the top of a subject's head.

Avoid cluttered backgrounds, and strive to make your main subject stand out clearly against a background of a *contrasting* rather than a matching color. A girl in a white dress, for example, will show up much better against a blue sky than against a beach of white sand.

4. VERTICAL OR HORIZONTAL? Try to decide whether your subject matter can be presented best as a vertical or a horizontal picture. In most cases, a picture of a tree or of one or two people standing close together looks best as a vertical picture. A landscape or a seascape generally looks best as a horizontal. Horizontal lines tend to be more peaceful as, for example, the gently rolling lines of a country scene. Vertical lines give a feeling of strength which is often depicted in bridge pillars, and the like. Sloping lines suggest action—a toboggan, or a diving plain. Don't hesitate to try a number of camera positions and angles before you snap a picture. Look for the kind of lines in the composition which help accentuate the thing you are trying to express about a subject.

5. PERSPECTIVE AND DEPTH. Perspective is gained by taking a picture of subject matter which stretches away from the camera in a long line. It may be achieved by showing a street, a long row of houses, railway tracks, or anything else that serves to give the picture a third dimension. It actually takes you into the picture. The photo here of a street in Paris has depth. The trees help to give it that quality. You can also obtain perspective by placing people properly. Two men at the end of a long table can give the picture depth. You can achieve depth, too, by placing objects in the foreground, middle ground, and background.

6. SIZE. The average *snapshooter* never thinks of using his camera at other than eye-level or waist-level. A *photographer* uses a camera at the level that will best interpret what he wants to say photographically about his subject. If you shoot down on a subject, you make it appear smaller and, in a sense, in an inferior position. A child, for example, appears smaller—and more "childish"— when you shoot down on him. Photographed at his own eye-level (not your eye-level), he becomes more of an individual of importance. A child can be interesting to photograph from a different angle. Hold the camera below the height of the child. It will make him look like a giant!

7. LIGHT AND DARK MASSES. Every picture is made up of a mixture of light and dark masses. In a simple

LIGHT AND DARK MASSES are divided in a manner that distinguishes this picture, aside from the startling action of the figure etched against the sky. The climbing rope—a streak of light—forms an interesting line in the composition.

DESIGN (below): A clear relationship exists in this picture between the cars which carry the eye harmoniously from below, sweeping up and to the left.

Courtesy of Eastman Kodak Co.

portrait, for example, the white oval of the face is balanced by the darker masses of hair and clothing. As a general rule, the most pleasing composition is obtained when the light and dark masses in a picture do not exactly balance one another. A picture of two tennis balls, one painted white and the other painted black, probably wouldn't be very interesting if there were nothing else within the picture frame to look at. They would be in static balance in regard to light and dark masses. Similarly, a landscape composed of exactly the same number of light and dark objects would very likely appear static. If a brooding sky (dark mass) dominated a small section of light-colored landscape, the picture would gain interest. The contrast in balance would give it mood.

JUXTAPOSITION: Without the men in the foreground, this would be just another waterfall.

RELATIONSHIP AND JUXTAPOSITION

There should either be a relationship or harmony, or conflict or juxtaposition within the subject matter of the picture you take. For example, you wouldn't show people wearing overcoats indoors unless you had a definite idea to present, such as houses without heat during a cold winter. If that is what you are

Relationship and Juxtaposition ■ **209**

trying to show, then the conflict presented by the idea would be effective. A picture of a slum house adjoining a fine apartment would depict the character of a city or street, to reveal social decay. The house in this case would be so much "out of position" that it would arrest and startle the viewer, and thus heighten the dramatic quality of the picture. This is juxtaposition or conflict and an excellent device to strengthen your point of view.

Relationship or harmony simply refers to the appropriate appearance of the subject matter.

TEXTURE

Texture can be described as that which "makes you want to reach out and touch it." You have often seen low slanting light which seems to pick out and highlight certain elements of a subject. That's texture. In order to emphasize texture, a light source generally has to either illuminate a subject from the side, or shine *through* the subject towards the camera. If the same subject is illuminated with direct light coming from the direction of the camera, the texture will probably not be seen.

With good textural lighting, the subject will appear to have a luminous property—as if the light source originates from within the subject itself. For good examples of textural lighting, study the magazine ads for carpets, towels and blankets. Often the photos in the ads will emphasize the nap. The light will slide across the top of the carpet in long shadows pointing up the individual woolen strands. How much more appealing and real than just showing a solid color without indicating the beauty of its weave!

Texture pictures have a way of bringing the viewer much closer to the subject so that he feels he can almost touch or smell the thing pictured. Grillwork, paint peeling off old houses, food, tree bark, water, grass, practically everything has texture which can be photographed. Hands, face and hair in portraits have good texture possibilities.

The three things to remember in order to photograph fine texture are: Choose a subject that *has* texture, check your lighting carefully, and find the camera angle which will bring out the best detail.

TEXTURE: What better texture than fishing nets? Doesn't this close-up give you a definite feel about the nature of fishing? The light must be just right to get your best texture shot. Study the light carefully before shooting.

Texture photos are easy to take because you can see the texture from the very start.

Most of what you learn about basic composition and lighting of textures will come as a result of experimenting, studying your results, and experimenting some more.

"A WAY OF SEEING"

Now that you know something about composition, let us take a step further and learn about "seeing." It is something that tells you what kind of a picture you will take even before you snap the shutter. It is a skill that gives you the "feel" of pictures. It directs your thinking and planning; it sharpens your approach so that after a while you are able to work with greater speed and self-assurance.

The first step in developing your ability to see photographically is to observe the world around you more closely than you have before. Don't just wait for the baby to smile. The picture *may* be better if you take it the moment *before* he smiles. Or it might be a more interesting picture if the baby cries instead! Don't be afraid to take chances. The faces of people watching a fire may be more dramatic than the burning building itself. Glimpses of people listening to a speech may make a better picture than a picture of the speaker. Think of all the pictures one might catch of the faces of people on a bus, people eating lunch, waiting in line to buy theatre tickets, faces at a game. In short, fine dramatic pictures are

A WAY OF SEEING: An audience reaction shot is often more interesting and revealing than a picture of the speaker.

all around you—waiting to be taken with an interpretative lens.

Watch what happens to light as it rounds a corner of a particular object, when it forms a silhouette, or when it reaches a subject from various levels and directions. Look for reflections in rivers, ponds, and lakes. Try experimenting with a cup and saucer, using only one light source. Turn the cup and saucer in all directions. Watch the lights and shadows form on it, and curve around the form. Try to see everything in terms of verticals, horizontals, diagonals, curves, and angles. The diagonals of a railway track, for example, may be more interesting in a picture if they make an extreme slant than if they form a gentle slant.

Practice selecting pictures in your mind. Do it at random during the day as you walk through the streets or ride in a car or bus. Say to yourself, "Would this make a good picture?" Then turn in another direction and view it from a different angle. Think about it.

DON'T LET COLOR FOOL YOU!

Color can be very misleading in a landscape scene. In your viewfinder, for instance, you are apt to see an autumn scene as a riot of colors with the trees painted bright yellow, orange, red and various tones of brown and green. But when all this is recorded on black-and-white film it is translated into black, grey and white. The bright colors you saw in the viewfinder are now fused together and you have a flat, uninteresting shot. So look for lots of contrast in *lights* and *darks,* but don't be misled by color!

With color film in your camera, it's quite a different story. You can capture emotion in a nature scene.

When a picture can evoke an attitude—something extra beyond the concrete composition—you have produced an above-average photograph, a photograph that people will want to see. Nature offers limitless ideas, images, symbols and patterns to photograph. There is a surprising amount of order and design in nature. All we have to do is see it: veins in leaves, ferns, branches, trees, tree bark, flowers, spider webs, seashells, grass, etc.

HOW TO GET THE ILLUSION OF 3-D

One of the chief hazards to good landscape pictures is a flatness and dullness in the final picture. Somehow this flatness did not show up when you viewed the scene through the viewfinder. As a matter of fact the scene looked good—that's why you took it!

Because the eye sees in three dimensions, while the ordinary camera records in only two dimensions, many scenes lose their punch when they appear on paper. That's why you deliberately have to *USE COMPOSITION* to produce a satisfying picture. You have to observe your vertical and horizontal lines, your large masses, your light and dark areas. You can emphasize depth with a line of trees, or long

AN ORIGINAL APPROACH: Statues and cleaning equipment are not exciting in themselves, but placed together in this arrangement you see something more.

rolling waves. It also helps create an illusion of "depth" in the foreground if your subject is in the middle or background. Shooting a mountain lake through trees which "frame" the foreground also produces a more interesting picture than a "depth-less" shot of a lake lying at a distance in the back-ground.

In photographing a landscape (or any other subject) don't confine yourself to having the light come only from behind you. As a matter of fact, it is generally better when it comes from either left or right. In this way you can achieve modelling and a roundness of forms you would otherwise miss. Half of your subject is then light, and gradually the other half assumes a darker tone, which gives it distinctive form.

If the sun is behind the camera everything appears bright, but without contrast—hence, the picture becomes flat.

If the light is *behind* the subject, the subject will then appear as a silhouette or near silhouette. Naturally you can't take this kind of picture unless the subject is exactly between the lens and the sun (or other light source) because direct light shining into the lens will spoil (flare) the film when the shutter is snapped.

ILLUSION OF DEPTH: Imagine this landscape with-out the fence! The fence produces depth and fine composition in what would otherwise be a flat scene.

HOW LIGHT "QUALITY" CHANGES

Notice how hard and brittle sunlight appears during the winter. Then observe, during the summer months, the sun's pearly softness in morning, its fullness and hardness around noon, its soft golden appearance in later afternoon and early evening. These are all changes in the "quality" of the light.

The quality of light also changes from day to day and hour to hour, as the sun and clouds move. At times you can even see how the changing quality of light alters the mood of a picture from one minute to the next. This is particularly dramatic when a sunny landscape changes with the approach of black storm clouds.

Generally early morning or late afternoon hours are the most favorable times for shooting black-and-white landscapes. During these hours, the slanting light produces long shadows, and emphasizes texture. Filters should be used to pick up clouds or to cut out haze and glare from snow scenes. A yellow filter should be used to correct blue skies or blue water;

otherwise they will have little tone. Filters are not necessary with overcast skies.

However, color pictures will come out truer if you avoid late afternoon light.

Water, sand and snow reflect more light than grass, so check your light reading carefully. For such scenes be sure the sun is low, and preferably at the side, so you will get longer shadows and so that details such as pebbles, snow flakes or water foam will be clear and sharp.

CANDIDS, ACTION AND SPORTS SHOTS

With the development of small, fast-lens cameras, mainly the 35 mm. miniature camera, a new type of photography came into being—the candid photo. In approach, the candid represents an attempt to interpret the unposed character of people.

Candid photography has become extremely popular. Pictures are taken in split-second time—usually with the subjects unaware of the camera. The resulting photographs thus emphasize realism—people eating, kibitzing, working and acting their normal selves.

Candid shots are especially effective in photographing children in their world of make-believe, or in recording their daily trials and tribulations. In sports, a whole new kind of photography has opened up. You can shoot the basketball player just ready to catch the ball, the boxer as he falls to the canvas, each at the right moment.

Successful candids require special approaches and techniques. Since most of the pictures are taken

LIGHT QUALITY: The low angle of the setting sunlight and the low angle of shooting have turned this piece of farm equipment into an unusual picture.

Courtesy of Standard Oil Co. (N.J.)

when the subject is unposed, a great deal depends upon the attitude of the subject before the picture is taken. If he has an idea that you are going to take his picture he may stiffen up and become self-conscious. So try to take it before he is aware of it, or at least when he isn't anticipating the click of your shutter. In terms of naturalness and purity of expression, the result will be far superior to the self-conscious photo of a subject who has "frozen" for the camera.

This doesn't mean, of course, that you have to hide your camera to take a candid. You can hold it in such a way that no one suspects you intend to use it immediately. Just be nonchalant. You'll find it's wiser than being furtive, or trying to sneak a shot when the subject isn't looking. Before taking the picture have everything ready, so you can work fast. Pre-set your shutter speed, exposure, and distance in your *preparation* for the picture. Then when your picture appears—simply raise the camera and shoot! Memorable candids of children can be taken in this way.

CANDIDS can be simple and humorous—nothing posed about this one.

To obtain candids of children play with them first, lead them in games, and stay long enough for them to get completely used to you and your camera. Then as they continue playing (as they always will), they gradually forget you to the extent that you are able to get shots.

RULES FOR SPORTS SHOTS

In order to take most fast action and sports pictures, you should use a camera with a shutter speed up to 1/500 of a second. This means that the lens in the camera must be fast enough to permit light to enter at that speed—in other words, it should be f/4.5 *or faster*.

Why take action shots when you can get a good posed picture? Just compare them, and you'll see the difference. In the action shot the person pictured

SPEED IN SPORTS can be shown effectively by using a blurred image. It is not always so successful as in this photo by Ronald McChesney, 17, of Gladewater, Texas, which won commendation in a Scholastic-Ansco Photographic Contest.

looks more natural—we rarely see people standing absolutely still.

To get better action shots, do two things: study your subject and get in the right position for the speed of your camera. A few rules should be kept in mind:

1. Movement across your path *is faster* (as far as the lens is concerned) than movement coming toward you. Imagine a track star breaking the tape at the finish line. From the sidelines, you would need a very fast lens to catch him clearly—probably 1/500 of a second from 25 feet. From in front of the runner, perhaps 1/100 would catch him.

2. The farther away a subject is, the less speed your camera will see. The nearer the subject, the faster its speed appears.

3. The best time to take a picture is at the climax of movement. For this, you have to know what your subjects are likely to do. For example, you know the runner is going to break the tape, and you know that that is the best moment to shoot. Taking a shot of him running midway down the track is usually going to be less interesting. When he is tearing through the tape, he shows more expression, too—his final lunge and burst of speed will be apparent in his face and in the strain and tension of his entire body.

To anticipate the most exciting moment to shoot, you must know the characteristics of the sport. If you look for certain situations in each sport you will be somewhat forewarned. Generally the best time to shoot is just before the action reaches its peak.

Try to compose all your pictures so there is no wasted space on the negative. However, don't worry about getting too much in, as you can crop and enlarge the center of action.

Light and weather conditions outdoors are variable factors you will have to reckon with. Indoor shots will require flash or speedlight. Use high-speed film both indoors and out for sports pictures.

ELECTRONIC FLASH helps greatly in getting spontaneous action, especially in candids of children.

SPEEDLIGHT

One piece of equipment that will help you get faster pictures is the "speedlight" or electronic flash. This is being used more and more by amateurs (who can afford to buy it) for sports, candid, wedding and baby pictures. It has a tremendous advantage over the simple flash, as you are able to get more than 10,000 flashes from a single bulb! This saves money in the long run, and eliminates the replacing of flash bulbs between shots. With the speedlight, you can obtain the equivalent of a shutter speed of 1/30,000th of a second—while the shutter is open the flash takes only that long! Make sure that your camera is synchronized for speedlight, or you won't be able to use one.

MOTION PICTURES

While we will not go into the technique and types of movie taking here, it is important to realize that the same fundamentals apply as in still-picture taking. Taking movies may seem easier, but to get good footage without a lot of waste movement is a science in itself. As your hobby becomes more absorbing to you, you will want to try your hand at motion pictures.

PICTURES AT NIGHT

Night pictures have a mood and excitement all their own. To make them you'll need high-speed film, a tripod and a cable release. In some cases you may want to take along a flash attachment to supply extra fill-in light.

For outdoor pictures with limited illumination, use a time exposure with your camera securely held on a tripod. Good "time exposure" subjects include night street scenes, fireworks, moonlight, campfires, lightning flashes, illuminated buildings, homes, industry, streets and bridges.

Many of these exposures will take several minutes, sometimes as much as 5 or 10, depending upon the amount of light on the subject. That is why you need a tripod to hold the camera. A trick of some photographers is to leave their shutter open for several hours on a night when the heavens are full of stars. The negative will show as streaks the lighted paths of the stars and meteors.

You can also record lightning flashes, and because the light given off is very intense, the shutter need be open only long enough to capture the lightning. Of course, your shutter might be open a long time before the lightning comes; if so, the lens should be pointed at a dark area of sky so that there will be no light flares from nearby buildings or passing cars.

While a large fire takes a short exposure, campfires generally need additional light such as a fill-in flash unless the people gathered around the flickering blaze can remain still for 8 or 10 seconds.

You will have to rely upon your own judgment regarding the proper exposure in night shots, because the light will seldom be strong enough to record on a photo-electric exposure meter. An exception might be a brightly lighted area, such as Times Square in New York City. Here, directly under a theatre marquee with its blazing light, it is often possible to shoot at 1/50 second with the camera hand-held and the lens aperture set at f/3.5.

You will learn that not all good day subjects make good night shots. At night, your picture depends a great deal upon the outlines made by your large mass objects such as bridges, buildings, campfires, etc., and what the light does to them.

NIGHT SUBJECT: Reflections in the water, quiet in the city, romance is in the air—it all sets the mood. This is Paris, but you can do the same thing with the bridge in your home town.

Courtesy of Standard Oil Co. (N.J.)

Pictures at Night ■ 215

Will your fireworks picture have gracefully drawn ribbons, or light with a few sparks, or will the pattern be confusing? A bridge can look drab and colorless during the day, yet at night under moonlight and lamps, with a languid river below, it can take on a mood of romance and drama.

You will soon observe, after studying a number of night pictures that the key to composition lies in the nature of the reflections that grow out of light—reflected light streaking across the sky, on the pavement, on the water, on a bit of glass, etc.

TRAVEL AND STREET SCENES

What kind of pictures do people take while travelling? Of course, they take what interests them. But too many people travel without knowing what they will find. With a camera at your disposal, it is important to know something about the country, the region, the people, and the culture, so that you can plan just what you'd like to photograph. This is the key to knowing what to look for and where to find it.

Let's assume you're going on a trip. What kind of camera should you take? The small cameras that are easy to carry are best for travel. You will want to carry your camera with you always—on your walks, rides, and explorations. You never know when a good shot will be coming up, so be prepared.

As a rule travellers are familiar with scenes and points of interest which are advertised on posters. You can start by photographing these, if you like them. But don't stop with that! There are byways, little hidden streets, and out of the way places in every region, every country, and what you will find there can often make much more interesting pictures. They will be fresher and more original than what you see along the beaten path.

Market places in foreign towns, the people, their clothes, their products, their expressions, the children

DOUBLE EXPOSURE PORTRAIT: This treatment gives double meaning to a head and bust study, but it must be carefully planned. This portrait won a prize in a Scholastic Magazines-Ansco Photographic Contest for Edward Ray, 18, of El Paso, Texas.

playing in the streets, all make good pictures. Churches, cobblestone alleys, graceful trees, archeological remains, political writing on the walls, all make stark exciting pictures, some beautiful, some tragic, but all true.

Street scenes are a kind of travel picture you can take right at home. As you walk along the streets observe people, children at play, storefronts, displays, buildings, etc. A number of interesting shots can be taken in New York City and other big cities. Many of the store windows and store fronts compose themselves into pictures.

PORTRAITS

Have you looked through any old family albums lately? If so, you probably notice that in photos taken about 50 years ago all the subjects look pretty much alike—as if the photographer had only a few standard ways of posing his subject. All of the hands appear in the same position, and the pictures were so carefully retouched that not a wrinkle or blemish shows.

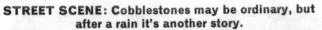

STREET SCENE: Cobblestones may be ordinary, but after a rain it's another story.

Courtesy of Standard Oil Co. (N.J.)

But with new cameras, new photographic paper and the influence of television and movies, portraiture became more natural. Today, portraits often show people at work or play—and the backgrounds are both natural and interesting. Instead of just faces, modern portraits often interpret the personality, mood and emotions of the subjects.

Emphasis is placed on the naturalness of the subject. The photographer tries to catch the subject's moods, even if a bit out of focus, or if his position violates some principle of composition. Backgrounds and foregrounds become important and casual. Often they suggest the vocation or hobby of the subject. If the subject is a dog fancier, a few dogs in the picture would help, or if the picture is of a girl who collects dolls then dolls would make the picture more interesting.

In informal portraiture the idea is to catch your subject in any mood, serious, tense, jolly, laughing, etc. Take candid portraits while your subject is doing something, perhaps talking, eating, smoking or just socializing. You will find that in this way your pictures will interpret a bit of your subject's personality.

Remember to consider your lighting carefully, but if you feel that by not following *all* the rules you can get a fine or unusual mood—go right ahead. It never hurts to experiment.

MOST COMMON PICTURE-MAKING MISTAKES

1. *Taking hackneyed subject matter without originality, feeling or thought.* Think twice before you snap the shutter. Ask yourself, "What is my purpose? Why do I want to take this picture?"

2. *Camera movement.* Hold the camera close to your eye or body, depending upon the kind of camera it is. Keep your arms steady, and move only the fingers that manipulate the camera. Hold your breath long enough to snap the shutter.

3. *Double exposure.* If you forget to advance your film to the next number then you will have a double exposure. Turn to the next number right after the last picture is taken.

4. *Subject movement.* You always have to adjust for subject movement. Even a portrait may move a little. Shoot portraits 1/50 of a second—babies faster.

5. *Tilted camera.* If you hold your camera at an angle, you will end up with a tilted skyline, building or person. Vertical lines in your subject matter should appear that way in your viewfinder, too!

6. *Poor composition and/or background.* Many pictures may have good ideas, or capture a fleeting or candid expression, and yet fail to be good pictures because of poor composition, or confusing background or foreground.

7. *Poor lighting.* Make the most of your available light. All objects look different when the light source changes position. For example, how does a portrait of a person look when the light comes from behind, from the front, side, both sides, front and side, front and back? Ask yourself these questions and try it out.

8. *Mechanical errors* occur when you don't compute shutter speed, exposure and distance accurately. Double check all your adjustments.

9. *Insufficient study of subject.* Look at the subject from different approaches. Study the angles. Observe the light change as you walk around it, and take several different pictures. You can always select your best ones later on.

MOOD: Without the fog, this picture would have been quite ordinary, but the mist lends a feeling of stillness. A special award in a National High School Photographic Contest was given to Bill Richards of Cranford, New Jersey, for this photo.

IDEAL DARKROOM: Here the photographer has ample storage space, fine plumbing, table and work space for enlarger and printing, and even a section (lower right) for drying prints.

PLANNING YOUR OWN DARKROOM

You can improvise a darkroom in your bathroom, kitchen or basement. This isn't the best idea, but if you have no other choice, it can be done. It means setting up your darkroom every time you plan to work, and this requires effort and time. You have to place newspapers over your breakfast table, pull out the enlarger from the closet, set up the trays and equipment, etc.

It is preferable to have a darkroom which is used for no other purpose, the enlarger always accessible. Then all you have to do is put on your apron and mix your solutions.

THE BASIC NEEDS

First of all a darkroom, whether temporary or permanent, must have a water supply, preferably hot and cold, electric outlets and—darkness. If possible, shelving and storage cabinets should be available for all the trays, chemicals and equipment. In addition to supplies listed on the next page, you need a sturdy table strong enough to support your enlarger or printer, and large enough for three trays (8×10 or 11×14) for printing. You can also use two tables; one for the enlarger, the other for the trays.

You should have enough working space to move around in freely, and a chair or stool.

Make windows light-tight by placing black oil-

cloth, a dark blanket, or cloth across them. The window shade or Venetian blind should be pulled down too. If you do most of your laboratory work at night, perhaps you will not have to be so concerned about light leaks. A room does not have to be absolutely light-proof for printing and enlarging. A little light under the door which does not find its way directly or by reflection to sensitive paper is permissible. But be sure it is a *very small amount* of light.

AN IDEAL SET-UP

If you live in a house and can convert a part of your basement into a darkroom, you have an ideal set-up. Basements usually have fairly constant temperatures in the neighborhood of the 65° to 75°F (18° to 24°C) required for photography. Basement windows are easier to black out and you can feel a little more relaxed if chemicals spill on the floor or spray on the walls. A beaverboard or thin composition board wall on one or two sides will give you the basic structure, and an old blanket can serve as a door.

Build shelves out of heavier lumber. If you can place the darkroom around the washtubs, or at least close to them, so much the better.

FILM DEVELOPING

A developing tank often has plastic reels which can be adjusted to accept several different sizes of roll or sheet film. In addition to a developing tank and the required chemical solutions (see page below) you should have a pair of metal or plastic film clips; a glass, rubber, or plastic stirring rod; a glass or plastic funnel; a photographic thermometer; and a small viscous sponge. A few clean glass bottles for storing solutions, and a clean, 1-lb. coffee can for washing your film, will just about complete your basic needs. Punch a few holes in the bottom of the coffee can and attach a wire handle to it so it can be hooked to the faucet when you are ready to wash your negatives after processing.

THE CHEMICALS YOU NEED

The shelves of any photo supply shop are loaded with different types of developers and processing solutions. Don't let them confuse you. Start with a very simple, very inexpensive "kit" of chemicals and stick with it until you have successfully developed several rolls of film. There will be plenty of time to experiment with bulk chemicals and prepared liquid solutions later.

A simple kit consists of a package of developing powder, a package of short-stop powder, and a package of acid hypo powder. All you do is mix them with water as explained on their labels.

These are the precautions you should take:

1. Be sure the packages will produce enough solution to cover your film adequately when you pour the liquid into the developing tank. If your tank requires more solution than one package of powder prepares, use two packages.

2. If the developer powder happens to come in two foil-wrapped packages of different colors marked "A" and "B" each package contains a different chemical. Mix them *only* in the order given in the instructions; in other words, don't mix powder B with water and then try to add powder A which should have been dissolved in water first.

3. Be careful *not* to transfer drops of one solution to another with your fingers or stirring equipment. Hypo or short-stop will contaminate (spoil) developer. Keep this in mind always: You get only

one chance to develop each roll of negatives properly. How well you develop them will partly determine the quality that can be obtained in your final prints.

Mix all your solutions *before* you start to process a roll of film. The temperatures of your solutions are important. The instructions will probably indicate that the developer should be used at a temperature of about 68°F (20°C). Place the bottle of mixed developer in warm or cold water so as to bring it to proper temperature. Use a photographic thermometer for checking the temperature. *All other solutions*, including the wash water from the faucet, should be within 3° or 4° of the same temperature as the developer.

film tank

safelight

LOADING THE FILM TANK

If you bought a film tank of the spiral reel type, it probably came with a blank roll of film to be used for practice loading. If it didn't, examine the reel and practice inserting old negatives in the spiral grooves until you are sure you know how the tank should be loaded. Practice in an empty tank.

The next step is going to be a bit of a strain. In a *completely* darkened room, with only an orange safelight on, remove the paper backing from your exposed roll of film. (If you are using a film pack or cut film, take the necessary steps to get at the negatives.) Handle the film gingerly by the edges, *not* letting your fingers touch the face or back of the film.

Insert one end of the roll of film in the spiral grooves of the reel exactly as you did when you were practicing with the dummy roll (or single negatives) in the light. The shiny or slick side of the film should be on the outside; the dull or emulsion side of the film should face the inside core of the reel. *Don't get panicky* if things go wrong. Remain cool and the film will eventually slip into place easily. All you do then is place the loaded reel in the empty tank, *slip the lid in place*, and go out into daylight or a lighted room with the tank.

DEVELOPING TANK

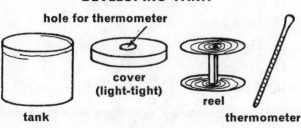

hole for thermometer

cover
(light-tight)

reel

tank

thermometer

If your developing solutions are of the right temperature, pour the required amount of developer into the tank. All of this can be done in a lighted room because the sensitive emulsion is safely covered when the tank lid is on. About every other minute, turn the wooden tank rod twice to agitate the solution. Continue this for the length of time specified in the instructions which came with the developer.

When development (by time) is completed, *do not* remove the tank lid. Instead, pour the developer out through the light-tight opening in the tank provided for this purpose. If you like, you can pour the developer into a green or brown bottle to be corked and saved for another developing session.

After the developing solution is poured out, rinse twice with water. Remember to keep all the temperatures fairly similar.

After you drain all the developer out of the tank with the lid still on, pour in the short-stop solution. Two minutes in the short-stop (with agitation) will "stop" all the action of the developer. The short-stop is cheap and expendable. Pour it down the sink after using it just once. *During all this process the tank lid is never taken off.* You pour through the light-tight opening.

Next, pour in the hypo. Ten minutes in fresh hypo will normally clear the film; you can judge this by noting if the margins are absolutely transparent. Hypo, like developer, can be stored and used again. If old hypo is used, the margins of the film may appear milky at the end of 10 minutes. You can check this by taking off the lid and inspecting the film with only the safelight on. If this happens, place the reel of film back in the hypo for another 5 minutes. Very old or exhausted hypo has a bad aroma and lacks the strength to clear a roll of film adequately. If after 15 minutes, the negatives are not completely clear, mix up a new batch of hypo and place the partially cleared negatives in this.

Now the negatives can be taken out of the tank into a lighted room for washing and drying.

The final step is to place the reel of film in the coffee can mentioned earlier (or in any receptacle that will allow a steady stream of fresh water to flood the film), and wash thoroughly. Hypo is not easily washed out of film; if allowed to remain it will stain and damage the negatives. If washed 20 to 30 minutes in running water, the film will be ready for drying.

To dry the film, attach a film clip to one end and gently slide (don't pull) the film out of the spiral reel. Suspend the film from a wire or cord by the clip, and attach another clip to the other end to provide enough weight to prevent curling. Then, with a viscous sponge that has been dampened and squeezed almost dry, wipe each side of the film *once* from top to bottom. *Do not* try to remove every tiny speck of water—but do get rid of the droplets. After wiping each side of the film just once, let it hang vertically in a dust-free spot to dry. It will curl a bit as it dries, then straighten out again. Don't touch for several minutes until completely dry. From then on, handle it gently and *only* by the edges.

CONTACT PRINTING AND ENLARGING

One of your greatest photography thrills is in printing and enlarging. Watching the image "come through" in the developing tray is a milestone in your photographic experience. Through the magic of chemistry, white sensitized paper will be transformed into the picture you created with your camera. This is the picture you found and composed out of your observation.

Now that your negatives are developed, you can go on to the subject of printing. Contact prints the exact size of the negatives are usually made to help determine what prints you may want to enlarge. This process helps save time when the negatives come out poorly.

EQUIPMENT FOR PRINTING AND ENLARGING

These are the essentials you will need:
1. Printing frame or printing box
2. Three or four trays (8 × 10 or larger)
3. Three print tongs (one for each solution—keep separate)
4. Stirring rods
5. Measuring cup
6. Clock
7. Contact paper or projection paper (check grades needed) (see p. 221)
8. 60-watt ordinary frosted electric light bulb
9. Safelight (amber or yellow)
10. Towels and apron
11. Scissors for cutting test strips
12. Enlarger
13. Blotter rolls
14. Syringe
15. Easel

Also, thermometer, developer, acid short-stop and

fixing solution (hypo) which you have from your developing kit.

CHEMICALS

Beginners will find it best to purchase chemicals in small kits, which contain packages of powdered developer, short-stop, and hypo fixer—in fact, they are often identical with the kits used in developing film. These are mixed with water, warmed or cooled to temperatures of between 65° to 75°F (18° to 24°C), and poured into three separate trays. The order of the trays from left to right are, of course: 1. Developer; 2. Short-stop; 3. Hypo.

Arrange to have part of your table top available for holding the contact printer (or enlarger), and the box of contact paper (or enlarging paper) you will be using. The amber safelight should be suspended or otherwise located at least 3 feet or more from the processing trays.

When everything else is in readiness, darken the room and turn on the safelight.

HOW TO MAKE A PRINT

Open the box of sensitized paper and take out one sheet, closing the box carefully afterwards to make sure it is light-tight. Place the emulsion (*dull*) side of the negative to be printed against the emulsion (*shiny*) side of the paper—then place both inside your printing frame with the negative on top. Light must pass from the 60-watt frosted light bulb through the negative to the paper for a given length of time in order to record an image on the paper.

The length of time the white light should be turned on will depend upon:

1. The *density* (darkness) of the negative.
2. The distance between the light and the printing frame.
3. The *grade* of paper you are using.

A dark negative naturally passes light more slowly than a medium density or a so-called "thin" negative. The closer the printing frame is to the light, the stronger the light will be upon the negative.

As for paper, there are at least 6 grades or "contrasts" of paper available but only 4 need be considered. The "normal" grade for negatives of average densities is called a No. 2 paper. No. 1 paper is generally used for negatives that are more contrasty than normal. No. 3 and No. 4 papers are for lower contrast negatives. Your first box of paper should be No. 2 paper; add other contrasts to your paper supplies only as you need them.

Begin by holding your printing frame about 2 feet

from the 60 watt bulb and snap on the white light for about 5 seconds. Then turn the white light off, remove the sheet of exposed paper from the printing frame, and place it face up in the tray of developer. Be sure that the face of the print is completely submerged in developer, then rock the tray gently so that fresh developer continually washes over the print. After a few seconds, what was a blank sheet of paper will begin to reveal an image. Keep track of the time the print has been in the developer and remove it at the end of the time specified in the directions that came with the developing powder. You may have to do a little experimenting and give the print more or less exposure than 5 seconds.

Don't become a print jerker! In other words, don't remove a print from the developer simply because the image seems to have become fully developed before the recommended length of developing time has expired. True, an image that "comes up" too fast will blacken out before the recommended developing time has elapsed. But, that is because the paper was over-exposed. You will have to make a new print then, giving it shorter exposure to white light, or holding the printing frame farther away from the light. In fact, you may have to experiment several times before you strike the right combination. It is absolutely impossible to get maximum tonal quality in a print before the developer has been given an opportunity to do its job. Allow 1 to 2 minutes.

However, never leave a print in developer more than a few seconds longer than the recommended maximum developing time. If the print is still too light—make a new print, giving it more exposure.

After removing a print from the developer, place it in the short-stop tray for a minute or two, then transfer it to the hypo (fixer) bath. Ten minutes or so in a fresh fixer bath will render the image permanent, provided it is properly washed in running water for 30 minutes to an hour afterwards. If you don't have running water available, place the prints in a tray of water which can be emptied and re-filled at least 6 times within an hour. In between times, rock the water tray so that fresh water is continually flooding the faces of the prints to carry away the chemical residues.

HOW TO FINISH THE PRINT

After washing, drying is the next process. You must dry your matt face prints in blotter rolls. Place the emulsion (dull) side so it faces the lined side of the paper. This kind of roll helps keep the print flat as it dries. Glossy emulsion prints have to be dried on a ferrotype tin to obtain the glossy surface. The emulsion face of the print is placed against the tin and rolled with a rubber roller. If you are not interested in a shiny glossy finish, you can dry glossy emulsion prints in a blotter roll. The unferrotyped glossy print produces a wide range of tones without the mirror effect of a ferrotyped print.

After some experience you will find that you can correct a poorly exposed film to some extent in the printing process. But never count on this while you are taking pictures. Always try to expose correctly in the beginning. That's the first step towards a technically good print.

HOW TO ENLARGE A PRINT

Since many of the steps of enlarging are the same as those described for making contact prints, only the new or different steps involved will be discussed in detail. The darkroom set-up is the same. Place the same chemicals and trays in the same order. Use projection paper instead of printing paper, and, of course, use an enlarger instead of a printer.

1. Place the negative in the enlarger carrier; use an ear syringe or bulb blower to clean the negative of dust.

2. Choose the grade of paper needed. See page 221 for types. Turn room light off and amber light on. Cut "test strips" of the projection paper you will be using—several inches wide and 3 or 4 inches long. These strips for testing are a short cut and a great help to calculating the amount of time that projection paper should later be exposed.

3. Move enlarger head up or down until the image projected on the easel is the *size* you want the final picture to be.

4. Compose picture, sliding easel around until you

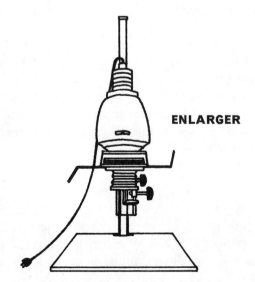

ENLARGER

are satisfied with what you see. You may use the entire negative, crop a little, or use only a part of the negative. Focus sharply.

5. Expose a test strip for several different intervals of time measured in seconds, i.e., 5, 10, 15, 20, 25 seconds. Put the test strips for 1½ minutes in the developer, then fix and check these exposures to find the one producing the most satisfactory image tones. The individual test exposures can be made by moving a piece of cardboard about one inch after each 5 seconds. Test strips only give clues to the proper exposure time, since the test strip is taken for only part of the picture, but it's a pretty good indication.

6. Expose full size sheet of enlarging paper, *dodging* if necessary. (See page 223.)

7. Develop to desired time, according to instructions which came with the developer you are using.

8. Dip in short-stop bath 20 seconds.

9. Place in hypo fixer 5 to 7 minutes, if hypo is fresh; 10 to 12 minutes, if hypo is used a few times.

10. Wash your print for one hour.

11. Dry in blotter roll, emulsion side against linen material or on ferrotype tins.

MORE ABOUT CHEMICALS

Stick to the simple kits of processing chemicals until you become accustomed to the technique of developing negatives and making prints. Then, if you like, try some of the more versatile chemicals available in either powder (to be mixed with water) or liquid (already mixed) form.

Different paper developers produce different tones of "warmth" or "coldness" in images. Different negative developers produce variations in what is known as "grain" size, developing time required, etc.

You will begin to understand the subtle differences inherent in different chemicals as you go along. Don't rush yourself or hop-scotch from one chemical preparation to another. Whenever you try a new preparation, stick with it long enough to find out why some manufacturer felt justified in placing it on a highly competitive market.

Large packages or bottles of prepared chemicals can, of course, save you money *if* you do a lot of darkroom work and *if* you can store the chemicals properly in tightly stoppered bottles as explained earlier. If you only do occasional darkroom work, it will pay you to mix fresh chemicals from small packages before each developing or printing session.

Short-stop consists of acetic acid highly diluted with water. It is short-lived, but cheap—therefore expendable. A bottle of acetic acid (in lieu of pow-

Courtesy of Standard Oil Co. (N.J.)

dered short-stop) will last for months. Many photographers nowadays have eliminated the short-stop bath from their technique and go straight from the developer to the hypo with, sometimes, a brief water rinse in between. (This applies to both negative and print development.) Try both methods—with and without short-stop—and settle for the method you feel gives you the most satisfactory results.

DODGING AND BURNING IN

When the shadow areas in a negative tend to print too dark on paper, you may have to *dodge*. This simply means that you will contrive to "hold back" some of the light so that the shadow areas will print in lighter tones of grey. In a twilight picture, water may reproduce too dark, but the sky may be rendered correctly. In this case, if you insert a piece of cardboard between the light source and easel, moving it over the water areas, it will cause these areas to print lighter—thus, more nearly matching the tone of the sky.

Thin areas of negatives usually need dodging. You can make a dodger by placing a small piece of cardboard on a thin wire. It should never be held still or it will print a shadow of the dodger or part of your hand. Dodging is easy once you get the hang of it, but don't waste time dodging too many areas on one picture. If possible, shoot the same picture over again—and this time try to get a better balance between your highlights and shadows.

The opposite of dodging is "burning in." This is performed when you have a very dense area in your negative which will make a chalky section or hot spot on your print. You can cut a hole in a piece of cardboard just large enough to allow a beam of light to reach the spot you want to "burn in," and correct the objectionable area. You will have to be skilful and confine the extra amount of light concentration only to the part you want to "burn in." The part to be "burned in" might be a light reflection that is too bright, part of a sidewalk that reflects too much sunlight, the searchlight of a train which is too bright, etc.

CROPPING

By cropping is meant eliminating the extraneous or unwanted areas of a picture. This leaves only that portion of the negative you want for the picture. Good cropping improves the composition and changes the emphasis in a picture. Often the areas to crop are the edges, the foreground or background of a picture.

You may also discover that some pictures contain more than one center of interest. In that case, cropping may give you two distinctly different pictures.

Cropping is best accomplished by using an en-

CROPPING: After this picture was taken, the photographer realized that the real picture was in the middle, as shown by the white lines. This got rid of the poorly lit areas and the grouped lights which were distractions. Although the player on the left foreground was well poised, he had to be sacrificed to the central action.

larging easel which has movable sides. Simply place the negative in the enlarger and move the sides of the easel in such a way as to crop out the undesirable parts of the picture. In eliminating unwanted areas you also shift the position and meaning of the subject; this is another important purpose of cropping. A subject in dead center can be moved to one side or the other by a little cropping on the sides. If the subject is too far away, cut away the foreground to bring the subject closer. If the subject is too close, cut off some of the background.

One of the things to keep in mind in cropping a picture, is the feeling or mood you want to convey.

If you want to study the physical structure of the lighthouse on page 223 without much concern for its relationship to the water, for example, you would crop off more water all around. As it has been printed, one gets the feeling of a lonely post in an immensity of water.

HOW TO IMPROVE PRINT QUALITY

We have talked a lot about developing your own point of view in an effort to "say something" in your pictures. Fine. But you should also know how to *show* your point of view. Your picture must meet technical standards. It should have a range of tones from light to dark. The blacks should be rich charcoal black, the whites should be brilliant and the colors should appear as clean shades of grey. Your highlights and shadows should have snap, and the details should not be "washed out" into nothingness. Print quality begins when you make your original exposure. It is much easier to control the quality of your print in the darkroom once you have taken the correct exposure and have a correctly balanced negative to work with.

When your print is not up to par, check with this list.

Light Print, dull and flat, little contrast

Expose longer in darkroom, keep print longer in developing tray or use warmer developer if cooler than directions call for. If above checks, then use harder contrast paper—No. 3, 4 or 5.

Dark Print, dull and flat, little contrast

Expose shorter in darkroom, develop shorter time in tray, use cooler developer, if warmer than directions call for. If above checks, then use harder contrast paper—No. 3, 4 or 5.

Grey Prints

Check possible light leaks in room, also check for an improperly mixed developer or outdated printing paper.

Extreme Darks and Lights, too much contrast without middle grey tones

Use a No. 1 soft paper to decrease contrast and bring out middle tones.

USING COLOR

Color photography is the same as black-and-white photography with the one main difference—color. Color film is very simple to handle, and requires no darkroom work on your part. All you do is take the exposed film back to the camera shop or mail it yourself to the manufacturer. In return you will get either color transparencies or positive color prints, depending on which type of film you use.

The *transparency type* gives you negatives, 35 mm. up to 8 × 10, that you can look at with an eye viewer or can project on the wall with a slide or special projector. Enlarged positive prints can also be made from transparencies. This is rather expensive, but if the photograph is a good one the result is worth it.

The color *print type* of film can be used on all cameras, even a box camera, and is usually the type chosen for less expensive cameras. Pictures taken with the print type film are $2\frac{1}{4} \times 2\frac{1}{4}$ size or larger, and are positives (no negatives). These prints sometimes do not have the faithful colors found in the transparency.

Color films are made for use *indoors* or for use in

PRINT QUALITY: This East Side New York City bakery window was taken with an 8 x 10 view camera, which accounts for the fine definition and print quality. The light was at an angle—7 a.m.—which brought forth good texture of the baked products.

Photo by Godfrey Frankel

Color Photography ■ **225**

daylight. Be sure you ask for the *kind* and *type* which fit your needs.

In taking color photographs, arrange your colors in such a way that you will achieve a pleasing picture. Do this as you would balance lights and shadows in black-and-white photography. Some experts will tell you that good color pictures should contain complementary colors (blue and orange, green and red, etc.). In general, good color pictures can also include any non-clashing combinations. Blending of three different shades of red, for example, may provide a pleasing impression in the final result.

Learn to think in color. When taking color portraits, make sure your subject wears colors that do not clash. When taking landscapes, street scenes and travel shots, let the arrangement of color help you select your picture. Brilliant flowers in a green meadow may give you just the color accent you are looking for. A mountain behind a town may give you just the contrast you need.

Avoid the most common mistake in color photography—improper exposure. There is less latitude in color film than in black-and-white. Follow rigidly the exposure chart on the instruction sheet which is packed with every roll of color film. You will find, for instance, that outdoor pictures should be taken between the hours of 10 in the morning and 4 in the afternoon to obtain true color reproductions. Before and after these hours the light will cast a reddish or orange glow on your film. Sometimes this "hot" glow can be used to advantage in early morning and twilight atmosphere pictures. So don't be afraid of this, if you have a subject which lends itself to this treatment.

Color adds an excitement all its own. Try it.

Now that you've learned the basics of photography, you should have a lasting hobby and many pleasurable moments.

Outdoor hobbies

FISHING

Angling is the most popular of all participating sports.

If you are interested in making fishing your hobby, learn all you can about angling, keep your mind, eyes and ears open and you will observe much that would otherwise pass you by. Be friendly but don't ask too many questions or act like a know-it-all. The locals will resent your presence and you will be the loser. You can't force anyone to tip you off if he doesn't like you. Some of the finest anglers will spend hours observing a new location before planning their own strategy. They study the stream, the anglers, and how they are fishing.

Some tips you get may be "as old as the hills" to you, but you may be hearing others for the first time. There are little tricks to every trade. Some of these are closely guarded "secrets" discovered after years of experimentation.

In some areas, some fishing methods are illegal but the same methods are legal and popular in other regions. Therefore, every angler should learn the fishing laws of every area he fishes in. It is best to support your local laws whether you are caught or not, because the laws were designed to protect the future supply of fish.

Fishing is one of man's oldest pursuits. Cave dwellers of France recorded such activities with drawings on their cave walls some 15,000 years ago.

The use of artificial flies was first described in a book printed in 1486. It later served as the basis of another book, "The Compleat Angler" by Izaak Walton (whom many regard as the first angling authority). Walton was a successful retired linen draper when his book was published in 1653.

An angler who fishes dry flies exclusively is referred to as a "purist" by other anglers. If the "purist" is a snob he refers to anglers using different methods as "meat hunters" and "non-sportsmen." Some "purists" begin by fishing with bait and later change to dry flies. Other "purists" who try a different technique sometimes become converts to the other method. Methods differ, but the sport is the same regardless of what techniques you apply.

All fishing can be fun. Of course you want to catch fish as well as enjoy the scenery and fresh air. Sometimes you will go home empty-handed, and other times you may catch fish in spite of yourself when everything is contrary to the rules. In any event, if you are a real angler, you will be back again the first chance you have to try your luck.

Luck frequently enters into one's fishing success, but knowledge of fish habitats and habits, of streams and of handling equipment and bait are more important than luck. Learn all you can about fish and perfect your casting ability. Join rod and gun clubs and read everything you can upon the subject. You may not agree with all any author has to say, but chances are you will learn a few important things anyway.

All fishing has one basic idea: you are trying to deceive a fish into taking your lure whether it is an artificial or live bait. Don't be afraid to try a technique usually reserved for other species. Trout are frequently taken by bass-finding methods and vice-versa.

Bear in mind that not all waters contain fish. You must learn the haunts of the fish, so keep a record or notes of just where you caught fish, in what type of water, and what conditions prevailed, and you will build up a great fund of angling knowledge.

HOW TO CATCH A FISH

Everyone has heard that a small boy needs only a can of worms, a willow pole and a bent pin to catch more fish than an adult expert angler with all his expensive tackle. Years ago that might have hap-

Condensed from "Fishing" by Gil Paust © 1961 by Sterling Publishing Co., Inc., New York

pened occasionally because most waters were not as heavily fished as they are today. Now it seldom happens, although people still believe the fable. It takes skill to catch most fish.

Sometimes some unusual tactics will deceive fish when established methods fail. It must be remembered that what worked best yesterday may not hook one fish today, so it's wise to vary your fishing methods once you know how.

CHARTS OF LAKES

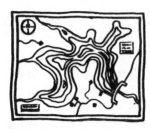

It is necessary to know a lake's bottom structure, location of channels, sandbars, weed beds, various depths, etc., to fish it best. Charts of some lakes are available and they are a great help in fishing such waters for the first time. Local tackle shops or lake officials may be able to supply charts or sources, if the lake has been charted.

Parts of a large lake may offer poor sport yet be excellent elsewhere.

THE BEST FISHING DEPTHS IN SUMMER

When the sun warms the top layer above 39.2°F (4°C) it becomes lighter in weight than the cold water below, so it stays above and the stagnation remains until turnover in the autumn. The middle dividing layer varies in depth with lake size and depth. This area of rapid temperature drop has the best combination of temperature and oxygen, so cold-water fish feed near the bottom within this layer.

Some shallow lakes may be deep enough to have areas below 39.2°F where cold-water fish feed on the bottom. Shallower lakes will have no *cold-water* fish in temperatures above 39.2°F unless there are cold spring holes or tributary streams for them. Such inlets usually supply the best fishing.

Warm water *without* cold inlets is suitable to large-

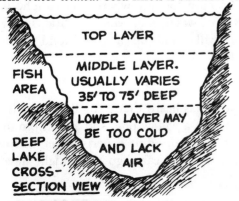

mouth bass, walleyes, pickerel and panfish. At 55° to 60°F (13° to 17°C) bass feed best from 10:00 A.M. to 4:00 P.M. between 5 and 10 feet deep under weeds, etc.

FLY-CASTING

Do you think you have to be a magician to cast a fly? It may look that way, especially when you're watching an expert do it. But fly-casting really is easy, although not as easy as spin-casting or bait-casting. And when you've mastered it, it will pay off in greater sport when your fish are the smaller species because fly tackle can be made lighter than any other kind and it gives your fish more of a fighting chance. You wouldn't be able to do much running if you were tethered to a flagpole and had a ball and chain tied to your ankle; similarly, a hooked fish can't do much fighting when the rod is stiff and he has to drag with him a bunch of heavy sinkers or a heavy lure! Some fly rods are so limber that a breath of air will bend them. Of course there are heavy-duty fly rods, too, but even these are "light" tackle compared to the 10- to 20-pound, and larger, fish they must fight.

THE FLY ROD

Split-bamboo fly rods are still preferred by expert casters in spite of the growing popularity of "glass," which is really fibreglass. Glass is too "soft" (not stiff enough) for casting long distances. The extra "backbone" (stiffness) of split-bamboo is what gives the rod its casting power. But split-bamboo rods, which are handmade of strips glued together, are much more expensive than machine-made glass ones! Until you become an expert, it may be wiser for you to pay the much lower price for the glass rod which is only slightly inferior to bamboo. Rod length is seldom important. Anglers used to think 9-footers were necessary for good casting; now even 7½ feet is not too short. The shorter rods are stiffer, too, and therefore more powerful. So are the heavier ones, but they'll tire your casting arm. Fly rods usually come in two or three sections which fit together by means of metal connections called "ferrules." Never twist the rod sections when putting them together or taking them apart since it might loosen these ferrules; always use a straight pull or push. The silk windings on a rod are pretty, but they don't make it any better. The fly rod's steel guides are called "snake" guides because of their twisted shape.

THE FLY REEL

The fly reel is the least important part of your casting outfit. All it does is hold the line; only when you fight very big fish do you have to turn it while "playing" them. Avoid large reels because they're heavy, unless you need the extra size to hold a lot of line, such as a "backing" line. This is 50 or 100 yards of cheap, strong nylon line tied to the end of your fly line so you'll have enough for a big fish that might run out a long distance. Your fly reel should have a simple "click" device so it won't unwind by itself.

THE FLY LINE

Your fly line is the most important item of your tackle. If you have the right one, casting is easy, even if you're just a beginner. The standard fly line is about 30 yards long, made of enamelled silk or treated nylon with a very smooth finish so it will slide through the rod's guides easily. And it must be heavy, because in fly-casting you don't really cast the fly—you cast the line. The fly just follows along! This weight, or thickness, is specified by letters of the alphabet from "A," the thickest and heaviest, to "G," the thinnest and lightest. It can be a "level" line, having the same thickness over its entire length, or a "double taper" which is thicker in the middle, tapering to thinner line at each end. Such a double taper is an "HEH," which is "H" thickness at the ends and "E" in the middle. The reason for its design is that it's thin and less visible on the end, which is the part the fish is most likely to see, but still heavy enough in its main section to have sufficient weight for casting. And when one end wears out, you can turn the line around on the reel and use the other end!

The third type of line is the real secret behind good casts; it's the "torpedo taper." It consists of three thicknesses in the same line: very thin on the fishing end (for about 3 feet), tapering to very thick and heavy line for the next 38 feet, then tapering to a medium-thick line for the remainder of 49 feet

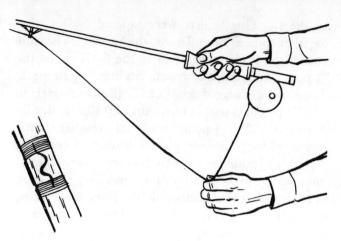

SNAKE GUIDE fastened to rod with windings of silk.

which is tied to your reel. Such a line is an "HCG." The torpedo taper's advantage? The thick, heavy part is right up front where it gives you a perfect weight concentration for casting. Lines made by different manufacturers may differ slightly in the lengths of the three sections, but the differences are insignificant. You must choose a torpedo taper to fit your rod, however. The stiffer the rod, the heavier the line needed. To solve this problem, ask your tackle dealer for help. By testing your rod, he'll know which line you should have.

Your fly line must be kept soft, pliable and free from cracks so that it will slide unhindered through the rod's guides. Lubricate it often with line dressing which you can buy at the tackle store. This dressing also helps the line to float, which is necessary when fishing dry flies. To be sure they'll float, some lines now are made with hollow cores. There's still another type designed for extra-long casting for fish that don't care if your line floats or not—a lead-core line. The purpose of the lead core, of course, is to add weight for the cast. Only exceptionally powerful, stiff rods will handle this type of line.

THE FLY LEADER

The purpose of a fly leader is to serve as a connection, as invisible as possible, between your fly and your line. The longer and thinner the leader, the more invisible it will be. But there are limits to its length; 12-foot and 9-foot leaders are difficult to cast because they lessen the weight up front. And thin leaders aren't very strong. In general, use as long a leader as you can cast satisfactorily. Leaders used to be made of gut; now nylon is preferred because it's stronger, more durable and can be tapered smoothly from a thick length where it joins the fly line to a spider-web thinness where it is tied

Light line on end　　　　　**Middle-weight line winds on reel**

Heavy line in center
TORPEDO TAPER LINE

to the fly. Gut leaders were tapered by knotting together pieces of different thicknesses. The fine end of the leader that's tied to the fly is called the "tippet," and its size determines its breaking strength. These sizes range from "OX" (2-pound-test) to "7X" ($\frac{1}{4}$-pound-test). The commonest size for dry-fly fishing is "4X" ($\frac{5}{8}$-pound-test); for wet-flies, "2X" (1-pound-test). Strong plastic leader material of incredible thinness recently became available to anglers. To make it even more invisible, it is dyed blue or ash color. Although fly lines must float, especially for dry-fly fishing, all leaders must sink. Since nylon is waterproof, leaders made of it must be rubbed with a special "sink" preparation before they're used.

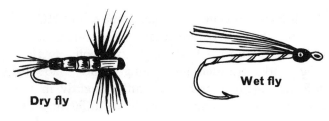

Dry fly   **Wet fly**

THE ARTIFICIAL FLY LURE

Artificial flies are intended to imitate insects and small fish. The dry fly resembles a live fly that has just hatched from the water or fallen on the surface; the wet fly is the drowned fly being swept downstream by the current. The small, less colorful dry and wet patterns look most real—and get the most strikes. The bright colors usually attract more fishermen than fish, but there are exceptions; when fish become "ornery" they seem to take the unreal patterns just for spite.

The streamer flies are intended to imitate small minnows on which the fish feed. They're more difficult to cast than dry or wet flies because they're bulkier, meeting greater air resistance which slows up your line during the cast and throws off your timing. Still another fly that fish love is the nymph. It imitates a fly that is still in its underwater larval stage before it hatches into a flying insect. Actually the hellgrammite is the nymph of a fly called the "Dobson." Trout depend largely on nymphs for food during the early spring days when other insects are scarce.

THE KNOT

The standard knot for tying a fly to a nylon tippet is shown in the drawing—after threading the hook's eye, twist the end around the leader several times, pass it through the loop formed just above the hook's eye, then pull it tight. To keep the knot from pulling loose, touch a lighted match to the end of the tippet; this will form a small blob of plastic which can't pull through.

HOW TO FLY-CAST

To get the "feel" of your fly tackle, assemble your rod, reel and torpedo line without a leader. The reel should hang below the rod's handle, or "grip." Stand in an open space and pull out about 20 feet of line beyond your rod tip. Grasp your rod with one hand; with the other, hold the line that hangs from the reel so no more of it will pull out. Now flip the line that extends from your rod tip from side to side in a constant motion, letting the whippy rod do the flipping. Don't move the rod tip very far from the vertical position. Flip the line with a wrist action while you hold your elbow close to your side. Note how the line will curl out one side in a loop, and then, if you wait until just the right moment—just before the loop has straightened—a slight snap of your wrist will pull it in and roll it out the other side. This is your "timing." Practice until it's perfect, then try casting a longer line. Next, turn your cast so it's front and back instead of side to side, and "feel" the timing instead of watching the line. In either a forward cast (when the loop is rolling out in front) or a back cast (loop rolling out in back), if you snap the rod in the opposite direction too soon or too late, the line will simply wrap around your neck. Your timing must be in a "1-2-3" count for both front cast and back cast—"1," the snap of the wrist that curls the line outward; "2," the hesitation until it uncurls just the right amount; and "3," the snap that brings it curling in the opposite direction.

Add a leader and a tuft of cotton to imitate a fly. The timing will remain the same. Only the length of line will alter that. Now, on one of your forward casts, let the line fall ahead of you. Just before it touches the ground, lift the rod tip a few inches so it tugs on the line slightly; the leader will curl ahead of the line and the cotton will fall first—just the way you'll want a fly to fall when you're fishing. To prepare for the next cast, pull in the slack line, raise your rod quickly and the line will lift over your head and curl behind you in a back cast. Notice

THE KNOT

Blobbed plastic

3 times round

Pass through loop near eye of hook

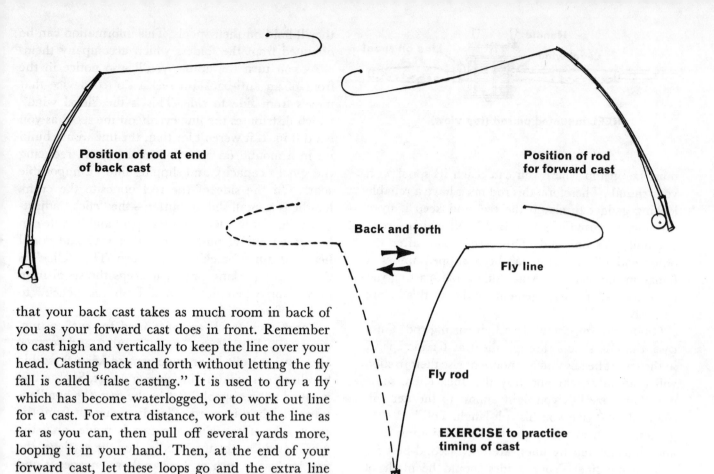

Position of rod at end of back cast

Position of rod for forward cast

Back and forth

Fly line

Fly rod

EXERCISE to practice timing of cast

Rod handle

that your back cast takes as much room in back of you as your forward cast does in front. Remember to cast high and vertically to keep the line over your head. Casting back and forth without letting the fly fall is called "false casting." It is used to dry a fly which has become waterlogged, or to work out line for a cast. For extra distance, work out the line as far as you can, then pull off several yards more, looping it in your hand. Then, at the end of your forward cast, let these loops go and the extra line will "shoot" out through the guides. Retrieve this extra line before picking up your regular length for the next cast. Retrieving a line is done with one hand; twist your hand back and forth, grasping a few inches of line and pulling it in with each twist. This is the way to work a wet fly. It's also how you retrieve slack line without letting go of it while you're playing a fish.

BAIT-CASTING

Bait-casting is the fishing method most sportsmen use. It's easy to learn and its tackle is inexpensive. And it isn't limited to catching small fish, as fly-casting and spinning are unless you're an expert. A big Cannibal Trout will hit your bait-casting spoon or plug. So will a hefty citizen of the sea such as a Striped Bass, and between these extremes there are hundreds of species willing to do the same. Accuracy is a great advantage of this tackle. Soon you'll be able to sight your casting rod the way you do a rifle and hit the target every time. Distance is another advantage; you can cast 150 feet or more with almost no effort—if you let your springy rod do the casting for you instead of trying to make your arm do all the work. Also, with bait-casting you don't need a lot of room behind you as in fly-casting.

THE BAIT-CASTING ROD

Your rod can be made of either fibreglass or split-bamboo. Both are suitable, but glass is better. Bamboo is more expensive and glass isn't as likely to snap when a big fish bends it in half. A long rod (6 to 7 feet) has more spring than a shorter one and with a light reel it will cast lures weighing as little as $\frac{1}{2}$ ounce, such as the ones you use for large pan-fish. For the $\frac{5}{8}$-ounce to 1-ounce plugs and spoons used to lure big Pike, Black Bass, and so forth, you'll need a stiffer rod of 5 or $5\frac{1}{2}$ feet. Although on a fly rod and spinning rod the reel hangs downward from the rod's handle, on a bait-casting rod the reel

BAIT-CASTING: Reel mounted on rod (side view).

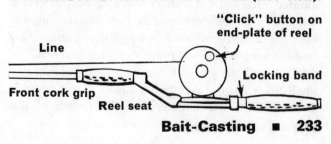

"Click" button on end-plate of reel

Line

Locking band

Front cork grip

Reel seat

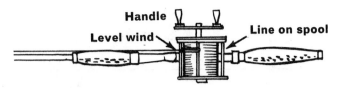

Handle

Level wind

Line on spool

REEL mounted on rod (top view).

must be on top where you can reach its spool with your thumb. Therefore, this rod must have a reliable locking gadget to clamp the reel and keep it from slipping. It's usually a threaded band which screws out and over one end of the reel's base after the other end of the base has been slipped under a flange in the reel-seat. Make sure a bait-casting rod has some locking arrangement similar to this before you buy it.

Guides are important on a bait-casting rod. On a cast, the line shoots through them at terrific speed, so they must be absolutely smooth or else their friction will gradually wear and fray the line. Then, some day that prize fish you fight almost to the net will snap off and give you his fish-laugh. Polished steel guides, which are all right for light spinning lines and slow-moving fly lines, are only second-best for bait-casting lines. Your guides should be made of uncracked agate, the genuine hard mineral, not ordinary glass. Or else they should be made of one of the new crackproof plastics. This is especially important for the tip guide over which the shooting line passes at an angle, generating the most friction and wear. To assemble your rod, hold its sections so their guides line up perfectly with each other, then push—don't twist—the rod sections together. Guides out of alignment will cause more line wear.

THE BAIT-CASTING REEL

The bait-casting reel is a tricky little gadget. Once you've learned to control it, the rest of bait-casting is a cinch because it's the main part of the whole operation. A fly-casting reel simply holds the line; a spinning reel just holds the line and then winds it in after it's been cast; but a bait-casting reel does three things—stores line, lets it out, and pulls it in. It fastens to the top of your rod handle, its double-handle crank on the right (left on left-handed reels). Turn this crank and note how the spool of the reel revolves. It turns faster, usually about four turns for each turn of the crank. It's a "multiplying" reel—it multiplies the turns of the crank handle so you can reel in a lure quickly at a small fish's natural swimming speed. Reels come in different sizes which determine the length of line

they'll hold on their spools. This information can be obtained from the folders which accompany them.

As you turn the crank, you'll also notice in the front of an anti-backlash reel a slotted device that moves from side to side. This is the "level wind" which distributes the line evenly on the spool as you wind it in. If it weren't for that, the line would build up in a mound on one spot on the spool, reducing the spool's capacity and slipping into an impossible snarl. On the side of the reel opposite the crank handle is a small sliding button—the "click" adjustment. Push it one way and the spool and handle can be turned freely; push it the other way and you'll hear a distinct "click" as they turn. This "click" is like a car's parking brake; it keeps the spool from unwinding when not in use. Push the "click" to "off" before casting.

Large reels, such as those used for surf-casting, necessarily have large, heavy handles and so they also have a built-in arrangement to keep these big handles from windmilling during a cast. Such a reel is called a "free spool." Before the cast, the handle is turned slightly forward. This disengages it from the spool. Therefore, when the cast is made, only the spool revolves, not the handle. For the retrieve, the first backward turn of the handle re-engages it and the line is reeled in as usual. Large reels also have an adjustable "drag," or brake, to protect the line. This drag allows the spool to slip and release the line before it breaks when a fish pulls too hard, even when the angler may still be reeling in with all his strength.

THE BAIT-CASTING LINE

Bait-casting line used to be made of silk until nylon, with its greater strength for its size, greater hardness and greater resistance to mildew, showed itself to be far superior. It comes in various strengths and lengths, dyed all different colors for camouflage. Green or black seems to be least visible to fish. For most fresh-water Bass casting, an 8-pound-test line is strong enough. Use as light a line as you can because the heavier it is, the more difficult it is to cast and the shorter your casts will be. However, for fish larger than Bass you'll have to settle for stronger, heavier line. In order to make casting as easy as possible, the line should fill the spool of your reel almost to its edges. But 100 yards of 8-pound-test only cover the bottom of a standard spool! The answer is to use a "backing"—more line to fill the spool partially before you wind your casting line on it. This can be an old or cheap line since it probably will never see action. As a safety measure, tie the backing tightly to the spool of your reel and after winding it on, make sure to tie it securely to your casting line.

THE BAIT-CASTING ARTIFICIAL LURE

There are thousands of lures for bait-casting—plugs that splash and gurgle, that perform on the surface and at all depths, and that imitate everything from small fish to swimming ducklings. Some recent ones look as though they might have come from Mars. There are also spoons of all descriptions that wobble fast and wobble slow, with and without hindquarters of colored feathers. They all catch fish and all are easy to cast. Spoons, especially, cast like bullets. Use them when you have to cast into a high wind. Use a "snap" (it looks like a small safety pin) at the end of your line to make changing lures easy—and change them often. With every snap there's a "swivel" to keep your line from being twisted by a revolving lure.

Swivel

HOW TO BAIT-CAST

For your first bait-casting attempt, cast a $\frac{5}{8}$-ounce rubber practice plug you can buy at your tackle shop. Assemble your rod and reel, being sure to pass the line through the level-wind slot of the reel before threading it through the rod guides. Tie the plug to the line and let it hang about 8 inches from the rod tip. Now, turn the rod so the reel is upright and grasp the rod handle with one hand, holding it so your thumb can rest on the spool of the reel. Holding the spool tight with your thumb, push the "click" button to "off" with your other hand. Next, release your thumb. The spool unwinds as the plug falls and pulls out line. But what happens when the plug hits the ground? The spool got started; there's nothing to stop it; it keeps right on turning. The line on it loosens and snarls. That, friend, is the curse of bait-casters—the "backlash"—but you have only a little one. Wait until you fumble a cast and get a king-size one! Straighten out your line, wind it in and do it again, but this time press your thumb on the spool as soon as the plug touches the ground to keep the spool from over-running. No snarl! That's what your thumb must do during your cast: it must act as a brake to keep the spool from unwinding faster than the plug is pulling out line, and it must stop the spool completely before the plug touches the water.

Now let's try a short cast. With your thumb on the spool and the plug hanging about 8 inches from the rod tip, raise your rod and swish the plug in a fore-and-aft direction directly over your head, moving the rod tip back and forth only a yard or so each time. Notice how the spring of the rod keeps the lure moving! Now, just as the rod tip snaps the plug forward and just before the plug reaches its forward position, release your thumb so it exerts only a very slight pressure on the spool. The plug will sail out farther than you think! And if you've remembered to use your thumb to stop the spool before the plug drops, you won't get a backlash.

Repeat this exercise, lengthening the casts by swishing a little harder until you've learned at which stage in the cast to release your thumb and when to start increasing the pressure on the spool again. For your next step, eliminate the swishing entirely. Point your rod tip ahead of you, sighting it at your target. Imagine there's an apple stuck on the tip and you're going to throw it. Bring the rod up and back sharply to your old swishing position, let the rod tip bend backward with the momentum of the plug, then bring the rod forward to about a 45-degree angle and release your thumb as the plug begins to pull forward—you know when from your swishing exercise. As the plug flies out, apply light thumb pressure to brake the reel slightly. When the plug is directly over the target, stop the spool so the plug will fall directly on it.

Sounds easy—and it is! The whole secret is to educate that thumb.

Once you've done this, there are a couple of additional tricks. When you cast, turn your rod on its side so the reel is vertical with its crank handle on top. This puts the weight of the spool on the end bearing so it will turn more easily, and you'll get more distance. Also, keep pointing your rod tip at the lure as it flies through the air, to lessen the line

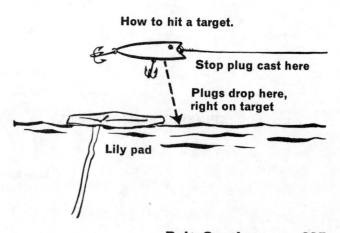

How to hit a target.

Stop plug cast here

Plugs drop here, right on target

Lily pad

friction at the tip guide. You might try some side casts, too, which come in handy when there are trees overhead. But overhead casting is most accurate—and safer—especially when you're casting with a companion in a boat.

When you get a backlash, don't yank the line from the spool in desperation. Pull gently while rolling the snarled line from side to side with your thumb and you'll gradually work it loose. To reel in a lure, or when playing a fish, switch hands. Take the rod in your other hand and turn the reel crank with your first hand. Now your other thumb must control the spool—acting as an adjustable drag when a fish wallops your lure and starts to run with it.

SPINNING

Spinning tackle is so easy to cast with that every angler becomes an expert. It's even simpler to use than bait-casting tackle, and in most cases can be used instead of it. Spinning tackle can also be used in places where fly-casting tackle can't, because a spinning rod doesn't require a lot of room for a cast. There is no back cast in spinning. It has one disadvantage, however. The size of spinning line is limited, and this limits its strength. Therefore spinning tackle isn't recommended for general fishing where there are lily pads, weeds and snags because the fish will break off easily. You'll lose too many.

THE SPINNING ROD

Spinning requires a special rod between 6 and 8 feet long with a very stiff tip. Before buying a spinning rod, test it by swishing it back and forth with a fast snapping motion. After each swish, the tip should snap straight again instantly with no lag. A rod made of split-bamboo will have a stiffer tip than one made of glass, but will be more expensive. Glass spinning rods perform almost as well and are cheaper. The advantage of a short rod (6 feet) is that it's easier to cast with when you're surrounded by bushes and overhead tree limbs. It doesn't need as much space for your casting swing. You can recognize a spinning rod by its cork "grip" or handle on which the reel fastens by means of two sliding metal bands. You can recognize it also by its first line-guide above the grip; it's huge, almost an inch in diameter. The line "spins" through it during the cast. The remaining guides, about 4, are smaller and vary in size. The tip guide is the smallest.

THE SPINNING REEL

The spinning reel is an amazing little machine, although it looks clumsy. Some anglers call it a "coffee mill" or "grinder," and it really does look like one with its big handle and its long post which makes it project almost 6 inches from the rod's grip. Its spool, which holds the line, is "fixed"—it doesn't turn during the cast. One end of this spool faces the front of the rod. During the cast, the line slips out over the edge, or "lip," of this front end of the spool with a "spinning" motion. This is the reel's secret! The line leaves it freely, with almost no resistance. It doesn't have to turn the spool and a handle as it goes. If it weren't for air resistance, your spinning reel would let you cast a lure a mile—almost! Also, you don't have to stop the spool and handle with your thumb at the end of a cast. When the lure hits the water and stops, the line automatically stops also. There's no overrunning of spool and handle to cause a backlash. You can't backlash a spinning reel. Your thumb is out of a job!

When you turn the reel's handle to retrieve the line, a wire loop called a "bail" (or a curved metal finger called a "pickup") snaps over the line, catches it and turns around the spool, winding it back on like magic. Since spinning reels are multipliers like bait-casting reels, each turn of the handle winds 4 or 5 turns of line on the spool. The reel also has an

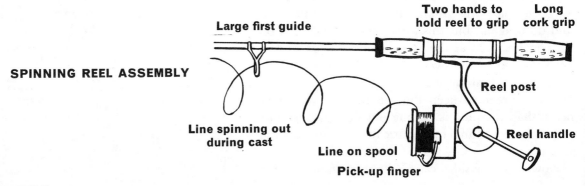

SPINNING REEL ASSEMBLY

Large first guide

Two hands to hold reel to grip

Long cork grip

Reel post

Reel handle

Line spinning out during cast

Line on spool

Pick-up finger

adjustable "drag," or brake. This protects the line from breaking when a fish pulls too hard. With the bail or pickup in place, the line can't uncoil from the spool when the fish pulls—but the brake allows the spool to slip and turn on its axis like a bait-casting reel's spool, and the line is pulled out in spite of the pickup. A better name for this brake would be "clutch" because it actually regulates the amount of pull required before the spool will slip and turn. Before fishing, you must set this drag so that it's less than the breaking strength of your line.

Before each cast, the bail or pickup is snapped out of the way so the line will be able to spin from the spool. Since nothing moves on the reel during the cast, there is no need for you to touch it with your fingers. The long base post holds it away from the rod grip where the line can spin off without interference. The reel is attached so it hangs below the cork grip. Where you place it on this long grip depends upon where you "feel" it balances best when you hold the rod. Most anglers prefer it just forward of the center position.

THE SPINNING LINE

Spinning line is made of monofilament (single-strand nylon), or of braided nylon strands, dyed blue, green or grey to make them invisible to a fish. This line must be light and fine, almost as thin as thread, so it will have no weight to slow up its spinning from the reel or to slow up the lure as it flies through the air during the cast. One of 3- or 5-pound-test is strong enough for most panfishing in open water. It can even hold a 10-pounder if you "baby" him and let your rod absorb his sudden twists and leaps. As the water gets weedier and the fish get large, however, it's best to use a heavier line, perhaps one of 10-pound-test, although it will shorten your casts slightly. Such a line should be powerful enough to hold more than a 10-pounder— if you have enough of it. The spool of a standard size spinning reel holds about 200 yards of medium-test line. This should fill the spool *almost* to its "lip," or edge. If the line on the spool is more than $\frac{1}{16}$-inch below this lip it will catch on the lip and won't spin off freely. If it's piled up higher than the lip it will slide off in coils and will snarl. When you have too much line, cut off the surplus. When you don't have enough, add some "backing" line as described in Bait-Casting. For very large fish, including the salt-water species, you can get a king-size spinning reel that will hold all the line necessary for their long runs. Such reels work well for surf-casting, too.

With a monofilament line, be careful of kinking, or accidentally knotting, since kinks and knots will reduce its strength to at least half. There aren't many knots you can use for tying a lure to monofilament without weakening it—the one described for attaching leaders in Fly-Casting is the best and safest. Although your spinning line won't backlash, it can cause you trouble in another way—it can get twisted by a lure that revolves steadily in the water, or you can accidentally give it a twist as you first wind it on your reel when it's new. Then it will form kinky loops instead of remaining straight and pliable. And these loops, spinning from the spool during a cast, will snarl and might catch in the guides, snapping the line. To avoid a twist when fishing, always use a swivel or two between your line and lure. If there is a twist on your line, remove the lure and let out all the line behind a moving boat; its motion through the water will untwist it. To avoid a twist when putting a new line on your reel, wind the line by hand and after every 10 windings turn over the original spool the line is wound on so it comes off first from one side, then from the other.

THE LURE FOR SPINNING

More lures are made for spinning than for any other kind of casting. They even outnumber the artificial-fly patterns. Fly-casters poke fun at them and call them "jewelry." Truthfully, some of them do look like fancy lockets or earrings. They certainly don't imitate anything a fish has ever seen in nature. Only half of them resemble minnows even slightly. But, mysteriously, they all catch fish! Maybe the fly-casters are just angry because a Trout can be so smart about flies, but so dumb about spinning lures.

With spinning tackle you can cast bait such as minnows, worms, frogs, and so forth. Most of these are heavy enough for use without any added weight, such as a sinker. A bobber can be used if desired. But the artificial lures catch almost as many fish and are more fun to use. Try spoons, plugs, wobblers, spinners or weighted flies—anything from $\frac{1}{8}$- to $\frac{3}{4}$-ounce, even most bait-casting lures. They all cast easily. You can even cast a dry fly or wet fly with spinning tackle, a fact that makes Trout fishermen very unhappy. Tie the heavy torpedo section of a torpedo-tapered fly line to the end of your spinning line, and add to the fly line the regular fly leader and fly. Then, with your forefinger holding the spinning line as usual, false cast (see Fly-Casting) the fly-line rig overhead with your spinning rod, timing it just as though it were a fly rod and you were getting ready to cast it that way. But, when you have the fly line looping back and forth with good timing, release your forefinger on a forward swing and out she'll fly. You'll get more distance with that fly than you ever did with conventional fly tackle. All the spinning rod needs is the slight extra weight to cast, and the fly line added to the fly supplies that.

HOW TO CAST WHEN SPINNING

Ready to discover why spinning is so easy? Assemble your rod sections by lining up the guides, then by pushing—not twisting—the ferrules together. Fasten the reel to the grip by means of the two sliding bands, thread the line through the guides and tie to its end a very light sinker (¼ ounce) or a spinning lure from which you've removed the hooks. Now grasp the rod grip just above the reel, your thumb along the top of the grip, your forefinger in front of the base of the reel and your remaining three fingers in back of it. With your free hand, crank the reel handle until the bail or pickup is at a bottom position, then reach downward with the forefinger of the hand that's holding the rod and hook that finger around the line. Lift the line with it and hold the line against the rod grip so the lure can't pull it out. Then, with your free hand, snap the bail or pickup out of the way. You're ready to cast—but first let's see how the reel works.

Point the rod ahead of you and release the line you're holding with your forefinger. The lure will fall and the line will spin out. But when the lure hits the ground and stops, the line will stop also. There'll be no backlash. Now for the retrieve. Crank the reel handle with your free hand. The bail or pickup will automatically snap back into position, hook the line and wind it back on the spool. Reel in the lure until it's about 8 inches from the rod tip and prepare for a real cast. Hold the line with your forefinger as before, snap the bail or pickup out of the way and swish the lure back and forth over your head. Note how the springiness of the rod tugs on the lure.

Select some target about 100 feet distant and on one of the forward motions of your rod, when it is pointed only slightly above this target, release your forefinger. (A large basket is a good target to practice on—or a hula hoop.) If you've released the line too soon, it will climb like a little space rocket and disappear over a treetop. This is what usually happens to an angler used to bait-casting tackle when he tries spinning for the first time, because the timing is different. A bait-casting lure must be

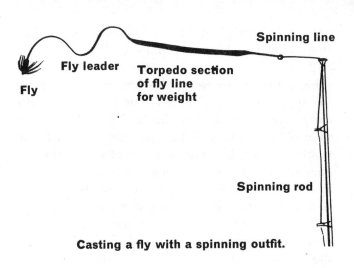

Casting a fly with a spinning outfit.

released sooner in the casting swing because it's slower getting started due to the drag of the reel spool and handle which it has to start turning. If you've released the line too late, however, as most beginners do on their first try, the lure will hit the ground at your feet. But after a few tries, you'll quickly learn the right timing. Then when you point your rod tip at a target (which might be the swirl of a big Bass), snap the lure over your head and let the rod tip snap it forward again, it'll shoot out for a bull's-eye every time. When you see that your lure is going to overshoot the spot you've aimed for—you've cast it too far—it's simple to stop it. Just grab the line with your free hand as it spins out, or crank the handle once so the pickup will hook the line and stop it. After you've learned the straight overhead cast, you can try the variations— side casts, underhand casts, bow casts, and the rest. They're all just as simple.

SPIN-CASTING

Spin-casting is not the same as spinning, although spinning is casting, too. Spin-casting is a technical term (to anglers) and it refers to a method that's really a combination of spinning and bait-casting. With it you use spinning line, either a spinning or bait-casting rod, and either spinning or bait-casting lures. It's made possible by a special little device called the spin-cast reel. And as you can guess, this reel is also a combination.

THE SPIN-CASTING REEL

The spin-cast reel mounts on a bait-casting rod exactly like a bait-casting reel. On a spinning rod it goes on just like a spinning reel except that you turn the rod upside down so the reel is on top instead of hanging down below the grip. Its handle is like that of a bait-casting reel. But the spool that holds the spinning line has one end facing the front like that of a spinning reel. And it is completely enclosed by a cover with only a small hole in its front center through which the line passes during the cast. Because of this cover, the spin-cast reel is sometimes referred to as a "closed-face" spinning reel. At the back of the reel is a button or lever within easy reach of your thumb. This controls the cast. The spin-cast reel also has a drag which works like that on the regular spinning reel.

THE SPIN-CASTING LINE

Since a spin-cast reel uses spinning line, there's a limit to the strength of the line you can use. You'll cast best with a light line of 10-pound-test or less. And avoid twisting it with revolving lures or when winding it on your spin-cast reel. Follow the instructions on twisted line spinning. You can remove the cover of the spin-cast line easily for hand-spooling. Regardless of line weight, your stiff bait-casting rod is best for casting heavy bait-casting lures, and your spinning rod is best for spinning lures.

HOW TO SPIN-CAST

Casting with it is so easy your baby brother can do it. With your tackle assembled, reel in the lure until it's a few inches from the rod tip. Grasp the rod in back of the reel and rest your thumb on the reel's button or lever. Press it and hold it in. Now raise the rod tip quickly to a position over your head and slightly behind, and bring it forward in a cast. At the position where, with a spinning reel, you would pull back your forefinger to release the line, on the spin-cast reel you simply lift your thumb from the button. This frees the line and out shoots the lure. If you want to stop the lure during the cast, push on the button once more. This brakes it. To retrieve the lure, shift the rod to your other hand and wind the reel handle with your casting hand as you do with a bait-casting reel. The hidden line-pickup is automatic. When playing a fish you don't have to thumb the line spool; the adjustable drag takes care of that.

SPIN-CAST REEL

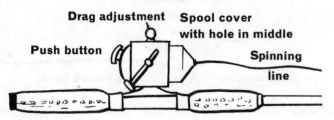

Drag adjustment **Spool cover with hole in middle**

Push button **Spinning line**

STILL-FISHING AND DOCK-FISHING

Seldom will any artificial fish-fooler beat a piece of natural bait on your hook when you want to catch the most fish and the largest. Moreover, lures must be kept moving or they won't fool anything because it's their motion through the water that gives them a lifelike action. Even a dry fly must be given a realistic twitch or two so that old Mr. Trout will think it's still kicking. And to make lures move, you must troll them, or cast and retrieve them. Bait can be trolled, or cast and retrieved, too, but it isn't necessary. You don't have to help a worm squirm. Just drop him overboard and he'll do it by himself. So will a frog, crawfish, grasshopper and all the others. This fishing without casting, while you let your bait do all the luring, is called "still-fishing," and it's the same whether you're dangling from a dock, or getting blisters from the hard seat of a rowboat, or lounging like Cleopatra on the soft cushions of a cabin cruiser.

RODS, REELS AND LINES

Still-fishing requires no special tackle, but don't use an ordinary string because it might not be strong enough. And don't use a bent pin because it has no barb on its point to hold either the bait or fish. Your tackle can be a fly-casting, bait-casting, spinning or spin-casting outfit, or a simple hand line which is a length of fish line wound on a wooden or plastic holder. A rod, of course, will let your fish fight harder when he's hooked; with a hand line all you do is haul him in hand-over-hand. And a rod will enable you to cast your bait farther from the boat or dock. Use the same line that's on your casting outfit—unless it's an expensive fly line. Then it's wiser to save it for its specialized job of fly-casting, and substitute a cheap bait-casting line. Nylon lines are best for both fresh water and salt water. And level leaders are stronger than tapered ones.

BOBBERS

A "bobber" is commonly used in fresh-water still-fishing. It's a float that attaches to your line and lets you know when a fish is tugging on your hook. In its simplest form, it's no more than a big cork with a slit in its side into which you wedge the line. Its distance from the hook determines how far the hook will sink. Bobbers sold in tackle stores are more elaborate but they work the same way. Some are pear-shaped and ride upright on the water. Other are long thin tubes that lie flat. Both types are brightly colored so you can see them clearly. The

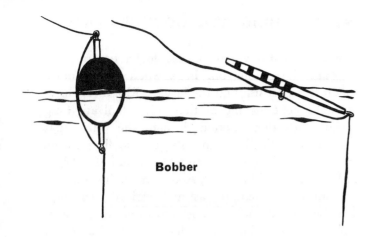

Bobber

pear-shaped kind bobs up and down when a fish nibbles, and when it starts to move away, or disappears completely, you jerk the line to set the hook because then you know the fish has a firm hold on the bait. The tube kind stands straight up in the air when a fish nibbles, and ducks out of sight when he runs with it. The disadvantage of a bobber is that when you're using it with a rod, you can't fish deep. Usually you can go no deeper than the length of your rod, because you can reel in only a certain length of line before the bobber strikes your top tip guide and stops. The only way you can get the hooked fish is to pull him in by hand. Some bobbers are made with hollow cores so they can slide down the line, but they're not easy to use. The salt-water still-fisherman, who almost always must fish deep, seldom bothers with a bobber.

HOOKS

Hooks for still-fishing with a hand line or with bait-casting tackle, either in fresh water or salt water, should be the "snelled" kind. These are eyeless hooks, each with a 10- or 12-inch nylon leader, or "snell," fastened to its shank. At the other end of the snell is a loop to which you tie your line. The purpose of the snell is invisibility; since the fish can't see it, they're less suspicious of your baited hook. Snelled hooks can be used with fly-casting, spinning and spin-casting tackle, also, but they're not necessary. With fly-casting tackle you already have an invisible leader, and the monofilament lines of spinning and spin-casting reels also are invisible. In these cases, eyed hooks will serve just as well. For fish with sharp teeth, always still-fish with hooks that are snelled with heavy, twisted nylon. The fish will bite through them anyhow, but not as often—and without snells you're not likely to get any bites at all on a heavy line.

Hooks come in many sizes. For practical use, No. 6/0 is the largest. Next smaller is 5/0, then

4/0, etc., down to 1/0, after which the sizes start downward from No. 1 to No. 16 which is the smallest. The size you need depends upon two things: the size of the fish's mouth and the kind of bait you use. The hook with bait on it obviously must be small enough for the fish to grab. From the standpoint of bait, however, you frequently have to take your chances with a small hook because a large one will kill your bait too quickly. Bass like grasshoppers, but how long will a grasshopper stay alive on a big No. 6/0 Bass hook? Here it is better to settle for a No. 2/0 hook, or use one slightly larger and tie the grasshopper to it with thread.

An objection anglers frequently have to small hooks for bait is that fish usually swallow them completely and so are hooked inside the stomach instead of the mouth. Then, when a fish is smaller than legal size, it can't be returned to the water unharmed because it's impossible to unhook it without fatally injuring it. Mouth wounds are almost never fatal, but a fish must be cut open for the removal of a hook from its innards. Fish biologists have come up with a startling remedy, however. They recommend that when a small fish swallows your hook, cut the snell as far down its throat as possible, then return it to the water with the hook still in its stomach. They've found that in most cases the hooks miraculously dissolve and the fish live.

SINKERS

Sinkers are made not only in different weights but also in different shapes because they have different purposes. Only one of these is to sink your baited hook down to where the fish are. Some sinkers are intended to supply a slight additional weight for casting. Others are used as small anchors to keep your hook from drifting with a strong current.

All sinkers are made of soft lead because this is the heaviest substance. The simplest shape is the split-shot, a small pellet (ranging from buckshot to BB size) which is split almost in half. For added weight in casting, you fasten it on your leader or monofilament line by squeezing the halves together.

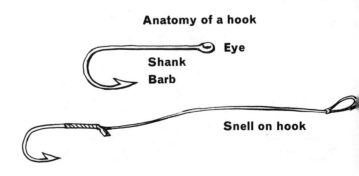

Anatomy of a hook

Eye

Shank

Barb

Snell on hook

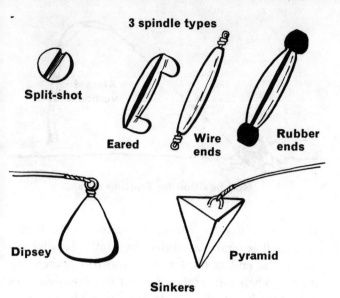

3 spindle types

Split-shot

Eared **Wire ends** **Rubber ends**

Dipsey **Pyramid**

Sinkers

Another light-weight, easy-to-fasten type is a "wrap-around." This is a thin strip of lead which you twist around your line or leader, instead of squeezing it on. These two are popular with users of fly-casting and spinning tackle. To add weight to a bait-casting lure, or just to sink a baited hook, the commonest sinker design is the "spindle," an elongated sinker with a slot in its side and a flap of lead on each end. To fasten it, you put the line in the slot and under the flaps, then squeeze down the flaps to hold it. A variation of this type has no slot or flaps, but a spring-fastener at each end to hold the line. The latest variation has rubber ears on its ends; a simple and easy twist fastens the line behind them. Sinkers which fasten at the end of your line and are designed chiefly for anchoring your baited hook, come in assorted shapes. The "dipsey" is a popular non-snagging one. It's shaped like a pear with a swivel-ring at the stem end. Another is the "pyramid" which has the connecting ring in its flat base.

HOW TO STILL-FISH

In still-fishing, you must get your baited hook down to a level where the fish on the bottom can at least see it. If you're fishing where a bobber will allow you enough line to do this (at least a length equal to the length of your rod), use it because it will keep your hook away from your boat or dock when you cast it, and the fish that see the hook won't also see you. But make sure you are able to tell whether the bobber signals "bite" or just "nibble." When it dances up and down on the surface, fish are nibbling. Reel in the slack line and get ready. When the bobber goes under, or almost goes under, strike! Lift your rod tip high, because there'll still be a lot of slack line you have to straighten before you can exert pull on the hook. If you miss the strike, don't reel in right away to put on a new bait. Let the hook rest a minute. Maybe the fish didn't get the bait, in which case he'll take it again. In still-fishing without a bobber, first lower a sinker to determine how deep the water is, then subtract 4 feet and measure off this distance on your fish line, tying a small slipknot in the line to mark it. When you cast out your baited hook, let out line to this mark, then let your hook gradually sink. When it's hanging straight down, it will be at just the right depth.

HOW TO DOCK-FISH

Dock-fishing is salt-water still-fishing, and it's part of a sport that ocean anglers refer to as "bottom-fishing." The principal difference between this and fresh-water still-fishing is that you don't have to worry as much about the bottom; it's usually sand with few places for your bait to hide. When bottom-fishing, always keep your line taut against the sinker that anchors it, and keep the line between two fingers. Your fingers will feel any vibration or tug that will indicate a bite. Reel in your hooks frequently to inspect them, because crabs and small fish will steal your bait continually.

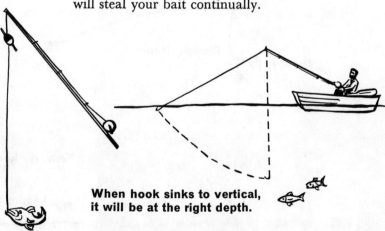

STILL-FISHING without a bobber: If you use too much line on your bobber, you can't reel in far enough to reach your fish.

When hook sinks to vertical, it will be at the right depth.

Still-Fishing and Dock-Fishing ■ 241

HOW TO FIGHT A FISH

To a sportsman, the fun begins when he's trying to fool the fish into taking his lure or bait. It ends with the fish on his dinner table. Between this beginning and end occurs that part of angling that makes it the most popular sport in the world—the contest between angler and fish. If this weren't so, all of us probably would be using hooks, worms, and hand lines, and hauling in our fish like bunches of bananas. An angler's success in this contest, of course, depends upon his skill with his tackle.

USING FLY TACKLE

A fish takes a floating fly (dry fly) on the surface where you can see him, and you must strike him immediately before he realizes he's been tricked and spits it out, which he can do in a split second. Only occasionally will he hook himself. In order to strike him, there should be only a small amount of slack line between your rod and the fly, and the rod should be extended forward at about a 45-degree angle so that by lifting the tip you can instantly straighten this slack line and put pressure on the hook. If your rod is too low, a fish that takes the fly and immediately runs will snap your leader; if it is too high, you won't be able to lift it any higher to straighten the slack. The same rod position is advisable when you're using a sinking fly (wet fly) although this fishing is more difficult because you can't see when the fish takes it. Neither can you feel him. You must watch the loop which connects your leader to your line. Strike when this loop makes a slight movement away from you, caused by the tug of the fish. Some anglers fish a

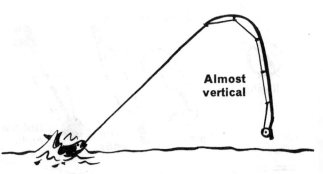

Rod position for fighting a fish.

wet with a dry-fly "dropper" (tied to the leader by a snell several feet above the "tail" fly which is tied to the end of the leader). And they watch this dry fly. When a fish takes the wet fly, the slight jerk will move the dry fly, too, telling the angler to strike.

The function of the rod, once the fish is hooked, is to tire him so he can be netted without danger of breaking the leader. Therefore, always hold the rod in a vertical position so that he fights its springiness. Your free hand controls the line at the reel—holding the line tight as long as the fish is making your rod bend, taking in line as the fish tires or when it runs toward you, and letting out line when the fish bends the rod so far that too much strain is being placed on the leader. When the fish tires, bring him in close, but never closer to the rod tip than the length of the rod itself. Hold the rod high over your head if necessary, transfer the line to your rod hand, hold your landing net under the water below him, lead him over it, then lower the rod so he drops into it head first. He may be only playing dead, however, so be ready to give him line if he wants to run again. The secret of fighting fish on fly tackle is: gentleness. Don't be a strongarm! That's why girls often make better anglers than boys; they're not as rough.

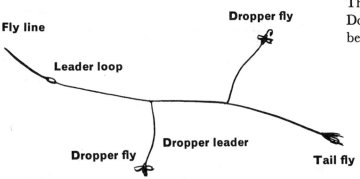

Fly line

Dropper fly

Leader loop

Dropper fly **Dropper leader** **Tail fly**

Rod position while retrieving.

Rod tip ready to be moved both ways

Always keep some slack in line

Rod held at about 45° angle

Fly **Leader on water**

USING BAIT-CASTING TACKLE

Gentleness pays off with a bait-casting rod, too. If you force a fish, you're apt to lose him because your line and leader may be strong enough but his mouth isn't, and the hooks will pull out. When retrieving a lure, hold your rod at a 45-degree angle as with fly tackle. And for the same reasons. As you wind in, keep your thumb on the bait-casting reel's spool, ready for action. When a fish strikes, clamp that thumb down for an instant as you lift the rod tip so that there's enough resistance to set the hook in his jaw, then release it slightly so he can run. Without your thumb pressure, his strike will make your reel backlash. Use your thumb as a brake; you might get a blister on it from a big fish, but that's a wound of respect. If you already have a blister on it, use a glove. Make the fish fight the bend in your rod, but give him line when he wants it! When he's tired, coax him in, never closer to your rod tip than the length of your rod, then lead him over your landing net, and drop him in head first. For fish that are too large for a hand net, anglers use a "gaff" which is a large barbless hook with a long handle. Another landing method you can use on smaller fish when you've forgotten your net is to grasp them by the lower jaw—but not if they have teeth like the Pike family. In their case you can sink the tips of your thumb and finger in their eye sockets and lift them aboard that way.

USING SPINNING AND SPIN-CASTING TACKLE

The rules which pertain to bait-casting also apply to this tackle, although with these reels you don't have as much control of your line and you'll lose more fish if you're not extremely careful. With spinning reels, hooking a fish is more difficult. Be extra certain to use needle-sharp hooks so they'll be sure to sink into the fish. The problem is this: you must adjust your spinning reel's drag before you start casting—and an adjustment that's loose enough to protect the line while you're playing a fish usually isn't tight enough to hook the fish. If you don't think the hook is set, release the reel handle for an instant, grab the line near the reel and, while holding it, bear back on the rod. While you're fighting the fish, of course, the drag adjustment determines whether or not you can reel in the line (and fish). If the pull is too great, the pickup will turn but the spool will unwind to nullify it. Frequently it is

Always keep a tight line.

When he jumps, pull rod back to turn him over.

necessary to tighten the drag as the fish becomes tired so you can put more pressure on him to bring him close. The change in drag adjustment is also necessary for a spin-cast reel, although with this type you won't have as great a hook-setting problem; just press down on the thumb button—this momentarily locks the line so you can exert a maximum pull on it. Netting with both spinning and spin-casting tackle is the same as with the bait-casting type.

No matter what tackle you use, there's an important rule to remember to keep a fish on your line once he's hooked—don't give him slack! Keep him fighting against the pressure of the rod. When a fish goes into his head-wagging act, either underwater or at the top of a leap, if you give him slack he'll shake loose your lure just as easily as you'd shake loose a grasshopper that's clinging to your hand. When he arcs up into the air, pull back on your rod and turn him over. Of course, no matter how careful you are, some clever fish will still throw your lure. But not as many!

And remember—be gentle! The rougher you are with a fish, the more likely you are to lose him!

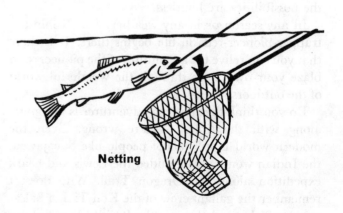

Netting

CAMPING AND BACKPACKING

Our cities are growing larger, our play areas smaller, and our recreations more mechanized, what with theatres, arenas, television and hi-fi's supplying almost all our entertainment. What is the result? Most of us are becoming flabby spectators watching the very few who are participants.

To break this vicious cycle, how about an active hobby, one that will take you out in the open air, a healthy hobby, a back-to-nature activity? Camping and backpacking is it. The camping ground remains *one* area where we are completely dependent upon ourselves, a place where the laws of the prairie rule, where we have to live like Robinson Crusoe or the Swiss Family Robinson, where we can make believe we are on the warpath like the Sioux on the Little Big Horn River or the Apaches from Salt River Canyon.

Wherever you live, you can find your own place to camp out. It might be a forested wilderness, but it needn't be. A park, a public picnic area—even your own back yard—can be transformed into a deserted island or Robin Hood's glen, and when you go farther afield, during summer holidays, perhaps, the possibilities are limitless.

In any season or in any weather, your Robinson-trapper-pioneer-redskin life begins there. It is there that you can relive the adventures of the pioneers and blaze your own trails through the wonderful world of the outdoors.

Do you think that playing adventurer is not going along with the times? You're wrong. Even the modern world is still full of people like Sacajawea, the Indian woman who guided the Lewis and Clark expedition along the Oregon Trail. Who doesn't remember the gallant crew of the Kon-Tiki, a balsa-wood raft that sailed across the Pacific? What about the courageous Englishman, William Stanley Moss, and his men? They parachuted into North Pole territory to see if survivors of a plane wreck could reach the nearest settlements in Greenland across the only usable route, a horrible distance of 600 miles. And there are the Australian aboriginals, whose ability to read tracks can shame even a well-trained police troop with all sorts of technical equipment. There are men like Admiral Byrd, and Albert Schweitzer, and the prospectors searching for uranium in northern Canada, and the technicians, scientists, and merchants for world organizations who help the underdeveloped nations and bring the assets of civilization to new areas. The age of pioneers and explorers dependent solely on their own skills for survival is still very much with us.

But you have not gotten quite that far. Not yet. For the moment, you are just going to the edge of the woods, or out to your back yard where you will start living like the pioneers, scouts, trappers, and Indians.

AROUND THE FIRE

From books and motion pictures we all know that Indians had the ability to maintain smokeless fires, and that trappers could blot out the sites of their fires without leaving the slightest trace behind. But we're not always able to imitate these models. We gaily follow the recipe: take some wood and light it . . . But there's far more to it than that.

FINDING THE RIGHT TYPE OF WOOD

Before you build a fire, you must first have a good supply of firewood on hand. It's embarrassing to realize that there's no more wood when your hot dog is only half done. For a smokeless fire you need

Condensed from "101 Camping-Out Ideas and Activities" by Bruno Knobel © 1961 by Sterling Publishing Co., Inc., New York, with some pages from "Bike-Ways (101 Things to Do with a Bike)" by Lillian and Godfrey Frankel © 1972, 1968, 1961, 1950 by Sterling Publishing Co., Inc., New York

completely dry, brittle wood. The driest branches are those that have lost their bark and never feel cold; cold wood is damp and heavy, and it is useless unless you want to dry it out at a fire first. You can find dry brittle wood even after a rain. Look for branches under dense shrubbery (that's a bit of old gypsy lore) or find the lowest dead branches of young pine trees, which are especially suitable for starting fires. Only a greenhorn would start a fire with wood that still has green leaves hanging on it. Such wood is usable only if you already have a strong fire. Thick, dead limbs of old oaks, dried roots and trunks make good heating material. In rainy weather, cut away the top layer of wet sticks; the center will be dry.

KINDLING A FIRE

This is almost like a game of skill. First, clean the site where you are going to lay your fire, and scrape the ground all around it so that you leave nothing that may be ignited by a flying spark. Then, start with paper, dried grass or reeds, dried leaves and twigs, birchbark or paper-thin shavings. Set up a little pyramid of the thinnest, driest twigs over this. Then, to get a strong flame, lay brittle softwood branches on top of the pile. Finally, to produce effective heat and a good glow, add pieces of root and thick hardwood sticks.

PYRAMID FIRE: An outer layer of bark will help hold the branches together.

The hardwoods include oak, beech, poplar, birch and hickory. Hazel, spruce, pine and fir are all softwoods. The paper-thin outer layer of birchbark is ideal for kindling.

Set fire to the core of the pyramid only when it is finished. If kindling piles are skilfully built, it is possible to light them with a magnifying glass—if the sun is out brightly. As long ago as 278 B.C. the inventive Archimedes saved the Sicilian city of Syracuse with this principle. He erected a huge reflector on the city wall and set fire to the enemy fleet with it. Soon the fleet was swimming in bright flames on the sea.

DIFFERENT TYPES OF FIRES

If you need a fire for cooking, add some heavy blocks of wood on top of the thicker branches as a final touch for a pile of strong, glowing heat. The best thing is a few short thick logs laid around the fire in the form of a star or the spokes of a wheel, so that only one end of each stick touches the flame. As the burning progresses, push the sticks further into the center and new glowing ashes will be formed.

FRIED EGG, camper's style.

Would you like to fry an egg in a primitive way? Use a flat, sun-heated stone from a dry stream bed as a hot plate, or you can even heat the stone in the fire. Remove the soft center from a slice of bread, so that you have a ring in the middle. Then lay this bread on the stone and break the egg into the ring. When the egg has cooked, you can eat it right off the stone.

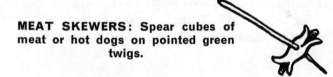

MEAT SKEWERS: Spear cubes of meat or hot dogs on pointed green twigs.

You can slice or notch hot dogs at the ends and spear them on a green twig, then cook them over the fire or the glowing coals. Don't ever hold meat directly in a flame, or you will char it.

Raw meat should be salted and wrapped up, first in butcher's paper and then in a few layers of damp newspaper or wrapping paper. Shove this package into the glowing coals, and continue to keep the fire going. In about an hour, a piece of beef that isn't too thick will be done. The damp paper keeps the meat from burning.

Even today certain islanders cook their meat this way, except that they use green plant leaves instead of paper. In this case, the moisture of the leaves protects the meat from charring.

CATERPILLAR FIRE: You can sleep alongside this type of campfire, but only if the wind doesn't shift.

A "caterpillar fire" is good for a campfire, because it needs little or no attention. However, you should build this kind of fire only when the wind direction is steady and there is no danger of rain. Build the wood pile as pictured here, beginning the pile in the direction of the wind. The supports underneath and at the sides should be *green* branches. The thickest support must always be under the middle of a log, and the thinnest under both logs. If there is a little wind, make the pile shorter by pushing the pieces further over each other.

In order to keep a fire overnight or for a longer period, cover it with a pile of ashes. This way it keeps glowing, and even after many hours you can rekindle it by blowing on it.

But only in the rarest cases should you ever leave a fire or glowing embers unwatched. On an empty sandy beach you might leave it untended for a short time, but always keep in mind that a strong rising wind can carry sparks from glowing coals. At best, you might escape with a few holes burned in your tent; at worst, you could start a forest fire.

For a fire that will dry wet clothing, you need a strong glowing mass of coals. Around it build a pyramid of sturdy, green, branchy tree limbs and hang your wet clothes on this. Turn the garments every few minutes. *And stay there* as long as there is still wood in the glowing mass. Glowing embers will spring into open flames in a rising wind.

DRYING CLOTHES on a fire requires a pyramid like this. Keep turning the garments every few minutes.

COOKING SITES

In the fall, when there's a tang in the air and the trees begin to shed their leaves, there's nothing so satisfying as a pot of hot soup or tea cooked over an open fire, with the unavoidable taste of wood smoke and the usually unwanted addition of pine needles.

You can invent and construct your stove on the spot. The type you build depends upon the circumstances and the available materials. Four possibilities are shown below.

But whatever kind of fire you use, there are some important precautions to take. Forest rangers and nature lovers do not like to see careless people building fires in the woods. And not without reason.

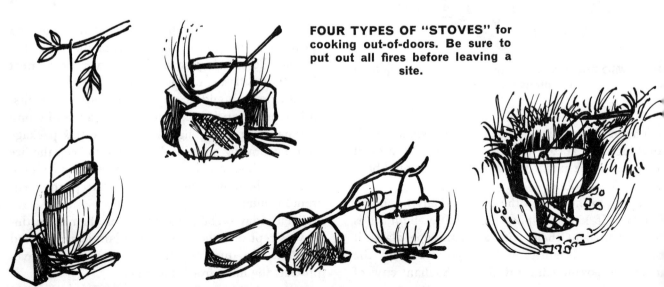

FOUR TYPES OF "STOVES" for cooking out-of-doors. Be sure to put out all fires before leaving a site.

Fires incompletely extinguished or sprays of sparks left unwatched have caused numerous, often devastating forest fires.

You should build your fire only in the middle of a clearing, in a pit, or on a stony spot. There should be nothing that can burn within 8 to 10 feet all round the fire site. Trees or bushes within this distance from the fire would be damaged by the heat.

You must completely extinguish the fire afterwards. It certainly is not too much for you to get some water for this from a nearby brook. If you merely want to stamp the fire out, at least leave yourself enough time for the job—it's really not so easy or fast. In addition, you are likely to burn your shoe soles doing this, although you may not notice it until later. Never scatter the fire in all directions so that the coals fly under leaves and are hidden from you somewhere. They keep on glowing!

OVERNIGHT SHELTERS

If you are to be truly at home in the out-of-doors, you won't use a sleeping bag, but you will learn how to build a shelter for yourself. There is no genuine trapper or ranger who has not spent at least one night sleeping under the sky. We've all read stories about the weary traveller who "dug a hollow for his hips in the soft ground and slept until dawn." Even this primitive sleeping arrangement calls for some knowledge of how to adjust to the prevailing conditions. Try lying down on the bare ground to sleep. You will notice quickly enough that the hip bone on whichever side you are lying is in your way. Dig out a depression, just big enough for your hip bone, and you will immediately notice how much more comfortable you are. You can go one step further, and cushion the hole with some fine sand, or you can place some slightly crumpled paper in the hollow for insulation against the cold.

RANGER'S OR GYPSY TENT

You can be even more comfortable if you put up a ranger's tent, which requires very few materials. All you need is a rectangular piece of cotton cloth, 6 or 7 feet long. To waterproof it, make a brew from the bark of an oak or birch tree, and let the cloth soak in it for two days. The ranger's tent can then be used as a rain shelter too.

In one corner make an eyelet large enough to run a thick cord through. At the other three corners, sew on small leather loops that you will attach to the tent pegs.

With this cloth, a solid cord 10 to 14 feet long, and a few pieces of branches from which you can cut

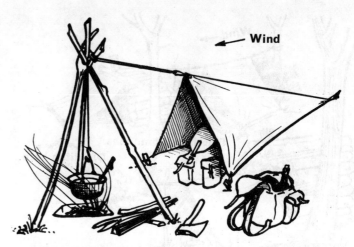

RANGER'S TENT: Keep the entrance open and the opening away from the wind, with the tent back narrow.

your own tent pegs, you will have sufficient equipment to sleep out pleasantly on even a cool summer night without having to worry about a cloudburst. Set the tent up as pictured in the illustration.

The way you pitch the tent is important. The entrance must remain open and the tent should narrow towards the rear, so you must always be careful to have the opening turned away from the windy or storm side. To keep out the cold, you can hang a raincoat or windbreaker in front of the opening, or put your backpack in front of it. There's an even simpler way: gather some leafy limbs and branches and, after you crawl into the tent, close off the entrance with them, sticking them in the ground like a fence in front of the opening. You can also do as rangers do. In cold weather they just light a fire in front of the tent entrance and lay a few thick, dry branches on the coals before going to bed. If the tent is set up right, the wind will carry the smoke away from it.

Gypsies also use similar tents, but they make theirs somewhat larger because several persons usually share a single tent. For two people the rectangle is about 7 by 10 feet. In this case too, the size and the addition of eyelets and leather loops depend on the particular needs. With this sort of tent, set up more or less like the ranger's tent, the open sides are closed off with bushes. A long branch stuck in a loose stone wall or in a wood pile stands as a roof beam to give the tent a solid support.

A tent of this type needs a little ditch around it just as more modern tents do. This ditch catches the rain water as it runs off the sides and carries it away.

GYPSY TENT: Bigger than the ranger's tent, this type can be more varied. Dig a ditch alongside for rainy weather.

Without the ditch, the water would seep into the ground around the bottom of the tent, soak it, and then run inside the tent.

It is always important to stretch the sides of the tent tightly, so that there are no folds. Even tightly woven cloth that has not been waterproofed will shed the rain if it is stretched taut. An umbrella is an example of this. However, the minute you bump against the side of such a tent during a heavy rain, it will start to drip at the spot you hit. If this happens, just press your finger against the spot and draw it straight down along the side of the tent to the ground—the water will flow off without bothering you any more.

Lay dry grass, reeds or branches on the floor of the tent, or perhaps you can get an armful of hay or straw somewhere. Even a layer of newspapers is useful. This will protect you from the coolness of the ground (unless you have decided to camp in the middle of a swamp—which is not recommended).

The choice of a camping site is important. The earth should not have too much clay, or it will keep the water from being absorbed. And don't camp in the middle of a hollow where the rain water can collect. Loose, sandy ground is warm and comfortable. It is pleasant to have a wooded area or a rise in the ground to protect you from the storm side. In northern latitudes, the storm side is the west, northwest, or southwest.

THE TEPEE

A tepee is very picturesque standing in a sunny forest clearing. It is also an exceedingly practical tent, with the advantage of allowing you to have a cooking fire inside it. And it is not particularly difficult to put up your own tepee.

First get a piece of sturdy cloth at least 7 feet by 14 feet. A larger size is all right as long as the length is twice the width. You can even make it by sewing several smaller pieces together. Then cut out a semicircle. From the cutout pieces make two smoke flaps, and sew them on at the spots shown in the illustration. Now bind all the edges of the cloth with heavy linen, or, better yet, with leather. Run a heavy cord round the bottom edge of the tepee, sewing it securely at about 4-inch intervals. Afterwards you will stick the tent pegs through the loops created this way to stretch the sides tight. The tent is not closed with buttons, but with wooden dowels and loops like those on duffle coats.

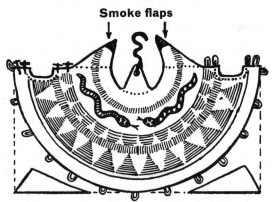

CLOTH FOR THE TEPEE: This is elaborate but authentic.

To set up the tepee, you need about ten poles as shown in the illustrations on the next page, or, if you like, branches cut as straight as possible.

Draw a circle on the ground with a diameter equal to the radius of the semicircle. Then set up three poles on the circle as shown, and tie them together at the height that the peak of the tent will reach. Lean the other poles against these three, putting three aside: two for propping open the smoke flaps and one to tie the top of the tepee to. By narrowing or widening the opening of the smoke flaps, you will get the "chimney flue" to draw. Naturally the opening must always be on the side away from the wind, for otherwise the smoke would be blown back into the tent. Secure the tepee in a strong wind by letting the cord which holds the poles together at the top extend to the ground, and fasten it there in the middle of the tent. In hot weather you can roll the front of the tepee up, holding it with strong forked sticks, to allow breezes to enter.

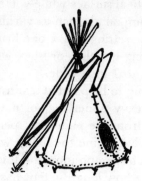

TEPEE CONSTRUCTION with 10 poles is simple, and the tent allows you to cook inside.

Painting the Tepee. Cave dwellers decorated their caves with drawings; the Indians painted their tepees, taking the motifs from their lives: hunting and war. They also drew their totem figures, the sun and the moon, and animals. You can decorate your tepee in the same way, and make your tent unique.

The Design. Designing consists of first making a drawing of, for example, an animal you are going to paint and then simplifying your sketch. If you are drawing a lion, first make a realistic sketch, then reduce it as far as possible to simple single lines, and finally intensify and stylize those lines.

In the same way, if you wish to paint an elk, first draw it. For your tepee decoration you don't need any perspective, so you can simplify the antlers and place the legs decoratively. Then further simplify all the forms, exaggerating those parts of the elk that are typical and distinctive. And you finish with a decorative pattern for painting.

You might like to make Indian shields, too, and paint them with the same motifs as your tepee. Be sure to adapt the design to the shape of the shield.

Another method is pure stylization. In the illus-

tration, the "photographic" image of an eagle is intensely simplified and the typical elements are completely exaggerated, but the bird is still recognizable as an eagle.

STYLIZATION: This eagle is simplified and its prominent features exaggerated.

The Painting Process. Use ordinary oil paints or acrylics, choosing pure tones and avoiding the mixed colors such as grey, purple, brown, light blue, and so forth. Use black, Prussian blue, red, and perhaps even green and chrome yellow. The paints should not be too thick or they will not penetrate well into the fabric. Thin the paint with turpentine (acrylics with water), but not so much that the paint is

INDIAN SHIELDS: Painted in reverse, the pelican and elk act as insignia for your tepee.

watery or runs down a vertical surface while you are painting. Add a drying compound, such as varnish, to oil paint to speed up the setting. Have one brush to use for each color—long-handled brushes with short bristles, $\frac{3}{8}$ of an inch to 1 inch wide.

Fasten the piece of tenting to be painted against a wall, first putting up a heavy underlayer of newspaper to protect the wall from the paint that penetrates through the material. Outline the figure with charcoal before painting. The composition and thickness of the paint determine how long the tent has to dry. It will probably take at least three days to a week. Be especially careful about putting on too thick a layer of paint—apply it just heavily enough so that the paint sticks together. Otherwise the layer of paint will break and crack when you fold the tepee.

Squirrel   **Rooster**

You can even add a bit of humor to your stylized drawings. For example, look at the squirrel. The eye, the pointed nose, and the ear give the whole picture an amusing touch. This is also true of the rooster, with its half-angry, half-proud expression. On the other hand, it's the arrangement of the wings and tail which gives the albatross its dash of caricature.

Albatross

HUTS

The bush hut is the simplest kind of shelter to build in the woods. It may not look like much when you start it, but it improves from year to year. Look for a bush that has long, pliable branches and thick foliage. Bend the branches down in an arch, and fasten the ends to the ground. You might use strong rope on

Bush hut

leather thongs attached to pegs. While you are doing this try not to crack any twigs or branches. Now, weave other leafy branches in between the arch so closely that the wind will be efficiently kept out. This hut has the advantage of actually growing. The network of branches will get thicker and thicker and will soon look so natural that anyone not in on the secret will not guess the existence of the hut. Unfortunately, the foilage does not completely keep out the rain, and the hut is a useful shelter only in the summer.

THE PYRAMID HUT

If you don't want to wait years until your hut gets roomy, and if you want a shelter that will protect you from the rain, you can erect a pyramid hut.

Find some long, solid branches, and set them up in the form of a pyramid. Weave smaller branches horizontally around the framework of the poles. Then weave branches with heavy foliage over this. Beech leaves are the best, for the branches from coniferous (cone-bearing) trees such as pine or fir are not able to keep out the rain. Work from the bottom up,

Pyramid hut

and extend every succeeding layer over the one below it. Only this way can the rain run from the peak down to the ground without leaking in. Be sure the opening of the hut faces away from the storm side. Don't forget to dig a ditch round the hut so that the rain water will run off. You can line the inside with dried moss, and add a couple of thick pieces of log to serve as stools. If you want additional furniture, look round you for ideas. There are many primitive but serviceable things you can build from materials you'll find at your camp site.

THE GABLED HUT

Setting up a hut is often time-consuming because you have to search for the suitable poles and weaving materials for the rough framework. Therefore, experienced hut builders always carry a net of tarred or waxed cord with them. The meshes have to be about 8 inches apart, and the whole net should be about 6 feet by 12 feet. With a net like this, you can build a gabled hut very quickly. Weave leafy branches between the meshes, or use grass, hay, straw, ferns, or large leaves if you are camping in a field—and, again, work from the bottom up and extend each layer over the previous one.

Gabled hut made with netting

REED HUTS

You can make both the pyramid hut and the gabled hut out of reeds. Reeds have the advantage of being rainproof and very warm as well. To be sure, you do need a great many reeds to make a good covering. The method you use depends on whether summer (green) or winter (dried) reeds are available. If you have pliable summer reeds, take a handful with the cut edges toward the top and the tips point-

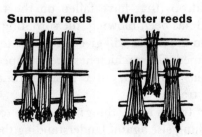

Summer reeds   Winter reeds

ing down, and bind them, once again starting at the bottom, over the first horizontal support, under the second, over the third, and so forth. Since the fresh reeds shrivel quickly and leave gaps, dry winter reeds are much better. Gather bundles of reeds by the armful, tie bunches together at the end, and then fasten them on the framework of the hut like roof shingles, pushed close to each other and overlapping.

Huts covered with dead leaves or reeds dry out quickly in the sun and become parched. Therefore, it is dangerous to have a fire in the hut or even to light a fire nearby.

THE TRAPPER'S ROOF

The trapper's roof lies about halfway between the gabled hut and the ranger's tent. It is usually rainproofed with reeds and intended as a nook to slide into on a rainy night—an emergency refuge—rather than a cozy shelter.

You can build a large, roomy trapper's roof in an afternoon, and then gradually improve it until you have built a regular hut.

You can move the trapper's roof around and place it where it will best protect you from the rain. In spite of its simplicity, it still offers good protection. It is also easily adaptable as a movable roof over cooking sites, but you'll have to be very careful that no sparks hit it.

First get two solid forked supports and stick them in the ground, then connect them with a horizontal pole. This is the crossbeam of the roof, where the upper edge will be bound. The lower edge rests on the ground or you can put it on a board, into a wood pile or against a rise in the ground. The different examples of gypsy tents shown on page 248 may

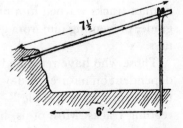

TRAPPER'S ROOF:
One type

7½'

6'

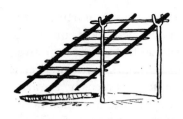
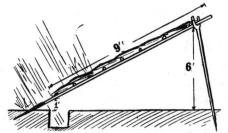
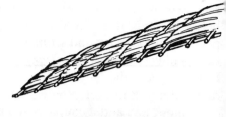

give you ideas for such constructions. The illustrations here show the roof sometimes resting in the ground, sometimes a bit above it.

It is best to cover the roof with reeds, using the same methods as for the reed hut. Complete the frame of the roof with a lattice of branches or cords, and then weave in the reeds. In an emergency, you can also use straw, ferns, and so forth, but you will have to make each layer much thicker than with reeds.

Since the slanted roof lacks side walls, you must carefully place it against the direction of the wind and rain. Set the roof at a steep or a gradual angle according to the angle at which the rain is falling.

Don't forget the ditches or drains or you'll quickly be flooded out. Since this airy hut has no walls, it's a good place to light a fire; the smoke can draw off freely. You can spend a comfortable night under this roof with a warming glow next to you.

This sort of hut has still another advantage: you can take it apart easily and set it up again in another spot. Some campers cycle out to a river in the country for swimming during the summer. The reed roof they set up there provides shade during the day and shelter at night. Before they start for home they dismantle their trapper's roof and store it away in a little shed at a nearby farmhouse. The next time they come, they simply pull it out again and set it up.

Very cautious people prepare more than one set of vertical supports so they can immediately shift the roof around in case the wind changes. This is also advantageous when you are using the roof as a sunshade, because you can always adjust it at any time to suit the position of the sun.

ON THE TRAIL

From the earliest times, reading tracks has been important to man. Animal tracks led him to food and human tracks warned him of enemies or served as a guide, preventing him from getting lost in the wilderness.

Those who have remained close to nature and are dependent on nature—today we often arrogantly call them "primitive peoples"—are highly skilled in reading tracks. Most of us, however, no longer have

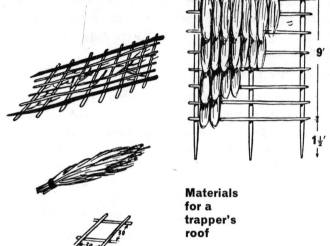

Materials for a trapper's roof

this ability. But while reading tracks is not something we grow up knowing how to do, we can develop and perfect the ability even today.

READING TRACKS

Begin your tracking lessons on a sunny day and face the sun, so that every uneven spot on the ground will cast a shadow. If you lose a track, mark the last impression, and search in a large circle for the continuation. Notice the peculiarities of the track you are following so you will be able to distinguish it from others you may come across. Mark the path you are following to keep from losing your bearings in an unfamiliar region while you are concentrating completely on the tracks.

The quality of the tracks depends primarily on the type of earth. Snow, loam and sand hold tracks best. But weather conditions can destroy even the best tracks. If you know what the weather in the area has been, you can determine when the tracks were made. For example, if it has rained you can examine the raindrops that have fallen on the tracks, or if the wind has been blowing, the sprouting grass seeds or dust in the tracks will give you a clue to when they were formed. Grass which has been stepped on lightly straightens up again after a short time. Sunshine hardens tracks.

Seeing tracks is one thing; being able to read them is something else again. Understanding the story told by tracks is primarily a matter of drawing conclusions.

During the War Between the States some soldiers looking for a lost comrade asked an Indian boy if he had seen the fellow they were seeking. The boy replied, "Do you mean a tall soldier riding a lame roan horse?"

But when the soldiers asked him *where* he had seen their lost friend, the Indian answered, "Oh, I haven't seen him at all." Instead, he led the soldiers to a tree where some roan horsehairs stuck to the bark at the spot where the horse had brushed against it. The hoof tracks showed that the horse had limped, because one hoof did not leave as deep an impression as the others, and the steps made with this hoof were not as long. The Indian observed that the rider had been a soldier from the boot prints he left when he dismounted, and concluded that he had been exceptionally tall because a tree branch had broken off at a height that a shorter person could not have reached.

HUMAN FOOTPRINTS

The human footprint lets you draw conclusions about many things. Frequently you can decide at first glance whether you are dealing with the print of a man's shoe or a woman's, especially if a woman was wearing high heels. From the size of the shoe you can make a rough guess about the person's height, and his weight may be revealed by the depth of the print in the ground. From the distance between the steps you can tell whether he was walking or running, still another clue to the energy of the person. Short steps and a deep imprint of the front part of the foot indicate that the person in question was carrying a load. The distance between the right and left foot tells you something about the person's width.

Every shoeprint has its characteristic features: the pattern of a rubber sole, missing nails, repairs or heel plates. A footprint rarely appears in isolation. Nearby impressions show if the person was using a cane or an umbrella. Matches, cigar or cigarette butts, the contents of an emptied pipe, or chewing gum wrappers characterize the person more closely.

Even something as impersonal as a bicycle track can reveal all sorts of things. Pebbles and bits of earth, or water and mud in rainy weather are thrown to the rear, supplying evidence of the direction in which a vehicle went. Similarly, a furrow or ridge of earth is pressed out broadly in the direction a bicycle is going. If a bicycle makes a curve, then the wheel tracks form a narrow angle to each other in the direction the bicycle turns.

Human footprints

TRAILING ANIMALS

You have to know a great deal about animals, about their habits, and about their individual traits if you are camping out in wild areas, and if you want to follow their tracks so as to come upon them unobserved. First, there are certain rules you must obey at all times:

When following the tracks of game, step lightly and learn how to walk silently on twigs and dried leaves.

Never look an animal in the eye, or it will run away.

Dress inconspicuously so that you do not stand out from the background and make your presence obvious.

Always be careful to sneak up on an animal against the wind. Even when you observe this precaution, don't come too close to an animal if you are sweating a lot. Animals have a very keen sense of smell when it comes to human perspiration. Bathe before going scouting and rub yourself with sorrel leaves to minimize the human scent.

We have talked about animal tracks, but this term is not strictly accurate. Woodsmen distinguish among traces, tracks and footprints, and only when they have made the distinction do they start to interpret the signs. *Tracks* are the marks left by big game, such as a moose, boar, antelope or a deer, whereas *traces* are the prints of a small game animal, such as a fox or a bird.

You may not always be lucky enough to find traces or tracks immediately. Often you will have to be content just to recognize a set of *prints*, as sportsmen call the imprint of all four feet of an animal. A set of prints calls for careful interpretation. Only occasionally do you have such a clear footprint in front of you that from the single impression you can tell with certainty what animal made it. When you are inter-

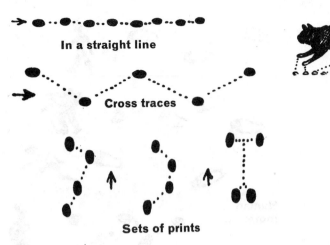

In a straight line

Cross traces

Sets of prints

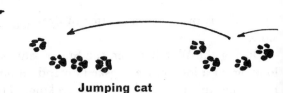

Jumping cat

preting tracks, first take in the whole picture, looking at them in their entirety, before concentrating on the details.

The tracks or traces animals make clearly show how they walk. Some small game animals, such as foxes and wildcats, are able, because of their size, to place one paw directly in front of the next, as if they were walking along a tightrope. Others, the big game animals, set their feet next to each other. These hoofed animals walk as if straddling a straight line, leaving what are called *cross traces*.

You will find such prints when the animal was moving along at an easy, comfortable pace. If the animal was running away or jumping, you'll find sets of prints at intervals. In the case of stags, the prints may be 25 feet apart. The prints of hoofed big game animals resemble the prints a rabbit makes.

Hopping rabbit

From the type of traces or tracks you find, you can determine whether you are dealing with a big or small game animal, and whether the animal was springing or just walking along easily. The length of the jumps or the side-to-side distance between hoofprints will tell you something about the size of the animal. The bigger, taller and older an animal is, the greater the distance from side to side (the cross trace). In general, female animals have a smaller cross trace.

Walking dog

ANIMAL FOOTPRINTS

You are not likely to come across the footprints of whole-hoofed animals—wild horses for example. The cloven-hoofed animals leave prints of their two-toed hoofs.

Small game animals, such as badgers, rabbits and squirrels, have paws. They walk on the soles of their feet as well as on their toes, and often leave clear imprints of the entire sole and toes.

When you find pawprints, look first to see if the animal has "toenails," that is, whether there are prints of its nails. Badgers and porcupines press their claws into the ground as they walk, but cats and lynxes do not.

Of the big game animals, the deer leaves the smallest tracks. If it is walking undisturbed and easily, the two toes of the hoofs leave a closed imprint. If it is fleeing and jumping (up to 15 feet), it leaves a "rabbit-jump" set of prints. The toes are pressed apart by the force of the jump and imprinted more deeply in the ground than usual. In fact, you will usually find an impression of the dew-claws, the "extra" toes or "false hoofs" higher up on the feet.

Landing from a jump

Suppose you find "rabbit-jump" prints. From the size of the set of prints, you can eliminate certain animals, but you might narrow your "suspects" to a fox, deer, or even a rabbit. If the two front footprints are larger, then it was a rabbit. But if all four prints are equally large, you have to search further. Perhaps you can find a print that is clearly impressed. If you see two toes of a hoof, it was a deer. If you see a paw-print, you have to conclude that it was a fox or a rabbit. The problem here will be solved if you can find a stretch with either straight line or straddling prints. If that is not possible, examine the individual prints. The paws of rabbits and foxes are so different

Trotting fox

(see illustrations of distinguishing characteristics), that it should be impossible to confuse them.

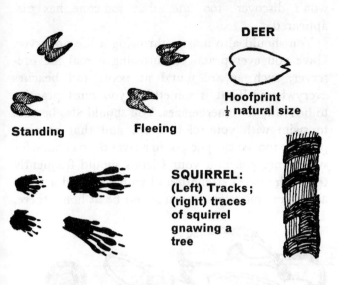

DEER

Standing   Fleeing

Hoofprint
½ natural size

SQUIRREL:
(Left) Tracks;
(right) traces
of squirrel
gnawing a
tree

TRACES OF BIRDS

You can find bird traces and wing marks only in the snow, soft sand, or on moist loam.

The *thrush* usually hops, leaving clawprints in pairs next to each other. Mincing short steps occur when it is waggling along directly towards something. When the thrush takes off from deep snow, it leaves marks with its wings because the large feathers hit the snow as the wings close.

The *crow* leaves larger traces than the thrush and is found more frequently. Since its legs are turned in somewhat, the crow waddles, and this can be seen in the traces. The marks made by the wings are also more pronounced than those of the thrush.

The *jay* leaves traces of about the same size as those of the thrush. They are found in pairs, at intervals of about five to six inches. Usually not many traces are found together, for the jay is not a ground bird. On the other hand, it often does leave traces of scratching, as it likes to dig for the squirrels' hidden provisions. The jay also drops feathers, and the blue plumage definitely reveals its presence.

The traces of the *partridge* approach those of the crow in size, but the toes are spread even farther apart. The partridge leaves cross-traced tracks and also flies up frequently, leaving wing marks which are especially pronounced since it beats its wings strongly when taking off and landing.

A *plucking* is the name given to a pile of feathers on which bits of skin, legs, or parts of the skull are still hanging. If you come across one, you will know that a bird of prey made the killing, since a martin, a pole-

cat or a fox would have dragged its prey into its den. You can guess at what sort of bird of prey it was by the size of its booty and by the feathers lost in the struggle. Larger birds, from the pigeon to the partridge, fall victim to the hawk. The buzzard eats mice.

GETTING LOST IN THE WOODS

Before you start out, it's a good idea to draw a simple map showing the area near your campsite, the groves of trees, clearings, streams, hills, large rocks and lakes. Indicate the trails you will take. Mark off the spot where you will set up headquarters for camping, resting or meeting other members of the group. With the help of your compass, mark off directions. Give each member of the group a copy of the map as well as a stick of chalk, a pencil, some small slips of paper, a few tacks, some safety matches and a compass. These items will be invaluable if anyone in your group gets lost.

If you camp in an area that is unfamiliar to you, you will have no map the first time you cover it. Here is another method of getting back to your meeting place without confusion or delay. As you ride along, make a chalk mark on the side of every fifth tree you pass. Your companions can also follow these marks, either to catch up with you or to explore the trail themselves.

If you decide to leave the path and veer off in an unmarked direction, scratch an arrow on a tree, rock or stump, or make one on the ground out of stones. If you don't have chalk, tack note paper to various trees. It is unwise to wander off the trail or path unless you are quite sure you can find your way back again.

Watch the sun for directions. For example, if the sun is setting, you can determine the direction of west. Then, when facing west, you will be able to ascertain the other directions. North will be to your right, south to your left, and east will be behind you.

WHAT TO DO IF YOU THINK YOU ARE LOST

1. Don't get panicky. Relax, but concentrate on remembering how you travelled. Mark a tree on four sides so you can see the mark clearly from any direction. Then walk straight out from the tree for about 75 feet, moving in a circle with the marked tree in the center. As you go round, study the trees, the ground and the surrounding area for familiar signs.

2. Leave a note for your friends telling the direction in which you are heading. Tack it to a tree, write it on a rock or spell it out on the ground with small stones.

3. Try to find a stream. Then follow it downstream. Streams flow into larger bodies of water, and eventually they will lead you to towns and people.

4. Look for high ground. You can see farther from a hill, mound, large rock, or tall tree. Climb up and try to see a familiar landmark—a road, a valley or a clump of trees that looks familiar. Try to call out from this high spot. Your voice will carry fairly well from high ground.

5. Follow such signs of civilization as telephone poles, power lines, cleared trails, sounds of trains or autos. These should lead you out of the woods.

6. Send up a smoke signal. Clear a large area of grass and brush and build three fires of semi-green wood, grass and mossy fern. Build them far enough apart so that they will send up three separate smoke columns. Someone will see them and come to your rescue. If it is cold, of course the fire will warm you.

7. If it is getting dark, stay where you are. Try to make yourself as comfortable as possible. Look for a dry shelter on high ground. Get behind a large rock or tree that will act as a windbreak.

Above all, don't lose your head. The clearer your thinking in any emergency, the better you will handle it.

AT WATER'S EDGE

The Indians, especially the tribes around the Canadian Great Lakes, were true water lovers and real artists at controlling their canoes, which they made for themselves out of barks and pelts.

The first essential for your activities in or near the water is, of course, knowing how to swim. In addition, you must know and obey all the safety measures that can prevent accidents. For example, never go swimming just after you've eaten or when you are very hot. Wait at least an hour after meals, and when you are overheated from the sun, cool off in the shade before entering the water. Never dive if you get earaches or dizzy spells from diving. If you are

enjoying the water with a group of friends, it is a good idea to use the buddy system, that is, to swim in pairs and watch out for your buddy. That way you won't discover—too late—that someone has disappeared.

You should also master throwing a life preserver. Have you ever practiced throwing a real life preserver, such as are found at pools and beaches everywhere? That is something you must practice to be ready for emergencies. You should also be able to swim with your clothes on, and that requires practice too. At the pool, or in a river deep enough for swimming, you and your friends should frequently test each other's strength and scuffle around a bit to accustom yourselves to water and be at home there.

SKIN DIVING

Indians are said to have stayed under water for hours to avoid pursuit, breathing through reeds, holding one end above the surface of the water.

Such stunts are no longer restricted to the warpath. Today they have become a sport, as diving masks with snorkels enable us to extend our roving expeditions even to underwater areas.

On the clear, sunlit bottom of a lake, pond or slow-flowing river, or at the edge of the sea, all kinds of things can be observed: you might see a pebbled bottom as colorful as a mosaic, growths of algae, and the fishes' hiding spots. There are seashells too, and even if the truly fantastic shells can only be found in the tropics, there are still enough snail shells almost everywhere, which are equally fascinating.

BOATBUILDING

Have you ever dreamed of owning a boat of your own, so that you could explore around the bend of a river, or just float lazily along a lake? Why not build the boat of your dreams?

As far as the appearance of your vessel is concerned, you don't have to be too particular. The important thing is its absolute seaworthiness. Perhaps it's too much to call these "boats"; for the most part,

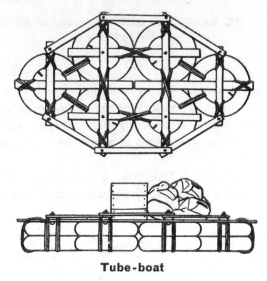

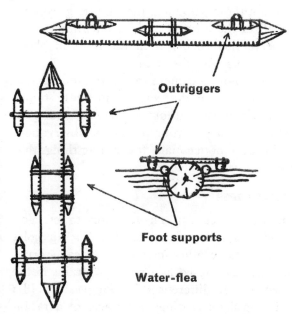

Tube-boat

they're actually rafts or floats, but they all serve the purpose of carrying you on the water. For example, here is a *tube-boat*. This is made of old tire tubes which are first carefully patched, then pumped up, and finally bound together with boards and ropes as the illustrations show. The ropes should be as thick as possible so they will not cut into the tubes. You can make paddles out of small boards nailed to short poles.

Outriggers

Foot supports

Water-flea

The *water-flea* is a different model, and to make it you first need a tree trunk. Fasten a pole crosswise at each end of the trunk and bind a small log or block of wood to the ends of each pole. This provides you with four floats which prevent the tree trunk from spinning on its own axis. Fasten blocks to serve as foot supports on both sides at the middle of the trunk. In order to reduce water resistance, the blocks and the trunk are pointed.

To make the *barrel-float*, you need a barrel, some poles, and two boards. The result will be a very unusual and individual boat.

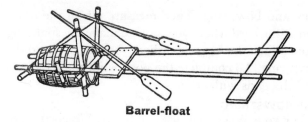

Barrel-float

A *tin-can raft* can be made in the same way as the tube-boat, with large cans such as oil drums instead of the tire tubes.

MAKING A BOW AND ARROW

Archery, a popular sport today, has been practiced by man for thousands of years. First used in the deadly pursuit of animals for food, the bow and arrow now provides fun and recreation.

The Indians used yew wood for their bows. Hickory, lemonwood or ash will serve equally well for making a bow.

THE BOW

Get a staff that is as tough and as evenly grown as possible. Its dimensions should be about 5 to 6 feet long, depending on the length of your arm span, fingertip to fingertip, and about $1\frac{3}{16}$ to $1\frac{1}{2}$ inches thick. The side opposite the bowstring should be sanded smooth, and the thickness should taper off towards both ends. However, the thickest point should not be in the middle (M in illustration), but about half the width of your hand below it. Although you will set the arrow at the exact center of the bow, you hold the bow at the thickest spot. When you are shooting, the lower limb of the bow will be longer than the upper limb.

At the ends of both upper and lower limbs are the *nocks*—notches in the wood that hold the bowstring. Make the nocks on the side opposite the bowstring and plane them slightly flat. (See the center cross section.) Now take a cord that is solid but not too thick, fasten it with a slipknot in one notch, and bend the bow to get the correct distance between the

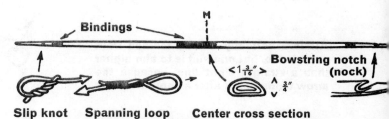

Bindings M **Bowstring notch (nock)**

$<1\frac{3}{16}"\!>$ $\frac{3}{4}$

Slip knot **Spanning loop** **Center cross section**

Making a Bow and Arrow ■ 257

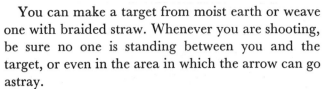
Distance from bow to bowstring (fistmele)

bow and bowstring. Then measure off on the other end of the cord where you have to make the spanning loop. When the loop is finished, you can hook up the bowstring. To complete the bow, wind the handgrip and the ends with cord.

THE BOWSTRING

For your bowstring, use unbleached linen thread.

Get three pieces of No. 12 Irish linen thread, wax each piece with beeswax, and braid the three together. Then twist the braided string and wax it again.

Length of arrow: 22"-30"

THE ARROWS

The length of your arrows can vary from 22 to 30 inches. The longer your bow, the longer your arrows should be. They should not be thicker than $\frac{5}{16}$ of an inch. Hardwood is preferred, but you can use a very tough softwood if necessary. To be sure that they will fly well, stabilize your arrows with feathers.

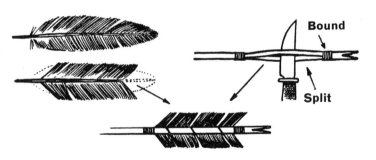

Bound

Split

AIMING

An arrow does not travel in a straight line for more than a very short distance. As it loses speed, it starts to fall in a slow curve. You must aim so that the arrow's path of flight, or trajectory, brings it to the target.

Aim as shown in the illustration.

AIMING correctly is only learned from experience, but one hint is to aim higher than a straight sight line, because the arrow tends to fall after a short distance.

You can make a target from moist earth or weave one with braided straw. Whenever you are shooting, be sure no one is standing between you and the target, or even in the area in which the arrow can go astray.

If you take care of your bow and arrows, protecting them from moisture, they will last a long time.

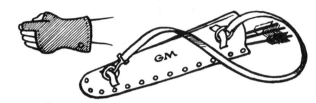

EXPLORING

Hunting in the woods is not confined to shooting game with a rifle or bow and arrow. You can spend your time in the out-of-doors far more enjoyably and constructively if you hunt with your head and eyes. All searching, tracking, and interpreting is really hunting, and the most patient and shrewdest hunters today are not those who hang their hunting trophies on the wall in the form of antlers, but rather those who preserve their booty from the hunt in photo albums—hunters with the camera.

Yet even without a camera there are innumerable things to hunt for in the woods and fields, things most people pass by without seeing. As you train your eyes and sharpen your powers of observation, you will begin to notice many fascinating things that you weren't aware of before.

LOOKING AT TREES

The marks on tree trunks have a story to tell. You might find traces of a mouse feeding (1); air holes made by a beetle or other insect(2); vertical, scarred tears or frost rips caused as a result of strains in the trunk because of differences in temperature (3); traces of a squirrel feeding (4); traces of a rabbit feeding (5). (See top of next column.)

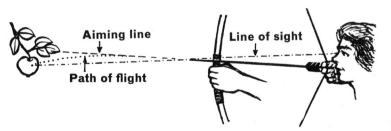

Aiming line   Line of sight

Path of flight

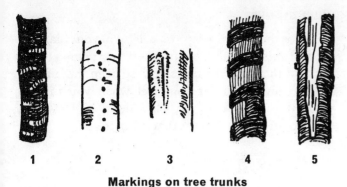

Markings on tree trunks

You frequently find galls, swellings of the tissues, on pine or oak branches and leaves. Galls result from the attacks of certain insects—gallflies, gall midges, and some aphids—that puncture the plant at a certain point and lay their eggs in the wound. The wound then grows into various shapes and the larvae grow up inside, feeding on the rapidly growing plant fibres.

OAK LEAVES: Round, spongy galls at the end of oak branches can get as big as apples, and are often called oak apples. Both the balls and the lens-shaped galls on oak leaves are made by two different types of gallflies or gall wasps. Ink can be made from such galls.

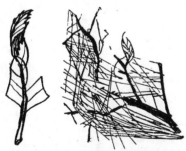

COBWEBS over leaves and branches indicate the leaves are already partially eaten. The cobwebs protect and support the caterpillars of different butterflies and moths.

  HAZEL NUTS: Hole made by mice (left) and small round holes (right) made by nut weevils or long-horned beetles.

ANIMAL TRACKS AND TRACES

You are already familiar with some tracks and traces of animals and you know that if you want to observe animals or photograph them you first have to track down their crossings, runs, and drinking and feeding places. Here are some more examples of the traces left by animals.

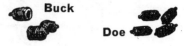

To the left are the droppings of a buck. The balls are drawn out at one end, pushed in on the other.

On the right are the droppings of a doe—smaller and drawn out at both ends.

 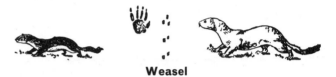

Weasel

Everywhere in the fields and woods, in stone piles, near holes in the ground, and around buildings there are tracks of the predatory weasel. The southern American weasel remains brown all year round, but there are other species whose fur in summer is reddish-brown on top, yellowish-white underneath, and changes in the winter to completely white except for the end of the tail, which remains jet-black. The body of this animal is about 16 inches long, the tail about 4 inches.

 **Otter**

You can easily recognize the pawprint of the otter by the webbed toes. Otters, found throughout the United States and Canada, live in burrows that have underwater entrances. Their droppings are full of fish scales.

BIRD WATCHING

Bird watching is a hobby that many people find absorbing. You too can spend fascinating hours tiptoeing through the woods hoping to glimpse the flash of a wing, or observing quietly from a window as birds cluster round a feeding station. (See pages 11–40.)

MOCCASINS, ETC.

These were the items of clothing worn by the Indians of old. Leather trousers are ideal for working in the woods, it's true, but ordinary old pants will do as well. Put some in your back pack. However, you can make cheap, long-lasting moccasins yourself.

Moccasins, etc. ■ 259

MOCCASINS, plain and fancy.

You need an old tire, preferably one on which the tread has not been completely worn off. This will make your moccasins skid-proof.

It is really simple to make them. According to your imagination and ability, you can make anything from simple slippers to magnificently embroidered moccasins. Cut out a piece of rubber that is the size and shape of your foot and remove the excess rubber sticking up on the sidewalls. You can use the excess as "leather" for the tops.

You can either sew the pieces together with twine or tarred cord, or cement or staple them together. Fasten them on your feet with laces drawn through the loops sewn around the top.

But moccasins are not the only thing you can make for yourself. You can make many things that will contribute to your ease, comfort and fun in the out-of-doors.

MAKING "SILVERWARE"

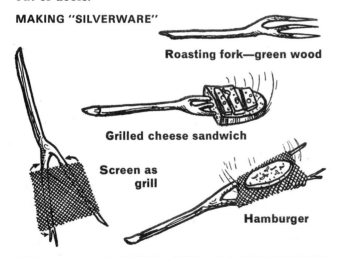

Roasting fork—green wood

Grilled cheese sandwich

Screen as grill

Hamburger

YOUR BLANKET

This is the way to wrap yourself up in your blanket: Lie along a diagonal. First turn in the corner over your feet and then fold the two sides. To keep the blanket from coming apart at your feet when you turn in your sleep, tie a cord or belt around it. However, this should not be so tight that it binds you.

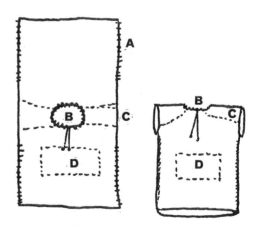

BLANKET WRAPPING: The proper way to stay wrapped.

RAIN PONCHO

Your outdoor adventures are not going to take place only when the weather is good, so you should be prepared for rain too. A raincoat is often clumsy, so why not make your own foul-weather gear?

The rain poncho illustrated here is modelled after a garment made by some Belgian scouts. Theirs was made of leather, but you can make yours of water-proofed cotton.

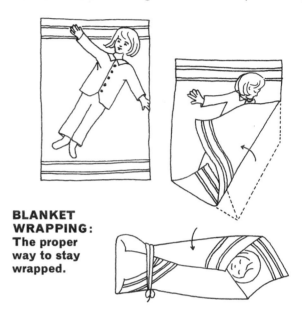

PONCHO: Sew as shown: A. Sew at these places. B. Opening for the head, with a cord for pulling it tight around the neck. C. Supports to strengthen the shoulder parts. D. Kangaroo-pouch pocket (yours might have a zipper). Make the armholes large enough so that you can pull your arms back inside the poncho.

THE LAW OF THE FOREST

In the woods and fields and camping grounds there are certain rules to be obeyed, certain laws to be respected. Like most rules and laws, there is a good reason for them. You already know that you must put out your fires completely and not trespass on private property, nor harm a living tree. As you feel more and more at home in the out-of-doors, you will be able to make your own list of do's and don'ts. But here are a few tips to help you improve your camping skills.

In northern temperate areas, the rabbit bears four to five litters of one to five young during the year, the first toward the end of February. The doe has one or two fawns in April. The badger has three to five young in February. Everywhere in the woods the young creatures cower in fear, and the older animals worry about their young. You should not frighten them by making noise and beating the bushes.

Don't close the openings of fox and badger burrows, and don't build a fire in front of the burrow. Closing up the openings means starvation for the young, and they would suffocate in the smoke.

Rabbits and deer bring their young into the thickest part of the underbrush for safety when there is a disturbance. For that reason leave these places alone.

Every Indian knows that animals always flee uphill when there is a disturbance. Therefore, if you have to make a lot of noise, do it along the streams and in the hollows. If a mother is forced to leave her young, the babies can easily fall victim to dogs and foxes when they are unprotected and helpless.

Be careful of trees of any age. You can damage a tree even by climbing on it with hobnailed shoes.

Woodpiles are the fruit of much hard work. Do not take some stranger's woodpile.

Light fires only in ditches, stony spots, paths, or sizable clearings.

DON'T attempt to feed wild animals. You will not be successful.

Route signs and no-trespassing posters were not put up as targets for stones.

Farmers spend a lot of time and money every year to keep their fences in shape, so do not use them for gym equipment.

If you find young animals out-of-doors, leave them where you find them without touching them. Attempts to raise them at home seldom succeed. As soon as you leave quietly, the mother will return to pick up her young.

When you prove, by following the rules of the woods, that you know how to be a considerate and sensible camper, you will have made friends of the farmers, foresters and all the people who love the forest. And this can only work to your own advantage.

BACKPACKING

What you take along when camping out depends on your trip—its duration, distance, the location of your campsite, the number of persons going and other factors. If you camp high up in the mountains, you will need many blankets, a good sleeping bag and warm clothes, because the temperature drops sharply at night. If you camp in summer near a lake, you will want mosquito netting.

Remember, everything you take on the trip should be light in weight and absolutely necessary. If you are in doubt about whether you will need an item, it's usually better to leave it at home. Here is a plan which some campers use to determine which equipment is essential. After returning from your trip, sort your equipment into three piles. In one pile put the things you didn't use at all. In the second pile place all the items you used only once or twice, and in the third put all the equipment you used every day. Then, on your next trip, take only those items from the third pile, and perhaps a few from the second pile. There is one very important exception to this method—a first-aid kit. Even if it is seldom or never used, always keep it in your backpack.

Here is a list of standard camping equipment and backpack supplies:

Sleeping bag (you can make one—see below)—or get one that weighs about 6 pounds—either kapok-filled or lined with detachable layers of woolen material)

Blankets (if you do not have a sleeping bag)

Pup tent—for shelter (unless you intend to make a tent)

Scout knife

Hunting knife with sheath for protection

Small ax with covering over edge

Cooking kit (frying pan, saucepan, tin cup, knife, fork and spoon)

Food bag (an old pillowcase will do)

Match box (waterproof)

Compass

Canteen

First-aid kit

Flashlight (and extra batteries)

Field glasses and camera (not essential but they help make trip more enjoyable)

Maps (road and topographical)

Toilet paper

Soap (face soap and laundry soap for washing and poison ivy precaution)

Towels

SLEEPING BAGS

Sleeping bags combine the comforts of a warm blanket and a cozy bed in one light, compact roll. That's why they are so popular with campers. The average sleeping bag weighs from $5\frac{1}{2}$ to 6 pounds, and there are about 100 varieties. Most of them are waterproof and these bags are filled with kapok,

TRAPPER'S BIVOUAC: Sleeping bag, ranger's tent and bivouac fire. These are enough to let you sleep comfortably through a cold night.

feathers or blanket material. They will keep you warm in weather as cold as 25°F (−4°C). Specially-built and rather expensive down-filled bags for use in Arctic regions are comfortable in temperatures as low as 40°F below zero (−40°C). These bags weigh only $2\frac{1}{2}$ pounds. However, most of the standard bags on the market are warm enough for the average camper. Some bags, usually those made with blankets, are put together in layers so that on warmer nights you can zip out unnecessary covers.

When rolled up, your sleeping bag should not measure more than 6 inches in diameter, 14-16 inches in width. Most people prefer mummy-shaped bags to rectangular ones. The "mummy" adherents say these bags are more draft-proof and fit more snugly than the others.

To carry your bag, roll it up and place it in your backpack. Bags are easier to handle than tents.

Use a waterproof ground cloth to keep the bag dry. Place the cloth on dry ground beneath the sleeping bag. The ground cloth can double as a waterproof cover for the sleeping bag while you are cycling, and you can also use it for a raincape or a picnic tablecloth. The best type of ground cloth is nylon.

HOW TO MAKE YOUR OWN SLEEPING BAG

Good sleeping bags are expensive, so you may want to make your own. Take an old down comforter and fold it in half the long way; it will measure about 33 by 84 inches. Sew up the bottom and then stitch halfway up the side opposite the folded edge. Now, attach "gripper" snaps to the unsewn upper half.

Presto! You've got yourself a sleeping bag as warm and light as many you can buy. Of course, it won't be waterproof, but waterproof sleeping bags have a disadvantage in that they don't "breathe." Moisture from your body condenses and remains inside a waterproof bag, making it cold and damp.

Here's how to make a sleeping sack to insert inside the bag:

1. Obtain an old single-sized sheet or two lengths of unbleached muslin.

2. Plan the sack to measure about 30 by 78 inches.

3. Bring down a 24-inch flap from the top part of the sheet to fold over the top of the bag. This will keep the area around your face clean.

4. A gusset at each side of the sack will give you roominess.

5. Place your comforter over the sack.

There you are—a lined sleeping bag!

TENTS

Sleeping bags are more popular than tents, but tents are still valuable. If you don't plan on making your own overnight shelter, on longer camping trips away from shelters, a small pup tent will give you important protection from rain and inclement weather. A steady downpour can destroy your provisions and also make you very uncomfortable if you have no tent.

The best type is the pup or mountain tent. The nylon variety is light, dries fast and folds down easily. It provides shelter for one or two people, weighs about 4 pounds, and costs very little. This tent has collapsible upright aluminum poles. The entire tent folds down into a neat bundle 1 foot by 2 feet, so it fits nicely into a backpack.

Remember not to touch the tent while you are inside it on a rainy day; water will leak through at the spot you touched. But if you accidentally bump again it, just press your finger against the spot you touched and draw it straight down along the side of the tent to the ground. The water will then flow off.

HOW TO CHOOSE A CAMPSITE

Of course, you will want a beautiful campsite, but in the final analysis, comfort and safety are more important. Although the view from a mountaintop may be awe-inspiring, a high, exposed campsite may get extremely windy at night. During the day it may be cool near a lake, but at night the mosquitoes will make you forget the loveliness of the lake.

Shady spots and hollows in dense forests are usually damp, making them hangouts for insects. A heap of stones may shelter a litter of snakes. Stately oak trees may have gnarled roots that will dig into your back while you are trying to sleep. Don't camp too near a creek. A rainstorm miles away can cause the creek to swell and flood your campsite. Above all, watch out for poison ivy!

This list of "bewares" is not intended to frighten you. But you must avoid these dangers if you want your trip to be safe as well as fun. Comfort and safety come first. Select a campsite on high, open ground. If the land slopes to the south, you will have maximum sunshine and your tent will be dry. Also, see that your tent is near a water supply and as close as possible to the wood you will be using as fuel.

Before setting up camp, decide where you want your fire. It should be far enough away from the tent for safety, yet not so far that it is inconvenient. Clear a six-foot circle of all grass, shrubbery and foliage that might burn, spreading the fire. After you have torn all these out, you are ready to build your fire. (See pages 244—247 on building a fire.)

If you are inventive, you can construct cranes and other means of supporting pots over the fire. Always remember that your pot handle is probably hot. Save yourself burnt fingers by being careful. If you have difficulty reaching the pots, your fire is too large.

Never go away and leave a fire—not even for a few minutes. A sudden gust of wind can spread the fire and turn a growing forest into a wasteland. Always be near your fire, watching it.

Burning the garbage should be your last act before putting out the fire. Be sure the fire is really out when you leave. Pour water over it; then stamp it out. If you have large smoldering logs, throw them into a nearby lake, or pour water over them until you are sure they will not start burning again. Cover your campfire with dirt, sand or gravel after you have drenched it with water.

Fire is a helpful servant—but a destructive master.

HOW TO PURIFY WATER

If you camp near farms or in regular camping areas, you will have no trouble getting fresh, pure water. Since water is needed for drinking, cooking and washing, you must have an easily reached supply. The nearer it is to your campsite, the better. Contrary to popular belief, water in a flowing stream may be as unsafe as water from a still pond. A flowing stream may carry down water from a contaminated source many miles away. Water found near a community is also likely to be contaminated. In a wilderness, chances are the water is relatively clean.

Boil all stream or river water for about 15 minutes before you drink it. Then allow it to cool. Toss it back and forth from one container to another. This process eliminates the flat taste which boiling gives the water. Water can also be purified by using "Halazone," a chemical tablet sold at most drugstores.

To "clear" water you will need a water purifier which sells at most camp supply stores. This is small and portable enough to carry. However, to be on the safe side, the tablets should be used along with the purifier in case there are bacteria present. This method may appear cumbersome, but if you are away from civilization, you will have to accept certain inconveniences. After using chemicals in water, let it stand for an hour to get rid of the chemical taste.

Remember always to carry an ample water supply in your canteen when you are away from your campsite.

BIKE-RIDING

With the current concern about saving the world from various forms of pollution, it is little wonder that bike-riding as a hobby is now enjoying a renaissance.

The bicycle is the simplest, most economical and most efficient method of transportation invented by man. It takes very little storage space when not in use, can carry as much as ten times its own weight, requires very little maintenance, moves noiselessly without fuel over almost any kind of road or narrow path, and is free from the useless accessories which have become characteristic of modern cars.

In this day and age its simplicity is amazing—two wheels, two pedals, a chain and sprocket, a frame, a seat and handlebars! Riding a bike is a simple task to learn, and safety rules are simple too!

There is no better way to get to know the land and feel a part of it. The sweep of the countryside, the layout of the city, the architectural achievement and even lack of achievement, are there to behold and ponder over in an intimate sort of way. All your senses are involved. The field of vision opens up to 180 degrees without dirty windshields and noxious smelling noisy engines. You are your own source of power, quiet power. And you get exercise the whole time.

With bike-riding as a hobby, you will enjoy spinning down a quiet country road, or the pure thrill of coasting down a steep hill, with the hum of the spokes and the whistling of the wind in your ears. What this section should do for you is give you some new ideas on how to pursue your bike holiday individually or in a group.

ORGANIZING A BIKE CLUB

If you are like most people, you enjoy sharing your interests with others. To get the most from bike-riding, you may want to form a bike club. Such a club can plan outings, go camping and hosteling, or organize such special events as a bike rodeo. Members can help each other repair their bikes and exchange information about equipment, trips, games and club business.

Another advantage of a club is that you can purchase bicycle parts and equipment very economically on a group plan. Your club may be able to get quantity discounts, resulting in substantial savings to each member. You may even be able to extend group purchasing to such items as cameras, small bike radios and clothing.

But first, how do you go about starting a club? Naturally, you will need a meeting place. Perhaps your club can meet in a community center, a "Y," or in a school or college. Club rooms are often available and a meeting place in an established institution will lend prestige to your group.

You may also have access to a mimeograph machine for turning out announcements and publicity. Moreover, an established organization is a good resource for recruiting members, and a channel for reaching out and becoming better known in the community. Your bike club can easily become part of other community center activities.

While you are searching for a meeting place, you should also spend some time recruiting members. Speak to your cycle friends to start the ball rolling. Many cyclists know each other from repeated meetings in the local bike repair shop. Here bike data and lingo are traded, and sometimes give-and-take between customers creates the atmosphere of an actual bike club meeting.

Where else can you find prospective members? Right in your own school and neighborhood. You can put up posters calling for interested cyclists in public buildings, such as social service agencies, "Y"s, schools, the city hall, the post office, and in the shops

Condensed from "Bike-Ways (101 Things to Do with a Bike)" by Lillian and Godfrey Frankel, © 1972, 1968, 1961, 1950 by Sterling Publishing Co., Inc., New York

HOSTEL: Travellers newly arrived at an AYH hostel in Holland check their bikes before getting set for the night.

of bike dealers and repairmen. Newspapers and radio stations will also assist in publicizing your invitation to prospective members.

Most local newspapers carry a column listing club announcements. Get in touch with the sports editor or sports columnist and ask him to print your news items. Knowing these writers will be invaluable later when you plan a bike rodeo or a race meet and want proper news coverage. Local radio stations will often accept spot announcements from nonprofit organizations, especially if the news is of civic interest.

HOW TO PLAN A BIKE PROGRAM

Once you have enough members to begin, you enter the second phase of club organization: setting a common goal. Everyone is interested in his bike and in bike activities, but what kinds of activities should your club plan? Six members may only be interested in racing; six others, with no interest in racing, may want to go on outings and tours.

It is best, of course, to include everyone's interest if you can. When there are differences in interest, the common club goal should include so many activities that the entire group will be pleased.

After some discussion your group may decide to limit its activities to racing and touring at the start,

and those members interested in other activities may be willing to postpone their choices till later. The central principle to keep in mind is that each member's tastes should be taken into consideration.

At the same time that you are all discussing the club's goal, it is wise to draw up a simple constitution or a set of bylaws, so your organization can govern itself smoothly. You will probably want to elect regular officers. In addition, you can form committees, each representing one phase of the club's activities. It often works out well if members volunteer for the committee they want to serve on.

The real key to the success of your group will be found in the spirit of the members and in the satisfaction they derive from their club experience.

The most highly organized national bicycle group is American Youth Hostels, Inc., described more fully on pages 273–276. It is a nonprofit agency which includes adults as well as younger members. It strives to cultivate a love for the countryside and a broad understanding of the world and of people. One of its goals is to encourage the use of hostels (overnight shelters), where face-to-face associations with people from different walks of life develop in a comfortable, natural manner. Here, local club members can meet cyclists from other communities and perhaps even from other countries, and share in simple living on overnight stays while touring. The AYH is a good source of ideas for your club program.

Once you have decided on a program, you will want to know how to carry out the activities you have planned. Why don't you start with a race meet? This event has several advantages. It will attract community attention—and probably new members—to your club and it will give you an opportunity to get your feet wet. You will learn how to run off races, how to enlist the cooperation of police and other community officials and how to obtain publicity for your club.

PLANNING A RACE MEET

First, locate a racing area. You can use a dirt track or an athletic field, a quiet street, even a fairground. Of course, if you use a street, you will have to get permission from the police department. Chances are, the police will rope off the street and assign one or two men to be present on the day of the meet.

After the rules for each event have been established, appoint judges, timers and starters. You may want to present awards or prizes to the winning contestants. Approach the owners of bicycle stores or hardware stores and ask them if they would be interested in giving bike accessories to the winners. In return, you will publicize the stores for presenting the awards.

The simplest race, and the easiest to run off, is the sprint. It is described more fully on page 270. For all short races, use a stop watch and time each cyclist individually. You may want to establish handicaps in relays or straight races if the participating riders are of widely varying abilities. For example, the handicapped team or contestant can start off 100 yards ahead of the faster one.

Many races are more elaborate than the sprint. What about including a 10-mile relay race? With 20 riders on each team, the first cyclist rides $\frac{1}{2}$ mile carrying a baton or small stick; he passes it to the next rider on his team and so on. With fewer riders, you can run off a 5-mile relay, for instance, with five cyclists on each team. The most important fact about relays is that they are more exciting and more competitive when opposing cyclists are fairly well matched in ability. You should always station the fastest member of each team in the final position.

A BIKE RODEO

How about organizing a bike rodeo? The rodeo games described here are exciting and challenging and, fortunately, do not require elaborate preparation. Obtain a permit from the police or parks department to set aside a street or an area in a city park that has a roadway. If you can find an unused area or a black topped schoolyard that is easily reached and for which no permit is necessary, all the better.

You can play any of the games described in this section at any time and, of course, you can make up your own scoring systems. When scheduled for a bike rodeo, however, these events should be scored as follows: If six people are competing, the winner receives 6 points; the remaining five contestants receive 5, 4, 3, 2, 1 points according to their positions. For relays, in which contestants are divided into two groups, scoring is different. If there are three on a

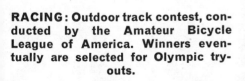

RACING: Outdoor track contest, conducted by the Amateur Bicycle League of America. Winners eventually are selected for Olympic tryouts.

Bike Rodeo ■ 267

team, *each* member of the winning team receives 6 points. This puts a premium on the relay and makes it an especially exciting event.

If your rodeo is organized so that two teams or clubs oppose each other in every event, score each individual separately. At the end of the day, add the individual scores for each side. You will end up with two total team scores. Always base the maximum number of possible points on the number of contestants. For example, if there are twenty entrants, the winner of an event receives 20 points.

You will find it easy to set up and run off these rodeo games. Let's start with three chalk-line games. Find an area at least $100' \times 30'$. It should be concrete or something similar so that the chalk will be visible. Let's play Parallel and Slalom.

PARALLEL

For the Parallel you will need 4 feet of string and a few sticks of white chalk.

Draw two parallel lines 75 feet long and 3 feet apart. This can be done by cutting off $3\frac{1}{2}$ feet of string and tying a stick of chalk to each end. Two people take the chalk, one at each end of the string, and walk in a straight line, drawing chalk lines on the ground while keeping the string taut. This method will produce parallel lines. One end is then marked "start"—the other "finish." A contestant who touches a line is disqualified.

Once your course is marked, you can use it for two races—a dash and a slow race. Watch the fun when entrants try to pedal as slowly as possible and still avoid the white lines!

SLALOM

For this race you will need 25 feet of string and a few sticks of white chalk.

The Slalom is named and taken from a famous skiing event in which racers follow a zigzag course down a hill. In the bike Slalom, the cyclist follows a course marked by two parallel zigzag chalk lines on a pavement. Prepare the Slalom by cutting a string $5\frac{1}{2}$ feet long and tying a stick of chalk to each end. The lines are to be 5 feet apart. As for the Parallel, two people draw lines with a stick of chalk, while both hold the string taut between them. Draw the lines parallel for 20 feet in one direction, then turn and go 20 feet in the other direction. The turn should be approximately 110 degrees, a little wider than a right-angle turn. Make as many turns as you have

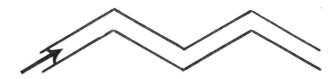

space for; generally four to five are the maximum. Naturally, the "start" and "finish" are marked at opposite ends.

Each cyclist is timed as he rides down and back the 5-foot-wide course. He is disqualified if he touches the lines or if his foot touches the ground. As in the Parallel event, you can run both fast and slow races.

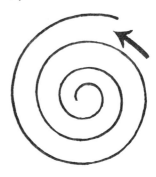

CIRCLE

For the Circle you will need a pencil, a stick of chalk and 15 feet of string.

Prepare the game by tying a stick of chalk to one end of a 15-foot piece of string and a pencil to the other end. This is how the spiral course is drawn: one person holds the pencil firmly in the center of the pavement while another, holding the string taut, walks in a circle around the man in the center. The person with the pencil-end gradually pulls in the string as his companion circles, thereby lessening the

CIRCLE: The contestant rides the spiral course from the outer lane to the center, trying not to touch any lines.

circumference on each round. In this way, a spiral course is automatically drawn, winding from the outer rim inward to the center, where the person with the pencil is standing. There should be 3 or 4 feet separating each inner circle.

You can use your spiral course for both fast and slow races. Time each entrant with a stop watch. As in the preceding two chalk games, a contestant is disqualified if he touches a line. Place the "start" at the opening of the outer circle; the "finish" at the center.

This is the most difficult of the chalk games, for it requires great control and co-ordination. The cyclist must operate his bike as perfectly as if it were a part of his body.

SEESAW

You will need one large brick and one plank of wood 18" wide × 12' long.

You can plan this simple event as part of a cross-country race, or you can set it up by itself as a demonstration event. Place a brick midway under a plank of wood about 18 inches wide and 12 feet long.

The entrant rides up one end of the plank. When he gets just past the center, the other end of the plank suddenly slams down. The rider must be ready for the quick change of position. Otherwise he will find himself off-balance and off-bike.

OBSTACLE DROP

You will need 4 bushel baskets and 4 old tennis balls or rubber balls the same size as tennis balls. Place the bushel baskets open end up in a straight line, about 15 feet apart on a pavement or some other level area. The cyclist attempts to drop one ball into each basket as he weaves around each one in order.

The "start" should be about 20 feet in front of the first basket; the "finish" about 20 feet behind the last basket. This event is timed with a stop watch, and only one entrant competes at a time. The cyclist who places balls in the most baskets in the shortest length of time wins. For example, a player who gets balls in three baskets will win over one placing balls in only two; if there is a tie, with two or more players having the same number of baskets, the one with the fastest time wins.

Remember that there are two objects to the game: accuracy and speed. If either has to be sacrificed, it should be speed. Practice handling a bike around

OBSTACLE DROP is a fine way to develop accuracy and speed on a bike—and it's fun besides.

the baskets; eventually you will develop enough skill to pitch or drop the balls into the baskets from almost any position.

BRAKING WITHOUT SKIDDING

All you will need is a piece of chalk.

Set off a 100-foot straightaway and draw a chalk line at about the 75-foot mark. Each rider works up speed until he reaches the chalk line and then brakes, attempting not to skid. If he brakes *before* he reaches the chalk line, he is disqualified. The cyclist who stops within the shortest distance beyond the chalk line without skidding places first; the one who stops within the next shortest distance is second, and so on. Run off the players separately. In this way, the judges can give full attention to skidding, and it will be easy to tell whether the cyclist applied his brake *at* the chalk line, not before.

It is usually left to the judges or other participants to decide whether a cyclist built up sufficient speed to deserve a second chance. An entrant who skids is also given another try, but no more than one extra chance should be allowed any player, or the game will proceed too slowly. If you enter this event, practice braking beforehand.

LEMON RELAY

Of course, the normal relay, explained on page 267, can be part of your rodeo. For this special relay, you will need 2 lemons, 2 tablespoons, and the ability to cycle with one hand. Divide your group into two equal teams, with each team lined up in single file. The two lines of teams should be at least 20 feet apart. Set a marker 100 feet in front of the first cyclist on each team.

At the signal the first cyclist on each team mounts his bike holding the spoon with the lemon in one hand. Suppose you have to lead off. Ride to the marker 100 feet away, turn around and ride back. Give the spoon (with the lemon still in it) to the next player, who repeats the same ride. If the lemon falls off the spoon, the rider must dismount, replace the lemon and go on from where he is. The relay continues until the last player has completed the run. Of course, the first team to finish the relay wins.

With relatively unskilled cyclists you may have to vary this game. If it becomes too difficult to pass the spoon to the next cyclist while you are on your bike, then dismount when you complete your run. Pass the spoon and lemon while you are standing on the ground.

BALLOON MAZE

You will need a piece of chalk and about 20 balloons. This game can only be played on a calm, windless day.

Black top school areas or large driveways are ideal, but if neither is available, chalk off either a circle or a rectangle approximately 30 square feet in area. This will accommodate from four to seven cyclists, but, of course, you can adjust the size of the game area and the number of balloons to the number of players. If you have fewer than four players in a 30-foot area, the game will be too easy. Now, blow up the balloons and place them in the chalked-off space.

The object of the game is for each rider to weave in and out around the balloons without losing his balance and falling, or breaking a balloon. You will have to station someone outside the ring to toss back the balloons if they are knocked out.

Since this is a game which emphasizes skill rather than competitiveness, you can keep your own score; each time you touch the ground with your foot or break a balloon one point is counted against you. Naturally, the player with the lowest score after all the balloons are broken or after a definite prearranges length of time is the winner. Fifteen minutes is a good time limit.

The Balloon Maze demands tremendous cycling skill! You have to avoid both the balloons and the other riders—all the while keeping your balance!

SPRINT: At the finish line, the victor breaks the tape.

SPRINT

The simplest event to arrange and perform is the sprint or fast race. You need a protected straightaway or oval track of 500 to 1,000 feet. It should be at least 30 feet wide. All entrants can make the dash simultaneously, or if the track is narrow or the group inexperienced, the race can be run off with two entrants at a time competing in an elimination contest. Each judge should watch one cyclist only, to determine accurately his place at the tape.

The sprint requires strength, energy, and easy bike acceleration. But you do not have to be an expert cyclist, or own a racer, to participate in it. Although a racer or a lightweight bike is best for the sprint, it is by no means a requirement. Anyone can enjoy a brisk race!

COASTING RACE

Test your skill and your bike's ability to coast. For this race your bike must be in top shape—cleaned, oiled, and stripped of extra equipment.

Select either a level straightaway, or one that starts out by being level and then rises gradually into an incline.

At the signal, pedal as fast as you can. At a predetermined point, marked by a flag, stop pedaling. Coast to the finish line.

Now, check the coasting distance of each bike. The longest coaster wins. Remember to station a judge at the point at which racers must stop pedaling.

You can run off this race several times so that each contestant can have a chance to improve his own record.

CROSS-COUNTRY

You will enjoy marking out this course for yourself. Plan the race over natural inclines, bridges, creeks, woods and parks. One cross-country event called on the racers to ford a creek, climb a hill, cross a bridge, ride through a thicket and dash the last 300 feet to the finish line. You should include as many natural obstacles as possible, but exactly which ones you use will depend on the topography in the area of your home. If you think it is necessary, you can invent your own obstacles. For example, cinders and loose earth can be piled up to make an interesting incline or a steep bank on a curve.

Although spectators see only a small part of a cross-country race, usually the end of the sprint, as a participant you will find the cross-country packed with thrills and adventures. Remember, though, that all the entrants should be taken over the course by a judge before the event begins. Everyone should be aware of the course and of its obstacles. Emphasize the interest rather than the difficulty of the race. There should not be too many large rocks in the streams you ford, and trails leading between trees should be wide enough for safety.

Use care in planning your cross-country course. It is a free-for-all, but it should not be dangerous.

HILL CLIMB

This event is modeled on a famous motorcycle race, but is it much less dangerous. The idea is to climb a steep hill with all the speed you can muster. You must choose a hill with enough straightaway leading up to it for the racers to build up speed. The steeper it is, the shorter it should be. Although you will want a challenging course, it must not be too difficult to negotiate.

You may have to search for just the right hill. Investigate nearby schools and parks, but stay away from embankments near highways. These are dangerous. Once you think you have found the right hill, give it a test climb.

CROSS-COUNTRY: You can enjoy the scenery along the way.

It is best to run off the contestants individually to avoid possible collisions. And, of course, you will need a stop watch with a second hand. On your mark!

NEWSPAPER RACE

It's natural to associate boys and bicycles with newspapers—so why not have a newspaper race? Sailing folded papers at a given target is always fun.

For this game you will need 2 upright poles, a wooden stake for a marker, an old blanket or sheet and 2 newspapers per player.

To prepare the event, tack the blanket or sheet to the upright poles—more simply, just drape the blanket over a low-hanging branch. The blanket is your target—big enough to see and big enough to hit —that is, if you're in good hurling shape. Thirty feet in front of the target, set a marker in the ground.

To fold the paper the way the newsboys do, first fold a complete section in half. Now, roll it horizontally and tuck in both ends. Remember, each player should have two folded papers.

With a paper under each arm, the contestant starts at a point 100 feet away from the target and rides toward the marker set 30 feet in front of the target. The cyclist must throw both papers *before* he reaches this marker.

A single hit is worth 1 point; two hits will earn 2 points. The game continues until someone accumulates 10 points.

BIKE BALANCE

Did you ever try to walk balancing a book on your head? It's easy, you say? Then try it while riding your bike!

The object of the game is to see how far you can ride before the book topples off. It's hard, but with a little practice you can master this balancing feat.

To warm up for this stunt, try walking with the book on your head. Then, when you become quite proficient, try it on your bike. Use a book you don't want any more; frequent falls will damage the binding.

This doesn't have to be a competitive event, but just a game of skill. Try it. You'll be surprised at the improvement in your posture.

Although race meets and rodeos are wonderful fun, you do not have to compete with others to enjoy riding your bike. Ever try competing with yourself? You can play many of the bike rodeo games alone. Test yourself on an event; run through it again. Did your performance improve? Now, try it again—and again. Challenge yourself; this is an

BIKE POLO is a fast, rough and tumble battle that has long been popular in England, and is rapidly gaining enthusiastic followers in the United States. Here the Grand Prix of the London polo tournament is being decided at Mitcham Football Ground.

excellent way to improve your skill in handling a bicycle.

BIKE POLO

This is a fast, energetic sport for two teams. Played from a bicycle saddle, the "sport of princes" is too young to have become part of the athletic tradition of the United States, but it is played enthusiastically in the eastern states. There are many bicycle-polo clubs in England and in Europe where this comparatively new sport is extremely popular.

The game is quite simple. It is played on a level field about 175 yards long and 75 yards wide, with a goal at each end, marked by posts 12 feet apart. You can use actual polo fields or football fields, if they are smooth enough.

The four players on each team attempt to hit a wooden polo ball through the opposing goal. Each player has a polo mallet 32 inches long, and a helmet for protection. There are four basic strokes: forehand and backhand with the right hand, and forehand and backhand with the left hand. Lightweight bikes with gear shifts are best for this game. Naturally, bike polo requires a great amount of team play, practice and facility with a bike. But, your effort will be rewarded. Few sports are as exciting as bike polo.

TRIPS AND TOURS

Planning a trip in advance will make it easier and more fun. First, decide whether you want to go alone as a family or with a group. Chances are, you will want company. Touring is more interesting if you can share your impressions and experiences with others. So your group should first agree on what it most wants from the trip—just a good ride, a swim in a nearby lake, a visit to an historical site, or hosteling. Once this has been decided, you are ready to lay out your course.

What sort of route will your group choose? Some riders enjoy taking main highways; others prefer side roads and byways. In fact, inexperienced riders should use relatively untravelled roads so that they can build up "bike legs" and develop a feeling of security in traffic. In planning your route, you will want to refer to maps. You can also get detailed contour maps of almost any area in the United States for 50 cents apiece by writing to your State Department of Conservation or to the U.S. Geological Survey in Washington, D.C.

Group travel is sometimes difficult unless riders are of approximately the same riding ability. Fast cyclists have a lonely time of it way up ahead, and beginners feel left out and discouraged if they find themselves hanging far behind the others. If your group has this problem, you may be able to get some of the faster members to take a rest now and then to wait for the others. Another suggestion is to divide the group according to cycling abilities. Assign a leader to "pace" each group.

After you have decided on your route, try to talk to other bike enthusiasts who have taken the same trip. Map information is invaluable, but it is a good idea to supplement it whenever possible with the advice of someone who knows the route. You can find out which are the best roads, the location of the most scenic areas, the best lakes and rivers for swimming, what spots of historical interest are along the way and where your group can find tourist homes or hostels. It's particularly important to get personal information if you plan to camp overnight.

You can keep your own touring records quite easily. Just ask each club member to write a brief report giving his impressions of the trip and all data he thinks would be valuable to a cyclist who had never before been over the route. Collect these reports. Whether you file them or keep them in a scrapbook, they will become a valuable part of your club records.

Once you've decided when and where you're going, set a starting time and place. Make sure all members of the tour have this information.

LOCAL TRIPS

Local trips are those planned for distances under 20 miles, round trip. Remember that if you live in a relatively flat rural area, your traveling time will be different from what it would be in an urban area. You can cover the same amount of ground in the country in less time than in the city. You will want to adjust the length of the trip to suit traffic and geographical conditions.

Local trips can be very exciting, but their secondary purpose is to get you in shape for longer tours. You will probably select for your destination an historical, geographical or cultural point of interest in or near your community. For example, city cyclists may want to visit homes of famous people, unusual buildings, zoos, museums, aquariums, parks, canals, rivers or bridges. Most parks, zoos and college or university campuses are crisscrossed with lanes and paths, making it quite easy for you to travel on your bike, observing the scenery. Of course, if you see signs prohibiting bicycles, you will observe them and you will remember to give pedestrians the right of way.

TOURING: Every part of the country has something to offer. Here, a couple on a tandem are enjoying the countryside.

PRACTICE TRIPS

The purpose of a practice trip is to get you in shape for a longer one. If you plan a tour longer than 15 miles, certainly you should take a practice trip first. Here is a simple ratio for establishing the length of a practice trip: the ratio is 3–1. For example, if you are training for a tour of 30 miles, your preliminary trip should cover 10 miles of terrain as similar as possible to that of the longer trip.

You'll be wise to practice carrying exactly the same equipment you plan to use on your big journey. This will help give you an accurate measure of your endurance. Start early in the morning, so you will be back by dark. If the weather becomes hot and humid, shorten the distance you plan to cover and take many rest breaks. (Generally you should rest 10 to 15 minutes every hour.) Try to stop in shady areas. Stretch out on the grass. Relax. If you are thirsty, take some water. Have a snack of cheese and crackers or fresh fruit.

The second purpose of a practice trip is to give you an idea of your cycling ability and endurance. Some riders can do 10 hilly miles a day, others only 5. Some find that they have to avoid hills altogether. By dividing your traveling time into the mileage covered, you will know whether you average 6 or 8 miles an hour, for instance, under certain specific conditions. If you don't have a speedometer to take with you, you can find out what mileage you covered from a map.

WHAT IS HOSTELING?

You must be wondering when you will be ready to take an overnight trip. You've got yourself in good physical condition; you've been on at least one practice trip and you know your average cycling speed. Just one thing more before you plan an overnight trip—you should be introduced to American Youth Hostels, Inc.

The privilege of joining the AYH and of using hostels is open to anyone of any race, religion or nationality, between the ages of 9 and 90. The only requirement is that you travel under your own steam, that is, by bicycle, canoe, skis or on foot. For membership details, apply to your local AYH council, of which there are 27 in the United States, or to national headquarters, 20 West 17th Street, New York, N.Y. 10011. Membership will entitle you to use any hostel in the world.

In the United States, hostels are sponsored by local groups interested in the movement and in establishing a hostel in their community. Shelters may be in barns, old houses, former Navy barracks, interesting lighthouses, or in similar buildings. Most accommodations are comfortable, and all are clean and supervised.

Sleeping quarters for men and women are separate, but each hostel has a community center where hostelers meet while cooking their meals. Some hostels have game rooms or common lounges equipped with phonographs and radios. There is often space for square dancing.

You will have no trouble meeting fellow hostelers.

There are more hostels in Europe than in America, as the movement started there.

NOVICE AND INTERMEDIATE TOURS

Novice tours include 30 to 50 miles of travel over a period of two days. You can camp out, stay at an AYH hostel or rent a room overnight. You and your friends will have to decide before you start out where you are going to stay, what route you will follow and whether maps and train schedules are necessary. In short, you will have to plan all the details of the trip very carefully.

Often, it is convenient to combine modes of transportation. You can save a great deal of time by travelling to your selected touring area by car, bus or train. However, if you use other types of travel for part of your trip, be sure to find out in advance whether you can bring your bicycle along.

Intermediate tours last less than a week, involve several overnight stops and an average of 20 to 30 miles between lodgings. You shouldn't attempt this type of tour until you have taken many practice trips, including at least one full-day cycling outing.

It is important that you know your average cycling rate: 10, 20 or 30 miles a day. If you do 25 miles a day, of course you will plan your trip on the basis of this rate. If you're about to take your first long trip, plan conservatively. Figure your daily mileage at slightly less than it usually is. Remember, too, to adjust the distances you think you can cover to the relative hilliness of the terrain. If you get to your destination ahead of schedule, you can always put the extra time to good use. Plan so that you can avoid feeling rushed.

If you are not acquainted with the area you're going to cover, try to learn something about the nature of the roads. Find out if they are hilly or flat, if they are in good condition, if they are gravel or paved. Is there heavy traffic? Are there parks and swimming areas? Are there any historical, cultural or scenic points of interest? Will you camp, stay at a youth hostel or at a guest home? These details should be arranged before you set out.

ADVANCED TOURS

Tours that are more than one week long, with an average of 25 miles or more between lodgings, are considered advanced. They require a great deal of training and experience. Your body has to be able to take the rigors of the road. You will need stamina and good lung power—both the results of serious practice. Do not undertake an advanced tour unless you are at least 15 years old, and no matter how old you are, don't take a long tour by yourself.

First, select the area you want to visit; list all the points of interest, available swimming facilities, camping, fishing and hiking areas along the way. Determine whether you will use only your bike, or other types of transportation as well.

If you use only your bike, plan to rest for a day or two after two or three days of steady touring. Otherwise, you will get very tired. The rest will refresh you, and also give you ample time to enjoy the countryside, city and whatever sights it has to offer.

The AYH plans and schedules all-expense advanced tours throughout the United States and abroad. A tour leader is assigned to every nine hostelers.

CYCLE TRIPS

Many cyclists, particularly those who live in cities, find it convenient to take a train to the area in

HOSTEL: The Youth Hostel on Nantucket Island, Massachusetts, offers warm hospitality at the end of a day of biking.

TOURING IN THE RAIN: For all-weather travel, bike riders should be equipped with lamps and ponchos.

which they want to ride. This enables them to avoid uninteresting territory and to save time.

Some railroads allow you to check your bicycle through to your destination for no extra charge. However, there is one vital precaution! Make sure your train has a baggage car. Then check as to whether you will be permitted to transport your bicycle on this train.

Other railroads may permit you to carry your bike with you onto the coach car, particularly if you can detach the front wheel from the frame so that it occupies less space. Of course, if you have a folding bike it will make it that much easier!

Of course, you can also transport your bike by auto. Just attach it to the back of the car and drive to the desired area. Some cyclists have cars with bike barriers built onto the rear bumper; some install simple toting devices. Other cyclists place their bikes directly on the back bumper of the car. Rest the bike upside down on the bumper, then tie the handle-bars and seat to the bumper. Now, pull the rope through the door of the luggage compartment and tie the bike firmly against the body of the car. To prevent scratching, put an old blanket between the bike and the car.

OVERSEAS TOURS

One of the finest travel experiences you can have is an overseas tour. Since so many arrangements are necessary, you will probably want to think in terms of a group tour. The best organization for this kind of program is the AYH, particularly if your budget is limited.

TRAVEL TIP: The Bike Toter can be attached to the rear bumper of almost every car. It will carry one or two fully assembled bikes (three in a pinch), and sells for less than $15.

Courtesy Bike Toter, Inc.
Box 888, Santa Monica, Calif. 90406

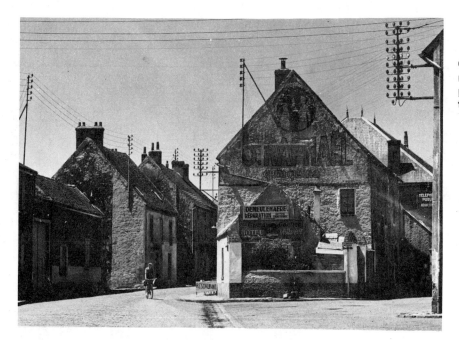

Each year the AYH conducts European tours. You will travel with a compatible group of young people, all of whom have important interests in common—cycling, love of travel and of the outdoors. For each group of nine travelers there is a trained leader. The minimum age for overseas touring is 16.

Overseas tours are educational as well as fun. You will get valuable experience in group living and in learning how to get along with others on a day-to-day basis. Compared with other overseas trips, AYH tours are very inexpensive. If you sign up for an AYH tour, you will receive a trip forecast giving the main points of interest in various areas.

HOW TO PREPARE FOR TOURING

Now that you know what kinds of tours your club can arrange, from short local excursions to extremely advanced European trips, you are probably anxious to pack and get started. But wait a minute! The surest way to spoil a tour is to set out before you are thoroughly prepared.

While touring, your bike is your "home," and you will have to know how to live safely and comfortably "on the road." Select the proper equipment and clothing and learn to protect yourself from illness and injuries—these are just two of the many things you must do before you can safely set out on a tour.

First of all, you must get yourself into excellent physical condition.

GETTING READY FOR YOUR TRIP

There is much more to preparation than riding.

For extended bike trips you must be in good physi-

cal condition. When you ride a bike, you are not a rider only. You are the engine as well. Your physical condition will determine how fast you can travel and how far you can go.

Do not overeat, however; keep your diet simple. There is no substitute for wholesome body-building foods. And get into the habit of eating a good breakfast.

Enough sleep is the second requirement for good health. If you want to be in good physical condition, you must give your body a chance to revitalize itself, which is what it does when you are asleep.

You must exercise to get into shape for your bike tour. Select exercises that will develop the muscles you will be using as you cycle. A very good one is the bicycle exercise. Lie down on your back. Raise the lower part of your body so that your buttocks and legs are in the air, your arms bent at the elbows. Rest your hands at your waistline so that your arms support your body. Now, bend your knees and move your legs as if you were pedalling a bike. Continue this motion as long as you can. The first day, try for 25 times. Each day increase the number of cycles.

Here is a good exercise to strengthen your arms and shoulders. Extend your arms as if you were holding the handlebars of your bike. First slowly draw your arms to each side until they are extended outward from the shoulder. Then bring them forward again. Continue doing this until they begin to ache slightly. You will find you can do this exercise for increasingly longer periods each day.

Develop good posture. For proper cycling you need strong lung power, and if you don't give your lungs room to expand, you will not breathe properly. Stand straight, and learn to breathe fully, so that your lungs completely fill up with air. You will find that proper breathing makes a great difference in your endurance as a cyclist.

As soon as your body is in good physical condition, you will be able to tackle that long bike tour without worrying about exhaustion. Touring will become a invigorating sport, never an arduous chore.

As for packing, it's best to use saddlebags that fit over your crossbar or rear wheel carrier. Or you can wrap your pack in a nylon, oilcloth or waterproof cover, and tie it to your metal carrier. Some riders carry their packs on their backs, but this may be uncomfortable and unsafe. Metal carriers, wicker or metal baskets have limited capacites, whereas saddlebags are roomier. Fast riders don't like baskets or other carriers on the front of their bike, because they offer wind resistance and slow down touring speed.

It isn't your bike that will be carrying the load. It will be you! So spare yourself as much weight as possible. Thirty pounds is the accepted maximum weight to carry on a touring bicycle. Divide things among your group so that the weight will be equally distributed. And in packing your individual load, make it as compact as possible. Cans that roll and rattle in your pack can be very annoying and may throw you off balance. So wrap cans securely in a woolen shirt or some heavy article of clothing.

Remember to take your tool kit and a tire-repair kit. If you ride at night, include a flashlight and a few extra batteries. Of course, you will always take a first-aid kit on any tour or camping trip.

Before setting out, see that your bike is in good condition. Inspect it a few days before the trip, so that if it needs any complicated work, you can consult your local bike shop. Check the brakes; oil the movable parts; inflate the tires to the proper pressure, tighten all loose nuts and bolts.

DOWNHILL AND MOUNTAIN BIKING

If you have ever ridden downhill for any distance at a great speed, you know how exciting it is. The experience is like flying. It's a wonderful free feeling, but you must be cautious or you may find yourself in trouble. Wind resistance becomes far greater—controls in stopping and steering become more difficult to apply.

Since most accidents seem to happen to tired riders, be sure you rest before taking a long drop or winding around a mountain. Be sure, too, that your bike is in top shape. Tighten all nuts, and tie down all gear. Stay at least 10 bicycle-lengths away from the rider ahead of you. If there's a motor vehicle ahead of you, stay at least 300 feet away to allow for quick stops and sudden turns.

Apply and release your brakes in a steady rhythm so that they won't wear out. There is another reason for this precaution; if you apply your brakes suddenly, you may be thrown over the handlebars. Watch for stones in the road. Slow down before every curve to be sure you can negotiate it at a certain speed. Once you are able to see around the curve, at

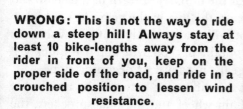

WRONG: This is not the way to ride down a steep hill! Always stay at least 10 bike-lengths away from the rider in front of you, keep on the proper side of the road, and ride in a crouched position to lessen wind resistance.

the same time controlling your speed properly, you can release your brakes.

In descending rapidly it is wise to maintain a crouched position so as to minimize wind resistance and lower your center of gravity.

HEALTH ON TRIPS

Carry a first-aid kit on all tours. And stay away from poisonous plants.

If you burn yourself while working around the fire, apply some of the burn ointment from your first-aid kit. If the burn appears serious, go to the nearest doctor or hospital for proper treatment. Never neglect any serious injury, even if getting to a doctor disrupts your trip and inconveniences members of your group. Good campers will be glad to co-operate when someone is hurt.

When cycling, you are completely exposed to the elements. Be prepared for the strong sun. Sunglasses are essential. If you sunburn easily, apply suntan lotion to your face, hands and arms (if exposed) *before* they get burned. Always wear a kerchief or thin cotton cap, preferably one with a visor. You must shade your eyes and nose. The nose in particular is extremely sensitive to strong sun.

A head covering will also protect you from sunstroke. If you have a throbbing headache, a rapid pulse and a dizzy feeling, get into a cool, shady place at once. Lie down and put cold, wet compresses on your head and on the nape of your neck. If you feel very sick, send someone for the nearest physician.

Heat exhaustion is as dangerous as sunstroke. This is why you should always plan to rest during the midday hours of a hot, sunny day. It's a foolish cyclist who continues riding when he has these symptoms: weakness; pale and clammy skin; a slow pulse. These result when body salts are lost through excessive perspiration. You can prevent heat exhaustion by drinking water frequently and by taking salt tablets, or plain table salt, when you perspire excessively. If you feel you are being overcome by the heat, get into the shade, lie flat on your back and take some salt. If you don't feel better after a while, go to the

nearest hostel or arrange to return home by train or bus.

When you pedal for a very long time, you may develop cramps in your legs or arms. Straighten out the affected limb and get off your bike. Massage the aching part to increase blood circulation. When you start cycling again, proceed slowly. Rest from time to time. When you reach your destination, take a hot bath or shower. This will ease your tired muscles.

RIDING WELL

GEARS

Gearing is a method of gaining wheel power on a bike. For example, when riding uphill you should shift to a lower gear; otherwise, the sprocket revolutions will slow down and you will find yourself tending to "stand up," trying to develop enough power to climb the hill.

In the early days of bike riding the pedal was attached to the large front drive wheel, which was about 70 inches in diameter. There were no gears; the power was applied to the pedals in the same way as on a child's tricycle. The drive wheel made exactly as many revolutions as the foot of the rider.

Today you can exert power on the standard 27-inch wheel, through the ratio of two sprockets and a chain, equal to the power of a wheel 70 inches in diameter. This increase in power is made possible by gearing. In other words, the modern 27-inch wheel can be pedalled by means of gears at the same ratio as that of the antiquated high wheelers, and with much greater ease.

For pleasant riding you should have gears. Most lightweight touring bikes have three-speed, five-speed or ten-speed gears, which help to "level off hills" in one gear and, in another, give you good pedal pressure on level or downhill runs. Some gears have as many as fifteen speeds which can be adjusted to suit your cycling skill and the terrain you are negotiating. The greater the variation in terrain, the greater should be the variation in available gears.

High gear is for fast riding. The greater the difference between the number of teeth in the chain and the rear sprockets, the higher the gear. At the higher gear, your foot will make relatively few revolutions for the speed obtained. You will not tire quickly if you use high gear on a level or declining slope.

The smaller the difference between the number of teeth in the chain wheel and the rear sprockets, the lower the gear. At the lower gear, your foot will make more revolutions than in high, and the number will more closely approximate the number of revolu-

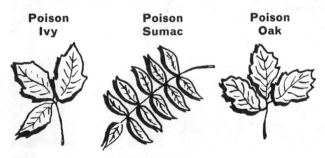

Poison Ivy   **Poison Sumac**   **Poison Oak**

tions made by the wheel. Low gear is best for hill climbing. In this gear your foot revolves quickly enough to give you the momentum necessary to accelerate uphill. Don't use low gear on level stretches or downhill; you will find your pedals revolving too quickly and you will rapidly become tired.

When going downhill or when developing speed on a level road, you should shift to high gear. This slows down the speed of sprocket revolutions. If you do not shift to high, your legs will be moving so fast you will not feel the pressure of the pedals against your feet.

On fairly level roads with a few easy hills, a three-speed gear should be adequate. However, if you are going through country which includes both mountains and level areas, you should consider getting a ten-speed gear.

For example, let's assume that 70 revolutions per minute is your normal pace on a level stretch. As you approach a hill, you will have to change gears to keep producing your normal, comfortable 70 revolutions. Although you could probably maintain 70 without changing gears, it would be such a strain that cycling would no longer be a pleasurable sport. With the gears, however, you can move smoothly along at the best cadence for you.

If you are riding over hills of varying steepness, you might want to use two lower gears. Again, this depends upon the terrain. Of course, on a bike with ten or twelve speeds you will be able to take all kinds of hills, but if the general direction of your trips leads you over fairly level country, you will be satisfied with only three speeds.

Find your own gear ratio by using this formula:
Number of teeth in your chain wheel sprocket..
Multiplied by the diameter of your wheel......
Divided by the number of teeth in your rear
    sprocket..............................
Equals your gear.

Example:
Number of teeth in your chain wheel sprocket..   48
Times the diameter of your wheel............   27
                         ———
                         1,296
Divided by the number of teeth in your rear
    sprocket...................................   20
                         ———
Equals your gear.......................   64.16

In the example given above, the gear was 64 plus. This is a useful road-climbing gear.

Select a bike whose gear ratio is the most comfortable for you. Try a number of bikes with different gear ratios before you decide on one. The most useful gears run from 60 to 80. Girls generally use the lower ones—50 to 70. These are the hill-climbing gears. Gears from 70 to 80 are best for level roads and downhill. Racers are geared from 80 to 90.

The gears we have been discussing are fixed. If your bike has hand brakes and no foot brakes, you can attach gears with different speeds. With variable three-speed gears, you can adjust to a normal speed at 64, shift into a low of 49 to climb a steep hill, or shift into a high gear of 85 on a level stretch. For the most pleasurable touring you need different gearing for uphill and downhill travel. A three-speed gear can be fitted to any bike equipped with independent hand brakes. For the most part, this means light-weights. Variable gearing, years ago invented in England, has now become widely used in America, and has had much to do with the growing popularity of biking.

BIKE SAFETY

Are you a "safety first" bike rider? Statistics put the responsibility for traffic accidents involving bikes squarely on the cyclist. Figures show that many bike accidents are caused by bikes in bad repair, and that many other accidents occur because the cyclist violates traffic rules.

CAUSES OF BIKE ACCIDENTS

1. Cyclist makes improper turn.
2. Cyclist fails to signal correctly.
3. Bike lacks proper controls (poor brakes, no head lamps, no rear reflectors, or rider fails to use them).
4. Carrying an extra rider.
5. Cyclist runs into open car doors.
6. Excessive speed.
7. Cutting in between cars.
8. Hitching a ride.
9. Riding against traffic.
10. Not coming to full stop when riding down driveway to street.
11. Riding when cyclist doesn't feel well or is tired.
12. Carrying a person on the handlebars.
13. Making repairs on the road.
14. Not riding on correct side of road.
15. Riding in busy sections.

The following rules were drawn up by a group of bike safety experts. If you observe them at all times, you probably will never be involved in an accident.

1. Observe all traffic regulations—red and green lights, one-way streets, stop signs.

2. Keep to the side and ride in single file. Keep a safe distance behind all vehicles.

3. Have a white light on the front and a danger signal on the rear for night driving. Wear white or light-colored clothing at night.

4. Have a satisfactory signalling device to warn of your approach. Always ride at a safe speed.

5. Give pedestrians the right of way. Don't ride on sidewalks.

6. Look out for cars pulling into traffic. Keep a sharp lookout for car doors that open suddenly.

7. Never hitch onto other vehicles. Never do stunts or race in traffic.

8. Never carry other riders—carry no packages that obstruct vision or prevent proper control of the cycle.

9. Be sure that your brakes are operating efficiently and keep your bicycle in perfect running condition.

10. Slow down at all intersections and look to the right and to the left before crossing.

11. Always use hand signals for turning and stopping. For a left turn, the left arm should be straight out; for a right turn the left arm should be extended, bent at the elbow with hand pointing upward.

12. Ride in a straight line. Do not weave in and out of traffic or move from side to side.

13. Avoid ruts, grooves or car tracks; if you must cross them, turn your wheels at right angles. Wet pavements may be slippery and gravel treacherous.

14. Avoid riding over curbs or other obstructions that might rupture your tires.

CARE AND REPAIR OF YOUR BIKE

Whether you are the owner of a custom-made racer or a standard balloon-tire model, your bike represents a considerable investment. Naturally, you will want to know how to care for your bike in the best possible way.

FIXING A FLAT TIRE

If the flat was caused by a tack or nail, you'll have a fairly easy job fixing it; you will not have to take off the wheel. Just mark the tire and the rim at the point of puncture. If there is still some air in the tube, let it out by pressing the valve. You will now need a pair of pliers and a screwdriver. Pry one side of the tire over the rim and pull out the part of the tube on which you marked the hole.

Use sandpaper or the scraper in a tire patch container to rough up the tube surface. Unless you do

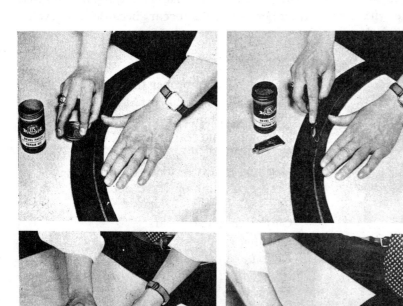

FIXING A PUNCTURED TUBE: (Top left) Clean and roughen the surface around the puncture. (Top right) Then apply cement and spread evenly with the unsharpened side of a knife or similar object. (Lower left) For the third step, remove backing from the patch. (Lower right) Roll the patch to force out all the air bubbles. Wait 15 minutes for the cement to dry, place tube in the casing and mount the tube and tire.

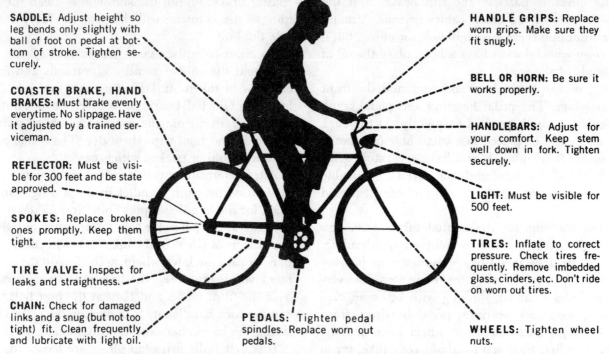

SADDLE: Adjust height so leg bends only slightly with ball of foot on pedal at bottom of stroke. Tighten securely.

COASTER BRAKE, HAND BRAKES: Must brake evenly everytime. No slippage. Have it adjusted by a trained serviceman.

REFLECTOR: Must be visible for 300 feet and be state approved.

SPOKES: Replace broken ones promptly. Keep them tight.

TIRE VALVE: Inspect for leaks and straightness.

CHAIN: Check for damaged links and a snug (but not too tight) fit. Clean frequently and lubricate with light oil.

PEDALS: Tighten pedal spindles. Replace worn out pedals.

HANDLE GRIPS: Replace worn grips. Make sure they fit snugly.

BELL OR HORN: Be sure it works properly.

HANDLEBARS: Adjust for your comfort. Keep stem well down in fork. Tighten securely.

LIGHT: Must be visible for 500 feet.

TIRES: Inflate to correct pressure. Check tires frequently. Remove imbedded glass, cinders, etc. Don't ride on worn out tires.

WHEELS: Tighten wheel nuts.

ALWAYS RIDE WITH CAUTION · TAKE GOOD CARE OF YOUR BICYCLE

Poster prepared by the Bicycle Institute of America, Inc.

this, the cement will not stick. Now, cement a patch over the damaged area.

If you can't find the hole on the tire, you will have to remove the wheel and take off the tire. It is best to begin by prying off the section of the tire opposite the valve, and work around until it is all removed. Inflate the tube and examine it closely for holes. It may be necessary to immerse the tube in water to locate the puncture. Any slight bubbling will indicate an air escape. Mark the hole and repair it as explained above. Your casing should then be cleaned of dirt, and any sharp particles which might have caused the damage should be removed.

CLEANING THE CHAIN

After considerable cycling, your chain will become gritty and clogged with small dirt particles. It is then time for a cleaning and lubricating job.

In order to do this, you will first have to remove the chain. Find the joint that binds the chain together. You will see a small spring connected to the joint. With a small screwdriver you can force this spring, and your chain will come off.

Place the chain in a quart bottle half filled with kerosene and shake the bottle around until most of the dirt falls off the chain. Now take the clean chain out of the bottle and allow it to dry overnight in the open air.

After it is dry, place the chain in a pan. Pour heavy motor oil—about SAE30—over the chain. Slosh the oil in and out of the links until you are sure the entire chain is covered with oil. You can use an old toothbrush to loosen stubborn dirt. After a few minutes take the chain out and wipe off the excess oil. Put the chain back on your bike and lubricate the links by rubbing them with a stick of graphite.

This special handling of your chain will provide smoother, quieter, and more efficient riding.

The chain should have no more than a one-inch slack when you move it up and down at its center. If your chain is too tight or too loose, you can adjust it by loosening the two nuts which hold the rear axle and either pulling in or pushing out the rear wheel, whichever is necessary to obtain the correct amount of tension.

CLEANING AND OILING

You can easily wipe dirt off a bike with a soft rag, mild soap and warm water. Use nickel polish on your handlebars, tire rims and other nickel or chrome areas.

For periodic oiling use a thin oil. It will help if you first turn your cycle upside down. It is best to begin oiling at one end of your bike, carefully working toward the other end. Examine each movable

Care and Repair of Your Bike ■ 281

part and oil it as you work along. At the front wheel, oil the movable parts of the rim brakes and the movable ends of the brake cables or rods. Usually at the front hub there is a small hole for oiling, but if your front wheel doesn't have a hole, place the oil at both ends of the hub.

Next, oil the handlebars and neck and the front fork bearings. The pedal bearings and pedal crank hanger should both be oiled frequently. At the back hub, oil should be placed in a small hole (similar to that in the front hub). If you have a variable gear, you should oil this part lightly too. Even the movable parts on accessories, such as bells and horns, should be oiled.

When it's time for the annual lubrication, you should also give your bike a complete overhauling. This can be done in spring, midsummer or just before putting your bike away for the winter. An overhaul includes cleaning, flushing with kerosene, and greasing the crank bearings, pedal bearings, front fork bearings, back and front wheel hubs and the chain. The first time you overhaul your bike, try to get someone who has done it before to work with you.

To clean your crank hanger, remove the pedal and the chain. With a strong wrench remove the hanger lock nut. As you take out each part, remember its position. Clean the shaft and other parts thoroughly with kerosene. Wipe them dry, and insert the crank back into the hub. Cover with light grease before you replace the other parts.

To overhaul the fork take out the handlebar stem. Turn off the head crown nut with your adjustable wrench. Remove the key washer and unscrew the cone. The fork will drop out of the head when it is raised. Now, remove the bearings. Thoroughly flush the head of the fork with kerosene and wipe it dry. Remove all the grit in the ball bearings. Grease the bearings and reassemble.

To clean the front wheel hub first take off both nuts and washers. Pull the fork apart with your hands and slip out one end of the axle. Place one end of the axle on a bench and unscrew one side of the hub. The other cone and side of the axle can be removed together. Be sure the ball bearings do not fall out. All these parts should be washed in kerosene, then wiped dry. Before reassembling the hub, pack it with grease.

To clean the rear wheel, first unscrew the hub nuts and washers. Take the fender arms off the axle. Undo the brake arm. Disconnect the chain by pushing the wheel in. Now, lift the wheel out of the frame. You can use an old toothbrush to clean fine particles of dirt out of the sprocket. If you have a coaster brake, do not use kerosene to clean the rear hub, as the kerosene will thin out the lubricant inside the hub.

To clean or replace your pedals, take off the nuts that hold the rubber treads. The treads and frame can now be taken off. Use care to see that you don't lose any of the ball bearings. Remove the lock nut and the key washer from the spindle. Wash all parts in kerosene, and then wipe them dry. The inside of the spindle should be packed with grease.

After determining your saddle height, you will be able to adjust your handlebars for riding comfort. Look for the handlebar post bolt. Now loosen it with a wrench and tap it so the taper plug comes out. Stand over the front wheel of the bike and twist the handlebars to raise or lower them, according to the adjustment you want. Keep the handlebars very straight over the front wheel and tighten the post bolt. You can tilt your handlebars by loosening the clamp bolt, tilting the handlebar, and then tightening it.

If your handle grips fall off or are loose, you can tighten them with bicycle rim cement. First, clean and rough up your bar with sandpaper or steel wool. Apply rim cement to the bar and to the inside of the grip. If the handlebar is too short for the grip, put a wooden plug in the bar to lengthen it. If you don't, the grip will come off. Turn the grip as you push it on the bar, and of course, keep the finger ridges on the underneath side. Wipe off any cement that seeps under the edges of the grips. You can clean off excess cement with alcohol or naphtha.

STRAIGHTENING HANDLEBARS and repairing tires should be part of every competent cyclist's skill.

TRUING THE WHEELS

In truing wheels your aim is to round out the rim. All you need are a spoke wrench and a nipple key. Turn your bike upside down so the wheels are free to turn as you test and work on them. Start with the spoke next to the valve so that you will be able to remember where you began. Now, test one spoke after another to see which are loose. When you come to a loose one, turn the spoke wrench on the nipple (the nut on the rim edge of the spoke). As you turn toward the left, you will see that the spoke becomes tighter.

If you find that the spokes are too long for the wheel, let the air out of the tires. Otherwise, the ends of the spokes may pierce the inner tube. Long spokes should be filed down at the ends.

You can pluck spokes as you would a musical string. When you hit a high note, you will know you have adjusted the spoke tight enough. Keep going until you have tightened all the loose spokes. Now, pluck all the spokes to see if all are of uniform sound, which means they have more or less the same degree of tension. Spin the wheel around and observe it carefully. Does it look round? Or does it seem to wobble? Apply your rim brakes if you have them to discover whether the brake pressure is even.

Uneven spoke tightness will make the wheel tend toward an egg shape. A wheel that is not round will wobble. Furthermore, if the cycle has rim brakes, the brake action will become uneven, as only certain parts of the rim will be reached by the brake.

WINTERIZING YOUR BIKE

If you are going to put your bike away for the winter, first follow these steps:

1. Lubricate all movable parts and bearings.
2. Deflate tires.
3. Check spokes, tightening them or replacing broken ones.

WINTERIZING: When you store your bike, put it away upside down.

4. Wipe spokes and all chrome parts with an oily cloth or vaseline.

5. Rub saddle soap into the seat. Work the soap in deeply, as this preserves the leather.

6. Store your bike by hanging it from the ceiling of your cellar, attic or garage. You can make hooks from half-inch iron rods attached to eye-hooks screwed into the ceiling. If you cannot hang your bike, turn it upside down so that it rests on its saddle and handlebars. Place paper or cloth over the wheels to protect them from dust.

7. Remember that winter storage should be in a cool place.

8. For a spring tune-up, repeat steps 1 and 3, inflate your tires to the proper pressure, check your saddle and handlebar adjustments as well as the operation of your lights and sounding device. Clean vaseline or excess oil off all chrome parts.

Performing hobbies

CHESS PLAYING

Chess, our oldest and most popular game, is played in every country in the world by people of all ages. Despite the fact that the game is so old, more and more people are turning to it as time goes on.

There are good reasons for the great popularity of chess. In the first place, the chess pieces themselves are so colorful and varied that they fascinate even those who know nothing about the game. The shapes of the Rook and Knight, for instance, make you curious to know how these pieces move and what they can do.

Each of these pieces has its own distinctive way of moving and capturing. This is one of the things that makes chess the thrilling struggle it is. No other game can equal chess for excitement, for constant surprises, for unexpected turns of play that leave you breathless with amazement.

There is always something new in chess. It is not like other games, which are so limited in their possibilities that you soon lose interest in them. Just think of it! There are no less than 169,518,829,100,544,-000,000,000,000,000 ways to play the first ten moves of a game of chess!

Nevertheless, you don't have to know more than a few of these patterns to play well, and you don't have to be an expert to enjoy this wonderful game. You will always be able to find opponents on your own level of playing strength. Because your fascination with chess will actually increase the more you play it, the game will give you a lifelong hobby. And, aside from the pleasure of playing, chess offers you many opportunities to meet interesting people and make new friends.

You may have heard that chess is most suitable for older people. This is far from the case. Chess is famous for its many child prodigies. Today, many schools in the United States, Canada and Great Britain have chess clubs and chess teams. Junior Championship tournaments attract skilled youngsters who often graduate into the ranks of experts. In fact, young people have distinguished themselves in tournament and match competition with the great masters of their time.

Among the child prodigies was José Raoul Capablanca, who learned to play at the age of 4 by watching his father at a chessboard with a family friend. At the second session, the little boy nearly earned a spanking by showing his father that he didn't know how to move his Knights properly! In time, this phenomenally gifted player became World Champion.

Paul Morphy, one of the greatest players ever produced in the United States, was beating the finest players of his time (the 1840's and 1850's) when he was so young that he had to sit on several fat books in order to see over the chessboard. Sammy Reshevsky, another famous child prodigy, gave exhibitions of his chess prowess all over Europe and the United States, playing 25 or more grown-up opponents at the same time—and beating all of them with ease!

Reshevsky, in turn, had to bow to a new prodigy in the 1958 United States Championship, when he lost his title to 14-year-old Bobby Fischer. Today, Fischer is widely acclaimed not only as World Champion, but as one of the greatest players who ever lived.

But, you don't have to be an expert to enjoy playing chess. Chess play has something to offer to every grade of player.

It is more than merely a pleasant way to spend spare time. For chess is a struggle that reflects the problems of making a living. It calls for many of the same qualities: alertness in taking advantage of opportunities; foresight rather than hasty, impulsive action; patience in difficult situations; determination in bringing a game to a successful conclusion.

Now, a word of caution. Never allow yourself to become so absorbed in chess that you neglect your work. Observe this caution, and you will get the greatest pleasure and benefit from the finest game devised by the brain of man.

Condensed from "Chess for Children" by Fred Reinfeld © 1958 by Sterling Publishing Co., Inc., New York

HOW THE CHESS PIECES MOVE AND CAPTURE

Each game has its special rules which you must know thoroughly in order to play properly. In chess, you can think of the two players as generals, each one in command of his own army. Just as an army has privates, corporals, sergeants, lieutenants, captains, majors, colonels, and so on, the chess forces at your command differ in their appearance, names and powers.

Each player has 16 pieces at the beginning of the game. The pieces on one side are light-colored, and are known as WHITE. The opposing pieces are dark-colored, and are known as BLACK. In books, these pieces are represented in diagrams by standard symbols. These symbols show you the make-up of the two opposing armies:

one KING
one QUEEN
two ROOKS
two BISHOPS
two KNIGHTS
eight PAWNS

(*Note*: ROOKS are the same as CASTLES, a term with which you may be familiar. But if you want to sound like an experienced chessplayer, always use the name ROOK.)

Now, what sort of battlefield do you set up these armies on? Diagram 1 shows how the pieces are placed at the start of a game. In this diagram, as in all chess diagrams, imagine the player of the White pieces sitting at the near or bottom end of the diagram; the player of the Black pieces is at the far or top end of the diagram.

The chessboard is made up of 64 squares arranged in 8 rows. These squares are alternately "white" (light-colored) and "black" (dark-colored).

Note that the right-hand corner square nearest each player is always a white square. This applies to chess diagrams and also to the way the chessboard must be placed between the players.

Now, to set up your chess pieces in the position of Diagram 1, you need a brief description of the pieces.

The King is always the tallest piece. It has a crown, which is generally topped by a cross. Each player has one King.

Diagram 1: The opening position in a game of chess.

The Queen is the next tallest piece. It also has a crown, generally with small notches. Each player has one Queen.

King's crown   **Queen's crown**

The Rook looks like a tower or a castle. Each player has two Rooks.

The Knight is topped with a horse's head, reminiscent of the days when knights fought on horseback. Each player has two Knights.

The Bishop, with a slit on top, gets its name from its resemblance to a bishop's hat, known as a mitre. Each player has two Bishops.

The Pawn, the smallest of the chess forces, has a ball on top. Each player has eight Pawns.

Photo 1—THE OPENING POSITION: The board is always placed so that the right-hand corner square nearest each player is a white square. Compare the photographed chessmen with the symbols for them in the diagram above.

Knight

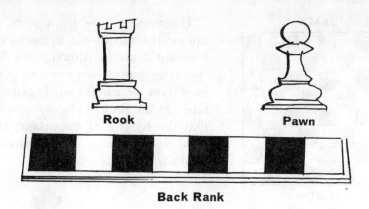

Rook

Pawn

Back Rank

File

Bishop

In setting out the pieces in the opening position, compare each piece to the descriptions just given. Then study the position of the symbols in Diagram 1 before placing the pieces on your board.

You will note that each player places his King, Queen, Bishops, Knights, and Rooks on the row nearest him. Such a row of squares, extending from left to right, is called a RANK.

Place the two White Rooks first in the two corner squares on White's side of the board. Then place the two Black Rooks in the two corner squares on Black's side of the board.

Next, place the two White Knights next to the two White Rooks, as in the position of Diagram 1. Do the same for the Black Knights. Note that the White Rooks face the Black Rooks across the board. (A row of squares running from one player to the other is known as a FILE.) Likewise, the White Knights face the Black Knights (on the Knights' files).

Place the White Bishops and Black Bishops on your board in the position of Diagram 1. These also face each other (on the Bishops' files).

Now take the White King—remember, this is the largest White piece—and place it on the empty *black* square on the rank with the other White pieces.

Place the Black King in the same row with the other Black pieces on the empty *white* square. The two Kings should face each other on the King's file.

Now place the White Queen on the remaining

empty (white) square on White's first rank. Then place the Black Queen on the remaining empty (black) square on Black's first rank.

To make sure you have placed the pieces correctly, check with the position in Diagram 1. Each player's back row, or rank, should now be filled completely.

Remember the useful rule of "Queen on its own color." The White Queen goes on a white square, the Black Queen goes on a black square.

Now set the eight White Pawns on the eight squares of White's second rank, the row directly in front of the White pieces you have already set up. Then set out the Black Pawns on Black's second rank, directly in front of the Black pieces on Black's back rank. Check the position with Diagram 1, and you are ready to play.

In chess, White always makes the first move. Then Black makes *his* first move, and the players continue to move in turn.

But before you can play, you have to learn how each piece moves and captures.

King

THE KING

The King moves one square at a time in any direction. It can move sideways, forwards, backwards or diagonally. (A diagonal is a row of squares of the same color which are joined to each other at the corners.)

White Queen on White Square

Black Queen on Black Square

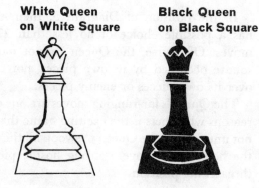

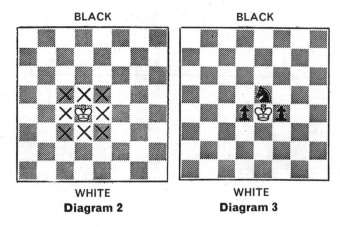

WHITE
Diagram 2

WHITE
Diagram 3

In Diagram 2, each cross indicates a possible square to which the White King can move. On any one move, however, the King can travel in only one direction at a time.

The King can capture any opposing piece that occupies any square to which the King can move. For example, in Diagram 3 the White King can capture the Black Knight or either Black Pawn.

All chess captures are made in the same way: you remove the hostile piece as you capture it, and you replace it *on the same square* with the piece which is making the capture. No two pieces, friendly or unfriendly, can occupy the same square at the same time. Your own piece cannot be captured by your own man.

Remember, then, that in chess you capture by displacing the captured piece.

The King cannot jump over hostile or friendly pieces. Since you cannot displace any of your own pieces, this explains why, in the position of Diagram 4, the White King cannot make any moves. (Incidentally, don't be puzzled by the absence of Black pieces in diagrams like this one. Many of the early diagrams in this book have been greatly simplified in order to emphasize a single point.)

Compare the situation in Diagram 4, where the King has no moves, with Diagram 2, where the King can choose from eight possible moves.

Diagram 4
BLACK

WHITE

The squares to which a piece can move are the squares it controls—the squares on which it can capture hostile pieces. Although the King's moving and capturing powers are not very great, it is the most important piece in the whole game! This is explained later; at the present stage you need only remember that the King is all-important, and that it cannot make any move or capture that will expose it to attack by any hostile piece.

Queen

THE QUEEN

The Queen is by far the strongest piece on the chessboard. Like the King, it moves sideways, forwards or backwards, or diagonally, but it can move any number of squares at one time. Diagram 5 shows the enormous range of control by the Queen, which can move to *any* of the squares marked with a cross. From this diagram you can see that the Queen has a choice of moving in eight different directions along any line of empty squares. But, on any single move it can move in only one direction, which you are free to choose.

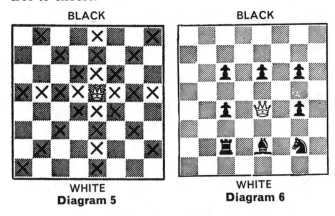

WHITE
Diagram 5

WHITE
Diagram 6

In the position of Diagram 5, then, the Queen has a possible choice of no less than 27 different moves. Of course, the Queen cannot move to any square occupied by its own pieces, nor can it leap over its own pieces or enemy pieces.

The Queen's far-ranging moves are one of the chief reasons why chess is the exciting game that it is. It is not unusual for the Queen to swoop all the way across the board to remove a strong hostile piece from a threatening position.

This is possible because the Queen captures the same way it moves. It can displace and capture any hostile piece that is within its moving range. It can of course capture only one piece on any given move. In the position of Diagram 6, the White Queen can capture the Black Rook or the Black Knight or the Black Bishop or any of the Black Pawns.

Rook

THE ROOK

Next in strength after the Queen is the Rook. The Rook can move in straight lines sideways, forwards and backwards. On any one move it can go in any one direction of your choice, along as many empty squares as you wish.

The Rook cannot displace any of its own pieces. It cannot leap over its own pieces or enemy pieces. In Diagram 7, the Rook can move to *any* of the squares marked with a cross.

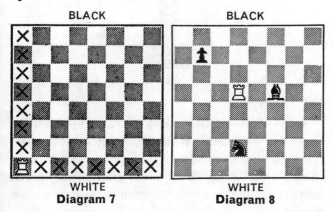

WHITE
Diagram 7

WHITE
Diagram 8

The Rook, with its great straight-line control, captures the same way it moves: it can capture (by displacement) any hostile piece that is inside its moving range. The Rook, of course, can capture only one piece at a time.

The White Rook can capture the Black Bishop in Diagram 8 (by moving sideways) or it can capture the Black Knight (by moving backwards). Note that the White Rook cannot capture the Black Pawn, which is outside its moving range; it cannot move diagonally; nor can it move in two directions on the same move.

THE BISHOP

The Bishop can move any number of squares at a time in only one direction on any one move but it can move only on diagonals—squares of the same

Bishop

color. In Diagram 9, the squares marked by crosses are all squares to which the Bishop has a choice of moving.

You see from Diagram 9 that the Bishop has great power and range along the diagonals.

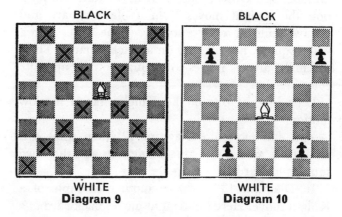

WHITE
Diagram 9

WHITE
Diagram 10

The Bishop cannot displace any of its own pieces. Nor can it leap over its own pieces or hostile pieces. But the Bishop can capture any hostile pieces (by displacement) inside its moving range. For example, in Diagram 10 the White Bishop has a choice of capturing any one of the Black Pawns.

Knight

THE KNIGHT

The way the Knight can leap around the chessboard gives rise to many of the surprises for which chess is famous. The Knight's powers differ from those of the other pieces. If you are alert to the differences, you will often score against an opponent who is less aware of the Knight's unusual powers.

One special quality of the Knight is that its move is *always of the same length*. In Diagram 11, the squares marked with crosses each indicate a possible move that can be made by the Knight.

What is the principle underlying these Knight

How Pieces Move and Capture　■　**291**

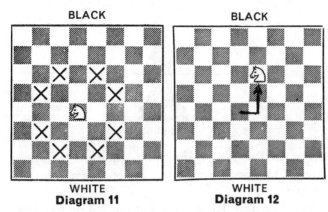

BLACK
Diagram 11

BLACK
Diagram 12

WHITE

WHITE

moves? In Diagram 11, note that each move is of the same length. Observe also that in the diagram position the Knight moves from a black square and always lands on a white square. (If he starts from a white square, he will land on a black square.) Thus, a Knight always moves to a square of the opposite color.

Let's look at one of the Knight moves in slow motion.

You can see from Diagram 12, then, that this knight has moved one square sideways and then two squares forward.

In Diagram 13 we have another example of a Knight move. Here the Knight moves backward one square and then two squares sideways.

Now, returning to Diagram 11, let's examine each Knight move. What do you find? That all the possible Knight moves come under one of these descriptions:

(a) one square to the left or right; then two squares forward or backward, or

(b) one square forward or backward; then two squares to the left or right.

These moves can also be described:

(c) two squares to the left or right; then one square forward or backward, or

(d) two squares forward or backward; then one square to the left or right.

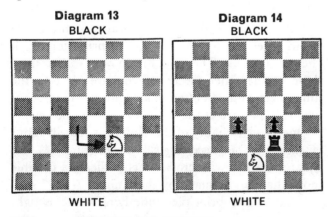

Diagram 13
BLACK

Diagram 14
BLACK

WHITE

WHITE

The result is always the L-shaped move which is the Knight's specialty.

A second way the Knight differs from the other pieces is that it *can* leap over its own pieces or hostile pieces. However, it cannot displace any of its own pieces, and it can capture only hostile pieces located on the final square it lands on. Diagram 14 shows how the Knight captures, and how it leaps over pieces.

The White Knight can capture either Black Pawn in the position of Diagram 14. It cannot capture the Black Rook, but it can leap over the Black Rook in making these captures.

In the position of Diagram 14, there are also four other possible moves that the Knight can make; all these other moves are to empty squares where no capture is achieved.

Later on, you'll find other ways in which the Knight uses its special powers. Of course, the Knight is like the other pieces, too, in a number of respects. It can move to only one square at a time. It can make only one capture at a time, and it captures by displacement.

Pawn

THE PAWN

Although the Pawn is the least powerful of all the chessmen, you cannot regard it lightly for it has certain qualities which add to its effectiveness and make chess more exciting. A thorough grasp of the special features of the Pawn will help you to become a good player.

The Pawn can move in only one direction: straight ahead. But it has a special way of capturing. Before going into this, let's give the Pawns their full names.

See the illustration here which shows you the opening position with all the Pawns on their proper squares awaiting the beginning of the game. Each Pawn is named for the file (vertical row) on which it stands. The King Pawn, for example, stands on the King file, in front of the King. The Queen Pawn stands in front of the Queen, on the Queen file, etc.

White Pawns always move toward the Black side. In diagrams, they move up the page.

Black Pawns always move toward the White side. In diagrams, they move down the page.

At *any* stage of the game, if a Pawn has not moved from its home square, its first move can be one square

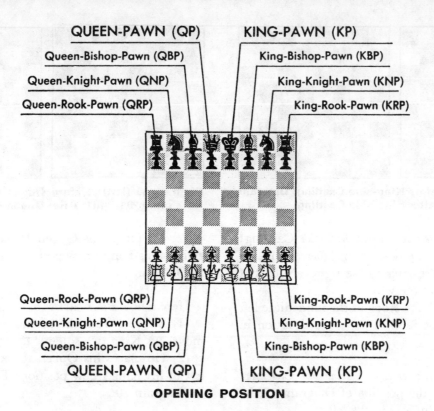

QUEEN-PAWN (QP)   KING-PAWN (KP)

Queen-Bishop-Pawn (QBP)   King-Bishop-Pawn (KBP)

Queen-Knight-Pawn (QNP)   King-Knight-Pawn (KNP)

Queen-Rook-Pawn (QRP)   King-Rook-Pawn (KRP)

Queen-Rook-Pawn (QRP)   King-Rook-Pawn (KRP)

Queen-Knight-Pawn (QNP)   King-Knight-Pawn (KNP)

Queen-Bishop-Pawn (QBP)   King-Bishop-Pawn (KBP)

QUEEN-PAWN (QP)   KING-PAWN (KP)

OPENING POSITION

ahead *or* two squares ahead. But once a Pawn has left its original square, it can move ahead only one square at a time.

Diagram 15 shows the position after White starts the game by advancing his King Pawn two squares and Black replies by advancing *his* King Pawn two squares. Now neither of these Pawns can move: they are blocking each other's way. Nor can either Pawn capture the other: their capturing method is different from anything you've seen so far.

The Pawn captures by taking the piece that occupies *either square diagonally ahead* of it. This means that it controls two squares. In Diagram 16 the White Pawn can capture the Black Knight *or* the Black Queen. It cannot capture the Black Pawn; nor can the Black Pawn capture the White Pawn.

When the Pawn captures, it *displaces* the piece captured, the same way all other chessmen do. In

Diagram 16, the Pawn would move to the next file left in capturing the Black Knight or to the next file right in capturing the Black Queen. When it captures, it assumes the name of the file it moves to. Thus, the Queen Pawn becomes the Queen Bishop Pawn if it takes the Knight here. If it takes the Queen, it becomes the King Pawn.

PROTECTING THE KING BY CASTLING

You have already learned that the King is the most important piece in chess. You must therefore be very careful to shield your King as much as possible from enemy attacks and threats.

One of the best ways to guard your King is by means of a special move known as CASTLING.

Castling is the only move in chess in which you move two pieces at a time—your King and a Rook. This is still considered a single move.

Castling is also the only move that a player can make only once during a game. You can Castle *only if* there is a clear space in your back row between the pieces to be moved.

There are two ways to Castle. You can Castle King-side (with the King and the nearest Rook, called the "King Rook"); or you can Castle Queen-side (with the King and the further Rook, called the "Queen Rook").

Diagrams 17 and 18 show the situation before and after King-side Castling.

Diagram 15   **Diagram 16**

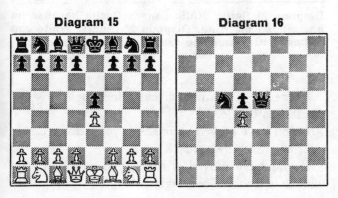

Castling ■ 293

Diagram 17 (left): Before King-side Castling. Diagram 18 (right): After King-side Castling.

Diagram 19 (left): Before Queen-side Castling. Diagram 20 (right): After Queen-side Castling.

Here is how *White* carries out *King-side* Castling:

(1) Starting from the position of Diagram 17, he moves his King *two* squares to the right. (Note that there are no pieces in the way.)

(2) He places his King Rook at the immediate left of his King's new position. This is the situation in Diagram 18.

Here is how *Black* carries out *King-side* Castling:

(1) Starting from the position of Diagram 17, he moves his King *two* squares to the left.

(2) He places his King Rook at the immediate right of his King's new position. This is the situation in Diagram 18.

Castling with the other Rook (the Queen Rook) is pictured in Diagrams 19 and 20.

Here is how *White* carries out *Queen-side* Castling:

(1) Starting from the position of Diagram 19, he moves his King *two* squares to the left.

Photo 2—CASTLING KING-SIDE: White has just moved his King two squares to the right, and then picked up his King Rook from its original square. He is about to put the Rook on the square to the immediate left of his King. This will complete his Castling move.

(2) He places his Queen Rook at the immediate right of his King's new position. This is the situation in Diagram 20.

Here is how *Black* carries out *Queen-side* Castling:

(1) Starting from the position of Diagram 19, he moves his King two squares to the right.

(2) He places his Queen Rook at the immediate left of his King's new position. This is the situation in Diagram 20.

How does this protect the King? It helps to get your King into a safe place, usually protected by a wall of Pawns. It also gets your Rook into a position nearer the center of the board where it will be more useful. Therefore, Castling is a valuable move and you want to Castle as early in the game as possible. Castling King-side is considered the safer of the two ways to Castle; so, *Castle early on the King-side.*

Diagram 21 (left): White cannot Castle because he has moved his King. Diagram 22 (right): White can Castle King-side; he cannot Castle Queen-side.

There are a number of cases in which it is not possible to Castle.

If you have moved your King, you cannot Castle later on. (See Diagram 21.)

If you have moved a Rook, you cannot Castle with that Rook. (See Diagram 22.)

Diagram 23 (left): White cannot Castle at this point because his King is attacked by a Black Bishop. (White's King is in check.) **Diagram 24 (right):** White cannot Castle at this point because the square on which his King would land is commanded by Black's black-square Bishop.

Diagram 25 (left): Black can Castle Queen-side, but not King-side, where his King would have to pass over a square controlled by White's black-square Bishop. **Diagram 26 (right):** White is unable to Castle, as the squares between his King and Rooks are not empty. Black, on the other hand, is free to Castle King-side.

If you have moved both Rooks, you cannot Castle at all.

There are several situations in which Castling is impossible for the time being; it *may* become possible later on.

For example, if your King is attacked (IN CHECK), you cannot Castle at that particular point. (See Diagram 23.) But you may be able to Castle later on.

You cannot Castle if the square to which you want to move your King is commanded by an enemy piece. (See Diagram 24.) But you may be able to Castle later if this enemy control disappears.

You cannot Castle if a square that the King has to pass over is commanded by an enemy piece. (See Diagram 25.) But you may be able to Castle later, if this enemy control disappears.

As mentioned earlier, you cannot Castle if any of the squares between your King and the Rook to be Castled are occupied—either by your own or enemy pieces. (See Diagram 26.) However, you can Castle later on if the squares become empty.

A final note on Castling: the Rook can pass over, or land on, squares that are attacked by the enemy.

HOW TO WIN CHESS GAMES

You win a game of chess by attacking the hostile King until he can no longer escape capture. When this final situation is reached, the King is said to be CHECKMATED. This ends the game. It does not matter how many pieces are left on the board.

Often a player who has a losing game will not wait to be checkmated. Instead, he admits defeat by surrendering at once; this is known as "resigning" the game. So, you win a game of chess when you checkmate your oponent's King, or when your opponent resigns.

CHECK

Directly attacking the King is known as GIVING CHECK or CHECKING the King. Whenever the King is in check, he must immediately be taken out of check—out of the range or line of attack.

In order to have a clear understanding of check and checkmate, you must keep two points in mind:

(1) You can never move your King into check.

(2) You can never move any of your pieces in a way that would expose your King to check.

In Diagram 27 White's Queen is checking Black's King. Black's King, as you know, has to get out of check. There are three ways in which this can be done:

(1) Move the King to a square where he will no longer be in check. (In Diagram 27, there are six possible King moves which will get the Black King out of check.)

(2) Interpose one of your Pawns or pieces in the line of attack. (In the position of Diagram 27, Black can interpose his Rook on the diagonal to stop the check.)

(3) Capture the hostile piece that is giving check.

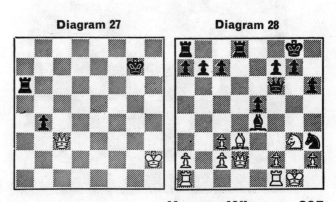

Diagram 27   **Diagram 28**

(In Diagram 27, Black applies this method by capturing the White Queen with his Pawn. Remember how the Pawn captures?)

In the position of Diagram 28, White is checked by the Black Knight.

White cannot capture the Knight; nor can he interpose any of his pieces (because the Knight is the one piece that can leap right over anything). Lastly, White cannot move his King, for moving to either square that is open would put his King inside the capturing range of Black's Bishop.

The situation, then, is that White's King is in check and has no way of getting out of check. White is checkmated; the game is over; Black has won.

Note that when a King is checkmated, he is never captured or removed from the board. As long as the King is trapped with no chance of escape, the game ends right then and there.

RELATIVE VALUES OF THE CHESS FORCES

Each man on the chessboard has a value. Since each piece's value is different, you have to know its worth in relation to other pieces so that you can avoid giving up a man of greater value for one of lesser value.

QUEEN	9	points
ROOK	5	points
BISHOP	3	points
KNIGHT	3	points
PAWN	1	point

In addition, if you capture an enemy unit without losing one of your own, you have to know the value of the material you have gained. To be ahead in the value of your material, to outnumber your opponent's forces, is an advantage with which you can almost always enforce checkmate sooner or later.

The table of values shown here should be memorized; it will help you to know when you are sufficiently ahead in power to win by careful play.

The King has no numerical value, as it cannot be removed from the board.

As Bishop and Knight have the same value, you may freely exchange one for the other. If you capture your opponent's Knight and lose your Bishop in return, you have made an even exchange.

To give up a Bishop or Knight (3 points) for a Pawn (1 point) is very bad play, and should eventually lose the game for you.

If, after an exchange of pieces, you have equal forces except that you have a Rook (5 points) when your opponent has just a Bishop or Knight (3 points), you are said to be THE EXCHANGE ahead. This is an advantage in material which should eventually win the game for you.

But material advantage is not all—you need a strong position, too.

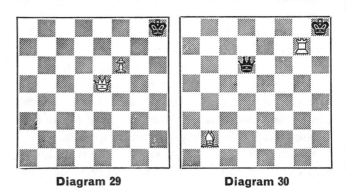

Diagram 29   **Diagram 30**

DISCOVERED CHECK

The usual way to give check is to move a piece or Pawn to a square from which it attacks your opponent's King.

In a DISCOVERED CHECK, however, you use a different method, In this case, you move a piece or Pawn that has been *blocking* a line of attack on the enemy King. When you move it out of the way, you let another piece, whose action has been blocked, proceed to "discover" check without having moved.

In Diagram 29, White can move his Pawn forward one square and let his Queen "discover" check.

Discovered checks generally come as a surprise, and sometimes they win valuable material.

In Diagram 30, White can give a discovered check

Photo 3—DISCOVERED CHECK: By moving his Rook, White will uncover his Bishop's diagonal, so the Bishop can give check. Such a move is called a discovered check.

by moving his Rook out of the diagonal row which his Bishop controls. If he's clever, he will kill two birds with one stone by moving his Rook three squares to the left, or one square backward. With either move, White not only gives discovered check but also attacks Black's Queen. As Black must move his King out of check (or interpose his Queen), he will lose his Queen on White's next move.

Diagram 31 (left): White can give discovered check by moving his Bishop. Diagram 32 (right): White is giving double check (with his Rook and also with his Bishop).

DOUBLE CHECK

This is a special case of discovered check: the piece that uncovers check also gives check at the same time. (See Diagram 32.)

The only way to answer a double check is to move the King. Double checks are so powerful that they often force a quick victory.

FORKING CHECK

The Knight's power of attacking in two or more directions at the same time (called a FORK) makes it a powerful weapon. When the fork is combined with a check, the effect can be deadly. For the attacked King must move out of check, so that the other forked piece has no time to escape.

In Diagram 33 White's Knight forks Black's King and Queen with check. Black must move his King out of check. (There is no way of interposing a piece to break up a check by a Knight.) White then captures the Black Queen with his Knight.

**Diagram 33:
Black to play.**

**Diagram 34:
The opening position.**

HOW TO READ CHESS MOVES

To read chess moves, you need to know the exact name of each chessman and the name of each square. You will recall from the illustration of the opening position that each Pawn gets named right at the beginning of the game. This name comes from the piece in front of which the Pawn is placed.

Starting with the back row for both White and Black and moving from the extreme left in the opening position across to the right, here are the names and abbreviations used for the pieces and Pawns:

Names of the Pieces	*Names of the Pawns*
QUEEN ROOK (QR)	QUEEN ROOK PAWN (QRP)
QUEEN KNIGHT (QN)	QUEEN KNIGHT PAWN (QNP)
QUEEN BISHOP (QB)	QUEEN BISHOP PAWN (QBP)
QUEEN (Q)	QUEEN PAWN (QP)
KING (K)	KING PAWN (KP)
KING BISHOP (KB)	KING BISHOP PAWN (KBP)
KING KNIGHT (KN)	KING KNIGHT PAWN (KNP)
KING ROOK (KR)	KING ROOK PAWN (KRP)

If you play in a tournament, you have to keep a written score of your game as you make your moves. Even if you are not a tournament player, you may want to write down some of your games so that you can study the moves afterwards.

But the most important reason for learning how to record chess moves is to enable you to read chess books and newspaper accounts of tournaments, so that you can follow games played by the masters of chess. This will help you to become a much better player and will greatly increase your enjoyment of the game as you become familiar with its many fine points.

NAMES OF THE SQUARES

The board consists of FILES (vertical rows of squares) and RANKS (horizontal rows of squares). Each file is permanently named for the piece that stands on it at the beginning of the game.

Each player numbers the ranks from his side of the board:

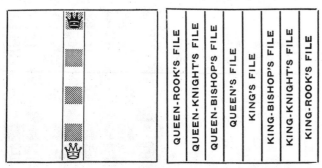

Diagram 35 (left): The Queen's file. Diagram 36 (right): The names of all the files.

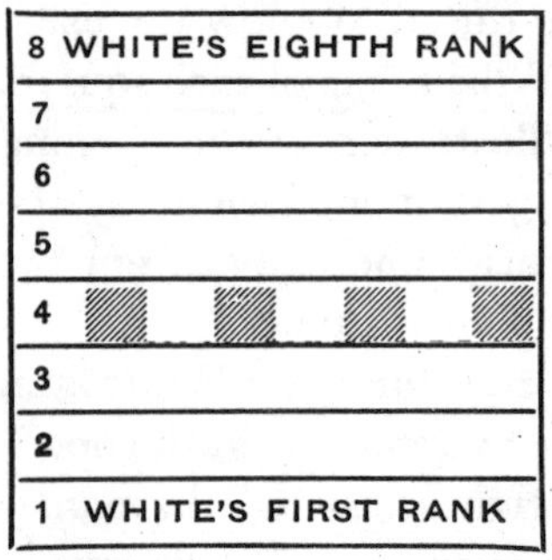

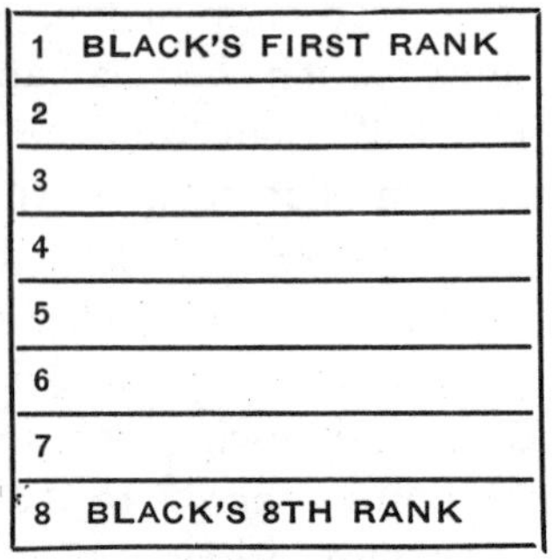

8	WHITE'S EIGHTH RANK		1	BLACK'S FIRST RANK
7			2	
6			3	
5			4	
4			5	
3			6	
2			7	
1	WHITE'S FIRST RANK		8	BLACK'S 8TH RANK

Diagram 37 (left): The ranks numbered from White's side of the board. Diagram 38 (right): The ranks from Black's side.

By combining the names of the files and the numbers of the ranks, a name is given to each square on the board. Here is how all the squares are named:

Diagram 39

BLACK

WHITE

Because the ranks are numbered one way from White's side of the board, and another way from Black's side, each square has two names.

As you look at any given square, the name at the bottom is White's name for that square. The name

printed upside down is Black's name for that same square.

When White makes a move to a given square, use the White name for that square. When Black makes a move, use the Black name for that square.

In writing down moves, use the abbreviated names of the pieces, Pawns and squares. The record of a move consists of the name of the piece or Pawn that makes the move, and the name of the square to which it moves. For instance, B—QB4: Bishop moves to Queen Bishop 4.

Here are some abbreviations that are commonly used:

moves to	—
captures	x
Castles	o—o
(o—o—o, Queen side)	
check	ch
discovered check	dis ch
double check	dbl ch
piece at certain square	(P/B7)
en passant	e.p.
(explained on page 300)	
good move	!
very good move	!!
bad move	?
very bad move	??

Here are some examples of notation:

PxB: Pawn takes Bishop.
R—Q7ch: Rook moves to Queen 7 giving check.
N—KB6?:   Knight to King Bishop 6. This is a bad move.

White's move always is stated first. Therefore, if you want to start with a move that Black has made, you put three dots before the move, such as 4 . . . P—K5; 5 Q—R5. This means that on Black's fourth move he advances his Pawn to King 5 and White replies on his fifth move with Queen to Rook 5.

SAMPLE GAME

The following brief sample game will give you practice in reading chess moves:

WHITE	BLACK
1 P—K4	P—K4

This gives us the position shown in Diagram 15.

2 B—QB4	B—QB4
3 Q—KR5	N—QB3??
4 QxBP mate (See Diagram 40.)	

Black's King cannot capture the White Queen, as this would put the Black King inside the capturing range of White's Bishop on Queen Bishop 4.

Diagram 40: Mating position.

Diagram 41 (left): Checkmate with the Queen.
Diagram 42 (right): Checkmate with the Rook.

Note that White's second move would ordinarily be written B—B4. It is not necessary to specify *which* B4 in this case, as the Bishop can go only to Queen Bishop 4.

Similarly, it would have been good enough to write White's fourth move Q—R5.

However, Black's third move is a different story. To write N—B3 would have been confusing, because Black's Queen Knight could go to Queen Bishop 3, while his King Knight could go to King Bishop 3. Hence we write N—QB3 in this case to avoid confusion.

If two Knights can move to the same square from a given position, then you might name the Knight, as KN—QB3. Also if a piece can be taken by either of two Pawns, or if two Pawns are under attack, you might write: QBPxP/Q4, which means Queen Bishop Pawn takes the Pawn at Queen 4.

HOW TO FORCE CHECKMATE

From the table of relative values (page 296) you learned what pieces to exchange so that you win more material than you give up in return.

Gaining material in an exchange gives you more attacking power than your opponent, and enables you to win still more material. Sooner or later, you will have an advantage in material so great that you can force checkmate no matter what your opponent does.

Sometimes, in order to win when you have a material advantage, you must try to make even exchanges just to clear the board. Then your advantage will be more firmly established. For instance, there are certain basic endgame positions for forcing checkmate against any resistance. You can aim for these positions when you have at least the following material advantages:

(1) King and Queen against King.
(2) King and Rook against King.
(3) King and two Bishops against King.
(4) King and Bishop and Knight against King.

In Diagrams 41 and 42, as well as in Diagrams 43 and 44, note that all the requirements for checkmate are fulfilled:

(1) The King is in check.
(2) The checking piece cannot be captured.
(3) It is impossible to interpose against the check.
(4) The King cannot move out of check.

Diagram 43 (left): Checkmate with the two Bishops.
Diagram 44 (right): Checkmate with Bishop and Knight.

Photo 4—CHECKMATE WITH THE TWO BISHOPS: This typical checkmating position reveals the great power of two co-operating Bishops. To win by this checkmate, you must force the hostile King into a corner.

It is important for you to be thoroughly familiar with these basic checkmate positions. Knowing them will enable you to win many endgames. Using this knowledge will prevent floundering in the middle game when you have a big advantage in material. You will seek to reduce your opponent's forces by even (or advantageous) exchanges until you are left with such an obviously superior force that your opponent resigns. If he does not, you can enforce checkmate.

SPECIAL POWERS OF THE PAWN

You know from the table of values that the Pawn has the least value of any of the chessmen. For this reason the beginner attaches little importance to Pawns; he gives them away without a thought and rarely bothers to protect them.

But this is a mistake, for the Pawn has a power that raises its value enormously.

PAWN PROMOTION

When a Pawn advances all the way down to the eighth (last) rank, you must promote it to a Queen or Rook or Bishop or Knight. In almost all cases you will choose a new Queen, as that is the strongest piece on the board.

Diagram 45 (left): White advances his Pawn from seventh to eighth rank and replaces it with a new Queen. Diagram 46 (right): Now White has "queened" his Pawn which gives him enormous material advantage.

Your choice is not limited. For example, if you still have your original Queen, you can nevertheless acquire a new Queen by promotion, and have two Queens at the same time.

To QUEEN a Pawn successfully is the same as winning your opponent's Queen for nothing. You can therefore see that promoting a Pawn is one of the strongest moves in chess.

This will teach you to have more respect for the

Pawns. You can never tell which Pawn may turn out later to be the one that becomes a new Queen.

Now, with your newly gained knowledge about the Pawn, you will see another way to win games. You already know you can win with a Queen ahead, but you can also win—most of the time—with only a Pawn ahead! For if you can turn this Pawn into a Queen, the result is such an enormous material advantage that checkmate can be forced.

There is still another way in which Pawns can be immensely important for winning purposes. If you come down to an ending of King and one Bishop against King—or King and one Knight against King—with no other forces left on the board, you cannot force checkmate.

But if you have a King and one Bishop (or Knight) plus a single Pawn against a lone King, you can win. You protect the advancing Pawn until it arrives at the eighth rank, and with the aid of the new Queen you force checkmate with ease.

CAPTURING IN PASSING

The Pawn which has reached its fifth rank has a special power called CAPTURING IN PASSING. This enables it to capture in a way that is an exception to the general rule about Pawn captures. Only a Pawn can be taken in this type of capture. Let's look at the position in Diagram 47:

White's Pawn is on its fifth rank. As Black's Pawn is still on its original square, it can advance one square or two. If it advances one square, White can capture it if he wishes (leading to the position of Diagram 49).

Diagram 47   Diagram 48

Diagram 49 (left): White has captured the Black Pawn in passing, or "en passant" (e.p. in the abbreviated notation).

But suppose that Black advances his Pawn two squares. Will he avoid capture?

No. On his next move only, White can capture the Black Pawn *as if it had advanced only one square.*

Note that you can capture in passing only if you want to: you don't *have* to capture in passing.

However, if you are to make the capture, you must do it in reply to the two-square advance of the enemy Pawn. If you don't capture in passing on your reply move, then you lose your chance for good.

WHAT TO DO IN THE OPENING

Playing the opening moves well is important, because your future prospects in a game depend on how you handle your forces in the opening. If you get a good start, you will have later opportunities for promising plans and powerful moves. If you play the opening badly, you will start off on the defensive, and all the winning chances will be on your opponent's side.

One basic rule to remember is to start the game by playing out the King Pawn two squares (1 P—K4) if you have White. If you have Black, answer 1 P—K4 by moving your King Pawn two squares (1 . . . P—K4).

By advancing this Pawn, you open up the diagonal of your King Bishop, so that you can bring out this piece quickly.

Another good idea is bring out your King Knight early (N—KB3), perhaps on the second or third move, if that is possible.

By playing out these two pieces quickly, you will clear the two spaces between your King and King Rook, so that you can Castle early and get your King to a fairly safe spot.

Throughout the opening stage, consisting of about the first ten moves on both sides, concentrate on *bringing out as many pieces as possible.* These pieces—aside from the King—are useless to you while they remain on their home squares. Once you bring them out ("develop" them), they will be ready for action —to attack and threaten the enemy.

Avoid two beginner's faults that lead to trouble in the opening. Don't keep moving the same piece continually; remember to develop new pieces all the time. The other fault is to play a great many Pawn moves, thus wasting time and creating weaknesses in the early stages. Once you have played 1 P—K4, play other Pawn moves sparingly. (The only other really essential Pawn move will be an advance of the Queen Pawn, to open the diagonal of your Queen Bishop.)

SOME STANDARD OPENINGS

As you study the game and become a better player, you will find that there are standard ways of beginning a game. These standard methods have distinctive names. Experts and specialists devote years of study to these openings, but at the present stage you need only be familiar in a general way with a few standard openings.

GIUOCO PIANO

	WHITE	BLACK
1	P—K4	P—K4
2	N—KB3	N—QB3
3	B—B4	B—B4

Photo 6—GIUOCO PIANO: The usual position in this opening after Black's third move. This is an opening recommended for beginners.

Photo 5—CAPTURING IN PASSING: Black has just advanced his Queen Pawn from his second rank to his fourth rank. In reply, White has captured Black's Queen Pawn in passing, with his own King Pawn, which was on his fifth rank. White's capturing Pawn is now on the sixth square of the Queen file.

The Italian name of this opening means "quiet game," and that is just what it is. Since there is small chance of difficult complications or dazzling surprises, this is a good game for beginners. It continues:

4 P—Q3	N—B3
5 N—B3	P—Q3
6 B—K3	B—N3
7 Q—Q2	B—K3
8 B—N3	......

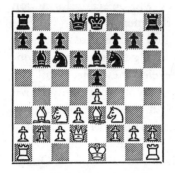

**Diagram 50:
Black to play.
Position after White's 8th move.**

Black will now Castle and White will follow his example. The position is even as you enter the middle game.

SCOTCH GAME

WHITE	BLACK
1 P—K4	P—K4
2 N—KB3	N—QB3
3 P—Q4	PxP
4 NxP	B—B4

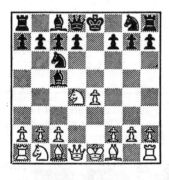

**Diagram 51:
White to play.
Position after Black's 4th move.**

White has opened up the game very rapidly and has a fine, free game for his pieces. But, since he has moved his Knight twice, he has lost time. Note that Black has played out two pieces, while White has developed only one.

In the position of Diagram 51, Black threatens to win a piece with ... NxN or ... BxN. So White protects his Knight by developing another piece.

| 5 B—K3 | Q—B3 |

This attacks White's Knight again and once more threatens to win a piece. Again White defends the Knight some more.

302 ■ CHESS PLAYING

6 P—QB3	KN—K2
7 N—B2	B—N3

The game is even at this point.

HOW TO WIN (OR LOSE) QUICKLY

People who don't play chess have an idea that a game takes a very long time. Actually, many games are over in jig time. If one of the players makes a bad mistake, his opponent can pounce on him and wind up the game with one or two powerful strokes. This is one of the features that makes chess such an exciting contest.

The following games will show some characteristic early mistakes which allow you or your opponent to win dramatically and quickly. You will find that you can apply all these ideas to win your own games in rapid order—or avoid embarrassing losses.

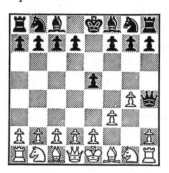

**Diagram 52:
"Fool's Mate."
White is checkmated.**

"FOOL'S MATE"

WHITE	BLACK
1 P—KB3?	P—K4
2 P—KN4??	Q—R5 mate

White's foolish, weakening Pawn moves opened the gates to the enemy. This is the quickest checkmate you can bring off in a game.

Photo 7—SCOTCH GAME: This is how the board looks after Black's fourth move. Black threatens to win a piece by capturing White's advanced Knight, which is attacked by two pieces and does not have enough protection.

"SCHOLAR'S MATE"

WHITE	BLACK
1 P—K4	P—K4
2 B—B4	B—B4
3 Q—R5	......

White threatens QxKPch, but what is much more important, he also threatens QxBP mate.

Black sees the first threat, but overlooks the second threat.

3	N—QB3??

The right way was 3 ... Q—K2, guarding his King Pawn *and* at the same time preventing the threatened mate.

4 QxBP mate

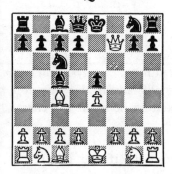

Diagram 53:
"Scholar's Mate."
Black is checkmated.

This mate is a good example of the suddenness with which a gross oversight in the opening can lead to a quick decision.

GIUOCO PIANO CONTINUATION

WHITE	BLACK
1 P—K4	P—K4
2 N—KB3	N—QB3
3 B—B4	B—B4
4 P—Q3	KN—K2?

Black's fourth move is a mistake. He should have played 4 ... N—B3, which is almost always the best way to develop the King Knight. In this case, 4 ... N—B3 would have prevented White's later Q—R5, which comes in at the proper time with terrific power. But first:

5 N—N5	......

Double attack against Black's weak spot, his King Bishop 2 square. Note how the winner (in this case, White) hammers away repeatedly at this weak spot in these games.

5	Castles

Black brings his King Rook to the defense. But it is too late now for satisfactory defense.

6 Q—R5!	......

Still another attack (with the third piece) bearing on Black's menaced King Bishop Pawn—and in addition White threatens QxRP mate. Now you can see

Photo 8—"SCHOLAR'S MATE": A tried and true checkmating technique that has caught unwary victims for centuries.

why Black should have played 4 ... N—B3—to stop this invasion by White's Queen.

6	P—KR3
7 NxP	Q—K1?

Black can fight on longer with 7 ... RxN, although after 8 QxRch White is sure to win, as he is the Exchange and a Pawn ahead.

8 NxRP dbl ch	K—R1

Photo 9—GIUOCO PIANO CONTINUATION—DOUBLE CHECK: This is the situation after White's eighth move. White is giving double check, with a Bishop and a Knight. Black's chances of escaping alive from such a check are very slight, as you can see.

**Diagram 54:
Black is
checkmated.**

9 N—B7 dbl ch   K—N1
10 Q—R8 mate

Black cannot capture the White Queen, as it is guarded by the White Knight; nor can he capture the White Knight, as it is protected by the White Bishop.

QUEEN'S PAWN OPENING

This is an acceptable opening for white but more difficult to play than a King's Pawn opening.

WHITE	BLACK
1 P—Q4	N—KB3
2 N—Q2	P—K4

Black gives up a Pawn in the hope of confusing his opponent. Thanks to White's careless play, this plan succeeds.

3 PxP   N—N5

Trying to regain his Pawn.

If White does not capture the impertinent Knight now, he loses his Queen.

5 PxN   ......

White has saved his Queen, but now he will be checkmated.

5 ......   Q—R5 ch
6 P—KN3   ......

**Diagram 55:
White to play.
Position after Black's
4th move.**

But now all that White has to do is play 4 KN—B3, developing a new piece and protecting his extra Pawn. If White plays this he will be a pawn ahead with much the better game. But he doesn't:

4 P—KR3??   ......

This careless move ruins White's game at once.

4 ......   N—K6!!

An amazing reply that forces victory.

If White had not played 4 P—KR3?? this Pawn would now be protected and he would not be subject to checkmate.

6 ......   QxNP mate

Again and again this type of quick, decisive attack is used to punish players who commit serious mistakes in the opening.

In these games you have seen typical mistakes in the opening which give you an opportunity to win quickly. As you study the moves carefully, you will become acquainted with many winning ideas and plans of attack which you can use in your own contests. They will make you a better and stronger player, and at the same time they will gradually open up your eyes to the many, many possibilities in each game of chess.

In this section you have learned all that you need to know in order to play chess. You can now go on to apply that knowledge in a number of ways. You can teach the game to your friends, and in this way you will have many happy, exciting hours at the chessboard.

Or, if you wish, you can join a chess club where you will find keener opposition. If you become a good enough player, you will be able to match your wits with players from other clubs in team matches and individual championships.

You may feel the urge to learn more about chess, to become a chess student and a stronger player, to enjoy going over the beautiful games played by great masters. Or you may go on to solving chess problems, which will challenge your skill and force you to think in new ways. Once you start to solve a chess problem, you will not be able to turn away from it until you have found the one perfect solution that completely clears up the mystery.

Perhaps you are unable to find any chess opponents. In that case you can still get a great deal of pleasure by reading chess books and learning more about the many beautiful sacrifices and combinations that give you the joy of discovery over and over again. Some people play chess by mail, sending the moves on post cards. There are organized groups of "postal chess" players, which you can reach through chess magazines.

The wonderful thing about chess is that there is always something new to be learned, to be enjoyed, to be used "the next time." That is why chess never loses it hold over chessplayers. It offers just as much pleasure as playing a musical instrument—but without all the drudgery. So whether you become an expert or play just for the fun of it, you will want to come back again and again to your chessboard.

HANDWRITING ANALYSIS

Here is a fascinating hobby that will help you gain insight into others and yourself. Many of us have in common the habit of labelling people. We pigeonhole our friends and enemies alike. It might surprise you to discover that your pat estimates of these people are not basically sound because you are judging them superficially. It is their *handwriting* which will give you the true picture. You can take a closer look at yourself in this way too.

Once you have learned all the fundamental techniques detailed here, you will have to learn to estimate carefully; to balance negative features against positive ones, strength against weakness. You may discover traits, attributes and talents you never suspected existed in your friends and associates. You also may discover potentials within yourself that you weren't aware of, characteristics to be strengthened or perhaps eliminated.

Read this section over; then if you have letters written by some of your friends, dig them out. Spread them in front of you as you might their photographs. The first thing you will see is how different one is from the other. There may be resemblances but there are no two exactly alike. You already know that these people differ in temperament, intellect, abilities. Now you can learn the cause of the differences and what they really mean. After some practice you'll begin to recognize the clues to their unique personalities, and this may cause you to drop your old labels and re-evaluate your friends. As your knowledge of graphology grows, you will gain more and more insight into what makes people tick.

The word *graphology* was coined from the Greek *graph* which means *writing* and the suffix *ology* which is applied to names of scientific studies. Over a period of many hundreds of years, men and women of intellect and intuition used handwriting as a means of judging character. From their intuitive findings a set of rules developed and it is by these that the student of graphology is guided today.

Early in the 20th century, a form of writing called the Palmer Method came into prominence and was taught in the elementary schools. It followed the ornate Spencerian hand—was, in fact, a refinement of it, and was designed to make the penmanship of school children legible and beautiful. The child who rebelled against schoolroom routine—or for that matter against any set rules laid down by authority—broke away from the set forms taught him and developed a characteristically individual handwriting of his own. Many children retained the Palmer formations of letters and words even into adulthood and we still see signs of them today.

Both the Spencerian and Palmer Methods of writing reflected the spirit, the style (even of dress), of their times. Then came a period of progress and greater cultural development, and this was reflected in manuscript writing which was being taught in progressive and private schools. This· method—a form of printing—is still in use today in such schools and reflects greater aesthetic development. (Printing usually points up the aesthetic and/or artistic elements in an individual's make-up.)

The *sex*—whether male or female—is not revealed in handwriting. Neither is the *age* of the writer.

What a person does—the work he is engaged in—does not usually show, although potentialities for what he can do are revealed. On the other hand, some occupations do influence handwriting (just as they influence the writers' points of view) and the expert often recognizes the handwriting of the bookkeeper, the engineer and the artist. Criminal tendencies will be revealed to the practiced eye of the graphologist, but the *criminal*, per se, cannot be detected.

Condensed from "The Psychology of Handwriting" by Nadya Olyanova, © 1960 by Sterling Publishing Co., Inc., New York

In an attempt to recognize a sexual difference in handwriting we might use an old measuring rod and tentatively say that female reasoning is *subjective* while male reasoning is *objective*, though we know that each sex can reason both ways. We are, therefore, somewhat in the dark. In analyzing handwriting, then, it is important to know the sex of the writer, rather than to guess. Even an expert—although an attempted guess might be correct—could be mistaken.

THE WRITER'S AGE

Although chronological age does not show in handwriting, what will be revealed are signs of maturity or a lack of it. Old age will usually be revealed in handwriting that is tremulous, with wavering strokes. It is not difficult to recognize. Yet it does not follow, all the time, that people of advanced years write such a hand. The nervous shaky handwriting should not be confused with the tremulous hand associated with old age. Such a writer may be suffering from shock to the nerves, as in the case of an excessive drinker, or he may have a tremor. Perhaps he was under great tension at the time the sample was written.

Try to find out your subject's age. A child's handwriting is usually easy to recognize because it is often a scrawl, done slowly. Frequently it slants downward because of the effort made when focusing attention on the letters and words. It is not wise to try to analyze the handwriting of a child under 12, unless you are an expert graphologist. A good rule to remember when you try to estimate maturity is: if the handwriting is very rounded, the person is childlike in many respects; where there is a great deal of angularity, this is a sign of development. But in any case, it is advisable to *know* the age of the writer.

Some people write quickly and smoothly one day and so shakily the next day, or even a few hours later, that they cannot read their own scribbling. That is why it is always best, when attempting to analyze a handwriting, to be sure the person is in a relaxed, comfortable position, using a pen he chooses.

DOESN'T AN INDIVIDUAL'S HANDWRITING CHANGE?

The answer is simple. A person who writes differently at different times is not only subject to changing moods but is also versatile. For instance: if your handwriting slants naturally to the right, it may take on a vertical angle when you are taking notes, since at such times you are not thinking spontaneously—you are taking down another person's thoughts. Or, your usual handwriting may be large or medium, and become very small when you are concentrating very hard on something. If you are very tense, your letter formations may become cramped, even illegible, though normally your writing is readable and flowing. Although handwriting specimens may look different, the essential character will be revealed. Even if you write a number of different ways, the real you will emerge in all the specimens.

FUNDAMENTALS OF ANALYSIS

It is the handwriting itself that is important to the graphologist, never *what* is written. Do not consider the text of the specimen, as it may mislead you. The writer may not mean what he is saying, or he may be quoting someone to leave an impression. Although there are instances when the text is helpful, the expert graphologist is not interested in it, but sees only the handwriting.

Since there are so many details to consider when analyzing a handwriting, it is best to systematize your approach. These are the fundamentals to be concerned with.

PEN PRESSURE: The pen pressure relates to the senses and to some extent reveals the vitality of the individual. It will be heavy, medium-heavy, "muddy," medium-light, light, or extremely light so that it appears hair-like. (Muddy pressure must not be confused with shaded writing; it is usually unpleasant to the eye while shaded writing often looks artistic.) Observe the writer's vitality—is he robust, athletic, delicate, supersensitive, unhealthy? If he is "out of this world" it will be indicated by extremely light writing, "spiritual" lack of pen pressure, corroborated by other signs in the handwriting.

SLANT: As Dr. Alfred Adler, the famous Viennese psychologist, said: "Handwriting points the way from me to you." It follows that the *slant* of an individual's handwriting will express whether his way is one of ardor, affection, reserve or withdrawal. There is the extreme rightward-flowing handwriting; the moderate right angle; the vertical, moderate backhand; and the extreme left-slanted backhand. In the slant (or slope) you discover whether the person is outgoing, extroverted, leaning toward people; or the opposite, which is reserved, introverted, unsocial or even antisocial. These are general categories, since more than the slant has to be considered in estimating the extent of extroversion and introversion in individuals.

SIZE: The size of the writing gives us clues to the individual's manner of approaching a situation. Does he generalize or observe details? The size really represents the kind of lens through which a person sees. Is it unusually large, large, medium-large? (All three sizes give a clue to a degree of exhibitionism.) Or is it "normal," which does not particularly strike the eye? This is the size most people write. The smaller the writing, the better the powers of concentration. Microscopic writing belongs to the specialist, the hermit, the introvert (no matter what the angle). The lens of the eye sees everything in minute detail as through a microscope.

BASIC LINE: Whether the lines run uphill, downhill or in both directions relates to the writer's point of view and his spirits. Is he optimistic, buoyant, cheerful, euphoric? Or skeptical, depressed, temporarily unhappy, suffering from melancholia, suicidal? Sometimes lines veer upward but words hang down either in the middle of a sentence or at the end of many sentences. You may see temporary or chronic depression, morbidity, hopelessness in these signs. The downhill writer is often the skeptic whose attitude arises from self-doubt. Here the basic line must be considered in conjunction with the t bars. Downhill writing is often a warning of depleted vitality, forerunner to a breakdown. Estimate very carefully.

MARGINS AND SPACING: The width or narrowness of margins and spacing between words determine the width or narrowness of a person's mind, his aesthetic reactions, whether he is a clear or muddled thinker, whether he is economical or extravagant. There may be wide spacing between letters in words, between the words, or between the lines. Or there may be no appreciable space between any of these. Perhaps there is a large margin on the right, on both right and left, or a margin that starts narrow and widens as the writer fills the page. The opposite may occur, where the margin starts wide and narrows as the page is filled. If the writing is poorly spaced in every respect so that it *looks* disturbed, you are probably dealing with a mentally and emotionally disturbed person. It will also be inconsistent in slant and pen pressure, and will have varying t bars and overly high upper loops. (Don't try to analyze it unless you are an expert. It might be the handwriting of a person who needs hospitalization, and you may have suspected it.)

SMALL LETTERS (*the abc's*): Observe these in conjunction with other signs. Are they printed, copybook style, open or closed, angular or rounded or both? They indicate conformity to rules, mental development, caution, generosity and other personality traits.

CAPITALS: Capital letters denote taste and pride. Are they ornate, simple, printed, old-fashioned, artistic, open at the top or closed tightly with a loop? Do they start with an incurve or an outgoing flourish; are they rounded or angular? Do capital letters appear where small ones would normally be?

LOOPS: Upper and lower loops have a special significance. Notice whether they are wide, narrow, compressed, ragged at the top, very high; whether the lower ones are exaggerated and run into the line below. Are they the outstanding feature in the entire handwriting? Do they have a "broken back" look? Or is there, instead of loops, a single stroke—the uppers in the letters l, h, k, the lower ones in y's and g's? Breaks in loops, both upper and lower, reveal the presence of a physical impairment.

ZONES: Divide the writing into three zones: upper, middle, and lower. The upper zone (loops especially) symbolizes the person's ideals, fantasy life, set of principles, standards; the middle zone concerns his approach to reality, how he deals with practical problems; the lower zone gives us clues to his physical demands, sexual potency, primitive impulses, materiality. Balance the three zones, as you would a mathematical problem. They will give you clues to more about the person than meets the eye.

INITIALS AND TERMINALS: Initial strokes, often unnecessary, show attention to detail. The terminals, too, give valuable clues. Are they long, wavy, curving upward or downward, abrupt, blunt, or do letters end with a long horizontal line that has a hook on it? The terminals (or finals) are clues to how much *give* the person has. Does he give of himself? Of his material possessions? Is he loquacious, generous, curious, possessive? Or sensitive, touchy, simpering, sadistic, outgoing or introverted? Does he have more "won't" power than will power? Taken in conjunction with other signs and strokes, terminals give us important clues to many traits of character.

SPEED (*rhythm*): Indicative of energy, it tells you how much the person expends in the way he does things as well as how he thinks—whether slowly or quickly. The person who thinks more quickly than his hand can record may leave out some letters in words or slur a word ending in *ing*. He writes as

1. 𝑡

2. 𝑡⁻

3. 𝑥 𝑞

4. 𝑡 𝑡

5. ▽

6. ⊤

7. 𝑋 𝑋

8. 𝐷

9. 𝑡

10. 𝑋

11. 𝑡

1. 𝑥 𝑥

2. 𝑡

3. 𝑋 𝑙

4. 𝑧

5. ▽ ⊀

6. 𝑡 (𝑡)

7. 𝑙

8. 𝑋 𝑥

9. 𝑏

t BARS: The way a person crosses or fails to cross his t's reveals much about his or her vitality and maturity, and if a variety of t bars appears in handwriting, special meanings can be found.

though recording his thoughts in shorthand. There are two kinds of speedy writing—distinct and indistinct. The distinct writer slows down his thinking in order to conform; the indistinct writer can't bother with conforming but goes ahead and expresses himself, later rearranging his thinking to make it fall into a comprehensible pattern. The slow thinker appears to draw every letter and the speed, therefore, is slowed down. He is also careful of punctuation, unless he is illiterate or negligent. *Uneven* speed produces letters lacking in uniformity and may be corroborated by other signs of disturbance in the writing. Writing that is too speedy shows anxiety, which is further revealed in a going over or patching up of letters or words. Words crossed

out in a messy looking specimen tell us the person is in an emotional mess. Writing in anger will show uneven pen pressure, blunt downstrokes, thick t bars, and the speed will be evident if you try to imitate the writing. When you have learned to estimate the speed of a person's writing you will know something about his energy output: whether he is lazy, indolent, indecisive because of tension, or, at the other extreme, whether he is a human dynamo.

i DOTS: The i dots, considered in combination with the t bars and other letter formations, show, among other things, retentiveness or lack of it, imagination, humor and critical faculties. Are the dots high, close to the letter, wavy, pointed, circled?

t BARS: They are extremely important in determining how much will power, drive, energy, determination (or a lack of these) the writer has and how much he uses. The t bars reveal whether he is aggressive, persistent, compulsive; or weak, timid, vacillating, indecisive, passive, neurotic. In the t bar you will see clues to emotional immaturity; to whether the writer lives in the past or drives his energy ambitiously toward the future. Many handwritings will show a variety of t bars, all of which have special meanings. The t bar, together with other horizontal strokes, shows the extent of the writer's balance—how he copes with life's situations. The vertical strokes are indicative of elemental forces and how much influence they have in his life. They also give us clues to sexual energy.

CONNECTING STROKES: A word is either connected in its letter forms or it is broken up. When the entire writing is connected, with even words joined together, consecutive reasoning or logic is revealed. The person may also be literal-minded. If breaks appear, this is the sign of intuition. Where the handwriting is entirely broken up, looking like printing but not printing, it is the "inspirational hand." Many poets, artists, and dancers print consistently. So do engineers. Connected writing combined with breaks in some words shows that the writer is capable of logic, yet possesses some intuition.

LEGIBILITY: While the legibility of the writing gives no real clue to the writer's mentality, it does indicate whether he has a desire to communicate his thoughts. Or does he seem to have something to hide?

PUNCTUATION: Careful punctuation indicates the writer's attention to details. Such care may be evident in the writing of an intelligent person. However, the person concerned with larger issues, with essences rather than details, may be careless in both punctuation and spelling, yet have a high intelligence rating. It is wise, therefore, to withhold judgment until the handwriting has been categorized according to which intellectual group the person belongs in. The meticulous person whose punctuation is flawless may also be a rigid, unimaginative one. One sure conclusion we can draw from the person who punctuates carefully is that he is obedient to the rules taught and often follows them to the letter. Careless punctuation, on the other hand, often shows a person who makes his own rules and can't be bothered with details, especially if

someone else demands they be followed. Where there are dashes, these often serve as a period, but they show, nevertheless, either a kind of mental twist or a desire to be original or different. (In graphology, the *intent* is considered more important than the form used to express the thought.) Any departure from established rules of writing tends to show the state of the mind at the time it was concentrated on the act of transferring thoughts to paper.

UNDERSCORING (*other than signatures*): This means a form of capriciousness, may mean delicacy of thought, but always indicates *emphasis*. Where there is too much underscoring under words, we are confronted with a type of emphasis which points to fanaticism. Who has not seen the religious fanatic's chalk writing on sidewalks or fences, underscored many times, quoting passages from the Bible?

SIGNATURES: The way a person signs his name gives an important clue to his personality. It is the face shown to the outside world, the façade that is presented, and it may be at variance with the *real* person. The signature may be entirely different from the rest of a person's writing, or it may be harmonious with it. People in the public eye often underscore their signatures. If a writer does this and is not a public figure, he either hopes some day to be or wishes to be noticed wherever he is. The underscored signature has the psychological connotation of an inferiority complex compensated by personality force. A signature that is involved and indecipherable tells us that the individual writing it wishes to be enigmatic, and makes no attempt to achieve a clear line of communication with the other fellow. The simple, legible signature tells us the person has no desire to hide anything, but wants to achieve clear communication with others.

RULES TO REMEMBER

A sign occasionally shown indicates an occasional trait;

When plentiful, it shows a habit;

When scarce yet evident, it reveals a tendency.

Even a sign that appears *once* in an entire handwriting is a clue to something that might develop under certain circumstances.

The way a person signs his name gives us a clue to the façade he presents to the world. Brilliant and truly great men often have plain signatures, although this does not always follow. People in the public eye usually sign their names with an underscore, giving emphasis to the personality. The great Sigmund

Freud, whose handwriting appears on the next page, signed his last name with a small "f."

When you have nothing more than a signature with which to work, you may, with diligent application, find in it many clues to the character of the writer, but it is better to have both the writing and signature for a complete analysis. There may be times, too, when a specimen is submitted for analysis without a signature. You may, if you are experienced, get clues to what the signature *might* look like from the rest of the handwriting, but you can't be sure unless you see it.

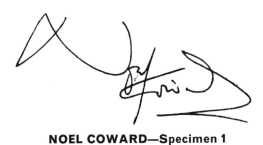

NOEL COWARD—Specimen 1

Specimen 1—Noel Coward is distinguished by its originality. It looks like a design. (Remember his play "Design for Living"?) We see in it an underscore that is a continuation of the last stroke. It is unlikely that we would hear his songs, see him act, or watch his plays without receiving a strong impression. His large capital N, certainly constructed with originality, shows that he is aware of his importance in the theatre.

JUAN PONCE de LEÓN—Specimen 2

Legend has it that Ponce de León discovered the "Fountain of Youth." His unique signature (Specimen 2), which looks like a design, gives us clues to his bizarre and interesting personality. We might describe this signature as having boundaries within which the writer functioned. We might even construe

the markings on both the left and right sides as foliage separating the island on which he lived from the rest of the world. (They also look like embellished dollar signs.) We see an elaborate underscore which tells us he was aware of his power and wanted others to recognize it too. Would he have been recorded in history if he hadn't been unusual? There is power, energy, fight, determination indicated all through the pen strokes. This signature was, no doubt, written at the height of his power.

Many people have tried to define the word genius and have come up with different answers. It is my feeling that when a person leaves a legacy of some kind—great books, great paintings, theories which are workable for the good of mankind—we may refer to him as a genius. Our concern here is not to ascertain whether or not men and women living today possess genius, but rather to examine the handwritings of those who have influenced our culture and added to our emotional and intellectual growth. What is the common denominator? We shall see.

Specimen 3 is the letter in which Freud proposed marriage to the woman who became his wife. It was written when he was 26 years old. It may be difficult to believe that the man who dealt so frankly with the primitive sexual urges of human beings was himself something of a prude! We view this in his capital M, the old-fashioned formation which means adherence to conventional forms as well as a paternal, protective instinct. To be sure, he wooed and won Martha Bernays with an ardor filled with jealousy, unreasonable demands, a passion bordering on frenzy, at times. Yet much of his wooing was done in writing, and he spent more time speaking of love than making love.

Within him was a terrific struggle between the dictates of turbulent emotions and a mind which could be clear and scientific in its reasoning. We see some rather long t bars revealing his drive and determination, and in his own words he was "tenacious and active." But he was also full of self-doubt as evidenced in some t bars which do not go through the stem of the letter (look at the specimen under a magnifying glass). Yet he could be aggressive in a querulous way, besieged by changing moods, some of which bordered on a temporary feeling of hopelessness. (This is evident in the word that hangs over on the end of the sixth line.)

His angular formations tell us that he could be exacting, demanding, efficient; that he was an ex-

SIGMUND FREUD—
Specimen 3

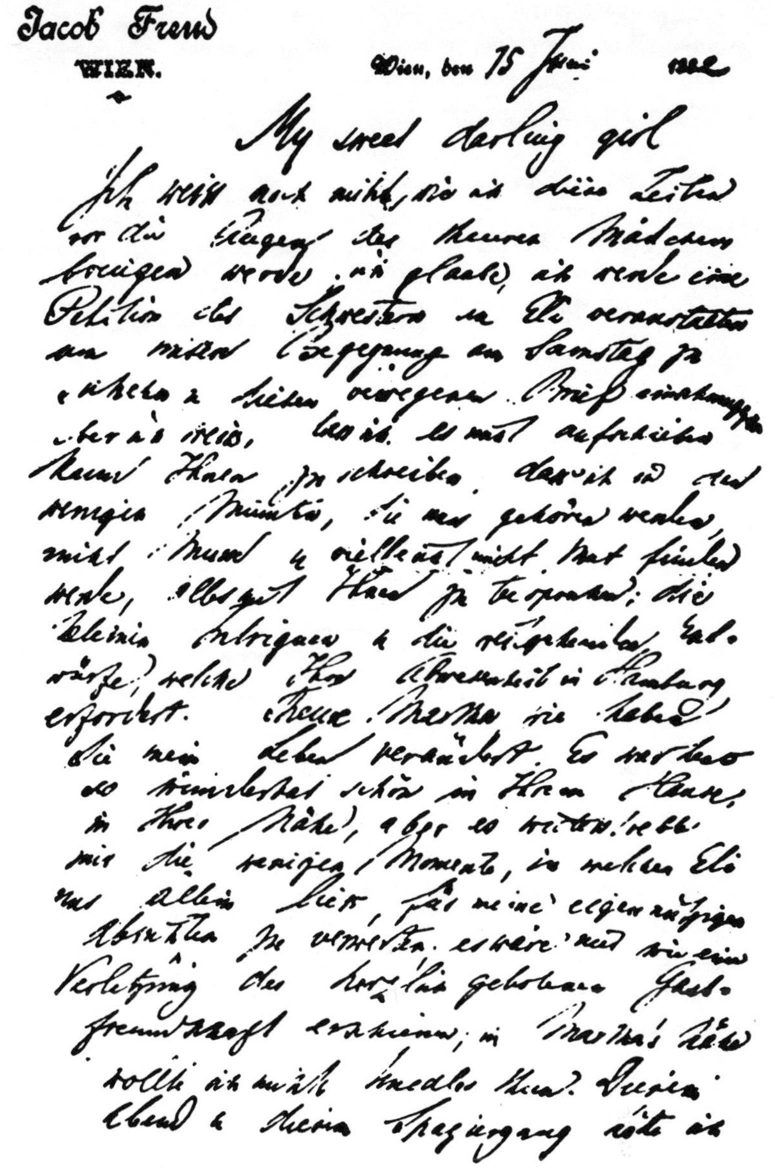

My sweet darling girl

[handwritten letter in German]

tremist who hated half-measures; that he drove himself and did things the hard way; that he was relentless in probing the truth to the bitter end, and this is what made him a great scientist. But he could be submissive when his emotions became involved, and he revealed a tenderness as sincere as his outbursts of fury.

Notice the altruistic g in the word "girl" in the salutation. This, in combination with the t bar which did not go through the stem, gives us clues to his occasional feelings of martyrdom, his masochism and his frequent feeling of being misunderstood. He fought against this as against his primitive impulses, but because of a need to make his contribution, he persisted in the face of opposition, criticism and feelings of rejection. He was essentially a reformer, a healer, an intensely social-minded being.

His intuition, revealed in the breaks between letters all through the writing, was uncanny, and he was forever analyzing motives, gestures, happenings —even during the most fervent period of his courtship. It was then that he ran through the whole gamut of emotions from ecstasy to despair, yet at the same time he could be calm, detached and coldly scientific in his work. Perhaps this is the combination that might be considered the essential feature of any great genius! Surely, Freud had it in full measure. His excellent memory persisted even in his latter years, when his handwriting began to show signs of disintegration.

In the handwriting of Michelangelo, sculptor, painter, architect and poet, we are struck at a glance with so many original formations. Specimen 4 is in Italian but its originality speaks a universal language. Look at the unusual way he forms his small c in the word "chromo" (first line) and in other words where a "ch" appears.

Intuition, without which the artist could not create, is shown all through the writing in breaks between letters. Pen pressure is uniformly heavy, telling us of his sensuousness to forms, colors, music. Even in the foreign language, we see a small g resembling the number 8 and we know, by now, that this is the "literary g." This is corroborated in

Specimen 6
(A on the barometer)

Enclosed handwriting as well

Specimen 7
(B on the barometer)

it. In view of my own opinion, I interested to read what you will ?

Michelangelo's handwriting by the Greek d. We know that he wrote sonnets and poems, and his paintings, too, told a story. He had many ways of communicating his thoughts, genius that he was.

Small letters, light pen pressure and simple formations in Professor Einstein's handwriting (Specimen 5) tell us he was an extremely sensitive man, modest and retiring, with many of the elements of the hermit-introvert. Capital letters are small. The A in his signature is a simplification of the old-fashioned formation, and tells us of his protective attitude toward the underprivileged and downtrodden. His prodigious memory is revealed in the careful dotting of his i's. The margins on both sides, coupled with clearly defined lines, indicate an aesthetic nature which made demands of him in a simple, unpretentious way. The rhythmic writing

itself, and the graceful final in the last word of the seventh line, are clues to his musical ability, while the t bar above the stem in his last name tells a story all its own. Here we have the clue to his world of fantasy, imagination, spirituality, and his desire to work for the good of humanity. He often curbed his personal desires to achieve his dreams. We may assume, therefore, that the destruction resulting from his scientific discoveries had a crushing effect upon him and contributed to his moods of depression. This depression is revealed in words which fall slightly over even though the basic line rises upward, revealing his underlying optimism. Perhaps in his simplicity lay the seed of his greatness, although he himself minimized it. Often he felt small and unworthy, and like most geniuses he felt isolated and alone. The capital D in the fifth line gives us a clue to a kind of mild frivolity in his make-up, and this

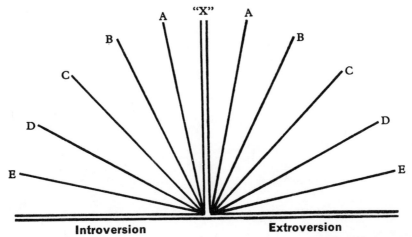

EMOTIONAL BAROMETER

Introversion   Extroversion

took the form of childlike indulgences in pleasures out of doors and close to Nature.

On the right side of this "Emotional Barometer" A and B belong to individuals writing at a *moderate* right slant. A is closer to "X" and is more re- served than B, and there is a tendency to write vertically when in certain moods. Specimens 6 and 7 correspond to A and B. They are the handwritings of individuals who moderately show what they feel.

[handwriting specimen]

SPECIMEN 8: The typical snob's handwriting. This can be seen in the vertical angle and t bar which flies upward. The writer does everything with formality.

[handwriting specimen]

SPECIMEN 9: The pressure is quite heavy and the backward slant (C) is pronounced. The writer is extremely emotional—but no one knows it, for he is detached and undemonstrative.

FORTUNE TELLING WITH PLAYING CARDS

From the dawn of their existence, cards have been credited with occult powers. It is interesting to note that, even in this day of scientific exploration into extra-sensory perception, the researchers at Duke University and other seats of learning have utilized cards as the best medium of experimentation.

Disputes, often acrimonious in nature, have raged over the centuries concerning the exact significance of the symbols.

We have no intention of entering into learned and scholarly controversies, but do want to point out that fortune telling by cards is not merely a game, and is more than a hobby. Properly used, popular playing cards can provide an introduction to a philosophy and wisdom more ancient than any of the Western religions.

THE VALUES OF THE CARDS

Probably no two people who have ever read the cards interpret the symbols identically.

In this section we have attempted to extract the basic meaning of each card and to present it in as simple and clear-cut a fashion as possible. Anyone who masters the material will be able to use the cards in forecasting his own future, or that of another, with a true understanding of the fundamentals underlying the symbolism of the cards.

To simplify matters, from this point on the person who reads the cards will be spoken of as the *Reader*. The person who consults the cards or seeks advice will be spoken of as the *Querent*. Use standard playing cards.

It should be stressed that fortune telling by cards is not based upon fatalism. It is rare indeed when the course of events cannot be changed. Most people have a series of problems with which they are wrestling. The sensitive Reader can bring these problems to the forefront. His task is not to dictate the actions of the Querent but to direct him into channels of thought which will clarify the nature of his problems and give him a deeper insight into his own personality and increased wisdom in dealing with the future.

PREPARING FOR THE READING

Few Querents will come to the cards with any knowledge of the ancient symbols they portray. In order to establish a rapport between the Reader and the Querent, it is frequently desirable to discuss briefly the significance of these symbols.

The cards are symbols of the life force, but symbols only. If the Querent approaches these symbols frivolously or with contempt, it may be well for the Reader to abandon the divination. Success in reading the cards depends largely on establishing a rapport in which the cards form a bridge linking the Querent and the Reader, so that temporarily they become part of a single entity.

It is common practice for the Querent to make a wish before the cards are spread out. The Reader may or may not conform to this custom but, if he does, he should be warned of its hazards. The wish is frequently frivolous and usually inadequately thought out, so that complications and ramifications occur which are likely to throw the reading off balance. The wish which is granted often proves disappointing and sometimes disastrous. Worst of all, the spread (of cards) which focusses about a specific wish, particularly a trifling one, must be interpreted in a somewhat superficial fashion.

Condensed from "How to Tell Fortunes with Cards" by Wenzell Brown, © 1963 by Sterling Publishing Co., Inc., New York

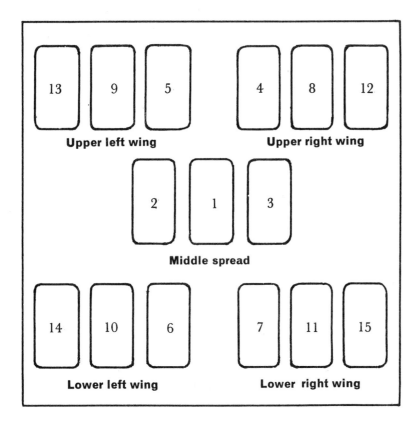

| 13 | 9 | 5 | | 4 | 8 | 12 |

Upper left wing   **Upper right wing**

| 2 | 1 | 3 |

Middle spread

| 14 | 10 | 6 | | 7 | 11 | 15 |

Lower left wing   **Lower right wing**

LAYING OUT THE SPREAD

The Reader should handle the cards before offering them to the Querent to shuffle. He instructs the Querent to shuffle the cards slowly, thoughtfully and for some period of time. The proper way is not to break and riffle the cards, but to shuffle them with a rhythmic motion of the hands.

The 15-card spread may seem like an extremely simple spread, but 7,921,834,931,684,532,415,560,000 variations are mathematically possible! Thus the likelihood of duplication is so infinitely small as to be virtually inconceivable.

The Querent is told that he may hesitate in the shuffling whenever he is so inclined, but the Reader makes the actual selection of the cards. He places the first card in the very middle of the spread, designated number 1 in the diagram.

The Querent continues shuffling the cards until he is ready for the second selection to be made. The Reader places this card in the position designated number 2 in the diagram. This continues until the entire 15 cards are laid out in the order shown.

No single card has a value all its own. It is influenced by the total spread and especially by those cards which are adjacent to it. Therefore the Reader should never comment on the individual cards as they appear, but should wait until he can get the *feel* of the entire spread.

THE POSITIONS IN THE SPREAD

By and large, the central card (number 1) represents either the Querent, his personality and the nature of his problems, or the primary influences which are moving through his life at the present moment. The cards which flank the central cards (numbers 2 and 3) are the next most important cards in the spread. They clarify the personality of the Querent and provide basic information regarding the situation in which he finds himself. A *face* card in the middle spread may represent the Querent or may represent an individual close to him who plays a dominating rôle in his life. The latter is more likely to be the case if the card ordinarily designates an individual of the opposite sex from the Querent.

The three cards in the upper right wing (numbers 4, 8, 12) indicate the course into which the Querent's life would normally flow unless checked by some positive action on his part.

The three cards in the upper left wing (numbers 13, 9, 5) offer the Querent an alternate route which he may follow if he so desires. This wing designates possibilities which are open to him. Whether this alternate route is desirable or one which will be dangerous to him depends upon the cards themselves.

The three cards in the lower left wing (numbers 14, 10, 6) are generally guide posts which will assist the Querent in making his decisions. However, where the Querent is elderly, or past middle age, this wing is likely to represent elements in his past which affect his present or future circumstances. In the youthful Querent, these cards are more likely to forecast future events and offer advice as to how to prepare for them.

The three cards in the lower right wing (numbers 7, 11, 15) usually represent specific forces at work outside of the Querent. While these forces cannot be controlled, the Querent can adapt himself to them, thus utilizing them for his own advantage.

A QUICK RUN-THROUGH OF A SPREAD

Before proceeding further, let us look at a sample spread in order to examine its more salient features. Many more details about the individual cards involved will appear in later pages, but a quick run-through of a spread will give a rough idea of the usefulness of the cards.

This spread, which has been selected from copious files, is that of a young actress who came to consult the cards at a critical point in her career.

The advice which the cards offer in this case is extremely clear-cut. The central card (the Jack of Diamonds) obviously represents the Querent, for this card may be a young person of either sex who is on the threshold of life. To the right is the Three of Diamonds which often signifies a contract or business opportunity. To the left is the Ace of Clubs, a card of dynamism and talent.

These three cards form the central core of the spread. In order to tell more of the character and personality of a Querent, the Reader must be familiar with the description of the Jack of Dia-

Sample spread of a young actress.

monds (page 330). To learn more of this particular Querent's talents, the Reader should consult the section dealing with the Ace of Clubs (page 333). These two cards will fuse together to give a picture of the Querent, and it is safe to assume that the contract or opportunity which lies open to her will be related to her skills and talents.

Next look at the upper right-hand wing of the spread. All the cards which appear there are beneficent and, grouped together in this fashion, promise wealth, fame, success, happiness and the achievement of lifetime ambitions. This wing represents the normal flow of the Querent's life. The advice here is for the Querent to continue on the path she is following and that, if she does so, she will have the opportunity to reap rich rewards.

Now examine the upper left-hand wing. This is an alternate route which she may take, but this route leads to failure! The warning is definite:

If the Querent fails to bend her energies in the direction which she has chosen and instead permits quarrels, petty misunderstandings and anger to influence her, they will divert her from the path of success. The Two of Spades represents a minor stumbling block which, badly handled, can have disastrous results. The Seven of Spades is a card of division, warning the Querent against discouragement and thoughtless actions. The Ten of Spades warns that neglect in concentrating on long-term objectives may result in unnecessary failures and disappointments. Obviously this alternate route must be avoided.

The next step is to examine the lower right wing of the spread. This wing represents outside influences which will affect the Querent's life. Here we see two Kings flanking the Ace of Diamonds. The Ace is a card of constructive power, symbolized by the magician, and often augurs success in the theatre or the arts. Usually Kings represent actual men, but the presence of two of them close together may indicate a group of people. The intimation here is that a number of individuals will be involved closely with the Querent and that they will give her assistance along the road which leads to success. Because these cards appear on the lower right wing of the spread and are joined to the central cards by a card of business (the Three of Diamonds), these men should not be interpreted in a romantic light, but rather as business associates.

The cards in the lower left wing of the spread warn that everything will not be smooth sailing. The two Fives suggest minor setbacks, tears, dis-

appointments and periods of anxiety. However, the Nine of Hearts at the end of the spread promises that, if these obstacles are met with determination and courage, the Querent will achieve happiness beyond her highest expectations.

Having examined the individual cards and their position in the spread, the next step is to note whether any one suit dominates the spread. In this instance, the suits are distributed fairly equally. Therefore this phase of the reading is irrelevant.

The next check should be for three or more cards of the same numerical value. In this spread three Aces occur. As explained later, three Aces, especially when accompanied by two Kings, promise unusual opportunities, much activity, changes, success, fame and the likelihood of mingling with many people in situations of unusual importance.

This is a first superficial reading of the spread.

The competent Reader must possess an intimate knowledge of each individual card in the pack so that it instantly flashes a message to him. It is important to know the significance of each card by heart, for the Reader who stops to look up a card or check it in the book risks losing the confidence of the Querent. He will find it hard to maintain the rapport essential to an adequate reading.

SIGNIFICANCE OF THE INDIVIDUAL CARDS

It should be stressed again that each card is shaded by those which surround it.

As the Reader becomes more expert in divining the future through the cards, he will discover that certain cards take on special meanings or shadings in his hands. This is completely valid.

THE JOKER

Where the Joker appears, the Reader must take especial care in interpreting the spread and beware of pitfalls wherein a literal reading of the cards may lead to a reversal of truth. The Joker is a card of duality that tends to shroud the future in mystery.

It may be advisable for the relatively inexperienced Reader to omit any Jokers from the spread as its appearance complicates the reading. Also, care should be taken not to introduce a Joker into a used pack of cards because its relatively untouched surface may tempt the Reader or the Querent to select it when otherwise it would be rejected.

When the Joker appears in the middle of the spread, the indication is that the Querent has attained in some degree, or seeks to attain, freedom from physical restraints, grandeur of vision and the superior wisdom which men term folly. He is no longer bound by conventions and he has rid himself of pettiness, jealousy and covetousness so that he rises above human tragedy, pain or adversity to find a perfect unity of mind and spirit.

When the Joker appears in the upper left wing of the spread, the indication is that the Querent will be faced with a choice of rejecting worldly goods to attain spiritual freedom, or of accepting material restrictions in order to assume social responsibilities.

On the lower wings of the spread, the Joker is likely to relate to more specific situations wherein the Querent may act in accordance with his highest ideals or may compromise with his conscience for personal profit, social acceptance or other practical reasons.

SPADES

THE ACE OF SPADES

There is a common superstition that the Ace of Spades augurs death or tragedy. This is not true. The Ace of Spades represents tremendous force, power and strength.

Some guidance as to the nature of this force may be found in the position of the Ace in the spread and the cards which adjoin it. With the Ace of Spades, high achievement becomes possible. If the strength is contained in the Querent, he can hold it in leash and find an inward power to face all obstacles in his path. He should look forward to the future with courage and surging hope.

The Ace of Spades does represent a danger, too. Uncontrolled, the force can explode and destroy the Querent and those close to him.

If the Ace lies in the middle of the spread, the force will dominate the subject's life. He has been granted great curative powers and should do well in medicine, nursing or allied fields. He has the capacity for leadership and should succeed in law, politics and other areas which demand dynamic energy. He is, however, likely to be plagued by narrow-mindedness, inflexibility and adherence to dogma. He should be encouraged to assume tolerant points of view and to dedicate his talents to his fellow men. He must curb his temper and his personal ambitions or else the force within him may become corrosive and bring about the enmity of other strong-willed individuals.

If the Ace of Spades lies in the upper right portion of the spread, it represents an external force which he will encounter. He should be prepared to cope with this force and use it for his own ends.

If the Ace lies in the upper left portion of the spread, the Reader should explore the capacities of the Querent to deal with new situations. If he is timid, fearful and vacillating, he should be discouraged from making radical changes in his life patterns. On the other hand, if he is bold, self-assured and adventurous, unusual opportunities lie ahead for him.

If the Ace of Spades lies on the lower wings of the spread, the Querent should brace himself to weather an emotional storm; to meet an unexpected, explosive situation; or to withstand pressures from an overbearing individual.

THE KING OF SPADES

The appearance of the King of Spades in the spread indicates the presence of a man of powerful and dominating personality. He is likely to be highly intelligent, stable, ambitious, honest and motivated by practicality and reason.

When the Querent is a woman, the King of Spades represents a dominant male in her life. He may be father, brother, husband, friend or a man who seeks her hand in marriage. When the King lies in the middle of the spread, this man has had long association with the Querent. If the card lies in the right wing, the man has already entered into the Querent's life, though not necessarily in an important rôle. If the King lies in the left wing, this man will become known to the Querent at some future date.

The King of Spades is likely to lack subtlety and to see things in terms of black and white. While he is well-intentioned, he may trample upon the sensitivities of others. He tends to be a good provider, astute in business affairs, well-liked and respected by his male associates. By his own code, he is generous, reasonable and kind. On the adverse side, he may be too sure of his own judgments, heavy-handed and either unwilling or unable to understand points of view which conflict with his own. He distrusts intuitive knowledge and tends to dismiss with contempt the artistic abilities, the soaring ambitions, the cherished dreams and idealism of those about him. Such attitudes may bring about domestic crises, create ill will in business, or antagonize friends.

If the spread indicates that the King of Spades is a man with whom the Querent must deal, he should be reminded of the many good qualities of the man, his staunchness, his loyalty, his uncompromising honesty. Open opposition or carping criticism will only strengthen his determination to have his own way, but when an appeal is made to his better instincts, he is highly responsive.

Such a man, in spite of his outward appearance of competence, strength and domination, has a great need for warm personal relationships and for a woman who will give purpose to his life. He does not like to be alone.

The female Querent who ponders marriage or a business relationship with such a man should be advised to examine her own personality and attitudes with great care. This is not a man whom she can change or wrap around her finger.

THE QUEEN OF SPADES

The Queen of Spades is a woman of unsuspected depths, whose immediate personality may be misleading. Such a woman, especially as she grows older, tends to conceal her emotions beneath a cloak of calmness which may make her appear unemotional and haughty or even shallow and unresponsive. This woman is not easy to know, but the cultivation of her friendship will be rewarding. Once this friendship is won she will offer unswerving loyalty and unselfish devotion. On the other hand, she may become an implacable enemy, ruthless and cruel.

Such a woman should be approached with complete sincerity, for she is highly intuitive and will be quick to recognize deceit or ulterior motives. Unless the Querent can meet her with frankness and a genuine desire to secure her friendship, it is best to avoid her.

While the Queen of Spades is a woman of deep emotional responses, her appearance in the layout rarely indicates romance. She is much more likely to play the role of mentor, advisor or confidante. However, where there is romantic attachment between her and the Querent, she will be a woman of endless surprises—passionate, possessive, inclined to jealousy.

Many successful people have a Queen of Spades in their lives and this is particularly true in the field of arts. She provides a practical, stabilizing influence upon whom the gifted may depend. She is frequently the source of inspiration, the spur to fame or success, the demanding critic who will not permit failure. She has the tendency to dominate and to appear aggressive and unfeeling but she can easily be won over by affection, good nature and respectful consideration of her views.

Conversely, if she is antagonized, she is a dangerous enemy. She finds ways to hurt, humiliate or injure the individual who has offended her.

The complexity of her nature will make her appear mysterious and enigmatic, driven by vagaries, subject to insights hidden from others and capable of contradictory actions. But she is a woman well worth cultivating.

THE JACK OF SPADES

The Jack represents a young person, but the sex is not indicated by the card itself.

If a Jack faces a Heart or Club, it usually means that the person is of the opposite sex of the Querent. If it faces a Spade or a Diamond, the Jack represents someone of the Querent's own sex. If the Jack is the end card on the middle line of the spread, the suit of the card above may determine its sex. If the Jack is at the extreme end of one of the wings and looks outward, the indication is that the individual represented will be going out of the Querent's life. Whether this departure is fortunate or not, will depend on the card closest to the Jack.

(NOTE: This explanation concerning the way the Jack faces is the same in all suits, so it will not be repeated in each case.)

The Jack of Spades represents a young and frequently immature person. The delineation of character cannot be as complete as in cards representing older persons. By and large, if is it determined that the Jack represents a male, he will develop characteristics somewhat similar to those of the King of Spades. Similarly, if the individual is female, she is likely to possess many of the personality traits of the Queen of Spades.

However, these characteristics are usually modified. The Jack of Spades is always a friendly person. If he is a young man, he tends to be dynamic, alert and often brilliant. He is restless and filled with nervous energy which may take the form of athletic prowess or intellectual curiosity. However, his interests tend to be short-lived and much of his energy may be wasted. The female Querent interested in such a youth should examine herself to see if she can offer a stabilizing influence. If she herself is unstable, insecure or given to quick temper, the alliance may be marked by quarrels, unhappiness and eventual separation. On the other hand, if she is able to leash his energies and direct them into constructive channels, so that a true alliance is formed between them, contentment and success may evolve from the union.

If the Querent has doubts, she should be advised to delay her decision. She should also be encouraged to discuss long-term plans with this young man. While he may appear to her in romantic guise, he is essentially practical and wants a helpmate who will implement his progress towards the goals which he has set for himself.

Where the Querent is a young man and the Jack of Spades appears in the spread in such a way as to designate a young woman, he will find that he is due for a series of surprises. Outwardly this girl may appear placid, but she will possess unexpected depths of character which will be revealed gradually. She is ardent, intuitive and inclined to be fiercely possessive. She will have many facets to her personality, some of which will appear contradictory. On the surface she may be wilful, capricious and given to flights of fancy. But her shifting moods cloak a determined character in which direct goals have been established. She is ambitious, skilled in directing others and her loyalty, once given, will never alter. She may achieve her ends by flattery, cajolery and subterfuge but, at the same time, she will be warm, generous and capable of tremendous sacrifices for those whom she loves.

Such a woman cannot be taken by storm. She must be wooed with diligence over a prolonged period.

THE TEN OF SPADES

The Ten of Spades symbolizes a wall or barrier. In spiritual matters it may mean the end of a delusion, the recognition of false goals, the surrender to the inevitable or the abandonment of long-cherished plans. The person who hurls himself recklessly against the wall, who blames others or who wallows in self-pity, may shatter his life. On the other hand, a calm appraisal of the situation may lead to a new and better set of values, to increased spiritual strength and to fresh pleasures.

When the Ten of Spades is the outer card in one of the wings of the spread, the indication is that some course of action which has appeared open will either close or lead to a dead end. Where this formation occurs, the Querent should be urged to review his plans for the future with the possible idea of revising them.

When the Ten of Spades lies in the middle of the spread, it is an indication of important news which will alter the course of the Querent's life. It is also likely that some person as yet unknown to the Querent will play a significant role in his future. The Querent's reaction to a frustrating and disappointing situation is the keynote to his enduring happiness. He need not know lasting defeat because

one passage is barred, but it may require wisdom and courage to seek a new pathway to happiness.

THE NINE OF SPADES

Traditionally the Nine of Spades spells catastrophe. It indicates changes through unexpected and unpredictable sources. But it may also destroy outworn patterns and free the Querent from the chains of customs which have bound him for so long that he has grown unaware of their weight and the restrictions which they impose upon him.

The Nine of Spades, when found in the middle of the spread, is a clear-cut warning that the Querent should broaden his horizons, seek out new friends, accept new ideas.

In the youthful Querent it may mark the first tenuous steps in leaving the shelter of family life. In the older Querent it may indicate the breaking up of the home, the loss of security and a radical revision of his life plan. Where this card appears in a prominent position in the spread, the Querent should be advised to seek out new interests. He should voluntarily cast off old prejudices and habits of thought which impede his progress. To continue without change may be calamitous.

On the other hand, if the Nine of Spades appears in either of the left-hand wings, he has a choice of maintaining his present course of life or of altering it.

THE EIGHT OF SPADES

The Eight of Spades is a card of contentment, of quiet pleasure, rest and relaxation. This calm joy may be found through the relationship with another person or it may be related to a place or some kind of activity, such as a hobby or sport.

However, the Eight of Spades represents only a facet of the Querent's life. It is not a total card. The comfort, the pleasure which lies within the Querent's grasp is a part-time thing, a segment of his life which is separated from the mainstream of his daily activities.

The Querent should be warned against too great a dependency on this quiet pleasure. The pleasure is there for the taking but to keep his refuge safe, he should wall it off from the rest of his life and remain vigilant.

THE SEVEN OF SPADES

The Seven of Spades is a card of division. It indicates partial success in the plans or aspirations of the Querent. It is also a warning of unexpected turns and twists of fate. Where the Seven of Spades appears, the Querent may find that objectives which he has successfully achieved do not bring expected satisfactions and rewards! The Querent should be advised to re-evaluate his plans and to view them with greater objectivity. He must expect setbacks but, if he can weather these disappointments, he can achieve some of his goals. He should be cautioned not to give up too easily. Above all he should not act in pique in such a way that he destroys future opportunities.

THE SIX OF SPADES

The Six of Spades is a card of anxiety. It usually marks a period of suspended motion in which the Querent can do little but wait. This may be a period of sickness either for the Querent or someone close to him. More often, however, it is a time during which the Querent awaits decisions made by others which he feels will be handed down to him. Because of this he is liable to feel trapped by circumstances and to cease his activities until he receives further information.

The Querent should be advised that, during the period of anxiety, he should examine all facets of the problem and make certain that he has done everything possible to bring about the desired ends.

THE FIVE OF SPADES

The Five of Spades is the card of separation. Its appearance in the middle of the spread is likely to mean that the Querent will break old ties, change employment, settle in a new location or travel extensively. Inherent in the Five of Spades is a sense of grief, sorrow and sometimes remorse.

When the Five of Spades appears in the upper right wing of the spread, it frequently means that someone close to the Querent will depart from his life or that a situation with which he has long been familiar will change. If the Five of Spades is flanked by Diamonds, the indication is a shift of business relationships. If the Five of Spades appears in the upper left wing, the separation will be optional. The two remaining cards of the wing will hint at the effects of the change should the Querent decide to follow this pattern.

If the Five of Spades appears in the lower wings of the spread, the indication is that the separation will be incidental to other matters. The person or situation removed from the Querent's life may be of importance only in that it affects his business, finances or social life.

Under no circumstances is the Five of Spades a card of death. At its worst this card may mean loss of friendships through quarrels, vituperation or anger.

It is unwise for the Reader to make positive recommendations.

THE FOUR OF SPADES

The Four of Spades is a card of recuperation or healing. It may mark the end of a period of sickness, prolonged anxiety or strife. On the surface this may appear to be a period of wasted time and energy, but in actuality it is a pause to renew strength.

THE THREE OF SPADES

The Three of Spades is a card of sudden resolution, the swift decision to take action in a seemingly minor matter. The decision may be, or appear to be, motivated by vindictiveness or spite, rather than sustained judgment.

If the Three of Spades appears in the middle of the spread, the Querent should be advised not to let personal animosity warp his critical faculties. In reacting too strongly to petty annoyances he may destroy the success of long-term objectives.

Where the Three of Spades occurs in juxtaposition to a face card he may be the victim of a slur or an unfair appraisal of his intentions by another person. He should be prepared to react with generosity and not to counter the injustice with angry denials, an exchange of accusations, threats or tears.

The Three of Spades may actually forewarn the Querent of a test or trial of his capacity to deal with unpleasant matters. Success in so doing may lead to improved conditions in business, better personal relationships and increased respect among his associates.

Whenever the Three of Spades occurs in the spread, it is wise to explore the situation more deeply.

THE TWO OF SPADES

The Two of Spades represents a minor stumbling block in one's path, sometimes no more than a trifling irritation or a brief delay. If impatience gives way to bad temper, obstinacy or vindictiveness, the original trifle may assume unreasonable proportions and even destroy carefully laid plans.

When the Two of Spades appears, and especially so if it is centrally located, the subject should be forewarned so that he will meet the block calmly and not come upon it unprepared.

HEARTS

THE ACE OF HEARTS

The Ace of Hearts is a card of pleasure. It promises joy, merriment, love and fertility. However, when badly placed in the spread, it can be a warning of dissipation, waste, and a sacrifice of spiritual values for transitory pleasure.

Like all Aces, it is a card of explosive force. It may predict strong, romantic attachment, birth or re-birth of spiritual faith and joy.

When found in the middle of the spread, the joy will be an integral part of the Querent's personality. If there are a number of face cards or tens in the spread, the Querent will have the opportunity for new, varied and pleasurable social contacts. He will be the hub of festivities and he will possess friends whose regard for him is much greater than he realizes.

If the Ace of Hearts is flanked by Clubs, the joy is likely to be more subdued, to be accompanied by peace and quiet joy. When there is a preponderance of Diamonds in the spread, there is a promise of business success and increased satisfaction in work.

When the Ace of Hearts lies in the lower left wing of the spread, the indication is that the Querent is an object of love, adulation or devotion of which he is not aware, or which he does not reciprocate. Especially where the central cards are Spades, the Querent may feel himself unloved because he has not taken time to cultivate the people around him or has failed to do so through shyness, cynicism, preoccupation with personal affairs or because he has underestimated his own capacity to win the love of others.

Whenever the Ace of Hearts appears it should be accepted as a challenge to share joy with others. It indicates that the Querent has not taken full advantage of the gifts with which he has been endowed.

Traditionally, the Ace of Hearts is the card of young lovers and gives promise of marriage and children.

Where the Ace of Hearts dominates the pack, the Querent should be advised to extend his circle of friends. He should do well in social work, the ministry, teaching or any other business or profession which brings him into contact with large numbers of people.

When the Ten of Spades stands between the Ace of Hearts and a face card, the indication is that a barrier exists which prevents a satisfying relationship with another person but that the barrier can be swept aside.

When the Nine of Spades lies beside the Ace of Hearts or blocks one of the wings, the Querent should be warned that a situation which imperils his happiness exists. Perhaps his joy has blinded him so that he has given unwitting offense to others or failed to take safeguards to protect himself from misfortune.

THE KING OF HEARTS

The King of Hearts represents a man of boundless good will and integrity. He is straightforward, dependable and mild-tempered. Outwardly he is uncomplicated and frequently conceals his feelings with gruffness; often he is inarticulate, his kindness being shown by deeds rather than words. Because of this, he may be regarded as insensitive and incapable of understanding the more intricate personalities of others.

When the Querent is a woman or a young man, the King of Hearts may appear as the father image or the symbol of authority.

The male Querent who finds the King of Hearts in the middle of the spread may aspire to develop the exterior calm and other characteristics which he admires in some older and more experienced man.

The female Querent, in the middle of whose spread the King of Hearts occurs, will find that her life is, or can be, intimately interwoven with such a man. He may be husband, father, devoted admirer or even, in some cases, a loving son.

When the King of Hearts appears in the upper left-hand wing, the indication is that such a man will enter the Querent's life in the not-too-distant future. Querent will have the choice of accepting this man's aid and loyalty, which may be coupled by restraints and obligations, or of rejecting him.

When the King of Hearts appears in the upper right-hand wing, he will become a potent force in the Querent's life. But his friendship can only be won through the integrity of the Querent. Should he be openly flaunted, he will strike back with courage, determination and sometimes with crushing force.

When the King of Hearts appears in the lower wings of the spread, he is more likely to be a man who will enter the Querent's life temporarily. He may pave the way for business promotion, sit in judgment of the Querent, or act as mentor or guide in domestic or social situations. He may provide financial assistance or emotional ballast in periods of stress.

The King of Hearts is admirably suited to teaching, judiciary posts, the ministry or any position which requires unswerving honesty, restraint and considered judgment.

Where the King of Hearts lies beside a jack—especially if the Querent is a woman—the indication is that the woman is seeking to instill strength of character, courage and a sense of responsibility in some younger person. This being so, inevitably the woman possesses some of the admirable characteristics attributed to this card. It may also be suggested that she should find some older man, symbolized by the King of Hearts, to guide and assist her.

The King of Hearts is rarely of a creative turn of mind, but he will possess a love of beauty and will find joy in simple things.

In all other suits but Hearts, marriage between the King and Queen of the same suit is likely to be disastrous. But the King and Queen of Hearts are admirably mated. Each will give to the other absolute love and trust.

THE QUEEN OF HEARTS

The Queen of Hearts offers pleasure, joy, unstinting and unquestioning love. She is deeply emotional, and acts through instinct rather than reason. Traditionally she is jolly, light-hearted, frivolous and gay. But she is fruitful too. While she may lack intellectual depths, she sparks ideas and serves as an inspiration to more talented people about her. She is highly sensitive to the moods of those who are fortunate enough to win her love and, through her trust and belief in them, encourages them to fulfil their desires, ambitions and aspirations.

She is attracted to the arts and has a deep sensitivity for beauty in any form. Although her judgments may be at fault, she errs on the side of generosity. She reponds quickly to kindness but is inclined to be easily hurt. She lacks aggression and is often impractical where her own affairs are concerned, but will show tremendous moral and physical courage in defending the objects of her love.

On the surface, the Queen of Hearts appears practical and primarily interested in creature comforts. She is a good home-maker, an excellent cook and a devoted mother. Beneath the surface, however, she may lead a secret life filled with fantasy, aspirations and soaring ambitions for those she loves. There is an undercurrent of melancholy which she rarely shows. Her love is paralleled by enduring grief for the misfortunes which befall others and the imperfections of life.

She is a champion of the underdog, a friend to the friendless, a crusader for justice. But she is frequently mistaken and easily imposed upon. She tends to overevaluate people, both in the matter of skill and character. She can see no flaw in those she loves. Her own lack of subtlety blinds her to duplicity in others. Her honesty impels her to move directly to a point and sometimes to be blunt and tactless. She is outspoken in anger, but easily appeased and never bears a grudge.

When the Queen of Hearts lies in the middle of the spread of a female Querent, the indication is that she possesses many of the characteristics symbolized by this card. Where the other cards in the spread represent hardship, deceit or danger, this is a warning that the Querent should proceed cautiously. She should be advised against too ready acceptance of others at their face values. If a Diamond appears at the right of the Queen, she must guard herself in financial matters. If the Ten of Hearts appears at her right, she will find deep joy in a younger person, possibly in the success of a son but more likely in her close relationship with a child.

If the Querent is a male and the Queen lies in the middle of the spread, it signifies that he is deeply loved. In this case the Queen may symbolize an entire family. If the Queen lies in the upper right or left wings of the spread, an opportunity for great happiness will soon be open to him. If the Queen lies in the lower wings of the spread, he will meet a woman who will offer him great comfort.

While the Queen is usually a mature woman, this may be a maturity of mind, not of years. The youthful Querent—regardless of sex—in whose spread the Queen appears, is promised the gift of a satisfying and rewarding love, though not necessarily in the immediate future.

THE JACK OF HEARTS

The Jack of Hearts is the card of romance. Also it is the card of folly and thoughtless abandonment to pleasure.

Where the Jack of Hearts appears, the Querent may expect a carefree interlude between the more serious pressures of life. This may mean an affair of the heart, but not necessarily so. It can represent a happy holiday, pleasant friendships, a round of parties or some other amusing break from the monotony of routine work.

When the Jack of Hearts lies in the middle of the spread, it may serve as a warning to the Querent to take life more seriously. The Jack of Hearts is easily tempted to excesses and tends toward self-indulgence. He is by nature generous and fond of people, so that he must take care lest he become involved in unpleasant situations through his impulse to please others.

If the Jack lies in the inner corner of any of the wings, the indication is that the Querent will meet a person whose gaiety will charm and disarm him. This association may be pleasant, stimulating and even valuable to the Querent, but he should not take the situation too seriously. If there is a romantic interlude, it should be entered into lightheartedly for the Jack of Hearts is likely to be here today and gone tomorrow. When the Jack faces a Spade, especially a Seven or Ten, there is a clear-cut warning of disappointment or heartbreak for the Querent if he dallies too long amid pleasures.

On the other hand, where the Jack of Hearts appears at the end of a wing, the Querent may look forward to a rewarding period of joy which will mark the success of some enterprise for which he has worked long and hard.

THE TEN OF HEARTS

The Ten of Hearts is a messenger and the news which he brings is usually good. The message, however, is likely to be a turbulent one, upsetting routine and raising havoc with carefully laid plans.

A clue to the nature of the message should be found in the cards close to the Ten. A King or Queen on either side of the Ten may mark a reunion with old friends. In the same way, Jacks or Eights indicate meetings with young people, or new friendships. Diamonds indicate that the message will relate to money, while a preponderance of Hearts in the spread augurs marriage, issue, or in the case of older people, grandchildren.

If the Two or Ten of Spades precedes the Ten of Hearts in the spread, the indication is that good news will follow news which was initially bad. Conversely, if the Ten of Spades follows the Ten of Hearts in the spread, the joyous news may prove to be false. If the Two of Spades is in this position, there may be a letdown or minor disappointment after the original elation which the good news has created.

THE NINE OF HEARTS

The Nine of Hearts represents happiness beyond all expectations. If the Querent has made a wish, the Nine of Hearts does not promise fulfilment of this wish as expressed in the Querent's mind. Instead, it represents something greater and more enduring, extending far beyond the realm of the Querent's imagination.

In many ways the Nine of Hearts is the most

joyous card in the pack. But, inherent in the Nine of Hearts is the warning that the happiness may be destroyed by greed, avarice, spite, envy or too great a preoccupation with material matters.

When the Nine of Diamonds appears in the same spread as the Nine of Hearts, the indication is that long-cherished ambitions or life-long aspirations will reach fruition.

When the Nine of Hearts is adjacent to a face card, the indication is that happiness may come through another person or be shared with him. If the Three of Diamonds separates the Nine of Hearts from a face card, there is a warning that the element of jealousy may be present.

When the Nine of Hearts lies in a spread in which Spades predominate, the Querent may find growth, increased stature, maturity and wisdom in the midst of difficulties or hardships. In this case, the Nine of Hearts is a symbol of victory over misfortunes, which will give the Querent strength, insight and recognition of himself as a person capable of facing adversity with courage and generosity.

THE EIGHT OF HEARTS

The Eight of Hearts represents a gift which causes pleasure. Whether the gift is received by the Querent or given by him to another depends upon the place of the card in the spread. The gift is not necessarily material. It may be the gift of love, restored health, spiritual knowledge, wisdom or ease of mind.

Where the Eight of Hearts lies in the middle of the spread, an exchange of gifts is indicated.

When the Eight is in the upper left wing of the spread, the Querent will be the recipient of a gift which will have deep meaning for him if he makes the effort to understand its significance. If he spurns the gift or treats it lightly, his action may be followed by regret, for the gift can be the forerunner of many good things that can come his way.

When the Eight of Hearts appears in the lower left wing of the spread, the gift is much more likely to have intrinsic value and to come from a source which is not intimately connected with the Querent's life.

When the Eight is in the upper right-hand wing, the Querent will be the donor of the gift. If he gives openly and freely, without expectation of material reward, he will receive much gratification from the act. On the other hand, if he is prompted by greed, the gift may backfire and do him injury.

When the Eight is in the lower left wing, the indication is that the Querent will be able to help, or do a service for, a relative stranger. By so doing, he will eventually be amply repaid.

However, a warning should be issued to the Querent that the Eight of Hearts, when badly placed in the spread, can refer to a bribe, either offered or received. Such a gift should be rejected firmly lest it bring disgrace and ultimate tragedy to the recipient.

THE SEVEN OF HEARTS

Traditionally the Seven of Hearts denotes a lover's quarrel. The quarrel may be no more than a tiff which can clear the air for a better understanding between the participants.

The phrase "lover's quarrel" should not be taken too literally. The card may indicate a disagreement between any two people who are devoted to each other, such as husband and wife, mother and daughter, or intimate friends. Where passions are unleashed the quarrel may become serious. The presence of the Nine or Ten of Spades or the Ten of Clubs close to the Seven of Hearts is a danger warning, signalling the Querent to guard his tongue.

Where the Seven of Hearts appears in the middle of the spread, the indication is that the Querent is too trustful, too content to let matters run their own course. He should not take friendships, family intimacies and continued love for granted.

When the Seven of Hearts appears in either left wing of the spread, the indication is that another person has need of the Querent's strength and cherishing. If the card is in the lower left wing, the person dependent upon the Querent may be shy, inarticulate or so in awe of the Querent that he or she is incapable of making his needs known. Because of this, such a person may cloak his affection with sharp words or criticism.

If the Seven of Hearts appears in the right-hand side of the spread, the situation is reversed. The Querent may have a deep affection for or a dependency upon another individual, which he attempts to conceal or to which he gives inadequate thought. In this case the Querent should be warned against carping criticism, nagging or other undesirable means of attracting the attention of the love object. Honest appreciation and frankness of purpose will serve the Querent better than more devious means of securing the rapport which he desires.

THE SIX OF HEARTS

The symbol of the Six of Hearts is a flight of stairs which leads to success, the fulfilment of ambition, or the achievement of enduring love.

The Six of Hearts marks gain, an advance towards a desired goal, but not its immediate accomplishment. Therefore the Querent may feel disappointment at the partial fulfilment of his desires. He should be cautioned against impatience, irritability and a sense of frustration. Should he seek an easier route to the end he desires, he risks total failure.

If the Six of Hearts lies in the middle of the spread, the Querent will be called upon to make a decision in the near future. If this card lies in the upper left wing, his decision will be optional and the Reader should examine the right-hand wing to test the advisability of an alternate route. If the Six of Hearts lies in either of the lower wings, the stairway may lead to a specific opportunity which is to the Querent's advantage although it will have only a temporary effect on his life.

THE FIVE OF HEARTS

The Five of Hearts is a card of disappointment, tears and vain regret. It may mark the end of a love affair or the abandonment of a cherished plan, but the sorrow seldom lies deep. He may grieve briefly but, even as he does so, he cannot be unaware of a sense of relief at his release from a self-imposed bondage.

The Reader should not belittle a sense of loss, especially if the Querent reacts emotionally. Instead, he should aid the Querent in placing the unfortunate incident in correct perspective, so that it will act as a stepping stone towards more enduring interpersonal relationships and sounder judgments in planning for the future.

THE FOUR OF HEARTS

The Four of Hearts offers an opportunity for happiness through work.

Its presence in the spread is indicative of opportunity, rather than the promise of increased pleasure. The rewards are unlikely to be financial, but a route will open by which the Querent can enrich his life through service to others. If the Four of Hearts lies in the middle of the spread, the opportunity is already present. It is probable that initial steps have been taken in this direction.

In some cases the Four of Hearts represents children or very young people. There is an intimation that work with youth groups, community enterprises or school organizations will give deep pleasure to the Querent.

As in most cards, there is a duality or reversal of

meaning. Thus the Four of Hearts may represent happiness through association with elderly people.

Where Diamonds flank the Four this new interest may lead to better business opportunities, increased salary or unexpected gifts. Where there is a preponderance of Clubs in the spread, the road will be open for new and treasured social contacts. If Hearts or face cards are closely linked with the Four of Hearts, new friendships will be established, a sense of added security may develop and there is the possibility of romance.

THE THREE OF HEARTS

The Three of Hearts represents a disappointment in love, a minor setback in one's plans or an error in judgment. The appearance of the Three of Hearts is a warning that the pathway ahead is not straight, that there are pitfalls lying there to trip the unwary.

The Three of Hearts may also warn of self-delusion. The Querent may have a subconscious knowledge that he is handicapping himself or causing himself unhappiness by his reluctance to make changes. If he is indolent, vacillating or indecisive, the difficulties will grow greater until they become an onerous burden.

The lover's quarrel may set things aright. The temporary setback may clear the pathway to greater success.

Where the Three of Hearts leads to the Nine of Hearts it has particular significance. The Querent should be advised to prepare himself to take rapid action to prevent catastrophe. The danger it presents is not so much one of making an error as of drifting into a situation from which it will be increasingly difficult to extricate oneself.

THE TWO OF HEARTS

Traditionally, the Two of Hearts is a love letter or a bit of good news.

Actually this card has far greater significance. It points out the possibility of unexpected pleasure, satisfaction or joy which can be found in the ordinary routine of life.

The Querent should be advised to examine his everyday life to see if he is deriving the maximum values from it. He may be missing opportunities, worthwhile friendships or social success because he is so intent on distant goals that he is oblivious of his immediate surroundings.

If the Two of Hearts lies next to a face card of the opposite sex from the Querent, the intimation is that there is someone at hand who would offer love and devotion if given the chance to do so. If a face card

of the same sex lies next to the Two of Hearts, it may mean that the Querent is overlooking a friendship which could be beneficial to him. If Diamonds flank the Two of Hearts, it should be suggested that the Querent search his surroundings for financial opportunities and promotion in business. Where Clubs predominate in the spread, channels for happier social relations lie open if the Querent will seek them out.

If the Two lies between Hearts, the Querent may be indolent or too preoccupied with the pursuit of pleasure to establish more enduring values.

DIAMONDS

THE ACE OF DIAMONDS

The Ace of Diamonds is commonly thought to represent money. Actually, the Ace of Diamonds may represent magic or wizardry, mathematical knowledge, engineering skill or a bent towards sciences such as astronomy, biology, archeology and especially architecture.

The Ace of Diamonds is not a card of ease, contentment or luxury, as sometimes supposed. It represents an unceasingly restless spirit and is the emblem of intellectual curiosity, energy and a dissatisfaction with life as it is.

At its best the presence of this card can indicate a selfless nobility of spirit dedicated to the welfare of humanity. At the opposite range of possibilities lies the self-seeking individual, clever and ruthless, able to turn every situation to his own advantage.

The Reader should guide the Querent into channels through which the greatest benefits may be derived from his talents. The youthful Querent should be encouraged to explore fields of science about which he is uninformed for he may find in such areas an absorbing lifetime interest.

The female Querent's "magical powers" may lie within the home. By nature she is a skilful organizer and may have the unrecognized capacity to influence others, especially in encouraging and developing the character, personality and skills of the young. She is an excellent teacher, but should be warned against a tendency to stress success instead of genuine accomplishment.

Where the Ace of Diamonds appears prominently in the spread of the adult male Querent, the indication is that he will soon have an opportunity to use his organizational skills to advantage. The "house" which he builds may be a business structure, the reorganization of a department, the amalgamation of companies or advancement of scientific knowledge.

When the Ace of Diamonds appears in the upper left wing of the spread, the Querent should be alerted to keep his eyes open for an opportunity which offers, or appears to offer, high advantage to him. Without this forewarning the opportunity may escape his notice. However, if the Nine of Spades, Ten of Spades or Seven of Spades lies to the left of the Ace of Diamonds, he should be advised to proceed slowly lest some precipitate action on his part bring about a catastrophe.

When the Ace of Diamonds appears on the upper right wing of the spread, the indication is that the Querent has either already embarked on some venturous plan or will do so shortly. In such case, the other cards on the wing should be examined with care. If the Two of Spades lies left of the Ace of Diamonds, there is a warning of delay. If the Ten of Spades lies to the right of the Ace of Diamonds, the Querent should be advised to consider other patterns of procedure. On the other hand, if Hearts or Clubs lie in close juxtaposition to the Ace of Diamonds, the promise is that some plan will have a happy and fruitful issue.

The Querent who seizes the opportunities offered by the Ace may find his life patterns changed. Usually these opportunities include financial benefits. However, embracing them may mean the sacrifice of values which, in the long run, are more deeply cherished.

THE KING OF DIAMONDS

The King of Diamonds represents a tremendously complex man, subtle, artistic, highly intelligent, with many hidden facets to his personality. He is prone to quick temper, though he may conceal this to forward his own ends.

This man is a creator. He is possessed of a driving, restless force that will give him no peace but which acts as a spur so that he is constantly seeking some fresh achievement. He is a skilled organizer, quick to see values especially in such fields as art, the theatre, literature, advertising or business enterprises which require vision and quick grasp of ambitious plans. His failings are lack of tact, disinterest in detail, impatience and a tendency to underestimate others.

He is mercurial in temperament. He can be suave, ingratiating and highly attractive to women. However, he is likely to be cursed with a streak of cruelty, to ride roughshod over those who stand in his way. When he is in the throes of some creative passion, he will be completely absorbed, seemingly indifferent or even callous in his relationship to his associates and even his family. Despite this he has a strong sense of family unity, especially if it concerns his children.

He is a master of subtlety, indirection and intrigue, but capable of generous gestures and lofty ideals. Despite his appearance of aggressiveness, he can be easily hurt and he craves acceptance and a circle of warm friends. His moods may shift with lightning speed. Elation may be followed by dark despair and overpowering depression. Beneath his external self-confidence is self-doubt and fear of inadequacy. He badly needs someone to bolster his ego and a confidante to whom he can impart his soaring ambitions. While he may lash out at such a person in a fit of anger or frustration, he will later be contrite and will seek to make redress with exaggerated praise, expensive gifts, cajolery or elaborate gestures.

He is a natural born actor, though he rarely is attracted to the stage because he dislikes to take direction. He prefers the world as his theatre and throws himself into rôle after rôle. He is likely to be a man of excesses and should be chary of overeating, drugs, alcohol and other stimulants.

Where the King of Diamonds appears in the middle of the spread of the male Querent, he should be cautioned to direct his talents into constructive channels, to guard his temper, to establish loyal friendships and to avoid excesses and a tendency to try to move ahead too rapidly. He may find the ideal helpmate in the Queen of Spades whose outer calm, intuitive powers and recognition of artistic leanings in others will give him ballast in his periods of discouragement and will add to his sense of accomplishment when he has been successful. However, he is likely to prefer the adoring Queen of Hearts of whom he may soon tire, or the more frivolous Queen of Clubs who is less likely to offer him the stability which he requires.

The female Querent who finds the King of Diamonds in the middle of the spread, is either in close contact with a many-talented and complex man, or will meet such a man in the near future. It may be that the presence of this card is a warning that she has not recognized the soaring aspirations, the dreams, the hidden skills and latent talents of a husband, son, suitor or companion.

When this card is in the upper left-hand wing, the female Querent may have a choice of linking herself to the King of Diamonds or of keeping clear of him. Does she wish to lead a turbulent, explosive life in which she must subjugate her own personality to that of another?

If the Querent is male and the King of Diamonds lies in the upper wings of the spread, the indication is of a close alliance between the Querent and a man of mercurial temperament. This may be a fruitful relationship and one filled with promise, but the Querent should be warned not to be bedazzled by his associate's brilliance. He must keep his own personality and integrity intact.

The King of Diamonds, when found in the lower wings of the spread, may spell opportunity or disaster. The other cards in the spread should provide the clues as to what the King of Diamonds may have to offer and whether or not it should be accepted.

When the King of Diamonds appears in these lower wings, he will enter the Querent's life for a brief period of time and then depart. If the Querent is a woman, she will not be able to hold this man, no matter how hard she may try. If the Querent is a man, he should beware of any impulsive action which may destroy the foundations of his business or his social or family life.

THE QUEEN OF DIAMONDS

The Queen of Diamonds is a fiercely passionate woman. She has great drive and energy. Her restless mind is constantly filled with plans, schemes, devices for making money, adding to her social prestige or controlling the destinies of others.

She is a woman who gets things done. The Queen of Diamonds can be an invaluable friend. With her agile mind, her indomitable spirit, her fierce loyalties, she is capable of directing those about her into constructive channels, to spur and goad them to success. She is an expert organizer, often interested in charity, social reforms or politics. She is aggressive and strongly partisan. She comes to the assistance of those in whom she believes with unstinting self-sacrifice.

She is shrewd and clever, but her judgments are frequently in error. Unless her materialism is leavened with idealism, she may waste her talents on petty details and schemes. While capable of grandiose visions, she may become involved in bickering, spite and gossip. She must avoid malice if the richness of her personality is to reach fruition. She is in danger of being side-tracked from high objectives by her resentment of criticism, personal dislikes or undue pride.

She will have to combat her quick temper, her passionate nature, her tendency to act too quickly and to have too many interests. She has an affinity for flame-red, and like the flame she can bring life into quick being, but she can also destroy. Unless she takes care, she may burn herself out, so that the declining years of her life will be empty. However, this need not be so. If she establishes enduring relationships and worthy objectives, she can accumulate interests which will give her lifelong pleasure.

The Queen of Diamonds is inimical to the Queen of Spades. Where both Queens appear in the spread, there is likely to be a clash of wills. Because the Queen of Spades is more subtle and intuitive, she is likely to come out the victor. When such a quarrel appears in the offing, the Queen of Diamonds would do well to guard her temper and humble her pride in order to achieve her ends.

There is an affinity between the Queen of Diamonds and the King of Clubs. She can bring out his best points, help him bring his dreams to fruition, give him practical guidance and assistance which will counterbalance his tendency towards impracticality.

When the Queen of Diamonds appears in the middle of the spread of a female Querent, it is likely to indicate her own personality. If the spread contains a preponderance of Clubs, the indication is that the Querent tends to use her skills well and for the benefit of others. Where there is a preponderance of Diamonds, there is danger of a too great preoccupation with money or other personal ambitions which may in the end impoverish her life. A preponderance of Hearts indicates an underlying gaiety and good will. Spades may indicate wasteful quarrels and a failure to achieve a maximum happiness because of involvement in matters of relatively small importance.

The male Querent who finds the Queen of Diamonds in his spread will be in contact with a woman of strong personality. She may be an invaluable ally, but she must be treated with consideration. She will be easily hurt, far more sensitive than she appears and, if she is offended, she can turn into a ruthless enemy whose skills may be employed to destroy him. The man who chooses the Queen of Diamonds for a wife cannot expect a calm or peaceful life, but he will rarely be bored.

Where the Queen of Diamonds appears in the outer wings of the spread, she is likely to be a woman whom the Querent will meet and who may play a significant rôle in his life. In such a case, the Querent should be advised not to offend this woman. She can be of great assistance in helping him achieve coveted goals and ambitions. But, if her anger is aroused, she may ply her skills to the Querent's disadvantage. When the Queen of Diamonds is in a wing and flanked by either the Nine or Ten of Spades, the Querent is warned of entanglement with a woman who will bring him sorrow or disgrace. When the Queen of Diamonds is flanked by the Nine of Diamonds or the Nine of Hearts, the indication is that the cultivation of a woman to whom the Querent is not quickly attracted may bring about the success of cherished plans or unexpected happiness.

THE JACK OF DIAMONDS

The Jack of Diamonds represents an individual who is at the crossroads of life. If the card appears in the middle of the spread this person may be the Querent or another individual who is, or will shortly be, dependent upon him for advice or guidance.

While the Jack of Diamonds is usually thought of as a young person, this is not necessarily so. However, he or she will be an individual torn with inner conflict, temporarily indecisive, whose outer appearance may be misleading.

This person may be of either sex. Outwardly he may appear brash, self-assertive or overconfident, but inwardly he is seeking new patterns of life.

This is a person of considerable talent who needs warm friendship and spiritual guidance, but who is likely to react to criticism by flying into a temper or rejecting the individual whom he feels misunderstands him. He is given to outwardly thoughtless actions, some of which may seem foolhardy or even cruel.

His position is a precarious one. He can expect to meet outspoken antagonism and even persecution which may crush his spirit and deprive the world of the good he may do.

Any attempt to force him into conventional patterns will be destructive. However, he can be directed towards more concrete goals and a balance which will help him to achieve his ambitions.

THE TEN OF DIAMONDS

The Ten of Diamonds warns of too great a preoccupation with making money or seeking material success at the expense of spiritual neglect. It may also advise change, not so much of place, but of attitudes. The Querent may be bogged down by boredom, routine, indifference or a lassitude of the spirits. He may feel that circumstances hem him in.

Inherent in the Ten of Diamonds is the promise of a richer and more rewarding future if the Querent will raise his eyes toward wider horizons. The Ten of Diamonds offers a choice of a journey over land or over water. This is not to be accepted in too literal a sense, although it often indicates an opportunity to travel. Plodding over land represents financial gain, economic security and acceptance of a limited life, and travel by water symbolizes purity of thought and inner vision.

When the Ten of Diamonds appears in the middle of the spread, there is an indication of world-weariness, along with an indication that a richer life is at hand.

On the lower wings of the spread, the Ten of Diamonds is likely to mean a pleasurable interlude from everyday living. This may come about through unexpected money which will ease economic worries, through travel or from an experience which will create new areas of interest.

THE NINE OF DIAMONDS

The Nine of Diamonds is a card of conflicting meanings. It has been associated with the moon whose pale light masks the truth and gives answers which, while literally true, are misleading.

Where the Querent approaches the ancient symbols which the cards depict with respect, and his wishes conform to acceptable patterns of arcane law, no misdirection will occur. The truth will lie in the spread. The Nine of Diamonds gives cognizance to the wish and indicates that in some degree it will be fulfilled. However, it does not promise that this will come about in the pattern which the Querent foresees, nor does it guarantee that the wish will bring satisfaction or happiness to the Querent.

If the Nine of Diamonds lies in the middle, the indication may be that the wish is either pressing, or of supreme importance to the Querent. If it lies in the upper right wing, the indication is that the wish will be fulfilled in the natural course of events. If it lies in the upper left-hand wing, the fulfilment of the wish is possible if the Querent will reject his current pattern of life. If it appears in the lower left-hand wing, the wish is likely to be incidental to more important factors in the Querent's life. If it is on the lower right-hand wing, outside forces beyond the Querent's control will be the decisive factors. If the Nine of Diamonds lies on the outer edges of the spread, the indication is that the wish will eventually be fulfilled but only after many delays or disappointments.

Where both the Nine of Diamonds and the Nine

of Hearts appear in the spread, there is a promise of happiness and good fortune which will extend far beyond the wish.

THE EIGHT OF DIAMONDS

The Eight of Diamonds is a card of balance, indicating a combination of skill in financial affairs and a spiritual insight which will prevent undue stress upon material success. This card represents a practical point of view in which all theories are weighed and tested objectively. It is a card of moderation, tolerance and balanced strength.

Where the Eight of Diamonds appears in the middle of the spread, it is likely to indicate the character and personality of the Querent. He may be strongly attracted to chemistry or other work which involves laboratory experiments. He can also be invaluable in government service or in executive posts in which careful decisions must be weighed. The female Querent should be capable in family budgeting, a thoughtful mother and considerate wife.

When the Eight of Diamonds appears in the upper wings of the spread, the indication is that a situation will arise in which careful judgments should be made. There is a warning to beware of impetuosity and not to take things at face value. If the Eight of Diamonds lies in juxtaposition to a face card, the indication is that it will be advisable to consult some authoritative person and to obtain additional information before some decision is rendered.

If the Eight of Diamonds occurs in a spread in which Diamonds predominate, the Querent should be warned against making judgments solely for monetary reasons lest he suffer from loss of more enduring values if he does. Where the Nine or Ten of Spades follows the Eight of Diamonds, there is a possibility that the Querent will be tempted into bad investments by the promise of quick wealth.

The presence of Clubs in proximity to the Eight of Diamonds indicates steady gain, tranquillity and the absence of pressing economic problems.

THE SEVEN OF DIAMONDS

The Seven of Diamonds is often a card of distress. Usually it involves finances although it may relate to domestic or business situations in which monetary matters are of secondary importance.

When the Seven of Diamonds lies in the middle of the spread it may represent a problem which casts a shadow over the Querent's life and is preventing his progress towards the goals he desires. It may be that the problem is not as difficult of solution as it appears. The nature of the problem will be suggested by the remaining cards in the spread.

Frequently the Querent is voluble in his desire to discuss his problem and presses the Reader for direct answers. When this occurs, the Reader should draw attention to the strong cards in the spread, those that indicate qualities such as generosity, courage in the face of adversity, the capacity to form friendships, etc.

Where the Seven of Diamonds appears on the upper wings of the spread, the indication is that a distressing situation may arise, but that it can be avoided or minimized if the Querent recognizes it in time. If the Seven of Diamonds is found in the lower wings of the spread, the problem may involve the Querent only indirectly. For instance, misfortune may befall a friend or circumstances may cause disturbances in his employment, his social activities or his business interests.

Inherent in the Seven of Diamonds is the possibility of advantageous solution. This card does not mark catastrophe, but a problem and the need to chart a course of action.

THE SIX OF DIAMONDS

The Six of Diamonds is a card of well-being, physical comfort and economic security. When it lies in the middle of the spread, it may emphasize the importance of these things to the Querent.

Frequently the appearance of the Six of Diamonds in the spread offers the Querent a choice between moderate financial well-being accompanied by security and ease of mind, or a more adventurous road which may be studded with pitfalls and uncertainties. This is particularly true if the Six of Diamonds is placed at the juncture of a wing.

If either of the upper wings shows routes leading to marked success or to misfortune, the Querent should be apprised of this. If the Six of Diamonds lies at the extreme end of the upper right wing, the indication is that if he continues on the route he is following, he will achieve satisfying results. If the Six of Diamonds lies at the extreme of the upper left wing, the indication is that an opportunity for change will arise which, if he so desires, may reward him with a calm, secure and comfortable life.

When the Six of Diamonds appears in the lower wings of the spread, the indication is that the Querent should be alert to take advantage of a situation which can be turned to his benefit. This may be a business deal which brings him a handsome profit, the sale of property or a chance episode which can bring him considerable pleasure. If a face card flanks the Six of Diamonds, it indicates that such an opportunity may arise through his association with an individual whom the face card depicts.

In the Six of Diamonds lies the suggestion that the benefits offered may come about through unpredictable sources, such as the seemingly chance meeting with an old friend, a social gathering, a call made through kindness.

THE FIVE OF DIAMONDS

The Five of Diamonds forecasts a clash of wills. This is not to be interpreted as a quarrel, a lover's spat or an enduring feud. It may be a conflict of spiritual forces in which two people, closely united, accept opposing standards of values and seek different patterns in their futures. Outwardly the two people may be in accord, but their ambitions, their dreams of the future and their moral judgments set them apart.

This may occur in a husband-wife relationship, a business partnership or in situations relating to parent and child. Money may be involved, but this is not the crux of the conflict and it should not be permitted to obscure more important issues.

Sometimes, especially when the Five of Diamonds appears in the middle of the spread, there is an indication that the warring factors lie within the Querent. He may have two sets of conflicting moral codes or be torn with indecision between two patterns of living.

Inherent in the Five of Diamonds is the power to adapt, to reach a state of concord, so that the two lives can flow in harmony, each with the other. This does not necessitate compromise. The misunderstanding may be, to a large extent, the result of a failure to communicate with those close to him.

THE FOUR OF DIAMONDS

The Four of Diamonds betokens concrete, measurable success in terms of finances, business or professional status. This is not a card of sudden fortune, good luck or sweeping changes. Instead it marks an advance earned by merit or hard work. This forward step may seem to have little importance in itself, but it will lay a foundation on which a series of other advances may be laid. The Querent may be inclined to dismiss his accomplishment as trifling, but actually it can bring him deeper satisfaction than he would achieve through more rapid progress towards his goals.

THE THREE OF DIAMONDS

The Three of Diamonds often represents a legal document such as a contract, a will, a lease, or papers related to sale or purchase of property. At times it may represent a dispute over finances, wherein no legal documents are involved. It can also denote legal contracts which are not directly related to finances, such as marriage, divorce, adoption or other legal procedures.

While the Three of Diamonds serves notice of financial or legal entanglement, in itself, it does not forecast the outcome. The card which lies just beyond the Three of Diamonds will give a clue to the conclusion of the proceedings. The Five of Diamonds in this position warns against acrimony and bitterness. The Seven of Diamonds indicates a solution to the situation which will be immediately displeasing to the Querent, but one which may serve his ends better than he thinks. The Nine of Diamonds lying beside the Three indicates that, while the Querent succeeds in his objectives, he may pay too heavy a price in achieving his ends. The Nine of Hearts promises happy issue from the contract. Minor Hearts indicate that the contract will be made in a friendly fashion, without dispute. Minor Clubs indicate that the contract will deal with business and offer increased opportunities to the Querent.

If small Diamonds flank the Three of Diamonds, the Querent should be warned of placing too much emphasis on details of finances. Because of his preoccupation with a lawsuit or dispute over money, he may lose opportunities of greater importance. In this case, the wings of the spread should be studied for alternate routes through which petty annoyances may be avoided.

THE TWO OF DIAMONDS

The Two of Diamonds augurs an unexpected communication concerning money or business. Usually it is a promise of a pleasant, though minor, surprise. The communication may contain a gift, a transfer of property, a legacy or an opportunity for a slightly better position. When blocked in by Spades, the message may indicate a happy surprise in the midst of adversity.

When the Two of Diamonds appears in any of the wings, it usually marks an isolated instance unrelated to the major influences in the Querent's life.

When prominent in the spread, it may mean that a relatively small expenditure of money can give permanent pleasure to the Querent, and he should be advised to examine the possibilities. Money spent in travel, education, hobbies, club membership, or in any other way that will broaden the horizons of the Querent, may enrich his life far beyond his expectations.

CLUBS

THE ACE OF CLUBS

The Ace of Clubs is a card of talent. It tells of high hopes and ambitions and denotes strong passions, imagination, energy and the power to communicate with others.

When centrally located in the spread, it intimates that the Querent has been given great gifts of artistic creation, intuitive power, forces that spring not only from the mind but also from mystic sources. His imagination will be vivid and he will have the power to express his images through authorship in the larger sense, which may include communication through the written word, art, music, the ministry and a variety of other channels.

However, the Ace of Clubs also warns of the possibility of chaos. Too many drives may nullify one another, preventing the success of any. Keenness of mind, sharp perceptions and vividness of imagery may fail to serve useful purposes unless they can be given concrete shape. For these reasons, the Querent should be urged to organize his activities and to perfect his plans lest he become a dabbler in the arts instead of a creative artist.

Indications are that the Querent who finds this card in his spread will enjoy travel, quick changes and variety, and that he will be deeply moved by beauty. Whether he controls these shifting forces or lets himself be carried willy-nilly through life depends upon the character and personality of the Querent.

The Reader should be guided in his advice to the Querent by the cards surrounding the Ace of Clubs. Where Hearts predominate in the spread, there is a warning of hedonism and a suggestion that the Querent may not have developed his talents because of his pleasures in daily living. Where Clubs dominate the spread, an interest and enjoyment in people and social activities may prevent full development of artistic skills. Diamonds indicate that material rewards may be gained by the exercise of latent talents. Spades may warn that the Querent is too easily discouraged by minor setbacks. A well-balanced spread promises increased pleasure and spiralling rewards through creative activity.

THE KING OF CLUBS

The King of Clubs represents a man of wide and diversified interests, outwardly sociable, but inwardly secretive and reserved. He may appear cynical, autocratic, harsh, or even unfeeling but, in his heart, he is a crusader, crying out against injustice and eager to help his fellow men.

This man will have many talents, some of which he may have developed secretly. Such a man will find routine employment or conducting a business boring and confining, but he may deliberately choose such work in order that his freedom be unencumbered during his leisure hours. He may even be very successful in enterprises which are distasteful to him, provided he has other interests to satisfy his intellectual curiosity and surplus energies.

The King of Clubs is often a lonely man. The sympathetic understanding of a woman will be vital to his happiness, but he will have difficulty in making his wants known. He is easily discouraged in matters of romance and, in consequence, often plays the passive rôle. He is susceptible to flattery and, although he will not admit it, tends to place a woman on a pedestal.

There is a natural affinity between the Queen of Diamonds and the King of Clubs. In her shrewdness, the Queen of Diamonds will bring out a man's good points and exploit his talents. Her restless drive will incite him to greater activity and her determination to live life fully will act as a challenge to his ingenuity and creative skill.

On the other hand, the Queen of Spades is inimical the King of Clubs. Her haughty manner and concealed passions will deter him from the use of his talents. Where such a mismating occurs, both partners will withdraw to their inner recesses until no genuine contact exists between them.

When the King of Clubs appears in the middle of the spread of a male Querent, the indication is that it represents his own character and personality. When this card appears in the wings, it is more likely to represent a close friend, relative or business associate of the Querent.

When the King of Clubs appears in the middle of the spread of a female Querent, the indication is that such a man is playing a dominant rôle in her life. On the wings, the King of Clubs is likely to represent a man who will be significant in her life, but to a lesser degree.

A spread which includes both the King of Clubs and the Queen of Spades is likely to augur a broken home, domestic unhappiness or a marital rift. This will be intensified if cards which designate quarrels or misfortunes lie between these two face cards.

THE QUEEN OF CLUBS

The Queen of Clubs possesses the social graces. She will command and beguile the hearts of men, but none will truly understand her. She will be warm, friendly, charming, an excellent companion but, beneath her light manner, is a calculating mind, an earthiness, a quality of shrewdness in matters pertaining to her own interests.

She may appear flirtatious, light-hearted and giddy, but much of this is a mask. She is sensitive, easily hurt and sometimes petulant. She can be moved to quick compassion, but her anger may flare up unexpectedly and seemingly without reason. She will take quick likes and dislikes. On occasion she may conduct herself outrageously but she will soon be contrite.

She will be fond of social activities, dancing, games, travel and parties. She will be vain of her appearance, interested in clothing and luxuries. But despite her gaiety and laughter, there will be an underlying sadness that may show itself in moodiness, tears or tantrums.

She will love beauty, but her artistic judgments may not always be sound. She will talk easily and well, but her cleverness may be paper thin. She establishes friendships with great ease, but often these do not endure. Admiration is important to her; she enjoys being the focus of attention and responds eagerly to flattery. But she cannot be deluded easily. She sizes men up quickly and, while she may enjoy a romantic interlude, her decisions are based on practicalities.

The man who falls in love with the Queen of Clubs may feel that he is following a will-o'-the-wisp. Her moods are so given to fluctuation that she may appear to be many women rolled into one.

In her relationship with other women, the Queen of Clubs tends to seek out her own kind. Such friendships tend to be brief and filled with petty quarrels. However, the Queen of Clubs and the Queen of Hearts have an affinity for each other. The Queen of Hearts will offer absolute devotion while the Queen of Clubs will bring excitement, gaiety and diversity into their lives. The Queen of Clubs and the Queen of Spades are instinctive enemies. The presence of both cards in the spread indicates conflict in which the Queen of Spades, with her greater subtlety and intuition is likely to emerge victorious.

When the Queen of Clubs lies in the middle of the spread of the female Querent, the card may be either a representation of her personality or the problems which she will meet. If another Queen or Jack also lies in the middle of the spread, the indication is that the personality of the Queen of Clubs will be moderated by the characteristics of the second card.

When the male Querent finds the Queen of Clubs in the middle of his spread, a woman with many of these character traits will play a dominant part in his life.

When the Queen of Clubs appears in the lower right wing of the spread of either male or female Querent, the indication is that such a woman will soon be involved in his or her affairs. If the Queen of Clubs is in the upper left-hand spread, the Querent may be forced into some decision in regard to such a woman. The remaining cards in the wing may guide him to wise judgment as to the rôle she should be permitted to play.

When the Queen of Clubs appears in the lower wings of the spread, there is a warning that a situation may arise in which appearances are deceptive. The Querent should be advised to avoid snap judgments and not to be influenced by personality until the facts in the case have been thoroughly examined.

When the Nine of Hearts lies beside the Queen of Clubs, the indication is that such a woman will bring great joy into the Querent's life.

THE JACK OF CLUBS

The Jack of Clubs usually represents a young or older innocent person who is hard-working, honest and sincere. This card rarely represents the Querent but someone who is devoted to him. To determine the sex of the Jack of Clubs, the Reader should follow the direction of the eyes portrayed in the card. If the eyes point toward the middle of the spread, the young person will be of the opposite sex to the Querent. If the eyes point away from the middle of the spread, the person will be of the Querent's own sex.

There is a suggestion that the Querent may underestimate the Jack of Clubs, considering him naive, dull or lacking in gaiety. In the eyes of the female Querent, the Jack may appear in the guise of a lacklustre suitor or unprepossessing female friend. For the male Querent, the Jack may be a girl whom he knows well but whom he has not considered in a romantic light; or a steady, reliable male companion whom he takes for granted.

The Jack of Clubs may act as a rein on the Querent, checking his impulsive actions and guiding him towards his highest possible achievement. As a whole, the Jack of Clubs counsels wisely and is rich in common sense. The Jack of Clubs is frequently lacking in tact. His natural honesty prevents him from the use of guile or subterfuge.

The presence of the Jack of Clubs in the spread is an indication that there is someone close to the Querent whom he does not fully appreciate. This person will promote the Querent's interests and work without remittance or expectation of reward to help him in the attainment of his ambitions.

THE TEN OF CLUBS

The Ten of Clubs takes the form of a youth, inexperienced, with a mind still filled with wonder at the earth's miracles. In this youth will be an admixture of lofty ambitions, uncertainty, an eagerness to experience life and a withdrawal from harsh realities. Because his character and personality are not fully formed, he will appear a mass of contradictions.

This youth does not represent the Querent but a person through whom the Querent may experience the fluctuating joys and sorrows of the young. Where the Querent has reached maturity, the youth may be a protégé, son or daughter, or even a grandchild. In the youthful Querent, the Ten of Clubs may represent a friend whose life is linked with his.

Through this youth, the Querent may enter into a whole new set of experiences, acquire fresh interests and re-awaken dormant ambitions and ideals. His life will be enriched but not all will be clear sailing. Misunderstandings will arise and clashes of personality. The relationship may appear one-sided yet, if this is so, it represents a failure on the part of the Querent.

The older Querent should be cautioned not to attempt to remake the youth into his own image but to respect the system of trial and error through which the youth seeks to secure dominion over himself.

The Ten of Clubs is symbolized by a figure with one arm reaching back to the past, the other stretching into the future. The indication is of a new life, built upon the foundation of the old, which will form a continuity between youth and the years which lie ahead.

THE NINE OF CLUBS

The Nine of Clubs represents satisfaction or success in work. It is also indicative of emotional adjustment, stability and progress. Where the Nine of Diamonds appears in the same spread, financial rewards are promised. If the Querent works in the field of arts, the indication is of an important sale or contract. If he is in business, this may be a promotion, or a better

position. When the Nine of Hearts appears in the same spread, the Nine of Clubs may represent recognition, acclaim or fame. The promise is happiness through achievement. Where the Nine of Spades appears with the Nine of Clubs, success is promised after many setbacks, strife and the threat of defeat.

When the Nine of Clubs appears in the upper left-hand wing of the spread, such success will depend on the immediate actions of the Querent.

In the lower wings of the spread, the promised success is more localized, indicating a specific situation which can be used to his benefit and through which he may win financial rewards, fame or recognition.

The cards in the same row as the Nine of Clubs should give clues as to the nature of the enterprise, the people who may be involved, the obstacles which may have to be overcome and situations which will assist the Querent in achieving the ends he seeks.

THE EIGHT OF CLUBS

The Eight of Clubs is a card of balance, harmony and quiet delight. It indicates a questing spirit in search of beauty which may be found in such simple things as flowers, sunsets, books or friends. This is the card of the gentle dreamer but it represents only one aspect, perhaps a hidden one, of the Querent's personality. This is not a card of social detachment or financial incompetence. On the contrary, it suggests a clear recognition of values but, at the same time, it indicates a growing inclination to sacrifice material comfort for the pleasures of the mind and soul. The Querent who finds the Eight of Clubs in his spread is fortunate. He possesses inner qualities which will guard him from many of life's vicissitudes.

The Eight of Clubs holds a promise of a happiness that will increase with the years. Its presence in the middle of the spread may bring into focus the Querent's need to rely on these inner forces. This holds especially true if Diamonds dominate the spread, for this is a warning that financial or business concerns may usurp the Querent's time to a point where the full appreciation of life's beauty is blunted.

THE SEVEN OF CLUBS

The Seven of Clubs warns of illusionary success, unstable effort and plans that may topple over backwards at the last moment because of carelessness, indifference or the too early assumption that all is well.

When the Seven of Clubs appears in the upper left wing of the spread, it indicates that some goal sought by the Querent is attainable but that he must exert vigilance, scrupulous care and unceasing energy in the enterprise.

In the upper right wing of the spread, the Seven of Clubs indicates that the Querent is in danger of suffering a loss through default or neglect.

The Seven of Clubs bespeaks high aspirations, but when it appears in the middle of the spread it may indicate weakness on the part of the Querent in implementing his ambitions. There is an indication that he starts many enterprises but does not follow through. The card warns him that apparent success must be bolstered by hard work or his efforts may be destroyed.

In the lower wings, the Seven of Clubs is more likely to relate to a specific situation than to the general attitude of the Querent. In conjunction with a face card, it may warn of the carelessness or indifference of associates or employees.

When the Seven of Clubs lies between Hearts, the suggestion is that business may be neglected for pleasure. If it lies between Diamonds, the Querent's security may be in the process of being undermined by financial chicanery or jealousy.

The Querent should be warned against disclosing plans indiscriminately to others and especially against announcing the success of his plans prematurely. His optimism may cause him unnecessary failure and exaggerate the blows of misfortune.

THE SIX OF CLUBS

The Six of Clubs speaks of opportunities for a burgeoning social life. Often it is referred to as the card of dancing and merriment but it does not represent thoughtless gaiety. The pleasures which it promises are partly of the mind and spirit, which can alter the Querent's outlook and change his life.

Usually the Six of Clubs is a card of good fortune in which spiralling social prestige brings with it other advantages such as financial benefits, increased security and the possibility of love.

If the Ten of Spades, the Two of Spades, or the Five of Diamonds lies beside the Six of Clubs, care should be taken to establish a proper balance between the quest for pleasure and the more serious aspects of life in order that they may be blended into a harmonious whole.

THE FIVE OF CLUBS

The Five of Clubs warns that care must be taken to avoid a rift between old friends. This is not a lover's tiff or a disagreement between husband and wife. The quarrel is much more likely to be between the Querent and a person of his own sex, unless a face card representing the opposite sex lies next to the Five of Clubs.

This card symbolizes rivalry, competition, strife and jealousy. Should the Five of Clubs appear in the middle of the spread, the Querent may find hidden hostilities among his associates which he does not suspect.

If the Five of Clubs appears on the upper wings of the spread, the quarrel is one which can be avoided. If it appears on the lower wings of the spread, the quarrel is likely to relate to a specific matter. In this case, the ill will of another, not necessarily an intimate, may cause the Querent to be disappointed in some project of a social nature which is of importance to him. In the lower left wing, this lack of success may spring from a set of circumstances for which no one individual is responsible.

THE FOUR OF CLUBS

The Four of Clubs is a card of strengthening friendships and increased social capacities. It suggests that the Querent is held in warm affection and high regard by those about him but that he is not fully aware of this.

There is a hint that the Querent may feel forlorn or abandoned, but, if so, his loneliness is self-imposed. The Querent should be advised that open friendliness on his part, together with a kindly interest in those about him, may open up gates to more rewarding social activities.

There is a suggestion that the Querent under-estimates himself and that he is capable of inspiring unexpected depths of friendship and of being deemed worthy of loyalties.

THE THREE OF CLUBS

The Three of Clubs indicates an unpleasant social episode. This may be a snub, a slight or a bit of malicious gossip. In itself, such an incident is unlikely to be important but the presence of the card in the spread, especially in a major position, is a warning to the Querent that his reaction to this unpleasantness may be out of proportion to the original harm done.

The slight may be unintentional or the gossip exaggerated as it is relayed to him. Particular care should be taken if Hearts lie at one side of the Three of Clubs and Spades at the other. Here a choice is indicated, showing that restraint and generosity will lead to a happy conclusion, while anger and unrestrained passions can inflame a minor unpleasantness until it threatens the Querent's happiness.

THE TWO OF CLUBS

The Two of Clubs represents a social invitation. This may be a bid to a club, an invitation to a social gathering or even a dinner engagement. On the surface this invitation may seem trifling, but acceptance of the invitation will play an unexpectedly important rôle in the Querent's life. When face cards appear close to the Two of Clubs, the indication is that this invitation will lead to new friendships. If a face card representing an individual of the opposite sex from the Querent lies directly above or below the Two of Clubs, there is a promise of romantic attachment.

If the Two of Clubs lies in a spread in which Diamonds predominate, the acceptance of this invitation promises financial rewards. Should the Ten of Spades block the path of the Two of Clubs, the Querent should be warned that the acceptance of the invitation may have unpleasant results and that refusal may be advisable. When Hearts predominate in the spread, the Two of Clubs suggests that this invitation will open a path to many things which the Querent has long desired. The presence of other Clubs close to the Two hints at gaiety, pleasure and social activity which result from the acceptance of the casual invitation.

THREE AND FOUR OF A KIND

When pairs of cards appear in the spread, there is usually little significance except that the importance of each card may be magnified to some degree by the presence of the other. However, when three or four cards of the same numerical value appear in the spread, a specific meaning may be attached beyond the significance of the individual cards, as follows.

4 Aces=Great power and force, dynamic action, radical changes.

3 Aces=Opportunities, movement, fresh interests, success beyond expectation in some enterprise.
(a) Lacking the Ace of Spades, these interests promise great pleasure, new friends, joy without regret.
(b) Lacking the Ace of Hearts, these activities do not relate to love or domesticity.
(c) Lacking the Ace of Diamonds, these activities will relate in a minor degree to business or finance.
(d) Lacking the Ace of Clubs, these activities will affect the Querent's social life very little.

4 Kings=For male Querent: New associations, an enlarged circle of friends or business acquaintances, prizes, respect, fresh responsibilities.
For female Querent: New and involved relationships with men, possibilities of domestic entanglements, jealousies.

3 Kings=For male Querent: Fresh business contacts, male pleasures. With three rather than four Kings: less likelihood of unpleasant involvements or burdensome duties, greater promise of enjoyment and increased success.
For female Querent: An enlarged circle of male friends, possibilities of romantic attachment, a heightened awareness of her own femininity. With three rather than four Kings: less likelihood of quarrels, jealousies and unpleasant entanglements; greater promise of permanent pleasure in new friends.

4 Queens=For male Querent: A situation which may be embarrassing, comic or even ribald. A suggestion that he will be involved in intense jealousies and he should be advised against taking himself too seriously. He may be torn by conflicting loyalties but can be saved by a sense of humor in regard to his own attraction for women.
For female Querent: Gossip. A warning that her affairs are a focus of interest among other women. She should be advised to treat what may appear as undue interference from friends with lightness and good humor for, if she is hurt by idle talk, she may cause herself great unhappiness.

3 Queens = Meetings with important people. Whether male or female, Querent should be advised to cultivate new acquaintances among the women he or she shall meet in the near future, for these contacts will be richly rewarding. Also an implicit warning that the virtues of these women will not be quickly recognizable, but through sincere interest in them as persons Querent can reap the rich rewards of loyalties they are willing to give.

4 Jacks=Association with young people, the rapid approach of unexpected situations involving youth.

3 Jacks=Correspondence, news, messages of various kinds.
(a) Lacking the Jack of Spades, the news will be altogether pleasant and joyful.
(b) Lacking the Jack of Hearts, the news will not relate to love or family.
(c) Lacking the Jack of Diamonds, the news will not relate to finances.
(d) Lacking the Jack of Clubs, the news will not alter the Querent's social life.

4 Tens=The Tens represent doors. The indication is that old patterns of life will close and new

patterns open. Querent is advised to adjust to different ways of life, to take advantage of fresh opportunities.

3 Tens=The meaning is the same as with four Tens but to a lesser degree.

(a) If the Ten of Spades is missing: no unhappiness in the loss of old friendships or familiar ways.

(b) If the Ten of Hearts is missing: no radical change in home or family.

(c) If the Ten of Diamonds is missing: no radical alteration of Querent's business or finances.

(d) If the Ten of Clubs is missing: no loss of friends or social activities.

4 Nines=The fulfilment of long-cherished dreams, hopes, ambitions, but a warning that this fulfilment may not bring the happiness expected. Querent should guard himself against unexpected disappointments.

3 Nines=Happiness coming from unexpected sources; wishes fulfilled. Perhaps a turn of fate which seems to threaten disaster will ironically end in pleasure and success.

4 Eights=Balance and adjustment in daily life, calm pleasure; a blending of material comfort and spiritual insight.

3 Eights=An increased capacity to deal with difficulties and still enjoy life. Forbearance. Strengthened character. Inward pleasure unaffected by chance or misfortune.

4 Sevens=Danger of conflict, quarrels, disappointments. A warning of the necessity for restraint, quiet courage and devotion to duty in the face of difficulty.

3 Sevens=Bickering, petty gossip, possibility of false accusations. Querent is warned not to be misdirected from high purposes, to ignore unfairness and jealousy, so that when truth is established, he may benefit by his own integrity.

4 Sixes=Slow, steady progress toward desired goals and suggestion that Querent is being tested; warn against impatience.

3 Sixes=Hidden opportunities. The indication is that judgment on Querent has been temporarily suspended, that if he acquits himself well in minor matters, his actions will terminate in more satisfying friendships, promotion in business or other benefits.

4 Fives=Orderliness, absorption in detail, rigid adherence to routine. An intimation that Querent may be deprived of many of life's pleasures unless he can break with established customs and seek fresh outlooks.

3 Fives=Revolt against authority, but unconsidered judgment may result in loss of prestige, waste of energy over trivialities. Querent should be advised to weigh any action to make certain his goals are worthy as well as workable.

4 Fours=Rest, peace, changelessness. An intimation that life will be uneventful with renewed satisfactions in daily living.

3 Fours=Hardships overcome. Rest after strife, sickness or misfortune. A philosophical acceptance of limitations which will result in increased pleasure and inner calm.

4 Threes=Dissatisfaction, resolutions, new beginnings. Querent should not give way to discouragement, but bolster his future plans with industry and scrupulous attention to detail, and take pleasure in establishing fresh interests.

3 Threes=Error in judgment, disappointment and discouragement. Querent should be warned against self-condemnation, encouraged to formulate fresh plans and resolutions, gain new knowledge.

4 Twos=Many small matters, some vexatious, some pleasurable. Delays, trifling gifts, brief visits. Pleasure in reading, nature, the arts, hobbies.

3 Twos=The same as 4 Twos except that:

(a) Lacking the Two of Spades, vexations will be minimized, small pleasures will fill the day.

(b) Lacking the Two of Hearts, pleasure will be found outside the home, especially in casual meetings with strangers, unexpected kindnesses from chance acquaintances.

(c) Lacking the Two of Diamonds, pleasures will be found in intangible things.

(d) Lacking the Two of Clubs, pleasure will rise from inner resources, increased awareness of beauty, renewed interests in neglected activities, spiritual insight.

PREPONDERANCE OF SUITS IN THE SPREAD

A marked preponderance of any suit in the spread has a significance of its own. This is particularly true when any suit is represented by five or more numerical cards. Inasmuch as the face cards usually indicate actual people, they should be omitted from the count unless all three of the suit are present.

A preponderance of SPADES heralds unexpected events. In general, Spades are associated with disappointment, regret and mysterious forces at work which are beyond the Querent's control. However, Spades should not be linked with misfortune, but with mystery, and courses into the unknown. Spades indicate activity.

A preponderance of HEARTS promises pleasure, gaiety, laughter and joy. Hearts are also cards of permanence, stability, good health and freedom from care. However, many Hearts in the spread can warn of indolence, self-indulgence, and indifference to the welfare of others. Hearts usually offer the Querent a choice between the calm inner joys of contemplation and self-abnegation or the more hectic pleasures of material gain.

A preponderance of DIAMONDS marks a preoccupation with money, business, success and prestige. The combination of Diamonds with unfortunate Spades indicates an unhappy outcome to the Querent's financial plans. On the other hand, a combination of Diamonds with Hearts indicates that plans proceed smoothly and culminate happily. Where more than Five Diamonds appear in the spread, the Querent should be warned against materialism and advised to cultivate a diversity of interests.

A preponderance of CLUBS promises a more interesting and rewarding life. Clubs are frequently cards of energy, enterprise, sociability and usefulness. Clubs indicate the presence of opportunities for new friendships, an enlarged social circle and the beginning of activities which will give added significance to the Querent's life. There is a danger, however, that too many plans may prevent the fruition of any one.

INTERPRETATION OF FACE CARDS

Usually the face cards represent actual people. Inasmuch as no two people are identical and the pack is limited to a small number of face cards, obviously any specific card will not be completely descriptive of the individual whom it wishes to designate.

If the Reader feels that a more minute description is desirable, he should ask the Querent to reshuffle the cards in the remaining pack. He should then select one or two cards from the pack and place them upon the face card. These cards should give him additional information about the individual characterized by the face card.

EXAMPLE No. 1: If the face card is the Queen of Hearts and the card drawn is the Three of Diamonds, the indication is that the Queen of Hearts is less naive than she appears, shrewder in business matters and possibly that she is prone to haggle over money.

EXAMPLE No. 2: If the Jack of Diamonds is covered by the King of Spades, the Jack is far less likely to represent a callow youth, but one who has already started on the road to maturity and has absorbed, to some degree, the stability, integrity and dependability characteristic of the King of Spades.

EXAMPLE No. 3: If the Queen of Spades is covered by the Nine of Hearts, the indication is that there is a light-hearted, gay or even frivolous aspect to her personality. The assumption can also be made that her attitude towards the Querent is friendly and that, given the opportunity, she will be valuable to him in the attainment of the ends which he desires.

SAMPLE READING: A YOUNG WOMAN

(See spread on next page)

A full reading of the cards usually takes about two hours. The Reader should prepare himself for the task of blotting out all personal concerns in order to dedicate himself to the welfare of the Querent.

The Querent in this case was an attractive woman in her mid-thirties, volatile, smartly dressed and filled with nervous energy. She shuffled the cards rapidly, almost violently, in spite of suggestions that she do so with thoughtful care. As each card was laid down she asked questions about it although it was explained to her that no divination could be made until the spread was complete.

The most notable feature of the spread was that the upper right wing was composed solely of Hearts. This was an immediate indication that the Querent's primary preoccupation lay in pleasure, romance and excitement, that she was more interested in temporary joy and passing delights than in calmer, more contemplative and more enduring pleasures. This surmise was strengthened by an examination of the individual cards composing the wing.

The Queen of Diamonds placed in the main line of the spread, facing the middle, was clearly the Querent herself. Moreover the traditional characteristics of the Queen of Diamonds fitted her. She was a woman of dynamic force, agile mind and fierce passions, who tended to dominate those about her and direct their lives. She was a good business woman, shrewd and clever, but, as the preponderance of Hearts in the spread indicated, she had a tendency to waste time in quarrels and to become too deeply involved in relatively unimportant details.

The Queen of Diamonds was looking directly at the Seven of Diamonds, a card of distress, indicating an unresolved problem concerning which the Querent was seeking advice. The other cards strengthened the impression that the problem did not relate to business or finances but was romantic in nature. The two face cards at the extremes of the upper wings indicated that she would soon be forced to make a choice between two men who were hostile to each other.

The inclusion of the Three of Spades on the main line of the spread, indicated that the Querent believed it necessary to make a swift, clear-cut decision which might cause bitterness and acrimony. It gave a warning for the need of tact and suggested that the Querent's actions were likely to be motivated by emotion rather than judgment. In conjunction with the Seven of Diamonds, it was clear that the Querent would remain in a state of inner turmoil until the matter was settled in her own mind.

The Querent's natural inclination was to select the road to the right which led to the Jack of Hearts, a card of romance which often indicates a temporary and unsatisfactory love affair. The Jack of Hearts,

when it represents a person, is likely to personify a likeable, pleasant but somewhat shallow and irresponsible man who is so intent on a good time that he neglects the more serious aspects of life.

The Seven of Hearts is a card of lovers' quarrels. The Five of Hearts is likely to be a card of tears and vain regrets. When these two cards are included in a wing which is made up solely of Hearts, as they are in this case, they forecast periods of intense pleasure interposed with unhappiness, remorse, feelings of guilt, anger and recrimination.

The alternate path, indicated by the upper left wing of the spread, is one which offers security, calm pleasure, contemplation and quiet joy. The King of Hearts at the end of the wing represents a solid, substantial man, mild-tempered and constant in his love.

The Eight of Spades suggests that this man can create a peaceful haven for the Querent in which she knows comfort and a state of well-being. The Eight

Sample reading of a young woman.

of Diamonds represents freedom from financial worries and a life of moderation, in which pleasure will be allied with responsibility. This will be a smooth, well-worn path, free of emotional upsets, quarrels, worries, duplicity and uncertainty.

In the lower left wing of the spread are found two women, facing each other as though in strong opposition. The intimation is that they offer conflicting advice to the Querent. The Queen of Hearts is likely to be a simple, uncomplicated woman, deeply devoted to the Querent, but her judgments tend to be faulty, dictated by emotion or sentiment rather than wisdom. The judgment of the Queen of Spades will be highly intuitive and perceptive, but her advice will be offered bluntly and without tact. Moreover, as the Queen of Spades is inimical to the Querent, who is represented by the Queen of Diamonds, it is likely that disputes will arise between them, resulting in acrimonious quarrels and eventual estrangement. However, the Querent was warned not to flaunt the advice of the Queen of Spades through pique or spite, for this woman can be of incalculable assistance to her if a true rapport can be established between them.

The Six of Hearts, standing alone at the end of the wing, would appear to be unrelated to the main problem of the Querent. It represents a specific opportunity for success or promotion in business to which the Querent may be blinded through her emotional entanglements. Because of the proximity of the Six of Hearts to the Queen of Spades, it may be that this opportunity will arise for the Querent through the offices of the Queen of Spades.

In the lower right-hand wing of the spread, the Ace of Clubs lies directly beneath the card depicting the personality of the Querent and would appear to supply further information regarding her. The Ace of Clubs denotes high skills, creative powers and vivid imagination, but it also suggests unrestrained passions, judgments marred by emotional reactions, impulsiveness and inner turmoil. When this card is linked with the Queen of Diamonds, there is danger of sensuousness, quick temper and uncontrolled passions which can lead to folly, despair and, in extreme cases, to a life thrown into chaos.

The Six of Spades represents a period of anxious waiting often accompanied by a feeling of hopelessness and inadequacy. The Querent may feel trapped by circumstances and should be warned against unconsidered action in a desperate attempt to break a seeming stalemate. The Eight of Clubs following the Six of Spades signifies that anxieties and dis-appointments which may appear bitter at the time, will later be recognized as tests of character, which will strengthen the inner resources of the Querent, and which will permit new and deeper pleasures that she will be able to evaluate with a higher degree of accuracy because she has escaped from a situation of danger and uncertainty. There is a promise here of a new self-recognition, an increased independence of spirit and a realization that happiness lies within the individual rather than in external circumstances.

This interpretation is further substantiated by the presence of three Eights in the spread. Eights, as a whole, are cards of balance. The presence of three Eights promises an ever-increasing capacity to deal with life's misfortunes with poise and equanimity. Especially when the Eight of Hearts is missing, there is an assurance of an ability to adjust and find happiness under any circumstances. There is also a promise of happiness in old age, a growing strength and a developing appreciation of beauty, especially in simple things.

The accuracy of the spread can probably be estimated most clearly by the Querent's reactions.

At the end of the reading she asked, "Even if I pick all the wrong routes, I'll have some good times, won't I? It won't all be bad."

SUMMING UP

Historically, the symbols from which those used on modern playing cards descend were used as decorations in the temples where the priest and priestesses convened. They were omnipresent reminders of the code of ethics demanded by those who lived within the inner circle.

SPADES were symbols of personal courage in the face of adversity, inner strength, self-abnegation and integrity. They demanded the growth of the spirit, uncompromising honesty and rigid self-control.

HEARTS were the symbols of universal love, stretching upwards to God, and outwards to embrace all mankind, cutting across all barriers of race, creed and nationality. They demanded gentleness, sympathy, kindness and the willingness to sacrifice for others. Through these symbols the priests sought to shrive themselves of pettiness, malice, envy, greed and all other unworthy attributes.

DIAMONDS were the symbols of achievement, ambition, scholarship and lofty ideals. They established worthy goals to which men could dedicate their lives. Diamonds represented constructive forces, admonishing men to create enduring edifices and to transfer their mental patterns and visionary concepts into concrete form.

CLUBS were the symbols of the humbler virtues. They taught modesty, the rejection of earthly power and glory for subservience to the will of the gods, truthfulness, balance, continence, endurance, and uncomplaining submission to the arrows of fate.

Many people will wish to use the cards as a daily guide. To forecast one's own future is far more difficult than reading the cards for another person. In this case the individual becomes both the Reader and the Querent. But it can be done.

Remember that fortune telling is a hobby. Some individuals may be tempted to use the information garnered here for personal profit. To do so is to debase the ancient, mystical symbols of the cards. Moreover, from a practical point of view, it is dangerous, for many communities have ordinances against forecasting the future where money changes hands.

MAGIC AS A HOBBY

This section will encourage you to make magic your hobby by sharing with you a few of the magician's secrets. Here you will learn about a number of magic tricks as well as about juggling and ventriloquism. You will also be given a few acting hints.

The magic here is easy to do! Included are tricks with everyday articles you have around the house and tricks that you can do without preparation.

Magic is surprisingly simple once you are "in the know." Sometimes the simpler the explanation of a trick, the more difficult it is for people to figure out.

If you know several good magic tricks, everyone will want to see them, and you will always be asked to bring along your "bag of tricks." Putting on a show for family and friends can provide great fun for everyone, but it will require a great deal of practice and concentration on your part.

Concentrate on learning just a few tricks to begin with. Once you get the knack, you'll want to include many more in your repertoire.

FUNDAMENTAL TRICKS

There are several things you should bear in mind when doing tricks. The surprise of not knowing what is about to happen makes people like magic, so never repeat the same trick for the same audience. Have another trick ready in case you are asked to show the first trick again.

Never tell what you are going to do before you start a trick, because if you do, it will be easier for your audience to see how you perform a trick, and that spoils the fun. Keep them fooled!

Don't expose the workings of a trick after you have done it, and don't tell on a fellow-magician either. It's more fun to keep your friends guessing, because magic isn't magic to people who know what methods you use.

You may present your magic in a natural, comic or mysterious way. In the natural way of presentation

you should strive to be yourself and not imitate anyone else. Be casual and easy-going. This is usually the best way to perform your magic before a group of people you know well.

The comedy style is used if you are performing before a larger group and have a natural flair for comedy. You should joke with your audience, but never poke fun at them—laugh with them—not at them. Remember, your audience is every bit as ready to be entertained as to be fooled. Comedy is a good form of entertainment. Remember though, not to be a show-off or act smart-alecky.

The mysterious style is usually best suited to a large stage and, as a rule, to an older person. If you are naturally very serious, and are really not the type to be funny, you may be able to present your show in a mysterious manner. Don't try to be too mysterious or you may end up being funny.

Don't mix the styles of presentation; either be natural, funny or mysterious.

"Patter" is the name magicians give to the running line of talk they use while performing a trick. It's a good idea for you to learn to keep up a continuous flow of chatter or patter as you perform because this will make your magic more interesting and entertaining.

You should not memorize what you are going to say. Just start with an idea of what you want to say as you perform. Then fill in with what comes to your mind as you go along. This will only come with practice. You may tell certain (not truthful) things that you will do, or call attention to the various articles you use. This is, of course, just the beginning. You must say other things in between so that your show will not have "dead spots" in it. All of your patter must be in the same style as your presentation: natural, comic, or mysterious. Some tricks have a story attached to them naturally, such as the Four Robbers Trick. Try most of all to be original in your

Condensed from "101 Best Magic Tricks" by Guy Frederick, © 1956 by Sterling Publishing Co., Inc.|Ventriloquism from "101 Best Stunts and Novelty Games" by Peggy and Robert Masters, © 1954 by Sterling Publishing Co., Inc.|Juggling from "Juggling" by Rudolf Dittrich © 1963 by Sterling Publishing Co., Inc., New York

stories and don't copy other magicians you may see. It is not only unfair to take someone else's patter, but it probably won't fit your style of magic.

If you are going to put on a complete show and not just a few tricks, arrange them into a suitable program. The opening trick is the most important because it introduces you to your audience and leads them either to expect to see a good magician—or one not so good. You should choose a trick that is quick, and attention-getting. Do not use a first trick which requires the use of spectators from the audience, but one that you can perform quickly, and that will baffle the audience.

The last trick should be fast and colorful (as well as mysterious) for it is the last time this audience will see you, and you want them to remember you as a pleasant person with lots of skill and talent.

Your dress is also important. Be neat and clean in your appearance, as this will make the audience like you better when they first see you. You will find coat pockets handy in many of the tricks, and also a high hat or magician's hat. Girls can wear slacks and a coat, or a skirt or a smock with pockets.

Magicians use a language all their own. You will find some of these terms useful and interesting, and they form the basis of a great many tricks. If you want to fool your audience you will have to practice certain tricks until you can do them without hesitating. You will find references to the following "Fundamental Tricks" throughout the rest of this section:

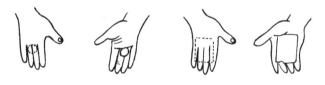

PALMING is holding something in your hand without the audience's knowing it is there. The easiest "palm" is called the finger-palm because the object is held in the natural curl of your two middle fingers. With a small object, such as a coin or a ball, held this way, you can move your hand freely and naturally. Your arm can be held in front of your body, or dropped to your side without the object's falling out.

Card to be forced

Force card

Portion cut by spectator

FORCING is causing a spectator to pick a certain card when he thinks he has a free choice. To "force"

a card, place the card you wish to force, on the bottom of the deck—that is, under the last card of the deck. Hold the deck on the palm of your hand, and ask the spectator to cut the deck at any point he wishes. Have him place the part he cut, and now holds, on the palm of his hand.

Place the portion you hold, crosswise on top of the portion in his hand. Ask him to pick up the top part of the deck (the one you have placed crosswise) and look at the bottom, or face-up card. To him it appears as if this was the card he cut to, but it is really the card that was on the bottom of the deck at the beginning—in other words, the "force" card.

This may sound very simple. It is, and because it is so simple, it really fools them. Try it and see!

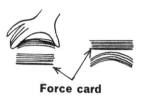

Force card

Another FORCE is the "bridge" force. Place the card to be forced on the bottom of the deck. Cut the deck at about the center, and bend the top packet along the ends in a concave "bridge." Now complete the cut and place the unbent portion on top of the bent portion.

Ask the spectator to cut the cards near the center, and glance at the card on the bottom of the packet to which he has cut. He will cut to the force card.

Before doing this, it is a good idea to notice whether he cuts the cards at the sides or the ends. This will work very well if he cuts at the sides, but if he cuts at the ends, you must bend the cards at the *sides* when you cut. Most people cut at the sides.

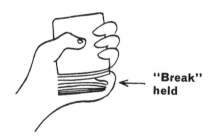

"Break" held

THE PASS is a very difficult but skilful trick which is used to bring a selected card to the top of the deck. This lets the spectator take any card from the deck, replace it, and lets you bring it to the top. This variation of the pass is very easy.

Fan the cards out and have someone select a card. Square up the deck and cut it at about the center. Ask the spectator to return his card, by placing it on top of the bottom pack, in your left hand. Hold the pack in the palm of your hand with the fingers curled around one side and the thumb on the other.

Replace the packet from your right hand on top of the one in your left, but as you do so, slip the tip of your left little finger in between the two packets. Riffle the outer ends of the cards a few times but keep looking right into the eyes of the spectator. *Do not look at your hands.*

Grasp the ends of the cards with your right fingers at the front, thumb at the back, and cut the cards at the break held by your little finger.

Now riffle shuffle the cards, being sure the top card on the packet held in your left hand falls on top. This will be the selected card. You can shuffle some more, but you can always locate the card very easily, as you will keep it on the top of the deck.

The spectator's card

THE ONE-WAY PRINCIPLE means using a deck which has a picture or figure on the back which is non-reversible. The back design has a definite top and bottom (rather than a pattern which looks the same in either direction) and you can tell if one of the cards is upside down.

To use this principle, arrange the cards so that the back designs face all one way. Fan the cards and have someone in the audience remove one. If you fan the cards in your left hand from left to right (top to bottom), and someone selects one, continue to close the fan in the same direction. If you use the left thumb and fingers as a pivot, you will find that when you square up the cards, you will have turned them completely around.

Have the card returned to the deck, and let the spectator shuffle them, or shuffle them yourself. Now fan the cards face-out toward the spectator, and have him make sure his card is in the deck. While he is looking for his card it is easy for you to find it too, as it will be the only one with an upside down pattern!

THE KEY-CARD PRINCIPLE is nothing more than using one card to locate another. To use this principle, note the bottom card of the pack. Have a spectator select a card.

While he is looking at it, cut the cards, and ask him to replace his card on top of the pile you have cut

from the deck. Now complete the cut. This puts the bottom card that you remembered, the key-card, directly over his selected card.

Now turn the deck face-up in your hands and look for your key-card. You will find the selected card to the right of your key-card.

Among the following, you will find tricks in which these principles are used, and also many others which you will find just as easy to do.

CARD TRICKS

Tricks with playing cards are the most popular magic tricks today. Many can be done without long hours of practice.

THE FOUR ROBBERS

Hold up four Jacks, which represent four robbers. Tell your audience that the Jacks decide to rob a house, which is represented by the deck. You will place the robbers in different parts of the house, but at the end of the trick they will all appear back together at the top of the house.

Before you start, all you need to do is place any three cards behind the Jacks before you fan them out to show them. Fan out only the Jacks, and keep the three extra cards hidden behind the Jacks.

Now start your patter. Say, "Here are four robbers named Jack, who decided to rob a house. We'll let the deck of cards represent the house." Place the Jacks, with the extra cards on top of them, on top of the deck, face down. Then continue. "The first robber entered the house through a window in the cellar." Take the top card from the deck (which everyone supposes to be a Jack) and push it into the deck near the bottom. Don't let anyone see its face. Push it all the way in, so that it is lost.

Now say, "The second robber went into the house by the front door." Take the top card from the deck (the second indifferent card) and push it into the deck near the center. "The third robber entered the house by the back door." Take the top card again and place it in the deck near the center. "The fourth robber stayed right here on the roof to act as the lookout." Pick up the top card and show it to the audience. Of course, this really is the first of the four Jacks. Now replace it on the top of the deck.

Continue your story. "The police came and the

lookout warned the other robbers, and, what do you know? Here are all four robbers back on the roof!" as you say this, deal the four Jacks, one at a time, from the top of the deck onto the table, face up, so that everybody can see them.

THE FOUR ACES

In this trick, you hand the spectator a deck of cards, and have him cut it into four equal piles. Then you ask him to transfer numerous cards back and forth from pile to pile and after the cards are seemingly lost and hopelessly mixed up, the spectator finds an Ace on top of each pile.

The preparation for this trick is very easy. Before you start the trick, place the four Aces on top of the deck. Now hand the deck to a spectator and make clear to him that he is going to do the trick; you won't even touch the cards.

Have him cut the deck into four equal piles. Most people cut from left to right, and in all likelihood the pile on his right will be the one with Aces on top. The only thing you must watch is to see where he puts the top pile. Now you try to confuse the spectator by having him move cards around from one pile to another in a seemingly aimless manner. However, you really keep track of the Aces as they are moved. What you want to do is to end with an Ace on top of each pile.

I won't give you any set way of moving the cards, because you probably won't do the trick exactly the same way any time you do it. It would be very hard to follow a pattern anyway, so just to give you an idea, let's call the pile to the spectator's left No. 1 and so on. Pile No. 4 will be the one with the Aces. Start by having the spectator take a card from No. 2 and put it on No. 3. Then take one card from No. 2 and place it on No. 1.

As you perform the trick, don't refer to the piles by number. Just point to them and say, "Take the card from the top of this pile and place it on that pile." You can have him move the cards back and forth as many times as you wish but be sure to keep your eye on the Aces. This may sound confusing, but try it and you will see how easy it is to do, and how baffling! But be sure to get an Ace on each pile before you finish the trick.

SOMETHING ON YOUR MIND

This is a "quickie" and is a gag as well as a trick.

Have someone select a card and get it to the top of the deck as explained in *The Pass*, page 344.

Have the spectator concentrate on his card. Hold the deck in your right hand and place the deck firmly against your forehead, card-faces toward the spectator. This will put the selected card against your head. Press the deck against your forehead hard, and push upward at the same time. Now tell the spectator that the card is on his mind, and it is also on yours. Remove the deck in an upward sweep, and his card will really be "on your mind," stuck to your forehead.

Usually, the card will stick by itself. It will stick better if you moisten your forefinger and get just a bit of moisture on the top card.

THE RED AND THE BLACK

In this trick you are able to predict the cards in certain piles dealt by the spectator, even though you never touch the cards. You will first write a prediction on a slip of paper and either place it in full view of the audience, or have another spectator hold it.

Hand a spectator the deck of cards, and have him shuffle them thoroughly. Now have him deal the cards in pairs face up onto the table. If he comes to two black cards, he is to place them in one pile; if he comes to two red cards, he is to place them in another pile. If he turns up a red one and a black one together, he is to discard them and lay them face down.

When he has finished dealing the cards, he is to count the red cards, and the black cards. When he reads your prediction he will find that you have written, "You will have two more red cards than black ones," and he does.

How does this happen? Before you hand him the deck, remove two black cards from the deck and secretly place them in your pocket. Then write the prediction as above. If you wish, you may remove two red cards, and then your prediction should read. "You will have two more black cards than red ones."

CARD FROM THE POCKET

A spectator deals three cards face up from the deck and selects one, mentally. You place the three cards in your pocket and then withdraw two. The spectator will name his card, which you will draw from your pocket. Then show that your pocket is empty.

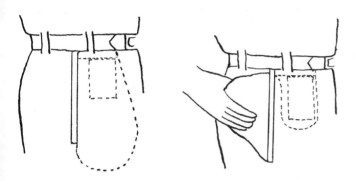

Before you start the trick, place any two cards in your right hand trouser pocket. Push the cards to the top inner corner of the pocket, and you will be able to pull out your pocket and show that it is empty. The cards should face toward your body.

Hand the spectator a deck of cards and ask him to shuffle them. After you have him deal any three cards face up onto the table, and he selects one just by thinking of it, you pick up the cards, and remember the location of each. The best way to do this is to pick up the one of highest value first, then the next lower one, and finally place the lowest value card on top, face down.

After showing that your pocket is empty, place the cards in it and appear to concentrate on the spectator's thoughts. Remove the two cards that you placed in your pocket before the start of the trick, and put them into the center of the deck without showing them.

Now ask the spectator to name his card aloud for the first time. Since you know the location of the cards in your pocket, it will be easy to pull out the one he names. The highest card will be closest to your body, while the lowest will be toward the spectator. Pull the card out quickly after it is named, without fumbling, because the audience believes that you have only one card in your pocket. Lay the card down on the table in front of the spectator, face down. Ask him to turn it over. Reach back into your pocket and push the two remaining cards up into the top of your pocket and casually show it is empty.

THE PUSH-THROUGH MYSTERY

Three cards are picked from the deck, and one of them is declared the favorite one. The three cards are placed half-way into the deck and pushed until they emerge from the other end. They are pushed through once more and the only projecting card remaining will be the favorite one selected.

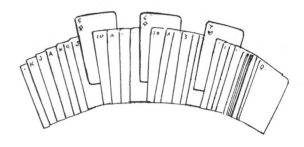

This trick works itself. You need to know the card selected by the spectator. Have him pick three cards from the deck. Now lay them face up on the table in front of him. Ask him to name his favorite card. Fan the deck face-up in front of you and place the first card half-way down into the deck. Now skip two or three cards and place the selected card half-way into the deck. Skip two or three more cards and place the last card half-way into the deck.

Square up the cards and you will have the three cards projecting from the top of the pack. Hold the deck firmly and tap the protruding cards into the deck. Some cards will project from the bottom. Quickly and firmly push these cards back up. The selected card will be the only one protruding from the deck. Remove it and show it to the spectator.

Another way to finish this is to tap the cards into the deck, then wrap the deck in a handkerchief, so that the top half protrudes. Now under cover of the handkerchief, push upward on the cards that project from the bottom and the selected card will rise from the center of the deck.

COIN TRICKS

Coin tricks are always interesting because everyone likes money. For these tricks you should use half-dollar-size coins, unless you are specifically told to use another size. If you wish, you can buy "palming coins" in a magic store. Most magicians use these for tricks done on the stage, when the audience can't see them closely. You might also use a "lucky piece" which lots of people carry. You could tell your audience that the coin, besides being lucky, has other magic properties.

THE FRENCH DROP

This is not really a trick in itself, but is the basis for many coin tricks. You can also use this principle for small objects other than coins, such as balls or keys. The *French Drop* is really an easy way to make a coin vanish. You seem to pass a coin from one hand to your other one, while really keeping it in the first hand.

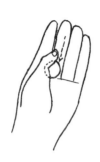

Hold the coin by its edges in your left hand between the tips of your fingers and thumb. The flat side of the coin should be parallel to your palm. Point the fingers of your left hand slightly upward so that the flat side of the coin is toward the audience. Hold your left hand still and move your right hand, palm down, toward your left hand as if you were going to take the coin out of your left hand. Your right thumb should go under the coin and your fingers above it, which hides the coin momentarily. When the coin is hidden, release it and allow it to fall back into your left hand where it should rest on the second joints of your left fingers. Hold it for a moment with your left thumb to keep it from falling.

Now bring your right thumb up along your left finger-tips. Close your right hand as if it held the coin. Move your right hand up and away from your left. As you do this, drop your left hand (with the coin) casually to your side. Be sure to keep your eyes on your right hand. Never look at your left hand. This is what magicians call "misdirection." Now get the coin into the finger-palm position. See *Palming*, page 344.

The movement of seeming to take the coin from your left hand should be one continuous motion. Don't hesitate, except just long enough to seem to take the coin into your right hand. This will require some practice, but it is not hard to do, and will be worth the trouble to learn.

Now, with your right hand held at eye-level, rub your thumb and fingers together. It will look as if the coin dissolved. In some other tricks, you will learn how to get rid of the coin in your left hand, so that you may show both hands are empty.

COIN THROUGH THE NAPKIN

You cause a borrowed coin to penetrate a borrowed napkin or handkerchief.

Borrow a coin and have the owner mark it if he wishes.

Hold the coin vertically by its flat side between thumb and forefinger of your left hand. Place the napkin over it so that the coin is under its center. Under cover of the napkin get a small fold of the napkin between your thumb and the coin. Now with your right hand lift the part of the napkin closest to the audience and drape it back on top of the other half, over your left arm, and show that the coin is still there. With a snap of the left wrist, cause both halves of the napkin to fall forward while still holding the coin and the napkin, in the center, in your left hand.

Twist the napkin to give the illusion that the coin is wrapped securely in the center of the napkin. Exert a little pressure on the edge of the coin and it will rise through the napkin. It looks as if it is slowly penetrating the napkin. Hand the coin back to the spectator and show that the napkin is unharmed.

MULTIPLYING MONEY

You count a number of coins into the hand of a spectator and apparently "catch" three coins from the air, and place them in the spectator's hand. When he opens his hand, he has three more coins than when he started.

You will need thirteen coins and a magazine the size of the *Reader's Digest*.

Before you start the trick, secretly place three coins under the cover of the magazine, so that they are hidden.

Hand the ten coins to a spectator and ask him to count them out loud, one at a time, and place them on the magazine. Hold the magazine so that the coins will not fall off. Stress the fact that you are using the magazine so that you do not touch the coins. After he has counted the coins onto the magazine, have him cup his hands together to catch the coins. Slightly curl the magazine to make a little trough, and pour the coins into his hands. (Of course the three duplicate coins that you hid under the magazine cover will fall into his hands, too.) Tell him to close his hands tightly so that nothing can get in or out.

Reach up into the air and pretend to grab an invisible coin. Hold it up as if you really see it, and ask the spectator if he can see the coin. Make a throwing motion toward his hand as if you were throwing the coin into his hand. Ask him if he felt the coin go into his hands. Ask him, too, if the coins are getting heavier. Repeat the throwing business two more times. Now ask him how many coins he had to start with. He will say ten. Have him open his hands and count the coins onto the magazine again. He will now have thirteen.

If you wish, you may use borrowed coins. Have a spectator count the coins from his pocket onto the magazine. If he has over seven coins, go on with the trick. If he has less than seven add three from your pocket. The reason for this is that if he has just a few coins to start with, he will be able to tell that you have added coins from the magazine. If you decide to use borrowed coins, have a penny, a nickel, and a dime concealed in the magazine at the beginning of the trick.

THE WARM COIN

You borrow several coins. One is scratched to mark it from the rest. The coins are placed in a hat or cap and mixed. Without looking, you are able to reach in and produce the marked coin.

First, stick a small pellet of beeswax on the tip of your thumbnail. Collect the coins and have someone select one, and make a mark or scratch on it for identification. As you take the coin back, press the wax to the edge of the coin and drop it into the hat. Drop the other coins in and have someone mix them by shaking the hat. Then have him hold the hat up above your eye-level so you cannot see into it. Reach in and feel for the wax. Take out the coin and scrape the wax off with your thumbnail before handing it to the spectators for identification.

THE DISSOLVING COIN

A spectator drops a coin in a glass of water while it is covered with a handkerchief. When the handkerchief is removed, the coin has vanished.

Hold a glass about half full of water on your left palm. Have someone place a coin in the center of a handkerchief and then pick up the coin through the handkerchief. Tell him to drape the handkerchief over the glass and drop the coin into the water on your signal. As he does this, tip the glass toward you so that the coin strikes the edge of the glass and falls into your fingers. The noise sounds as if the coin fell into the glass.

Now have the spectator let go of the handkerchief and as you remove it from the glass, allow the coin to slide directly under the center of the glass. Remove the handkerchief and allow him to look directly into the glass and see that the coin is still there.

Cover the glass with the handkerchief again and pick up the glass with your right hand, through the handkerchief. Turn you left hand over so that the coin does not show and finger-palm it (see *Palming*, page 344). Then, still holding the coin in your left hand, lift the handkerchief from the glass and show that the coin has disappeared.

COIN IN THE KNOT

A handkerchief is tied in a knot, and when it is untied by a spectator, a coin is found to be inside.

You may use this method to reproduce a coin which you have made vanish by any of the above methods. Palm a coin in the finger-palm position, and borrow a handkerchief. Allow the coin to slide to the tips of your fingers and hold it with your thumb and fingertips, unseen.

Fold the handkerchief by the two opposite corners, and place the coin unseen at one of the corners, beneath the folds, and hold it in place with your thumb. Pull the handkerchief taut, and twirl it so that it becomes like a hollow rope or tube. Bring the corners together and hold them with one hand. Release the pressure on the coin and it will roll into the folds of the handkerchief and stay at the center.

Coin falls to here

Shake the handkerchief once or twice to be sure the coin is at the loop. Tie a knot, and hand the handkerchief to a spectator to hold. Make a magical pass towards the handkerchief and ask the spectator to untie the knot. He will find the coin inside.

IMPROMPTU TRICKS

These tricks look impromptu. They are called "close-up" tricks, because they are good for small groups. They will all seem to be done on the spur of the moment, without active beforehand preparation. You might also call them "pocket tricks" because the items you will use for them can all be carried in your pocket. These tricks are good when a group of friends are sitting around and someone says, "Show us a trick."

THE MAGNETIC TOOTHPICK

You rub the end of a wooden toothpick on your sleeve, and hold it close to some small bits of paper on the table. The paper will fly away from the toothpick as if it were magnetized.

Put a few small scraps of paper on the table. Rub the toothpick on your sleeve. Bring the toothpick slowly towards the paper. As you do this, blow gently through your mouth towards the paper. This is what makes the paper move. No one must see you blow, of course. Anyone else who tries to do this trick won't be able to "magnetize" the toothpick. Instead of a toothpick, you could use a pencil.

THE MAGIC SAFETY PINS

Get a spectator to link two safety pins together. The trick is to separate them by pulling them apart without opening either one.

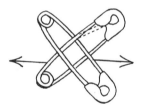

Take the pins from the spectator, and hold one pin in your left hand with your thumb and forefinger, by the small end, with the opening of the pin facing upward. Turn the other pin around the end so it hangs from the upper bar of the left hand pin, small end at the top, both sides over the lower bar, and the left side over the upper bar. The pins should form an X.

With the pins in this position, hold them tightly and pull your hands apart quickly. The pin moving to the right will slip through the catch of the other pin without forcing it to spring open.

A large blanket pin is the best size to use.

THE THREAD AND THE STRAW

Run a threaded needle through a drinking straw. The ends of the thread should be held by two spectators. Cut the straw in two with a pair of scissors and the thread will not be harmed.

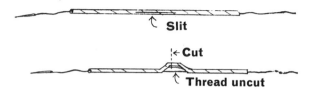

Before you start, make a slit about 1½ inches long in the center of the straw, lengthwise, with a razor blade. Hold the straw, and have a spectator push the needle through it, pulling the thread through the straw. Have each end of the thread held by spectators. Bend the ends of the straw slightly downwards above the slit which must face *towards* the floor. This pulls the straw away from the thread. The thread will be underneath the straw. Insert your scissors between the straw and thread, scissors above the thread. Cut through the straw, and you will appear to be cutting the thread as well. Separate the pieces of straw, and let them hang on the thread showing that the thread is unharmed.

THE BROKEN TOOTHPICK

You wrap a toothpick in a handkerchief and get a spectator to break it. When you unwrap the handkerchief, the toothpick falls out unharmed.

Beforehand, take a handkerchief with a fairly wide hem and force a wooden toothpick into the hem where it won't show.

Show another toothpick to the audience and place it in the center of the handkerchief. Wrap it up very carefully, and ask a spectator to feel it through the handkerchief. What he feels is the toothpick in the hem, because you have folded that corner of the handkerchief up under its center. Be sure not to let the loose toothpick fall out.

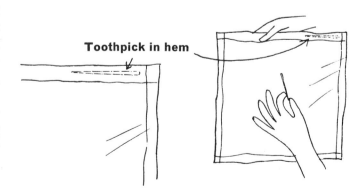

Toothpick in hem

Ask the spectator to break it in two (He, of course, breaks the one in the hem.) The audience can hear it snap. After making several passes over the handkerchief, flick it open and let the centered toothpick drop out—unharmed.

THIMBLE VANISH

You place a thimble on your right forefinger and make it vanish. Then you throw the thimble up in the air, and it vanishes.

Practice this move, because it is the basis of all thimble tricks. Place the thimble on your right forefinger. Bend down your finger, so the thimble is gripped in the fork of the thumb and forefinger. When you extend your finger, holding all of your fingers apart, your hand will appear empty. You leave the thimble in the crotch of your thumb on the palm side of your hand.

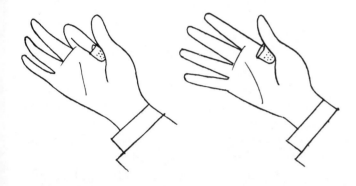

Now bend your forefinger down again and pick up the thimble on it. If these motions are done quickly, and your hand is kept in motion, the thimble will appear to vanish and reappear right before the eyes of your audience.

To do the "Throw-Vanish" trick, start with the thimble on your right forefinger, the back of your hand towards the audience. Make a throwing motion upward. The eyes of the audience, as well as yours, follow the imaginary flight of the thimble. As you make the motion, quickly "thumb-palm" the thimble, as described above. The thimble has vanished. You may reproduce it from anywhere you wish, by quickly reaching behind your left elbow, or right ear, under the table, or from anywhere you desire.

AFTER-DINNER TRICKS

These tricks are designed for you to do after dinner, right at the table. All the things you will need are found at the table, or in the pockets of your audience.

THE VANISHING SUGAR

You make a lump of sugar vanish and cause it to pass right through the table.

Secretly get a lump of paper-wrapped sugar, the kind you find in most restaurants, and carefully unwrap it, so the paper remains intact. Close up the end of the paper so it looks as if it still contained sugar. Keep the piece of real sugar in your lap.

Show the paper and handle it as if it were a real lump of sugar. Place this make-believe piece of sugar on the table. Call attention to it. Raise your right hand above the paper, and bring your palm down sharply on the table and flatten the paper. Let your audience see that the sugar is gone. Then reach under the table with your left hand, and take the piece of real sugar out of your lap. Lay it on the table, showing that the sugar has apparently penetrated the table.

THE MAGIC KNIFE

You pick up a small butter knife and place specks of paper on its blade. The spots vanish, re-appear, and jump on and off the knife.

Slightly moisten two small pieces of paper napkin or newspaper. Stick these to one side of the blade of the knife, about an inch apart.

Practice holding the knife between the thumb and index finger of your right hand and making what is called the "Paddle-Move." Although it may sound difficult it is really very easy to do: you appear to show both sides of the knife while actually you show only one.

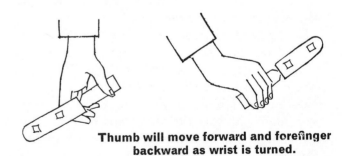

Thumb will move forward and forefinger backward as wrist is turned.

With the tip of your right thumb on the right edge of the handle, and the tip of your forefinger on the left edge of the handle, the blade of the knife should point to the right as it is held horizontally. Your palm should be facing slightly upward.

You will seem to show the other side of the knife if you turn the knife over now so that your palm faces downward. Move the tip of your thumb forward, and the tip of your forefinger backward, turning the knife over between your thumb and forefinger. This turnover is done at the same time you turn your hand over. Practice this motion until you have it perfect.

Show the knife (which really has two spots on only one side) spot-side up and call attention to the fact that it has spots on one side (pretend to turn it over using the method described above) and also spots on the other side. Now place your left hand over and around the blade of the knife, spot-side up, and pretend to wipe the spots off. What you really do is to turn the knife over under cover of your hand and wipe the clean side. Using the same method you can show that both sides are blank. Be sure to show your audience that your left hand is empty. Now place your left hand over the knife again, and show that the spots have come back.

Then remove one of the spots, and show how the spot from the other side vanishes also. You will apparently have only one spot on each side. Now remove the last spot, and by turning the knife over, you can show that the spot on the other side has also vanished. Place the knife on the table, so that anyone who cares to, may examine it.

THE PAPER NAPKIN BALLS

You make some small paper balls from a paper napkin. They multiply, vanish, and re-appear in a surprising way.

Before you start, place a small paper ball made from ⅓ of a paper napkin into your right coat pocket. When you are ready to start the trick, take a fresh paper napkin and, in front of your audience, tear it into three parts. Roll each part into a paper ball, and place them on the table.

To start, just ask someone how many balls he sees and, as you talk, casually reach in your pocket and get the extra ball in your right hand in the finger-palm position (page 344). Your right hand is palm-down on the table and your left hand palm-up. Reach over with your right hand and pick up a ball with your thumb and forefinger. Place it into your

left hand and say, "One." Pick up another ball and place it, along with the palmed ball, in your left hand saying, "Two." Quickly close your left hand. Pick up the third ball with your right hand and say, "This one I'll place in my pocket." Place your right hand in your pocket, but finger-palm the ball and bring your hand out again with the ball, and place your hand, palm-down on the table.

Now say, "How many balls are in my left hand?" Someone answers: "Two." Open your left hand and let three balls drop on the table. "You're not paying attention. I'll do it again. Watch! I'll place one in my left hand." Pick up a ball with your right hand and place it (and the palmed ball) in your left hand. Close your left hand so that the extra ball won't be seen. Pick up another ball and place it in your left fist, through the top (thumb up). "This one I'll place in my pocket." Pick up the third ball and leave it in your pocket.

Now ask, "How many balls in my left hand?" Someone answers: "Two." Open your hand and show that you have three balls.

Say, "Now we'll use just two balls." Place one ball in your pocket. Say, "I'll hold one and I'll place the other one in your hand. When I do, I want you to close your hand very tight—quickly so that nothing can get in or out."

Pick up one of the balls and pretend to place it in your left hand but really keep it in your right one.

Pick up the other ball in your right hand, adding it to the ball you apparently placed in your left hand. Slightly squeeze the balls together so they appear as one and place them in the spectator's hand. Ask him how many he has, and how many you have. He will say you each have one. Open your left hand and show it is empty.

Ask the spectator to open his hand. He has two balls.

THE TRAVELLING SUGAR

You place four lumps of sugar on the table, and cover them with your hands. You can make them jump around and finally make all four lumps appear together.

You will need five lumps of sugar, but the audience must be aware of only four. The four lumps are laid on the table so that they form a square. Here is how they look:

3   4

1   2

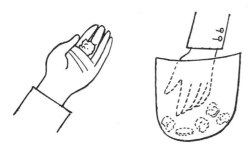

The extra lump is thumb-palmed (page 348) in your left hand. Now you are ready to start.

Place your right hand over 2, your left hand over 3. With a wiggle of your fingers, your right hand thumb-palms 2, while your left hand leaves the extra lump at 3. Raise your hands slightly, and show that lump number 2 has vanished, and there are two lumps at 3.

Cover 1, with your left hand, and your right hand goes to 3. Wiggle your fingers, lift your hands, palming the lump at 1, in your left hand. Your right hand leaves the lump it has brought over from 2.

Your right hand, which is empty, covers 4, while your left hand covers the three lumps at 3. When you lift your hands, your right hand picks up the lump at 4, and your left hand leaves the fourth lump at 3.

Now the process is reversed. Your left hand covers the four lumps and palms one, while your right hand leaves a lump at 4. Place your left hand over 1, leave a lump there, while your right hand covers, and removes a lump from 3. Place your right hand over 2, leave a lump—and your left hand picks up one of the two lumps at 3.

Now if you lift your left hand an instant before you do your right, the eyes of the audience will go to your right hand, which gives you a chance to drop the extra lump from your left hand into your lap.

ODD TRICKS

In this group you will find tricks in which all kinds of objects are used. Most of them can be found around the house. By doing tricks with different things you will add variety and interest to your act.

THE APPEARING HANDKERCHIEF

In this trick, you show that both hands are empty, and when you pull up your sleeves, a handkerchief appears in your hands.

The best kind of handkerchief to use in all magic tricks is silk. Magicians, who use all sizes, call them "silks." You will find that a silk about a foot square is the best size to use. A bright color shows up well. You can use a scrap of dress material, or a silk scarf. You should hem the edges so that they won't unravel, unless you buy your silks already hemmed.

To make the handkerchief appear, fold it into a small bundle and place it in the bend of your *left* elbow. Pull a fold of your coat sleeve over it to hide it. Now show that your hands are empty, and pull up your right sleeve. Keep your arms bent all the

time, to keep the silk from coming out. Now, pull up your left sleeve, and as you do so, get the silk into your right hand and palm it.

Bring your hands together, away from your body, and move them slowly up and down, letting the silk unfold. Now separate your hands, and show the silk. It looks as if it materialized out of thin air.

This trick is best used as the first in a program, because you must keep your arm slightly bent. The first trick in a magician's program is called the "opener." This is a good opener because it is quick, surprising, and attention-getting.

THE VANISHING HANDKERCHIEF

You pull up your sleeves and roll a silk in your hand. The silk seems to grow smaller and finally vanishes altogether.

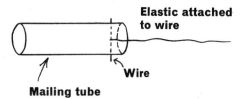

Elastic attached to wire

Wire

Mailing tube

Once again, use a 12-inch-square silk. You can use the one you have just produced in the above trick. You also will need a "pull." You can make a pull very easily from a piece of mailing tube about an inch in diameter. Cut a piece of tube about 2 inches long, and paint it black. By means of a piece of wire (paper clip, or hairpin, bent to shape) or a piece of string run through the tube at the end, attach a piece of elastic cord. The elastic should be about a foot long.

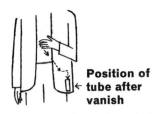

Position of tube after vanish

Tie or pin the free end of the elastic to the center of your trousers in the back. You can tie it to your belt-loop; or tie it to a safety pin and then pin it in place. Run the pull through the next belt-loop on your left side. The pull should then hang down along your left hip, but should not show below your coat. Lengthen or shorten the elastic so the pull will hang in place.

Now take the pull and place it either in your left trouser pocket, or tuck it in the top of your trousers on the left side so that it may be reached easily.

Hold the silk in your right hand and wave it up

and down a couple of times to draw attention to it. Turn slightly so that your left side is away from the audience and get the pull in your left hand. Turn to the front and place your hands together. Roll your hands slowly up and down, meanwhile stuffing the silk slowly into the pull.

When it is all the way in, turn once again to the side so that your left side is away from the audience. Open your hands very slightly, whilst still moving them up and down as before, so that the pull will fly under your coat out of sight. Face front once again, and continue with the motion of your hands. Slowly, with a wringing motion, open your hands and show that the silk has vanished.

HERE AND THERE

This is another method of vanishing or producing a silk. It uses a principle in magic that most people don't realize. That is, you can place a silk in your pocket, and still pull the pocket out to show it is empty.

Put a silk in your pocket and push it up to the top and towards the center of your body. You will find a space large enough to conceal a silk or a small object. If you pull your pocket out, the silk won't show.

You can make the silk re-appear or you can produce the silk by the method in "The Appearing Handkerchief," and make it disappear in your pocket. After you say a magic word, pull out your pocket and show that the silk has vanished. You can then produce the silk from that same pocket by pulling it down with your thumb as you push your pocket back in. Again, you can vanish it by the method shown in "The Vanishing Handkerchief."

KNOT HERE!

You hold a handkerchief by its corner and let it hang down. When you shake it, a knot appears tied in its corner.

Tie a knot in the corner of a silk handkerchief. Hold the knot between the thumb and forefinger of your right hand.

Show the silk, and take the corner that is hanging down, between the thumb and forefinger of your left hand. Shake the silk several times and on the final shake (a hard snap), open the fingers of your right hand and let go of the silk. The knot appears on the silk held in your left hand. This gives the illusion that the knot shakes itself into the corner of the handkerchief.

EGG FROM NOWHERE

You show a pocket handkerchief, fold it up and produce several eggs which you drop into a hat. The hat, when inspected, is empty.

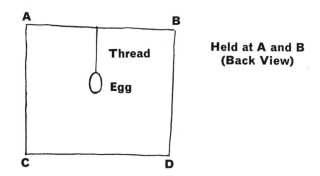

Use a fake wooden egg, or a small solid rubber ball for this trick. Push a thumbtack into the end of the egg. You will also need a man's large handkerchief. Attach a short length of black thread to the egg or ball by tying it around the thumbtack. Attach the other end of the thread to the center of one edge of the handkerchief, so that if the handkerchief were held up by the two corners of that edge, the egg would hang in the center of the handkerchief. Lay the handkerchief on the table, in such a way that you can pick it up by the corners causing the egg to hang out of sight.

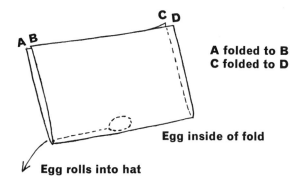

Take your magician's hat and place it on the table. Pick up the handkerchief so that the egg hangs behind it and is not seen by your audience. Bring the two top corners together and hold them between the thumb and forefinger of your right hand. Grasp the two corners that are hanging down with your left hand. Now bring your right and left hands to a horizontal position. Tip one end of the handkerchief, so that the egg will roll along the inside center of it and fall out the other end into the hat. Drop the handkerchief on the edge of the hat, reach in and show the egg by lifting it from the hat. Drop it back into the hat, and pick up the handkerchief by the four corners, two in each hand. Produce another egg in the same way, by letting it roll into the hat. Make sure the audience can see the egg as it drops in. Repeat this several times, until it appears as if you have produced almost a hatful of eggs.

Now ask a spectator if he would like to have the eggs. Place the handkerchief (with the egg wrapped inside) in your pocket. Pick up the hat and hand it to the spectator. The hat is empty.

VENTRILOQUISM

If you are under the impression that being a ventriloquist requires special vocal chords, you are wrong. *Anyone* can become a ventriloquist—that is, anyone with just a little skill who will practice a great deal!

Ventriloquism is simply creating the illusion that your voice (or a voice slightly different from your normal voice) is coming from a different place than your own mouth. No one can "throw" his voice—he can only give that illusion. The reason that ventriloquists usually have dummies is to *misdirect* the attention of the audience.

The performer bends his head slightly over the dummy, appearing to watch the dummy's face, as in ordinary conversation. This not only helps to cover up the ventriloquist's lip movements, but also serves to focus the attention of the audience on the dummy. Many professional ventriloquists actually move their lips and can't perform without doing this.

To make your study easier, get yourself some kind of temporary dummy—even a hand monkey will do, so long as it has a mouth that you can manipulate with your fingers. Hold the dummy on your lap, or at least lower than your own eye level, so you can look down at him. Practice until you can make the dummy's head and mouth move without your having to concentrate on it. Therefore, when choosing a puppet or doll, choose one that is easy to manipulate. Your hand movements are going to be almost as important as your voice in ventriloquism.

Before learning voice techniques, you must first determine which "alternate" voice comes most naturally to you and will be easiest for you to use—that of a little boy, a little girl, an old man, an old woman, a duck, some other animal, a farm boy, or someone else. Here's how to find out:

Take a long wooden pencil and clench it between your teeth. Stand in front of a mirror and watch to see that your lips don't move but stay slightly parted as you speak. Say the vowels (a, e, i, o and u). What does your voice sound like? Without shaping your lips, your voice may sound slightly cracked and higher in pitch. Repeating, you will soon begin to *feel* your vocal chords.

To help in repeating these sounds over and over, touch your tongue to the roof of your mouth near the back of your upper front teeth. Take a deep breath. Let it out slowly, making a groaning sound as you let out the air, putting a steady pressure on your vocal chords. The groan will be like a prolonged "ah." Repeat this until you finally produce a clear, humming sound like the buzzing of a bee.

Now, vary the pressure on your vocal chords as you repeat this, and you will note a change in the tone of your humming. When you have mastered the hum, go back to saying the vowels in the same way. You are beginning to develop a dummy voice. Every person has a natural alternate voice, and this can be further developed to become easily distinguishable from your trained speaking voice. It took years to train you to speak, and it will take much less time to train yourself to be a ventriloquist.

Armed with the knowledge now of what your dummy voice will sound like, you are ready to practice what is called "near" ventriloquism. Notice that when you have the pencil in your mouth, you can move your tongue without moving your jaw or lips. You should by now be thoroughly familiar with the vowels. So practice saying the major consonants (t, d, g, l, n, k, r and s). Of these, the *s* sound will be the most difficult and require the greatest use of the tongue. The other consonants (b, p, f, v and m) are impossible to pronounce without moving your lips. Remember this when you choose a performance script, and avoid those sounds as much as possible.

Practice the vowels and consonants that can be pronounced and don't waste effort on the others.

Practice with a pencil between your teeth.

When you hit a difficult sound you will either have to slur over the sound or move your lips. But your face will be turned away from your audience, and so your performance will not be marred greatly.

In your alternate voice now, try to read from a book (any book) and *mimic* and sing in the voice of your character (little boy, girl, old lady, or whatever voice you've chosen) so that it sounds peculiar. Talk in a stilted fashion as you read, or a baby-like fashion, or in any manner that is different from your normal way of speaking. You want to make your dummy character not only different in age, but different in manner.

Developing an interesting dummy character is half of the battle. The reason for your success may be due to the humorous character of your dummy who might be a dressed-up boy with a raucous voice who says everything that pops into his head. In contrast, your own character might be mild, gentlemanly and subdued. The greater the contrast between performer and dummy the better.

Thus, the emphasis in developing a voice for your dummy should be on making it different. If your own speech is rapid, then the dummy should speak slowly and painfully. If you are naturally methodical, your dummy should be frivolous. Try reading rapidly with the pencil between your teeth. After some practice you will be able to read faster and faster, stressing those words which come through easiest and clearest. This in itself gives a slight artificiality to your dummy's character. With experience, you will find which words sound funny to your audience and your script can be built around them.

After you become fluent in reading and singing in your dummy voice, try reading alternate paragraphs in your natural voice with the pencil removed. Choose for this work a novel with a great deal of dialogue, or a play. Keep using the pencil for your dummy voice, so you will remember to change character. After perhaps two weeks of daily practice, you can omit the pencil.

Keep your lips slightly parted (otherwise the sounds can't come out) and read without the pencil, still looking in the mirror occasionally. Repeat the words you are uncertain of. (Some performers keep their lips pursed but parted when talking in the dummy voice, and you may prefer to do this.) Move your lips and head when speaking in your natural voice, and let the dummy sit quietly, with his head tilted to watch you. When in the dummy voice, keep your own head, as well as your lips, still. Movement draws attention and you want your audience to shift

Developing an interesting dummy character is half the battle.

attention to the speaker, whether it's you or your dummy.

After you become facile at switching and moving, you are almost ready to put on a performance. Now you will choose your permanent dummy. The hand monkey may do if you want your dummy voice to be animal-like. If your dummy character is to be a little girl, you will want a doll you can sit on your lap or slip over your hand. The dummy should *look like* (not contrast with) the character your dummy voice is mimicking. You may wish to make a funny-looking hand puppet, or you can purchase an appropriate one at a toy shop.

If you don't want to use a hand dummy, you can use a screen or curtain with a pair of shoes showing under it to represent the dummy. Then you can talk to the "person" behind the screen and answer in your dummy voice. The illusion is not as great as with a dummy, but this can be performed on the spur of the moment when you may not have a dummy with you.

For your first public appearance, choose a few friends or your family and try out your act on them. Use a play or dialogue as a basis for your script, and tailor it to your tastes and character, perhaps adding a song. Then, after memorizing an act about 5 minutes long, put on the show in your living room. Have as much light as possible shining on your dummy and sit so that your face is more or less in shadow. You are trying to create an illusion and the more aids you get from the setting the better.

If this act goes over well, you will be ready for a bigger performance. Ask your audience to give you *constructive* criticism after you finish. Run through the act a second time, if necessary, to find the spots to improve. There are bound to be some slips in any performance and you can iron out the difficulties later in practice sessions before the mirror.

When tailoring your script, try to keep the sentences of both the dummy and yourself fairly short. Interrupting in the middle of a speech adds interest to a script and gives greater illusion than routine switching at the end of a sentence. Learn to imitate the sounds of musical instruments, animals, the wind, sawing wood, etc., as you can spice your script with these, and they are easier to master than words.

Another trick most ventriloquists use is to alternate between a whisper and a loud voice in the dummy. Whispering holds an audience's attention more than anything else, because people have to be quiet to hear you. If you can master whispering, musical and animal sounds, and interrupting in your script, you will be a star performer. You want to be able to interrupt in the dummy voice so rapidly that your audience will get the illusion of two people talking *simultaneously!* The whisper-switch-interruption needs practice, but is the most effective. Work your script around this.

The illusion of distance ("throwing" your voice) is not necessary to master unless you want to put on a stage performance of "distant" ventriloquism, but you should know some of the principles. You can create this illusion by holding your dummy at arm's length and letting him speak softly, then drawing him closer and raising the volume of the dummy voice at the same time. With some practice, you can seem to be throwing your voice to distant parts of the room simply by lowering or increasing the strength and tone of your dummy voice. If a ventriloquist wants the voice to come from a cupboard across the stage, he talks as a person would from the inside of a cupboard, and *looks* at the spot. Easier than this, he may put his dummy in a trunk and walk away. Then you hear a small voice seeming to come from the trunk, crying "Let me out!" The performer carries on a conversation this way, perhaps with his back or side to the audience, varying the volume of his voice ("voice modulation" is what this is called). You can do this too, practicing continually before a mirror with or without your dummy. But learn "near" ventriloquism first.

After your first tryout, you can judge better *what* in a script is most amusing. Figure that almost all audiences are likely to react the same way your family and friends do. A performance at a big gathering is no different from performing before your family. In fact, it is easier, because most of the crowd is not close to you—the first row should be about 10 feet away. Your voice will not be strong enough to carry to the far corners of a big room unless the acoustics are excellent, so try out the room empty first if you have an opportunity, and *don't* perform under unsatisfactory circumstances. Straining your voice will destroy the illusion.

If you are learning ventriloquism with a friend, it is a fine idea to put on a combined performance, with both of you and your two dummies. In this case, a staged argument usually creates a sensation, with the dummies bickering and the performers trying to keep them apart.

Remember that in all ventriloquism the misdirection of attention is of primary importance. Your act should always aim at diverting attention towards the dummy and away from yourself when you are in the dummy voice. Remember always to do this and your hobby of ventriloquism is bound to be a success.

JUGGLING

Juggling seems mystifying to people who have never learned the art, but it is really quite easy to learn if you have just a small amount of manual dexterity—the ability to move your hands quickly and accurately.

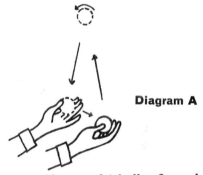

Diagram A

To start, get yourself a set of 4 balls of equal size and weight. These can be rubber or tennis balls. (Later on, you may want to use wooden balls or special silver-plated hollow brass balls which can be purchased at a magic shop.) Begin with one ball. Toss it straight up in the air with your right hand and catch it with the same hand. Repeat this over and over, throwing it about a foot high and as straight vertically as you can. Then do the same with your left hand, and keep repeating it. When you can throw the ball uniformly with either hand and catch it unerringly each time, you are ready for the next exercise.

Now throw the ball up the same distance, but with a slight left arch, with your right hand; catch it in your left, and toss it over to your right hand. (Left-handed people would start with the left hand.)

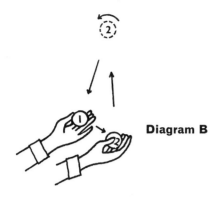

Diagram B

Keep repeating this cycle rhythmically until you perform it perfectly time after time, with the ball going to exactly the same height each time. See Diagram A.

Take 2 balls now, and hold one in each hand with your elbows fairly close to your sides. With your right hand toss the ball in the air (same distance as before), and at exactly the same time toss the ball that is in your left hand into your right hand. As soon as you catch the first ball with your left hand, you throw the second ball up with your right hand. Keep the cycle going, as in Diagram B. Just remember to hold your hands fairly close in toward your body so your eyes can see the balls in flight easily. As you gain skill in throwing and catching, your rhythm will gradually improve, and juggling 2 balls will be second nature to you.

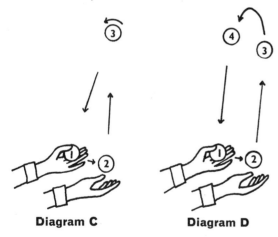

Diagram C   **Diagram D**

With 3 balls now, hold 2 in your right hand and the third in your left. Toss one from your right hand into the air, and just as it reaches the *top point* of its flight, toss the second ball from your right hand into the air. At the same moment, toss the third ball from your left hand into your right. By the time your left hand has done this and come back into position, the first ball will be ready to be caught by your left hand. As you catch this in your left, you toss the third ball up in the air with your right hand.

When you are juggling with 3 balls, two balls are always in the air, as in Diagram C. You will find it more convenient to throw the balls higher in the air with 3 than with 2, for it will give you a longer time between moves and help your rhythm.

Juggling 4 balls requires you to throw the balls still higher, but otherwise the procedure is the same. You start with 2 balls in each hand. You toss the first ball with your right hand, and before it reaches the peak of its height, you toss the second ball with your right hand. At the same time you pass one ball from your left hand to your right. You now have 2 balls in air and one in each hand. Before the first ball comes down, you have to toss the third ball with your right hand, and pass the fourth from left to right, thus releasing your left hand to catch the first ball. See Diagram D. Now you have the rhythm, and it is a fairly easy matter to keep the balls going. As you practice, you will come to know exactly how high to throw the balls and exactly at what instant to toss and catch. Keeping rhythm will allow you to continue juggling without difficulty for as long as you want.

When you have had enough practice, you can put on a performance for your friends. When juggling in public, just forget that anyone else is present and follow your routine automatically.

Juggling silver balls will give a glittering impression, and for stage performances these are often used. Plates (either enamel over metal, or china) will be easy to handle once you have mastered juggling with balls, and they give audiences an even greater thrill. You always toss plates so that the flat surface is almost parallel to your body. It's a good idea, of course, to practice with the metal plates before starting on the family's good china! After you develop the correct rhythm of movements, you will be able to juggle with *anything*.

On the stage, you have no doubt seen jugglers handling bottles with ease. These are not ordinary bottles, of course, or they would not always come down neck first. You will remember the physical law that gravity has the greater pull on the heavier part of an object. Applying this to a bottle, you will find that an ordinary bottle is heavier at its base than at its neck, and therefore when you throw it in the air, it will come down base first. The juggler's bottle has lead in its neck and this extra weight causes it to fall neck first, thus making it easier to grasp. You can weight your own bottles by sealing lead into a hollow cork if you want to learn bottle juggling. The system and rhythm are exactly the same as with balls, and you handle the bottles by their necks, flipping the bases up in the air.

Indian clubs (similarly weighted) and even umbrellas and parasols are used by stage jugglers. The umbrellas and parasols have weights in their handles, and usually, also, they have buttons which allow you to open them out easily while juggling, to end the act in spectacular fashion. Don't attempt umbrella juggling in a low-ceilinged room!

After you have developed skill in juggling, you may want to add some comedy to your routine. This is done by throwing a ball too high, out of its regular path, or tossing behind your back, or something similar, and then making the catch by reaching, and going on with the regular rhythm. At the end of your act, you may toss a ball to a spectator and catch him unawares.

You may also want to dress up in costume to perform for an audience, or talk gibberish while you juggle. Don't you want to be the life of the party?

BIBLIOGRAPHY

BIRD WATCHING

Adler, Helmut E., Ph.D. BIRD LIFE FOR YOUNG PEOPLE. 1962. New York: Sterling Publishing Co.

Bruun, Bertel. BIRDS OF EUROPE. 1970. Middlesex, England: Golden Pleasure Books.

Bruun, Bertel, and Robbins, Chandler S., and Zim, Herbert S. BIRDS OF NORTH AMERICA. 1966. New York: Golden Press.

Chapman, Graeme. COMMON AUSTRALIAN BIRDS OF TOWNS AND GARDENS. 1970. Melbourne: Lansdowne Press.

Hickey, Joseph J. A GUIDE TO BIRD WATCHING. 1943. Garden City, New York: Garden City Books.

Peterson, Roger Tory. A FIELD GUIDE TO THE BIRDS. 1947. Boston: Houghton Mifflin Co.

Peterson, Roger Tory. HOW TO KNOW THE BIRDS, 2nd edition. 1957. Boston: Houghton Mifflin Co.

Schutz, Walter E. HOW TO ATTRACT, HOUSE AND FEED BIRDS. 1970. New York: The Bruce Publishing Co.

Thomson, A. Landsborough (ed.). A NEW DICTIONARY OF BIRDS. 1964. New York: McGraw-Hill Book Co.

TROPICAL FISH

Axelrod, Herbert R. and Vorderwinkler, William. COLOR GUIDE TO TROPICAL FISH. 1955. New York: Sterling Publishing Co. London and Sydney: Oak Tree Press.

Axelrod, Herbert R. and Vorderwinkler, William. TROPICAL FISH IN YOUR HOME. 1956. New York: Sterling Publishing Co. London: Ward Lock.

Coates, Christopher W. TROPICAL FISH AS PETS. 1962. New York: The Macmillan Co.

Hoedeman, J. J. and Van den Nieuwenhuizen, A. NATURALIST'S GUIDE TO FRESH-WATER AQUARIUM FISH. 1973. New York: Sterling Publishing Co. London and Sydney: Oak Tree Press.

Walker, Braz. TROPICAL FISH IDENTIFIER. 1971. New York: Sterling Publishing Co. London: Blandford Press.

INDOOR GARDENING

Bechtel, Helmut. HOUSE PLANT IDENTIFIER. 1973. New York: Sterling Publishing Co. London and Sydney: Oak Tree Press.

Borg, John. CACTI: A GARDENER'S HANDBOOK FOR THEIR IDENTIFICATION, 4th edition. 1972. New York: International Publications Service.

Bulla, Clyde R. FLOWERPOT GARDENS. 1967. New York: Thomas Y. Crowell.

Culpeper, Nicholas. CULPEPER'S COMPLETE HERBAL. 1654. New York: Sterling Publishing Co. London: W. Foulsham.

Doole, Louise Evans. HERB MAGIC AND GARDEN CRAFT. 1972. New York: Sterling Publishing Co. London and Sydney: Oak Tree Press.

Fox, Helen Morgenthau. GARDENING WITH HERBS FOR FLAVOR AND FRAGRANCE. 1971. New York: Sterling Publishing Co. and Dover Publications.

Guilcher, J. M. and Noailles, R. H. THE HIDDEN LIFE OF FLOWERS. 1971. New York: Sterling Publishing Co. London and Sydney: Oak Tree Press.

Higgins, Vera. CACTUS GROWING FOR BEGINNERS. 1972. New York: International Publications Service.

McDonald, Elvin. THE WORLD BOOK OF HOUSE PLANTS. 1972. New York: Popular Library.

Meyer, Joseph E. THE HERBALIST. New York: Sterling Publishing Co.

Raskin, Edith. FANTASTIC CACTUS: INDOORS AND IN NATURE. 1968. West Caldwell, New Jersey: Lothrop, Lee, Shepard Co.

Stevenson, V. INDOOR GARDENING: A GUIDE TO PLANTS IN THE HOME. 1971. Elmsford, New York: British Book Center.

STAMP COLLECTING

Hobson, Burton. GETTING STARTED IN STAMP COLLECTING. 1972. New York: Sterling Publishing Co. London and Sydney: Oak Tree Press.

MINKUS NEW 1973 AMERICAN STAMP CATALOG. 1973. New York: Minkus Publications.

MINKUS NEW 1973 WORLD WIDE STAMP CATALOG. 1973. New York: Minkus Publications.

COIN COLLECTING

Arnold, P. and Steinhilber, D. and Kuthmann, H. CATALOGUE OF GERMAN COINS. 1972. New York: Sterling Publishing Co. London and Sydney: Oak Tree Press.

Friedberg, Robert. APPRAISING AND SELLING YOUR COINS, 7th edition. Friedberg, Jack (ed.). 1973. New York: Sterling Publishing Co.

Freidberg, Robert. GOLD COINS OF THE WORLD, 3rd edition. 1971. New York: Sterling Publishing Co.

Hobson, Burton. CATALOGUE OF SCANDINAVIAN COINS, 2nd edition. 1972. New York: Sterling Publishing Co. London and Sydney: Oak Tree Press.

Hobson, Burton. COIN COLLECTING AS A HOBBY. 1972. New York: Sterling Publishing Co.

Hobson, Burton. HISTORIC GOLD COINS OF THE WORLD. 1971. Garden City, New York: Doubleday and Co.

Hobson, Burton and Reinfeld, Fred. PICTORIAL GUIDE TO COIN CONDITIONS. 1968. Garden City, New York: Doubleday and Co.

Reinfeld, Fred. HOW TO BUILD A COIN COLLECTION. 1970. New York: Sterling Publishing Co.

Reinfeld, Fred. TREASURY OF THE WORLD'S COINS. 1955. New York: Sterling Publishing Co. London and Sydney: Oak Tree Press.

ROCK COLLECTING

Bottley, Percy. ROCKS AND MINERALS. 1969. New York: G. P. Putnam's.

Deer, William A., et al. INTRODUCTION TO THE ROCK FORMING MINERALS. 1966. New York: John Wiley.

Fay, Gordon. ROCKHOUND'S MANUAL. 1972. New York: Barnes and Noble.

Gallant, Ray A. and Schuberth, Christopher J. DISCOVERING ROCKS AND MINERALS. 1967. New York: Natural History Press.

Pough, Frederick. A FIELD GUIDE TO ROCKS AND MINERALS. 1953. Boston: Houghton Mifflin Co.

Sinkankas, John. GEMSTONE AND MINERAL DATA BOOK. 1972. New York: Winchester Press.

Tennissen, Anthony C., Ph.D. COLORFUL MINERAL IDENTIFIER. 1972. New York: Sterling Publishing Co. London and Sydney: Oak Tree Press.

SHELL COLLECTING

Abbott, R. Tucker. THE KINGDOM OF THE SEASHELL. 1972. New York: Crown Publishers.

Dance, S. Peter. SHELL COLLECTING: AN ILLUSTRATED HISTORY. 1966. Berkeley: University of California Press.

McMichael, Donald F. SOME COMMON SHELLS OF THE AUSTRALIAN SEASHORE. 1962. San Francisco: Tri-Ocean Books.

Murray, Sonia J. SHELL LIFE AND SHELL COLLECTING. 1969. New York: Crown Publishers.

Wagner, Robert J. and Abbott, R. Tucker (eds.). VAN NOSTRAND'S STANDARD CATALOGUE OF SHELLS, 2nd edition. 1967. New York: Van Nostrand Reinhold Co.

DRAWING

Alkema, Chester Jay. ALKEMA'S COMPLETE GUIDE TO CREATIVE ART FOR YOUNG PEOPLE. 1971. New York: Sterling Publishing Co. London and Sydney: Oak Tree Press.

Bridgman, George B. BRIDGMAN'S COMPLETE GUIDE TO DRAWING FROM LIFE. 1952. New York: Sterling Publishing Co. London and Sydney: Oak Tree Press.

Bridgman, George B. CONSTRUCTIVE ANATOMY. 1971. New York: Sterling Publishing Co. London and Sydney: Oak Tree Press.

Calder, Alexander and Liedl, Charles. CALDER'S ANIMAL SKETCHING. 1972. New York: Sterling Publishing Co. London and Sydney: Oak Tree Press.

Faustle, Alfred. DRAFTING TECHNIQUES FOR THE ARTIST. 1973. New York: Sterling Publishing Co. London and Sydney: Oak Tree Press.

Gollwitzer, Gerhard, Ph.D. ABSTRACT ART, 2nd edition. 1962. New York: Sterling Publishing Co. London and Sydney: Oak Tree Press.

Gollwitzer, Gerhard, Ph.D. DRAWING FROM NATURE. 1970. New York: Sterling Publishing Co. London and Sydney: Oak Tree Press.

Gollwitzer, Gerhard, Ph.D. EXPRESS YOURSELF IN DRAWING. 1967. New York: Sterling Publishing Co. London and Sydney: Oak Tree Press.

Greco, Simon. ART OF PERSPECTIVE DRAWING. Brooks, Walter (ed.). 1968. London: Golden Press.

Guptill, Arthur L. DRAWING WITH PEN AND INK, revised edition. 1961. New York: Van Nostrand Reinhold Co.

Nicolaides, Kimon. NATURAL WAY TO DRAW. 1941. Boston: Houghton Mifflin Co.

Laning, Edward. ACT OF DRAWING. 1971. New York: McGraw-Hill Book Co.

Rines, Frank M. LANDSCAPE DRAWING WITH PENCIL, 4th edition. 1967. New York: Sterling Publishing Co. London and Sydney: Oak Tree Press.

PAINTING

Carlson, John F. CARLSON'S GUIDE TO LANDSCAPE PAINTING. 1971. New York: Sterling Publishing Co. London and Sydney: Oak Tree Press.

DiValentin, Maria, and DiValentin, Louis. COLOR IN OIL PAINTING. 1966. New York: Sterling Publishing Co. London and Sydney: Oak Tree Press.

Guptill, Arthur L. OIL PAINTING STEP-BY-STEP, revised edition. 1965. New York: Watson-Guptill Publications.

Hawthorne, Charles W. HAWTHORNE ON PAINTING. 1938. New York: Dover Publications.

Kampmann, Lothar. CREATING WITH POSTER PAINTS. 1968. New York: Van Nostrand Reinhold Co.

Mayer, Ralph. ARTIST'S HANDBOOK OF MATERIALS AND TECHNIQUES, 3rd edition. 1970. New York: Viking Press.

Poore, Henry Rankin. COMPOSITION IN ART, revised edition. 1967. New York: Sterling Publishing Co. London and Sydney: Oak Tree Press.

Shumaker, Philip G. PAINTING THE SEA. 1966. New York: Crown Publishers.

Smith, Jacob Getlar. WATERCOLOR PAINTING FOR THE BEGINNER, revised edition. 1967. New York: Sterling Publishing Co. London and Sydney: Oak Tree Press.

Torche, Judith, Ed.D. ACRYLIC AND OTHER WATER-BASE PAINTS, revised edition, 1969. New York: Sterling Publishing Co. London and Sydney: Oak Tree Press.

Van Ingen, J. AQUARELLE AND WATERCOLOR COMPLETE. 1972. New York: Sterling Publishing Co. London and Sydney: Oak Tree Press.

Wood, Paul W. PAINTING ABSTRACT LANDSCAPES. 1969. New York: Sterling Publishing Co. London and Sydney: Oak Tree Press.

PHOTOGRAPHY

Caulfield, Patricia. BEGINNER'S GUIDE TO BETTER PICTURES. 1964. New York: American Photographic Book Publishing Co.

Daniels, Dan. PHOTOGRAPHY FROM A TO Z. 1968. Philadelphia: Chilton Book Co.

Epstein, Samuel and DeArmand, David W. HOW TO DEVELOP, PRINT AND ENLARGE, revised edition. 1971. New York: Grosset and Dunlap.

Frankel, Godfrey. SHORT CUT TO PHOTOGRAPHY, third edition. 1957. New York: Sterling Publishing Co.

Feininger, Andreas. COMPLETE PHOTOGRAPHER. 1965. Englewood Cliffs, New Jersey: Prentice-Hall.

PHOTOGRAPHER'S HANDBOOK. 1970. New York: Time-Life Books.

FISHING

Bauer, Erwin A. FISHERMAN'S DIGEST, 8th edition. 1971. Chicago: Follett Educational Corp.

Bergman, Ray. FISHING WITH RAY BERGMAN. Janes, Edward C. (ed.). 1970. New York: Alfred A. Knopf.

Brooks, Joseph W. Jr. WORLD OF FISHING. 1964. New York: Van Nostrand Reinhold Co.

McClane, A. J. (ed.) McCLANE'S STANDARD FISHING ENCYCLOPEDIA AND INTERNATIONAL ANGLING GUIDE. 1965. New York: Holt, Rinehart and Winston.

Paust, Gil. FISHING. 1961. New York: Sterling Publishing Co.

Sharp, Hal. SPORTSMAN'S DIGEST OF FISHING. 1953. New York: Barnes and Noble.

CAMPING AND BACKPACKING

Cheney, Theodore. CAMPING BY BACKPACK AND CANOE. 1970. New York: Funk and Wagnalls.

Gould, Heywood. THE COMPLETE BOOK OF CAMPING. 1972. New York: New American Library.

Hillcourt, William. GOLDEN BOOK OF CAMPING, revised edition. 1971. London: Golden Press.

Johnson, James R. ADVANCED CAMPING TECHNIQUES. 1967. New York: David McKay Co.

Knobel, Bruno. 101 CAMPING-OUT IDEAS AND ACTIVITIES. 1961. New York: Sterling Publishing Co.

Luce, William P. FAMILY CAMPING: A SELF INSTRUCTION GUIDE TO CAMP SKILLS AND SITES. 1965. New York: The Macmillan Co.

Merrill, W. K. HIKER'S AND BACKPACKER'S HANDBOOK. 1970. New York: Winchester Press. Sydney: Oak Tree Press.

Ryalls, Alan. ENJOY CAMPING HOLIDAYS. 1963. New York: International Publications Service.

BIKE RIDING

Asa, Warren. NORTH AMERICAN BICYCLE ATLAS, 2nd edition. 1972. New York: Crown Publishers.

Baranet, Nancy N. BICYCLING. 1972. Cranbury, New Jersey: A. S. Barnes and Co.

Frankel, Godfrey and Frankel, Lillian. BIKE-WAYS (101 THINGS TO DO WITH A BIKE), revised edition. 1973. New York: Sterling Publishing Co. London and Sydney: Oak Tree Press.

McIntyre, Bibs. THE BIKE BOOK: EVERYTHING YOU NEED TO KNOW ABOUT OWNING AND RIDING A BIKE. 1972. New York: Harper and Row.

CHESS PLAYING

Cozens, W. H. THE KING-HUNT IN CHESS. 1971. New York: Sterling Publishing Co. London: G. Bell and Sons.

Hanauer, Milton. CHESS MADE EASY. 1967. Hollywood, California: Wilshire Book Co.

Horowitz, I. A. and Reinfeld, Fred. FIRST BOOK OF CHESS. 1973. New York: Sterling Publishing Co. London: Faber and Faber.

Reinfeld, Fred. ATTACK AND COUNTERATTACK IN CHESS. 1958. New York: Barnes and Noble.

Reinfeld, Fred. CHESS FOR CHILDREN. 1972. New York: Sterling Publishing Co. London: World's Work.

Reinfeld, Fred. CHESS FOR YOUNG PEOPLE. 1961. New York: Holt, Rinehart & Winston. London and Sydney: Oak Tree Press.

Reinfeld, Fred. CHESS IS AN EASY GAME. 1972. New York: Sterling Publishing Co. London: Lutterworth Press.

Reinfeld, Fred. CHESS SECRETS REVEALED. 1970. North Hollywood, California: Wilshire Book Co.

Reinfeld, Fred. COMPLETE BOOK OF CHESS OPENINGS. 1957. New York: Sterling Publishing Co. London and Sydney: Oak Tree Press.

Reinfeld, Fred. THE COMPLETE CHESS COURSE. 1959. Garden City, New York: Doubleday and Co.

Reinfeld, Fred. HOW TO WIN CHESS GAMES QUICKLY. 1957. New York: Barnes and Noble.

Reinfeld, Fred. IMPROVING YOUR CHESS. 1960. New York: Barnes and Noble.

Reinfeld, Fred. WINNING CHESS FOR BEGINNERS. 1973. New York: Grosset and Dunlap.

HANDWRITING ANALYSIS

Martin, Renee. INSTANT HANDWRITING ANALYSIS. 1972. New York: Bantam Books.

Olyanova, Nadya. THE PSYCHOLOGY OF HANDWRITING. 1960. New York: Sterling Publishing Co.

Roman, Klara G. HANDWRITING: A KEY TO PERSONALITY. 1952. New York: Pantheon Books.

FORTUNE TELLING

Brown, Wenzel. HOW TO TELL FORTUNES WITH CARDS. 1968. New York: Sterling Publishing Co.

Leek, Sybil. SYBIL LEEK BOOK OF FORTUNE-TELLING. 1969. New York: The Macmillan Co.

Martin, Kevin. COMPLETE GYPSY FORTUNE-TELLER. 1970. New York: G. P. Putnam's.

Showers, Paul. FORTUNE TELLING FOR FUN. 1971. Hollywood, California: Newcastle Publishing Co.

MAGIC, VENTRILOQUISM, AND JUGGLING

Dittrich, Rudolf. JUGGLING MADE EASY. 1967. Hollywood, California: Wilshire Book Co.

Permin, I. B. HOKUS POKUS. 1969. New York: Sterling Publishing Co. London and Sydney: Oak Tree Press.

INDEX

368 ■ INDEX